COMPOSERS OF THE TWENTIETH CENTURY

ALLEN FORTE, *General Editor*

THE MUSIC OF
IGOR STRAVINSKY

PIETER C. VAN DEN TOORN

Yale University Press
New Haven and London

Made possible in part by a grant from *The Martha Baird Rockefeller Fund for Music, Inc.*

Designed by Nancy Ovedovitz and set in Baskerville type by A-R Editions, Inc., Madison, WI. Printed in the United States of America by Vail-Ballou Press, Binghamton, New York.

Library of Congress Cataloging in Publication Data
Van den Toorn, Pieter C., 1938–
 The music of Igor Stravinsky.

 (Composers of the twentieth century)
 Includes bibliography and index.
 1. Stravinsky, Igor, 1882–1971. Selections.
I. Title. II. Series.
ML410.S932V36   780.924   82-2560
ISBN 0-300-02693-5   AACR2

10   9   8   7   6   5   4   3   2   1

In memory of
Nadia Boulanger

CONTENTS

ACKNOWLEDGMENTS   xi

INTRODUCTION   xiii

ONE   **THE FIREBIRD (1910)**   1

Introduction   10
"Danse infernale"   17
"Danse infernale" and Finale: Rhythmic-Metric Implications   25
"Khorovod"   29

TWO   **PETROUSHKA (1911): An Introduction to the Octatonic Pitch Collection and Its Deployment in Stravinsky's Music**   31

The Lists   42
The Models   48
Some Useful (and Useless) Explanatory Notions   61
The Familiar Orientation Categories or Periods   66

THREE   **PETROUSHKA: The Diatonic Pitch Collection in the Music of Stravinsky's "Russian" Period**   73

Pitch Relations in the First Tableau   73
Russian Folk Music in "Russian" Music   90
Repercussions   96

FOUR   **LE SACRE DU PRINTEMPS (1913)**   99

Pitch Relations   100
Conclusions   131
Some General Considerations   133
Rhythmic-Metric Implications   137

FIVE   **THREE PIECES FOR STRING QUARTET (1914)**   144

Some General Considerations   147
Pitch Relations   149
Conclusions   152

SIX   **LES NOCES (1917)**   155
Pitch Relations   164
Conclusions   176

SEVEN   **HISTOIRE DU SOLDAT (1918)**   178
Pitch Relations   178
Looking Ahead: Two Neoclassical Examples   193
Some General Considerations   197

EIGHT   **RHYTHMIC (OR METRIC) INVENTION**   204
Rhythmic (or Metric) Invention (I)   214
Histoire du soldat (1918) and *Renard* (1916)   218
Rhythmic (or Metric) Invention (II)   224
Repercussions   238

NINE   **THE NEOCLASSICAL INITIATIVE**   252
Change of Life   256
Some General Considerations   258
Pitch Relations   261

TEN   **(0 3 4/3 4 7/3 6 7) "MINOR-MAJOR THIRD" EMPHASIS**   271
"Basle" *Concerto in D* (1946)   275
Symphony in Three Movements (1945): Nos. 112–18   284
Danses concertantes (1942)   288
Babel (1944)   290
Symphony of Psalms (1930): Third Movement, Nos. 0–3   295
Oedipus Rex (1927): Nos. 166–70   298
Orpheus (1947)   305
Conclusions   317

ELEVEN   **OCTATONIC "PROGRESSIONS"**   321
The (0 4 7 10) "Dominant-Seventh" Complexes   323

TWELVE   **THE DOMINANT-TONIC RELATION**   330
Octet (1923)   332
Symphonies of Wind Instruments (1920)   337
Symphony of Psalms (1930): First Movement   344
Symphony in Three Movements (1945)   351
Oedipus Rex (1927): Act 1, Nos. 27–45   366

THIRTEEN   **THE SERIAL PERIOD (I)**   372
Change of Life   378
Agon (1953–1957)   390
Canticum Sacrum (1955)   414

FOURTEEN   **THE SERIAL PERIOD (II)**   427
The Flood (1962)   436
Abraham and Isaac (1963) et al.   445
A Conclusion   452

NOTES   457

BIBLIOGRAPHY   501

INDEX   506

ACKNOWLEDGMENTS

Few contemporary composers have exerted a more conspicuous musical presence than Igor Stravinsky. And this is quite naturally to the benefit of all those with an interest in his music: not only are a great number of Stravinsky's works widely and frequently performed, but the immense acclaim accorded a handful of them has ensured the publication (and recording) of just about everything Stravinsky composed. There are, to be sure, a few early pieces that were lost during the Russian Revolution, and some of the more extensive of the revisions of pre-1931 works have posed some problems in that, for financial or artistic reasons, the old versions continue to be performed along with the new. But these are comparatively minor items. Virtually the whole of his oeuvre is intact, in print, readily serviceable.

Moreover, Stravinsky's sketchbooks reveal little in the way of unfinished works or unused material. He was ever tidy and punctual in his craft, almost clerklike. Once assured of an "auditive shape," he carefully gauged its potential and plunged through with alarming—if at times intense—regularity. (*The Nightingale*, *Les Noces*, the *Mass*, and *Agon* are among notable exceptions in this regard.) Indeed, from what may presently be gathered from the sketches themselves, many are not really sketches at all, but resemble abridged drafts. Having catalogued those sketchbooks in Stravinsky's possession in 1948, Robert Craft was startled to find so frequent a lack of "struggle"; that so much material had apparently been born "full grown." Some of this may be owing to the fact that Stravinsky orchestrated while he composed, timbre having been inseparable from the inception and projection of a musical idea. Not only did he compose at the piano (a muted piano), but he improvised during the preliminary stages, often at great length. (Schoenberg would later protest that such were not the manners of a "real composer"; that "real" composers did not play first and write later, but composed wholly within their imagination, without use or need of an instrument. But these distinctions are, insofar as Stravinsky is concerned, hardly valid. Apart from the chance delights of improvisation, Stravinsky relished the immediate, physical contact of his instrument. Before committing their ideas to paper, both Stravinsky and Schoenberg appear often to have sorted matters out in detail. The difference is that Stravinsky did much of this sorting at the piano, whereas Schoenberg did not.)

Then, too, there is a wealth of biographical material. The six Stravinsky-Craft books, along with Craft's diaries and later publications, are known to both musicians and the general public; and they contain valuable information on attitudes, working habits, and conditions attending the conception of many of the works. There are, in addition, the recollections of close associates: apart from Craft's own studies, those by C. F. Ramuz, Nicolas Nabokov, and Paul Horgan come readily to mind. Indeed, the career has been sumptuously chronicled in a recent Craft collaboration with Vera Stravinsky, *Stravinsky in Pictures and Documents*. Of course, these accounts are rarely, if ever, technical in nature. But even in analysis and theory the field has not lacked its enthusiasts. Several entries are of the highest calibre, offering genuine insight into the intricacies of musical structure. And so it is inevitably to these circumstances that the present volume is most heavily in debt. The perspective it offers is necessarily its own, but a foundation has been laid with established assumptions from which it has been possible to depart.

On the other hand, there was assistance of an immediate kind, without which the task would not merely have been arduous but very nearly impossible. In particular, Allen Forte, general editor of the Yale series on composers of the twentieth century, offered his knowledge, skill, and patience; Dennis Libby made a very thorough reading of the final draft; and Melvin Wildberger furnished superb engravings of the musical illustrations.

Moreover, there were others who, if somewhat removed from the immediate scene, offered their encouragement and advice: Henry Mishkin, formerly of Amherst College; Elaine Barkin of the University of California, Los Angeles; and Benjamin Boretz of Bard College.

I am also grateful for assistance in matters practical and no less consequential: Word Processing Specialists of Novato, California, proved immensely resourceful, as did C. Bianchini of the Novato Secretarial Service. Odds and ends were often attended to by Cornelia van den Toorn, Virginia Duys, C. Miller, and W. H. van den Toorn. And a word of thanks, as well, to Cattarina, Anna Marie, and Linnea.

INTRODUCTION

I have had to survive two crises as a composer, though as I continued to move from work to work I was not aware of either of them as such, or, indeed, of any momentous change. The first—the loss of Russia and its language of words as well as of music—affected every circumstance of my personal no less than my artistic life, which made recovery more difficult. Only after a decade of samplings, experiments, amalgamations did I find the path to *Oedipus Rex* [1927] and the *Symphony of Psalms* [1930]. Crisis number two was brought on by the natural outgrowing of the special incubator in which I wrote *The Rake's Progress* [1948–51]. . . . The period of adjustment [i.e., with serial techniques] was only half as long this time, but as I look back on it I am surprised at how long I continued to straddle my "styles." [Igor Stravinsky and Robert Craft, *Themes and Episodes*, p. 23.]

I am not a believer in *ex nihilo* explanations of art, and in my own case I know positively that reactivated springs from my past work have continually nourished the present—which is one reason why I think my work deserves to be considered as a whole. [*Themes and Episodes*, p. 45.]

To identify the structural functions of Stravinsky's harmony is very difficult; to demonstrate them conclusively may be impossible—or may be the task of some future generation. Conventional harmonic analysis is not enough, even when its notions are extended to the utmost. [William W. Austin, *Music in the 20th Century*, p. 260.]

Stravinsky's music has seemed stubbornly to resist binding analytic-theoretical legislation. This is curious because of the conviction voiced by those familiar with his music that there *is* a consistency, a remarkable identity or distinction in "sound" that certainly *ought* to lend itself to such legislation. Curious, too, because the attention, analytic-theoretical, historical, and critical, accorded this music over the past fifty years could scarcely have been more insistent. In the realm of analysis and theory alone, for example, the elusive (if at times highly suggestive) imprint of major-scale tonally functional relations has been circumvented in appeals to a "basic-cell" rationale, in which "coherence" is attributed to the unfolding of some intervallically conceived cohesiveness; Stravinsky's neoclassical works, stretching roughly from *Pulcinella* (1920) to *Agon* (1953–57), have been juxtaposed with models drafted from Baroque and Classical major-scale literature in an effort to track down the contamination, the departure from traditional (tonal) form, or the "impurities" or "wrong notes" for which Stravinsky has so often been cited. Roy Travis, with reference to the first pages of the Introduction to *Le Sacre*, has suggested that, by substituting "tonic sonority" for "tonic triad," we might find techniques analogous to those of tonal (major-scale) practice (as interpreted by Heinrich Schenker); and Allen Forte has subjected the whole of *Petroushka* (with its sizable "chunks" of diatonic material) to a Schenker-type analysis.[1]

But it is questionable whether the methods in even the most revealing of these and similar endeavors are appropriate to the bulk of Stravinsky's oeuvre (or to a concern for consistency, identity, and distinction in his work "considered as a whole," to use his own phrase quoted earlier). Further, one may question whether the transfer of terms and concepts intimately associated with the tonality of Baroque, Classical, or Romantic major-scale literature to a music which is at least problematic in this respect does not confuse rather than illuminate, while at the same time jeopardizing any binding, particularizing understanding that this conventional (tonal) analytic-theoretical reckoning affords the music for which it was intended. Moreover, apart from the philosophical or psychological understanding to which some have addressed themselves, comprehensive attempts to bind in technical terms have been unfruitful; indeed they have led to a dialogue so misleading, so contradictory and indiscriminate as to stupefy, frighten, or otherwise offend the most conscientious readers. The confusion that permeates the pages of Paul Collaer's discussion is exemplary in this respect.[2] Here, a bewildering succession of descriptive terms and explanatory notions (e.g., "key," "C-major," "tonality," "bitonality," "polytonality," "atonality," "pantonality," "pandiatonicism, "polyharmony," "polychordal," "superimposition"), invariably left undefined or underdefined, deprives the undertaking of all meaning and consequence. Stravinsky's music, everywhere and at once, is made to embrace every conceivable musical technique.

The comprehensive studies by Alexandre Tansman, Roman Vlad, and Eric Walter White invite similar criticism.[3] When venturing beyond the purely descriptive (or beyond the specious or trivial), these texts are of little assistance because the meaning or relevance of the technical or semi-technical terms introduced, both traditional and new, is never adequately explored. Consequently, many of the terms and explanatory notions associated with Stravinsky's music may now seem symptomatic of confusion rather than of any substantive understanding or "coming to terms": "pantonality" and "pandiatonicism" appear, in the presence of diatonicism, merely to suggest the absence of major-scale tonally functional relations; and "bitonality" and "polytonality" (the simultaneous unfolding of separate "tonalities" or "keys") have already been widely dismissed as too fantastic or illogical to warrant serious consideration.[4]

So we take heed of these discomforting signs. It may be that Stravinsky's music, with its diverse orientations or "stylistic" trends, its position sandwiched between the pillars of major-scale tonality and twelve-tone ordering procedures (pillars which, admittedly, might eventually prove not as pillarlike as they now seem), is incapable of yielding (or succumbing to) a truly useful set of binding analytic-theoretical propositions. Moreover, as long as this music continues to attract the kind of attention that it has in the past, the likelihood of such a design seems, ironically, all the more improbable. In our quest for a theoretical framework and accompanying analytical approaches that will satisfy our binding instincts—substantiate, that is, our sense of a distinctive presence—and prove effective in dealing with specificity in individual works or groups of works, we may have to contend not with a single consistency, identity, or distinction, but with multiple ones which may or may not correspond to the three widely acknowledged orientation categories or "stylistic" periods (these being—with much overlapping or "straddling"—the "Russian" period from the very beginning to the *Symphonies of Wind Instruments*, 1920, the neoclassical period from *Pulcinella*, 1920, to *Agon*, 1953–57, and the serial period from the *Cantata*, 1952, to the *Requiem Canticles*, 1966).[5]

This brings us to Arthur Berger's classic discussion of pitch organization in Stravinsky.[6] Here, "binding theoretical legislation" is wisely forsaken (or left to some future date) in favor of a method of classification that deals with what appear to be usefully definable consistencies, identities, or distinctions: (1) octatonic writing—music accountable to the octatonic pitch collection, a collection of eight distinct pitch classes (instead of the familiar seven of the diatonic collection) which, in scale formation, yields a symmetrical interval ordering of alternating half and whole steps; (2) diatonic writing—music accountable to the diatonic pitch collection, but in which Stravinsky's articulation may implicate interval orderings other than those defined by the familiar major and minor scales of Baroque, Classical, and Romantic musical literature; (3) octatonic-diatonic interaction—the interaction or interpenetration of these two distinct collections of reference (for never, in pieces of considerable duration, do we find a referential commitment to but one of these cohesive frames of reference).

And so in matters of pitch organization generally, this inquiry will be confronting the question of consistency, identity, and distinction in Stravinsky's music as it imposes itself in regard to these octatonic and diatonic classes of writing. This has meant confining detailed scrutiny to a series of works stretching from *The Firebird* to *Abraham and Isaac* (i.e., *through* the abovementioned orientation categories or "stylistic" periods).

1. *The Firebird* (1910)
2. *Petroushka* (1911)
3. *Le Sacre* (1913)
4. *Three Pieces for String Quartet* (1914)
5. *Les Noces* (1917)
6. *Histoire du soldat* (1918)
7. *Symphonies of Wind Instruments* (1920)
8. *Octet* (1923)
9. *Oedipus Rex* (1927)
10. *Symphony of Psalms* (1930)

11. *Symphony in C* (1940)
12. *Babel* (1944)
13. *Symphony in Three Movements* (1945)
14. "Basle" *Concerto in D* (1946)
15. *Orpheus* (1947)
16. *Canticum Sacrum* (1955)
17. *Agon* (1953–57)
18. *Epitaphium* (1959)
19. *The Flood* (1962)
20. *Abraham and Isaac* (1963)

Much peripheral acknowledgment is also accorded the remainder of Stravinsky's works, pieces like the *Scherzo fantastique* (1908), *Pribaoutki* (1914), *Renard* (1916), the "Dumbarton Oaks" *Concerto in E♭* (1938), *Danses concertantes* (1942), *In Memoriam Dylan Thomas* (1954), *Movements* (1959), and the orchestral *Variations* (1964).[7]

While this scrutiny ignores much music that might be deemed significant (e.g., *Apollo*, 1928; *Perséphone*, 1934; *The Rake's Progress*, 1948–51), this is not generally because of an absence of octatonic, diatonic, or octatonic-diatonic writing (or an absence of the consistency, identity, or distinction to be inferred on behalf of this reference classification). Often, additional detailed analyses seemed likely to duplicate much that had been proposed concerning the works ultimately selected and listed above. And with an eye (and ear) toward a sound, manageable format, the preference was to probe a nucleus of Stravinsky's works (or parts thereof) with meticulous care and to discuss the remaining works whenever revealingly pertinent to the issues at hand, rather than to treat each of the hundred-odd works individually and equally—and on what seemed likely to be a somewhat indiscriminate, piecemeal basis.

Critical, however, is the fact that this octatonic, diatonic, octatonic-diatonic reference classification overlaps the familiar "Russian," neoclassical, and serial orientation categories. This may be in keeping with current trends in analytic-theoretical, historical, and critical discourse. There has been a tendency in recent years to de-emphasize these orientation categories, whose apprehension, earlier in the century, had seemed essential to a proper grasp of Stravinsky's "stylistic development." On the other hand, this reference classification need not undermine the legitimacy of these categories. On the contrary, our contention is that they continue to embody useful distinctions in musical thought.

Thus, in regard to Stravinsky's octatonic writing: consistency, identity, or distinction may be defined in his work "considered as a whole" by means of two models of partitioning. But within these "Russian," neoclassical, and (at least early) serial orientation categories, there are preoccupations that are very nearly exclusively "Russian," and others that seem peculiarly neoclassical. The same holds for Stravinsky's diatonicism. "Russian" works (e.g., *Petroushka, Le Sacre, Renard, Les Noces*) exhibit processes of diatonic articulation that differ from diatonic articulative habits of neoclassicism.

And so this whole question of consistency, identity, or distinction (or of *a* consistency, identity, or distinction) is not just *context-bound* (e.g., put forward here on behalf of Arthur Berger's classification as to reference), but *relative* (i.e., varying in accord with the scope of our perspective). What might seem pertinent to a hearing and understanding of "Russian" musical thought (as regards, say, Stravinsky's octatonic contexts) may seem irrelevant to neoclassicism. We apprehend in this relativeness the classic seesaw effect of analytic-theoretical pursuit (or, indeed, of perception itself, with which this pursuit seeks to cope): the further we tilt toward the unexceptional, toward regularity on a literaturewide basis, the less direct or immediate is our preoccupation with the particulars of a given context; and the closer we draw toward the particulars of a given context (perhaps both with respect to local events and a long-term, global attitude), the less this specification is likely to apply to the literature as a whole. (Although, of course, the broader perspective "covers" or "encloses" the specification; specificity will not conflict with our covering definition(s) of collective regularity.) Then, too, the interdependence of the strategy: our choice of a broad perspective (i.e., "the music of Igor Stravinsky," consisting generally of the framing of some theoretical model—and, of course, put forward here on behalf of the classification indicated) can come only by way of a consciousness of detail from one context to the next; and a demonstration of this detail (i.e., *what* it is that we *choose* to regard in this light) hinges on our definition of the unexceptional, the consistent on a comprehensive, literaturewide basis.

For example, had we elected to situate Stravinsky's music within the general context of Baroque or Classical major-scale musical literature, our observations in regard to specificity—from one piece to the next—would have been quite different from what they are. Such a "situation" would have entailed discussion of how relations deemed critical to a hearing and understanding of Stravinsky's music comply with the tonal functionality of this major-scale literature (as interpreted, say, by Heinrich Schenker), a pretension whose likely consequence—in the eyes and ears of this observer—would have been the collapse of this tonal category, of its legitimacy as a cohesive system or frame of musical thought, invention, and reference. But we elected not to so situate Stravinsky's music, principally because the symmetrical (nontonal) implications of his octatonic material, as well as of his diatonic material (especially of the "Russian" period, but also of the later neoclassical variety), seemed fundamentally at odds with the tonality of Baroque, Classical, or Romantic literature (from the beginning of the seventeenth century to the end of the nineteenth). Too persistently, Stravinsky's articulation, whether referentially octatonic, diatonic, or octatonic-diatonic, seemed devoid of those tonally functional relations (e.g., the familiar harmonic progressions, the modulations, the definitions of key and cadence) that we readily associate with this particular "slice" of Western music. Then, too, the unvarying—and, of course, highly revealing—presence in individual pieces of more than one distinct collection of reference (i.e., the octatonic and the diatonic), and the relationship of this referential variability to certain general methods of procedure (e.g., triadic superimposition, abrupt "block" juxtaposition, ostinatolike repetition), as well as to certain distinctive melodic, formal, instrumental, and rhythmic-metric features, seemed equally injurious to a tonal reading. These considerations provided a further reason to adopt Arthur Berger's method of classification (based on this critical question of reference), and to propose a hearing and understanding of consistency, identity, and distinction accordingly. This is not to suggest that Stravinsky's diatonicism ("Russian" or neoclassical) is not ultimately a species of diatonicism generally; that his neoclassical diatonicism is not often a form of major-scale diatonicism (of which the tonal variety might be reckoned as one particular type); that certain major-scale tonally functional relations do not, in however parenthetical or contaminated a manner, impose themselves at times; and hence, ultimately, that there are not other useful classes or categories of musical reference that intersect with Berger's, or broader categories (e.g., "diatonicism," "Western music") that are in turn implicated by our perspective on Stravinsky's work. (For our concern here is not merely with *any* regularity or consistency, but with typicality, with identity and distinction, which naturally presupposes a reckoning of just such intersecting or broader—even "outside"—frames or categories of musical reference. Indeed, it is because of the necessary intersection of these broader or "outside" categories of reference that our discussion assumes a historical or critical bent as crucial as its analytic-theoretical bent.) Only, it seemed essential not just to extricate Stravinsky's diatonic articulation from past modal and tonal considerations, but also to free his neoclassical (major-scale) diatonicism from the tonally functional relations with which the major-scale ordering of the diatonic collection is closely identified.

On a more broadly defined basis, it is not to be denied that our general analytic-theoretical attitude, however elementary to virtually all fields of inquiry, has met with resistance. Analysis, in the sense of "impoverishing the immediately given,"[8] has seemed, when applied to music, peculiarly suspect, a perverse kind of intellectualism, an act of desecration. There may be some confusion here between analytic-theoretical study as a musical (auditive) endeavor (in which all musicians participate), and the effort to transmit verbally or graphically a hearing and understanding—a misunderstanding, then, of the nature or objectives of formal analysis. (We can think of no explanation other than this for the skepticism voiced by Stravinsky in these matters: a suspicion that formal reckoning represented a kind of thinking *about* music rather than a thinking *in* music (the conceptual-perceptual dichotomy, or the theory-practice relation), or a suspicion that, unlike composition or performance, such reckoning was not fundamentally auditive.) Or perhaps it is not generally supposed that what formal analysis abstracts, what it acknowledges as orderly and consistent, is not as much a part of that "immediately given" as is uniqueness or novelty—wholeness, a totality of relations as something quite different from the mere sum of its (abstracted) parts. The classic responses to these complaints run like this: (1) it is in the quest itself, in the actual seeking to hear and understand, that the benefits or rewards of analytic-theoretical study accrue; (2) "Reading criticism, otherwise than in the presence, or with the direct re-collection, of the objects discussed is a blank and senseless employment—a fact which is concealed from us by the cooperation, in our reading, of many non-critical purposes for which the information offered by the critic is material and useful."[9] Or: some have found the business of verbally and/or graphically coping with their musical thought processes useful and stimulating; others, obviously, have not.

Here is an itemization of the stages which, in retrospect, appear to have initiated this particular venture:

1. An attraction for a handful of Stravinsky's works (e.g., *Le Sacre, Les Noces,* the *Symphony of Psalms*, the *Symphony in Three Movements*) manifests itself. Apart from recordings, these scores are studied and restudied, and certain passages played and replayed at the piano.

2. At some point, *identity* (in relation to the works of other composers or other known literatures) imposes itself. A conscious effort is made to pursue the question of consistency, identity, or distinction.

3. A reading of the *Symphony in Three Movements* prompts an awareness of the octatonic pitch collection. As a consequence, other known Stravinsky works are reheard and reinterpreted in the light of this distinct—and evidently distinctive—frame of reference. Also, an apprehension of *routine* in octatonic articulation prompts some musical notetaking.

4. The available analytic-theoretical, historical, and critical record is scanned. In particular, Arthur Berger's "Problems of Pitch Organization

in Stravinsky" is found to contain much useful information about the structure of the octatonic scale and its deployment in Stravinsky's music.

5. The analytical—but still principally nonverbal—note-scribbling becomes feverish. "New" works are studied and restudied. The effort is now clearly to examine Stravinsky's octatonic articulation as it relates to his diatonic articulation, and to hear and understand the relationship of this referential interaction to certain general methods of procedure (e.g., superimposition, "block" juxtaposition, repetition) and to traits in melodic, formal, instrumental, and rhythmic-metric design.

6. A decision is made to communicate. All of Stravinsky's works are now studied, as are his books of "conversation" with Robert Craft and many of the hundreds of books and articles on his music. (For there can be little point in merely repeating what has already been said or written.) Of these latter books and articles, several by Edward T. Cone, Wilfrid Mellers, Arthur Berger, Pierre Boulez, Allen Forte, and Benjamin Boretz are helpful. But the reading extends well beyond the musically oriented. For an uneasiness develops in response to the lack of any (conscious) knowledge or understanding of the nature of perception (which prompts much reading in the works of the early Gestalt psychologists, Wolfgang Köhler, Kurt Koffka, and Max Wertheimer) and of the sticky problems of "historical explanation" (which, in turn, prompts much reading about historical reasoning). All this becomes time-consuming.

7. Since the preoccupation is with a perspective on Stravinsky's work as a whole, a book seems logical. But the writing gets bogged down. Questions arise as to presentation, the inclusion of biographical detail—in short, how to limit the scope.

8. The book is temporarily discarded in favor of two or three essays focusing on specific issues.

9. Upon completion of these essays (which are submitted for publication),[10] the broader perspective is again confronted, the biographical detail again assembled and filtered, and the book completed within a few years. (While this book addresses itself to the *music* of Stravinsky—to the "sound," so to speak—it nonetheless attempts to record some of the circumstances surrounding the conception of the works under discussion; to record Stravinsky's published reflections on these circumstances; to report, occasionally, on his whereabouts; to afford—secondhand, necessarily—some insights into the musical personality; and to provide his music with a general historical framework or setting. This peripheral staging would not have been possible without Stravinsky's six books of "conversation" with Robert Craft, to which extravagant reference is made throughout this inquiry.)[11]

Now, the present writer has no intent to belittle verbal and/or graphic interchange in musical analysis and theory. But it would certainly appear that at one of these stages—perhaps at or during stage 6—the project became "intellectual." This does not mean that the verbal and/or graphic communicative effort was not prompted by an initial and ongoing hearing and understanding and that it was not always directed at a reliable account of this hearing and understanding, but only that the immediate and overriding concern became increasingly literary: words, words, words. And not only literary, but methodological: how best (linearly) to classify, systematize, exclude. While it has been argued that this formal act of communication adds immeasurably to one's hearing and understanding (principally an auditive, mental, nonverbal experience), this observer remains skeptical: he questions the extent to which the initial and ongoing hearing and understanding (aided by some musical note-scribbling, possibly unintelligible to all but the scribbler) was substantially enriched by the literary effort—ultimately the most time-consuming part of the venture. For the musician becomes a writer (however reluctantly), and in matters of communication in music there can be no substitute for a face-to-face confrontation—with the piano in easy reach.

Of course, advantages of the formal communiqué are not lightly dismissed. Writing itself is challenge. And one seeks, after all, a wider audience, an audience that can share, react, and respond. And there is then the possibility (although not the true ethical justification for the musician turned writer, since this resides in the calling itself, the doing, the "challenge") that, just as he/she might have benefited from someone else's communication, so might someone else benefit from his/hers. (Although such benefits are largely owing to the efforts of the recipient. For just as with harmony or counterpoint, learning becomes a matter of applying oneself musically, of engaging one's musical—and principally auditive—faculties to the fullest extent, and hence only superficially a matter of "understanding" certain rules and regulations.) But it would still seem that the practical (and, of course, private) benefits of this investigation, benefits which appear to have directly affected the conduct of this musician as a listener, composer, performer, or teacher, had been reached by—or in the midst of—stage 6, before the effort to commit the hearing and understanding to words, before the musician became a (somewhat reluctant) writer and designer of communicable graphic displays.

Still, none of this "intellectualism" need hinder the reader's musical participation. The language may assume its customary—and essential—transparency, and whatever is written or graphically displayed may take on musical (auditive) significance. But, as should by now be apparent, this is a circumstance for which the writer can regrettably offer no direct assistance—and certainly no assurances. All that can reasonably be expected is the guarantee of a certain sensitivity to the "problem." And this alone may enable us to turn a bit more confidently to the business at hand.

ONE
THE FIREBIRD (1910)

Concert Suite (1919)
   I. Introduction
  II. "L'Oiseau de feu et sa danse"; "Variation de l'oiseau de feu"
 III. "Khorovod"
  IV. "Danse infernale" (Kastchei section)
   V. "Berceuse" (Lullaby)
  VI. Finale

I had begun to think about *The Firebird* when I returned to St. Petersburg from Ustilug in the fall of 1909, though I was not yet certain of the commission (which, in fact, did not come until December, more than a month after I had begun to compose; I remember the day Diaghilev telephoned me to say go ahead, and I recall his surprise when I said that I already had started). Early in November I moved from St. Petersburg to a *dacha* belonging to the Rimsky-Korsakov family about seventy miles southeast of the city. I went there for a vacation in birch forests and snow-fresh air, but instead began to work on *The Firebird*. Andrei Rimsky-Korsakov was with me at the time, as he often was during the following months; because of this, *The Firebird* is dedicated to him. The Introduction up to the bassoon-and-clarinet figure at measure 6 was composed in the country, as were notations for later parts. I returned to St. Petersburg in December and remained there until March, when the composition was finished. . . .

I was flattered, of course, at the promise of a performance of my music in Paris, and my excitement on arriving in that city, from Ustilug toward the end of May, could hardly have been greater. . . .

The first-night audience glittered indeed. . . . I sat in Diaghilev's box, where, at intermissions, a path of celebrities, artists, dowagers, aged Egerias of the Ballet, writers, balletomanes, appeared. . . .

I was called to the stage to bow at the conclusion, and was recalled several times. I was still on stage when the final curtain had come down, and I saw coming toward me Diaghilev and a dark man with a double forehead whom he introduced as Claude Debussy. The great composer spoke kindly about the music, ending his words with an invitation to dine with him. . . .

Ravel, who liked *The Firebird*, though less than *Petroushka* or *Le Sacre*, ex-

1

plained its success to me as having been paved, in part, by the musical dullness of Diaghilev's last new production, *Pavillon d'Armide* (Benois-Tcherepnin). The Parisian audience wanted a taste of *avant-garde*, and *The Firebird* was just that—according to Ravel. To this explanation I would add that *The Firebird* belongs to the styles of its time. It is more vigorous than most of the composed folk music of the period, but it is also not very original. These are all good conditions for a success. . . .

The orchestral body of *The Firebird* was wastefully large, but I was more proud of some of the orchestration than of the music itself. The horn and trombone glissandi produced the biggest sensation with the audience, of course, but this effect, at least with the trombone, was not original with me. . . . But how am I to talk like a confessing author about *The Firebird* when my feelings towards it are purely those of a critic?—though, to be honest, I was criticizing it even when I was composing it. . . . I have already criticized *The Firebird* twice, however, in my revised versions of 1919 and 1945, and these direct musical criticisms are stronger than words.

Am I too critical? Does *The Firebird* contain more real musical invention than I am able (or willing) to see? I would this were the case. It was in some respects a fecund score for my own development in the next four years, but the few scraps of counterpoint to be found in it—in the Kastchei scene, for example—are derived from chord tones, and this is not real counterpoint. . . . If an interesting construction exists in *The Firebird*, it will be found in the treatment of intervals, for example in the major and minor thirds in the *Berceuse*, in the Introduction, and in the Kastchei music. . . . Rhythmically, too, the finale might be cited as the first appearance in my music of metrical irregularity—the 7/4 bars subdivided into 1, 2, 3; 1, 2; 1, 2/1, 2; 1, 2; 1, 2, 3 etc. But that is all. . . .

I should add that *The Firebird* has been a mainstay in my life as a conductor. My conducting debut occurred with it (the complete ballet) in 1915, at a Red Cross benefit in Paris, and since then I have performed it nearly a thousand times, though ten thousand would not erase the memory of the terror I suffered that first time. And, oh yes, to complete the picture, I was once addressed by a man in an American railway dining car, and quite seriously, as "Mr. Fireberg." [Igor Stravinsky and Robert Craft, *Expositions and Developments*, pp. 145–52.]

The Firebird is readily identified with trends in nineteenth-century Russian music. Stravinsky himself acknowledged the ties: "The two strains of Rimsky(-Korsakov) and Tchaikovsky appear in *The Firebird* in about equal measure. The Tchaikovsky element is more 'operatic' and more 'vocal'. . . . The Rimsky strain is more pronounced in harmony and orchestral color."[1] Indeed, perhaps as a reflection of these ties, disaffection set in at the time of its conception: "I was more proud of some of the orchestration than of the music," Stravinsky recalled (see quotation above). "I was criticizing it even when I was composing it."

The specifics of this identification may be all too apparent or already too familiar to require much attention. But consider, for a moment, the orchestra. "Wastefully large" wrote Stravinsky in 1962—it was, of course, trimmed to more modest proportions in 1919 concert suite and the 1945 "ballet suite." (Reference here and in the analysis is to the 1919 concert suite. The concert suite is better known, and its score more accessible than that of the original ballet or the later "ballet suite." And the six selections it contains—Introduction, "L'Oiseau de feu et sa danse," "Khorovod," "Danse infernale" (Kastchei section), "Berceuse," Finale—suffice for our purposes.) More to the point, the instrumentation—along with the "effects" of which Stravinsky was so proud at the time—is geared to the kind of coloristic virtuosity that identifies closely with the music of the Russian "Five," Rimsky-Korsakov, Balakirev, Borodin, Moussorgsky, and Cesar Cui. Then, too, a preoccupation with "accompaniment" manifests itself, with figures and quasi-scale patterns often of a rather perfunctory nature. Stravinsky was to rid himself of this instrumental "fill" or deadweight in *Petroushka* (1911), replacing it with the dry, open, crisp, soloistic approach which his invention suddenly spawned, and which would subsequently become the trademark of his own orchestral or instrumental "touch."

Moreover, the material, its "chromaticism" on the one hand and its harmonization of borrowed diatonic Russian folksongs on the other, is typical of the schizoid approach encountered in the operas and symphonic poems of Stravinsky's predecessor and teacher, Rimsky-Korsakov.[2] Thus, on the diatonic-folksong side of this approach, "harmony"—or "harmonic progression"—is "straight." The diatonic folk melodies of *The Firebird*'s "Khorovod" are arranged in a manner consistent not only with Rimsky-Korsakov and his "school" but with the nineteenth century generally. They implicate the familiar interval ordering of the major scale, and as such adhere to a functionality that is unambiguously tonal (as codified in nearly every textbook on the subject of Western harmonic practice). Consequently, the diatonicism of the "Khorovod"—and that, to an extent, of the "Berceuse" as well—is a tonally functional major-scale diatonicism which is to be distinguished from the diatonic—or partially diatonic—passages of Stravinsky's ensuing "Russian"-period works. In *Petroushka* (1911), *Le Sacre* (1913), *Renard* (1916), and *Les Noces* (1917), the articulation implicates interval orderings (scales) for the diatonic collection other than that defined by this major-scale ordering, and tonally functional relations fail to materialize. But a tonally functional major-scale diatonicism has to be distinguished, as well, from the major-scale settings of Stravinsky's neoclassical ventures, for it unfolds without the contamination, the "wrong notes," or "impurities" that mark neoclassicism, Stravinsky's later "discovery" and reinterpretation of Baroque, Classical, and Romantic idiosyncrasy.

All these factors naturally point to the customary role of tradition in Music History. *The Firebird* is written *within* a living—though, in retrospect, dying—tradition. Its reference is the immediate past, its models the works of Stravinsky's immediate predecessors. And the implications of this immediacy are as we have suggested: *The Firebird* relates more readily to established trends in Russian music of the nineteenth century than it does to Stravinsky's "Russian"-period works from *Petroushka* (1911) to the *Symphonies of Wind Instruments* (1920)—or to his neoclassicism from *Pulcinella* (1920) to *Agon* (1953–57), that later unearthing of the (more) remote past.[3]

And so *The Firebird* may seem profoundly uncharacteristic, profoundly out of step with the bulk of Stravinsky's oeuvre. That felt continuity of an immediately inherited tradition, that adherence to what was at the time a universally shared language—the language of tonality and the major scale (in the "Khorovod," especially)—separates it from all subsequent work both "Russian" and neoclassical, giving it, in effect, a nineteenth century flavor that is true, authentic, "straight"—not tampered with, "impure," or *Stravinskian*, as is, for example, *Le Baiser de la fée* (1928), where Tchaikovsky's melodies are reinterpreted in accord with the developed manners of the neoclassicist. So, too, a touch of irony envelops the public exposure accorded this music. Enormous popularity has been the response to a work in which the preoccupations that were to engage Stravinsky for long stretches of time, preoccupations in one way or another associated with his familiar "Russian," neoclassical, and serial orientation categories, are either absent or overshadowed by the habits of this older and soon-to-be-abandoned nineteenth century musical tradition. (Stravinsky would later refer to *The Firebird*, contemptuously, as "that audience lollipop.") Scarcely anyone familiar with these general orientations and the breadth of his yield, so to speak, would be inclined to fancy *The Firebird* as "representative."

Indeed, before pausing to rebut this line of thought—the impertinence, always, of confronting a work of art solely as a piece of History, an artifact—we might pursue it scanning Stravinsky's material where it embodies essentials of this immediate but soon-to-be-discarded heritage. And, as a conspicuous precedent for *The Firebird*, we might again cite the schizoid arrangement of Rimsky-Korsakov's operas and symphonic poems, the musical distinction drawn there between the magical scenes and characters and the real or natural ones by complementing the former with music that was "chromatic" or instrumentally "decorative," and the latter with Russian folksongs (borrowed or pseudo) that were diatonic and set rather simply in comparison.

The "chromaticism" Rimsky favored was of a type quite different from that of, say, Richard Wagner. It consisted of figures and patterns designed to impart an exotic or oriental flavor; seldom did it spring from the kind of complexity in triadic progression we have come to associate with the author of *Tristan und Isolde*. Indeed, this "chromatic" figuration was occasionally derived from—or may occasionally appear to implicate— scales neither tonal nor modal but symmetrical, with interval orderings delineating a partitioning of the octave that is symmetrical or "equal" rather than asymmetrical like the scales available to the diatonic pitch collection. For example: the *whole-tone scale*, a scale consisting of six distinct pitch classes instead of the familiar seven of the diatonic scales, these pitch elements forming an interval ordering of successive whole steps (whole tones), steps defined by the interval of 2. Or, presently to be discussed, the *octatonic scale*, a scale consisting of eight distinct pitch classes forming an interval ordering of alternating half and whole steps, steps defined by alternating intervals of 1 and 2 (or 2 and 1).[4] In "chromatic" music of this type, heard logic naturally became a matter not of major-scale tonal functionality but of the symmetrical or circular "pull" exerted by the figuration. And the mechanical element, always to be expected from symmetry of this kind, was magnified in Rimsky's case—at least in this observer's estimate—by a rather routine or unimaginative approach. Rimsky then interlaced this "chromatic" figuration with diatonic Russian folksongs arranged in as tonally functional a manner as their contours would permit. (As authentic folksongs, these melodies were neither tonal nor rhythmically "square," but became so—to a degree—in the westernized versions compiled and arranged by Tchaikovsky, Balakirev, Rimsky-Korsakov, Liadov, and others.)

Stravinsky adopted this formula. In the 1919 concert suite, the "chromatic" patterns of the Introduction, of "L'Oiseau de feu et sa danse" at No. 7 and the "Danse infernale" (Kastchei section) are not only similar to Rimsky's but were also designed to complement the magical element, the Firebird and King Kastchei; the borrowed diatonic folksongs of the "Khorovod" and Finale relate to the real or sentimental implications of the plot. Into this scheme, however, Stravinsky introduced a technique of his own. From the opening six-note ostinato pattern of the Introduction—the first music to be composed, according to his recollection quoted above—he fashioned nearly all the magical or "chromatic" music of the ballet, with the result that *The Firebird*—or its "chromatic" component—may be heard and understood as a kind of "basic-cell" composition. Indeed, through this "basic-cell" process of thematic transformation—a process wherein the encompassing tritone interval of the Introduction's ostinato pattern is retained as the interval or relation of enclosure while the number, order, or priority of the pitches and intervals contained within it is varied—the Introduction's ostinato pattern, or one of its several derivatives, appears in all sections of the 1919 concert suite.

(A derivative of the ostinato surfaces in the "Khorovod" at No. 14 and in the Finale at Nos. 16 and 20, although these sections are devoted primarily to the diatonic side of the schizoid arrangement.)

And so we might begin our analysis of *The Firebird* by identifying the ostinato pattern of the Introduction as the Principal Theme or "basic cell" for the "chromatic" figuration, and by designating all subsequent modifications or transformations *derivatives*. (We proceed, then, according to Stravinsky's testimony: the "chromatic" figuration was *derived* from the first six measures, the first music to be composed.) There are two of these derivatives, each consisting of four pitch elements, which occur with such persistence that we single them out for special attention in Examples 1, 2, 2a, and 2b.

The first of these, Derivative I in Example 1 (see brackets), need not detain us here, however. It consists of the first two pitch elements of the ostinato pattern (paired as a "major third," the interval of 4, defined by four semitones) and its fourth and fifth elements (paired as a "minor third," the interval of 3, defined by three semitones), these two intervals jointly spanning the interval of 6, the tritone. Derivative I figures prominently in the Introduction, parts of which will presently be subject to analysis.

The second derivative, Derivative II in Example 2 (see brackets), is the more pervasive of the two, and may have been intended as a leitmotiv for the Firebird. It consists of the first four pitch elements of the ostinato pattern; these elements again span the interval of 6, the tritone, their original order being permuted in subsequent appearances by means of inversion, retrogression, and retrograde inversion. In the 1919 concert suite, it appears as part of the Introduction's ostinato pattern (its first four pitch elements), in "L'Oiseau de feu et sa danse" at No. 7, in the "Danse infernale" (Kastchei section) at No. 5 (Example 2a), throughout the "Berceuse," and in the Finale at Nos. 16 and 20. In Example 2a from the Kastchei section, this second derivative is followed in quick succession by its inversion at the interval of 6, the tritone, so that the oscillation or back-and-forth movement first defined by the ostinato in the Introduction is retained as an in-

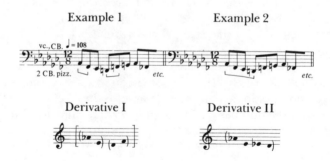

Example 1   Example 2

Derivative I   Derivative II

Example 2a: "Danse infernale"

Example 2b: "Supplication"

variant factor in the transformation process. Indeed, for the listener, this oscillating motion at the tritone may well constitute the most valuable clue in apprehending all derived material. Yet, so extensive are the changes from one section to the next in harmonic, rhythmic, and instrumental lay-out, that even so telling a mark may not always guarantee recognition. Compare the Kastchei passage in Example 2a with "L'Oiseau de feu et sa danse" at No. 7; or, consulting the original ballet score, compare these renditions to the elaborately embellished version of the second derivative in the "Supplication" scene (Example 2b). Such changes radically alter the "musical sense" of the "basic cell," the ostinato and its several derivatives. And the invention they entail is, needless to say, scarcely appreciated by wrenching the contours of these derivatives from their contexts and tak-ing note merely of the slight deviations in interval content and/or order. Methods of thematic transformation (or of the "basic-cell" process) can be appreciated only with an ear to the varying total (or more global) situations, which, to take but one example, enable Derivative II to function almost ton-ally in one setting (the "Berceuse"), and nontonally, by way of symmetrical patterning, in another ("L'Oiseau de feu et sa danse" at No. 7).

But a thorough investigation of these matters lies beyond the scope of this inquiry. However conspicuous the weight of the nineteenth century, we are committed to the study of those peculiarities which, in one way or another, were to remain characteristic of Stravinsky's music. This means that we will be operating somewhat selectively here at the outset—although not without regard for the varying "total situations." Happily, the context of the Introduction offers a convenient set of circumstances: "chromatic" figuration with a frame of reference which, while reminiscent of Rimsky's "chromaticism," was to remain characteristic of Stravinsky for years to come.

But we return, briefly, to correct possible distortions of an overzealously applied historicism. For it is only in retrospect, only in view of the abrupt departures from the tonal tradition that composers like Schoenberg, Webern, Bartok, and Stravinsky were to initiate early in the twentieth century, that *The Firebird* is lightly dismissed as a nineteenth-century cliché. Despite its ties, the music is no more *like* Rimsky (or Tchaikovsky) than, say, Beethoven's string quartets are *like* Haydn's. (Hence the historically misleading implications of Stravinsky's explanation of *The Firebird*'s immediate success, which he attributes to its having been au courant or "of the styles of its day," as if this were a circumstance inherently disadvantageous or not in accord with precedence in Western music generally; as if an "explosion" like *Le Sacre* were normal; or as if, too, historical reckoning, any more than analytic-theoretical reckoning, could effectively cope with the vicissitudes of public taste and appeal.) [5]

Indeed, evidence suggests that *The Firebird*, far from having labored as an underprivileged cliché, a bundle of conventions, was in its day deemed a novel, highly personal endeavor. In a revealing document, Tamara Karsavina, who first danced the role of the Firebird, has recalled how new and different this music was at the time of its debut (especially its rhythmic aspect) and how difficult the process of assimilation, a process concluded only after many hours of private rehearsals with Stravinsky patiently at the piano.[6] Then there is S. L. Grigoriev, *régisseur* of the Russian Ballet, who offers the following account of those weekly encounters at Serge Diaghilev's apartment during the winter of 1909–10 in St. Petersburg:

> From now on Stravinsky began to be present at our committee meetings, and so I met him for the first time. He was rather short, with prominent features and a very serious expression. He took active part in the discussions, especially those on the production of *L'Oiseau de Feu*. His composition of the score went ahead rapidly and he sometimes played passages over to us. We all listened attentively but, apart from Diaghilev, expressed no opinion. Nouvel [Valentine Nouvel, an official of the Imperial Court and an associate of Diaghilev's] did not share Diaghilev's taste for Stravinsky's music, and as for the General [General Bezobrazov, a patron of the arts], he declared quite frankly that he disliked it and that it was unsuitable for dancing. Diaghilev had certainly been right when he warned us that we should find Stravinsky's music new and unusual.[7]

About the rehearsals, Grigoriev recalled the following:

> Fokine began rehearsals with *L'Oiseau de Feu*, since it was clearly the most difficult of the various works; and Stravinsky was then first introduced to the

company. Fokine started on a passage near the middle of the score: the great ensemble called by Stravinsky "The Unholy Revels" [Kastchei section]. From the moment they heard the first bars the company were all too obviously dismayed at the absence of melody in the music and its unlikeness to what they were used to dancing to at the Mariinsky. Some of them indeed declared that it did not sound like music at all. Stravinsky was usually present to indicate the tempo and rhythms. Now and again he would play over passages himself and, according to some of the dancers, "demolish the piano." He was particularly exacting about the rhythms and used to hammer them out with considerable violence, humming loudly and scarcely caring whether he struck the right notes. It was invigorating to watch such a display of temperament, which certainly inspired Fokine in his work. Also the extraordinary music led Fokine to the invention of original steps, which the dancers could not but enjoy and be amused at. This ensemble accordingly progressed apace and was soon finished. Other passages in the first part of the ballet, such as the Lullaby ["Berceuse"] and the dance of the Twelve Princesses, were more melodious and did not present the same difficulties.[8]

And still later, with the orchestra in Paris, the following:

After the production of *Giselle* all that remained for us was to show our most important and difficult work, *L'Oiseau de Feu*. The company rehearsed intensively and did their utmost to "dance themselves into" the unfamiliar choreography, all of us being eager to exhibit the ballet to the best advantage. Diaghilev invited the well-known Parisian conductor Gabriel Pierné to take charge of the orchestra. Stravinsky attended the orchestra rehearsals and endeavoured to explain the music; but energetically though the musicians attacked it, they found it no less bewildering than did the dancers.[9]

If these artists are not to be trusted as the most musically literate or progressive-minded of the day, there is Stravinsky's own account of Ravel's reaction quoted earlier. Ravel thought it avant-garde!

Of course, it is understandable that by 1962 Stravinsky, far removed in years and experience, found himself unable to appreciate any of this. He would concede that the stretch of 7/4 bars in the Finale at No. 17 was the first instance of "metrical irregularity" in his music. And, yes, the score was in many ways a "fecund" one. When pressed for details (by Robert Craft), he offered the following:

If an interesting construction exists in *The Firebird*, it will be found in the treatment of intervals, for example in the major and minor thirds in the *Berceuse*, in the Introduction, and in the Kastchei music.[10]

"Interesting" is a poor substitute for genuine delight. But we shall presently be witnessing in the Introduction these "major and minor thirds" (the two intervals of Derivative I) confined to a symmetrically cohesive collection of eight distinct pitch classes, the octatonic pitch collection, a confinement that may well have prompted Stravinsky's abiding "interest" in "the treatment of intervals." For this is a collection of reference that for some fifty years remained so fundamentally a part of his musical thought that it has claims to being at the root of much that has persistently been dubbed "characteristic," "typical," or "distinctive."

INTRODUCTION

These referential implications should be apparent from a glance at the analysis of the Introduction in Example 3. Here, the material at mm. 1–10 and 18–20 is first compressed into a sequence of "events." Then, just below, these "events" are in turn stripped of their rhythmic identity, a stripping which allows the articulative groupings to stand in semi-isolation and hence to become more readily apparent.[11] Finally, below the stripping, the articulative groupings yield, through a totaling of the pitch-class content, the octatonic reference collection indicated.

Thus, as the first in this sequence of "events," the A♭–E–E♭–D–F–G ostinato pattern is forwarded, and the embedded "major and minor

Example 3: Introduction

thirds," the intervals of 4 and 3 of Derivative I in terms of (E A♭) (D F), are again bracketed. (Note that A♭ and D, which define the A♭-D (0–6) tritone relation, are elements of enclosure with respect to the ostinato and its embedded (E A♭) (D F) Derivative I, and are metrically accented as well.)[12] Then, in the trombones at mm. 5-7, Derivative I is disengaged and transposed "down" into the complementary D–A♭ tritone relation in terms of (B♭ D) (A♭ B), this transposition being superimposed over the ostinato. The "major and minor thirds" of Derivative I are paired vertically at this point, a pairing that will remain characteristic of these intervals throughout *The Firebird*—except, of course, for their linear A♭–E–D–F delineation within the ostinato itself. The disengaged (B♭ D) (A♭ B) derivative at mm. 5–7 appears in reverse order on the first and third beats (retrograde at A♭, the (A♭ B) "minor third" preceding the (B♭ D) "major third"). Thus, original interval order and retrograde delineations crisscross each other between the ostinato pattern and the disengaged derivative. But the back-and-forth oscillation of the figuration, together with the vertical pairing of the "major and minor thirds," eventually obscures the distinction between original order (as stipulated by the ostinato) and retrogression, the distinction becoming exclusively metric. Hence, to avoid confusion we dispense with the retrograde designation, referring to the disengaged derivative at mm. 5–7 merely as a transposition of the original order, concerning ourselves henceforth merely with original interval order and inversion.

The unified or compound configuration at mm. 5–7 may be summarized as follows: the octave at A♭ is halved at the interval of 6, the tritone (at D), each half or complement of this two-part symmetrical (0,6) tritone partitioning of the octave delineating Derivative I at A♭ and at D in terms of (E A♭) (D F) and (B♭ D) (A♭ B). Furthermore, the compound configuration, the superimposition of the disengaged derivative over the ostinato pattern in the manner described, results in the octave reinforcement and metric accentuation of A♭ and D, these pitch elements assuming a kind of priority. Indeed, the compound configuration, the A♭–D–A♭ tritone orbit at mm. 5–7, acquires the character of a "home base" to which the music returns in recapitulation at m. 9 and again at m. 18.

Then, in the clarinets and bassoons at mm. 7–9, the figuration, assuming a new rhythmic guise, entails further transpositions of Derivative I. But within the new B♭–E–B♭ tritone orbit, these transpositions are *inversions* of the original interval order. And, significantly, these inversions, while momentarily shifting the tritone orbit from A♭–D–A♭ to B♭–E–B♭, remain confined to the initial octatonic collection (A♭ G F E D C♯ B B♭ (A♭)). (Only inversions at B♭ and E ensure this confinement; literal transpositions at B♭ and E would have transgressed the collection.) Moreover, these inversions effectively exhaust the (A♭ G F E D C♯ B B♭ (A♭)) collection, its C♯ having been absent at mm. 1–7. Accordingly, not only are the ostinato and Derivative I referentially octatonic with respect to fixed local identity in pitch and/or interval content but also transpositions and transformations at mm. 1–10 and 18–20 are pursued with unmistakable reference to the collection. And so we conclude that this first music to be composed in the Introduction is *referentially octatonic*; that the opening ostinato and its disengaged derivative, a design from which nearly all the ensuing "chromatic" figuration of *The Firebird* is derived, was conceived within an octatonic framework.

In Example 4 the various transpositions and transformations of Derivative I—four in all—are reassembled, these groupings again yielding the octatonic reference collection indicated. And in Example 5 a structural-level format is applied, the idea here being to reconstruct the Introduction at mm. 1–10 and 18–20 in such a way that the levels express, in terms of the groupings or partitionings of the collection forwarded, kinds of determinacies for the material (proceeding, generally, from a least determinate stage—that, say, of the pitch-class priority exercised by A♭ and D here—to a most determinate stage—that, say, of the articulative Derivative I here), these groupings or partitionings once again yielding, through

Example 4

Example 5

a totaling of the pitch-class content, the (A♭ G F E D C♯ B B♭ (A♭)) collection.[13] ("Level 1" is omitted since it will in future formats signal (single) pitch-class priority. The structural-level approach in analysis—or its particular application to Stravinsky's music in this inquiry—will be discussed in greater detail in chapter 2).

All of this is not to suggest, of course, that exclusive rights are exercised by the octatonic collection over the contextual arrangements subsequently assumed by the ostinato's assortment of derivatives, or that when *The Firebird* is viewed in its entirety the collection is not but one of several references with respect to which this assortment finds a suitable bearing. Indeed, in the Introduction at mm. 10–12, confinement to the collection is terminated by a rising sequence of "major and minor thirds"— Derivative I in sequence. (See Example 6.) But the culminating (A♯/C♯–C/ E) (F♯/A♯–E/G) tremolo in the flutes and clarinets at m. 12 is a transposition of the configuration at mm. 5–7, accountable to a different octatonic collection. And following this culminating tremolo, a third octatonic collection of distinguishable pitch content may be inferred over the barlines at mm. 13–14 and 20–21. And this third collection is implicated not only by Derivative I in terms of (B D) (A♭ C) and (A♭ C) (F♯ A), but by succes-

Example 6: Introduction

sions of (0 4 7 10) "dominant-seventh" complexes. And these "dominant sevenths" at Ab, D, and F constitute—obviously—a different kind of articulative partitioning than that defined by Derivative I. Indeed, as indicated in Examples 6 and 7, these "dominant sevenths" are available to the (Ab Gb F Eb D C B A (Ab)) reference collection at Ab, F, D, and B. Hence, quite apart from Derivative I, the octatonic collection may be partitioned by (0 3 7/0 4 7) "minor" and "major" triads and (0 4 7 10) "dominant sevenths" a "minor third" apart, triadic complexes related by the interval of 3. (Or, to rephrase this, (0 3 7/0 4 7/0 4 7 10) triadic complexes related by the interval of 3 are referentially octatonic.)

Now then. The "events" recorded in Examples 3 and 6 unfold in an orderly fashion. And in the future, with the reader better acquainted with the methods of this inquiry, some of this verbal reporting can doubtless be eliminated. Still, we ought not to dismiss the preceding as an enumeration of "facts," as information processed in some impersonal, absent-eared fashion from the score, free or detached from auditory guidance or even from peripheral speculation as to what might at the time (*in the act*, so to speak) have constituted immediate, conscious concerns. Despite the "descriptive" bent here with its appearance of "objectivity" (so easily misunderstood), the account is not without its interpretative framework, a perspective through which, it contends, the music has been heard and understood. And it has been determined that pitch organization, at a more-or-less "foreground" surface-articulative level, involves the identity of the ostinato pattern and its embedded Derivative I, as well as transpositions and transformations of the latter, and that logic and/or coherence (at a more-or-less "foreground" surface-articulative level) lie within the perception of these identities and operations, which are conditioned referentially by their confinement to a select, symmetrically defined collection of eight distinct pitch classes, the *octatonic pitch collection*.

This conception tallies with earlier remarks regarding the "chromatic" invention of Rimsky's scores, in which certain melodic patterns, yielding a mechanical sort of logic founded on a symmetrical partitioning of the octave (of which, referentially, the octatonic collection was but one of several sources), circumvented tonal procedure. The Introduction figures as an example of this kind of musical behavior.

Still, the concept of major-scale tonality may still prove useful, if only as

Example 7

a foil.[14] Introducing its specter may yield insights to illuminate our substitution here of a symmetrically conditioned partitioning of the octatonic collection (by Derivative I) for the tonal functionality associated with the C-scale (or major-scale) ordering of the diatonic collection.[15]

Consider "harmonic progression." "Harmony," conceived as a set of (0 3 7/0 4 7) triads progressing according to functions derived from the diatonic C-scale, has no relevance here. In perception and analytical review, simultaneity consists, quite simply, of a verticalization of the "major and minor thirds" which comprise the articulative Derivative I. And movement, a sense of motion beyond oscillation, is a matter of transposing or transforming (by inversion) the derivative in a way consistent with its structure and referential implications, and then of returning to a kind of A♭–D–A♭ (0–6–0) "home base." True, exceptions may be found over the barlines at mm. 13–14 and 20–21. And these successions of (0 4 7 10) "dominant-seventh" complexes, while accountable to the single octatonic collection indicated (see Examples 6 and 7), do prompt a sense of over-the-barline progress, relieving the listener momentarily of that back-and-forth oscillation, a paralysis immobilizing all factors of musical enterprise. Indeed, as suggested already, these successions constitute a different kind of partitioning of the octatonic collection than that defined by Derivative I. And since this (0 4 7 10) "dominant-seventh" partitioning is destined to figure prominently in Stravinsky's octatonic perspective, it is one to which we shall be turning in chapter 2 for further study. (In chapter 11 we shall again return to these over-the-barline successions of (0 4 7 10) "dominant sevenths" to examine their C-scale tonally functional implications, specifically, their status in tonally functional C-scale literature as irregular resolutions of the dominant-seventh chord.)

But between these points the material scarcely lends itself to traditional (tonally inspired) modes of description. Even the (0,6) tritone-related (0 4 7) "major" triads outlined by the ostinato and its superimposed derivative in the configuration at mm. 5–7—(0 4 7) "major" triads at E and B♭ in terms of (E G♯ B) and (B♭ D F)—are not tonally motivated. Instead of progressing they merely oscillate, as they do in the transposition of this configuration, the tremolo at m. 12. Indeed, at mm. 5–7 these (0 4 7) triadic outlines are obscured by the linear identity of the ostinato and its derivative, which more readily attract the attention of the listener at the "foreground" surface-articulative level of perception. This attraction is consistent with the fact that, at mm. 1–7, it is not really E and B♭—the roots of the (0 4 7) "major" triads—but A♭ and D which, as pitch elements of metric accentuation and fragmental enclosure vis-à-vis the ostinato and Derivative I, assume a degree of pitch-class priority.[16] This non-correlation between the elements of priority (A♭ and D) and the roots of the (0 4 7) triadic outlines (E and B♭) naturally accounts for the distinction in the articulative partitioning of the octatonic collection (noted in the analysis) between the configuration at mm. 5–7 and the (0 4 7 10) "dominant-seventh" complexes at mm. 13–14 and 20–21. These complexes are exposed because of the suspension of oscillation, the over-the-barline succession (or progress) momentarily defined.

The tritone relation which encompasses these articulative identities imparts none of the urgency or tendency toward "resolution" one might ordinarily expect were its surroundings tonal. The configuration first encountered at mm. 5–7 and then transposed at m. 12 is curiously frictionless. The two-part (0,6) tritone, symmetrical (or numerically equal) partitioning of the octave at A♭ by D allows each of the complementary intervals, A♭–D and D–A♭ (each encompassing Derivative I), to "oppose" each other as "equals," to balance each other out, as it were, by virtue of their similitude or "equality." The same holds for the individual pitch classes A♭ and D. A♭, to which "a kind of priority" has been assigned, is not a "tonic." Nowhere is its priority (or centricity) defined by C-scale tonally functional means. Thus, the E♭ in the ostinato pattern—the hypothetical "dominant" here—serves merely as a (metrically "weak") passing tone lying outside the reference collection between E and D; these two pitch elements are ultimately of greater structural weight because of their inclusion in the embedded and soon-to-be-disengaged derivative. A♭ is always identified with—or is always qualified by—the D, deriving its priority from octave reinforcement, metric accentuation, delineation of enclosure, and as a point of departure and return—by means other than tonally functional ones. Similarly, the D is in no way active as, say, a traditional (tonal) V-of-V tendency tone vis-à-vis the A♭, but is felt, in its coexistence with the A♭, as exerting an independence or "equality" similar to that expressed by the complementary tritone intervals, A♭–D and D–A♭. Thus, while A♭ may seem to outweigh the D—owing, perhaps, to precedence or to its positioning on the first and third beats of the measures in question—it has seemed advisable, as a more reliable account or reckoning of affairs, to acknowledge the exhibition of this symmetrically defined "equality" on the part of these (0,6) tritone-related elements: pitch number 0 encompasses the assertion of priority on the part of A♭, but pitch numbers 0 and 6, the A♭ and D, are interchangeable, given the "equality" or "independence" exhibited.

And so the A♭-minor key signature becomes irrelevant. Indeed, the signature is dropped at m. 18 with the return of the mm. 5–7 configuration and its A♭–D–A♭ tritone orbit.[17] As here interpreted, this music has nothing to do with the "key of A♭ minor," that is, with the interval orderings stipulated for the diatonic collection by the A or C-scales on A♭ (these orderings or scales serving in a referential capacity), or with any of the tonally functional behavior associated with the referential ordering of the C-scale (on A♭ here). Consequently, some further hearing and under-standing rests with an examination of the structure of the octatonic col-lection (or scale), to which we shall be addressing ourselves in chapter 2.

"DANSE INFERNALE"

Am I too critical? Does *The Firebird* contain more real musical invention than I am able (or willing) to see? I would this were the case. It was in some respects a fecund score for my own development in the next four years, but the few scraps of counterpoint to be found in it—in the Kastchei scene, for example—are derived from chord tones, and this is not real counterpoint.

In the "Danse infernale" or Kastchei section (whose syncopated rhythmic scheme proved so hazardous to musicians in 1910), the material at Nos. 0–3 and 9–11 is partially octatonic, although the interference with the collection—a question of one or two pitch elements in the Kastchei theme—is slight. There is, of course, at the outset of this section little to recommend an inference of the octatonic scale: the Kastchei theme's (0 3 6 9) diminished-seventh outline in terms of A–C–E♭–F♯ is virtually unac-companied. (See Example 8a.) Indeed, there is insufficient evidence at Nos. 0–2 to determine which of the three different octatonic collections might pertain, since the theme's A–C–E♭–F♯ diminished-seventh outline is applicable to two of them (as, indeed, are each of the three (0 3 6 9) diminished-seventh chords).[18]

However, with the transposition of the Kastchei theme's B–C–A–C–E–E♭ outline to E♭–E–C–E–G–F♯ at No. 2 (with a slight change in interval content favoring octatonic inference), confinement to the (A B♭ C D♭ E♭ E F♯ G (A)) collection becomes unmistakable. (Only the B at Nos. 0–2 lies outside the collection.) Moreover, this referential com-mitment is later underscored by upsweeping B♭–C–E–F♯ arpeggios in the flutes, bassoons, piano, and harp at No. 4 + 3. And so our analytic-theoretical conclusions here at Nos. 0–3 in the Kastchei section, as re-corded in Example 8a, are similar to those proposed for the Introduction: the Kastchei theme—doubtless Stravinsky's initial material in this section (and perhaps the most widely known of all the work's themes, certainly the most popular)—is *referentially octatonic*; it is conceived within an octa-tonic framework, with transpositions and transformations pursued with unmistakable reference to the collection.

Still, we are not unmindful of the diatonic A-scale-on-A (or possibly C-scale-on-C) alternative to this octatonic determination, according to which the transposition of the Kastchei theme at No. 2 would signal a transposi-tion from an (A C E) triadic outline at Nos. 0–2 to a (C E G) outline at No. 2, while E♭ and F♯, in lieu of their referential commitment to the (A B♭ C

Example 8a: "Danse infernale"

Db Eb E F♯ G (A)) octatonic collection (to which, of course, the (A C E) and (C E G) triads are also accountable), would figure as chromatic tendency tones or "melodic leading tones" to the fifth degree of the (A C E) triad, the E, and to the third and fifth degrees of the (C E G) triad, the E and the G. (See the "diatonic side" to our analysis in Example 8a, occupying the right-hand side of the dotted line.) Then, too, the theme's A–C–Eb–F♯ diminished-seventh outline could be construed as the chord of the "raised supertonic" in relation to this diatonic A-scale-on-A (or possibly C-scale-on-C) alternative, a verticalization, properly speaking, of these Eb and F♯ chromatic tendency tones. Significantly, too, interactions of this type between a partitioning of the octatonic collection and certain chromatic inflections of tonal C-scale literature figure prominently in many of Stravinsky's neoclassical works. The only problem here, however, is that

Eb and F# are not really operative as classically conceived chromatic tendency tones, and that the A–C–Eb–F# diminished-seventh outline, of which Eb and F# are vertically (or harmonically) a part, scarcely behaves in the manner of a "raised supertonic"—or, alternatively, in the manner of a V-of-V diminished-seventh chord. Instead of "tending" (chromatically) to E and G (on which they become chromatically dependent), Eb and F# assert themselves rather more forcefully as independent elements (or, articulatively, as members of the Kastchei theme's A–C–Eb–F# diminished-seventh outline), an independence warranting accountability at the collectional level, an accreditation which neither the A-scale on A nor the C-scale on C can properly confer. And so we opt instead for a hearing and understanding primarily in terms of the (A Bb C Db Eb E F# G (A)) octatonic collection or in terms of some form of *interpenetration* of the octatonic (A Bb C Db Eb E F# G (A)) collection and the diatonic A-scale on A, with the shared (A C E) and (C E G) triads, along with Eb and F#, as points of between-reference intersection. And not only because of prior commitments in this (octatonic) direction, or because of the convenience such a hearing and understanding might render our perspective on Stravinsky's music "considered as a whole," but also because this initial commitment of the Kastchei theme at Nos. 0–3 foreshadows another such commitment at Nos. 9–11.

Thus, further along in the canonic drama that unfolds at Nos. 9–11 (quite possibly "the few scraps of counterpoint" to which Stravinsky refers above), the (0 3 6 9) diminished-seventh outline of the Kastchei theme is again referentially octatonic, principally as a result of the instrumental "fill" introduced as an accompaniment to the thematic statements. But reference at Nos. 9–11 is to the (Ab Bb B C# D E F G (Ab)) octatonic collection, the collection of the Introduction at mm. 1–10, rather than to the (A Bb C Db Eb E F# G (A)) collection of the Kastchei theme at Nos. 0–3. The directions for inference, illustrated in Example 8b, run as follows:

Level 2: The passage at Nos. 9–11 comprises two canonic initiatives. The first begins at one measure before No. 9 with the Kastchei theme on Bb (with Ab–B–D–F diminished-seventh emphasis), and the second at one measure before No. 10 with the theme on E (with D–F–Ab–B emphasis)— a transposition at the interval of 6, the tritone. But it is not Bb and E but rather Ab and D which, as partitioning elements of priority, articulate this transposition and (0,6) tritone partitioning at a "background" level by virtue of the following instrumental-"fill" conditions: (1) the Ab–D dyad punctuated throughout in the bassoons, oboes, and violas; (2) the octatonic scale passages in the violins accentuating Ab at No. 9 and D at No. 10 (passages in which, incidentally, there occurs not a single transgression of the octatonic reference collection); (3) the harp simultaneities beginning

Example 8b: "Danse infernale"

two measures after No. 10. The passage is indeterminate with respect to (single) pitch-class priority, there being insufficient evidence for a ruling in favor of either the A♭ or D. Hence the setting realizes the (numerical) equality noted earlier with respect to (0,6) tritone partitioning. The selection of A♭ as pitch number 0 merely reflects the arrangement of the Introduction.

Level 3: "Foreground" articulative partitioning is recognized in terms of the Kastchei theme at A♭ and its transposition to D, pitch number 6, at No. 10. At level 4 this articulative grouping, assembled along with the instrumental "fill," yields the reference collection at level 5.

The reference collection is identical to that employed at the opening of the Introduction, as is (0,6) tritone partitioning in terms of A♭ and D. But again, as in the Introduction, partitioning at the surface-articulative level fails to comply with the (0 3 7/0 4 7/0 4 7 10) and (0 2 3 5) articulative partitioning schemes that become, subsequent to *The Firebird*, fundamental to Stravinsky's perspective.

The origin of the octatonic collection remains obscure. But Stravinsky undoubtedly inherited it from his teacher, Rimsky-Korsakov. And while we might credit *The Firebird*'s Introduction and Kastchei section with ideas of greater consequence and with a deployment of the collection already more compelling than any in the brief and scattered passages by Rimsky (for whom, perhaps, the collection was never more than a colorful "device"), Stravinsky's intentions in *The Firebird* are not very different from his predecessor's. He too, as we have indicated, associated octatonic passages with the magical or supernatural element in the dramatic action, interlacing these and other "chromatic" sections with borrowed diatonic melodies harmonized in as tonally functional a manner as their contours would permit, and designed to accommodate the real or human element in the action.

More significantly, the instrumental "fill" or accompaniment figuration for which the (Ab Bb B C♯ D E F G (Ab)) octatonic collection is summoned in the Kastchei section at Nos. 9–11 (Example 8b) bears little resemblance to those future structural arrangements in which the collection would assume a more constructive role. Compare the decorative scales (or "fill") in Example 8b with those in Example 9a from the sixth tableau of Rimsky's opera *Sadko* (1897). The resemblance is remarkable; the collections are even identical. (Stravinsky has assured us that he was intimately familiar with all of Rimsky's music at the time; indeed, in 1935 he would consider *Sadko*—not the opera, but the symphonic poem of 1867, from which portions of the opera were drawn—one of the few works of Rimsky worth salvaging for an all-Russian program.)[19]

Apart from Nos. 9–11 in the Kastchei section, there are in the whole of Stravinsky's music only two instances where the octatonic collection is decorative, introduced ornamentally as a scale passage similar to that in *Sadko*: (1) at No. 60 + 3 in the second tableau of *Les Noces* (1917), where the (E F G Ab Bb B C♯ D (E)) and (A B C D Eb F F♯ G♯ (A)) collections and orderings in Pianos II and III and in the xylophone are superimposed in a climactic flurry terminating the lengthy passage or "block" at Nos. 59–61 (Example 9b); (2) at No. 158 in Act II of *Oedipus Rex* (1927), where Oedipus ends his aria "Nonne monstrum" with a descending F E D C♯ B Bb Ab

Example 9a: *Sadko* (Rimsky-Korsakov)

Example 9b: *Les Noces*

Example 9c: *Oedipus Rex*

G (F) scale passage, in "chromatic" imitation of an earlier diatonic (C-scale-on-F) flourish just prior to No. 157 (Example 9c).

Moreover, the Introduction's Derivative I and the Kastchei section's theme are not the sort of themes, fragments, chords, or motives (articulative groupings or partitionings of the octatonic collection, as we have here preferred to call them) that would, subsequent to *The Firebird*, typify Stravinsky's octatonic settings. True, the (0 4 7) triadic outlines at mm. 5–7 in the Introduction and the (0 4 7 10) "dominant-seventh" complexes which follow at mm. 13–14 and 20–21 prefigure a coming regularity in articulative partitioning.[20] And the practice of *oscillation*—the suspension of steady, tonally functional, C-scale (0 3 7/0 4 7) harmonic progress (a progress which, beyond some radically local reckoning, cannot really obtain under conditions of octatonic confinement)—will remain characteristic. (See, in Example 10a, the tremolo of the "*Petroushka* chord" at No. 51 in the second tableau; in Example 10b, the oscillating (0 4 7 10) "dominant sevenths" related by (0, 3) "minor thirds" at G and B♭ in the *Symphony of Psalms* (1930), first movement; or, in Example 10c, the similarly related (0 4 7 10) "dominant sevenths" at C and E♭ in the *Symphony in Three Movements* (1945). These passages occur within sections or "blocks" in which reference to the collection is unimpaired and hence explicit.) But certain

Example 10a: *Petroushka*

Example 10b: *Symphony of Psalms*

other methods or practices, later to become characteristic, are not yet part of Stravinsky's octatonic imagination. These include registrally fixing articulative groupings of the octatonic collection; assigning varying rhythmic-metric periods to these reiterating, and registrally fixed components; and placing the resulting "blocks" in abrupt juxtaposition with other "blocks" of varied referential implications.

Nor, for that matter, can we speak in *The Firebird* of superimposition, but only of succession (albeit an oscillating succession). For while the disengaged Derivative I at mm.·5–7 in the Introduction is indeed superimposed over the ostinato, the effect is "harmonious" (or frictionless): the triads stemming from this superimposition *succeed* one another (in oscillation). And the practice of superimposition—or its appropriateness as an

Example 10c: *Symphony in Three Movements*

explanatory notion—will always refer to the simultaneous imposition of such groupings, where a quality of "opposition" or of "confrontation" (and hence of internal friction or "dissonance") manifests itself. Thus, in Example 10c, the oscillating (0 4 7 10) "dominant sevenths" at C and E♭ are superimposed over an A–C–A ostinato in the bass; *superimposed* because the A of this ostinato, while accountable to the octatonic collection in question, is not shared by the oscillating (0 4 7 10) complexes above. Indeed, in the Kastchei section's canonic drama at Nos. 9–11 (Example 8b), it is because of the absence of this kind of (0 3 7/0 4 7/0 4 7 10) triadically conceived and, of course, symmetrically defined, referentially octatonic superimposition (an absence which is in turn owing to the (0 3 6 9) diminished-seventh articulative partitioning of the octatonic collection by the Kastchei theme) that this passage assumes its frictionless, non-dissonant quality; or, as Stravinsky puts it, that these "few scraps of counterpoint" are "derived from chord tones," and hence define no "real counterpoint"—or no real Stravinskian "dissonance."

These same general observations pertain to Stravinsky's works preceding *The Firebird*. While the octatonic collection figures prominently in the *Scherzo fantastique* (1908) and *Fireworks* (1908), its deployment, although often (0 3 7/0 4 7/0 4 7 10) triadic in conception, similarly lacks practices or methods of procedure associated with his post-*Firebird* music.[21]

Consequently, while a referential commitment to the octatonic pitch collection seems unmistakable in *The Firebird*'s Introduction and Kastchei section, it will not be until *Petroushka*—or perhaps even *Le Sacre*—that we can begin to witness a potential that Stravinsky was rather more consistently to exploit, as well as some of the practices or general methods of procedure (e.g., superimposition, abrupt "block" juxtaposition) that relate to this potential.

"DANSE INFERNALE" AND FINALE:
RHYTHMIC-METRIC IMPLICATIONS

Rhythmically, too, the Finale might be cited as the first appearance in my music of metrical irregularity—the 7/4 bars subdivided into 1,2,3; 1,2; 1,2/1,2; 1,2; 1,2,3 etc. But that is all.

Nor, for that matter, can we detect in the rhythmic-metric patterns of the "Danse infernale" (Kastchei section) much that is typical or characteristic of the Stravinsky to come. Observers have pointed to the "compulsive," "incisive," "explosive," "hypnotic," "demonic" character of the Kastchei theme's syncopation, and to its incessant, hammerlike repetition. The percussive effect here, along with the repetition, is no doubt idiomatic. Indeed, the dry, crisp, percussive character of Stravinsky's articulation—always intricately linked to harmonic, melodic, formal, and instrumental procedures—may still overwhelm in the Kastchei section, as it did in 1910, continuing to represent what is most immediately striking in Stravinsky's rhythmic-metric patterns. (We are reminded of S. L. Grigoriev's account, cited earlier, of the first *Firebird* rehearsals in St. Petersburg. Endeavoring to indicate the proper "tempo and rhythms," Stravinsky would "hammer" these out "with considerable violence, humming loudly and scarcely caring whether he struck the right notes." He was observed by some of the dancers to "demolish the piano" in the process.) Moreover, this hammerlike action is reinforced instrumentally. From the very start, a staccato (*secco*) accentuation of the Kastchei theme in the fourth horn crisply punctuates, in unison doubling, the legato accentuation of the theme in the bassoons and second horn. (See Example 8a.)[22] The percussive punctuation of the theme's syncopation by the xylophone, piano, and harp at No. 3 (not shown in Example 8a)—indeed, the use of the piano and harp as percussive instruments here—is likewise typical of Stravinsky's orchestral or instrumental "touch."

On the other hand, syncopation, however "incisive" or percussive, is scarcely a novelty. In itself it cannot even be considered typical of or peculiar to Stravinsky's music. (Indeed there are contexts where the very notion of syncopation might legitimately be deemed anachronistic or irrelevant.) More to the point, in its repetition, with all the parts synchronized unvaryingly in vertical (or "harmonic") coincidence, the Kastchei theme has always the same syncopated rhythmic-metric identity. And this, quite definitely, is not at all characteristic of Stravinsky. In other words, the peculiarity of Stravinsky's rhythmic (or metric) invention often derives from

the curious, even fiendish, manner in which the rhythmic-metric implications of his material, once introduced and defined as to upbeat/downbeat
or off-the-beat (syncopated)/on-the-beat identity, are subsequently displaced, contradicted, or reversed. There is none of this Stravinskian
"play," none of this intricacy in the Kastchei theme's repetition. Even the
outward appearance of this "play" is missing: there are no rapidly changing meters, and there are no superimpositions of registrally and instrumentally fixed fragments repeating according to "separate" or "independent" rhythmic-metric periods or cycles. As a result, the repetition of the
Kastchei theme may be characteristically "incisive," "explosive," and
"hypnotic," but it is also uncharacteristically unvarying and monotonous,
at least in a rhythmic-metric sense.

(What *is* definitely characteristic in the Kastchei theme's repetition is its
formal design, consisting of two alternating "blocks"; successive entrances
of the theme are placed in abrupt juxtaposition with—or are punctuated
or spaced by—a single simultaneity, the (A E) "fifth" played tutti. Of many
later passages related in character, see the conclusion of *Les Noces* (1917) at
Nos. 133–35; the punctuating (E G B) "*Psalms* chord" in the first movement of the *Symphony of Psalms* (1930), Example 10b above; the punctuating (F F♯ A) "minor-major third" complex in the introductory passage of
the "Basle" *Concerto in D* (1946), Example 58a in chapter 10; or, in the later
serial works, the Te Deum music at mm. 18–45 in *The Flood* (1962), Example 88 in chapter 14.)

Somewhat similar observations pertain to *The Firebird*'s Finale at Nos.
17–20. (See Example 11.) Stravinsky would later cite this stretch of 7/4
bars as the first instance of "metrical irregularity" in his music. But here
again, "irregular" 7/4 bars are not, comparatively speaking, typical of or
peculiar to Stravinsky's music. And Stravinsky can scarcely be credited
with having invented "irregular" measures—or, better, "phrases," since,
as he later confessed, he barred "according to phrasing" during the "Russian" period, until 1921, when his "performance experience" led him "to
prefer smaller divisions."[23] Consequently, if there is something peculiar in
this stretch of 7/4 bars (and their dotted-line divisions), it cannot rest with
the "metrical irregularity" as such.

The *true* irregularity has to do, crucially, with *what it is* that Stravinsky
subjects to this stretch of 7/4 "metrical irregularity"—with the coordinated interplay between this "irregularity" and the material itself. Viewed
from this perspective, this music does indeed exhibit peculiarities well
worth mentioning. First, the harmonically static, ritualistic, incantatory—
and, of course, highly percussive—repetition of the borrowed folk melody, a melody of limited range and content. Second—and ultimately of
greater consequence—the horn's upsweeping glissando to the first F♯ of
the melody. This glissando, a typical upsweeping upbeat, has here been

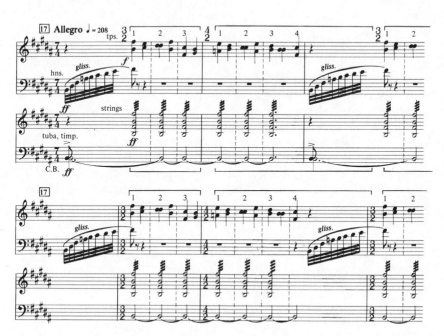

Example 11: Finale

forced onto the downbeat. In other words, what would in relation to the upbeat/downbeat routine of the tonal, C-scale tradition most certainly have been conceived and barred as an upbeat to the melody's first F♯ (and, indeed, has already been repeatedly treated in this way earlier) is here suddenly displaced, contradicted, and reversed. This reversal is reinforced not only by the glissando in the horn (instrumentally, of course, a Stravinskian "effect," and one, as noted, of which he was particularly proud at the time), but also by a timpani-tuba blast *on* the upsweeping downbeat. And when properly executed, with no undue stress on the melody's first F♯ (with the accentuation evenly distributed, in other words), the impact is stunning: it uplifts, liberates the harmonically static repetition, and propels it forward with exhilarating effect. On the other hand, it harbors, as suggested, this potent contradiction or reversal of an established (and possibly ingrained tonal, C-scale) upbeating sensibility; and to an extent that we shall eventually be discovering, a profoundly static—rather than progressive, forward-moving, or developmental—implication.

The brackets in Example 11 offer a more conventional rhythmic-metric interpretation. This alternative bars the horn glissando as an upbeat, while the melody's first F♯ becomes a downbeat. The imposition of this 3/2 + 4/2 rhythmic-metric scheme eliminates the "irregular" 7/4 bars altogether. Indeed, only when the second of the 7/4 measures—or "phrases"—is omitted from the repetition transposed to G at No. 18 (not shown in Example 11), may the "irregular" 7/4 measure become necessary to a conventional interpretation. Even then, a 4/4 + 3/4 pattern might be applied. And, of course, the conventional or traditional impulse would still be to commence the 7/4 measures with the melody's opening F♯ on the downbeat, not, as in the Stravinskian contradiction or reversal, on the second beat (with the horn glissando as a downbeat).

The reversal here, the downbeating of a conventional or traditional upbeat, has far-reaching implications with respect to material of both the "Russian" and neoclassical categories, implications to which we shall therefore be directing our attention more thoroughly in succeeding chapters. In the meantime, however, we note (1) that these rhythmic-metric innovations at Nos. 17–20 in the Finale coincide (by no means coincidentally) with a nontonal, non-major scale partitioning of the diatonic collection that is typically "Russian," and that anticipates *Petroushka*'s first tableau (and to which we shall therefore be returning briefly in chapter 3);[24] and (2) that these early innovations partially explain the frequent dubbing of Stravinsky as a "downbeat composer," a superficial characterization in that the downbeating masks, as we have observed, this potent contradiction or reversal of a conventional or traditional upbeat, in which, of course, lies its point.

"KHOROVOD"

The "Khorovod" contains little of an anticipatory nature. Along with the Finale it represents the other side of the schizoid approach Stravinsky inherited from Rimsky-Korsakov, the borrowing and arranging of Russian folk material to accommodate the real or natural scenes and characters of the scenario.

Useful to the present discussion, however, is the startling contrast the "Khorovod" affords listeners acquainted not only with the diatonicism (which is seldom C-scale tonally functional) of Stravinsky's ensuing "Russian"-period works, but also with the celebrated "impurity" of his C-scale (or major-scale) neoclassicism. For the "Khorovod" is not just diatonic, it is tonal, almost routinely tonal. And seldom shall we again be confronting in Stravinsky's music such compliance with tonally functional processes of (0 3 4/0 4 7) triadic progression and voice leading, relations that so unequivocally partake of that soon-to-be-abandoned universal language of C-scale tonality.

Two melodies have here been abstracted from collections well known at the time. Stravinsky's arrangements of these appear back to back at Nos. 1 and 2, and again at Nos. 5 and 6.[25] The second melody is repeated on each occasion at Nos. 3 and 8, and reoccurs again at No. 10 and at No. 12 (− 4). In Example 12a we reproduce the repetition of this melody as it unfolds at No. 3, and to it apply, without the slightest hesitation, the familiar analytic-theoretical symbols, the codification of tonally functional behavior.

In Example 12b there is an unadulterated, unequivocal augmented-sixth chord *progressing*, with conventional voice-leading intact, to the second inversion of the tonic triad in E major. This progressing is authentic, conceived without the slightest trace of "recomposition," of the reinter-

Example 12a: "Khorovod"

Example 12b

pretation of neoclassicism. There is nothing quite like this in the whole of Stravinsky's music. A true believer here. The writing is not even peculiar to the nineteenth century. Haydn and Mozart, uncontaminated.

Our purpose is not (absurdly) to argue the merits of Stravinsky's pending habits over the tradition of C-scale tonality. The skill or beauty of his arrangements in the "Khorovod" may be beyond contention. And were we to follow Gerald Abraham's example of comparing Stravinsky's arrangement of the first of these melodies (at Nos. 1 and 5) with that of Rimsky-Korsakov in the slow movement of the latter's *Symphonette*, this skill or beauty might seem all the more compelling.[26] (The slight alteration in the harp chords accompanying this melody, an alteration that invests its first appearance at No. 1 with an "open" quality, its second at No. 5 with a "closing" quality, is particularly striking.)

But two critical (and highly convenient) distinctions arise in the "Khorovod": that between the piece's C-scale tonally functional diatonicism and the non-C-scale diatonicism of Stravinsky's ensuing "Russian"-period works, and that between this same C-scale diatonicism and the C-scale settings of Stravinsky's neoclassical ventures.

As with Stravinsky's partitioning of the octatonic collection in the Introduction and Kastchei section, we shall have to await *Petroushka* (in this case, the first tableau) before we can begin to confront a diatonic articulation that will reflect partitioning schemes that become inferable in "Russian" pieces like *Le Sacre, Renard, Les Noces,* and *Histoire du soldat.*

TWO
PETROUSHKA (1911)
An Introduction to the Octatonic Pitch Collection and Its Deployment in Stravinsky's Music

First tableau: The Shrovetide Fair   Nos. 0–48
Second tableau: Petroushka's Cell   Nos. 48–62
Third tableau: Blackamoor's Cell   Nos. 62–82
Fourth tableau: The Shrovetide Fair   Nos. 82–End

Before tackling the *Sacre du printemps*, which would be a long and difficult task, I wanted to refresh myself by composing an orchestral piece in which the piano would play the most important part—a sort of *Konzertstück*. In composing the music, I had in mind a distinct picture of a puppet, suddenly endowed with life, exasperating the patience of the orchestra with diabolical cascades of arpeggios. The orchestra in turn retaliates with menacing trumpet blasts. The outcome is a terrific noise which reaches a climax and ends in the sorrowful and querulous collapse of the poor puppet. [Igor Stravinsky, *An Autobiography*, p. 31.]

Of course, the *Konzertstück* to which Stravinsky refers above was never completed as such. Sergei Diaghilev persuaded him to reinterpret his vision as a ballet scenario. This first music to be composed (in September 1910, following performances of *The Firebird* in Paris) swiftly became the second tableau of *Petroushka*, with brief reappearances in the third tableau at Nos. 76–81 and the fourth and final tableau at No. 125. (Unless otherwise indicated, reference in this inquiry will be to the original 1911 version of the score.)

And the illustrious "*Petroushka* chord," the nucleus of the piano's "diabolical cascades of arpeggios" and of the orchestra's "menacing" retaliation, consists of the two (0,6) tritone-related (0 4 7) "major" triads rooted on C and F♯—(0 4 7) triadic subcomplexes, then, of the "chord" itself, the compound sonority or configuration. The "chord" complements the quirky antics of the half-real, half-mechanical puppet, a Petroushka grossly maligned but, through his "chord" in the final measures of the fourth tableau, jeering at the cheap, hypocritical sentimentality of the real

31

world of the Moor, the Ballerina, and the Crowd (the public). (The borrowed Joseph Lanner waltz tunes in the third tableau depict insipid—or otherwise standardized—sentimentality. Stravinsky later expressed a particular fondness for the final exposition of Petroushka's "chord" in the trumpets at No. 132, fourth tableau: "I wanted . . . to show that his ghost is still insulting the public."[1])

Still: given the role of the octatonic collection as a constructive or referential factor in Stravinsky's music for some fifty years; given the manner in which, by means of models or schemes of partitioning, this role may be comprehensively defined; given the sharp definition afforded certain general practices (or some of the most useful of explanatory notions associated with this literature) through these octatonic schemes of partitioning, it is a matter of some consequence that *Petroushka*, like *The Firebird*, should have been conceived with material that is referentially octatonic.[2] Let us briefly compare the configuration at mm. 5–7 and at m. 12 in *The Firebird* Introduction (Example 13) with the "*Petroushka* chord" at Nos. 49, 50, and 51 in the second tableau (Example 14), and then with a passage from Rimsky-Korsakov's *Sadko*.

Now the configuration at mm. 5–7 in *The Firebird* Introduction was interpreted in terms of Derivative I, a derivative "built into" the ostinato pattern, transposed "down" into the complementary tritone interval D-A♭, and superimposed over the ostinato pattern. But in combination, as a configuration, this superimposition yields (0 4 7) "major" triads at E and B♭ in terms of (E G♯ B) and (B♭ D F), (0,6) tritone-related triads all the more conspicuous at m. 12, in terms of (F♯ A♯ C♯) and (C E G), where the additional ostinato passing tones are omitted. So with this triadic perspective in mind, the correspondence between the configuration at mm. 5–7 and the "Petroushka chord" should be obvious: the configurations are identical in interval content and order (discounting the ostinato's passing tones, the E♭ and the G).

The resemblance extends to treatment as well. The tremolo of the "*Petroushka* chord" at No. 51 ("Curses of Petroushka") is oscillation (the configuration at mm. 5–7) at a frenzied pace, a pace, indeed, anticipated by the climactic tremolo at m. 12. Furthermore, at m. 12, the resemblance is all the more remarkable owing to the identity in pitch content, the mm. 5–7 configuration having been transposed into the collection inferable from the "*Petroushka* chord." (In the models and analyses we shall be iden-

Example 13: *The Firebird* (Introduction)

Example 14: *Petroushka* (second tableau)

tifying this particular collection as Collection III, the third of the three octatonic collections distinguishable in content.) And so at m. 12 the only difference is trifling: accentually, the (E G C) first-inversion triad follows the (F♯ A♯ C♯) root-position triad, while the triadic roles are reversed, the first inversion triad being rooted on C and the root-position triad rooted on F♯. Hence the illustrious "*Petroushka* chord" appears to have had as its origin the Introduction of *The Firebird*, Stravinsky's inspiration for the later work transcending its conceptual boundaries in the earlier, both inspirations referentially octatonic.

Still, the similarities disclosed here between the configuration at mm. 5–7 and m. 12 in *The Firebird* Introduction and the "*Petroushka* chord" may seem superficial. Environmental conditions are overlooked, conditions that prompt a different sense of priority and a different partitioning of the octatonic collection. In *The Firebird* Introduction it is the ostinato pattern and Derivative I that attract the attention of the listener as "foreground" articulative groupings, with respect to which the (0 4 7) triads stemming from their superimposition at mm. 5–7 and m. 12 seem almost incidental. And since, at mm. 5–7, A♭ and D predominate in defining these patterns, these pitches and not E and B♭, the roots of the (E G♯ B) (B♭ D F) triads, serve as pitch numbers 0 and 6 (or as pitch numbers 6 and 0, assuming, as we have, that an identity or numerical equality is realized on behalf of the tritone relation, so that pitch number 0, insofar as it encompasses the assertion of pitch-class priority on the part of A♭, becomes interchangeable with pitch number 6, the D).[3] But in *Petroushka* the (0 4 7) triadic implications are the more immediate attraction, the configuration being conceived far more directly as an aggregation of two (0,6) tritone-related triadic subcomplexes, this aggregation establishing itself as the central idea from which the succeeding material flows. In *Petroushka* it will be the (0 4 7) triadic subcomplexes of the "chord" (or of the compound configuration) which define the articulative partitioning; and it will be the roots of these (0,6) tritone-related (0 4 7) triadic subcomplexes, C and F♯, which assume a degree of pitch-class priority as pitch numbers 0 and 6 (or again, as pitch numbers 6 and 0, assuming that these (0 4 7) triads and their roots take on the previously noted symptoms of "equality" by virtue of the tritone relation which defines their coexistence.) In effect, then, identical relations in interval content and/or order—identical from a strictly local standpoint—yield, with larger contextual considerations taken into account, a different sense of pitch-class priority and a different articulative partitioning of the octatonic collection. And so the trifling variances alluded to above point, on the one hand, to the articulation of Derivative I in *The Firebird* Introduction and, on the other, to the more explicit (0 4 7) triadic composition of the "*Petroushka* chord" (and to the dyadic composition of the "chord" as well, the first of these dyads at Nos.

49, 50, and 51, A♯–C, referring to relations of significance in *Petroushka's* first tableau).

Accordingly, what surfaces inobtrusively in *The Firebird* from the super-imposition of Derivative I over the ostinato becomes the point of departure for a new work (the abandoned *Konzertstück*) and then, in *Petroushka*, for the second tableau. The transformation may be viewed, it would seem, in terms of realignment of the earlier configuration at mm. 5–7, resulting in a new "hearing" or ordering of the collection in which the (0 3 7/0 4 7) "minor" and "major" triads of the collection lie exposed with their roots positioned as (0,3,6,9) symmetrically defined partitioning elements. It is this adjustment that must in some fashion have occasioned all that vigorous and pleasureful improvisation at the piano.

For what more natural than for the "refreshment" of *Petroushka* to have presented itself in the form of an earlier configuration? A configuration whose (0,6) tritone-related (E G♯ B) (B♭ D F) triads, by having been viewed from a slightly altered octatonic perspective, had suddenly acquired a new and startling potential? What more natural than to strike out by transposing the configuration "up" to (F♯ A♯ C♯) (C E G), where the black and white keys of the keyboard (the analogy of black and white to (0 4 7) triads at opposite "ends" or "poles" of the "circle of fifths" may have figured in the refreshment) ensured the pianist a convenient location for "diabolical cascades of arpeggios"? And then, after the lush, sumptuous textures of *The Firebird*, to delight in the directness or harshness of the configuration conceived in this manner? A conversion had taken place whose principal offering lay in some fuller recognition of the (0,3,6,9) symmetrically defined succession of triads available to the octatonic collection (and, as we shall presently be indicating, of the 1,2,1,2,1,2,1,(2) interval ordering implicated by this succession). Stravinsky's later partiality for a (0 3 7/0 4 7/0 4 7 10) triadic partitioning of the octatonic collection may well have sprung—or received a substantial boost—from *Petroushka*.

Yet this transformation of the configuration at mm. 5–7, this fuller recognition of (0 3 7/0 4 7/0 4 7 10) triadic partitioning of the octatonic collection, cannot be the whole of it. For in our analysis of *The Firebird* Introduction such recognition seemed apparent from the successions of (0 4 7 10) "dominant-seventh" complexes over the barlines at mm. 13–14 and 20–21. And if we glance, in Example 15a, at the opening ten measures of the second tableau of Rimsky-Korsakov's opera *Sadko* (1897), we witness not only a gradual (and unimpaired) unfolding of the (0,3,6,9) symmetrically defined succession of (0 4 7/0 4 7 10) triads and "dominant sevenths" at C, E♭, F♯, and A (Collection İII), but also an initial emphasis on the (0,6) tritone-related (0 4 7) triads at—or rooted on—C and F♯. (Rimsky's collection in Example 15a is thus identical to that of the "*Petroushka* chord.") Indeed, in Example 15b, a passage from Stravinsky's *Scherzo fantastique*

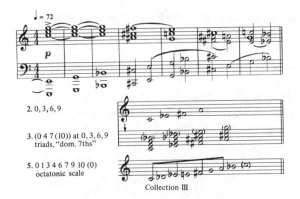

Example 15a: *Sadko* (Rimsky-Korsakov)

Example 15b: *Scherzo fantastique*. Used by permission of European American
Music Distributors Corporation.

(1908), a gradual (and unimpaired) unfolding of this same (0,3,6,9) symmetrically defined succession of (0 4 7/0 4 7 10) triadic complexes at C, Eb, F♯, and A is apparent.⁴ (And note some additional similarities between these two passages in Examples 15a and b: In *Sadko*, Collection III's E–G–Bb–C♯ "diminished-seventh" component ascends as a bass line, providing each of the (0,3,6,9) symmetrically defined (0 4 7) "major" triads at C, Eb, F♯, and A with (0 4 7 10) "dominant-seventh" supplementation; this same C♯–Bb–G–E component descends as an inner voice in the horns at No. 75 + 1 in the *Scherzo fantastique*, similarly providing each of Collection III's (0,3,6,9) symmetrically defined (0 4 7) triads with its "dominant-seventh" outline.)

The distance separating Rimsky's passage or the early *Scherzo fantastique* from the second tableau of *Petroushka* may seem rather slight. We can, quite justifiably, trace the origin of the "chord" to *Sadko* (perhaps via *The Firebird* Introduction at mm. 5–7 and m. 12, or via the *Scherzo fantastique* at No. 75). But what dramatically distinguishes the invention in *Petroushka* from these earlier examples is the superimposing of these (0,6) tritone-related (0 4 7) triads (or, more generally, any of the four (0 3 7/0 4 7/0 4 7 10) triadic complexes available to the single octatonic collection).

Thus, in *Petroushka*'s second tableau, the (0,6) tritone-related (0 4 7) triads in the clarinets at No. 49 and in the horns and trumpets at No. 51 no longer *succeed* one another (as they do, harmlessly, in *Sadko* or in *The Firebird* Introduction). They are now imposed *simultaneously*.⁵ And the "bite" of this invention, from which the most startling implications were to accrue in pitch organization (and, as a consequence, in melodic, formal, instrumental, and rhythmic-metric design as well) opens up a new universe, a new dimension in octatonic thought, one that Stravinsky was to render peculiarly his own.

The distance separating Rimsky's passage from *Petroushka* suddenly becomes enormous. Play through—or hear through—the passages from *The Firebird*, *Sadko*, and the *Scherzo fantastique* (Examples 13, 15a, and 15b), and compare them with the "bite" at Nos. 49 and 51 in *Petroushka* (Example 14). Or, in Example 16a, compare these *successions* with a passage at No. 56 in *Danses concertantes* (1942), where, over thirty years later, Collection III's (0,6) tritone-related (0 4 7) "major" triads at C and F♯ are again superimposed in a manner resembling their appearance at Nos. 49 and 51 in *Petroushka*; or, in Example 16b, with an improvisation on these same (0,6) tritone-related triads in the manner of the "Jeu du rapt" in *Le Sacre*;⁶ or, indeed, in Example 16c, with an extract from the "Jeu du rapt" itself (in which, conveniently, the collection—Collection III—is identical to that inferable from the preceding examples, and in which all four of its (0,3,6,9) symmetrically defined (0 4 7/0 4 7 10) triadic complexes are present not only in succession in the oboes and english horn, but are also

Example 16a: *Danses concertantes*. Used by permission of European
American Music Distributors Corporation.

Example 16b

superimposed). These illustrations should bring this universe to mind
and provide an indication of relations and general practices that, in one
way or another, were to become Stravinskian.

The "refreshment" of *Petroushka* may thus not have been prompted so
much by a fuller recognition of (0 3 7/0 4 7/0 4 7 10) triadic partitioning of
the octatonic collection as by a new method of procedure, that of superimposition. This method, like that of oscillation, will very often supersede
conventional (tonal, C-scale) processes of harmonic progression and development. Along with abrupt "block" juxtaposition—that peculiarly
Stravinskian conception of form or architecture—and the habit of registrally fixing reiterating articulative fragments (to which varying rhythmic-
metric periods may be assigned), superimposition becomes intricately a
part of those relations—or of those octatonic partitioning processes—
readily identified with this oeuvre. A hearing and understanding of con-

Example 16c: *Le Sacre* ("Jeu du rapt")

sistency, identity, and distinction thus hinges on a hearing and understanding of the resulting interplay—of how each of these practices
(interpretable harmonically, melodically, formally, instrumentally, or
rhythmic-metrically) supports, reinforces, or "prompts" the other. Indeed, whether viewed as methods of procedure or simply as useful explanatory notions, oscillation, superimposition, abrupt "block" juxtaposition, repetition, registral fixity, and the allocation of varying rhythmic-
metric periods of reiterating fragments all become applicable to certain of
Stravinsky's diatonic partitioning schemes as well—not withstanding the
perhaps more striking nature of their appearance in (or applicability to)
octatonic construction.

Then, too, while we have in the foregoing confined our discussion to
forms of (0 3 7/0 4 7/0 4 7 10) triadic articulation, the distinctions that have
been drawn between earlier pieces and *Petroushka*'s second tableau pertain to alternative schemes of partitioning as well. In Example 17a from
the *Scherzo fantastique*, the (F E♭ D C B A G♯ F♯ (F)) octatonic collection—
the second of the three octatonic collections distinguishable in content—is

Example 17a: *Scherzo fantastique*. Used by permission of European
American Music Distributors Corporation.

partitioned articulatively not by its four (0,3,6,9) symmetrically defined (0
3 7/0 4 7/0 4 7 10) triads and "dominant sevenths," but by its four (0,3,6,9)
symmetrically defined (0 2 3 5) tetrachords at F, D, B, and G♯ [A♭], descending in terms of (F E♭ D C), (D C B A), (B A G♯ F♯), and (A♭ G♭ F E♭).
But here this (0 2 3 5) tetrachordal partitioning is introduced as a succession: the (0 2 3 5) tetrachords are not superimposed, but merely succeed
one another (notwithstanding the dissonance of the accompanying trem-
olos in the strings, which also refers to Collection II). On the other hand,
in Examples 17b and 17c from "Jeux des cités rivales" in *Le Sacre* (1913)
and "Le Vieux et le lièvre" of the "Russian" song cycle *Pribaoutki* (1914),
superimposition does materialize. At No. 64 in *Le Sacre*, the (0,6) tritone-
related (0 2 3 5) tetrachordal fragments in terms of (G F E D) and (C♯ B A♯
G♯) are superimposed, one on top of the other, while in *Pribaoutki*, the (D
C B A) tetrachordal fragment in the voice and clarinet is superimposed
over its (0,6) tritone-related G♯ in the violin and the F in the bassoon, again
implicating a (0,6) tritone-related (0 2 3 5) tetrachordal grouping and ordering, but in terms of (D C B A) (G♯ F♯ F E♭). (Of course, the more traditionally inclined might contend that *Pribaoutki*'s pitch content, (D C B A)
(G♯ F), is accounted for in terms of the hybrid-diatonic harmonic minor
scale on A. The problem with this, however, is that G♯ is in no way functional as a leading tone to A, but stands in a static, superimposed "opposition" to (D C B A) fragment, while F scarcely behaves in the manner of a
"flatted sixth degree," but stands likewise in a fixed "opposition" to (D C B
A). And so we opt instead for this (D C B A) (G♯ F♯ F E♭) tetrachordal
partitioning of the octatonic collection, and here again (as with *The Firebird*'s "Danse infernale" in chapter 1) not only because of the advantages
that this determination affords a hearing and understanding of Stravinsky's music "considered as a whole" (the question of its identity and distinction), but also because this octatonic reading can better account for the

Example 17b: *Le Sacre* ("Jeux des cités rivales")

Example 17c: *Pribaoutki* ("Le Vieux et le lièvre")

articulation in *Pribaoutki* than can the diatonic—or, in this case, the C-scale, tonally functional hybridization of the diatonic A-scale, the harmonic minor scale on A and all its, in *Pribaoutki*, irrelevant implications.)

Thus, with *Petroushka*'s second tableau at hand, we turn to a preliminary survey of Stravinsky's works: (1) to a listing of the "blocks," passages, and sections that are referentially octatonic; (2) to a comprehensive definition, by means of two models, of Stravinsky's partitioning schemes and the two interval orderings (or scales) implicated by these schemes; (3) to some brief mention of certain practices or explanatory notions, and the relationship of these practices or notions to these octatonic schemes of partitioning; (4) and finally, to the general implications of this octatonic routine insofar as the "Russian" and neoclassical orientation categories are concerned. With this survey as a frame of reference, we can in forthcoming chapters proceed to examine those more specific relations that obtain from one context or piece to another.

THE LISTS

That pitch relations accountable to the octatonic collection occur with remarkable consistency in the works of Stravinsky is a proposition no longer in need of any special act of confirmation. Indeed, what may seem curious is that this should have remained largely undetected for nearly half a century, that of the hundreds of articles and books devoted to Stravinsky and his music there should be but few, all comparatively recent, containing any mention of it at all.[7] Stravinsky was of no assistance in this matter. Not once did he broach the subject in his six books of "conversation" with Robert Craft. And while we are familiar with his indifference toward most forms of analytic-theoretical reckoning and with the sharp distinction he drew between "hindsight" and the behavior of composers *in the act* ("I am not an intellectual, and therefore problems of explanation are of no very great interest to me"),[8] his commentary was not always of a nontechnical nature,[9] and, given the evidence, it seems inconceivable that he could somehow have been unaware of the collection as a cohesive frame of reference, or of its very considerable role in his music as a constructive or referential factor.[10]

And so it would seem that anyone engaged in tracking down consistency, identity, or distinction in pitch organization would at some point confront the numerous passages of octatonic confinement, selecting those wherein the dependency is explicit (that is, of substantial duration, relatively unimpaired by outside interference, with the collection complete or nearly so; see List 1), and determining from these the regularities to be considered in a definition of Stravinsky's approach(es). For the special attraction of these passages—apart from their handy accountability to a symmetrically cohesive "background" reference set—is that they can be found scattered throughout Stravinsky's work. They are unmistakable already in the *Scherzo fantastique* (1908), *Fireworks* (1908), and *The Firebird* (1910); abundant in the succeeding "Russian"-period works from *Petroushka* (1911) to the *Symphonies of Wind Instruments* (1920); less frequent but nonetheless significantly evident in the neoclassical works from the *Octet* (1923) to *Agon* (1953–57); and still quite distinct in some of the serial (or partially serial) works like *Canticum sacrum* (1955), *Agon,* and *Threni* (1958). And since few if any composers have been known to employ relations attributable to the collection as extensively or in as varied a manner as Stravinsky, it follows that a definition of his approach(es) would contribute significantly to just such a hearing and understanding of consistency, identity, and distinction (about which there has been such insistence in the 1960s and 1970s, somewhat ironically in the wake of Stravinsky's gradual adoption of twelve-tone ordering procedures).[11]

Still, even if these passages of explicit reference (List 1) do respond favorably to such a definition (and Stravinsky's form or architecture, his method of abruptly juxtaposing blocks of explicit octatonic reference with blocks distinct not only in instrumentation, dynamics, and rhythmic-metric design, but in referential character as well, does lend itself to a selective analysis, this method of block juxtaposition conveniently investing the blocks or passages of explicit octatonic reference with an unusual degree of stability, distinction, and insulation), analysis is seldom a dead end, seldom exceptionally tidy or accommodating. By this is meant that the ear, having digested the passages of explicit reference (List 1) by way of all the various testing devices known to musicians (transposing, inverting, altering a given registration or pitch distribution: in short, improvising as a means of "getting into" the material), can be expected to assume a bias in this direction, so that it would take an observer exceptionally deliberate were he/she not at some point to apprehend, beyond explicit reference, the still more numerous passages exhibiting degrees of octatonic influence, passages where the collection, given some prior familiarity with it, might reasonably be inferred, even with interference from conflicting sets (or systems) of reference: List 2.

The evidence of inference in such cases might be slight, or, with the collection complete or nearly so, entail considerable interference. For example, there are passages where inference might be drawn on the basis of only four or five octatonic intervals, but with these intervals encountering little or no interference (Nos. 1, 5, and 6 in Les Noces, 1917; or Nos. 0–5 in the "Basle" Concerto in D, 1946). There are also numerous passages that suggest a form of interpenetration between the octatonic and diatonic collections, in which elements or relations attributable to the octatonic collection could be viewed as infiltrating or "subverting" diatonic contexts (or the reverse). From such a diatonic (or even tonally functional C-scale) perspective, many of the "chromatic" (or "dissonant") irregularities, many of the "wrong notes" or "impurities" for which Stravinsky has so persistently been cited in his neoclassical works (but in his "Russian" works as well) could handily be viewed as the octatonic side to this octatonic-diatonic intermingling. So the role of the octatonic scale in Stravinsky's music—or, more precisely, the extent to which inference can reasonably be drawn under these circumstances—appears very large. And we are inclined to agree with Arthur Berger that the Stravinskian stamp is advantageously defined with reference to the octatonic pitch collection, whether inferred singly or in terms of some kind of octatonic-diatonic interpenetration.[12]

The two lists in this chapter indicate "the extent to which octatonic in-

LIST 1

1. *Scherzo fantastique* (1908) — Nos. 7, 20–22, 23, 32, 47–49, 50–52 + 1, 56–64, 74–76, 93–94 + 3.

3. *The Firebird* (1910) — Introduction: except mm. 10–12, 16–18.

4. *Petroushka* (1911) — Second tableau: Nos. 48–52. Third tableau: Nos. 77–81. (1911 version.)

6. *Zvezdoliki* (1912) *(Le Roi des étoiles)* — Nos. 0–1 + 3, 9.

7. *Le Sacre du printemps* (1913) — Part I: Introduction, Nos. 6 (and near repeats), 8; "Danses des adolescentes," Nos. 16–18, 22–24; "Jeu du rapt," Nos. 38–40, 40 + 6–43, 44. Part II: Introduction, Nos. 82 + 2–83, 87–89; "Action rituelle des ancêtres," Nos. 131–35, 138; "Danse sacrale," Nos. 157–62.

8. *The Nightingale* (1914) — Act III: No. 108.

10. *Pribaoutki* (1914) — Song IV: mm. 1–14 (and near repeats at mm. 17–30 and 50–conclusion).

11. *Renard* (1915) — Nos. 9 + 1–11, 20–26, 41 + 1–43, 53–56.

12. *Les Noces* (1917) — First tableau: Nos. 1 (and near repeats at Nos. 5, 6), 11. Second tableau: Nos. 35–40. Third tableau: Nos. 68–72, 82–87.

15. *Symphonies of Wind Instruments* (1920) — Nos. 0–6 (and near repeats at Nos. 9, 26, 37, and 39). (1947 version.)

17. *Oedipus Rex* (1927) — Act I: Nos. 41–43. Act II: Nos. 158, 167–69.

19. *Symphony of Psalms* (1930) — First Movement: Nos. 0–2, 3–6, 7–9.

21. *Danses concertantes* (1942) — Second Movement: Nos. 31, 33, 53–55, 56. Third Movement: Nos. 125–27. Fourth Movement: Nos. 149–51, 152.

22. *Ode* (1943) — Second Movement: Nos. 24–26.

23. *Babel* (1944) — Nos. 0, 16–24.

24. *Scènes de ballet* (1944) — Nos. 0–2.

25. *Symphony in Three Movements* (1945)	First Movement: Nos. 5–16, 22–38, 88–96. Second Movement: Nos. 125 + 1–130, 131. Third Movement: Nos. 152–54, 156–57 + 1, 161–64, 191–94.
26. *Concerto in D* "Basle" (1946)	First Movement: Nos. 0–5.
28. *The Rake's Progress* (1948–51)	Act II, Scene III: Nos. 189, 191.

LIST 2

1. *Scherzo fantastique* (1908)	Nos. 7–10, 20–27, 32–37, 47–64, 74–76, 93–conclusion.
2. *Fireworks* (1908)	Nos. 0–9, 16–21.
3. *The Firebird* (1910)	Introduction; Kastchei section: Nos. 0–3, 9–11.
4. *Petroushka* (1911)	Second tableau: Nos. 48–52, 59–62. Third tableau: Nos. 77–81. Fourth tableau: No. 124–conclusion. (1911 version.)
5. *Two Poems of Balmont* (1911)	Poem No. 2, "The Dove."
6. *Zvezdoliki* (1912) *(Le Roi des étoiles)*	Nos. 0–2, 3–5 + 2, 8–10.
7. *Le Sacre du printemps* (1913)	Part I: except "Danses des adolescentes" at Nos. 28–30, and "Rondes printanières" at Nos. 48–57. Part II: "Glorification de l'elue;" "Evocation des ancêtres"; "Action rituelle des ancêtres;" "Danse sacrale."
8. *The Nightingale* (1914)	Act III: Nos. 108–12.
9. *Three Pieces for String Quartet* (1914)	Piece No. 1.
10. *Pribaoutki* (1914)	Songs I, II, and IV.
11. *Renard* (1915)	Nos. 9–11, 20–26, 41–56.
12. *Les Noces* (1917)	First tableau: except Nos. 9, 12–16. Second tableau: Nos. 29, 31–40, 53–62. Third tableau: Nos. 67–72, 78–80, 82–87. Fourth tableau: Nos. 87–106.

13. *Histoire du soldat* (1918) Music to Scene II. "The Devil's Dance."

14. *Ragtime* (1918) Nos. 4, 6, 8–13, 19.

15. *Symphony of Wind Instruments* (1920) Nos. 0–6 (and near repeats at Nos. 9, 26, 37, and 39). (1947 version.)

16. *Octet* (1923) *Tema con variazioni*: Nos. 24–55.

17. *Oedipus Rex* (1927) Act I: Nos. 2–11, 19–22, 27–30, 40–45, 61–69. Act II: Nos. 158–70.

18. *Capriccio* (1929) First Movement: Nos. 0–8.

19. *Symphony of Psalms* (1930) First Movement. Third Movement: Nos. 1–6, 8, 15–20, 29.

20. *Concerto in E♭* "Dumbarton Oaks" (1938) Third Movement: Nos. 52–58.

21. *Danses concertantes* (1942) Second Movement: Nos. 30–34, 52–61. Fourth Movement: Nos. 148–53.

22. *Ode* (1943) Second Movement: Nos. 24–28.

23. *Babel* (1944) Nos. 0–8, 16–30.

24. *Scènes de ballet* (1944) Nos. 0–5.

25. *Symphony in Three Movements* (1945) First Movement: Nos. 0–38, 58–69, 88–97, 105–12. Second Movement: Nos. 112–18, 125–40. Third Movement: Nos. 142–64, 191–95.

26. *Concerto in D* "Basle" (1946) First Movement: Nos. 0–5, 27–48.

27. *Orpheus* (1947) Nos. 4–77, 125–43.

28. *Mass* (1948) Credo: Nos. 33–43.

29. *The Rake's Progress* (1948–51) Act II, Scene III: Nos. 189–93.

30. *Canticum Sacrum* (1955) First Movement: mm. 10–16 (and near repeats at mm. 26–31, 41–45). Second Movement. Fifth Movement: mm. 307–12 (and near repeats).

31. *Agon* (1953–57) Prelude: mm. 122–45. Interlude: mm. 254–77 (and near repeat at mm. 387–410). "Bransle simple": mm. 278–309. "Bransle gay": mm. 310–35. "Bransle double": mm. 336–86. "Pas de deux": mm. 411–62.

32. *Threni* (1958) Mm. 1–7; mm. 35–44 (and near repeats); mm. 204–17.

33. *Epitaphium* (1959)

34. *The Flood* (1962) Mm. 7–45 (and near repeat at mm. 552–82).

ference can reasonably be drawn" in Stravinsky's music. List 1 is composed of blocks or passages of material where reference to the collection is explicit: blocks or passages "of substantial duration, relatively unimpaired by outside interference, with the collection complete or nearly so." List 2 consists of those more numerous and sizable "chunks" of material only partially accountable to the collection. These latter, often encompassing the smaller, explicitly octatonic blocks of List 1, reflect octatonic-diatonic interaction, which imposes itself through a highly abrupt form of block juxtaposition (octatonic blocks being rapidly and repeatedly juxtaposed with diatonic blocks), or, more generally, through a fusion, blending, or intermingling of elements or relations attributable to the octatonic and diatonic collections. This interaction naturally entails the coming together or simultaneous assertion of elements or relations *not* held in common: "passages where the collection, given some prior familiarity with it, might reasonably be inferred, even with interference from conflicting sets (or systems) of reference."

The criteria applied in this classification and selection allow for considerable flexibility in the drawing of inference, because of the extent and variety of the material at hand. Then, too, selection is subject to the extent to which the ear, prompted by certain objectives, is conditioned by an octatonic frame of reference. Hence, interpretation. And it follows: (1) that the lists should be regarded as comprising works and passages that tend *in the direction of* the classification indicated (since, obviously, even the question of explicit reference is a question of degree); and (2) that the lists should not be regarded as complete, since it will always be possible to infer further or differently in respect to the classification indicated or to attain some slightly altered perspective. It is therefore inevitable that certain works or passages will be found to have been ignored (or overlooked), and some of those listed found to be questionable—at least at this stage—as to their octatonic credentials.

To illustrate some of the reasoning behind the classification and selection: the middle section of the second movement of the *Symphony in Three Movements* (1945), Nos. 125 (−1)–130, is octatonic (accountable to Collection I, Models A and B partitioning), except for the interference of a single pitch class, G♭, which is first articulated in the harp as part of a (G♭ B♭ D♭) triad, second inversion. In order to acknowledge octatonic hegemony but to account at the same time for the slight, here-and-there interference of the G♭ and the (G♭ B♭ D♭) triad it articulates (of which, however, the B♭ and D♭ refer to Collection I), it seemed appropriate to includes the passage on both lists. The same holds for Nos. 22–38 on List 1 from the first movement of this work. This passage is octatonic (Collection I; Model A partitioning) except for an interfering E♭ at Nos. 22–28 which is articulated as part of a (E♭ G B♭) triad (of which, however, the G and B♭ refer to

Collection I). The same holds for Nos. 48–52 in *Petroushka* (Collection III; Model A partitioning), which includes the aforementioned "*Petroushka* chord" at Nos. 49, 50, and 51, but also, at No. 50, interference with Collection III in the form of a (G B D) triad which could not be overlooked.

On the other hand, a more determined effort to isolate octatonic passages of explicit reference (List 1) from those exhibiting interference, partial reference, or octatonic-diatonic interpenetration (List 2) was made in the case of the *Scherzo fantastique* (1908), *Le Sacre* (1913), *Les Noces* (1917), and the *Symphony of Psalms* (1930), works heavily endowed with lengthy "chunks" of octatonic concentration. Thus, while the entire Introduction of *Le Sacre* was included on List 2 as a case of partial accountability (or, with respect to the accumulatively climactic Nos. 10–12, a case of obvious octatonic-diatonic interpenetration), only certain rehearsal numbers or blocks of this section were included on List 1. And with respect to questionable credentials, the reader might well find the inclusion on List 2 of Nos. 52–58 from the third movement of the "Dumbarton Oaks" *Concerto in E♭* (1938) a bit farfetched, because of the opening unimpaired diatonic reference to the E-scale on G, and because of the unmistakable (but parenthetical?) tonally functional overtones of those (0 4 7 10 1) "dominant-minor-ninth" complexes at G and B♭ at No. 55—complexes that relate, in this (parenthetical?) tonally functional sense, to the subtle assertion of C and E♭ as pitch classes of priority. But the peculiar spacing and exchange of these complexes—the (0 4 7 10 1) "dominant-minor-ninth" partitioning at G and B♭—and, above all, the eventual transposition of the opening passage from an E-scale-on-G reference to an E-scale-on-B♭ reference at No. 56 (a change from a G pitch-class priority to a B♭ pitch-class priority) point just as unmistakably to octatonic guidance and penetration (Collection I), a penetration rather obvious in view of the *Symphony of Psalms* (1930) and subsequent work during the 1940s. Similarly, the inclusion on either of the lists of the introductory passage of the "Basle" *Concerto in D* (1946) might be found questionable at this point. But these matters of accreditation lie at the heart of this discourse, and will therefore be subject to scrutiny in the analyses subsequently to be undertaken.[13]

THE MODELS

We proceed now with the structure of the octatonic collection, and with a comprehensive definition, by means of two models, of Stravinsky's partitioning schemes. This model-definition is intended to cover *both* Lists 1 and 2. Some preliminary observations:

1. The octatonic scale may be defined as any collection of eight distinct pitch classes which, when confined to the octave and arranged in scale for-

mation, will exhibit the interval ordering of alternating half and whole steps or alternating whole and half steps (alternating intervals of 1 and 2 or 2 and 1).

2. When a particular passage is held accountable to the collection, the collection may be designed to incorporate essential data regarding pitch and/or complex priority. With this in mind, one should always distinguish between the *reference collection* (the total pitch-class content inferable from a given passage) and the *referential ordering of intervals* that the collection will assume on the basis of the pitch class to which priority is assigned. (The pitch class of priority, pitch number 0, will also determine, in semitonal count, the numbering of the remaining seven pitch classes.)

3. Given the symmetrical nature of such a collection of alternating half and whole steps, *it follows that there are but three collections distinct with respect to total pitch-class content*; or, to put it another way, the collection is limited to three transpositions.[14] Thus were we to continue transposing beyond the initial transposition from E to F and F♯ in Model A, these further "transpositions," beginning at pitch number 3, would merely duplicate the initial statements with respect to pitch content and interval ordering.

4. In addition, *it follows that such an arrangement of alternating half and whole steps yields but two possible interval orderings,* one with its second scale degree at the interval of a half step (semitone) from the first, the other with its second scale degree at the interval of a whole step (whole tone): 1,2,1,2,1,2,1,(2), as in Model A (ascending), and 2,1,2,1,2,1,2,(1), as in Model B (descending).

At this point the critical distinction arises. For it is on the basis of these competing interval orderings—or, more precisely, on the basis of differences in the partitioning of the collection that are referable to (or may, in turn, be inferred from) these orderings—that Models A and B have been constructed as comprehensive representations of two distinct schemes of partitioning that emerge from an examination of the literature.

With respect to the symmetrical discipline in the interval orderings of the scale exhibited by Models A and B:[15]

1. The alternating half and whole steps (or whole and half steps) divide the octatonic octave into four numerically equal partitions at pitch numbers 0, 3, 6, and 9. Pitch number 6, the fifth scale degree and at the interval of a tritone (6 semitones) from 0, is an axis around which the two halves of the octave are symmetrical. Pitch numbers 3 and 9 form another axis around which two quarters of the octave (halves of the tritone) are analogously symmetrical.

2. But the interval ordering initiated at 0, 3, 6, and 9 in Model A is 1,2, while that in Model B is 2,1. Hence it is this variance in the interval order-

0, 3, 6, 9

(0 1 3 4) at 0, 3, 6, 9
tetrachords

(0 3 7/0 4 7/0 4 7 10 (1)) at 0, 3, 6, 9
triads, "dom.7ths", "dom. minor 9ths"

0 1 3 4 6 7 9 10 (0)
octatonic scale

Model A

	i	ii	iii	iv	v	vi	vii	viii	(i)
Collection I:	E	f	G	ab	Bb	b	Db	d	(E)
Collection II:	F	f#	Ab	a	B	c	D	eb	(F)
Collection III:	F#	g	A	bb	C	db	Eb	e	(F#)
pitch numbers:	0	1	3	4	6	7	9	10	(0)
intervals		1	2	1	2	1	2	1	(2)

ing that permits, beyond the more "background" (0,3,6,9) partitioning common to both models, the distinction between Models A and B to become readily apparent at the "foreground" surface-articulative level: *(0 3 7/0 4 7) triadic partitioning of the scale at 0, 3, 6, and 9 in Model A, and (0 2 3 5) tetrachordal partitioning of the scale at 0, 3, 6, and 9 in Model B.* In Model A, pitch numbers 0, 3, 6, and 9 are bequeathed not only the interval of 7 (the "supporting fifth"), but are roots of (0 3 7/0 4 7) "minor" and "major" triads as well as of (0 4 7 10) "dominant-seventh" and (0 4 7 10 1) "dominant-minor-ninth" chords, the entire succession of pitch classes, with much overlapping, still referable to any given collection. So the assertion of Model A in any particular passage will naturally reflect a preoccupation with (0 3 7/0 4 7) triadic partitioning. (Traditional terminology is

Model B

	i	ii	iii	iv	v	vi	vii	viii	(i)
Collection I:	E	d	C♯	b	B♭	a♭	G	f	(E)
Collection II:	F	e♭	D	c	B	a	G♯	f♯	(F)
Collection III:	F♯	e	E♭	d♭	C	b♭	A	g	(F♯)
pitch numbers:	0	2	3	5	6	8	9	11	(0)
intervals:		2	1	2	1	2	1	2	(1)

here invoked in a supplementary manner for purposes of identification, there being no intent to implicate C-scale tonally functional relations.) On the other hand, pitch numbers 0, 3, 6, and 9 in Model B are bequeathed the interval of 5 and the (0 2 3 5) tetrachord with interval order 2, 1, 2, so that the assertion of Model B in any particular passage will in turn reflect a preoccupation with (0 2 3 5) tetrachordal partitioning at the articulative level.

With respect to pitch-class and/or pitch-complex priority in Models A and B:

Within any given octatonic collection . . . the first element of any of the partitions of the octave at 0, 3, 6, and 9 has the potentiality of being the pitch class of priority in an identical ordering referable to the same given octatonic collection. . . . That is to say, not only is each of the partitions a "transposition" of the other, in a sense, but the interval ordering of the total collection defined in relation to the first element of each partition is also identical; hence, each of the four possible orderings is also a different "transposition" of the octatonic scale. (Strictly speaking, this is really "rotation," since the collection has only three transpositions. . . .) Therefore, in the interval ordering of the scale. . . , there are, loosely speaking, four potential "tone centers" of equal weight and independence.[16]

This means that, given the (0,3,6,9) symmetrically defined partitioning and the reproduction in content and interval ordering of the scale when "transposing" from pitch number 0 to 3, 6, and 9 ("rotation"), there exists an identity or, with respect to (0,6) tritone partitioning, a numerical equality between the elements of this partitioning, so that in order for one pitch class and/or pitch complex to assert priority over the others it must eliminate this identity, equality, or potential for "equal weight and independence." Such elimination—the assertion of pitch-class and/or pitch-complex priority—will occur by means of contextual articulation (persistence, octave reinforcement, metric accentuation, influence of surrounding material, etc.), C-scale (or major-scale) tonally functional relations being unavailable to these octatonic partitioning elements, "potential priorities," or "accented tones." [17]

Already it may be possible to envision here, as exemplified by the "*Petroushka* chord" or in Examples 3–17c, a condition peculiar to Stravinsky's octatonic contexts, one in which two or more of these four symmetrically defined partitioning elements or "potential priorities," generally with (0 3 7/0 4 7) triadic or (0 2 3 5) tetrachordal "support," assert themselves to such a degree that relations assume a deadlocked character. This occurs particularly in cases where emphasis is placed on the (0, 6) tritone partitioning of the scale; then these relations impose themselves all the more forcefully in the form of an inert, self-contained, tension-clinched *complexe sonore* within which no selection of pitch-class priority seems legitimate, and, indeed, the search for one somewhat beside the point. Berger, in a brief analysis of the "*Petroushka* chord" at Nos. 49 and 51 of the score, invoked Stravinsky's use of "polarity" in describing the nature of these contexts, a term which seemed to him to reflect an awareness on the composer's part

> of the special properties of the tritone which make it possible for pitches at 0 and 6 (capable of graphic representation as "poles" in a circle of fifths, whether or not one accepts the assumption on which this circle is predicated), by virtue of similitude or equal and thus independent weight, to remain in equilibrium or—to the end that a tone center is asserted by neither—to stand in a certain opposition. This speculation might easily take flight in a direction which would establish, as a necessary condition of "polarity," the denial of priority to a single pitch class precisely for the purpose of not deflecting from the priority of the whole *complexe sonore*. [18]

So given the octatonic scale's inherent ability to foster (0,3,6,9) symmetrically defined multiple priorities—and, naturally, the tendency for Stravinsky's material to reflect this ability—attempts to determine (single) pitch-class and/or pitch-complex priorities in contexts referable to the scale will entail certain hazards. Even when a pitch class or complex does

appear to assert priority, it will still be the sense of deadlock that is immediately striking and hence deserving of analytical attention. Consequently, with the symmetrical nature of the scale in mind, we might feel
inclined to attach special significance to (0,3,6,9) "background" partitioning when examining a particular passage, or to consider a recognition of
the pitches or complexes that delineate a two-, three-, or four-part partitioning far more critical than any designation of the most likely candidate
for priority status according to the criteria noted above (persistence, octave reinforcement, metric accentuation, etc.).

Moreover, the four (0,3,6,9) partitioning elements or "potential priorities" in these displays (C, E♭, F♯, and A for Collection III, for example) are
interchangeable with respect to pitch-class and/or pitch-complex priority.
While allowing for the assertion of priority, these models are, by
definition, comprehensive or panoramic, providing the reader with the
full potential of (0 3 7/0 4 7) triadic and (0 2 3 5) tetrachordal partitioning as
reflected in the literature. And they are adaptable with respect to the
number of partitioning elements that might actually pertain to a given
passage. For Stravinsky's octatonic settings, while frequently approaching
a realization of the potential for "equal weight and independence" among
two or more of the (0,3,6,9) partitioning elements—or their (0 3 7/0 4 7)
triadic or (0 2 3 5) tetrachordal complexes—seldom encompass all four at
the same time, and then seldom on an equal footing: configurations tend
to gravitate around two or three of these elements within any significant
period of time.[19] Thus, in regard to Nos. 48–52 in *Petroushka* (and, in particular, the "*Petroushka* chord" at Nos. 49, 50, and 51), were we to accept
the interpretation of this "chord" as containing two (0 4 7) triadic subcomplexes at C and F♯; to recognize (0,6) tritone partitioning of "equal weight
and independence"; to disregard interference in the piano figuration at
No. 50 (the (G B D) triad being foreign to Collection III) and the vertical
dyads at No. 49 (the A♯/C dyad being conspicuous, since it refers to
significant relations in the first tableau and might therefore have
prompted, with respect to a more global attitude, a different kind of
"background" partitioning) then the following structural-level format
might apply (corresponding to those of Examples 5, 8a–b, 10a–c, 14,
15a–b, 16a–c, and 17a–c) stipulating (0,6) tritone partitioning of Collection III in terms of C and F♯, Model A, where pitch numbers 3 and 9 are
inoperative as partitioning elements, and, indeed, are absent from the
configuration:

Level 2: 0,6
    3: (0 4 7) at 0,6
    4: (10 1 6) (0 4 7)
    5: 0 1 (3) 4 6 7 (9) 10 (0)

Then, were we to include in this account the previously noted transposition of the "*Petroushka* chord" at No. 77 in the third tableau to the remaining—and, at Nos. 49–52, omitted—tritone-related partitioning elements of Collection III, E♭ and A (as pitch numbers 3 and 9), the following format might apply, stipulating (0,3,6,9) "background" partitioning of Collection III in terms of C, E♭, F♯, and A, Model A, where the selection of (single) pitch-class priority at level 1 is again deemed illegitimate (or may again seem beside the point), and is omitted from the record:

Level 2: 0,3,6,9
    2a: (0,6) (3,9)
     3: (0 4 7) at 0,3,6,9
    3a: ((0 4 7) at 0,6) ((0 4 7) at 3,9)
     4: ((10 1 6) (0 4 7)) ((10 3 7) (9 1 4))
     5: 0 1 3 4 6 7 9 10 (0)

Or, in pitch lettering:

Level 2: C, E♭, F♯, A
    2a: (C, F♯) (E♭, A)
     3: (C E G) (E♭ E B♭) (F♯ A♯ C♯) (A C♯ E)
    3a: ((C E G) (F♯ A♯ C♯)) ((E♭ E B♭) (A C♯ E))
     4: ((A♯ C♯ F♯) (C E G)) ((B♭ E♭ G) (A C♯ E))
     5: C C♯ E♭ E F♯ G A B♭ (C)

This passage has already been outlined in pitch notation in Example 14.

The underlying rationale of the structural-level approach in analysis as it applies to the varying octatonic settings briefly examined here may now be apparent. To follow Benjamin Boretz in this regard:

> The construction of "structural levels" in music consists of making inferences of relations on a more than "one element–one element" scale, which thus *groups* sets of pitches (however minimally) so that "larger-scale" complex-unit ("thing") structures are assertible *as well as* a unit-to-unit structure.[20]

Thus, in the structural-level format advanced for the "*Petroushka* chord" (or those sketched in Examples 5, 8a–b, 10a–c, 14, 15a–b, 16a–c, and 17a–c), "making inferences of relations on a more than 'one element–one element' scale" (structural-level reconstruction) consists of proceeding from a most "background" level (*least determinate* in the sense that a relatively large group of passages or pieces might apply: e.g., pitch-class priority) to a most "foreground" surface-articulative level (*most determinate* in the sense that relatively few other passages or pieces, if any, might qualify as instances of this partitioning). A first stage—least determinate—might be that of the (single) pitch-class priority; a second stage, "background" partitioning of the octatonic collection in terms of the (0,3,6,9) partitioning elements of Models A and B; a third stage, the surface-articulative complexes, possibly (0 3 7/0 4 7) triadic or (0 2 3 5) tetrachordal, "based," of course, on the partitioning elements at level 2, a stage at which the partitioning identity of Models A and B and the interval ordering of the scale are generally recognized; and a fourth stage, the assembling of all "foreground" partitioning (possibly as presented), which, at level 5, yields the reference collection, which may be designed to incorporate some of the aforementioned stage-data: pitch-class and/or pitch-complex priority (if any), and, by means of beams, "background" partitioning as defined at level 2. (While the total pitch content stipulated by the partitioning generates or yields the reference collection, structural-level reconstruction is undertaken with reference to this collection.)

Thus each level of the structural-level format constitutes a (re)interpretation of the passage or piece in terms of the proposed entity, grouping, or partitioning, a (re)interpretation added to or superimposed on preceding (or succeeding) levels of interpretation (rather than replacing or superseding them), so that, in moving from "the background" to "the foreground," we never eliminate or "lose sight of" the sense or respect in which elements or "sets of pitches" assigned to a new or more determinate grouping are operative or noticeable at a more "background" and less determinate level, this being "the essential basis of that *functional multiplicity* exhibitable by musical entities."[21]

Moreover, each level constitutes a (re)interpretation of the entire content of the passage or piece in terms of the entity, grouping, or partitioning forwarded:

> for the notion here is just that the "levels" constitute—each individual level as well as all the levels collectively—*a model of (all) the distinguishable data* of the composition, such that each level specifies a particular *degree of* (and *kind of*) *determinacy* for that data. . . . So the "Schenker graph" or any other structural-level-notational model is meaningful insofar as it is regarded at every stage as laid against the data, as a model of a particular (and presumably significative) *determinate thing-stage* with respect to that data. . . . Thus, both "the background" and "the foreground" are just *relatively determinate* ways of hearing "the piece." And so there is no discernible sense to the dichotomy asserted by some theorists between "going from the background to the foreground" and the reverse procedure as a way of hearing, describing, or understanding a piece.[22]

Still, it is to be anticipated that the signification of the structural levels or the structural-level format will undergo modifications from one analysis to the next, because we shall at times be dealing with relations exclusively on a local basis (blocks, passages, or sections; e.g., *The Firebird* Introduction, or the "*Petroushka* chord"), and at other times with relations on both a local and a long-term, global, or continuously operative basis (e.g., *Le Sacre* in chapter 4). These complementary bases will prompt varied formats (although successive local reconstructions are generally to be understood as constituting successive local interpretations or realizations of the more global or continuously operative format). Then, too, Stravinsky's diatonic material, even when interacting with the octatonic relations, prompts still more varied applications of structural-level reconstruction. (As always, the epistemic problems that so subtly arise while seeking efficient analytical representation are awesome, and the reader cannot expect an anticipation and clarification of every conceivable ambiguity, although the analysis will attempt to foresee and "plug" as many as possible. He/she must, with the music at hand, attempt to "feed" the conceptualization "back" into the musical experience as effectively as possible, a task which, as indicated, cannot be that of the analyst.)

In regard to improvisation or the "feeding back" into the musical experience of analytic-theoretical reckoning, it should be cautioned that while the (0 3 7/0 4 7) triads of Model A and the (0 2 3 5) tetrachords of Model B are complexes or composites of pitches (with specifics of interval complementation and order ignored in any given instance), the interval of 7 (the "fifth") at pitch numbers 0, 3, 6, and 9 in Model A, and of 5 (the "fourth") at these pitch numbers in Model B, will generally be indispensable insofar as the identity of these models is concerned.[23] (Pitch numbers 0, 3, 6, and 9 cannot really serve as "potential priorities" in the partitioning sense indicated by Models A and B without them.) Thus it will generally be necessary for the first and last pitches of the (0 2 3 5) tetrachord (its pitch numbers 0 and 5) to articulate the interval of 5 (the "fourth") at 0, 3, 6, and/or 9, and hence acquire a degree of priority as elements of fragmental enclosure, if Model B is to apply in some significant sense. (And such is indeed invariably the case with the (0 2 3 5) tetrachord in Stravinsky's music. As the principal melodic fragment in material of the "Russian" category, it spans the interval of 5, the "fourth," and hence is articulated in the closest or "tightest" arrangement possible. See in this connection the (0 2 3 5) tetrachord fragments in Examples 17a, b, and c.) Thus there are qualifications of the notion of complex, certain limits on the extent of interval complementation and hence on the extent to which those "testing" devices alluded to earlier might prove apropos. Octatonic identity *with respect to these models* will tend to hinge on the assertion of at least two of the (0,3,6,9) partitioning elements as "accented tones" or pitches of priority by means of articulative "support," at the very least, in the form of the interval of 7 (for Model A) and 5 (for Model B).

The "conflict of interest" between pitch numbering, pitch lettering, and pitch notation in the documentation of "relations on a more than 'one-element—one-element' scale" is, of course, quite legitimate. Apart from the fact that the documentation is always to be "laid against the data" (against a specific passage, piece, or group of pieces), pitch numbering, pitch lettering, and pitch notation are best understood as relatively determinate or relatively abstract ways of hearing, understanding, interpreting, or describing such "relations on a more than 'one-element–one-element' scale." Thus, pitch numbering, the numerical quantification of intervals by means of semitonal count, may seem the more abstract of the three, particularly in reference to complexes of pitches (the (0 3 7/0 4 7) triads and (0 2 3 5) tetrachords of Models A and B, for example, where not only interval complementation and order are ignored, but pitch identity as well). It aims at greater generality in musical thought, and to this end may circumvent pitch identity, interval complementation, and order—as may, of course, the terminology of tonal, C-scale (or major-scale) analysis and theory, terms like triad, major scale, tonic, dominant seventh, leading tone—while it transcends, or is unbiased toward, theories, systems, "styles," orientations, literatures. Its usefulness in this inquiry is therefore twofold: (1) it handily identifies and labels intervallic relationships (cohesive groupings or complexes of intervals) above and beyond the pitch, interval complementation, or ordering implications of any given instance; (2) it skirts the terminology of tonal, C-scale analysis and theory which may be exceedingly awkward when, as with Stravinsky's octatonic or octatonic-diatonic contexts, the functional behavior identified no longer applies.

Take, for example, the "background" (0,3,6,9) symmetrically defined partitioning elements of the octatonic collection. In moving from one octatonic or octatonic-diatonic context to the next, this (0,3,6,9) partitioning, stipulating the intervallic relationship defined by the various triads and tetrachords of Models A and B, is always the same in respect to the three possible octatonic collections. The convenience of this (0,3,6,9) label is that it identifies and exposes this invariance, while relieving us of the necessity, in our comparisons from one context to the next, of having always to begin anew. (As should be evident, then, we ask of pitch numbering far less than is customarily expected of traditional terminology: only that it classify and label *routine* from one passage or piece to the next.) And while this (0,3,6,9) relationship equates with the familiar (0 3 6 9) diminished-seventh chord of tonal, C-scale music, its significance in Stravinsky's octatonic contexts has no relation to the functional behavior of the diminished-seventh chord in tonal, C-scale contexts. The same is true of the (0 4 7 10) "dominant-seventh" complex of Model A. The numbering here identifies and labels this cohesive entity whatever its pitch identity, registral spacing, and order, while at the same time freeing it from irrelevant tonal, C-scale implications. (Even with the common "irregular resolutions" of the dominant-seventh chord duly considered, seldom, in Stravinsky's octatonic or octatonic-diatonic contexts, is this chord treated in a manner resembling its C-scale, tonally functional appearance in music of the seventeenth to nineteenth centuries.)[24] In marked contrast to pitch numbering, then, pitch lettering and pitch notation, by taking pitch identity more readily into account, may seem closer to the music at hand—although, just as with pitch numbering, pitch/interval classes and complexes of pitches are invariably implicated in analysis and theory.

Moreover, any accommodation afforded these varying ways and means of documentation (pitch numbering, pitch lettering, and pitch notation) will naturally reflect analytic-theoretical concerns and objectives. Thus, with respect to the initial statements of Models A and B where relations are numbered on the left hand side: pitch numbering here would have sufficed. However, to facilitate the use of these models as a reference with which to check specific passages; to encourage improvisation or an application of the various "testing" devices alluded to above; and hence to familiarize the reader in a more direct fashion with the implications (in regard to pitch-class identity) of these model-statements for each of the three possible octatonic collections, it seemed advisable to supplement pitch numbering with pitch notation. And while pitch/interval classes and complexes of pitches are implicated by the concept of a comprehensive or panoramic model, this pitch-notational supplement spares us the dreary abstractness that can result from a too heavy reliance on numbering. Consequently, what is ultimately sought is a medium that can suitably reflect, on the one hand, a concern for *routine*—for the constancy or persistence of relations from one passage or piece to the next (often best served by pitch numbering)—and, on the other a concern for specificity—for the unique element in those same relations (often best served by pitch lettering or pitch notation).

But quite apart from these general considerations, there are even more pressing reasons for the adoption in this volume of some form of pitch numbering, however limited and supplementary in scope. For while a conventional term like triad (indeed, nearly all of conventional terminology) bypasses pitch identity, interval complementation, and order, a fixed interval content is generally implied (the "minor" and "major" triads, for example, which are always "minor" and "major" triads whatever the specifics in pitch identity, registral spacing, and order). But terms like tetrachord and hexachord carry no such fixed intent. A tetrachord is merely a grouping or complex of four pitches with any possible interval content; and a hexachord one of six pitches with no fixed interval content. And so if we are to identify and label that particular tetrachord—the (0 2 3 5) tetrachord with interval order 2,1,2 (with octatonic implications defined in Model B)—which figures so persistently as a melodic fragment in Stravinsky's "Russian"-period material (imposing itself through all manner of reiterating folkish tunes), or, in turn, to identify that particular hexachord—the (0 2 3 5 7 9) hexachordal segment—which figures so persistently in "Russian" material as a cohesive diatonic frame of reference, pitch numbering seems the most practical solution. (We are dealing, in other words, not merely with a pitch-numbering supplement to an often irrelevant tonal, C-scale terminology, but with articulative groupings for which there are no familiar labels. Moreover, this "Russian" (0 2 3 5) tetrachord is to be distinguished from the (0 1 3 4) tetrachord of Model A, which figures more conspicuously in neoclassical works. The (0 2 3 5) tetrachord, with its 2,1,2 interval order reflecting Model B's 2,1, whole-step–half-step scale, spans the interval of 5, the "fourth," while the (0 1 3 4) tetrachord, with interval order 1,2,1 reflecting Model A's 1,2 half-step–whole-step scale, spans the interval of 4, the "major third.") When the numbering of these groupings is mirrored by a numbering of the appropriate reference collections as scales (for which, in the case of the two octatonic scales of Models A and B, no conventional labels are available), the whole process becomes doubly advantageous as a means of recording, from one context or piece to the next, groups of relationships that prevail more widely in Stravinsky's work. On the other hand, pitch numbering is here nearly always introduced in a supplementary fashion, often in conjunction with conventional terms (whenever possible or appropriate), or in reference to specific contexts (where pitch lettering and/or pitch notation is provided). Apart from the separate intervals, the numbering will refer to but a select handful of articulative groupings and scales, in large part already covered by these first two chapters. It is hoped that by occasionally setting aside a few moments for reflection in this regard, readers unfamiliar with the approach will not find it a constant stumbling block. The instruction it affords, particularly when dealing—as we are here—with matters of consistency, identity, and distinction for a body of works, should be apparent.[25]

Still, an awkwardness of pitch numbering may be that, in committing itself to a pitch number 0 (which may or may not implicate priority), it must also, to remain intelligible, commit itself to either an ascending order from pitch number 0 or a descending order. This commitment will mean that, when referring to complexes of pitches (or, more determinately, to the interval order stipulated by a given complex), the numbering will at times conform to a given design vis-à-vis interval complementation and at times conflict with it, an irregularity often rather irritating (even though, again, the documentation is always to be "laid against the data"). Hence the general preference in this discourse for a looser type of documentation (e.g., (0 4 7) "major" triad at 0, 3, 6, or 9) instead of the exotic (and needlessly confusing) pitch numbering that exact specification entails with respect to (0 4 7) triads at 3, 6, and 9.

But more significantly, Model B's (0 2 3 5) tetrachordal articulation, prevalent in octatonic settings of the "Russian" period, lends itself most advantageously to a descending scale and pitch numbering (a reading-down situation), a formula obviously in conflict with the customary ascending approach advanced on behalf of Model A (a reading-up situation). The advantages of the descending formula in cases of (0 2 3 5) partitioning arise from the following: (1) it is, more often than not, an "uppermost" pitch or "uppermost" (0 2 3 5) tetrachord that presents itself in Model B settings as the likeliest candidate for priority status (according to the criteria noted above), a priority or centricity that is conveniently correlated with the pitch numbering by resorting to the descending or reading-down formula; (2) the descending pitch numbering for Model B's (0 2 3 5) partitioning allows the (0,3,6,9) symmetrically defined partitioning elements to be identical for Models A and B in each of the three octatonic collections (Eb, C, A, and F♯ for Collection III in both Models A and B, for example), an identity or link between these models often critical to a hearing and understanding of octatonic relations in Stravinsky's "Russian"-period material; (3) this "uppermost" pitch or "uppermost" (0 2 3 5) tetrachordal predominance in Model B settings of the "Russian" period becomes applicable to many of the diatonic D-scale settings with which these (0 2 3 5) octatonic settings interact, so that the descending approach (the reading-down situation) can properly record, in the pitch numbering, the various (0 2 3 5) tetrachordal connecting links or "threads" that prevail (possibly with a degree of priority on a global or continuously operative basis) in moving or shifting from octatonic settings to diatonic D-scale settings, or to some form of octatonic (Model B) and diatonic (D-scale) interpenetration. And while a certain awkwardness may be felt in using a descending numbering when referring to Model B's (0 2 3 5) tetrachords and then the customary ascending numbering for Model A's (0 3 7/0 4 7/0 4 7 10) triads and "dominant sevenths," the greater illumination the descending formula affords in exposing (0 2 3 5) partitioning and the connecting links in the octatonic-diatonic interaction in Stravinsky's "Russian"-period material outweighs any awkwardness incurred by the discrepancy. Moreover, the switch (or even a constant switching) from the descending to the ascending formula is far less burdensome or problematic than might be expected. For the symmetry that underlies Model B's (0 2 3 5) tetrachordal partitioning extends to the (0 2 3 5) tetrachord itself, its 2,1,2 interval order and consequent (0 2 3 5) pitch numbering being the same whether descending or ascending. Indeed, the D-scale, so prominent in "Russian" contexts as a diatonic frame of reference, conveniently exhibits similar properties: its 2,1,2,2,1,2(2) interval ordering and consequent (0 2 3 5) (7 9 10(0)) pitch numbering is also the same, whether descending or ascending. Accordingly, in cases of octatonic (Model B) and diatonic (D-scale) interaction, we extend Model B's descending formula to the diatonic D-scale as well.

SOME USEFUL (AND USELESS)
EXPLANATORY NOTIONS

Although introduced in earlier writings without reference to the octatonic partitioning that may be inferred from the blocks, passages, or sections of Lists 1 and 2 and comprehensively defined by Models A and B, it is from being brought into relation with this partitioning that the most useful explanatory notions (e.g., "harmonic stasis," "polarity," "superimposition," "juxtaposition") achieve their sharpest definition. Indeed, while accountability to the octatonic collection is consistently ignored (or, more probably, overlooked) by their proprietors and propagators, these terms are nevertheless invariably invoked in discussions of the referentially octatonic blocks and passages of Lists 1 and 2 (passages whose relations are just as invariably dubbed "characteristic," "typical," or "distinctive").[26]

The notion of "polarity," following its appearance in Stravinsky's *Poétique musicale*, reappears in Pierre Boulez's celebrated discussion of rhythmic organization in *Le Sacre*. There Boulez conceives it in terms of an anachronistic subdominant-tonic-dominant relation (octatonic activity not only abounds in *Le Sacre*, but is as unsullied by C-scale tonal implications as any in the literature).[27] It emerges again in Berger's discussion, interpreted in terms of the (0,3,6,9) symmetrically defined partitioning elements of the octatonic collection, elements which assume, as regards "polarity," a degree of "equal weight and independence" and "stand in a certain opposition." Briefly to supplement this latter interpretation of "polarity": at the articulative level, maximum "opposition" or "polarity" (maximum content differentiation) is achieved, in Model A, by the (0,6) tritone-related (0 3 7/0 4 7) triads—as in the "*Petroushka* chord," Example 14—and, in Model B, by the (0,6) tritone-related (0 2 3 5) tetrachords—as at No. 64, "Jeux des cités rivales" in *Le Sacre*, Example 17b. Lest this descriptive terminology prove confusing, it should be borne in mind that, pursuant to the underlying rationale of structural-level reconstruction, the "reconciliation" or subsumption of "polarized" pitch elements (or articulative fragments) in terms of the symmetrically cohesive octatonic reference collection *does not eliminate* the respect in which, at another level of determinacy, separate entities in the partitioning of this collection—or, in the case of (0,3,6,9) symmetrical partitioning, degrees of "opposition" or "polarity" evidenced by these entities—are recognized. The levels of a structural-level conceptualization constitute (re)interpretations of the passage or piece in question in terms of the particular entity or grouping forwarded (expressions of particular kinds and degrees of determinacy), (re)interpretations which are added to or superimposed on (rather than replacing or superseding) preceding (or succeeding) levels of interpretation, all this constituting, in Boretz's words, "the essential basis of that *functional multiplicity* exhibitable by musical entities."

Terms like "superimposition" and "juxtaposition" bring similar case histories to mind. In the writings of Pierre Boulez, superimposition is viewed, contemptuously, as an "irreducible aggregation," a "coagulation" which creates for the "superimposed" fragments a "false counterpoint," all of this "eminently static in the sense it coagulates the space-sound into a series of unvarying stages . . . and in the sense that it annuls the entire logic of the development."[28] But this "coagulation" is attributed—anachronistically again—to "complexities grafted onto the old organization," these "complexities" constituting a mere "surcharge of an existent [tonal] language."[29] This perspective was perhaps not wholly unpredictable, since the (0 3 7/0 4 7) triads and (0 4 7 10) "dominant sevenths" of Model A are, as regards vocabulary, not only a part of that "existent [tonal] language," but their (0,3,6,9) symmetrical definition, given proper voice-leading, may also be considered as having been available *at least in succession* (although, in *Le Sacre*, implications of this sort are completely irrelevant, so that any attempt to define these "complexities" along tonal lines—something Boulez eschews beyond the casual equation of "polarity" with the subdominant-tonic-dominant relation—would most assuredly confuse rather than illuminate). But this perspective fails to consider the referential status, the (octatonically conceived) symmetrical nature of the deadlock, "coagulation," or "superimposition." For superimposition, viewed as a method of procedure or simply as a handy explanatory or descriptive notion, can only be superficially (or partially) understood as the grafting of reiterating fragments which, in typically Stravinskian fashion, remain fixed in registral distribution. Superimposition will seem conspicuous—or apt as an explanatory notion—to the extent that "a certain opposition" or "polarity" is defined in a content which, octatonically, projects this "opposition" or "polarity" among the fragments being superimposed—possibly (0 3 7/0 4 7) triadic or (0 2 3 5) tetrachordal ones—in the (0,3,6,9) partitioning sense indicated. And so Boulez's lively discussion of superimposition is best interpreted with reference to Models A and B, there being, manifestly, nothing in Stravinsky's music quite so conducive to the production of "superimpositions" that "coagulate the space-sound" than the (0,3,6,9) symmetrically defined (0 3 7/0 4 7/0 4 7 10) triads and (0 2 3 5) tetrachords of Models A and B (Boulez's neglect of these referential implications in *Le Sacre* notwithstanding).

Finally, abrupt block juxtaposition raises the issue of octatonic-diatonic interaction. For the reader will have noted that List 1 (of explicit octatonic reference) is composed merely of blocks and passages of material, which are generally subject to repeats (or near repeats) in their respective contexts, and which exhibit, upon successive (near) repeats, an unusual degree of stability, distinction, and insulation. Quite so. For as here defined, (0,3,6,9) symmetrical construction within blocks defies internally motivated "progress" or "development" along traditional tonal lines (the sense of harmonic progression, resolution, or cadence associated with tonality and the diatonic C-scale). Change, "progress," or "development" is possible only by abruptly cutting off the symmetrically conceived deadlock, only by terminating activity and abruptly juxtaposing it with something new in the collectional reference or in its partitioning (through which, however, some relation, possibly continuously operative, might be left "hanging" as a connecting link or "thread"). In other words, juxtaposition, like superimposition, is no mere formality, no mere architectural curiosity to be heard and understood solely in terms of "form," or in terms of the abrupt or sudden "discontinuities" or "breaks" which, admittedly, tend to affect all dimensions of musical discourse (instrumentation, dynamics, tempo, rhythm, and meter).[30] Abrupt block juxtaposition is *content-motivated*, prompted (one might say necessitated and brought into being) by the static, non-progressive nature of the balance, "polarity," or locked confrontation of Stravinsky's octatonic settings.[31] The results are discernible, in the most conspicuous of cases, in terms of "pitch-collection change,"[32] in terms, that is, of an abrupt shifting in the collectional reference (possibly from octatonic to diatonic or the reverse), each of the juxtaposed blocks acquiring, in the process, a collectional identity. (In other words, the rationale for such juxtaposition is to be found in the static, non-progressive nature of pitch organization generally.) And while we shall presently find all these methods of procedure—or all these explanatory notions or descriptive terms—transcending their specific applicability to octatonic partitioning and becoming applicable to certain of Stravinsky's diatonic partitioning schemes as well, octatonic material seems nevertheless to propel the most incisive formulation (or exemplification).

Naturally, all these procedures—or all these explanatory notions or descriptive terms—interrelate. Symmetrically conceived relations forge conditions of "coagulation," "harmonic stasis," "balance," "polarity," or deadlock; these conditions prompt a "method" of abrupt block juxtaposition; and reiterating fragments at fixed registral points (to which varying rhythmic-metric periods might be assigned) reinforce the general effect of superimposition. (Indeed, at so fundamental a level of construction did Pierre Boulez consider superimposition, juxtaposition, and repetition— and at so fundamental a level did these methods conflict with his own conception of a proper "progress" and "development"—that he ventured to suggest that to juxtapose in the manner of Stravinsky was not really to compose at all.)[33]

Furthermore, it is to be understood that questions regarding the "bitonality" or "polytonality" of certain passages in this literature can no longer be taken seriously within the context of this inquiry. Presumably implying the simultaneous (C-scale tonally functional) unfolding of separate "tonalities" or "keys," these notions—real horrors of the musical imagination—have widely (and mercifully) been dismissed as too fantastic or illogical to be of assistance.[34] Thus, Arthur Berger writes concerning the "*Petroushka* chord":

> Since the entire configuration [the "*Petroushka* chord"] may now be subsumed under a single collection with a single referential order, i.e., the octatonic scale, the dubious concept of "polytonality" need no longer be invoked; nor does such an interpretation make it impossible to acknowledge a certain compound nature of this configuration, since this can be done entirely within the referential collection of the octatonic scale, by means of the partitions.[35]

In other words, it becomes more accurate to speak of the "compound nature of the configuration"—or of the "opposition" or "polarity" that this "compound nature" projects—in terms of the oscillating or superimposed (0,6) tritone-related (0 4 7) triads of the octatonic collection. And while Stravinsky, in 1962, would continue to refer to the "chord" (or, more precisely, to the second tableau of *Petroushka*) as having been "conceived . . . in two keys" (presumably, C and F♯), there is, in actuality, no simultaneous (tonally functional) unfolding of "two keys," but merely this oscillation or superimposition of the (0,6) tritone-related (0 4 7) triads of Collection III at C and F♯.[36] (Stravinsky's conception of "two keys" may have been prompted by the (G B D) triad from outside Collection III which substitutes occasionally for the (C E G) triad. [See, for example, the piano arpeggios at No. 50 in the second tableau, Example 14.] But in place of initiating a tonally functional definition of the "key of C-major," the (G B D) triad merely prompts surface tendency-tone behavior on the part of F♯, A♯, and C♯ of the (F♯ A♯ C♯) component in relation to G, B, and D; that is to say, the F♯ tending to the G, the A♯ to the B, and the C♯ to the D. Indeed, a similar case can be made in regard to the "*Petroushka* chord" itself: namely, that the peculiar disposition of the "chord," the manner in which, as a tremolo at No. 51, its (A♯ C♯ F♯) component in first inversion precedes its (C E G) component in root position, allows F♯ to be heard and understood as something like a chromatic V-of-V tendency tone to the G of the (C E G) triad. But these, surely, are the limits within which the conventions of tonal C-scale practice may reasonably be inferred, or within which such conventions may be said to interact with a Model A partitioning of the octatonic collection. For the context of "*Petroushka* chord," at Nos. 48–52 in the second tableau and at Nos. 76–78 in the third, is securely octatonic. It is prefaced at No. 48 by a G–C–G–F♯–E–E♭ contour in the woodwinds and piano, and just prior to its initial appearance at No. 49 by a (E♭ G B♭ D♭)–(C E G) succession in the piano. This peripheral articulation extends Collection III's (C,E♭,F♯,A) symmetrically defined presence beyond C and F♯ to include, within its cohesive grip, E♭ and the (E♭ G B♭ D♭) "dominant seventh." At No. 77 in the third tableau the "chord" itself is transposed to the remaining—and at Nos. 49–52 omitted—(0,3,6,9) symmetrically defined partitioning elements of Collection III, E♭ and A in terms of a (E♭ G B♭)–(A C♯ E) tremolo.

Of course, if we ignore the (F♯ A♯ C♯) triad entirely at Nos. 48–52, some crudely drawn "key of C-major" is conceivable. But the overall effect does not admit such an interpretation. Aside from the inherent contradictions posed by the notion of "bitonality," a simultaneous unfolding of separate "tonalities" or "keys" is not a part of our perceptual experience. (Indeed, to include the "*Petroushka*-chord" context and the countless others like it in Stravinsky's music within the tonally functional C-scale compound of earlier music would be to invite so crippling a degree of qualification as to render the inclusion nearly incomprehensible. On the other hand, without such qualification, the meaning and significance of C-scale tonally functional analysis and theory would be so stretched as to render them, in turn, useless as a set of binding propositions for the music for which, after all, they were intended.) We are struck, first, by "the compound nature of the configuration," by the separate (0,6) tritone-related triads "rooted on" C and F♯, a separateness underscored in the instrumentation and by the variance in disposition, the (C E G) triad being in root position, the (F♯ A♯ C♯) triad in first inversion. And we are struck, second (and nonetheless), by the unified, cohesive effect of the configuration or "chord," by the (0,6) tritone relation or "equal" partitioning of the octave, which allows the oscillating or superimposed triads to assume "equal weight and independence" and stand in a fixed, polarized "opposition," and hence to assume, in place of the conventional forms of harmonic progress, the inert, deadlocked character alluded to, a self-enclosed sufficiency unto itself.

And we are struck, finally, by referential character: that a vocabulary of (0 3 7/0 4 7) "minor" and "major" triads, of (0 4 7 10) "dominant sevenths" and—however peripherally—of chromatic tendency tones (a vocabulary so familiar to the music of the seventeenth to nineteenth centuries) should here be so subtly transformed, acquiring a new complexion attributable not only to techniques of triadic oscillation and superimposition, but also to the new octatonic or octatonic-diatonic mold of which this vocabulary is now felt to be a part. (All of this pertains to octatonic and octatonic-diatonic contexts of the neoclassical works as well, of course, even though, on the diatonic side of the referential coin, the familiar C-scale may often be inferred, so that the transformation has not merely to do with vocabulary *tout court*, but also with an occasional yielding, in however parenthetical or "impure" a manner, to the functional behavior with which it identifies in the music of the Baroque, Classical, and Romantic eras.)

And so we have come, by means of the "*Petroushka* chord" in this preliminary, roundabout, frame-of-reference fashion, to an initial understand ing of the general appearance of much of Stravinsky's music: an abrupt juxtaposition of blocks of material, these blocks exhibiting, upon successive (near) repeats in their respective contexts, an unusual degree of stability, distinction, and insulation in instrumental, dynamic, and rhythmic-metric design; these blocks at times referentially octatonic (as comprehensively defined in Models A and B), at times referentially diatonic (a term as yet to be defined), and at times exhibiting an interpenetration of these two distinct reference collections. Moreover, abrupt block juxtaposition offers an invaluable clue to analytical method. For confronted with the kind of "discontinuity" it imposes, the "sudden breaks" which so often affect all dimensions of musical discourse (but, most profoundly, referential character), why burden ourselves with tonal C-scale schemes of "continuity" or "coherence" which, if not entirely inapplicable, cannot be the most advantageous since they ignore this most conspicuous feature?[37] Why not accept this conception of form (so tellingly Stravinskian), accept the relative stability, distinction, and insulation of these blocks upon successive (near) repeats in their respective contexts, accept the referential implications of this formal or architectural condition (in terms of "pitch-collection change"), and proceed accordingly? And if, by so doing, we afford ourselves, in comparison with the analysis of a tonal, C-scale piece, little with which to contend on a global or continuously operative basis (possibly in the way of between-block or between-reference connecting links or "threads"), what of it? We shall have penetrated far more persuasively matters of consistency, identity, and distinction.

THE FAMILIAR ORIENTATION
CATEGORIES OR PERIODS

When Stravinsky's music is viewed as a whole, a partiality for Model A's (0 3 7/0 4 7/0 4 7 10) triadic or (0 1 3 4) tetrachordal partitioning of the octatonic collection is revealed. This partiality is doubtless owing to the length of the neoclassical period, encompassing the bulk of Stravinsky's output, Model A's (0 3 7/0 4 7) triads and (0 1 3 4) tetrachords having constituted—evidently—a more favorable foundation for accommodation in this neoclassical respect than the (0,3,6,9) symmetrically defined (0 2 3 5) tetrachords of Model B. Thus, while Model B's (0 2 3 5) tetrachordal scheme of partitioning prevails in many "Russian" pieces like Le Sacre and Les Noces (notwithstanding the "Petroushka chord" and Le Sacre's "Jeu du rapt"; see Examples 14 and 16c in this chapter), this (0 2 3 5) preoccupation is scarcely evident during the neoclassical and serial periods, when octatonic partitioning invariably "hooks up" to Model A and the 1,2 (ascending) interval ordering of the scale.

Moreover, a change of this sort relates to changes in the diatonic writing. In many "Russian" works, Model B's (0 2 3 5) articulative partitioning of the octatonic collection coincides with a (0 2 3 5) partitioning of the diatonic collection that rather consistently implicates the interval ordering of the D-scale, or of a diatonic hexachordal segment. But in the neoclassical era, the partiality for Model A's (0 3 7/0 4 7) triadic or (0 1 3 4) tetrachordal partitioning relates to a partitioning of the diatonic collection that frequently implicates the interval ordering of the C-scale, a reference almost nonexistent in lengthy "Russian" works. And, naturally, this neoclassical C-scale implication harbors references not only to certain conventions, inflections, and gestures of (tonal) C-scale literature, but, occasionally, to certain tonally functional relations as well (conceived in however adulterated, "impure," or parenthetical a manner).

Thus, in regard to the *Symphony of Psalms* (1930), we might generally describe the first movement as a piece in which octatonic blocks referable to Collection I (Model A, with a generally (0.3,6) "background" partitioning in terms of E, G, and B♭) interact with—or are placed in juxtaposition with—diatonic blocks referable to the E-scale on E. Throughout this, however, the (E G B) triad (the "*Psalms* chord") acts as a punctuating element; it is the principal connecting link, articulatively shared between these distinct collections of reference and the interval orderings implicated. But a gradual ascendancy of G and its (G B D F) "dominant-seventh" articulation (also shared) becomes unmistakable in view of "half cadence" on G that concludes the first movement, a conclusion that prepares, in dominant-toniclike fashion, for the quasi-C-minor fugue of the second movement. Moreover, a critical interpenetrating circumstance (stemming from the coming together or simultaneous engagement of a pitch element *not* held in common) materializes earlier in the first movement to reinforce this tonally incriminating conclusion: a non-octatonic C asserts itself at Nos. 3 and 6, so that the dominant-toniclike "resolution" concluded by the second movement, complementing the "half cadence" on G in the first, may be said to have been anticipated by an earlier suggestive "feel" in this direction.

Similar tonally incriminating (long-term or global) conditions govern many of Stravinsky's neoclassical ventures. In the *Symphony in Three Movements* (1945), the opening material of the first movement is octatonic, accountable to Collection I and "hooking up" to Model A with a generally (0,6) "background" partitioning in terms of G and D♭. But this material is superimposed over an interpenetrating C-scale-on-C reference in the trombones at No. 1, and interpenetrating C-scale passages in the strings at Nos. 4 and 16–20, so that the (tonally incriminating) "C-ending" to which this Collection-I material resigns itself in the final measures, in the form of a (C E G) triad (riddled, to be sure, with a most telling peculiarity or "impurity": a B positioned so as to preserve the earlier, octatonically conceived assertions of priority on the part of both G and, at No. 29, E), may also be said to have been anticipated by an earlier suggestive "feel."

But octatonic-diatonic interaction in neoclassical works—often in the form of an accommodation between Model A's (0 3 7/0 4 7/0 4 7 10) or (0 1 3 4) partitioning of the octatonic collection and certain conventions and inflections associated with (tonal) C-scale literature—need not provoke tonally functional substantiation—however "impure" or parenthetical—of the dominant-tonic relation. Nor, obviously, is octatonic-diatonic inter- action limited to the neoclassical category. The whole of this music is satu- rated with varied exhibitions of it, discernible already in *Fireworks* (1908) at Nos. 0–9 and 16–21, and subsequently in non-C-scale, nontonal works like *Le Sacre* (1913), *Renard* (1916), and *Les Noces* (1917). Even later, when this interaction is of the neoclassical Model-A–C-scale variety, it need not prompt tonal functionality in the manner of the *Symphony of Psalms*, first movement. And so it will be useful here to ponder (and correct) some mis- conceptions in Arthur Berger's remarks concluding his "Problems of Pitch Organization in Stravinsky." These misconceptions betray a neo- classical or Model-A bias not wholly unpredictable (since this orientation encompasses the bulk of Stravinsky's output, with Model A predominat- ing), but, by dismissing the role of Model B's (0 2 3 5) tetrachordal parti- tioning of the octatonic collection in Stravinsky's "Russian" music, contra- dict findings critical to this inquiry (and so conveniently bring these findings to the fore):

> The [(0 2 3 5)] tetrachord with interval order 2,1,2 . . . is one that proliferates in manifold folktune-derived motives and melodic fragments throughout Stravinsky's "Russian" period. . . . What could be more natural than a merger of two predilections—the other being his well-known one for the tritone— out of which would issue a new scale: D,e,F,g; G♯,a♯,B,c♯, two tritone-related tetrachords thus bringing the D-scale into the orbit of the octatonic scale? The answer to this question is fundamental: if such were the case the octa- tonic scale would suffer a severe loss of identity. Thus, in terms of the impor- tant first degree (or of each "accented" element of the disjunct dyads in the normal representation of the scale), the succession of consecutive scale de- grees would yield nothing different from any referential ordering of inter- vals in the familiar white-note vocabulary until the fifth degree were reached—and even this, in terms of Classical practice, could be a so-called "tendency tone." It is the new "rhythm," in the ordering of intervals, that defines the uniqueness of the relations Stravinsky employed, namely, an or- dering that gives up its secret, not at the fifth, but at the *fourth* degree, defining a [(0 1 3 4)] tetrachord whose first and fourth elements are related by the interval of 4 semitones.[38]

Berger's conclusions notwithstanding, the "blocks" and passages of Lists 1 and 2—especially those of the "Russian" era, as we have suggested—provide evidence of frequent analytical assertions of Model B with respect to (0 2 3 5) partitioning ("the tetrachord with interval order 2,1,2") and the 2,1 whole-step–half-step interval ordering of the scale implicated. Relations in *Le Sacre*—which one can only assume to be as uniquely Stravinskian as any in the literature—frequently exemplify (0 2 3 5) articulative partitioning by way of the "two tritone-related tetrachords" mentioned by Berger. These (0,6) tritone-related (0 2 3 5) tetrachords in terms of (0 2 3 5) (6 8 9 11) span the interval of 11 (the "major seventh"), an 0–11 vertical interval span that not only accounts for much of the static "vertical chromaticism" in the piece but is also very nearly continuously operative. The elements of this 0–11 interval span assert, from one block or section to the next, degrees of priority, of "equal weight and independence," and stand in a fixed, polarized "opposition." As two of many obvious examples, see, in Example 17b of this chapter, No. 64 in "Jeux des cités rivales," where the "upper" (G F E D) complete (0 2 3 5) tetrachord in the strings stands "in opposition" to the "lower" (C♯ A♯ G♯) incomplete (6 8 9 11) tetrachord in the tubas; or see, in Example 27 of chapter 4, No. 134 in "Action rituelle des ancêtres," where the "upper" (C♯ B A♯ G) tetrachord stands "in opposition" to the "lower" (G F E D) tetrachord, the (0,6) defined (C♯ B A♯ G♯) (G F E D) partitioning in both these blocks referring to Collection I, Model B, and representing, in pitch content, precisely the one to which Berger refers. (The "uppermost" pitch and the "upper" of the two (0,6) tritone-related (0 2 3 5) (6 8 9 11) tetrachords, complete or incomplete, generally preside in *Le Sacre*, the "lower" of these tetrachords being less persistently pursued and often represented merely by pitch number 11. This predominance is—as indicated already above—just one of the many reasons why, in cases of (0 2 3 5) tetrachordal partitioning, we subscribe to a descending scale and pitch numbering, a reading-down instead of the customary ascending approach.) Moreover, at Nos. 13–30 in "Danses des adolescentes" (Example 27 in chapter 4), the octatonic contribution, conspicuous at Nos. 14–18 and 22–24, is accounted for in terms of Collection III, a (E♭,C) "background" partitioning with (E♭ D♭ B♭), representing an incomplete (E♭ D♭ C B♭) tetrachord, standing "in opposition" to the (C B♭ A G) tetrachord and (C E G) triad. To the extent that the elements of this (E♭ D♭ C B♭ A G F♯ E) Collection-III contribution gradually give way to an unimpaired diatonic (E♭ D♭ C B♭ A♭ G♭ F (E♭)) D-scale-on-E♭ reference at Nos. 28–30 (where the (E♭ D♭ C B♭) tetrachord serves as the principal connecting link, as that which is shared between Collection III and the D-scale on E♭), the transaction is manifestly one in which, in Berger's words, "the D-scale is brought into the orbit of the octatonic scale." There can be no more accurate description of these "Danses" proceedings.

With respect to any "loss of [octatonic] identity" incurred by (0 2 3 5) partitioning and the 2,1 interval ordering of the scale (as mentioned by

Berger), we may note that, as the collection stands engaged, Model A's 1,2 ordering, implicated by the various (0 3 7/0 4 7/0 4 7 10) and (0 1 3 4) articulative complexes, is far more vulnerable with respect to tendency-tone behavior. There are numerous instances of octatonic reference, particularly in Stravinsky's neoclassical ventures, where the (0 1 3 4) complex is conceived in terms of (0 3 4/3 4 7/3 6 7) "minor-major third" emphasis, and where pitch numbers 3 and 6 of this 1,2 ordering, irrespective of their potential for "equal weight and independence" in the (0,3,6,9) symmetrical partitioning of the collection outlined in Model A, are more conventionally conceived as tendency tones or "melodic leading tones" to pitch numbers 4 and 7 (the "major third" and "fifth") of the (0 4 7) "major" triad, this tendency-tone potential being available to each of the (0 4 7) "major" triads at 0,3,6, and 9 of Model A.[39] In other words, it will often be useful to hear and understand cases of "minor-major third" emphasis— the (0 3 4/3 4 7/3 6 7) "clash," perhaps the most persistently pursued of all neoclassical "impurities," certainly the most frequently cited—as octatonically conceived, as a species of octatonic-diatonic interaction. Thus, in the C-scale-on-D (or D-major scale) reference at Nos. 112–18 in the second movement of the *Symphony in Three Movements* (Example 59 in chapter 10), pitch numbers 3 and 6, the F and G♯, may serve conventionally as tendency tones to 4 and 7 of the (0 4 7) "tonic" triad (the F♯ and A of the (D F♯ A) triad), but also as intruding "impurities" in this C-scale-on-D setting. Here, the (0 3 4/3 6 7) "clash" in terms of (D F F♯/F F♯ A) signals the elevation of these pitch classes—and particularly of F—from "dependency tones" to independent elements on a par with their neighbors, thus warranting accountability at the collectional level, an accreditation which the C-scale (on D) cannot properly confer. And so we would interpret this passage in terms of an interpenetration between the C-scale on D and Collection II, noting: (1) that D assumes priority and serves, with its (D F♯ A) triad, as the principal connecting link (that which is shared); and (2) that a duality is manifested in the functional behavior of pitch numbers 3 and 6, but that, with respect to the octatonic (Collection II) contribution, the F and G♯, while asserting independence, do not really act as symmetrically defined partitioning elements with a degree of "equal weight and independence" in relation to the D in the sense demonstrated in Model A, there being no (0 3 7/0 4 7) triadic "support" at F or G♯ to implement this potential. This naturally undermines the identity of the contribution, placing Collection II at a rather severe disadvantage vis-à-vis its diatonic counterpart, the C-scale on D.

Among countless similar neoclassical examples, the introductory passage from the "Basle" *Concerto in D* (1946) seems exemplary in these respects. The total (0 3 4 7 9) pitch content inferable at Nos. 0–5 in terms of (D F F♯ A B) is as octatonic (Collection II) as it is diatonic (C-scale on D), but diatonic, of course, *only* by virtue of the tendency-tone interpretation of F, pitch number 3. (See Example 58a in chapter 10.) Here again, the point of the passage would seem to rest in the dual nature of E♯ [F] as pitch number 3. This pitch is occasionally articulated as a tendency tone to the F♯, the "major third" of the (D F♯ A) "tonic" triad, and occasionally as an intruding "impurity" by virtue of the (F F♯ A) "clashes" and the (D F F♯/F F♯ A) "minor-major third" figuration, pursued without the slightest trace of C-scale (on D) tonally functional behavior. And so, in addition to tonal functionality in the manner of the *Symphony of Psalms*, the (0 3 4/3 4 7/3 6 7) "minor-major third" phenomenon appears as just another way in which octatonic partitioning (Model A) and traditional C-scale or major-scale conventions or inflections interrelate. Were we to investigate from a diatonic perspective, we could credit the interpenetrating octatonic collection with systematically "subverting" the C-scale with (0 3 4/3 4 7/3 6 7) "impurity"; or, from an octatonic perspective, acknowledge the manner in which Model A is modified by a neoclassical concern for C-scale conventions and tendency-tone inflections. The attraction of this perspective is that it allows for a hearing, understanding, and definition of certain neoclassical phenomena in terms of a lifelong preoccupation with octatonic partitioning, resulting in a consistency, identity, or distinction that overlaps the considerable changes in general "stylistic" orientation from *The Firebird* (1910) to *Agon* (1953–57). By extending accountability to these phenomena, the broad perspective allows, at the same time, for a better grasp of peculiarity in the exhibition of these phenomena from one period (or from one passage or piece) to the next.

But to return to the "Russian" era. The neoclassical or Model-A bias underlying Berger's conclusions may have been prompted by his commitment to the familiar ascending approach in scale representation and pitch numbering. Thus, at Nos. 35–40 and 82–87 in *Les Noces* (containing explicit octatonic reference: List 1), Berger infers (0,6) "background" partitioning in terms of (A,E♭). And given the pitch content (Collection III), this approach naturally yields the 1,2 interval ordering for the scale at A or E♭: A–B♭–C–D♭–E♭–E–F♯–G–(A). But the problem with this determination (and with the pitch numbering it implies) is that it obscures the essential 0–2 whole-step reiterations and the (0 2 5) "basic cell" articulated by (A-G) (E♭-D♭) and (A G E) (E♭ D♭ B♭) (reading down, with the uppermost pitch generally presiding as the more insistent). These (0 2) and (0 2 5) groupings are very nearly continuously operative in *Les Noces* with respect to both diatonic and octatonic activity, and the only means of recording both (0,6) tritone partitioning in terms of (A,E♭) *and* this global (0 2 5) articulation (at A and E♭ here) would be via a descending formulation which, far more conveniently than the ascending form, would expose the priorities, associative factors, and connecting links discernible "above" the blocks of varied referential implications: A–G–F♯–E–E♭–D♭–C–B♭–(A), reading down (or, from E♭, also reading down).

It is apparent, then, that questions regarding the "identity" of the collection or the "uniqueness of the relations Stravinsky employed" are not as clearcut or as easily defined as Arthur Berger would have us believe. Obviously, the comprehensive survey of this chapter, with its inclusion of a (0 2 3 5) tetrachordal format (Model B), reflects—or can cover— considerable diversity in octatonic or octatonic-diatonic thought, a diversity which Berger seemed unable or unwilling to acknowledge.

And so, as we now turn to a study of individual passages or pieces, our interest will lie not only in how efficiently (or how cleverly) instances of octatonic partitioning substantiate the comprehensive definition of Models A and B, but also in how efficiently (or how usefully) this comprehensive coverage allows for a detection (a satisfying hearing and understanding) of peculiarity both in such individual instances and in the familiar orientation categories. So, too, our inquiries will constitute a kind of hovering over what might, with respect to our comprehensive coverage, be deemed unexceptional (routine), and what might, with respect to this same coverage, be deemed exceptional.

THREE
PETROUSHKA
The Diatonic Pitch Collection in the
Music of Stravinsky's "Russian" Period

Curiously, the octatonic beginnings of *Petroushka*—as a *Konzertstück*—were to become part of a framework that is overwhelmingly diatonic. There are no blocks or passages of explicit octatonic reference (List 1) in the lengthy first tableau. And in the final appearances of the (referentially octatonic) "*Petroushka* chord" toward the close of the (ostensibly diatonic) fourth tableau, its referential complexion is altered from that at Nos. 48–52 in the second tableau. Hence, this continued discussion of *Petroushka* inevitably becomes a discussion of the diatonic collection, and of the partitioning—perhaps typically "Russian"—that may be inferred on its behalf.

Still, at Nos. 0-30 in the first tableau, "chromatic" (nondiatonic) pitch elements and intervals may be heard and interpreted as referentially octatonic, as prompting a form of diatonic-octatonic (Model B) interpenetration—again, perhaps typically "Russian." And so our concern here rests not only with the diatonic collection, but also with how the partitioning of this collection relates to these "intrusions" of referentially octatonic (nondiatonic) material, and how the consequent octatonic (Model B) and diatonic interpenetration may be distinguished from the neoclassical octatonic (Model A) and diatonic C-scale (major-scale) variety briefly alluded to in the final pages of the preceding chapter (a variety to which, of course, we shall be returning for further study in chapters 9, 10, 11, and 12). For it is a matter of consequence that these octatonic "intrusions" in the first tableau refer to Collection III, and therefore anticipate the (more) fully committed Collection-III framework of the "*Petroushka* chord" in the second tableau.

PITCH RELATIONS IN
THE FIRST TABLEAU

In *Petroushka*'s first tableau attention will be drawn to the D-scale with a pitch numbering of 0 2 3 5 7 9 10 (0) reading down (see Example 18), and to the diatonic hexachordal segment with a pitch numbering of 0 2 3 5 7 9 (0) also reading down (see Example 19).[1] And while these references—or the partitioning manifesting them—may occasionally be apprehended in diatonic material of the neoclassical persuasion, like (0 2 3 5) partitioning of the octatonic collection and the 2,1 interval ordering of the scale implicated (Model B), they are nonetheless characteristic of "Russian" musical thought, doubtless because of Stravinsky's addiction at the time to all manner of (0 2 3 5) folklike fragments with interval order 2,1,2 (some of these genuine, most ingeniously pseudo). Indeed, were the "Russian" label to wield a legitimacy transcending the preoccupation with these (0 2 3 5) folkish fragments (and with Russian popular verse), this legitimacy would have to reside in this partitioning of the diatonic collection (often implicating the D-scale or the (0 2 3 5 7 9) hexachord), and in the regularities governing diatonic-octatonic (Model B) interaction. Some of this between-reference, connecting-link regularity is perhaps already vaguely discernible from the pitch numbering.

Moreover, while the integrity of the six-note (0 2 3 5 7 9) diatonic hexachord naturally hinges on the absence (or peripheral behavior) of a seventh pitch element—a possible closing of what might be called the (0 2 3 5 7 9) hexachord's 9-0 "gap," with pitch number 10 (reading down) completing the diatonic collection—it harbors a partitioning strategy that often ensures it a measure of referential cohesion even when such an element does insinuate itself. Indeed, a circumstance tending to underscore (0 2 3 5 7 9) integrity is the flexibility often found in the

		i	ii	iii	iv	v	vi	vii	(i)
0 2 3 5 7 9 10 (0) D-scale on E:		E	D	C♯	B	A	G	F♯	(E)
pitch numbers:			0	2	3	5	7	9	10	(0)
intervals:				2	1	2	2	2	1	(2)

Example 18

(0 2) (7 9)

(0 2 3 5) (7 9 0)
tetrachords

(0 3 7 / 0 4 7)
triads

0 2 3 5 7 9 (0)
hexachord

		i	ii	iii	iv	v	vi	(i)
0 2 3 5 7 9 (0) hexachord on E:		E	D	C♯	B	A	G	(E)
pitch numbers:			0	2	3	5	7	9	(0)
intervals:				2	1	2	2	2	(3)

Example 19

identity of the seventh pitch class. Of the two pitch elements that might close its 9–0 "gap," the "intrusion" of pitch number 10 (reading down) would render (0 2 3 5 7 9) surroundings fully diatonic, by tending to implicate the D-scale's (0 2 3 5 7 9 10) interval ordering, but with the hexachord's partitioning formulae intact; and pitch number 11 (reading down) results in a (0 2 3 5 6 8 9 11) octatonic (0 2 3 5 7 9) diatonic interpenetration. This flexibility in turn allows many (0 2 3 5 7 9) contexts to act as "go-betweens" with respect to more fully committed diatonic, octatonic, or octatonic-diatonic frameworks, with the elusive seventh pitch element acting as a kind of pivot. (Only the (0 2 3 5 7 9) hexachord's pitch number 7 resists the (0 2 3 5 6 8 9 11) octatonic order, Model B; and only the absence of pitch number 10 thwarts a fully accredited diatonic collection.)

Thus, in Examples 18, 19, and 20 the reader will find both the (0 2 3 5 7 9 10 (0)) D-scale and the (0 2 3 5 7 9 (0)) diatonic hexachord descending from E in terms of (E D C♯ B A G (F♯) E). This collection has been selected from the twelve available because it figures in the opening blocks of *Petroushka*, *Les Noces*, and *Histoire du soldat*. In Example 19, the partitioning formulae to be inferred on behalf of the (0 2 3 5 7 9) hexachord (on E here) are demonstrated: first, (0 2) (7 9) partitioning in terms of (E D) (A G); second, (0 2 3 5) (7 9 0) tetrachordal partitioning in terms of (E D C♯ B) (A G E), where the "lower" (A G E) tetrachord is (7 9 0) incomplete, but might be rendered (7 9 10 0) complete with the D-scale's pitch number 10, the F♯ here; third, (0 3 7/0 4 7) triadic partitioning in terms of the two (0 4 7) "major" triads related by the interval of 2 at A and G, (A C♯ E) and (G B D), and in terms of the (0 3 7) "minor" triad at E, (E G B); fourth, these groupings yielding the (0 2 3 5 7 9) hexachordal collection in terms of (E D C♯ B A G).

In Example 20, a possible closing of the (0 2 3 5 7 9) hexachord's 9–0 "gap" (at G-E here) is demonstrated (see the arrows): the "intrusion" of the D-scale's pitch number 10, the F♯ here, would complete the diatonic collection as well as the "lower" incomplete (7 9 0) tetrachord in terms of (A G F♯ E); and the ("chromatic") "intrusion" of the octatonic Collection I's pitch number 11, the F here, would signal the intervention of octatonic

Example 20

relations, possibly a form of Collection I (Model B) and diatonic (E D C♯ B A G) interpenetration, this F defining the interval of 11, an 0–11 or "major-seventh" interval span with pitch number 0, the E. Still, it is to be noted that the (0 2 3 5 7 9) hexachord's "missing" seventh pitch element may "intrude" pivotlike elsewhere, although its 9–0 "gap" is most vulnerable in this respect. Thus, in moving from a (0 2 3 5 7 9) diatonic hexachordal context to a (0 2 3 5 6 8 9 11) octatonic context—or to some form of (0 2 3 5 6 8 9 11) octatonic and (0 2 3 5 7 9) diatonic interpenetration— the (0 2 3 5 6 8 9 11) octatonic collection's pitch number 6, the B♭ in the (E D C♯ B A G) hexachord in Example 20, might "intrude" to signal this intervention. This referentially octatonic pitch number 6, the B♭ in Example 20, defines the interval of 6, the tritone, with pitch number 0, the E, these (0,6) tritone-related elements generally assuming the previously noted symmetrically defined conditions of "equal weight" and standing in a fixed, polarized "opposition."

We begin our analysis with a passage in which the credentials for (0 2 3 5 7 9) hexachordal inference are impeccable: the opening block of *Petroushka* at Nos. 0–2 and its subsequent abbreviation at No. 2 + 3. (See Example 21.) For here, the omission of a seventh pitch element—indeed, the adverse consequences that accrue from any "forced" closing of the G–E "gap" with an F or F♯—testifies to (0 2 3 5 7 9) integrity in terms of the (E D C♯ B A G) collection, foreclosing any referral of this block to the A-scale on D or the "key of D-minor" (in the sense, perhaps, of an "ascending D-minor scale" at No. 1 and of a "descending D-minor scale" at No. 2). There are, in addition to this very critical absence of a truly unthinkable F, no C-scale (or major-scale) tonally functional transactions.[2] (F as the "missing" seventh pitch element—pitch number 11 with respect to the (0 2 3 5 7 9) numbering at No. 0–2—does not appear until No. 3 where the (0 2 3 5) articulation in terms of (C B♭ A G) accentuates G rather than D (or A). These circumstances implicate the D-scale on G rather than the A-scale on D, and thus provide the opening (2–0) (7–9) whole-step reiterations, D–E and A–G, with a new referential framework and pitch numbering.)

Indeed, of the two pitch elements that might close the G–E "gap" at Nos. 0–2 and 2 + 3, F♯ seems by far the more "thinkable." But if either the F or the F♯ is hypothetically inserted into these (E D C♯ B A G) surroundings, the effect is manifestly ruinous. And so, straightaway, we perceive in this critical withholding of a seventh pitch element the "open" quality Stravinsky means to impart with respect to any potential leanings toward a more fully accredited diatonic, octatonic, or octatonic-diatonic framework. It is left for future blocks to implement this potential and to decide the (0 2 3 5 7 9) hexachord's fate, very often by closing its 9–0 "gap" with an "intruding" seventh pitch element.

Example 21: First tableau

Of course, F does appear on the first beats of subsequent (near) repeats of the No. 0 block (at Nos. 8+4 and 11+5, and in the instrumental "fill" accompanying the final (near) repeat at No. 27). And this imposition of F does alter the referential implications. For not only does F, or the (D F A) triad intervene, but the (0 2 3 5) tetrachord in terms of (E D C♯ B), articulated by the cello at Nos. 1 and 2+5, is omitted. Moreover, in these subsequent (near) repeats, the F, or the (D F A) triad, may clearly be apprehended as a continuation of the material of the No. 8 block, material which invariably precedes these No. 0 block (near) repeats, and in which a (D F A)–(G B D) triadic oscillation implicates the (D C B A G F) hexachordal collection. Consequently, in respect to these subsequent No. 0 block (near) repeats, we interpret referentially in terms of the (D C B A G F) collection—or, possibly, the D-scale on D.

But before concluding that the (0 2 3 5 7 9) hexachord in the first tableau is the referential "norm" or "home base" from which subsequent blocks diverge—often, as we have indicated, by way of a seventh-pitch "intrusion"—we might retreat to a somewhat more long-term, global, or

Example 21 *continued*

continuously operative perspective. For it is illuminating to interpret *Petroushka* as a piece in which two simultaneities oscillate or move back and forth (accordianlike, as so many have observed), a movement by no means limited to *Petroushka* (as should be apparent from the illustrations in chapters 1 and 2), but which may nonetheless seem unusually conspicuous and persistent there. The two simultaneities very often number six pitch elements, three to each. (Thus, in this global, number-of-elements approach, the (0 2 3 5 7 9) hexachord of the first tableau appears as just one of several hexachordal collections or orderings.) Either "on top" or "on the bottom" (or both), the simultaneities are often related by the interval of 2, a whole step. Of the three D–E, A–G, and B♭–C whole-step reiterations which define the two (B♭ D A)–(C E G) oscillating simultaneities at Nos. 2 and 3 and at subsequent (near) repeats of these blocks, at least one of these whole-step dyads survives globally (on a more or less continuously operative basis), especially in material of the first, second, and fourth tableaux.

Still, in regard to the global attitude, we ignore for the time being inferences regarding (pitch-identity) dyadic "survival," and merely record,

Example 21 *continued*

from one block to the next in Example 21, the two oscillating simultaneities. Thus, at Nos. 0–2 and 2 + 3, these simultaneities are (D A)–(G E),
numbering four elements, not six. Beneath this surface, a partitioning is
forwarded on behalf of the (0 2 3 5 7 9) hexachord in recognition of the
following circumstances: (1) the 2–0 and 7–9 whole-step reiterations, D–E
and A–G in the horns, which are in turn articulated as a series of 5s or
"fourths," A–D, E–A, and D–G, in the accompanying flute melody; (2) the
(0 2 3 5) tetrachord in terms of (E D C♯ B), articulated in the cello at No. 1;
(3) these articulative groupings jointly yielding the (0 2 3 5 7 9) hexachordal collection in terms of (E D C♯ B A G). (We leave local or sectional
assertions of pitch-class and/or dyad priority to the commentary, reserv-
ing for analytical representation the articulative partitioning and the consequent referential implications. These constitute the focus of our concern even though local definitions of priority are critical to our
deliberations and may *sometimes* be inferred from the assigned scale representations and pitch numbers. *Sometimes*, because E is not the most likely
candidate for pitch-class priority status as pitch number 0 at Nos. 0–2 and

Example 21 *continued*

2 + 3; D is actually in that position, owing perhaps to metric accentuation and "fifth support." However, the two pitch classes which encircle the (0 2 3 5 7 9) hexachord on each side (four in all: the D–E and A–G reiterations, (2–0) and (7–9) in the (E D C♯ B A G) hexachord at Nos. 0–2 and 2+3), will be found, from one "Russian" diatonic context to the next, to exercise a uniquely (0 2 3 5 7 9) conceived life of their own with respect to the assertion of pitch-class priority, an exercise often foreclosing rulings as to (single) pitch-class priority even on a strictly local basis.)

At No. 2, the oscillating (B♭ D A)–(C E G) simultaneities number six elements. A B♭–C reiteration is here added to the D–E and A–G reiterations (which serve as between-block or between-reference connecting links); this B♭–C unit thus replaces the (C♯ B) dyad of the cello's opening (E D C♯ B) tetrachord. These three 2s or whole steps, together with the (0 2 3 5) tetrachord now articulated in terms of C–B♭–A–G in the lower strings, yield the (E D C B♭ A G) collection, a retrograde inversion of the opening hexachordal ordering, so that the reference collection is altered with respect to pitch-class content and referential ordering.

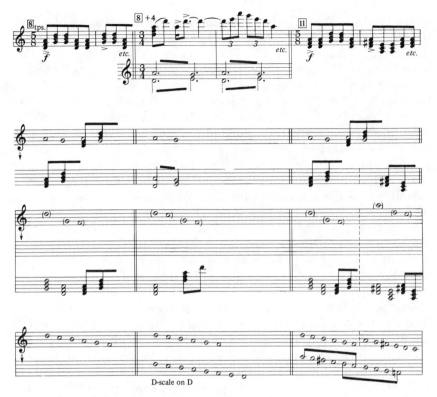

D-scale on D

Example 21 *continued*

Then, following the (near) repeat of the opening block at No. 2+3, F, withheld as the "missing" seventh pitch element (pitch number 11 with respect to the two preceding referential orderings), is introduced at No. 3 in an extension of the C–B♭–A–G tetrachordal fragment of the No. 2 block. This imposition completes the diatonic collection, the articulation accentuating G and implicating the D-scale on G with respect to referential ordering. We extend this D-scale-on-G determination to the following block at No. 5 as well; the G–C–B♭–A–G–F–A–G folk melody bursts forth here as a culmination, a final destination with respect to which the preceding blocks assume a preparatory character.[3]

Still, we might consider the tonal alternative to our interpretation of the No. 5 block in Example 21. For an observer could claim that the presiding G here is as readily identified with the (C E G) triad as it is with (G B♭ D), and that this identification with the (C E G) triad suggests a harmonization of the borrowed melody "in the key of F-major" (with "added notes"): vi–IV–V–vi–IV(ii)–V. And, indeed, such a reading may not be entirely unwarranted: the (B♭ D A)–(C E G) oscillating simultaneities, introduced by the blocks at Nos. 2 and 3, reinterpreted at No. 5 in terms of a "half cadence" or IV (ii)–V progression "in F."[4] The only problem, however, is that the (F A C) "tonic" triad, which must in some sense underlie such a perspective and be at least conceivable at some point, if not actualized, is not only scrupulously avoided but seems as unlikely or as "unthinkable" in these surroundings as was the "missing" seventh pitch element, the F or F♯, in the opening (E D C♯ B A G) and (E D C B♭ A G) preparatory blocks at Nos. 0–2, 2, and 2 + 3. And so this tonal reading seems predicated on an entirely local (No. 5 block) reckoning of affairs.

Furthermore, were we to extract from the harmonization at No. 5 three triads as the foundation of the display, we might discover in their referential implications probable cause for the inconceivability (or undesirability) of the (F A C) "tonic" triad: the (G B♭ D) triad and the oscillating (B♭ D F)–(C E G) triads "underneath" yield the (G F E D C B♭) collection with respect to (0 2 3 5 7 9) hexachordal reference, and thus provide the setting with a (0 2 3 5 7 9)-conceived "harmonic stasis" (derived from the incapacity of (0 2 3 5 7 9) for real harmonic progress beyond static oscillation or the accordion effect), similar to that realized in the opening passages or blocks. In other words, from within the framework of the (completed) diatonic D-scale on G at No. 5, we may infer a foundational (G B♭ D) (C E G) (B♭ D F) triadic articulation accountable to the (G F E D C B♭) hexachord, in which G may be identified with the (G B♭ D) triad or with the (C E G) triad, or may simply be regarded as centric with respect to the (G B♭ D/C E G) compound simultaneity punctuated throughout at No. 5+8, + 12, + 15, and + 17 as a point of departure and return. (Notice, too, the (G C E) second inversion of the (C E G) component, which would seem to underscore G as *the* pitch class of priority.) This foundational triadic partitioning of the (G F E D C B♭) hexachord at No. 5 is also of consequence in that it may again be inferred at Nos. 8 and 11, in terms of the (D C B A G F) and (A G F♯ E D C) hexachordal collections.

Thus, the "breaking-up" passage at No. 7 (see Example 23) is interpreted in terms of the (A G F♯ E D C) hexachord in which B♭—not F— serves as the "intruding" seventh pitch element as pitch number 11. (We infer C from the (C E G) triad which directly precedes the "breaking up" at No. 7, and from the E–D–C grace-note sequence. And, with respect to B♭ as the seventh pitch element in relation to the (A G F♯ E D C) hexachordal collection, we shall presently be discussing the octatonic implications of the "intrusion" of this "chromatic" pitch number 11 when we turn briefly to No. 35 in the "Danse russe"of this first tableau.)

Then, at No. 8 (Example 21 again), the oscillating simultaneities in terms of (D F A)–(G B D), numbering the usual six elements, three to each triad, yield the (D C B A G F) hexachord. And at No. 11 this oscillation alternates with identical relations expressed in terms of the (A G F♯ E D C) collection—a (A C E)–(D F♯ A) triadic oscillation. These (D F A)–(G B D) and (A C E)–(D F♯ A) oscillations, yielding the (D C B A G F) and (A G F♯ E D C) hexachordal collections respectively, are, as indicated, anticipated by the punctuating (G B♭ D/C E G) compound sonority at No. 5; these two triads,(G B♭ D) and (C E G), constitute a superimposition of the triadic relationship defined by these subsequent oscillations at Nos. 8 and 11.

The (0,7) "fifth"-related adjacency of these (D C B A G F) (A G F♯ E D C) hexachords at No. 11 effects a (D F F♯/F F♯ A) "minor-major third" play with respect to F/F♯, but one quite different in "feel" from that of the neo-classical examples briefly alluded to in the latter part of chapter 2. This difference pertains to the question of reference generally; the "minor-major third" phenomenon here at No. 11 is triggered by this simple "fifth"-defined overlapping of (0 2 3 5 7 9) hexachords, while in the neo-classical examples it derives from a species of octatonic-diatonic interpen-etration, in which the referential ordering of the diatonic collection is that of the C-scale (or major scale) interacting with Model A's 1,2 interval or-dering of the octatonic scale. This distinction is just one of the many that can be drawn between phenomena that are identical from a strictly local standpoint in material of the "Russian" and neoclassical categories. It re-lates to the critical question of reference, or, more precisely, to the parti-tioning formulated on its behalf.

More critical to our deliberations, however, is the clue this (D C B A G F) (A G F♯ E D C) overlapping at No. 11 affords as to overall (0 2 3 5 7 9) hexachordal planning in the first tableau at Nos. 0–30. For we may now assemble the four (E D C♯ B A G) (A G F♯ E D C) (D C B A G F) (G F E D C B♭) hexachords inferable from this section, and, owing to their (0,7) "fifth"-related adjacency, arrange them according to the chain or "spread" of overlapping (0 2 3 5 7 9) hexachords suggested by No. 11. (See Example 22a.) And, in regard to this compression of (0 2 3 5 7 9) strategy, we can begin to confront in the consequent exemplification the three key issues regarding (0 2 3 5 7 9) activity in the "Russian" period generally: (1) the (0 2) (7 9) encircling units, the (0 2 3 5) (7 9 0) tetrachords, and the three (0 3 7/0 4 7) triads that may be inferred in relation to the single (0 2 3 5 7 9) hexachord (as outlined already in Example 19); (2) the exercise in pitch-class priority unique to the (0 2 3 5 7 9) hexachord in which the pairs

0 2 3 5 7 9 hexachords

Example 22a

of 2s or whole steps that encircle it—(0 2) (7 9), each of these defining the point of overlap with respect to (0,7) "fifth"-defined adjacency—may be rearranged as an 0–7–2–9 series of 7s or "fifths," or a 9–2–7–0 series of 5s or "fourths"—this rearrangement, articulated by the flute in the blocks at Nos. 0–2 and 2 + 3, allows insight into the question of "harmonic stasis" (the stability or balancing effect of these "fifths" or "fourths"), and hence into the seeming irrelevance of (single) pitch class-priority rulings in many (0 2 3 5 7 9) contexts (but a rearrangement will not always deprive the encircling (0 2) (7 9) units of a certain whole-step cohesion, as evidenced in *Petroushka*'s opening blocks by the (2–0) (7–9) reiterations in terms of D–E and A–G which encircle the (E D C♯ B A G) collection at Nos. 0–2), Example 22b; (3) the regularities governing octatonic-diatonic interaction or interpenetration with respect to (0 2 3 5) partitioning of the D-scale, the (0 2 3 5 7 9) hexachord, and Model B's (0 2 3 5 6 8 9 11) octatonic scale (Examples 23, 24a, and 24b). While we defer, momentarily, the question of pitch-class priority, Nos. 7 and 35 in the first tableau do afford an opportunity to examine octatonic-diatonic interaction in which the above-discussed seventh pitch element—B♭ as the "chromatic" pitch number 11 in relation to the (A G F♯ E D C) hexachordal collection and ordering at Nos. 7 and 35—signals, pivotlike in place of the diatonic pitch number 10, a "leaning" toward octatonic-diatonic interpenetration. This "intrusion" of pitch number 11 constitutes a first regularity in octatonic-diatonic interaction, with the between-reference connecting link discernible in terms of the (0 2 3 5) tetrachord, (A G F♯ E) here.

For with respect to these blocks at Nos. 7 and 35 and the inferred (A G F♯ E E♭ D♭ C B♭) octatonic and (A G F♯ E D C) diatonic interpenetration (Example 23), it is instructive to consider how very close we are here to the illustrious "*Petroushka* chord" at Nos. 49, 50, and 51 of the second tableau.[5] This compound simultaneity contains, as we have indicated, (0,6) tritone-related "major" triads at C and F♯ (six elements in all, accountable to Col-

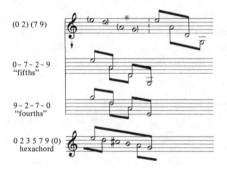

Example 22b

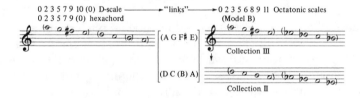

Example 23: First tableau

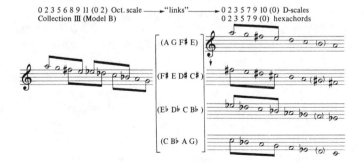

Example 24a

Example 24b

lection III), in which the (F♯ A♯ C♯) triad is (A♯ C♯ F♯) first inversion, thus preserving the B♭–C (or A♯–C) whole-step reiteration found in the first tableau. (*Petroushka* was, after all, conceived with this Collection-III material of the second tableau.) Only the D of the (A G F♯ E D C) hexachord at Nos. 7 and 35 resists the interpenetrating (A G F♯ E D♯ C♯ C B♭) octatonic Collection III (however critical this D is to (A G F♯ E D C) identity, since it constitutes, with the C, one of the pairs of 2s which encircle the (A G F♯ E D C) collection); and with the referentially octatonic (Collection III) B♭ (A♯ in the "*Petroushka* chord"), only C♯ is missing. (So we have, then, in this interpenetration of (A G F♯ E D♯ C♯ C B♭) Collection III and the (A G F♯ E D C) diatonic hexachord at Nos. 7 and 35, at least a hint of coming attractions.) In Example 24a we summarize this first, and typically "Russian," regularity in moving from a diatonic to an octatonic or octatonic-diatonic context: Model B's "chromatic" pitch number 11 "intrudes," while the connecting link between these (0 2 3 5) (7 9 (10) 0) diatonic and (0 2 3 5) (6 8 9 11) octatonic orders (that which is shared between these interacting collections of reference) is realized in terms of the "upper" (0 2 3 5) tetrachord, (A G F♯ E) here.

But note, in Example 24a, that the "lower" (7 9 (10) 0) tetrachordal unit of the (0 2 3 5) (7 9 10 (0)) D-scale or (0 2 3 5) (7 9 0) hexachord may serve as the connecting link to still another octatonic collection: (D C (B) A) of the (A G F♯ E) (D C B A) D-scale or (A G F♯ E) (D C A) hexachord may implicate Collection II. In this second possibility, pitch number 6 (the E♭ here) often becomes the "intruding" seventh pitch element. (Still, in re-structuring the octatonic scale accordingly, this number 6 merely becomes another pitch number 11. And apart from the interval of 11, what is immediately striking in these referentially octatonic "intrusions" of pitch number 11 is the tritone relation defined by pitch numbers 5 and 11—with an "intrusion" of pitch number 11—and by pitch numbers 0 and 6—with an "intrusion" of pitch number 6. Furthermore, note in Example 24a that an "intrusion of pitch number 6 may implicate Collection III as well as II.) Accordingly, with respect to any given (0 2 3 5) (7 9 (10) 0) tetra-chordal partitioning of either the D-scale or the (0 2 3 5 7 9) hexachord, two of the three octatonic collections—(0 2 3 5) partitioning, Model B—may be implicated in octatonic-diatonic interaction. If we reverse this procedure by commencing with an octatonic framework (Example 24b), any given octatonic collection may implicate, through its four overlapping (0 2 3 5) tetrachords, four D-scales or (0 2 3 5 7 9) hexachords in interacting proceedings. (We note this reversal in anticipation of *Le Sacre*.)

Moreover, in reviewing these "Russian" octatonic-diatonic summaries of Example 24a and b with additional reference to Example 20, we may note that the (0 2 3 5) (7 9 10 0) D-scale, the (0 2 3 5) (7 9 0) hexachord, and Model B's (0 2 3 5) (6 8 9 11) octatonic scale each contain—or may be partitioned by means of—two distinct (0 2 3 5) tetrachords (as indicated by the

parentheses), one of these "upper," the other "lower." (The "lower" (7 9 0)
unit of the (0 2 3 5) (7 9 0) hexachord is naturally incomplete because of
the 9–0 "gap," the "missing" seventh pitch element. Model B's octatonic
scale actually contains four overlapping (0 2 3 5) tetrachords, of which we
consider here only the two disjunct ones.) In the two diatonic scales, the
two adjoining (0 2 3 5) (7 9 (10) 0) tetrachords are joined by 5–7 numbering, forming the interval of 2, a whole step, and are hence (0,7) "fifth"-
related; in the octatonic scale, on the other hand, the (0 2 3 5) (6 8 9 11)
tetrachords are joined by a 5–6 numbering, forming the interval of 1, a
half step, and are hence (0,6) tritone-related. Consequently, in moving
from a diatonic to an octatonic context (or to some form of octatonic-
diatonic interpenetration), one of these "upper" or "lower" (0 2 3 5) (7 9
(10) 0) tetrachords will "survive" as the connecting link between references, while it is most often—or most conspicuously—Model B's "chromatic" pitch numbers 6 and/or 11 which "intrude" to signal this intervention. And indeed we apprehend in this transaction one of the deepest and
most elemental "secrets" pervading Stravinsky's "Russian" musical
thought generally, from *Petroushka*'s first tableau, through the whole of *Le
Sacre* (1913), *Renard* (1916), *Les Noces* (1917), and a host of smaller, subsidiary works, to the music to Scene II of *Histoire du soldat* (1918): the single (0
2 3 5) tetrachord, as the principal melodic fragment of the "Russian" period (imposing itself by means of all manner of reiterating folkish fragments; see, for example, in Example 21, the reiterating (E D C♯ B) fragment in the cello at Nos. 1 and 2+3, and the C–B♭–A–G fragment in the
lower strings at No. 2, or, in Example 25b, the reiterating (D C B A) fragment in the solo violin at No. 42), may in its referential implications be
either octatonic (Model B), diatonic, or octatonic-diatonic, serving, by way
of this neutrality, as the principal shared, connecting link between successive blocks of distinct referential character.

Still, at Nos. 7 and 35 in *Petroushka*'s first tableau, the tonally inclined
observer could interpret the B♭ as the "flatted sixth degree" in relation to
the (D F♯ A) triad (presumably implicating the G-scale on D), an interpretation perhaps particularly apropos at No. 35, where conventional voice-
leading may be inferred on behalf of this B♭. And, again, we are not
wholly unsympathetic to such a reading. For if we turn to the Finale of *The
Firebird*, we discover a harmonization of a borrowed folk melody that is
similarly accountable to the (0 2 3 5 7 9) hexachord, but in terms of (F♯ E
D♯ C♯ B A). (See Example 25a.) This (F♯ E D♯ C♯ B A) hexachordal reference is implicated by an oscillation between the two (0,2) whole-step related (0 4 7) "major" triads at B and A, (B D♯ F♯) and (A C♯ E). Preceding
this block at No. 17 in *The Firebird*'s Finale, a similar flexibility manifests
itself with respect to seventh pitch class identity, involving the closing of
the (F♯ E D♯ C♯ B A) hexachord's A–F♯ "gap" with a G♯ or a G; and, indeed, as pitch number 11, G does behave more or less as a conventional

Example 25a: *The Firebird* (Finale)

"flatted sixth degree," a resolution to the F♯ of the (B D♯ F♯) triad being quite unmistakable over the barline at No. 14 (See Example 11 in chapter 1.)

But tonally conceived voice-leading of this sort is irrelevant at No. 7 in *Petroushka*; the "low" B♭ stands, rather, in an unresolved, fixed, or polarized "opposition" to the "upper" (A G F♯ E) tetrachord or (D F♯ A) triad, a deadlocked situation. It is therefore fitting to interpret Nos. 7 and 35 in terms of a (A G F♯ E) (E♭ D♭ C B♭)–(A G F♯ E) (D C (A)) interpenetration, not only because B♭ behaves unconventionally in relation to tonal, C-scale conventions (and cannot, without reference to such conventions, be accounted for in terms of the diatonic collection), but also because its behavior is suitably accounted for in terms of the symmetrically defined (A G F♯ E) (E♭ D♭ C B♭) tetrachordal partitioning of Collection III (Model B), a partitioning that anticipates, to some extent, the more fully committed octatonic (Collection III) framework of the "*Petroushka* chord" in the second tableau.

Finally, Example 25b acknowledges continued reference to the (0 2 3 5 7 9) hexachord at No. 42 in the "Danse russe" of the first tableau. Indeed, along with the No. 35 block (also belonging to the "Danse russe"), this block at No. 42 conveniently exemplifies all the conditions associated with (0 2 3 5 7 9) hexachordal reference as set forth at the outset of this chapter: The instrumental "fill" (in the piano here) completes the diatonic collection, with a pitch number 10 (the E here) implicating the D-scale (D-scale on D here); but (0 2 3 5) and (0 3 7/0 4 7) partitioning of the single (0 2 3 5 7 9) hexachord—the (D C B A G F) collection here—remains intact. Thus, a reiterating "upper" (0 2 3 5) tetrachord in terms of (D C B A) in the solo violin and oboe combines with a (D F A)–(G B D) triadic oscillation (as at the earlier No. 8 block) to implicate the (D C B A G F) hexachord; and this

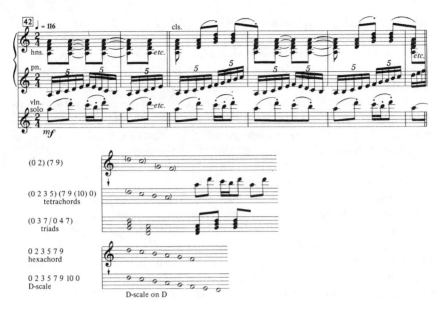

Example 25b: First tableau

cohesive (D C B A G F) reference becomes inferable *from within* the fully accredited framework of the diatonic D-scale on D. And so, manifestly at No. 42, the (0 2 3 5 7 9) hexachord harbors a (0 2 3 5) tetrachordal and (0 3 7/0 4 7) triadic articulative routine that ensures it a measure of referential cohesion even when an outside seventh pitch element—in the form of pitch number 10 here, the E—completes the diatonic collection.

Still, the concept of "added notes"—or, more specifically, of an "added sixth degree"—may seem relevant to the "Danse russe" at Nos. 33–47 in a way in which, earlier at Nos. 5–7, it did not. Thus, an A—interpreted as "added sixth degree" in the C-scale on C—may seem to attach itself persistently to a (tonally functional, C-scale on C) V–I–V reiteration in terms of ((G) B D F)–((G) C E G)–((G) B D F). This reiteration reaches its climax at Nos. 44–47 and subsequently "resolves" with an abrupt (C-scale on C) ii–V–I cadence to conclude the first tableau. In accord with this tonally functional C-scale-on-C interpretation, the predominance of G or (G B D F)—with the "added" A—figures in the "Danse russe" as a kind of sustained dominant in preparation for this abrupt ii–V–I cadence.

But this tonally functional C-scale-on-C perspective is overshadowed—or is at least complemented—by nontonal considerations equally deserving of attention. Thus, of consequence in the harmonization of the "Danse russe" at No. 33 is the articulative affiliation of A—the "added sixth degree" of the C-scale-on-C interpretation—with G, an articulative affiliation which yields the sustained or fixed (A G) dyad "above" the oscil-lating (B D F)–(C E G) simultaneities, and which naturally relates to the A–G whole-step reiteration in *Petroushka*'s opening measures. When the oscillation at No. 33 is transposed at No. 34 by the interval of 7 (a "fifth"), this fixed (A G) dyad becomes a fixed (E D) dyad "above" oscillating (F♯ A C)–(G B D) simultaneities. This transposition in turn reflects the (pitch-identity) "survival" of the second of *Petroushka*'s opening whole-step reit-erations, D–E. Then, too, the opening (A♯ C) dyad of the referentially oc-tatonic (Collection III) "*Petroushka* chord" in the second tableau at No. 49 may be heard and understood in terms of the (pitch-identity) "survival" of the B♭–C reiteration introduced at No. 2.

Consequently, the abrupt (tonally functional C-scale-on-C) ii–V–I ca-dence of the "Danse russe" may seem, as a consequence of these fixed dy-adic "survivals" (and of the static triadic oscillation "underneath"), a bit forced, alien, or "out of place." Indeed, only the persistence of A—or of the (A G) unit—in the concluding (C E G A) simultaneity saves this hack-neyed ii–V–I (obviously, a kind of terminating convenience here) from being entirely incongruent, a very curious turn of "events."

RUSSIAN FOLK MUSIC
IN "RUSSIAN" MUSIC

Like *The Firebird*, *Petroushka* makes reference to authentic Russian folk melodies. And while Stravinsky could no longer recall (in *Memories and Commentaries*, 1960) which of the standard, westernized collections avail-able to him at this time might have served as immediate sources, there are at least five such folk melodies in the first and fourth tableaux that are traceable as follows:[6]

1. The G–C–B♭–A–G–F–A–G tune at No. 5 in the first tableau (burst-ing forth here after much A–G and C–B♭–A–G anticipation; see Example 21) is an Easter song, and appears as No. 47 in Rimsky-Korsakov's collec-tion of *100 Russian National Songs* (1876).

2. The tune in the piano at No. 41 in the first tableau (anticipated by much (0 2 3 5) tetrachordal articulation in terms of (A G F♯ E); see No. 35 in Example 23; or, for a subsequent D-scale-on-D or (D C B A G F) hexa-chordal setting, see No. 42 + 4 in Example 25b) is a St. John's Eve song, and appears in the Istomin-Diutsch collection of 1894.

3. The tune first introduced at No. 90 in the fourth tableau to accom-pany the "Danse of the Nursemaids" (undoubtedly the most familiar of all these borrowings) is entitled "Down St. Peter's Road," and appears in both Rimsky-Korsakov's collection of forty Russian folksongs (1882) and the Tchaikovsky-Prokunin collection of sixty-five folksongs (1898).[7]

4. The tune at No. 96 in the fourth tableau may be found in E. L. Swerkoff's collection of *50 Russian Folk Songs for Voice and Pianoforte* (1937).

5. The tune introduced at No. 109 in the fourth tableau to accompany the "Dance of the Coachmen and Grooms" appears in the Tchaikovsky-Prokunin collection of 1898.

In addition to these Russian folksongs—all doubtless of distant origin—there is a Russian "street song" or popular chanson at Nos. 9, 12, and 15 in the first tableau; a French chanson, "Elle avait un' jambe en bois," at Nos. 13 and 15 in the first tableau (Stravinsky pegged this from a hurdy-gurdy while composing the first tableau; as he later explained, it "struck me as a good tune for the scene I was then composing"); and two Joseph Lanner waltz melodies at Nos. 71 and 72 in the third tableau, the scene of the Moor. These waltz tunes are introduced to accompany the Ballerina's entrance in the third tableau. At Nos. 72–74, Stravinsky ingeniously superimposes the second of these 3/4 waltzes over the Moor's earlier 2/4 dance. And so what ultimately emerges at this point is a kind of superimposition of the insipid, dull-witted Ballerina (in her sweet little waltz tune in the flutes and harp) over the artless, vain, dull-witted Moor (in his lumbering 2/4 dance in the clarinet and bass clarinet). The effect of this awkward, disjointed non-synchronization is spectacularly grotesque, so much so that the passage must surely rate among the seamiest, the most delectably sleazy in twentieth-century music.

The extent and variety of the borrowing in *Petroushka*, the manner in which incongruent or vastly diverse "styles" of music—diverse in relation to conventional or orthodox sentiment—are welded together, points to an eclectic spirit. This eclecticism, however, is different in kind from the many "influences" that pertain to neoclassicism, and to which we shall be directing our attention a bit more thoroughly when considering *Histoire du soldat* in chapter 7.

Critically to be noted, however, is the fact that Stravinsky's initial ties with Russian folk music were founded on the nineteenth-century Western (tonal, C-scale) tradition of Tchaikovsky and the so-called Russian "Five," on the songs compiled and arranged by Tchaikovsky, Liadov, Rimsky-Korsakov, Balakirev, and others. Only very peripherally can he be imagined, during the "Russian" period, as an "ethnomusicologist" (or, alternatively, an anthropologist, presumably of the "hunting and gathering" type). True, the texts to pieces like *Renard* (1916), *Les Noces* (1917), and *Histoire du soldat* (1918) are derived from Russian popular verse (specifically, from the anthologies of Afanasiev and Kireievsky, the "two great argosies of the Russian language and spirit," as Stravinsky later called them). And all of Stravinsky's "Russian"-period works naturally reflect an awareness not only of popular verse, ritual, and art, but of Russian chant and folksong as well. But Stravinsky did not consciously pursue the question of authenticity, nor did he consciously seek to familiarize himself with the true, authentic nature of Russian chant and folksong (the latter, in particular, with its extraordinary wealth and diversity in polyphonic elaboration).[8] For it has long since been established, in the collections published by Melgunov, Istomin and Diutsch, Liapunov, Linieva (Lineff), and others, that the earlier, westernized editions greatly distorted the melodic, harmonic, and rhythmic-metric character of the Russian folksong, which, although diatonic, was not generally oriented toward the C-scale (major scale) or tonally functional, and which further displayed a remarkable intricacy in polyphonic variation largely ignored by early editions.[9] Indeed, subsequent to *Petroushka*, conscious use of Russian folk music by Stravinsky becomes increasingly rare. Apart from the opening bassoon melody in *Le Sacre* (extracted from an anthology of Lithuanian folk music), and a single melody introduced in the fourth tableau of *Les Noces*, there is no conscious borrowing at all in *Le Sacre* (1913), *Three Pieces for String Quartet* (1914), *Pribaoutki* (1914), *Berceuses du chat* (1916), *Renard* (1916), *Trois histoires pour enfants* (1917), *Four Russian Peasant Songs* (1917), *Les Noces* (1917), *Histoire du soldat* (1918), and the *Symphonies of Wind Instruments* (1920)—in short, the heart of the "Russian" period. "If any of these pieces *sounds* like aboriginal folk music," Stravinsky was later to remark, "it may be because my powers of fabrication were able to tap some unconscious 'folk' memory"—not, in other words, because of any direct borrowing or pursuit of authenticity.[10]

On the other hand, if the substance of Stravinsky's "Russian" musical thought transcends conscious affiliation with Russian chant and folksong, neither is this substance, following *The Firebird*'s "Khorovod," all that reflective of the Western folksong tradition inherited from Tchaikovsky, Liadov, Rimsky-Korsakov, and others. To demonstrate this divergence, this emerging of what Stravinsky himself called a uniquely designed "fabrication" of Russian musical thought (the "Russian" period itself, of course), we might briefly compare the borrowed Easter song at No. 5 in *Petroushka*'s first tableau to Rimsky-Korsakov's transcription in his *100 Russian National Songs* (1876). (See Example 26.)

Now the No. 5 block in *Petroushka* was interpreted, in Example 21, in terms of an overall G or (G B♭ D) centricity, implicating, given the pitch-class content, the diatonic D-scale on G. More articulatively, however, this D-scale on G was partitioned, first, by its (0 2 3 5) (7 9 10 0) tetrachords, (G F E D) and (C B♭ A G), and, second, by its embedded (0 2 3 5 7 9) hexachordal segment, a foundational (G F E D C B♭) hexachord implicated by the superimposition of (G B♭ D) on the (C E G) and (B♭ D F) triads. Critical, however, was the relationship of this articulation to abrupt block jux-

Example 26

taposition. The D-scale on G, No. 5's referential identity, pertained to the block at No. 5, but not necessarily to preceding or succeeding blocks (although, of course, the D-scale does reappear in subsequent blocks or sections, most notably at No. 42 as the D-scale on D; see Example 25b). Accordingly, were we in Example 21 to envision the (A G) dyad as a between-block or between-reference connecting link at Nos. 0–6 (among other possibilities in respect to connecting links), the following condensed scheme would apply: (1) in the opening block at Nos. 0–2, the A–G whole-step reiteration is affiliated referentially with the (E D C♯ B A G) hexachord, with respect to which it defines a pitch number 7–9 reiteration; (2) in the block at No. 2, this A–G reiteration is affiliated with the (E D C B♭ A G) hexachord, with respect to which it likewise defines a pitch number 7–9 reiteration; (3) and in the block at No. 5, this same A–G reiteration identifies referentially with the D-scale on G, with respect to which it delineates the G–C–B♭–A–G–F–A–G Easter song's over-the-barline, upbeat-downbeat terminating succession on A–G. (Indeed, the A–G reiteration of the preparatory blocks preceding No. 5 is in this respect a long, drawn-out anticipation of this terminating succession of the Easter song.) Moreover, at no point did the articulation in these successive blocks—or in their respective (near) repeats throughout the first tableau—appear to implicate the interval ordering of the C-scale (or major scale) and at no point did this articulation materialize in the form of C-scale tonally functional relations. While referentially diatonic, these blocks seemed conspicuously non-C-scale (or non–major scale), and conspicuously nontonal. Hence, the tonally functional C-scale-on-F alternative at No. 5, the possibility of a terminating IV (ii)–V "half cadence" for the Easter song's A–G terminating succession, seemed irrelevant. And primarily because the dominant-tonic relation in this C-scale on F reading and the (F A C) "tonic" triad itself were not only scrupulously avoided but seemed nearly inconceivable within No. 5's securely fastened D-scale-on-G or (G F E D C B♭) hexachordal framework.

However, in Rimsky-Korsakov's westernized (tonal, C-scale) version of the Easter song, it is precisely this tonally functional C-scale-on-F alternative, this "in-the-key-of-F-major" alternative, that is pursued unambiguously. Thus, Stravinsky's (G B♭ D/C E G) compound sonority, used as a punctuating point of departure and return at No. 5, is heard and understood with reference to a (G B♭ D) centricity, and hence with reference to the D-scale on G and its embedded or foundational (G F E D C B♭) hexachord. But in Rimsky's setting this (G B♭ D/C E G) compound sonority— instead of superimposing the two triads (G B♭ D) and (C E G)—is conceived, rather, as an actual (G B♭ D)–(C E G) succession, as a progression "in the key of F-major," and hence as a ii–V half cadence which resolves deceptively to a (D F A) triad, and then, in the final measure of the piece, to a (F A C) tonic triad. (The melody's concluding F is ignored in *Petroushka*. On the other hand, the F may have been Rimsky's, part of that westernizing, C-scale, tonally functional prejudice.) And so the Easter song's (or Rimsky's) concluding F or (F A C) tonic triad, inconceivable in *Petroushka* (where the successive blocks and their subsequent (near) repeats must in some sense remain "open" or inconclusive, where within-block relations, whether octatonic, diatonic, or octatonic-diatonic, cannot really admit to any C-scale, tonally functional conclusiveness, a conclusiveness withheld, indeed, until the final measures of the first tableau, where the abrupt C-scale-on-C tonally functional ii–V–I "cadence" surfaces as a terminating convenience), becomes part of a tonally functional C-scale-on-F framework in Rimsky-Korsakov's *100 Russian National Songs*. And to it we apply, with little hesitation, the familiar analytic-theoretical symbols representing the codification of C-scale (on F) tonally functional behavior.

We might note, too, the instruments of transformation here. The ii–V half cadence of Rimsky's version, the (G B♭ D)–(C E G) progression "in F," is at No. 5 in *Petroushka* a punctuating (G B♭ D/C E G) superimposition, which is subsequently transposed at Nos. 8 and 11 to the (D C B A G F) and (A G F♯ E D C) hexachordal collections, where the encompassed triads appear in back-and-forth oscillation. Hence, the referential character of the configuration (or of the Easter song itself), although diatonic in both versions, is altered radically. Thus these techniques of triadic superimposition and oscillation, first introduced with reference to certain of Stravinsky's octatonic contexts in chapters 1 and 2, become as diatonic as they are octatonic in conception.

Still, if we momentarily ignore the song's (or Rimsky's) terminating F, Stravinsky is remarkably loyal to its general contour. Of special interest in this connection is the melody's irregular 3/4 measure, preserved in the adaptations of both composers. Of course, the metric irregularity here is not really the point. It harbors (and conceals) a displacement, a contradiction or reversal in the downbeat-upbeat-downbeat accentuation of the melody's F–A–G terminating succession. Or, more precisely: were we to pursue the 2/4 rhythmic-metric pulse *through* the irregular 3/4 measure (as the brackets indicate in Example 26), we would then discover that the downbeat-upbeat-downbeat rhythmic-metric identity of the melody's terminating F–A–G succession is contradicted and reversed by this irregular 3/4 measure's extra beat, becoming an upbeat-downbeat-upbeat identity. (As indicated earlier in chapter 1 in connection with *The Firebird*'s Finale, this is a maneuver with vast implications for the whole of Stravinsky's music.) But a contradiction or reversal of this type is evident already at the outset of the No. 5 block. Here, the descending (C E G)–(B♭ D F)–(A C E)–(G B♭ D) triadic succession, underneath the (G B♭ D) reiteration of the folk melody, would most certainly, following the rhythmic-metric conventions of tonal, C-scale literature, have been introduced as a downbeating triadic succession. But Stravinsky displaces this conventional approach. The succession is introduced on the upbeat, on the second beat of the 2/4 measure. And with the consequence that when the conventional downbeating does fall into place at No. 5+5, the original upbeating scheme is contradicted and reversed, allowing a degree of titillating doubt or uncertainty to prevail as to the "true" rhythmic-metric identity of the succession (or of the Easter song itself at No. 5+5). And so the block at No. 5 harbors rhythmic-metric displacement of the sort examined earlier in *The Firebird*'s Finale. (Except, of course, in reverse—for in *The Firebird*'s Finale at No. 17, a conventional upsweeping glissando in the horns was forced onto the downbeat, while in *Petroushka*, a conventional downbeating succession

commences on the upbeat, on the second beat of the 2/4 meter, and is subsequently reversed, the conventional downbeating falling into place at
No. 5 + 5.)

REPERCUSSIONS

Notes: 1. My arrangement of "Three Movements from *Petroushka*" for piano
solo dates from August 1921. Artur Rubinstein, to whom I had dedicated my
Piano Rag Music [1919], . . . paid me the generous sum of 5,000 francs for it.
(Diaghilev had given me only 1,000 rubles for the whole ballet.) . . .

2. I rewrote *Petroushka* in 1947 with the dual purpose of copywriting it and
adapting it to the resources of medium-sized orchestras. Ever since the first
performance of the score I had wanted to balance the orchestral sound more
clearly in some places, and to effect other improvements in the instrumentation. The orchestration of the 1947 version is, I think, much more skillful,
though many people consider that the original music and the revised version
are like two geological levels that do not mix. [*Expositions and Developments*, p.
159.]

Those who imagine that my works make me rich do not realize that everything I composed before 1931 (I became a French citizen in 1934, and this
citizenship extended authors' rights retrospectively for three years) was and
is unprotected in the United States: the United States and the U.S.S.R. failed
to sign the Berne copyright convention. I do not receive performance rights
for *The Firebird*, which as one of the most popular pieces of music composed
in this century, would have made me a "millionaire" (though, of course, for
the good of my soul, I do not aspire to be any such thing). *The Firebird*, *Petroushka*, and *Le Sacre du printemps* were pirated in the United States and have
been performed there free for the last thirty-five years. . . . When I became
an American citizen in 1945 I prepared a new version of almost all the music I
had composed before 1931. These versions vary from complete rewritings,
like *Petroushka* and the *Symphonies of Wind Instruments* [1920], to the mere correcting of printers' errors—as in the case of the *Capriccio* [1929], and *Symphony of Psalms* [1930]. But the three popular and lucrative early ballets are
still far more commonly played in the old, pirated editions. [*Memories and
Commentaries*, p. 90.]

Stravinsky's 1947 revision of *Petroushka* should be acknowledged. True,
Stravinsky notes above that this 1947 version figured among many revisions of pre-1931 music undertaken during the 1940s. While all of these
revisions (or "revisions") doubtless afforded an opportunity to correct
"printers' errors," to simplify the notation, or to clarify the articulation
with additional dynamic and tempo markings, their prime motivation was
economic: everything composed before 1931 was "unprotected in the
United States"; Stravinsky received no royalties for any of this pre-1931
music, a circumstance perhaps doubly painful in relation to "the three
popular and lucrative early ballets" (*The Firebird*, *Petroushka*, and *Le Sacre*),

which, even after the publication of their revisions (or "revisions"), were "still far more commonly played in the old, pirated editions."

But the 1947 revision of *Petroushka* is real enough, and stretches well beyond the mere correcting of "printers' errors" or adjustments in notation, embodying changes in instrumental layout on a scale more extensive than anything that can be found in the remainder of these revisions of pre-1931 music. Most noticeable is the 1911 orchestra's reduction in size. (Like the "old" 1910 *Firebird*, the "old" 1911 *Petroushka* might well have seemed, throughout its long and distinguished career, "wastefully large.") For example, the second harp is eliminated, with much of its material assigned to the piano, which assumes a far more conspicuous role in the 1947 version. The "old" groupings of four in the woodwind section are replaced by more modest groupings of three. The ultimate effect of this simplification is to render the "new" apparatus not only more compact but also, as Stravinsky notes, more compatible "with the resources of medium-sized orchestras."

More significantly, however, this reduction in size seems to have triggered some fundamental rethinking in orchestral sound (as many have noted), aimed primarily at sharpening the punctuation.[11] The means to this end are diverse and apparent on the very first page. They range from the added staccato doubling of the first flute's A–D–E–A–G–E–D–(A) melody in the opening block at Nos. 0–2 (a percussive measure perhaps to be expected at this stage; see Example 21), and the piano's percussive doubling of the G–C–Bb–A–G–F–A–(G) figuration in the flutes, oboes, and trumpets at No. 4 ($+2$)–5, to the rather startling substitution of trumpets and clarinets, all staccato, for the "old" flowing, legato accompaniment in the bassoons at No. 90 in the fourth tableau ("Dance of the Nursemaids"). Then, too, whatever "waste" or "fill" might have penetrated the original version (and this was sparse indeed in comparison with the original *Firebird*) is either eliminated or reconstituted with a more polished contrapuntal framework. Particularly striking in this regard is the string writing.[12] In the original block at No. 7 (first tableau; see Example 23), the strings merely reiterate the (E/D) dyad; while in the 1947 revision they partake of the A–G–F♯–E–D articulation above this sustained reiteration, an articulation which had earlier been confined to the woodwinds.

Consequently, changes of this type have not unexpectedly been found unacceptable by large groups of *Petroushka* admirers. Early Stravinsky conductors like Pierre Monteux and Ernest Ansermet would continue with the "old" rather than the "new" (quite apart from the question of "performance rights"), perhaps finding in the "new" a somewhat "cold," "heartless" distortion of what had always seemed a soft, warm-blooded musical experience. On the other hand, those with no particular ties to the "old"—among whom this observer would include himself—might find the precision, economy, the more compact or less wieldy circumstances of the "new" *Petroushka* refreshing and a definite advantage. Preference need not necessarily reflect taste (rather than habit), and it seems possible to prefer "old" or "new" without necessarily considering the other unpalatable (even if reflecting "geological levels" which, as Stravinsky suggests above, "do not mix").

The *Petroushka* of 1911 was yet another immediate, overnight success. Stravinsky attributed this to Diaghilev's Russian Ballet, and specifically to the dancing of Vaslav Nijinsky, whose Petroushka appears, by all accounts, to have marked one of the most electrifying events in the history of modern ballet. That Nijinsky was to prove himself less capable as the chief choreographer of the first *Sacre* did not pass unnoticed, however, or unforgiven. To the very end, Stravinsky lamented Nijinsky's lack of musical training, complaining that he "never understood musical meters . . . and had no certain sense of tempo," and that he consequently made of the first *Sacre* a "rhythmic chaos." But there was no dismissing Nijinsky's gifts as a dancer and his contribution to the stage:

> If Nijinsky was the least capable musically of my choreographic collaborators, his talent was elsewhere—and one talent such as he had is enough. To call him a dancer is not enough, however, for he was an even greater dramatic actor. His beautiful, but certainly not handsome, face could become the most powerful actor's mask I have ever seen, and as Petroushka he was the most exciting human being I have ever seen on a stage.[13]

But the success was musical too, and this seems to have been important at the time. In Stravinsky's words, "The success of *Petroushka* was good for me . . . in that it gave me the absolute conviction of my ear just as I was about to begin *Le Sacre du printemps*."[14]

FOUR
LE SACRE DU PRINTEMPS (1913)

PART I ("L'Adoration de la terre")

Introduction	Nos.	0–13
"Danses des adolescentes"	Nos.	13–37
"Jeu du rapt"	Nos.	37–48
"Rondes printanières"	Nos.	48–57
"Jeux des cités rivales"	Nos.	57–67
"Cortège du sage"	Nos.	67–72
"Danse de la terre"	Nos.	72–79

PART II ("La Sacrifice")

Introduction	Nos.	79–91
"Cercles mystérieux"	Nos.	91–104
"Glorification de l'élue"	Nos.	104–21
"Évocation des ancêtres"	Nos.	121–29
"Action rituelle des ancêtres"	Nos.	129–42
"Danse sacrale"	Nos.	142–End

The idea of *Le Sacre du printemps* came to me while I was still composing *The Firebird*. I had dreamed a scene of pagan ritual in which a chosen sacrificial virgin danced herself to death. This vision was not accompanied by concrete musical ideas, however, and as I was soon impregnated with another and purely musical conception that began quickly to develop into, as I thought, a *Konzertstück* for piano and orchestra, the latter piece was the one I started to compose. . . .

In July 1911, after the performances of *Petroushka*, I traveled to the Princess Tenichev's country estate near Smolensk, to meet with Nicolas Roerich [who was responsible for the decor] and plan the scenario of *Le Sacre du printemps*. . . .

I became conscious of thematic ideas for *Le Sacre* immediately after returning to Ustilug, the themes being those of *Les Augures printanières* [*Danses des adolescentes*], the first dance I was to compose. Returning to Switzerland in the fall [1911], I moved with my family to a *pension* in Clarens and continued to work. Almost the entire *Sacre du printemps* was written in a tiny room of this house, in an eight-feet-by-eight closet, rather, whose only furniture was a small upright piano which I kept muted (I always work at a muted piano), a table, and two chairs. I composed from the *Augures printanières* to the end of the first part and then wrote the Prelude [Introduction] afterward. . . .

The dances of the second part were composed in the order in which they now appear, and composed very quickly, too, until the *Danse sacrale*, which I could play, but did not, at first, know how to write. The composition of the whole of *Le Sacre* was completed, in a state of exaltation and exhaustion, at the beginning of 1912, and most of the instrumentation—a mechanical job, largely, as I always compose the instrumentation when I compose the music—was written in score form by the late spring. . . .

That the first performance of *Le Sacre du printemps* [May 29, 1913] was attended by a scandal must be known to everybody. Strange as it may seem, however, I was unprepared for the explosion myself. The reactions of the musicians who came to the orchestra rehearsals were without intimation of it and the stage spectacle did not appear likely to precipitate a riot. . . .

Mild protest against the music could be heard from the very beginning of the performance. Then, when the curtain opened on the group of knock-kneed and long-braided Lolitas jumping up and down [*Danses des adolescentes*], the storm broke. Cries of "Ta gueule" came from behind me. I heard Florent Schmitt shout "*Taisez-vous garces du seizième*"; the "*garces*" of the sixteenth arrondissement were, of course, the most elegant ladies in Paris. The uproar continued, however, and a few minutes later I left the hall in a rage. . . . I arrived in a fury backstage, where I saw Diaghilev flicking the house lights in a last effort to quiet the hall. For the rest of the performance I stood in the wings behind Nijinsky holding the tails of his *frac*, while he stood on a chair shouting numbers to the dancers, like a coxswain. [*Expositions and Developments*, pp. 159–64.]

PITCH RELATIONS

In *Le Sacre* the situation in regard to pitch organization is conspicuously the reverse of that encountered in *Petroushka*'s first tableau. In place of *Petroushka*'s pervading diatonicism, a "vertical chromaticism" is likely to attract our attention from the opening 0–11 or "major-seventh" interval span between the bassoon's high C and the horn's C♯ (at m. 2 in the Introduction), with respect to which we might view subsequent blocks of unimpaired diatonicism—such as at Nos. 28–30 in "Danses des adolescentes" and at Nos. 48-57 in "Rondes printanières"—as subsidiary or as diverging.[1] This static "vertical chromaticism" manifests itself in the following manner: (1) With remarkable persistence it is composed of an 0–11 or "major-seventh" interval span, which is vertical and interfragmental in the sense that, rather than being linear, melodic, or fragmental in character, it habitually defines (harmonically) the vertical interval span between pitches of unmistakable priority among superimposed, reiterating fragments.[2] (2) With equal consistency, this 0–11 vertical interval span is octatonic (or octatonically conceived, "hooking up" to Model B) in that, reading down, the span very often contains (or is articulated by means of) an "upper" (0 2 3 5) tetrachordal fragment—which may be (0 2 3 5) complete or (0 2 5/0 3 5) incomplete—that stands in a static, polarized "opposition" to a "lower" pitch number 11—with the "lower" of Model B's (0,6) tritone-related (0 2 3 5) tetrachords, (6 8 9 11), less frequently in evidence.[3] (3) This octatonically conceived (0–5,11) articulation interacts, by block juxtaposition or interpenetration, with a diatonicism most often accounted for in terms of the (0 2 3 5) (7 9 10 (0)) D-scale, where, as indicated by Examples 24a and 24b in the previous chapter, a shared (0 2 3 5) tetrachord serves as the between-reference connecting link.

In other words, a "chromatic" pitch number 11 with respect to Model B's (0 2 3 5) (6 8 9 11) tetrachordal numbering (reading down) is with us from the very start in *Le Sacre*, and is inferable—at least insofar as octatonic activity is concerned (the pervading "vertical chromaticism")—on a long-term, nearly continuously operative basis. And so in marked contrast to the diatonicism of *Petroushka*, *Le Sacre* is generally octatonic, with the collection inferred singly or in terms of some form of octatonic-diatonic interpenetration. While we may still infer the single (0 2 3 5) tetrachord—complete or (0 2 3/0 3 5) incomplete—as that which is articulatively shared between successive blocks or sections of varied octatonic, diatonic, or octatonic-diatonic content, it is thus the perspective afforded by Example 24b in chapter 3—that of moving from a predominately octatonic to a diatonic framework—that will apply: the octatonic collection, through its four (0,3,6,9) symmetrically defined (0 2 3 5) tetrachords, may implicate four D-scales in interacting proceedings.[4]

Indeed, to demonstrate this reversal, we might briefly examine Example 27's analysis of "Danses des adolescentes" from the No. 13 block to the one fully committed to the diatonic D-scale on E♭ at Nos. 28–30. Here, the reader will find the analysis divided into three stages: (1) A first (global) stage recognizes the (0 2 3 5) tetrachord—again, complete or (0 2 5/0 3 5) incomplete—as that which is articulatively shared between blocks or sections of varied referential implications, as therefore more-or-less globally determinate or continuously operative with respect to the whole of *Le Sacre*, and therefore also (as yet) indeterminate with respect to varied (octatonic or diatonic) referential implications. (2) A second (global) stage recognizes the attachment of this (0 2 3 5) tetrachord to Model B's 0–11 and (0–5,11) partitioning formats, a partitioning which defines that pervasive "vertical chromaticism" of *Le Sacre*, but which is not quite globally determinate, since it pertains only to the octatonic or octatonic-diatonic blocks and sections, not to the few blocks of unimpaired diatonicism. (3) A third (local) stage recognizes the structure of individual blocks, block reconstruction which is to be understood as encompassing successive local inter-

Example 27

pretations of the globally determinate (0 2 3 5) unit, or, when referentially octatonic or octatonic-diatonic, of Model B's 0–11, and (0–5,11) partitioning formats.

Accordingly, the first stage in "Danses" at Nos. 13–30 is accounted for in terms of (E♭ D♭ B♭), a mostly (0 2 5) incomplete (0 2 3 5) tetrachord which serves as the principal between-reference connecting link.[5] The second stage interprets Model B's 0–11 interval span and (0–5,11) formula in terms of E♭–E and (E♭ D♭ B♭) (E), with both E♭, as pitch number 0, and (E♭ D♭ B♭), as the "upper" (0 2 5) incomplete (0 2 3 5) tetrachord, standing in a fixed, polarized "opposition" to the "lower" pitch number 11, the E here. The third stage recognizes individual blocks, generally a (E♭,C) "background" partitioning of Collection III in terms of the (E♭ D♭

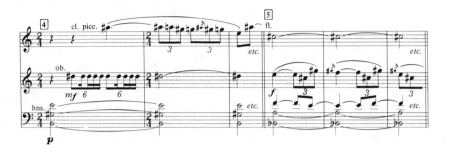

Example 27 *continued*

B♭) incomplete tetrachord and the (C B♭ A G) tetrachord and (C E G) triad. The point at Nos. 13–30 is that, in contrast to the diatonic framework of *Petroushka*'s first tableau (where, at Nos. 7 and 35, the "chromatic" pitch number 11 could be construed as an occasional octatonic "intrusion"), "Danses des adolescentes" is primarily octatonic to begin with (as is the preceding Introduction). The unimpaired diatonic D-scale on E♭ in the block at Nos. 28–30 is reached by the gradual elimination of an already persistently present pitch number 11–the E, referable to Collection III—and its substitution, anticipated already at No. 25, by pitch number 10, the F, as well as by the substitution of the remaining octatonic elements not part of the D-scale on E♭, A and G, by A♭ and G♭.

Example 27 can shed some additional light on the descending approach

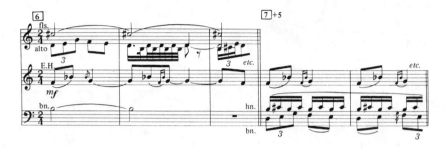

Example 27 *continued*

in scale formation and pitch numbering, as it so very appropriately applies to Stravinsky's "Russian" (0 2 3 5) tetrachordally oriented music,
whether octatonic or diatonic. For the question arises here in "Danses des
adolescentes": How do we stand with respect to pitch-class and/or (0 2 3 5)
tetrachord priority? For pitch number 11 (the E), while encompassing a
degree of "equal weight and independence" and standing "in opposition"
to pitch number 0 (the E♭), is not among the (E♭,C,A,F♯) symmetrically
defined partitioning elements of Collection III, Models A or B. Consequently, once the E♭–E interval span is acknowledged and its pitches assumed to encompass priority, should either assert priority over the other
while conforming to this 0–11 or (0–5,11) format, the resultant (0,3,6,9)

Example 27 *continued*

symmetrically defined partitioning, beginning at E♭ or E, would be different in each case.

This "problem" is not apparent in the Introduction. For there is insufficient evidence for a settlement in favor of either pitch number 0 or 11 with respect both to individual blocks and the section as a whole. And so pitch number 0 is simply the "upper" pitch element in the 0–11 interval span or (0–5,11) partitioning. The successive blocks realize the potential for "equilibrium," "opposition," or "equal weight and independence" with respect to pitch numbers 0 and 11; priority extends no "further" than varying realizations of the (0 2 3 5), 0–11, or (0–5,11) partitioning formulae—or, with respect to the Introduction as a whole, no "further"

Example 27 *continued*

than the intervals defined by these formulae. (The same holds for *Le Sacre* as a whole, of course. Global determinacy may be inferred in terms of (0 2 3 5), 0–11, or (0–5,11) intervallic relations, so that, in the global stages of the analysis, pitch notation merely records realizations of these intervallic relations with varying local pitch identity.)

But at Nos. 13–30 in "Danses des adolescentes," at Nos. 37 and 39–44 in the (Model A) triadically oriented "Jeu du rapt," and certainly in the first part of "Rondes printanières," there is little doubt that the uppermost pitch and, at Nos. 13–30 in "Danses," its "upper" (E♭ D♭ B♭) incomplete tetrachordal articulation acquire a sectional and even intersectional advantage, one that should properly be taken into account. Beginning at No. 13, this uppermost pitch advantage is assumed by E♭ (as pitch number 0).

Collection III

Example 27 *continued*

For already at No. 16—and certainly in the "block" of diatonic D-scale on
Eb at Nos. 28–30—its priority is assured, becoming less assertive in "Jeu
du rapt," but unmistakable again in the first part of "Rondes printanières."

But were we now, in "Danses des adolescentes" at No. 13, to recognize
Eb as pitch number 0 (and to recognize the extra "weight" of the "upper" (Eb Db Bb) incomplete tetrachord owing to its persistence or "survival" as a connecting link), the scalar interval ordering, given the customary ascending approach in scale formation and pitch numbering, would
be the 1,2 half-step–whole-step triadic form of Model A: Eb–E–F♯–
G–A–Bb–C–Db–(Eb). For the time being, however, this "triadic ordering" is out of the question. The (0 2 3 5) tetrachord predominates un-

Example 27 *continued*

til "Jeu du rapt", and is only obscured by resorting to Model A's ascending 1,2 interval ordering. So if we are to account for (0 2 3 5) tetrachordal
partitioning by means of Model B, to account for Collection III *and* the
gradual ascendency of E♭ and the (E♭ D♭ B♭) "upper" incomplete tetrachord at Nos. 13–30, the only proper means of representation is a *descending* 2,1 whole-step–half-step scale beginning on E♭ at No. 13. By descending from E♭ the symmetrically defined partitioning elements are E♭, C, A,
and F♯ (as stipulated by both Models A and B for Collection III), not E, G,
B♭, and D♭ as they are when ascending from E. The descending scale is a
most appropriate and telling representation by virtue of the following circumstances: (1) the unmistakable assertion of C as a partitioning element

Example 27 *continued*

in the reference collection (Collection III), owing, among other items, to the (C B♭ A G) tetrachordal articulation in the flutes at Nos. 16–18, and the sustained octave Cs in the oboes and bassoons; (2) without tetrachordal support (the A and F♯ being relatively inactive at Nos. 13–30), the reduction in intensity (except for the block at No. 13 and its near repeats) of E as a potent "opposition" element to the "upper" (E♭ D♭ B♭) incomplete tetrachord (the (0–5,11) partitioning), a weakening which coincides with E's gradual affiliation with a (C E G) triad at Nos. 14, 16–18, and 23 (scrupulously (E G C) first inversion, however, with E metrically accented in the bass to sustain, however minimally, the 0–11 articulation); (3) the mostly (Model A) triadically octatonic "Jeu du rapt" at No. 37 and 39–44 will re-

Example 27 *continued*

fer to Collection III (excepting one block at 40 + 6), in which the symmetrically defined partitioning elements via Model A are, of course, E♭, C, A, and F♯. Hence, a descending 2,1 scale beginning at No. 13 would allow the content connection between (0 2 3 5) tetrachordal partitioning in "Danses des adolescentes" and (0 4 7/0 4 7 10) triadic partitioning in "Jeu du rapt" to be defined with respect to the reference collection (Collection III) *and* the four "accented" partitioning elements, E♭, C, A, and F♯.[6]

Needless to say, those passages or sections indifferent to the temporary expressions of priority found in "Danses" and "Jeu du rapt" (e.g., No. 6 in the Introduction) are not in the least misrepresented when, for purposes of uniformity, this descending (0–5,11) global determination is extended

Example 27 *continued*

to the whole of *Le Sacre*. (In other words, the determination may at certain points reflect local or sectional priority on the part of pitch number 0, but, more often than not, merely a globally persistent (0–5,11) registral distribution or vertical interval span, with respect to which priority extends no "further" than varying local realizations of the *relations* expressed by this grouping.)

Accordingly, in "Jeu du rapt" at No. 37 (see Example 27), we note, first, the return to Collection III and local (E♭,C) partitioning (as inherited from "Danses"); and, second, that the articulation of this (E♭,C) partitioning alters (or reinterprets) the appearance of the 0–11 and (0–5,11) global units in terms now of a thoroughly (0 4 7 10) "dominant-seventh" orienta-

Example 27 *continued*

tion (Model A). Thus, the "upper" (E♭ D♭ B♭) incomplete tetrachord of
"Danses" is now part of a (E♭ D♭ B♭ G) "dominant seventh" in the trumpets; and E's affiliation in "Danses" with the (C E G) triad is fully
confirmed by the (C E G) root position in the horns.

Still, while this (0 4 7 10) "dominant-seventh" orientation in "Jeu du
rapt" obscures the (0 2 3 5) tetrachordally oriented 0–11 and (0–5,11)
units, note how carefully preserved—and thus reaffirmed—are the 0–11
and (0–5,11) spans of these units at No. 37; the first-inversion articulation
of the (E♭ D♭ B♭ G) "dominant seventh" at No. 37 preserves, in simultaneity, the "upper" (E♭ D♭ B♭) incomplete tetrachord of "Danses," which still
stands "in opposition" to the "lower" pitch number 11, the E of the (C E G)

Example 27 *continued*

triad. Indeed, we apprehend in this special chordal disposition at No. 37 a
certain logic behind the persistent incompleteness of the "upper" (E♭ D♭
B♭) tetrachord. For it is by virtue of its (E♭ D♭ B♭) incompleteness—with
the C omitted—that (E♭ D♭ B♭) may adapt itself to both (0 2 3 5) tetrachordal and (0 4 7 10) "dominant-seventh" blocks and sections, E♭, D♭, and B♭
merely becoming, in the process of transformation, the root, seventh, and
fifth of the (E♭ D♭ B♭ G) "dominant-seventh" complex. This point seems
apropos with respect to Stravinsky's "Russian" period generally: (0 2 5)
incompleteness renders the (0 2 3 5) tetrachord more flexible, so that, in
adapting itself to both Model B's (0 2 3 5) tetrachordal and Model A's (0 4
7 10) "dominant-seventh" partitioning of the octatonic collection, it may

Example 27 *continued*

define not only the connecting link in octatonic-diatonic interaction, but also the link connecting these differing modes of articulative partitioning of the single octatonic collection. (It may also explain the preponderance, in octatonic contexts of the "Russian" period, of Model A's (0 4 7 10) "dominant sevenths" in place of this model's (0 3 7/0 4 7) "minor" and "major" triads. Indeed, when extended to include the "lower" (7 9 0) incomplete (7 9 10 0) tetrachord of the (0 2 3 5 7 9) hexachord, (0 2 5) "incompleteness" may be envisioned, even when inferred on a relatively "foreground" articulative level (as here in "Danses" with the (E♭ D♭ B♭) tetrachord; or later as the "basic cell" of *Les Noces*), as reflecting something fundamentally distinctive about "Russian" musical thought.)

Example 27 *continued*

Thus, in moving from the opening block of "Danses" at No. 13 to No. 37 and 39–44 in "Jeu du rapt," the following pattern emerges: the (0 2 3 5) tetrachord, mostly in its (0 2 5) incomplete form at (E♭ D♭ B♭), is first part of a (E♭ D♭ B♭ G) "dominant seventh" in the strings; second, a D♭–B♭–E♭–B♭ ostinato figure in the english horn at No. 14, the trumpet at No. 23, the first violins at No. 25, and the trombone and timpani in the block of diatonic D-scale on E♭ at Nos. 28–30); third, a B♭–C D♭–E♭–D♭–C–B♭ melodic fragment in the trumpets at Nos. 28–30; and, finally, part of a (E♭ D♭ B♭ G) "dominant-seventh" complex in the trumpets at No. 37. In Example 28a, a summary of this sequence of "events" is sketched from the vantage points of this (E♭ D♭ B♭) between-reference

Example 27 *continued*

connecting link. And we note, in this conceptualization, that the (E♭ D♭ C B♭) tetrachord "passes through" the (E♭ D♭ B♭) or (E♭ D♭ B♭) (E) incomplete—and (nearly) globally determinate—stage before it branches off toward the committed (0 4 7 10) "dominant-seventh" framework (Model A) of "Jeu du rapt."

But to return briefly to No. 37 in "Jeu du rapt." Collection III's local (E♭,C) partitioning (the (E♭ D♭ B♭ G) "dominant seventh" superimposed on the (C E G) triad) is here extended to (E♭, C, A, F♯), owing to the F♯ in the timpani, and then to the (A G F♯ E) tetrachord of the interpenetrating fragment of the (A G F♯ E) (D C B A) diatonic D-scale on A in the flutes. Hence, notwithstanding Collection III's predominance, the block refers

Example 27 *continued*

to both Collection III and the D-scale on A. (See the dotted line in Example 27, which, as always in the analytical sketches of this volume, signifies octatonic-diatonic interpenetration. Collection III's contribution appears on the left-hand side of the line, while the right-hand side refers to that of the diatonic D-scale on A. Points of intersection—such as the shared, between-reference (A G F♯ E) tetrachord here—are marked off by brackets.) Then, in the succeeding climactic block at No. 42, this (E♭, C, A, F♯) extension of Collection III is realized in terms of (0 4 7 10) "dominant sevenths" at E♭, C, A, and F♯, and in the oboes and pizzicato strings in terms of ascending successions of (0 4 7) "major" triads at these four symmetrically defined partitioning elements. Furthermore, this climactic

Example 27 *continued*

(E♭,C,A,F♯) partitioning of Collection III is at No. 44 transposed into Collection II, with (0 4 7 10) "dominant sevenths" at F, D, B, and A♭: a Collection-II, F–E♭–D–C–B–A–A♭–G♭ framework. At No. 46, this Collection-II block is in turn succeeded by a "block" of unimpaired diatonic D-scale on F (in which the initial D-scale-on-A fragment in the flutes at No. 37 reappears, transposed to the D-scale on F). In this final moving from Collection II to this reference to the (F E♭ D C) (B♭ A♭ G F) diatonic D-scale on F at No. 46, it is the (F E♭ C) incomplete tetrachord of Collection II's presiding (F E♭ C A) "dominant seventh" at No. 44 which serves as the shared, between-reference connecting link. And in Example 28b we sketch a summary of these concluding blocks at Nos. 44–47 in "Jeu du rapt," where Collection II's (0 4 7 10) "dominant sevenths" on the left-

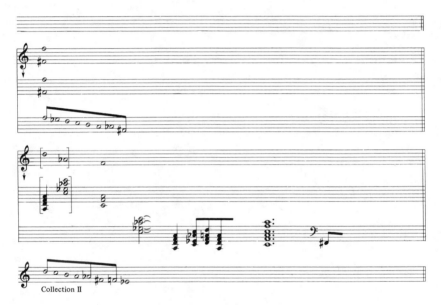

Example 27 *continued*

hand side *move through* the (F E♭ C) connecting link "slot" in the middle to the references to the diatonic D-scale on F and C on the right-hand side. Then, the summary of Example 29 resorts to pitch numbering to facilitate general application. Still, the (0–5,11) global unit of *Le Sacre* is retained in Example 29's final pitch-numbering summary of octatonic (Model B) and diatonic interaction in recognition of those instances where, in moving from right to left (from a diatonic to an octatonic or octatonic-diatonic context), it is most often pitch numbers 6 and/or 11 which "intrude" to signal the intervention of octatonic relations.

Thus, with respect to all the varied octatonic-diatonic summaries sketched in chapter 3 and here in regard to *Petroushka*'s first tableau and the "Danses" and "Jeu du rapt" sections of *Le Sacre*, we may note that Ex-

Example 27 *continued*

ample 24a in chapter 3 demonstrates the regularities governing octatonic (Model B) and diatonic interaction in moving from a (0 2 3 5) (7 9 10 0) D-scale or (0 2 3 5) (7 9 0) hexachordal context to a (0 2 3 5) (6 8 9 11) octatonic one, where any content-realization of this transaction will allow, by means of the two adjoining (0 2 3 5) (7 9 (10) 0) tetrachords of the D-scale or the (0 2 3 5 7 9) hexachord, two possibilities for octatonic penetration (coming often by way of the "intrusion" of a "chromatic" pitch number 6 and/or 11). Example 24b examines these same regularities—the (0 2 3 5) connecting link remains the same—but in moving from an octatonic to a diatonic context, so that, of the four overlapping (0 2 3 5) tetrachords available to any given octatonic collection, four possible D-scales or (0 2 3 5 7 9) hexachords may be implicated. Finally, the point of Examples 28a, b,

Example 27 *continued*

and 29 is the exhibition of these regularities from the standpoint of the (0 3 5/0 2 5/0 2 3 5) connecting link itself, so that, in moving from left to right or conversely (from an octatonic to a diatonic passage or conversely), we need merely realize the connecting link in order to activate the conceptualization. And so each summary demonstrates the same type of linkage in octatonic (Model B) and diatonic interaction or interpenetration from a slightly different angle. When "laid against the data," they jointly afford a fair indication of what Stravinsky's "Russian"-period material is all about.

Finally, as we approach detailed comment on Example 27's analysis, it will be noted that certain sections are ignored in it: in Part I, "Danses des adolescentes" at Nos. 30–37 and "Rondes printanières" and "Danses de la terre" in their entirety; then, Part II in its entirety excepting "Action ri-

Example 27 *continued*

tuelle des ancêtres." These omissions are generally owing to the near repetition of relations covered in one way or another elsewhere in the analysis. But they also reflect an intent to confront the selected blocks and
sections with meticulous care, a care which, applied to the whole of *Le Sacre*, might well have resulted, in the interests of preserving a manageable
format, in the farcical consignment of the remainder of Stravinsky's
works to a footnote. Rarely, then, are these omissions indicative of any
pronounced inability to trace (0 2 3 5) or octatonically conceived 0–11 or
(0–5,11) partitioning. (See Lists 1 and 2 of chapter 2. More specifically, see
"Danse de la terre" at No. 75, where the C–F♯ reiteration in the timpani
and strings, along with a (E♭ D♭ C B) tetrachordal articulation, refers unmistakably to relations encountered earlier in "Danses des adolescentes"
and "Jeu du rapt." Indeed, the C –D–E–F♯–G♯–A♯ ostinato in "Danse de

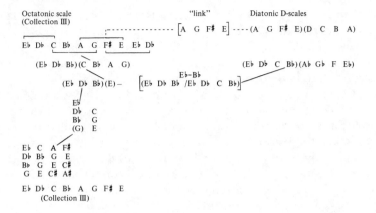

Example 28a: "Danses des adolescentes," "Jeu du rapt," Nos. 13–43 ("summary")

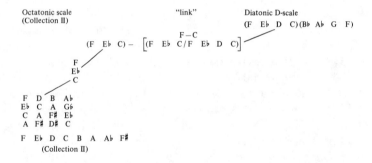

Example 28b: "Jeu du rapt," Nos. 44–47 ("summary")

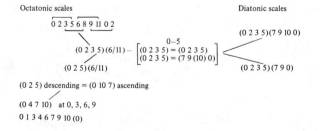

Example 29

la terre" prompts an octatonic (Collection III) and whole-tone interpenetration with respect to local (block) reconstruction.) "Cortège du sage" (primarily octatonic, Collection I) is also ignored except for a brief acknowledgment of certain obvious links. These omissions should not prove disadvantageous and are often clarified in the commentary.

As a final note, the reduction and condensation is extensive here, an imperative in view of this score's length and complexity and the long-term or global nature of the analytical pursuit. A degree of familiarity with this music is taken for granted, the reader being expected to find him/herself in the articulative groupings assembled at the local levels of the analytical sketches. To compensate for the reduction and condensation, the articulative groupings at these local levels are assembled pretty much as presented in registration and interval content. As always, study is most advantageously pursued with a score, piano, and/or recording within easy reach.

Introduction: The material here offers but a suggestion of pending octatonic confinement. The (0 2 3 5) tetrachordal fragment of the opening bassoon melody, (D C B A), is not affiliated with (0,11;0–5,11) partitioning, there being no "lower" pitch number 11 (E♭) "in opposition." Nonetheless, as a (0 2 3 5) complex, the fragment represents the most persistent articulative grouping in *Le Sacre*. And its presented contour, C–B–A–D–A, anticipates the D♭–B♭–E♭–B♭ contour of the (0 2 5) incomplete (0 2 3 5) tetrachordal ostinato of the succeeding "Danses des adolescentes," the predominating (0 2 3 5) fragment of this succeeding section.

Nos. 1–4: Here, the (C/C♯) simultaneity (or C–C♯ vertical interval span) first encountered at m. 2 submits to (0,11) octatonically conceived global partitioning. Moreover, reference is to Collection III, the reference collection of "Danses des adolescentes" at Nos. 13–24 and of "Jeu du rapt" at Nos. 37 and 39–44. But the incomplete (6 8 9 11) tetrachord attached to this (0,11) partitioning (or vertical interval span) is the "lower" of Model B's (0,6) tritone-related (0 2 3 5) (6 8 9 11) tetrachords, (6 9 11) in terms of (F♯ D♯ C♯) in the english horn, not the (0 2 3 5) "upper" one so much more prevalent in *Le Sacre*.

Nos. 4–5: Nos. 4 and 5 provide evidence for (0,11;0–5,11) octatonically conceived global partitioning, although outside interference is considerable: the A♭ at No. 4 and the A at No. 5. (But notice how very conspicuous is the semitonal transposition of the 0–11 interval span from E♭–E at No. 4 to E–F at No. 5.)

No. 6: At No. 6 and succeeding repeats (or near repeats) of this block at Nos. 7 + 3 and 7 + 5, outside interference elements are eliminated, and we encounter, for the first time, unimpaired octatonic partitioning in the (0,11;0–5,11) global manner indicated. Thus, the "lower" of Model B's (0,6) tritone-related (0 2 3 5) (6 8 9 11) tetrachords at No. 2 in the english

horn ((6 9 11) incomplete) has now become (0 2 3 5) "upper" within the
0–11 interval span ((0 3 5) incomplete in the global (0–5,11) partitioning
unit), where it stands "in opposition" to the "lower" pitch number 11 (the
B here), and where, with changes in content, it will remain predominately
"upper" in "Danses des adolescentes" and in succeeding sections as well.
Consequently, (0,11;0–5,11) global partitioning is realized in terms of
((B♭,B); (B♭ G F) (B)), Collection I.

   No. 8: No. 8 is wholly octatonic (Collection I), although the global
(0,11;0–5,11) partitioning is missing owing to the omission of the "upper"
(B♭ G F) incomplete (0 2 3 5) tetrachord of the english horn.

   No. 9: Three new diatonic fragments are here introduced. The first, a
continuation of the alto flute's (G F E D) tetrachordal fragment at Nos. 6
and 8, delineates the (0 2 3 5 7 9) hexachord in terms of (A G F♯ E D C).
The other two, in the oboe and clarinet piccolo, implicate an incomplete (0
2 5) (7 0) D-scale on F in terms of (F E♭ C) (B♭ F)—reading down, as always
in our analysis of Stravinsky's (0 2 3 5) tetrachordally oriented music. The
connecting link between the preceding Collection I ((B♭,B); (B♭ G F) (B))
blocks—and between the climactic block at Nos. 10–12 which follows—is
thus realized in terms of the (B♭ F) unit, the lower "fourth" or incomplete
(7 0) tetrachord of the (F E♭ C) (B♭ F) D-scale, which connects with Collection I's (B♭ (A♭) G F) tetrachord in the english horn.

   Nos. 10–12: Finally, Nos. 10–12 represent a climactic accumulation of
nearly all previously introduced fragments. This accumulation is principally an interpenetration between the octatonically conceived global
(0,11;0–5,11) partitioning, accountable to Collection I in terms of ((B♭,B);
(B♭ A♭ G F) (B)), and the diatonic (F E♭ C) (B♭ F) D-scale-on-F units introduced at No. 9 in the oboe and clarinet piccolo (now in the trumpet and
clarinet piccolo). Thus, octatonically speaking, the "upper" (B♭ A♭ G F)
tetrachord in the english horn, now (0 2 3 5) complete, perseveres in static,
fixed, or polarized "opposition" to the "lower" pitch number 11, the B;
and the "lower" of Model B's (0,6) tritone-related (0 2 3 5) (6 8 9 11) tetrachords, (6 8 9 11), is also in evidence in terms of (E D B), (6 8 11) incomplete. Still, this "lower" (E D B) incomplete (6 8 9 11) tetrachord is part of a
sustained (0 4 7 10) "dominant-seventh" complex at E in the strings—
revealingly (7 10 0 4) second inversion, however, so that the "lower" pitch
number 11, the B, is not only "lower" but "lowest," and is doubled. And so,
in view of this (0 4 7 10) "dominant-seventh" articulation and its accompanying bassoon fragment, we might be tempted, from a local standpoint,
into a partial (0 4 7 10) triadic (Model A) interpretation of the octatonic
contribution (Collection I).

   The interpenetration of octatonic Collection I ((B♭, B); (B♭ A♭ G F) (B))
and the diatonic D-scale at Nos. 10–12 is of an exceptional variety. Here,
nearly all octatonic (Collection I) fragments from the blocks at Nos. 6 and

8 are assembled in a final, tutti summation. This Collection I assemblage interacts with the two D-scale fragments introduced earlier at No. 9. And while the between-reference connecting link lies exposed in terms of Collection I's "upper" (B♭ A♭ G F) tetrachord in the english horn (which represents, respectively, the "lower" (B♭ F) "fourth" of the clarinet piccolo's (F E♭ C) (B♭ F) D-scale-on-F fragment and the "upper" (B♭ A♭ G F) tetrachord of the high trumpet's (B♭ A♭ G F) (E♭ D♭ C B♭) D-scale-on-B♭ fragment), this interpenetration yields an extraordinary richness in sound at Nos. 10–12, owing perhaps as much to the rhythmic-metric individuality of the reiterating, superimposed fragments as to the specifics of the interpenetration. The whole octatonic (Collection I) orchestra is made to stand, as it were, in a fixed "opposition" to this diatonic D-scale articulation in the clarinet piccolo and high trumpet.

Accordingly, conditions of (content-defined) "opposition" or "polarity"—generally to be understood with reference to superimposition or reiterating fragments at registrally fixed points—are never entirely "lost" or reconciled at the collectional level in cases of octatonic-diatonic interpenetration (even with a between-reference (0 2 3 5) connecting link). These conditions are applicable not only to (0,3,6,9) symmetrically defined partitioning of the single octatonic collection—or to certain partitioning formulae realized on behalf of the diatonic collection—but also to instances of octatonic-diatonic interpenetration, with respect to which they are merely reinterpreted in terms of interpenetrating reference collections that exhibit a degree of incompatibility (elements or relations *not* held in common) and a degree of coalescence (elements or relations held in common).

But note, at the same time, that the F–B♭–C–E♭–F fragment (reading up) in the oboe at No. 9 and clarinet piccolo at Nos. 10–12 is identical in interval content to the flute melody in the opening block at Nos. 0–2 in *Petroushka*: A–D–E–G–A. And so the question arises: why interpret this oboe–clarinet piccolo fragment in *Le Sacre* referentially in terms of the (F E♭ C) (B♭ F) incomplete D-scale on F, and the same diatonic articulation in *Petroushka* in terms of the (0 2 3 5 7 9) hexachord, (E D C♯ B A G)? The answer is that, in *Le Sacre*, the (F E♭ C) (B♭ F) fragment anticipates complete D-scale articulations at No. 37 in "Jeu du rapt" in terms of (A G F♯ E) (D C B A), and later at No. 46 in terms of (F E♭ D C) (B♭ A♭ G F), while, on the other hand, the critical omission of a seventh pitch element, together with the (E D C♯ B) tetrachordal articulation in the cello at No. 1, render the (E D C♯ B A G) hexachord referentially unmistakable at Nos. 0–2 in *Petroushka*'s first tableau. Differing contexts, or different global situations, suggest different referential categories for diatonic fragments which, in *Le Sacre* and *Petroushka*, are nonetheless identical in interval content.

"Danses des adolescentes," Nos. 13–30: In contrast to the Introduction, (0 2 3 5) or (0,11;0–5,11) *global partitioning* is here relatively stable in content: (E♭–B♭) or ((E♭,E);(E♭–B♭) (E)). The celebrated simultaneity at No. 13 is of consequence here as a reaffirmation of the (0,11; 0–5,11) global partitioning unit, a verticalization of the "upper" (0 2 5) incomplete (0 2 3 5) tetrachord, (E♭ D♭ B♭), which stands "in opposition" to pitch number 11, the E.

However, *local (block) partitioning* repeatedly alters the articulative appearance of the (0,11;0–5,11) global unit. Thus, at Nos. 14, 16, and 23, the E, as pitch number 11, becomes affiliated with a (C E G) triad—(E G C) first inversion, however, with E metrically accented to sustain, however minimally, the (0,11) articulation. And, coinciding with this affiliation: (1) the potency of E as an element of "opposition" to the E♭ ((0,11) partitioning) or to the "upper" (E♭ D♭ B♭) incomplete tetrachord ((0–5,11) partitioning) steadily subsides despite repeats of the No. 13 block, and is dropped altogether at Nos. 24–30 in favor of the D-scale on E♭ at No. 28, where only the "upper" (0 2 3 5) tetrachord, (E♭ D♭ C B♭), is retained; (2) E♭ gradually assumes a degree of overall pitch-class priority; (3) the C, pitch number 3, asserts priority as a partitioning element, a local (0,3) partitioning of Collection III in terms of (E♭,C) that will continue into "Jeu du rapt." This (0,3) "localized" partitioning is anticipated at No. 12 + 3 in terms of E♭ and C, and even earlier in the Introduction at No. 6 in terms of B♭ and G, by the tetrachordal fragments in the english horn and alto flute, (B♭ F G) and (G F E D), Collection I.

With the exception of the No. 13 block, "Danses des adolescentes" is (0 2 3 5) tetrachordally oriented, and the (0 4 7/0 4 7 10) triadic implications noted at Nos. 13, 14, 16, and 23 will not really come to the fore until "Jeu du rapt" at No. 37. However, with respect to these implications, note again the logic behind the persistent incompleteness of the "upper" (0 2 3 5) tetrachord. It is by virtue of its (0 2 5) incompleteness that this tetrachord ((E♭ D♭ B♭) here) readily adapts to both (0 2 3 5) tetrachordal and (0 4 7 10) triadic partitioning of the octatonic collection, its pitch numbers, in the process of transformation, merely becoming 0, 10, and 7 (reading up) of the (0 4 7 10) "dominant seventh." Thus, incompleteness renders the (0 2 3 5) tetrachord more flexible with respect to articulative partitioning, so that, in adapting itself to both (0 2 3 5) tetrachordal (Model B) and (0 4 7 10) triadic (Model A) partitioning, it may often define not only the connecting link in octatonic (Model B) and diatonic interpenetration, but the connecting link with respect to these differing modes of articulative partitioning of the single octatonic collection as well.

"Jeu du rapt," Nos. 37–48: (0 2 3 5) and (0,11;0–5,11) *global partitioning* perseveres, but, being (0 2 3 5) tetrachordal in conception rather than (0 3

7/0 4 7) triadic, it is less conspicuous here than in previous sections. (For example, the E at No. 37, pitch number 11, is now persistently a member of the (C E G (B♭)) triad, root position.) Still, at No. 37 and subsequent transpositions of this material at Nos. 38, 40 + 6, and 44, note how carefully preserved and thus reaffirmed is the registral distribution or vertical interval span of the (0,11;0–5,11) global unit, how the (4 7 10 0) first-inversion articulation of the "upper" (0 4 7 10) "dominant-seventh" complex ((E♭ D♭ B♭ G) at No. 37) preserves, in simultaneity, the "upper" incomplete (0 2 5) tetrachord which still stands "in a certain opposition" to the "lower" pitch number 11, the E at No. 37.

In regard to content, accountability alternates between Collections III and II, between a ((E♭,E); (E♭–B♭) (E)) partitioning of Collection III at Nos. 37, 39, and 41–44 (inherited from "Danses des adolescentes"), and a ((B,C);(B–F♯)(C)) or ((F,F♯);(F–C)(F♯)) partitioning of Collection II at Nos. 38, 40 + 6, and 44–46. And note that when the (0,11) global unit at No. 37 in terms of (E♭,E) is transposed "down" into Collection II in terms of (B,C) at Nos. 38 and 40 + 6, the latter B–C relation is reinforced in the timpani, horn, and bass clarinet by a fragment reiterating these pitches. (This is one of the few instances where the vertically conceived global (0,11) partitioning becomes linear or fragmental.)

Local (block) partitioning radically alters (reinterprets) the articulative appearance of the global units in terms of a thoroughly triadic (0 4 7 10) "dominant-seventh" orientation (Model A). Thus, local (0,3) partitioning continues from "Danses des adolescentes" at Nos. 37, 38, 40 + 6, and 44, but is now articulated by means of (0 4 7 10) "dominant-seventh" complexes (rather than (0 2 3 5) complexes) at pitch numbers 0 and 3. (Thus, too, the accompaniment affiliation of E, pitch number 11, with the (C E G) triad in the preceding "Danses" at Nos. 14, 16, and 23 is here fully confirmed—in terms of (C E G (B♭)) at Nos. 37, 39, and 41–43.)

Furthermore, local (0,3) partitioning is extended to (0,3,6,9) at No. 37 because of the (A G F♯ E) tetrachord of the superimposed, interpenetrating (A G F♯ E D C B (A)) D-scale fragment introduced by the flutes and the high trumpet, and the F♯ in the timpani. At climactic points, such as at Nos. 42 and 44, this (0,3,6,9) partitioning is articulated by means of (0 4 7 10) "dominant-seventh" complexes.

But with "Jeu du rapt" we can begin to see how the articulative appearance of the (0,11;0–5,11) global unit or of the "upper" (0 2 3 5) complete or incomplete tetrachord in this unit is successively altered or reinterpreted from one block or section to the next by means of changes in the collectional reference or in the articulative partitioning, so that, in moving from the Introduction to "Jeux des cités rivales" with this "upper" (0 2 3 5) tetrachord in mind, the following pattern emerges: (1) at No. 6, the "upper" (B♭ G F) incomplete tetrachord balanced against the "lower" B (Collection I); (2) at No. 13, the "upper" (E♭ D♭ B♭) incomplete tetrachord, conceived as part of a (0 4 7 10) complex at E♭, balanced against the "lower" E; (3) at Nos. 14, 16, and 23, the "upper" (E♭ D♭ B♭) incomplete tetrachord balanced against the "lower" E, which is now articulated as a part of a (C E G) triad; (4) at Nos. 28–30, the "upper" (E♭ D♭ C B♭) tetrachord with no pitch number 11 "in opposition" (D-scale on E♭); (5) at No. 37, the "upper" (E♭ D♭ B♭) incomplete tetrachord, now part of a (0 4 7 10) complex at E♭, balanced against the "lower" E, now part of a (C E G (B♭)) complex (Collection III); (6) at No. 57 + 2, the interval of 5 which spans the "upper" (0 2 3 5) tetrachord, F–C reading down, balanced against the "lower" F♯ (Collection II); (7) at No. 64, the "upper" (G F E D) complete tetrachord balanced against the "lower" G♯ (Collection I).

Finally, "Jeu du rapt" is almost entirely octatonic, with interference or diatonic interpenetration from the (0 2 3 5 7 9 10 (0)) D-scale. Thus, in the (A G F♯ E D C B (A)) D-scale fragment superimposed "above" the compound ((E♭ D♭ B♭ G)(C E G (B♭)) simultaneity from Collection III at No. 37, the D conspicuously conflicts or "clashes" with the E♭ and D♭ of Collection III, while the between-reference connecting link is realized in terms of its "upper" (0 2 3 5) tetrachord, (A G F♯ E). This diatonic D-scale fragment is subsequently transposed to (F E♭ D C B♭ A G (F)) at No. 46, and to (C B♭ A G F E♭ D (C)) at No. 47, where it presides to conclude this section.

"Jeux des cités rivales," Nos. 57–64: (0 2 3 5) and (0,11;0–5,11) global partitioning is conspicuous, although the timpani-brass block at No. 57 introduces a new (vertical) disposition, namely, B–C–F♯ (reading down), which, transposed to F–F♯–C at No. 57 + 2, persists at subsequent repeats of these blocks. However, the block at No. 57 + 4 restores the normal (0–5,11) registral distribution, F–C–F♯ here, reading down.

The content refers to Collections II and III; there is a ((B,C);(B–F♯)(C)) and ((F,F♯);(F–C)(F♯)) partitioning of Collection II at Nos. 57 and 57 + 2 (and subsequent repeats), and a ((E♭,E); (E♭–B♭)(E)) partitioning of Collection III at No. 62. These varying realizations of the (0,11;0–5,11) global unit are identical to those of "Jeu du rapt" and "Danses des adolescentes" at Nos. 13–48. More specifically, the ((B,C);(B–F♯)(C)) realization at No. 57 is anticipated by the No. 38 block in "Jeu du rapt" (which likewise refers to Collection II; see, especially, the timpani fragment); the ((F,F♯); (F–C) (F♯)) realization at Nos. 57 + 2 and 57 + 4 is anticipated by Nos. 44 and 47.

Local (block) partitioning at Nos. 57–64 naturally continues to alter (reinterpret) the articulative appearance of the (0,11;0–5,11) global unit, primarily by means of a generally (0 3 7/0 4 7) triadic orientation and "outside" diatonic penetration. Thus, at No. 57 + 2, reference is to Collection II and, possibly, the F-scale on F. The octatonic side to this interpenetration is defined, of course, by the ((F,F♯);(F–C),(F♯)) global unit articulated by the reiterating F♯/C fragment in the bassoons and, in the horns, by two conflicting superimposed fragments. The first "upper" fragment delineates an A–F–D–B outline with F presiding, the second a (0 4 7 10) "dominant-seventh" outline at G♯, in (4 7 10 0) first inversion, with F♯ presiding (rather than G♯ because of metric accentuation and the bassoon's F♯/C fragment). The diatonic side is defined primarily by the first "upper" A–F–B–D horn fragment, which implicates the F-scale on F, the connecting link or associative factor between these interpenetrating references (Collection II and the F-scale on F) discernible in terms of the F, the (F A C) triad, and the A–F–D–B outline of the first "upper" horn fragment.

It is highly revealing that F as pitch number 0 (which stands "in opposition" to the "lower" G♯–F♯ reiteration and the (4 7 10 0) "dominant-seventh" outline at G♯ at Nos. 57 + 2 and 57 + 4) *reverses* (inverts), in terms of (F,G♯), the local (E♭,C) articulation of the global unit in "Danses des adolescentes" (at Nos. 14, 16, and 23, for example) and "Jeu du rapt" (at No. 37, for example). For on these former occasions it was the E♭–D♭ reiteration or the root of the (4 7 10 0) "dominant-seventh" complex, E♭, which presided ("on top") as pitch number 0 over the "lower" (C E G) triad (C as pitch number 3). Hence, the G♯–F♯ reiteration has the E♭–D♭ reiteration of the (E♭ D♭ B♭) incomplete (0 2 3 5) tetrachord or of the (4 7 10 0) "dominant seventh" at E♭ in the preceding "Danses" and "Jeu du rapt" sections very conspicuously as its origin.

No. 64: (0 2 3 5) and (0,11;0–5,11) global partitioning is here highly conspicuous owing to the return (already anticipated at Nos. 60 and 61) to local (0 2 3 5) tetrachordal articulation. Indeed, as in the Introduction, priority extends no "further" than the Collection I ((G,G♯);(G–D)(G♯)) content realization of the global unit, with pitch number 0, the G, standing "in opposition" to pitch number 11, the G♯. The "lower" (6 8 9 11) tetrachord is also present here ((C♯ A♯ G♯) incomplete), so that this "opposition" is expressed at the more articulative level in terms of Model B's (0,6) tritone-related (0 2 3 5)(6 8 9 11) tetrachords, (G F E D♮ and (C♯ A♯ G♯), which are enclosed within (and which thus articulate in this fashion) the global unit.

However, reference to Collection I is qualified by the diatonic (0 2 3 5)(7 9 10 (0)) D-scale in terms of (G F E D) (C B♭ A (G)). And so an octatonic-diatonic interpenetration may again be inferred with the connecting link between these two references again discernible in terms of the "upper" (0 2 3 5) tetrachord, (G F E D) here.

"Action rituelle des ancêtres," Nos. 131–35: Finally, Nos. 131–35 acknowledge the persistence of (0,11;0–5,11) global partitioning in Part II. While the "lower" pitch number 11, the D in the C♯–D global interval span here, appears to predominate at first, the introduction of the "upper" (0 2 3 5) tetrachord in terms of (C♯ B A♯ G♯) at Nos. 132, 134, and 138 (as well as the C♯–D reiteration in the alto flute at No. 131, in which C♯ is metrically accented over the "lower" D) fully confirms (0,11;0–5,11) global partitioning with respect to a thoroughly (0 2 3 5) tetrachordal articulation.

The content refers to Collection I, a ((C♯,D); (C♯–G♯) (D)) specification of the global unit. While the "lower" Model B's (0,6) tritone-related (0 2 3 5) (6 8 9 11) tetrachords, (6 8 9 11) in terms of (G F E D), is not fully accounted for at Nos. 131–34 (the G is missing), the tutti eruption at No. 134 exposes it (in the flutes and violins) as a cohesive articulative unit "in opposition" to the "upper" tritone-related (0 2 3 5) tetrachord in terms of (C♯ B A♯ G♯).

CONCLUSIONS

In this fashion *Le Sacre* is approached globally with a between-block or between-reference (0 2 3 5) tetrachord—complete or (0 2 5/0 3 5) incomplete—and with an octatonically conceived 0–11 and (0–5,11) partitioning formula. While this latter 0–11 or (0–5,11) partitioning of the octatonic collection is (0 2 3 5) tetrachordal in conception—articulated by means of Model B's (0,6) tritone-related (0 2 3 5) (6 8 9 11) tetrachords, but with a generally greater emphasis on the "upper" of the two—it lends itself to a Model A (0 4 7 10) "dominant-seventh" articulation as well, because of the frequently articulated (0 2 5) incompleteness of the (0 2 3 5) tetrachords. It is also in this fashion that Model A's (0 4 7 10) "dominant sevenths" surface appendagelike within a predominately (0 2 3 5) tetrachordal context: in the process of transformation, pitch numbers 0, 2, and 5 of the (0 2 3 5) tetrachord, reading down, merely become pitch numbers 0, 10, and 7 (the root, seventh, and fifth respectively) of the (0 4 7 10) "dominant-seventh" complex (as with the (E♭ D♭ B♭) incomplete tetrachord in "Danses des adolescentes" and its subsequent articulation as a (E♭ D♭ B♭ G) "dominant seventh" in "Jeu du rapt" at No. 37). We apprehend in these transactions an underlying rationale for the frequent (0 2 5) incomplete articulation of the (0 2 3 5) tetrachord in Stravinsky's "Russian"-period material (so evident in *Les Noces*, for example, as well as *Le Sacre*), and for the partiality so often exhibited for Model A's "dominant-seventh" complexes—in place, that is, of this model's (0 3 7/0 4 7) "minor" and "major" triads.

The "dissonance," "vertical chromaticism," or "primitivism" associated with *Le Sacre* is thus octatonically conceived but is qualified at points by octatonic-diatonic interpenetration or by blocks of unimpaired diatonicism, often accounted for in terms of the D-scale. Moreover, while the first of *Three Pieces for String Quartet, Pribaoutki, Renard, Les Noces,* and *Histoire du soldat* continue to exhibit a preoccupation with (0 2 3 5) partitioning of the octatonic collection and the 2,1 interval ordering of the scale implicated (Model B), never, in these ensuing works, does this preoccupation manifest itself with such persistence.[7] And so, finally, whatever else *Le Sacre* may be presumed to represent, it can unquestionably be regarded as the most extensive and varied account of Model B partitioning in the literature, perhaps in *any* "literature."

Indeed, to continue in a somewhat exploratory vein, it may very well be owing to the persistent and pronounced exposure of Model B's (0 2 3 5), 0–11, and (0–5,11) tetrachordal partitioning of the octatonic collection that *Le Sacre*, for all its novelty and acknowledged "revolutionary" aspects, has no "true descendants" (as Boulez has remarked).[8] So uniquely embedded is the persistence of these Model B partitioning formulae—and, of course, the links forged with Model A's (0 4 7 10) "dominant-seventh" complexes—that to tinker with these formulae in an improvisational or compositional fashion is invariably to invoke the whole "sound-world" of *Le Sacre*—and to provoke, at the same time, all the melodic repetition and rhythmic-metric intricacy that relate to this "sound-world" (to which, of course, we have yet to address ourselves in detail).

Of course, in another sense *Le Sacre* has many "descendants," many derivatives: the piece may be situated within the general confines of Stravinsky's "Russian" musical thought—as has indeed been here our intent—so that it may tellingly be heard and understood to wield an influence over a host of succeeding works (neoclassical as well as "Russian"). And *Le Sacre*'s ostinati and instrumental "effects" did influence a great many composers, although this influence may now seem a bit superficial in that it failed to encompass the work's complexities in pitch organization, architecture, and rhythmic-metric construction.[9]

Hence while *Le Sacre* may be new, different, or "revolutionary" (and highly influential, at least for Stravinsky himself), it did not become "consequential" by spawning a succession of "true descendants" among Stravinsky's contemporaries (or descendants) in the same sense as did, say, Arnold Schoenberg's serial or twelve-tone innovations. But we are at the same time reminded that those of us truly and honestly affected by a musical composition are seldom swayed by retrospective or historically oriented propositions of influence or "consequentiality" (or by the "promise" thereof, as Stravinsky would later put it);[10] indeed, influence or consequence may oftentimes be found lurking in the most improbable, random, offhand, or freakish of circumstances. History teaches us, for instance, that the music of Bach could scarcely have been less consequential in its day, and apart from a few critical encounters in the late eighteenth century (Mozart comes to mind), lay dormant for a hundred years. Even since the mid-nineteenth century, the real measure of its consequence—apart from the pedagogical uses to which it has been put—has been diverse, scattered, and unpredictable; along with Schumann, Brahms, Reger, and Hindemith, certain of Stravinsky's neoclassical ventures (especially the *Octet*, 1923; the *Piano Sonata*, 1924; and the "Dumbarton Oaks" *Concerto in E♭*, 1938) readily come to mind. And so we can never be quite sure about the question of consequence or "consequentiality" (about which, at any rate, composers had perhaps best not concern themselves), especially with a piece like *Le Sacre*, which, as Stravinsky so quaintly put it, has so disadvantageously had to withstand over half a century of "destructive popularity" (along with *The Firebird* and *Petroushka*).

SOME GENERAL CONSIDERATIONS

What are the implications of pitch organization insofar as the general appearance of *Le Sacre* is concerned? How is it that our analysis and commentary specify—*presuppose*, to an extent—features in the formal, instrumental, melodic, and rhythmic-metric domains (or subdomains)?

The preceding pages afford a meticulous account of what may yet be deemed *Le Sacre*'s most striking attribute: the persistent and pronounced harshness of the "dissonance" or "vertical chromaticism," based on the 0–11 or "major-seventh" vertical interval span sustained statically and very nearly continuously throughout. This is quite naturally an articulation in which rhythmic-metric emphasis and instrumental procedure are critical. Scanning the successive blocks and sections of Example 27 (or those to be examined in "Jeux des cités rivales" and "Cortège du sage," Examples 30a and b), one notes the incessant, hammerlike downbeating that so frequently accentuates this "dissonant"0–11 interval span (E♭/E at the No. 13 block or G/G♯ at No. 64 in "Jeux des cités rivales"). The pitch elements of this span, while interfragmental in the sense of being a part of separate, superimposed, reiterating fragments, are pitted against each other in a registral and instrumental fixity, or in that vertically conceived "polarity" or "opposition" alluded to in earlier chapters, thus a conception as rhythmic-metric as it is "harmonic." And the agony of this "dissonant" drone, of this static, hypnotic 0–11 "polarity" or "opposition," is an instrumental conception. For apart from the question of "fixity" (the manner in which reiterating fragments remain fixed both registrally and instrumentally, with little or no developmental "dialogue" or exchange between parts), it is often the case that the pitch elements of this span are reiterated in strained, awkward instrumental registers. For example: the high C in the bassoon at m. 2 in the Introduction, pitted against the lower C♯ in the horn (very nearly the first simultaneity in *Le Sacre* and a very telling one); or the G in the violins at No. 64 in "Jeux des cités rivales," pitted against the tuba's G♯ or G♯–A♯–C♯–A♯–(G♯) incomplete (6 8 9 11) tetrachord (see Example 27). These registers guarantee the 0–11 interval span a strained, often shrill effect, producing a natural instrumental tension which is thus built into the whole 0–11 or (0–5,11) globally defined structure. And these registers ensure, as well, the emphatic exposure of the 0–11 span or (0–5,11) partitioning from one block or section to the next.

(In matters of instrumentation, however, it is generally to be conceded that, excepting a few soloistic passages or sections (most notably the Introduction), *Le Sacre*'s orchestra is heavy, often loaded with octave and double-octave doublings, a thick instrumental "fill" not to be found in the earlier *Petroushka*. The material may have warranted such an approach, of course, and Stravinsky later confided that Diaghilev encouraged it by promising him an immense ballet orchestra for the 1913 season, including eight horns, eight trumpets, and four tubas. "I am not sure my orchestra would have been so large otherwise."[11] But the instrumentation in *Petroushka*, even in the original 1911 version before the revision of 1947 drastically curtailed orchestral size, is on the whole far more characteristic of Stravinsky's "touch," with its light, bouncy, crisp, soloistic textures.)

Were we to draw more specific implications affecting the formal, melodic, and rhythmic-metric components, the several linkages might be summarized as follows (but not necessarily in the order indicated, since it is the coordinated interplay to which our attention is drawn, and with respect to which these components—or coordinates—are interdependent, with a hearing and understanding of one hinging, however peripherally, on a hearing and understanding of the others):[12]

1. *Le Sacre*'s (0 2 3 5), 0–11, and (0–5,11) globally defined framework is conceived primarily in terms of a partitioning of the (0 2 3 5 6 8 9 11) octatonic collection (Model B) and of the (0 2 3 5 7 9 10 (0)) diatonic collection (D-scale), in which the (0 2 3 5) octatonic partitioning relates to a (0 4 7 10) "dominant-seventh" partitioning (Model A) by means of the frequent (0 2 5) incomplete articulation of the (0 2 3 5) tetrachords.

2. These octatonic, diatonic, and octatonic-diatonic relations, being symmetrical and hence inherently static, non-progressive or inconclusive in some tonally conceived progressive, developmental, or cadential sense (being "coagulated stuff," to return to the commentary of Pierre Boulez, "irreducible aggregations"),[13] are linked to—or may be said to prompt—a form constructed with relatively stable, self-contained blocks of material. These blocks are often abruptly cut off (without "resolution" or cadential formulation) and subjected to (near) repeats in their respective contexts, at which point(s) they acquire that unusual degree of distinction and insulation marked not only in instrumentation, tempo, dynamics, and/or rhythmic-metric design, but perhaps most critically in referential character.

3. This abrupt juxtaposition of blocks of material (a formal construction which replaces the familiar tonal, C-scale schemes of the Baroque and

Classical traditions) is in turn linked to a melodic construction which consists of reiterating fragments, often registrally and instrumentally fixed in ostinatolike repetition. These fragments are very often of limited range and content, and delineate the (0 2 3 5) tetrachord (which may be referentially either octatonic, diatonic, or octatonic-diatonic).

4. This melodic construction is in turn linked to a rhythmic-metric construction which imposes itself either in the form of stretches of rapidly changing meters (when this happens, the blocks are of relatively short duration, with all the superimposed, reiterating fragments sharing the same rhythmic-metric periods as defined by the shifting meter), or in the form of a steady or a steady varying meter, in which the reiterating fragments repeat according to "separate" or "independent" periods, time spans, or cycles (all becoming ostinati in this respect), but in which one of these reiterating periods will reflect the steady or steady varying meter and thus serve as a "pedal" in relation to the other, superimposed rhythmic-metric periods "above" and/or "below."

First, the melodic component: in incantatory fashion, it consists of a stretch of superimposed reiterating fragments; these fragments are fixed registrally and instrumentally (locked in repetition, so to speak), each being generally of limited range and content, and very often delineating the (0 2 3 5) tetrachord, complete or (0 2 5/0 3 5) incomplete. But we are scarcely content with an account of "melodic invention" in *Le Sacre*—or in Stravinsky's "Russian" period generally—that merely acknowledges the profusion of (0 2 3 5) folklike melodies. Stravinsky can scarcely be credited with having invented the (0 2 3 5) tetrachord as melody; nor was he this century's only composer to exploit its folkish potential. For example, such (0 2 3 5) material may frequently be found in the music of Bela Bartok, where it is frequently subject to some form of repetition. Bartok's Third String Quartet (1927) offers an opportunity for comparison in this connection. In the opening section or *Prima parte*, the (0 2 3 5) tetrachord, generally (0 3 5) incomplete (reading down, as in our analysis of Stravinsky's (0 2 3 5) tetrachordally oriented music, whether octatonic or diatonic), figures as the principal articulative grouping, as a kind of "basic cell." But more significantly, Bartok was fond of symmetry, not only in the formal layout (as in the archlike shape his movements or pieces often assume), but also in pitch relations. He was fond of the (0,6) tritone relation "between fragments," for example. Thus, in the Third Quartet, an (0 2 3 5) tetrachord, incomplete in terms of (F♯ D♯ C♯), is introduced as an ostinato in the viola at No. 4, and is immediately superimposed over its (0,6) tritone-related (6 8 9 11) tetrachord, incomplete in terms of (C A G) in the cello. These superimposed ostinati yield (0,6) tritone-related (0 2 3 5) (6 8 9 11) tetrachords, incomplete in terms of (F♯ D♯ C♯) (C A G), accountable to Collection III. Further along at No. 11+3, similar interfragmental (0,6) tritone relations materialize: a sustained (D G) "fourth" in the first violin is superimposed on its (0,6) tritone-related "fifth" in the cello, (C♯ G♯), and this sustained superimposition accompanies an incomplete (0 2 3 5) tetrachordal articulation in terms of (G E D) in the second violin and viola, these relations jointly yielding the (G A♭ B♭ B C♯ D E F (G)) octatonic collection, Collection I.

Still, it is the constant infusion of non-octatonically derived chromaticism in Bartok's music, along with the many imitations, transpositions, and inversions of fragments which, apart from a few interfragmental (0,6) tritone relations, are not octatonically motivated (pursued with reference to the octatonic collection) that renders those octatonic implications that may occasionally be inferred—as here in these few measures in the *Prima parte* of the Third Quartet—fleeting and of little consequence. Difficult to apprehend on a scale approaching its role as a constructive or referential factor in Stravinsky's music, the octatonic collection is of little assistance in coming to terms with Bartok, with relationships which, local or global, pertain fundamentally to the question of identity and distinction. Even the interfragmental—or "between-fragments"—(0,6) tritone relation, so characteristic of Stravinsky's octatonic thought (with each of the collection's eight pitch elements tritone-related), is not generally octatonic in conception in Bartok's music. And this is because, unlike the incomplete (0 2 3 5) (6 8 9 11) tetrachordal articulation at Nos. 4 and 11+3 in Bartok's Third Quartet, the fragments themselves are not generally octatonic, but are either diatonic or fused with an abundance of chromatic detail, circumstances which tend to invest this interfragmental (0,6) tritone symmetry with a referential complexion different from that—typically octatonic—found in Stravinsky.[14] (Interfragmental (0,6) tritone relations—or (0,3,6,9) relations— are, of course, invariably octatonic in Stravinsky's music, if not explicitly octatonic, then at least octatonic-diatonic. In diatonic contexts they signal, as we have seen already in *Petroushka*'s first tableau, the "intrusion" of octatonic relations. With certain modifications in specification, these transactions pertain to neoclassical and early serial works as well.) All of this need not suggest, of course, that nontonal, symmetrically forged conditions of "polarity," "opposition," "harmonic stasis," or deadlock—a descriptive terminology introduced in chapter 2 in regard to Stravinsky's octatonic settings—are not also in some sense pertinent to symmetrical relations in Bartok's music—specifically, the (0,6) tritone relation—but only that the referential character of this symmetry is not generally octatonic, and hence differs from that characteristic of Stravinsky.

We may note, as well, the close imitation of which Bartok was so fond, an imitative part-writing which is often thoroughly progressive and developmental in the Classical sonata-form tradition, tending also to prompt formal and rhythmic-metric considerations of a sort quite different from those typical of or peculiar to Stravinsky. Indeed, it is precisely this developmental "style" of the Classical sonata form that seems to run so fundamentally counter to Stravinsky's musical thought processes, that seems so conspicuously at odds not only with the special conditions of pitch organization in his music, but also with all the formal, melodic, instrumental, and rhythmic-metric features that intimately accrue. Apart from some fugues (or fugatos) and canons of the neoclassical and serial periods (which, of course, relate more directly to Baroque conventions and certain peculiarities of Webern's contrapuntal "style"), perhaps the closest we come to this Classical developmental "style" is in the first movement of the neoclassical *Concerto for Two Pianos* (1935)—composed, as Stravinsky later acknowledged, when the composer was for a short while basking in the piano sonatas and variations of Beethoven and Brahms—or perhaps in the first movement of the *Symphony in C* (1940). But even in these and similar endeavors, neoclassicism takes its toll, and the Classical formal designs so fondly resurrected are often only superficially apparent, or may seem only crudely relevant, with their rationale—which lies, ultimately, in pitch relations of the tonally functional, C-scale variety—severely undermined by Stravinsky's uniquely designed modes of accommodation.

And so, quite obviously, we draw closer to the specifics of melody in *Le Sacre*—or in the "Russian" period generally—once the (0 2 3 5) tetrachord's referential identity through its affiliation with the octatonic (Model B) and diatonic (D-scale or (0 2 3 5 7 9) hexachordal) collections is properly acknowledged, once this (0 2 3 5) tetrachord is recognized as a partitioning of these collections of reference, a partitioning which, from one block or section to the next, may serve articulatively as the between-block or between-reference connecting link (since the single (0 2 3 5) tetrachord is in this respect neutral, and may be octatonic, diatonic, or octatonic-diatonic in referential character).

RHYTHMIC-METRIC IMPLICATIONS

We draw even closer to *Le Sacre* and the "Russian" stamp once the question of melodic repetition is linked to the rhythmic-metric issue. This brings us to Pierre Boulez's remarkable analysis of rhythm in *Le Sacre*, a skillful and revealing document notwithstanding its nearly total neglect of pitch organization (which prompts some misleading conclusions about the "separateness" or "independence" of the rhythmic-metric component, to which we shall be turning for further comment in our discussion of rhythmic (or metric) invention in chapter 8).[15] And while to repeat or paraphrase what has already been demonstrated in a thorough and efficient manner is a senseless endeavor, there are some general observations which tie in nicely with our preliminary remarks on rhythmic-metric innovation in *The Firebird's* Finale (chapter 1), and which, at the same time, point in a more general way to the whole of Stravinsky's music, "Russian," neoclassical, and serial.

There are in *Le Sacre*—and in Stravinsky's music generally—two usefully distinguishable kinds of rhythmic-metric construction (viewed as extremes, of course, with numerous blocks, passages, or pieces partaking of both in one way or another). The first has to do with a changing (often rapidly changing) meter in which the fragments, lines, or parts, fixed registrally and instrumentally in repetition, share the same irregular rhythmic-metric periods as defined by the changing meter, and are hence synchronized unvaryingly in vertical (or "harmonic") coincidence. (In reality, this is often a kind of rapid block development, with all the reiterating fragments proceeding en masse, and with the blocks of relatively short duration.) Typical examples of this construction are the "Danse sacrale," as examined in detail by Boulez, or the closing section of "Jeu du rapt" at Nos. 46–48, also examined by Boulez. But here we turn to the opening blocks of "Jeux des cités rivales" at Nos. 57 and 58. (See Example 30a.) Notice, first, that all superimposed fragments share, in repetition, the same irregular rhythmic-metric periods as defined by the shifting meter, and hence coincide unvaryingly in vertical coincidence. These superimposed, reiterating fragments remain fixed registrally and instrumentally upon successive (near) repeats of the blocks in question (labeled A, B, and C in Example 30a). While the meter changes and thus subtly either lengthens or shortens the periods of these reiterating fragments, the blocks retain their individual referential identities. Finally, it is really this subtle lengthening and shortening of the rhythmic-metric periods of

Example 30a

these reiterating fragments—upon successive (near) repeats of the blocks in question—that account for "development," within-block relations making for an essentially static, symmetrically defined, "coagulated" stuff. And so in the first of these rhythmic-metric types, construction proceeds in strict block formation: the horizontal fragments, lines, or parts proceed all together, synchronized unvaryingly in vertical coincidence.

The second usefully distinguishable rhythmic-metric construction is less prevalent in material of both the "Russian" and neoclassical categories. It consists, in marked contrast to the first, of a steady meter—or possibly of a steady varying meter—which will generally reflect the stable rhythmic-metric period(s) of one of the reiterating fragments. Then, "above" and/or "below" this stable "pedal" (or ostinato, often basso ostinato), other reiterating fragments are superimposed, in the sense that they repeat according to "separate" or "independent" rhythmic-metric periods, time spans or cycles (thus also becoming ostinati). Consequently, these superimposed rhythmic-metric periods ("rhythmic cells," as Boulez calls them) are not synchronized unvaryingly in vertical coincidence, but effect a coincidence that is constantly changing.[16]

The first of the *Three Pieces for String Quartet* (1914), presently to be examined in chapter 5, offers a stunning illustration of this type of construction, as does the last movement of the *Symphony of Psalms* at No. 22 (Example 30c in this chapter).[17] Here in *Le Sacre*, however, we focus our attention on "Jeux des cités rivales" at Nos. 64–71, a passage which flows without interruption into the "Cortège du sage" at Nos. 67–71. (See Example 30b.) We note, first, a steady meter: 4/4 from No. 64 in "Jeux des cités rivales" to No. 70 in "Cortège du sage," and 6/4 at No. 70. This stable metric scheme is to a degree reinforced by a G♯/D basso ostinato in the bassoons and contrabassoons at No. 66, which is subsequently embellished by a host of complementary ostinati in the flutes, oboes, clarinets, and lower strings (constituting a thick instrumental "fill," largely ignored in Example 30b). On the other hand, these steady 4/4 and 6/4 meters, together with the pulsating ostinati underneath, provide a stable background for three superimpositions, consisting of three registrally and instrumentally fixed reiterating fragments, each highly differentiated in rhythm-meter: (1) the (G F E D) tetrachordal fragment in the strings at Nos. 64–66; (2) the G♯–G, G♯–F♯, and (C♯ A♯ G♯) (0,6) tritone-related tetrachordal reiterations in the tubas, which enter below the (G F E D) articulation in the strings at No. 64, and continue to the close of "Cortège du sage" at No. 71; (3) the D and A–D–C–D reiterations in the horns, which enter at No. 65 + 2, and, along with the tuba fragment, continue to the close of "Cortège du sage" at No. 71.

Now what distinguishes this display at Nos. 67–71 (and, indeed, *Le Sacre* as a whole from the remainder of Stravinsky's works, with the possible ex-

Example 30b

ception of a few passages in *Three Pieces* and *Les Noces*) is the extraordinary "mobility" (to use Boulez's term) exhibited in the repetition of the rhythmic-metric periods of these reiterating fragments. In other words, we do not find here a steady meter together with "separate" rhythmic-metric periods which, while conflicting with this steady meter, nonetheless repeat according to periods that are in themselves stable. (An example of this is the steady 3/2 meter with a conflicting rhythmic-metric period of four half-note beats that remains stable throughout, found at No. 22 in the final movement of the *Symphony of Psalms*, Example 30c in this chapter.) Rather, the rhythmic-metric periods which define the repetition of each of the three reiterating fragments at Nos. 64–71 are irregularly spaced, being of unequal duration. The duration of the horn's D and A–D–C–D entrances, detached by rests until No. 70, is constantly altered. As bracketed in Example 30b, the first entrance at No. 65+2 defines a rhythmic-metric period of six quarter-note beats; the second entrance at No. 65+5, a period of eight beats; the third, a period of thirteen beats, which is repeated twice; and, finally, at No. 68+2, there is a further stretching of this period duration to seventeen beats (cut off just before No. 70). The same "mobility" pertains to the rhythmic-metric periods of the reiterating tuba fragment, beginning at No. 64. For while the periods of this tuba fragment may be subdivided into "equal" groupings of four and eight quarter-note beats to reflect the steady 4/4 meter, the number of G♯–G or G♯–F♯ reiterations, which precede the G♯–A♯–C♯–A♯–(G♯) reiteration, is constantly varied (until No. 67): this number is sometimes one, sometimes two, most often three. And so the "mobility" of these periods in the horns and tubas here at Nos. 64–71 renders the second of our two rhythmic-metric types exceedingly intricate, to a degree possibly unequaled, as has already been suggested, in the remainder of Stravinsky's works.[18]

On the other hand, of no less consequence in this passage at Nos. 64–71 is the eventual cessation of "mobility" at No. 70. At No. 67, the periods of the tuba fragment attain the stable sequence of three G♯–G or G♯–F♯ reiterations to one G♯–A♯–C♯–A♯–(G♯) reiteration, a period totaling sixteen quarter-note beats; while at No. 70 the periods of the horn's D and A–D–C–D reiterations define a stable sequence totaling eight quarter-note beats. Consequently, as the "Cortège du sage" draws to a close, this conflict is resolved; the rhythmic-metric periods of the horn and tuba fragments, "mobile" or irregularly spaced at Nos. 64–70, unite and are stabilized, tending also to confirm the steady 4/4 design of the meter. (The change to a 6/4 meter at No. 70 accommodates some conflicting accentuation in the percussion, producing a thickening of the texture at this point. Otherwise, all reiterating fragments at No. 70 reflect a continuing 4/4 meter.) But significantly, this is a resolution steadfastly restricted to the rhythmic-metric domain, one in which pitch relations fail to take part. For to the very end, the symmetrical confinement of these relations remains at an impasse, with the principal fragments in the horns and tubas locked in an unresolved (or unresolvable) confrontation (principally a D/G♯ (0,6) tritone symmetry), pitted against each other in a static, superimposed "polarity" or "opposition." And so there is no "progress" here, no "resolution," no "cadence," no finality. Like the gears of a giant locomotive, the repetition merely grinds to a halt, with the block at Nos. 64–71 abruptly cut off, silenced by a grand fermata.

But compare, now, these rhythmic-metric intricacies at Nos. 64–71 in *Le Sacre* (or the synchronized block development at No. 57 in regard to the first of our two rhythmic-metric types), with the unvarying repetition of *The Firebird*'s Kastchei theme (Example 8a in chapter 1), or the unvarying stretch of 7/4 measures in *The Firebird*'s Finale (Example 11), in which there is no change of meter (type 1), and no superimpositions of reiterating fragments whose rhythmic-metric periods conflict and vary "separately from" or "independently of" one another (type 2). While doubtless providing an indication of the origin of these intricacies, these comparisons point all the more strikingly to the enormous distance traveled in some two years via *Petroushka*. And were we to compare the block at Nos. 64–71 in *Le Sacre* with the passage in Example 30c from the *Symphony of Psalms* (which likewise adheres to the second of our two rhythmic-metric types, although in a way that is simpler and on the whole more characteristic of Stravinsky), we afford ourselves an even more telling demonstration of this intricacy. In *Psalms*, the reiterating E♭–D–C–D–(E♭) fragment defines a rhythmic-metric period of three half-note beats (to which the steady 3/2 meter is adjusted); this period conflicts with the rhythmic-metric period of four half-note beats as defined by the E♭–B♭–F–B♭–(E♭) basso ostinato below. But there is no "mobility" or irregular spacing in the periods of these two superimposed fragments; they remain stable unto themselves. And so while these "separate" or "independent" periods conflict with one another, the inconstancy, irregularity, or variance in vertical (or "harmonic") coincidence is short-lived, "sabotaged" in the long run by the E♭/E♭ coincidence, which is registered as a point of departure and return. Then, too, as indicated already in chapters 1 and 3, an absence of "mobility" becomes subtly linked to regular metric periodicity: Stravinsky's rhythmic (or metric) invention, conforming either to the first or second of our two rhythmic-metric types, becomes subtly linked to upbeat/downbeat of off-the-beat/on-the-beat displacements in fragmental repetition (which necessarily hinge, for their apprehension, on a steady meter).

Example 30c: *Symphony of Psalms*

Indeed, in even so highly "mobile" a display as at Nos. 64–71 in *Le Sacre*, this simplistic reduction of the rhythmic-metric scheme is apparent. Set against the pulsating ostinati and the reiterating tuba fragment (whose periods, while "mobile," may nonetheless be subdivided into "equal" groupings of four and eight quarter-note beats to equate with the 4/4 meter), the horn's A–D–C–D reiteration may first be heard and understood, at No. 67, as an upbeating succession (entering on the fourth quarter-note beat of the 4/4 measure); then, at Nos. 67 + 3 and 69, it is contradicted and reversed as a downbeating succession (entering on the first and then the third quarter-note beat); and finally, at No. 70, it resumes its initial rhythmic-metric identity as an upbeating succession (entering on the second quarter-note beat, and certainly in keeping here with the resolution of the rhythmic-metric conflict).[19] That Stravinsky might have been conscious of this subtle upbeat/downbeat duplicity seems indicated by the stress and slur markings. These markings are identical for each repeat of the A–D–C–D succession, whether barred as an upbeating or downbeating succession—identical, it would seem, precisely in order to further confuse this upbeat/downbeat ambiguity by giving each repeat, in opposition to the barred upbeat/downbeat duplicity, a "sameness" in rhythmic-metric identity. The result a nearly meterless display. But Stravinsky—who always insisted that his barline was "much, much more than a mere accent" (and could not, indeed, be "simulated by an accent")—elected *not* to shift his meter in accord with the horn fragment's duplicity in upbeat/downbeat accentuation.[20] He chose, as "foreground," to hear the regular metric periodicity of the stable 4/4 and 6/4 meters, and hence, ultimately, to hear and feel this duplicity, this contradiction or reversal in the upbeat/downbeat accentuation of the horn fragment's rhythmic-metric periods. It may at this point appear as if he had actually wished it both ways, to hear both the contradiction or reversal in upbeat/downbeat accentuation and a rhythmic-metric "sameness" in the repetition of the A–D–C–D fragment.[21] Indeed, this "both ways" is typical of Stravinsky's rhythmic-metric schemes, a feature by no means limited to *Le Sacre*. Displacement, contradiction, and reversal (producing ambiguity in the rhythmic-metric identity of a reiterating fragment) often seem elevated to this "higher" level of perception, where tonal, C-scale notions of rhythm and meter are no longer relevant, or seem disconcertingly beside the point.

And so we have in the foregoing touched on certain intricacies of rhythm and meter in *Le Sacre*. But our purpose has quite definitely been to situate this intricacy within the context not only of Stravinsky's "Russian"-period material, but also of his music "considered as a whole." This is a "situation" that will advantageously allow us to cope with some of the consequences of *Le Sacre* in succeeding works, "Russian," neoclassical, and serial in origin.

FIVE

THREE PIECES FOR STRING QUARTET
(1914)

As to its reception [Stravinsky's opera, *The Nightingale* (1914)], the "advanced" musicians were genuinely enthusiastic—or so I thought. That Ravel liked it, I am certain, but I am almost as convinced that Debussy did not, for I heard nothing whatever from him about it. I remember this well, for I expected him to question me about the great difference between the music of Act I [1909] and the later acts, and though I knew he would have liked the Moussorgsky-Debussy beginning, he probably would have said about that, too, "Young man, I do it better." [*Memories and Commentaries,* p. 124.]

Debussy was only slightly taller than I am, but he was much heavier. He spoke in a low, quiet voice, and the ends of his phrases were often inaudible—which was to the good, as they sometimes contained hidden stings and verbal booby traps. The first time I visited him in his house, after *The Firebird,* we talked about Mussorgsky's songs and agreed that they contained the best music of the whole Russian school. He said he had discovered Mussorgsky when he found some of the music lying untouched on Mme von Meck's piano. He did not like Rimsky, whom he called "a voluntary academic, the worst kind." Debussy was especially interested in Japanese art at that time. I received the impression, though, that he was *not* especially interested in new things in music; my own appearance on the musical scene seemed to be a shock to him. I saw him rarely during the war, and the few visits I did pay him were extremely painful. His subtle, grave smile had disappeared, and his skin seemed yellow and sunken; it was hard not to see the future cadaver in him. I asked him if he had heard my three pieces for string quartet—they had just been played in Paris. I thought he would like the last twenty bars of the third piece, for they are some of my best music of that time. He had not heard them, however, and, indeed, he had heard almost no new music at all. I saw him last about nine months before his death. This was a *triste* visit, and Paris was gray, quiet, and without lights or movement. He did not mention the piece from *En blanc et noir* he had written for me, and when I received this music in Morges, late in 1919, I was very moved by it, as well as delighted to see that it was such a good composition. I was moved, too, when I composed my *Symphonies* [*of Wind Instruments,* 1920] to the memory of my old friend and, if I may say so, they, too, are "a good composition." [*Expositions and Developments,* pp. 158–59.]

I was handicapped in my earliest years by influences that restrained the growth of my composer's technique. I refer to the Saint Petersburg Conservatory's formalism, from which, however—and fortunately—I was soon free. But the musicians of my generation and I myself owe the most to Debussy. [*Conversations with Stravinsky*, p. 50.]

Though the *Four Etudes* [orchestrations of the *Three Pieces* (1914) and the *Etude for Pianola* (1917)] were not performed until 1930, the orchestrations of the first three of them date back to 1917. The fourth piece, originally the *Etude for Pianola*, was orchestrated in 1928 or 1929, at which time I gave it the name *Madrid* and added titles to the other pieces as well. The first is a *Danse* for the woodwinds. They repeat a four-note chant over and over—"The *Four Fingers*" one could call it—but at varying rhythmic distances. The second, *Excentrique*, was inspired, as I have said before, by the eccentric movements and postures of the great clown, Little Tich. The third is called *Cantique* or *Canticle* because the music is choral and religious in character, but *Hymne* would have been as good a title. [*Themes and Episodes*, pp. 32–33.]

Incidentally, these pieces were not influenced by Schoenberg or Webern, as has been said—at least not to my conscious knowledge. I knew no music by Webern in 1914, and of Schoenberg only *Pierrot Lunaire*. [*Memories and Commentaries*, p. 89.]

Stravinsky was immensely fond and proud of these *Three Pieces* at the time of their conception, considering them—particularly the third—his "best" or most "advanced" music to date (however inconceivable this might now seem, in light of *Le Sacre*). And so we can well imagine his disappointment at finding his friend and colleague Claude Debussy ill and indifferent at what was to mark one of their final encounters during the war (see quotation above).[1] For it had been only four years since Debussy had so graciously introduced himself to Stravinsky onstage following the premiere of *The Firebird*, and barely two since these giants, in November 1912, had seated themselves at a Pleyel piano to rummage through Stravinsky's latest—and at the time not yet fully orchestrated—creation, *Le Sacre du printemps*. (Stravinsky's original four-hand piano version of *Le Sacre* has recently been revived, becoming a favorite with several duo-piano teams.) Claude Debussy died, *musicien français*, on 25 March 1918.

As for any substantive influence Debussy's music might have had on Stravinsky, we remain largely unconvinced. True, both composers had by 1914 created "languages" which, implicating pitch collections and/or orderings other than that of the familiar diatonic C-scale or major scale (e.g., Debussy's famed—and symmetrically defined—whole-tone scale; Stravinsky's symmetrically defined octatonic scales), defied the familiar tonal C-scale conceptions of harmonic progression, modulation definition of key, cadence, and formal design. But apart from this defiance or break with tradition—and apart from some early and rather obvious borrowings (e.g., in *Faune et bergère*, 1906; in the early Act I of *The Nightingale*, 1909, with its reminiscence of *Nuages* from Debussy's *Nocturnes*, 1890; at No. 26 in the Kastchei section of *The Firebird*, 1910; and, possibly, in the Introduction to Part II in *Le Sacre*), these "languages" are more striking for the dissimilarity they project than for any apparent likeness.[2] And it is perhaps especially the rhythmic-metric aspects that seem so conspicuously at odds. (To use a highly descriptive terminology, Debussy's rhythmic-metric instincts are typically inconspicuous, vague, passive, and "loose", while those of Stravinsky are habitually severe, stiff, rigid, insistent, and percussive.) Consequently, Stravinsky's acknowledged—but unspecified—debt to Debussy ("The musicians of my generation and I myself owe the most to Debussy"; see quotation above) may have been primarily philosophical or psychological in nature. For like Stravinsky, Debussy was a rebel and an anti-academic, and the example Debussy had so forcefully set as a composer charting his own, independent, inimitable course, together with the encouragement so thoughtfully provided in regard to *The Firebird*, *Petroushka*, and *Le Sacre*, must have afforded Stravinsky a powerful stimulus.[3] Indeed, it was with artists like Debussy, and in the general milieu of Parisian musical life, that Stravinsky quite suddenly and for the first time felt at ease. And to an extent that, after the *Firebird* performances in 1910, he was stunned to find the St. Petersburg of his youth, a city which he had known a few months previously as the grandest of them all, "sadly small and provincial."[4] So varied, restless, and far-reaching had his artistic inclinations suddenly become that it seems unlikely, judging from his own recollections, that he would under any circumstances have set up permanent residence in his homeland following The Great War, however injurious and brutal the irrevocable break—"Lenine" and the Russian Revolution—must ever have been.[5]

Neutral Switzerland became Stravinsky's home during the war years, and hence the birthplace of much of his "Russian" music (e.g., *Pribaoutki* (1914), *Berceuses du chat* (1916), *Renard* (1916), *Four Russian Peasant Songs* ("Saucers") (1917), *Les Noces* (1917), *Histoire du soldat* (1918)); this was a period to which he would later refer, affectionately, as his "Swiss years." He moved back to France after the war, living usually in the southern regions near the Mediterranean (but also in Paris, especially during the 1930s), and became a French citizen in June 1934. Then, at the outbreak of hostilities in 1939, he moved to the United States (which he had visited on concert tours in 1925, 1935, and 1937),[6] and soon after to the Mediterranean climate of Southern California.

Stravinsky lived in Hollywood until the final months of his life. He died in New York City on 6 April 1971, at the age of eighty-eight. His body was transported to Venice, where, following a performance of his *Requiem*

Canticles (1966), he was laid to rest on the island cemetery of San Michele.[7] His grave lies but a few yards from that of his early patron, collaborator, and compatriot, Sergei Diaghilev.

SOME GENERAL CONSIDERATIONS

In the first of the *Three Pieces for String Quartet* we encounter a construction wherein all the various "harmonic," melodic, formal, instrumental, and rhythmic-metric features examined in *Le Sacre* are very much in evidence. (See, especially, the preceding chapter's concluding sections, "Some General Considerations" and "Rhythmic-Metric Implications.") Of course, there is no abrupt block juxtaposition here. Piece No. 1 is possibly too short. But superimposition and repetition, the already examined implications of these general methods of procedure with respect to harmony, melody, instrumentation, and rhythm-meter, are highly conspicuous (or, as explanatory notions, singularly apropos).

We are dealing, first of all, with the second of our two usefully distinguishable rhythmic-metric constructions outlined in the preceding chapter. But instead of a steady meter (as at Nos. 64–71 in *Le Sacre*, Example 30b), we are here afforded a steady varying meter of 3/4 + 2/4 + 2/4. (See Example 31a.) This metric scheme reflects the rhythmic-metric period of the viola's reiterating pizzicato D and the cello's reiterating E♭–D♭/C–D♭

Example 31a: *Three Pieces for String Quartet*, No. 1

fragments; both of these reiterations thus define a stable rhythmic-metric period of seven quarter-note beats, which is repeated fourteen times throughout, and in which the smaller "rhythmic-cell" division is $3 + 2 + 2$ quarter-note beats. Superimposed on this stable "pedal" in the viola and cello is another ostinato in the first violin, a reiterating (G A B C) fragment (Stravinsky's "The *Four* Fingers"; see quotation above); this defines a "separate" (but nonetheless stable) rhythmic-metric period totaling twenty-three quarter-note beats, which is repeated four times throughout, and whose smaller "rhythmic-cell" division is $11 + 6 + 6$ quarter-note beats. Finally, against the stability exhibited in the repetition of these "separate" or "independent" linear rhythmic-metric periods (which, however, produce instability, inconstancy, or variability insofar as their union or coincidence is concerned), the second violin's reiterating (0 2 3 5) tetrachord, F♯–E–D♯–C♯, is rhythmic-metrically "mobile" (as Boulez would say), in that it exhibits no stable definition as to period, but intrudes abruptly (double forte and *sur le sol du talon*), and generally at terminal points of the three "rhythmic cells" which comprise the first violin's $11 + 6 + 6$ period.[8]

Moreover, apart from this rhythmic-metric differentiation, the individuality of these reiterating fragments is enhanced melodically and instrumentally. Each of the four fragments remains fixed registrally and instrumentally, resulting in a static superimposition with no developmental "dialogue" or exchange between parts. Each fragment is accorded a different mode of attack (e.g., *avec toute la longueur de l'archet* for the first violin; *ff* and *sur le sol du talon* for the second violin; pizzicato for the cello, etc.). Indeed, all of this constitutes, it must be conceded, a regimentation exceedingly stiff, rigid, and mechanical.

Consequently, the attraction of this material would seem to rest with that curious kind of "development" defined by the second of our two types of rhythmic-metric construction, a "development" in which the "separate" or "independent" rhythmic-metric periods conflict so as to effect a degree of inconstancy or variability in vertical (or "harmonic") coincidence. Indeed, here in the first of these *Three Pieces* (as at Nos. 64–71 in *Le Sacre*), this degree of inconstancy is *absolute*: owing to the length and "inequality" of the first violin's $11 + 6 + 6$ rhythmic-metric period, and to the persistent "mobility" (irregularly spaced entrances) of the second violin's F♯–E–D♯–C♯ reiteration, rhythmic-metric or vertical coincidence is absolutely irregular. This inconstancy triggers, in turn, a dizzy (but perhaps titillating) uncertainty as to the "true" (stable) rhythmic-metric identities of the reiterating, superimposed fragments (however stable and unvarying their individual rhythmic-metric periods are when considered independent of each other—excepting, of course, the "mobile" period(s) of the second violin). Hence, a norm in coincidence with respect to the "separate" or "independent" rhythmic-metric periods of these four reiterating fragments would be difficult to ascertain, a difficulty perhaps deliberate, perhaps precisely "the point." There is no norm. Or there are no norms in coincidence (or in synchronization).[9] Or there is (are) no "true" rhythmic-metric identity(ies).

Still, the (G A B C) theme of the first violin is quite obviously the center of attention. And so it is likely to be with reference to the steady 2/4 meter that may here vaguely be discerned (vaguely because this "background" 2/4 periodicity is ultimately contradicted by the 11 + 6 + 6 period), as well as to all the rhythmic-metric habits brought about by the theme's terminating A–G reiteration at mm. 4, 7, and 10 (a reiteration which could be construed as an A–G cadential figure in terms of the C-scale on G or G-major scale, with A as downbeating appoggiatura to the G) that the listener will feel the threat of coincidal dislocation, of uncertainty as to the rhythmic-metric identities of the reiterating fragments in the second violin, viola, and cello fragments.

(The "background" duple meter of the first violin's (G A B C) fragment begins with the first beat of its first 3/4 measure as an upbeat to the first B, and persists through the 11 + 6 + 6 period at mm. 1–10. Moreover, doubt or uncertainty as to the "true" (stable) rhythmic-metric identities of the various instrumental parts in combination is naturally triggered, at least in part, by the surfacing of such (possibly tonally conceived) rhythmic-metric habits, by regular 2/4 metric periodicity, in other words. This surfacing is in turn linked to the suggestion of the C-scale on G or G-major scale in the first violin—specifically, to the terminating A–G reiteration construed as a conventional cadential figure with A as a downbeating appoggiatura to the G. And while "purists" might contend that such inferences constitute an arbitrary imposition on what is essentially an absolutely irregular or variable rhythmic-metric construction, this observer finds the suggestion of the C-scale on G, and the A–G reference to C–scale conventionality, unmistakable. Indeed, the reference to past C-scale conventionality seems deliberately designed to invoke past rhythmic-metric habits of regular metric periodicity, and hence to provoke titillating doubt and uncertainty as to some "true" (stable) rhythmic-metric identity for the entire complex of reiterating fragments. Although briefly noted already in our discussion of rhythm-meter in *Le Sacre*, these implications of Stravinsky's rhythmic (or metric) invention will be subjected to further scrutiny in chapter 8.)[10]

PITCH RELATIONS

But superimposition is not merely heard and understood in terms of registrally and instrumentally fixed fragments which exhibit, in repetition, "separate" or "independent" rhythmic-metric periods. Superimposition, as it applies to the content of Stravinsky's music, manifests itself in terms of an "equilibrium," "opposition," "polarity," "harmonic stasis," or dead-lock. And it should in this connection be apparent that this content-defined "equilibrium" in the first of these *Three Pieces* is linked to a parti-tioning of the octatonic collection (Collection III here), a partitioning that interacts with a diatonic articulation implicating either the (A G F♯ E D C) hexachord or, possibly, the C-scale on G (the G-major-scale in tonal terms).

Thus, in Example 31b, a critical point of coincidence among the first violin, second violin, and cello fragments is encircled where confinement to the octatonic collection (Collection III) is unmistakable. The A–G (0–2) whole-step reiteration in the first violin—earlier interpreted as a cadential figure in relation to the C-scale on G—stands in an octatonically conceived—and hence symmetrically defined—(0,6) tritone-related "op-position" to the "lower" E♭–D♭ (6–8) reiteration in the cello. The second violin's Collection III (F♯ E D♯ C♯) tetrachord intrudes precisely at that point where its D♯–C♯ component "doubles" the E♭–D♭ (6–8) reiteration of the cello. So with the A–G (0–2) reiteration in the first violin, the point of connection yields the following octatonic (Collection III) pitch succes-sion: A–G–F♯–E–D♯–C♯–C. The octatonic contribution, "hooking up" to Model B, may be interpreted by means of Example 31b's structural-level format, to which the following comments are added:

Level 2: In the octatonic model, (0,6) tritone partitioning of Collection III is recognized in terms of (A,E♭).

Level 3: Again in the octatonic model, this (0,6) tritone partitioning in terms of (A,E♭) is articulated by the first violin's A–G (0–2) reiteration, which stands "in a certain opposition" to the cello's "lower" E♭–D♭ (6–8) reiteration. These (0,6) tritone-related (0–2) (6–8) reiterations are poised in static "equilibrium" and exhibit the previously noted octatonically con-ceived symptoms of "equal weight and independence," "polarity," and deadlock. And note the special nontonal implications of this reference: pitch number 8, the D♭ of the cello's (E♭–D♭) unit, is in no sense functional as a V-of-V "tendency tone" to the sustained D in the viola (with respect to the possible interpenetrating reference to the diatonic C-scale on G). Rather, D♭ is articulatively affiliated with E♭, this E♭–D♭ (6–8) unit thus assuming, given the nature of the (0,6) relation and of the collectional ref-erence, a degree of "equilibrium," "independence," and "opposition" vis-à-vis the "upper" A–G (0–2) unit.

Level 3a: The F♯–E (3–5) unit of the second violin's (3 5 6 8) tetrachord in terms of (F♯ E D♯ C♯) is included at this partitioning level.

Level 4: In the octatonic model, (0,6) tritone partitioning of Collection III is recognized with respect to an "upper" (0 2 3 5) tetrachord in terms of (A G F♯ E)—with the (F♯ E) component "borrowed" from the second vio-

Example 31b: *Three Pieces*, No. 1

lin's (F♯ E D♯ C♯) tetrachord, which stands "in a certain opposition" to the cello's "lower" (6 8 9 11) tetrachord in terms of (E♭ D♭ C), (6 8 9) incomplete. Thus, Model B's pitch number 11, the B♭ here in relation to the A–G (0–2) reiteration, is missing, there being, in its place, a pitch number 10, the B of the first violin's (G A B C) theme, which identifies with the interpenetrating diatonic collection.

Level 4a: The second violin's (3 5 6 8) tetrachord in terms of (F♯ E D♯ C♯) is added to this level's (0 2 3 5) tetrachordal partitioning of the octatonic collection.

Level 5: All the various (0 2) and (0 2 3 5) fragments are assembled as presented, yielding, at level 6, the reference collection (Collection III) in accord with Model B's 2, 1 interval ordering.

On the other hand, these octatonic relations collide with a diatonic reference, conspicuous in the first violin and viola. (See the right-hand side of the dotted line in Example 31b, which represents the diatonic side to the octatonic-diatonic interaction.) This interpenetrating diatonic contribution may be interpreted with reference to the (A G F♯ E D C) hexachord, or, alternatively, with reference to the C-scale on G, in which respect the G, as the first violin's point of departure and return, appears to assert a degree of pitch-class priority, and to which the non-octatonic, sustained D in the viola lends "fifth support." So, too, the octatonically conceived A–G (0–2) whole-step reiteration assumes the guise of a cadential figure, with A as a downbeating appoggiatura to the G. (The tonally functional overtones of this C-scale-on-G reference are very parenthetical—the first violin's A–G reiteration merely suggests a slight reference to tonally conceived cadential conventionality, while the (G B D) triadic outline of the first violin and viola is sustained statically throughout with virtually no evidence of tonally functional harmonic progressions.) Note the connecting links in the octatonic (Model B) and diatonic-C-scale-on-G interpenetration sketched in Example 31b: the A–G (0–2) reiteration—or the C-scale-on-G cadential figure—and the A–G–F♯–E succession between the first and second violins. Then, note the elements of "opposition" (elements or relations *not* held in common): the sustained diatonic D in the viola, and the diatonic B in the first violin, neither contained in Collection III. (There is a similarity here with No. 37 in *Le Sacre*, where the D of the superimposed (A G F♯ E D C B (A)) D-scale fragment likewise conflicts or "clashes" with the E♭ and D♭ of the interpenetrating Collection III.)

CONCLUSIONS

And so No. 1 of *Three Pieces* is interpreted as a piece in which octatonic relations (Collection III, Model B partitioning) interpenetrate with the diatonic (A G F♯ E D C) hexachord or the C-scale on G; this interaction exhibits a degree of fusion or blending (in the elements or relations held in common), and a degree of "opposition" or incompatibility (in the elements or relations not held in common). So, too, as in all cases of octatonic-diatonic interpenetration, a quality of "opposition" is not entirely lost or reconciled at the collectional level (as it is in cases of unimpaired, explicit octatonic reference), but is merely reinterpreted in terms of conflicting (but to some degree coalescing) collections (or systems) of reference.

Finally, should these conclusions seem contrived or defective in one way or another, the reader may peruse the supplementary illustrations furnished by Examples 32a, b, and c. In all these passages, the octatonically conceived (0,6) tritone-related (0–2) (6–8) whole-step reiterations in terms of (A–G) (E♭–D♭) are identical to those of No. 1 in *Three Pieces*, all naturally referring to Collection III and "hooking up" to Model B. In Ex-

Example 32a: *Le Sacre* ("Danses des adolescentes")

Example 32b: *Renard*

ample 32a from "Danses des adolescentes" in *Le Sacre,* the G–A reiteration in the second violin's and in the horn's theme stands in a (0,6) tritone-related "opposition" to the D♭–E♭ unit of the first violin's D♭–B♭–E♭–B♭ ostinato; in Example 32b from *Renard,* the A–G reiteration in the flute stands in like "opposition" to the E♭–D♭ reiteration of the cello; and in Example 32c from *Les Noces,* E♭–D♭ in the soprano stands in "opposition" to A–G in the bass. True, the mustering of bits and pieces in support of an interpretation concluded on behalf of a different context is hazardous and perhaps not generally to be recommended. Long-term global conditions may be ignored. But abrupt block juxtaposition—the unusual degree distinction and insulation afforded blocks or passages in their respective contexts—renders this comparative maneuver more legitimately instructive (or less problematically instructive) than is generally the case in perception and analytic-theoretical review.

Then, too, we are dealing, after all, with a literaturewide perspective

Example 32c: *Les Noces* (second tableau)

here, specifically, a "Russian" perspective. The time span of these passages is five years, five years within a nearly sixty-year, nonstop yield. And it is precisely because the comprehensive coverage allows for a grasp of specificity from one context to the next that this specificity is never heard or understood in a void.

"Russian" pieces are littered with 0–2 whole-step reiterations, stretching, on the diatonic side of the referential coin, from the (D–E) (A–G) reiterations in the opening blocks of *Petroushka* to the (0 2 3 5 7 9) hexachordally conceived ostinati of *Histoire*'s Soldier's March and Music to Scene I. And so, pursuant to the various summaries sketched on behalf of *Petroushka* and *Le Sacre* in chapters 3 and 4, these 0–2 reiterations implicate all manner of folkish (0 2 3 5) tetrachordal fragments. The (0 2 3 5) tetrachord relates, diatonically, to a (0 2 3 5) (7 9 (10) 0) tetrachordal or (0 3 7/0 4 7) triadic partitioning of the D-scale or of the (0 2 3 5 7 9) diatonic hexachordal segment; and, octatonically, to a (0,3,6,9) symmetrically defined (0 2 3 5) partitioning of the (0 2 3 5) (6 8 9 11) octatonic collection, Model B. When (0 2 5) incomplete, the tetrachord may in addition implicate Model A's (0,3,6,9) symmetrically defined succession of (0 4 7 10) "dominant sevenths", its pitch numbers 0, 2, and 5 (reading down) merely becoming pitch numbers 0, 10, and 7 (the root, seventh, and fifth respectively) of the (0 4 7 10) "dominant-seventh" complex. Such, truly, is the nature of "Russian" thought. And exceptions to this hearing and understanding—exceptions like the interpenetrating C-scale-on-G (or G-major scale) reference here in No. 1 of *Three Pieces*—are just that: exceptions. Manifestly, No. 1 of *Three Pieces*, along with Nos. 2 and 3 as well (although not examined here), figure in the "Russian" nutshell.

SIX
LES NOCES (1917)

PART I

First tableau: With the Bride   Nos. 0–27
Second tableau: With the Bridegroom   Nos. 27–65
Third tableau: The Bride's Departure   Nos. 65–87

PART II

Fourth tableau: The Wedding Feast   Nos. 87–End

I became aware of an idea for a choral work on the subject of a Russian peasant wedding early in 1912; the title, *Svádebka, Les Noces,* occurred to me almost at the same time as the idea itself. As my conception developed, I began to see that it did not indicate the dramatization of a wedding or the accompaniment of a staged wedding spectacle with descriptive music. My wish was, instead, to present actual wedding material through direct quotations of popular—i.e., non-literary—verse. I waited two years before discovering my source in the anthologies of Afanasiev and Kireievsky, but this wait was well rewarded, as the dance-cantata form of the music was also suggested to me by my reading of these two great argosies of the Russian language and spirit. *Renard* and *Histoire du soldat* were adapted from Afanasiev, *Les Noces* almost entirely from Kireievsky.

Les Noces is a suite of typical wedding episodes told through quotations of typical talk. The latter, whether the bride's, the groom's, the parents' or the guests', is always ritualistic. As a collection of clichés and quotations of typical wedding sayings it might be compared to one of those scenes in *Ulysses* in which the reader seems to be overhearing scraps of conversation without the connecting thread of discourse. . . .

Individual roles do not exist in *Les Noces,* but only solo voices that impersonate now one type of character and now another. Thus the soprano in the first scene is not the bride, but merely a bride's voice; the same voice is associated with the goose in the last scene. . . . Even the proper names in the text such as Palagai or Saveliushka belong to no one in particular. They were chosen for their sound, their syllables, and their Russian typicality. . . .

At the first performance, the four pianos filled the corners of the scene, thus being separated from the percussion ensemble and the chorus and solo singers in the pit. Diaghilev argued for this arrangement on aesthetic grounds—the four black, elephantine shapes were an attractive addition to the *décors*—but my original idea was that the whole company of musicians and dancers should be together on the stage as equal participants.

I began the composition of *Les Noces* in 1914 (a year before *Renard*) in Clarens [Switzerland]. The music was composed in short score form by 1917, but it was not finished in full score until three months before the *première*, which was six years later. No work of mine has undergone so many instrumental metamorphoses. I completed the first tableau for an orchestra the size of that of *Le Sacre du printemps*, and then decided to divide the various instrumental elements—strings, woodwinds, brass, percussion, keyboard (cimbalom, harpsichord, piano)—into groups and to keep these groups separate on the stage. In still another version I sought to combine pianolas with bands of instruments that included saxhorns and flügelhorns. Then, one day in 1921, in Garches, where I was living as the guest of Gabrielle Chanel, I suddenly realized that an orchestra of four pianos would fulfill all my conditions. It would be at the same time perfectly homogeneous, perfectly impersonal, and perfectly mechanical.

When I first played *Les Noces* to Diaghilev—in 1915, at his home in Bellerive, near Lausanne—he wept and said it was the most beautiful and the most purely Russian creation of our Ballet. I think he did love *Les Noces* more than any other work of mine. That is why it is dedicated to him. [*Expositions and Developments*, pp. 130–34.]

Enthusiasts of Stravinsky's music harbor a special fondness for *Les Noces*. "*Svadebka* (*Les Noces*) ranks high in the by no means crowded company of indisputable contemporary masterpieces," writes Robert Craft.[1] Even Constant Lambert, cranky and scarcely an enthusiast (however astute), found *Les Noces* uniquely compelling: "*Les Noces* is one of the masterpieces of this ["Russian"] period and possibly the only really important work that Stravinsky has given us."[2]

It may be, too, that this miracle of miracles, whether perceived as a piece of "pure" music—its battery of percussion with four "elephantine" pianos—or as a musical-dramatic spectacle—its "cantata-ballet" scheme—still offers today's listeners something startling, something new and different. Certainly the prolonged indecision in instrumentation was uncharacteristic of Stravinsky (who generally orchestrated while he composed, whatever the preliminary sketch routine), and may therefore suggest novelty (even for the composer of *Le Sacre*), a musical or musical-dramatic inspiration for which there was no ready settlement along lines even remotely traditional. Then, too, this indecision may seem all the more extraordinary given the self-imposed interruptions for *Renard* (1916), *Histoire du soldat* (1918), *Pulcinella* (1920), and the *Symphonies of Wind Instruments* (1920), pieces all of considerable duration and diversity. For Stravinsky was loath to delay, to postpone. Once assured of a

"find," a melodic or rhythmic idea of some sort, his instinct was to persevere from start to finish, without interruptions, particularly in the composition. As he later explained, the future seemed never to furnish the certainty of the present; ideas were best encouraged when new and fresh.

To condense Robert Craft's documentation (in the essay referred to
above) of the at times intricate circumstances surrounding the making of
this settlement: work on the libretto commenced in May or June of 1914.
A need for additional texts prompted a trip to Russia (Ustilug and Kiev) in
July 1914, at which time Stravinsky acquired P. V. Kireievsky's volume of
Russian wedding songs (compiled in 1911), which would serve (apart
from Stravinsky's own modifications) as the principal source for the libretto. Then, "back in Switzerland" (Stravinsky's residence during the
war years), "the song cycle *Pribaoutki* [1914] came first." But by October
1914, a first version of the libretto was "pieced together." And by the end
of November, "Stravinsky had drafted some, possibly most, of the music
of the first tableau."

Much of 1915 passed with *Les Noces* and *Renard* "incubating" in what
Craft describes as Stravinsky's "amazingly compartmented mind." In January 1916, he accepted a commission for the "chamber opera" *Renard*,
and *Les Noces* was set aside for seven months. Not until April 1917 was the
whole of *Les Noces* "unveiled" for Diaghilev (to whom the music is dedicated), and not until October of that year was the sketch-score complete.[3]

There then followed nearly five years of experiments with varied instrumental ensembles along with lengthy interruptions for *Histoire du
soldat* (1918), *Pulcinella* (1920), the *Concertino* (1920), the *Symphonies of
Wind Instruments* (1920), *Mavra* (1922), and an assortment of smaller
works. The final score—with its four pianos—was not completed until
April 1923. From the time of its conception to its completion there had
passed nearly a decade. Indeed, "of all Stravinsky's works," Craft notes,
"*Les Noces* underwent the most extensive metamorphosis." (Craft estimates that *Les Noces* may not only have preoccupied Stravinsky for the
longest time, but may also, "in aggregate," have taken the longest time to
compose.) Then, too, each interruption, each excursion altered Stravinsky's perspective(s); each diversion "left him greatly changed." This
appears especially to have been the case with *Histoire*, the preoccupation
with percussion and small ensemble in that work dramatically reducing
the sizable orchestral cloak with which Stravinsky had first envisioned his
material.

Still, if this prolonged insolvency is indicative of novelty, of musical or
musical-dramatic ideas incapable of succumbing to a ready settlement, it
might at the same time be viewed in a somewhat different light: namely,
that this vast and cumbersome undertaking, stretching through the heart
of the "Russian" period, affords the observer a decisive formulation of

this period's uniquely conceived preoccupation with the substance and rhythm of Russian popular verse, and with all the peculiarities in pitch organization to which we have in these pages been addressing ourselves. It presents the listener, indeed, with a kind of stem, initially so rich and varied in its implications (musical as well as musical-dramatic), that its future growth could be assured only by systematically divesting it of some of these implications, a weeding-out which was gradually to result, to the benefit of all enthusiasts, in a prodigious, diversionary harvest of suckers—the "Russian" period itself. (For the springboard role *Les Noces* assumes for much of "Russian" music—the supplementary, suckerlike quality of *Pribaoutki, Berceuses du chat,* and portions of *Renard* and *Histoire*—is unmistakable.)[4] Indeed, the prolonged indecision in instrumentation is itself symptomatic of an important development in Stravinsky's "Russian" musical thought: from 1914 onward, a shift occured from the immense orchestral resources harnessed on behalf of the *Scherzo fantastique, The Firebird, Petroushka, Zvezdoliki, Le Sacre,* and *The Nightingale* (all reflecting, as Stravinsky later noted, "the Russian orchestral school in which I had been fostered")[5] to the "solo-instrumental style" of the more modest, chamber groups assembled for *Pribaoutki* 1914), *Berceuses du chat* (1916), *Renard* (1916), *Four Russian Peasant Songs* ("Saucers") (1917), and *Histoire* (1918). *Les Noces* was originally conceived for an orchestra roughly equivalent to that of *Le Sacre.* In addition to a subsequent version combining "pianolas with bands of instruments that included saxhorns and flügelhorns" (noted by Stravinsky in the quotation at the outset of this chapter), numerous scaled-down versions preceded the "perfectly homogeneous, perfectly impersonal, and perfectly mechanical" settlement of 1923, the most extensive of these having been an arrangement for two cymbaloms, harmonium, pianola, and percussion requiring only five players in all, composed during the winter of 1918–19 in Morges, Switzerland (after *Histoire*). (The manuscript of this arrangement has been preserved, and is complete until the end of the second tableau.)[6] Then, if we disregard "Russian" peculiarity in *Les Noces* altogether, there is little question but that pitch organization along with certain general practices indelibly project the Stravinskian stamp. And so, quite frankly, the chances of any musician, modestly informed of a handful of Stravinsky's works, mistaking *Les Noces* for anything but Stravinskian seem remote. Novelty in instrumentation aside, *Les Noces* seems about as "Russian" and as uniquely Stravinskian as ever might reasonably be expected from any such conception.

We are confronted at the outset—and in a highly conspicuous manner—with general practices or methods of procedure detailed in earlier chapters: a very abrupt form of block juxtaposition manifests itself, along with superimposition and repetition. In the first tableau (the first music to be composed; the scene of *La Tresse,* in which the bride, surrounded by a chorus of intimates, prepares in ritualistic—Russianstylized—lament for the wedding ceremony), the opening blocks at Nos. 0 and 1 acquire, upon successive (near) repeats at Nos. 4,5,6, and 8 + 2, an unusual degree of stability, distinction, and insulation; melodic fragments of limited range and content repeat ostinato-like in conjunction with a changing meter; and this fragmental repetition at registrally fixed points reinforces the element of superimposition—of "coagulation," "equilibrium," "harmonic stasis," and deadlock—conditions obviously as much a question of pitch organization as they are of form, melody, or rhythm-meter.

Nor, as we have indicated, is abrupt block juxtaposition a mere formality, an architectural curiosity heard and understood solely in terms of "form," in terms of the abrupt or sudden departures in texture, tempo, dynamics, and rhythmic-metric design. Juxtaposition often entails a shifting in the collectional reference, each of the blocks thus acquiring a collectional identity. Typically, these blocks are either octatonic, diatonic, or accountable to some form of octatonic-diatonic interpenetration.

Then, if we focus a bit more specifically on the "Russian" category (with reference to *Le Sacre* and certain sections of *Petroushka*'s first tableau), the (0 2 3 5) tetrachord surfaces again as the principal melodic fragment—indeed, in its (0 2 5) incomplete form, as a kind of ever-present "basic cell."[7] And since this (0 2 5) incomplete tetrachord—or "basic cell' in *Les Noces*—may be referentially either octatonic or diatonic, it serves once again as the principal link connecting the blocks of varied referential implications, hooking up variously to a Model B (0 2 3 5) tetrachordal partitioning of the octatonic collection, to a (0 2 3 5) (7 9 (10) 0) tetrachordal and/or (0 3 7/0 4 7) triadic partitioning of the diatonic D-scale or the (0 2 3 5 7 9) hexachord, or to a form of interpenetration between these distinct collections (and orderings) of reference.

Still, where in *Le Sacre* we found an octatonically conceived "vertical chromaticism," *Les Noces* may seem primarily diatonic.[8] The "chromatic" pitch number 11 in Model B's (0 2 3 5) (6 8 9 11) tetrachordal numbering (the 0–11 or "major-seventh" interval span of this scale, reading down), is not persistently or conspicuously with us here at the outset. It may seem, as in *Petroushka*'s first tableau, to "intrude" occasionally. Consequently, the analytical perspective adopted on behalf of *Petroushka*'s first tableau is tempting: that, broadly speaking, of moving from a securely fastened diatonic framework to a variety of octatonic or octatonic-diatonic contexts. The regularities governing this transaction will be those stipulated by Example 24a on behalf of *Petroushka*'s first tableau in chapter 3: the D-scale or the (0 2 3 5 7 9) hexachord, by means of their adjoining "upper" and "lower" (0 2 3 5) (7 9 (10) 0) tetrachords, may implicate two of the three octatonic collections in octatonic-diatonic interaction. This moving from a securely fastened diatonic framework to a variety of octatonic or octatonic-diatonic contexts (the reverse of *Le Sacre*) will naturally entail *a reading from right to left* in the various connecting-link summaries sketched for *Le Sacre* in chapter 4 (Examples 28a, 28b, and 29).

For example: the present analysis addresses itself at length to a (0 2 3 5 7 9) diatonic hexachordal passage at Nos. 10, 16–18, and 20+3 in the first tableau, and then at No. 67 in the third tableau. (See Examples 35, 36, 37, and 38.) As in certain parts of *Petroushka*'s first tableau, this (0 2 3 5 7 9) passage—however uniquely conceived in the form of an octatonic (Collection II) and (F♯ E D♯ C♯ B A) hexachordal interpenetration—serves as a mediating transition from a diatonic block to a variety of octatonic-diatonic settings. And, in lengthy passages at Nos. 58–65 and 80–87 in the second and third tableaux (Examples 41 and 38 respectively), the (0 2 3 5 7 9) hexachord in terms of (A G F♯ E D C) is the referential "home base," with respect to which a closing of its A–C "gap" with a seventh pitch element may render the surroundings fully diatonic with a B as pitch number 10 (tending to implicate the D-scale on A, but with the hexachord's partitioning formulae intact), or signal the intervention of octatonic relations with a "chromatic" B♭ as pitch number 11, implicating Collection III in terms of (A G F♯ E E♭ D♭ C B♭). (See, especially, the B♭ at No. 82 in Example 38, which pivots the (A G F♯ E D C) diatonic hexachordal blocks at Nos. 78–82 to the fully committed octatonic (Collection III) block at Nos. 82–87.)

But already the first page of *Les Noces* offers a stunning illustration of these maneuvers (indeed, a stunning illustration of all the various "Russian" summaries plotted in chapters 3 and 4): the reiterating (E D B) fragment of the soprano solo (the (0 2 5) "basic cell" here), "open" and uncommitted at No. 0 even with respect to (0 2 3 5 7 9) identity because of its (0 2 5) incompleteness, becomes octatonic at No. 1 with the "intrusion" of the "chromatic" pitch numbers 6 and 11, the B♭ and the F in Pianos II and IV. In this moving from a diatonic—or referentially "open"—framework to an octatonic arrangement at No. 1 (Collection I in terms of (E D C♯ B B♭ A♭ G F)), it is thus (E D B) which serves as the connecting link. (See Example 33.) The B♭, as pitch number 6, defines the tritone in relation to E of the (E D B) unit, while the F, as pitch number 11, defines the 0–11 or "major-seventh" interval span in terms of E–F. In Example 34 we insert (E D B) into the (0 2 (3) 5) connecting-link "slot" for a "Russian" summary along the lines sketched for *Le Sacre*, noting, however, that the present circumstances call for a reading from right to left, a moving from the diatonic scales on the right-hand side, through the (E D B) connecting-link "slot" in the middle, to the octatonic Collection I scale on the left.

Example 33: First tableau

While B♭ and F jointly articulate, in relation to (E D B), Collection I's (0,6) tritone-related (B♭ D F) triad or "fifth" in place of the (B♭ A♭ G F) tetrachord or "fourth," Model B's descending scale is retained so as not only to correlate pitch number 0 with the E, but more determinately to identify and expose, in the scale and consequent pitch numbering, (E D B) as the (0 2 5) connecting link in this between-block octatonic-diatonic interaction at

Octatonic scale
(Collection I)

Diatonic scales

E D C# B B♭ A♭ G F

(B A G# F#)(E D (C#) B)
(E D (C#) B)(A G (F#) E)

(E D B)(B♭/F) [(E D B)]

Example 34

Nos. 0 and 1, as that which is articulatively shared between–or sustained "above"—these two blocks of varied referential implications.

Notice, too, how the changes in tempo and dynamics at No. 1 underscore the sense of a collectional shift at this point. The metronome marking for the eighth-note beat, 80 at No. 0, is doubled to 160 at No. 1. The dynamics at No. 0 are *ff*, while the reiterating (B♭ F) "fifths" in Pianos II and IV enter *p, subito*. Moreover, the rhythmic-metric designs of these blocks are in telling compliance with the first of our two types of rhythmic-metric construction, as examined in chapter 4: all fragments, lines, or parts, registrally and instrumentally fixed in ostinatolike repetition, share the same irregular rhythmic-metric periods as defined by the shifting meter, and are hence synchronized unvaryingly in vertical (or "harmonic") coincidence. (Thus, in the first block at No. 0, the accompaniment in Pianos I and III moves in unvarying synchronization with the stressed, over-the-barline D–E succession of the soprano solo's (E D B) fragment, while the xylophone reiterates only that one particular D which, over the barline, is succeeded by E as the point of departure and return. Hence the fragments proceed together, with "development" hinging on the lengthening and shortening of the jointly sustained periods, as acknowledged by the shifting meter.)

But as is so often the case with schemes of this type, regular metric periodicity subtly imposes itself. As bracketed in Example 33 (and rebarred accordingly below): a 3/8 meter for the opening block at No. 0, a 2/4 meter at No. 1. It is with reference to these "background" 3/8 and 2/4 periodicities that displacements, contradictions, or reversals in the rhythmic-metric identity of the reiterating fragments are revealed.

Accordingly, in the opening two measures of the first block, the stressed D-E succession of the (E D B) fragment falls on the third beat, with D–E assuming an over-the-barline, upbeat-downbeat identity. But in subsequent repeats one and four measures later, this identity is reversed. For in accord with regular 3/8 metric periodicity (as bracketed in Example 33 and rebarred below), the D in this succession falls on the second beat at m. 3, and on the first beat at m. 6. But note—and this is highly revealing—that this "background" 3/8 meter emerges "on target" with Stravinsky's "foreground" metric irregularity in the final measures of the block. In other words, if we pursue the steady 3/8 meter *through* Stravinsky's irregular meter, we find these "foreground" and "background" meters aligned as the block draws to a close at No. 1. This "targeting" neatly allows E–D to resume its initial identity as an over-the-barline, upbeat-downbeat succession. (The E–D succession is repeated twice in these final measures, as if to confirm the resumption of its upbeat-downbeat identity.) And so there is here exhibited, all in accord with "background" regular 3/8 periodicity, a carefully patterned cycle of displacement: the D of the D–E succession is introduced on the third beat, subsequently displaced to the second and first beats, and then, in the completion of the cycle, displaced yet another notch back to the original third beat, at which point D–E resumes its over-the-barline, upbeat-downbeat identity. So, too, this cyclical displacement intensifies the insulation and self-enclosure of this opening block in juxtaposition with its successor at No. 1. For it invests it with a sense of departure from—and eventual return to—3/8 periodicity at the "foreground" level.

But there are additional subtleties here. Note that while Stravinsky's metric irregularity in the opening block would seem directly to implicate displacement in (E D B) or D–E repetition, such is not actually the case, or the whole case. For the shifting meter here *preserves* the over-the-barline, upbeat-downbeat identity of the D–E succession. In other words, in accord with Stravinsky's shifting meter, the D–E succession has always the same over-the-barline, upbeat-downbeat identity, with E falling always on the downbeat of the 3/8 and 2/8 measures. And so the purpose of the shifting meter would seem to be to intone a kind of rhythmic-metric "sameness" in D–E repetition, a "sameness" in direct opposition to the displacements which hinge, for their apprehension, on regular 3/8 metric periodicity. Such, indeed, is habitually the case with Stravinsky's rhythmic-metric designs, conforming either to the first of our two rhythmic-metric types (barred metric irregularity) or to the second (a steady meter). There is, on the one hand, a form of displacement, a contradiction or reversal in the rhythmic or metric accentuation of a reiterating fragment, and, on the other, an effort to press nonetheless for a rhythmic-metric "sameness" in repetition. So, too, this opening block of *Les Noces,* with its elaborate metric irregularity seemingly at such odds with simple and direct intent, harbors a remarkable design in rhythmic-metric effect. While the irregularity conceals a carefully patterned cycle of displacement in (E D B) or D–E repetition (in accord with regular 3/8 metric periodicity), it subverts this displacement by effecting a counteracting "sameness" in rhythmic-metric identity. The double edge of these cross-purposes lies critically at the root of melodic or fragmental repetition in Stravinsky's music. And this is an issue to which we shall therefore be turning at greater length in chapter 8 on "Rhythmic (or Metric) Invention."

We return now to matters of pitch organization. It is the experience of *Le Sacre* that prompts us to view the (0 2 5) "basic cell" of *Les Noces*—(E D B) at Nos. 0 and 1, for example—as an incomplete (0 2 3 5) tetrachord, incomplete in the same (0 2 5) fashion as the persistent D♭–B♭–E♭–B♭ (E♭ D♭ B♭) ostinato figure in "Danses des adolescentes." For here, as in *Le Sacre*, this (0 2 5) incompleteness will constitute not only the principal link in octatonic-diatonic interaction, but also the link between Model B's (0 2 (3) 5) tetrachordal partitioning of the octatonic collection and Model A's (0 4 7 10) "dominant-seventh" partitioning, its pitch numbers 0, 2, and 5 merely becoming, in this process of transformation, pitch numbers 0, 10, and 7 (the root, seventh, and fifth respectively) of the (0 4 7 10) "dominant-seventh" complex. (Or, to hypothetically realize this transaction on behalf of (E D B): in moving from a Model B (0 2 (3) 5) tetrachordal context to a Model A "dominant-seventh" framework, E, D, and B become the root, seventh, and fifth of the (E D B G♯) "dominant-seventh" chord, Collection I. Again, see *Le Sacre*'s "Danses des adolescentes" and "Jeu du rapt" in Example 27, chapter 4. And review this material in conjunction with the summary diagrams sketched in Examples 28a, 28b, and 29.)

PITCH RELATIONS

The transition passage briefly noted above occurs four times throughout the first and third tableaux: at Nos. 10, 16–18, and 20+ 3 in the first, and at No. 67 in the third. In the three occurrences furnished by the examples (Nos. 16–18 in the first tableau are omitted), the passage serves to unite a diatonic block at Nos. 9, 20, and 65 (where (F♯ E C♯) in the vocal parts is the (0 2 5) "basic cell") with a fully committed octatonic framework at Nos. 11 and 68 (Examples 35 and 38), and with an octatonic-diatonic framework at No. 21. But the transition is itself (0 2 3 5 7 9) hexachordal, with the (F♯ E D♯ C♯ B A) hexachord presiding on top. And so in all three examples it is the "lower" (B A F♯) incomplete tetrachord of this (F♯ E D♯ C♯B A (F♯)) hexachord that serves as the connecting link to the fully committed (B A G♯ F♯) (F E♭ D C) Collection II blocks at Nos. 11 and 68, and to the Collection-II–D-scale-on-A block at No. 21. (Thus, for example, at No. 11 in the first tableau, Example 35, the octatonic Collection II delineation is as follows: a reiterating G♯–A–F♯–B fragment in Pianos I and III, comprising the (B A F♯ G♯) tetrachord, is superimposed over its "lower" (0,6) tritone-related (F E♭ (D) C) tetrachord in the bass solo. And with an accompanying (C G♯ A)–(B) reiteration in Pianos I and III also referring to Collection II, the context is wholly octatonic (explicit octatonic reference, List 1 in chapter 2). Indeed, the context is uniquely "Russian" in conception, and very close to *Le Sacre:* Model B's (0,6) tritone-related (0 2 3 5) (6 8 9 11) tetrachords are locked in superimposition, with the entire framework enclosed within this scale's 0–11 or "major-seventh" interval

Example 35: First tableau

span, from the B of the (B A G♯ F♯) fragment to the low C of the bass solo's (F E♭ C) fragment.)

But as the successive analyses of the transition passage indicate, this mediating "go-between" is only partially accounted for in terms of the presiding (F♯ E D♯ C♯ B A) diatonic hexachord. For while (F♯ E D♯ C♯ B A) presides on top (or is central to the activity, especially when, at Nos. 10 and 67, the preceding tenor fragment is included), the setting actually contains three superimposed (0 2 3 5 7 9) hexachords: (F♯ E D♯ C♯ B A), (D C B A G

Example 36: First tableau

F), and (A G F♯ E D C), reading down from top to bottom. (See Example 37.) Each of these superimposed (0 2 3 5 7 9) hexachords is represented triadically by its two (0 4 7) "major" triads related by the interval of 2, a whole step apart: the (B D♯ F♯) and (A C♯ E) triads of the presiding (F♯ E D♯ C♯ B A) hexachord; the (G B D) and (F A C) triads of the (D C B A G F) hexachord; and the (A C♯ E) and (G B D) triads of the (A G F♯ E D C) hexachord, a total of six triads, each in second inversion. (Each of these pairs of (0,2) whole step–related (0 4 7) "major" triads naturally exhausts that particular (0 2 3 5 7 9) hexachord to which it refers. Thus, the (B D♯ F♯) and (A C♯ E) triads, totaling six pitches, complete the (F♯ E D♯ C♯ B A) hexachord.)[9] These three superimposed (0 2 3 5 7 9) hexachords could naturally implicate any of the three octatonic collections in moving, through the transition, to an octatonic context. Indeed, Collection III seems favored in this respect, owing to the (F♯ E D♯ C♯) and (A G F♯ E) "upper" (0 2 3 5) tetrachords of (F♯ E D♯ C♯ B A) and (A G F♯ E D C). But Collection I is also implicated, by the (G F D) unit and the (G B D) triad of the (D C B A G F) hexachord; and, subsequently at No. 18 (not shown), the transition does proceed to a Collection I passage.

And so the question arises: Why Collection II at Nos. 11, 21, and 68? The answer would seem to be primarily that it is the triadic articulation of

Example 37

these three superimposed (0 2 3 5 7 9) hexachords, the succession of six second-inversion (0 4 7) "major" triads rooted on D, C, B, A, G, and F, that tips the balance in favor of Collection II; and partly that the transition itself is an interpenetration of (B A G♯ F♯ F E♭ D C) Collection II and the (F♯ E D♯ C♯ B A (F♯)) hexachord, with the seeds of the succeeding Collection II settings thus firmly imbedded. In other words, three of the six (0 4 7) "major" triads, (B D♯ F), (D F♯ A), and (F A C), refer to Collection II; and the triadic succession is flanked by Collection II's (0,6) tritone-related triads, (B D♯ F♯) and (F A C). Moreover, that Stravinsky was conscious of this transitional commitment to Collection II seems evident in the (near) repeat at No. 20 + 3 (Example 36): a (A♭ C E♭ G♭) "dominant seventh" is outlined in Pianos II and IV to complete a "background" (B, A♭, F, D) symmetrically defined partitioning of this collection in terms of (0 4 7/0 4 7 10) triads and "dominant sevenths" at B, A♭, F, and D. So in all three examples the transition is an interpenetration of (B A G♯ F♯ F E♭ D C) Collection II and the (F♯ E D♯ C♯ B A (F♯)) hexachord with the between-reference connecting link discernible in terms not only of (B A F♯), but also of the (B D♯ F♯) triad, which is also shared. (See the dotted line at Nos. 10, 20, and 67 in Examples 35, 36, and 38. The left-hand side refers to the (F♯ E D♯ C♯ B A) diatonic hexachord, the right-hand side to the octatonic Collection II material. The (0 2 3 5) tetrachords or triads held in common as shared, between-reference connecting links are, as always, marked off by brackets, or may be inferred by their inclusion on both sides of the line.)

The octatonic setting at Nos. 68–70 in the third tableau (Example 38) merits further consideration. For while the instrumental contribution at Nos. 68–70 refers to Collection II (explicit octatonic reference, List 1 in chapter 2: the G♯–F–B–D basso ostinato of Piano IV articulates the (B, G♯, F, D) symmetrically defined partitioning elements of Collection II, these elements constituting the roots of the reiterating (0 4 7 10) "dominant sevenths" introduced by Pianos I and III), the vocal ensemble introduces a succession of (0 2 5) incomplete tetrachords at E, C♯, B♭, and G. And while pitch numbers 2 and 5 of these (0 2 (3) 5) tetrachords are accountable to Collection II— and are, indeed, metrically accented in this particular version of the (0 2 5) "basic cell," a version first introduced by the diatonic blocks at Nos. 9, 14, 20, and 65 in terms of (F♯ E C♯)[10]—pitch number 0 as

Example 38: Third tableau

E, C♯, B♭, and G lies *outside* Collection II. In fact, this vocal (E, C♯, B♭, G) symmetrically defined succession of (0 2 5) incomplete tetrachords is, in its entirety, a Model B (0 2 (3) 5) tetrachordal partitioning of Collection I. The succession is introduced in terms of (E D B) in the bass solo at No. 68, which is subsequently transposed to (C♯ B G♯) in the soprano at No. 68 + 2, and then, although not shown in Example 38, to (B♭ A♭ F) in the bass at No. 69 + 2, and to (G F D) in the soprano at No. 69 + 4. Thus this octatonic block at Nos. 68–70 refers to *both* Collections II and I: along with the tremolo in Piano II, the (B, A♭, F, D) symmetrically defined "dominant sevenths" in Pianos I and III implicate Collection II, while the (E, C♯, B♭, G) symmetrically defined succession of (0 2 (3) 5) tetrachords in the vocal parts implicates Collection I.

Moreover, the G♯–F–B–D basso ostinato of Piano IV is the link connecting these two octatonic collections. For quite apart from the partitioning

Example 38 *continued*

schemes outlined by Models A and B, each of the three octatonic collections contains—or may in addition be partitioned by means of—two
"diminished-seventh" chords, with the pitches of one of these constituting, in each case, the (0,3,6,9) symmetrically defined partitioning elements. The two "diminished-seventh" chords of Collection II are (B G♯ F
D) and (A F♯ E♭ C), while those of Collection I are (B G♯ F D) and (B♭ G E
C♯). Hence, Piano IV's G♯–F–B–D "diminished-seventh" outline is shared
by these two interpenetrating octatonic collections of reference—
although G♯, F, B, and D do not constitute, for Collection I, the "background" (0,3,6,9) symmetrically defined partitioning elements that they
do for Collection II. Hence, too, the block at Nos. 68–70 moves very
smoothly into the fully committed Collection I block at Nos. 70–72, where
this G♯–F–B–D basso ostinato of Piano IV may persevere as the shared
"diminished-seventh" chord between Collections II and I.[11]

Example 38 *continued*

We might pause for a moment to consider how impressively this block at Nos. 68–70 demonstrates the (0,3,6,9) octatonically conceived conditions of balance, "opposition," "harmonic stasis," "polarity," and dead-lock. The poised equilibrium exhibited by the "separate" or "independent" rhythmic-metric periods of the reiterating fragments (Piano IV's G♯–F–B–D basso ostinato, which defines a stable rhythmic-metric "pedal" of four quarter-note beats, set against the "mobile" or irregularly spaced entrances of the (0 4 7 10) "dominant sevenths" in Pianos I and III) is exquisite, a triumph of the octatonic imagination. Indeed, few passages in the literature can match the invention here, the subtle play of symmetrical confinement that unfolds through a superimposition of reiterating fragments whose rhythmic-metric periods vary "separately from" or "independently of" one another, and effect a vertical (or "harmonic") coincidence that is constantly changing. (The block thus adheres to the second

Example 38 *continued*

of our two rhythmic-metric types of construction, as examined in chapter 4 at Nos. 64–71 in *Le Sacre* (Example 30b), and then in chapter 5 in the first of the *Three Pieces for String Quartet* (Example 31a): a steady meter, with the fragments, lines, or parts repeating according to varying rhythmic-metric periods, which may in themselves remain stable or exhibit a degree of "mobility." Here at Nos. 68–70, the stable period of four quarter-note beats in Piano IV reflects the stable 2/4 metric design, while the entrances of the reiterating "dominant sevenths" in Pianos I and III, varying "independently of" this four quarter-note beat "pedal" in Piano IV, are rhythmic-metrically "mobile," being irregularly spaced.)[12] It is with such passages that a study of Stravinsky's octatonic routine(s) is most advantageously initiated, passages which, like "Jeu du rapt" in *Le Sacre* and others of List No. 1, are not only explicitly octatonic (unimpaired reference), but also demonstrate a full—or nearly full—realization of (0,3,6,9) symmetri-

Example 38 *continued*

cally defined partitioning, Models A or B. Indeed, here at Nos. 68–70, not
only is there a full (0,3,6,9) symmetrically defined partitioning of Collection II in terms of Model A's (0 4 7 10) "dominant sevenths" (the instrumental contribution in Pianos I and III), but also a full (0,3,6,9) symmetrically defined partitioning of Collection I in terms of Model B's (0 2 (3) 5)
tetrachords (the vocal contribution). As a result, the octatonicism is here
exceptionally rich, varied, and intricate. Indeed, with two of the three collections imposed simultaneously—along with Models A and B, also simultaneously deployed—there is an intricacy possibly unmatched by the remaining blocks and passages of Lists 1 and 2.

In the concluding blocks of the third tableau at Nos. 78–87 (Example
38), the (A G F♯ E D C (A)) diatonic hexachord may be inferred as central
to the articulation. A closing of the hexachord's C–A "gap" with a pivoting

seventh pitch element may render the surroundings fully diatonic with B as pitch number 10 (tending to implicate the D-scale on A, but with this hexachord's partitioning formulae intact), or signal the intervention of octatonic relations with the "chromatic" pitch number 6 and/or 11 of Model B's (0 2 3 5) (6 8 9 11) tetrachordal ordering.

Thus, at Nos. 78–80, the reiterating G–F♯–E–D–A–(G) fragment in Pianos I and III and the vocal ensemble refers to the (A G F♯ E D C) hexachord. But as earlier at Nos. 68–70, Collection II's (0 4 7 10) "dominant sevenths" at B, F, and D intervene (off the beat here in Pianos II and IV, *sforzando*), so that the block refers to both the (A G F♯ E D C) hexachord and the octatonic Collection II, a diatonic-octatonic (Collection II) interpenetration in which both the hexachord's "lower" (D C A) incomplete tetrachord and its (D F♯ A) triad serve as connecting links. (Note the C–G–D–A ostinato accompanying the G–F♯–E–D–A–(G) fragment in Pianos I and III, in which the (A G) (D C) encircling units of the (A G F♯ E D C) hexachord are exposed as a series of 5s or "fourths.") Then, in the following block at No. 80, the G–F♯–E–D–A–(G) fragment is harmonized in terms of the (A G F♯ E D C) hexachord's two (0 4 7) "major" triads at D and C, (D F♯ A) and (C E G). This (D F♯ A)–(C E G) harmonization is superimposed on a third triad, (A C E) in Piano IV. (As mentioned earlier, the (0 2 3 5 7 9) hexachord yields three triads; with respect to (A G F♯ E D C), these are the two whole step–related (0 4 7) "major" triads at D and C, (D F♯ A) and (C E G), and the (0 3 7) "minor" triad, (A C E).) Finally, at No. 82, the "diatonic B" in the vocal parts as pitch number 10 is replaced by an "octatonic B♭" as the "chromatic" pitch number 11 in Model B's (0 2 3 5 6 8 9 11) ordering; and the (A G F♯ E D C) diatonic framework of Nos. 78–82 gives way to a fully committed octatonic (A G F♯ E E♭ D♭ C B♭) Collection III framework at Nos. 82–87 (explicit octatonic reference, List 1 in chapter 2). In this final move to an octatonic Collection III framework at Nos. 82–87, it is thus A and the (A G F♯ E) tetrachord that prevail as shared, between-block (and between-reference) connecting links. So, too, in this lengthy concluding block of the third tableau (which celebrates the departure of the bride), the two mothers of the bride and bridegroom are gathered in hushed lament (*lamentando* and *p, subito*), murmuring their mournful farewells. This sorrowful lament is thus sung to this A–G–F♯–A♯–C♯–C–B♭–G–(A) fragment which, wholly octatonic and accountable to Collection III, is systematically transposed to the remaining (0,3,6,9) symmetrically defined partitioning elements of Collection III, D♯[E♭] at No. 83 + 3, F♯ at No. 83 + 4, and finally C in terms of C–B♭–A–C♯–E–D♯–C♯ at No. 84. (The soprano and mezzo soprano here impersonate the two Russian mothers, but as Stravinsky remarks (see the quotation prefacing this chapter), the soloists in *Les Noces* do not identify with particular characters throughout—or, in fact, with characters as such, but only with character types. Thus, while the soprano soloist is a Russian mother at the conclusion of the third tableau, she had been the Russian bride in the first.)

The entire concluding section of the third tableau at Nos. 78–87 exemplifies, in a most telling fashion, the summary of Example 24a in chapter 3: the D-scale or (0 2 3 5 7 9) hexachord, through their two complete or incomplete (0 2 3 5) (7 9 (10) 0) tetrachords, may implicate two of the three octatonic collections in octatonic-diatonic interaction. Here, the "lower" (D C A) unit of the (A G F♯ E) (D C A) hexachord implicates Collection II at Nos. 78–80 in terms of this collection's "intruding" (0 4 7 10) "dominant sevenths" at B, F, and D, while the "upper" (A G F♯ E) tetrachord implicates Collection III at Nos. 80–87 by means of an "intruding" pitch number 11, the B♭. To accommodate these transactions, we may insert these (D C A) and (A G F♯ E) connecting links in the connecting-link "slot" of Example 29 (chapter 4) for a "Russian" summary, noting that Nos. 78–87 constitute *a reading from right to left*, where the (A G F♯ E D C) diatonic framework moves toward—or is "intruded upon" by—octatonic relations. (See Examples 39 and 40.) We note, too, that the between-

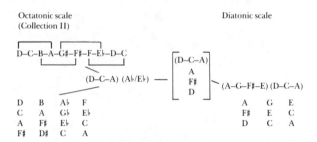

Example 39

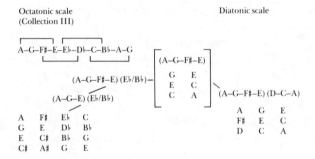

Example 40

reference (0 3 7/0 4 7) "minor" and "major" triads would have to be included in these insertions, so that, at No. 82, the connecting-link "slot" would include, as that which is articulatively shared between Collection III and the (A G F♯ E D C) hexachord, not only A and the (A G F♯ E) tetrachord but the (C E G) and (A C E) triads as well.

Finally, the reader should find the interpenetration of (A G F♯ E E♭ D♭ C B♭) Collection III and the (A G F♯ E D C) hexachord at No. 58 in the second tableau (Example 41) reminiscent of the blocks at Nos. 7 and 11 in *Petroushka,* first tableau. For, at No. 11 in *Petroushka,* the (A G F♯ E D C) hexachord is implicated by (0 3 7/0 4 7) triadic partitioning: the principal melodic fragment outlines a (D F♯ A)–(A C E) triadic reiteration. And, as

Example 41: Second tableau

at No. 7 in *Petroushka*, the (D F♯ A) triad of this reiteration stands "in oppo-sition" to the "lower" octatonic pitch number 11, Collection III's B♭. While we may note the inclusion of pitch number 10, the B, in an accompanying tremolo at No. 58, this inclusion in no way undermines (A G F♯ E D C) hexachordal identity. For the principal fragment's (D F♯ A)–(A C E) artic-ulation remains central to the activity at No. 58, with respect to which pitch number 10, the B, assumes a peripheral role. The simultaneous im-position of both pitch numbers 10 and 11, the "diatonic B" and the "octa-tonic B♭," underscores the previously noted (in chapter 3) "flexibility" re-served for seventh pitch class identity in (0 2 3 5 7 9) hexachordal contexts, the closing of the (0 2 3 5 7 9) hexachord's 9–0 "gap" with a pitch number 10 and/or 11. (And note the (E♭ G B♭ D♭) "dominant seventh" just prior to No. 59, which enhances Collection III's contribution to this octatonic-diatonic interpenetration.)

At No. 59, a Collection III (C–A–A/B♭/C♯–A) basso ostinato is intro-duced by Piano IV and persists in the lengthy passage at Nos. 62–65 (which concludes the second tableau), interpenetrating with the (A G F♯ E D C) hexachord implicated by both the vocal ensemble and the material in Pianos I, II, and III. This material consists—as in the third tableau at No. 80—of an alternation or back-and-forth movement between the (A G F♯ E D C) hexachord's (0,2) related (0 4 7) "major" triads, (D F♯ A) and (C E G), and an outlining of its (A C E) "minor" triad. In the lengthy vocal passage at Nos. 62–65 (not included in Example 41), there occurs not a single transgression of the six-note (A G F♯ E D C) diatonic hexachord; not even a peripheral pitch number 10, the "diatonic B," may here be inferred.

CONCLUSIONS

When coupled with those prior summaries of octatonic-diatonic thought compounded on behalf of *Petroushka* and *Le Sacre* in chapters 3 and 4, the analysis of *Les Noces* concluded here continues to reflect matters of consis-tency, identity, and distinction in "Russian" thought. And our conclusions regarding pitch organization, together with whatever traits this organiza-tion presupposes in formal, melodic, and rhythmic-metric design, will therefore resemble those put forward for *Le Sacre* in chapter 4 (notwith-standing the securely fastened diatonic framework here which, although deceptive—since most of *Les Noces*, including the fourth tableau, is oc-tatonic-diatonic in conception—might still contrast sharply with the pro-nounced "vertical chromaticism" of *Le Sacre*):

1. The (0 2 3 5) tetrachord, principally (0 2 5) incomplete in articulation, figures prominently as an articulative "basic cell" in *Les Noces* (as it does, indeed, for much of Stravinsky's "Russian" music), and hence as the prin-

cipal between-block or between-reference connecting link. In this capacity it relates, in diatonic blocks and passages, to a (0 2 3 5) (7 9 (10) 0) tetrachordal or (0 3 7/0 4 7) triadic partitioning of the D-scale or the (0 2 3 5 7 9) hexachordal segment; and, in octatonic or octatonic-diatonic blocks and passages, to a (0,3,6,9) symmetrically defined (0 2 (3) 5) tetrachordal partitioning of the (0 2 3 5 6 8 9 11) octatonic collection, Model B; and, with pitch numbers 0, 2, and 5 becoming pitch numbers 0, 10, and 7 of the (0 4 7 10) "dominant-seventh" complex (the root, seventh, and fifth respectively), to a (0,3,6,9) symmetrically defined (0 4 7 10) "dominant-seventh" partitioning of the (0 1 3 4 6 7 9 10 (0)) octatonic collection, Model A.

2. Because of the symmetrical and hence inherently static, inconclusive nature of this diatonic, octatonic, or octatonic-diatonic articulation, pitch relations in *Les Noces* prompt a form or architecture constructed with relatively heterogeneous blocks of material, which exhibit, upon successive (near) repeats, an unusual degree of distinction and insulation in instrumental, dynamic, rhythmic-metric, and referential character. These blocks effectively replace the traditional tonal, C-scale (or major-scale) forms of the Baroque, Classical, and Romantic eras.

3. This abrupt block juxtaposition is linked to a melodic construction which consists of reiterating fragments registrally and instrumentally fixed in ostinatolike repetition (with little or no developmental "dialogue" or exchange between parts or registers). These fragments are very often of limited range and content, and delineate the (0 2 (3) 5) tetrachord (which, as indicated, may in its referential implications be either octatonic, diatonic, or octatonic-diatonic).

4. This melodic construction is in turn linked to a rhythmic-metric construction in which we typically find stretches of rapidly changing meters with all the reiterating fragments sharing the same irregular rhythmic-metric periods as defined by the shifting meter (as in the opening blocks at Nos. 0 and 1 in the first tableau, Example 33); or, on the other hand, a steady meter which will generally reflect the stable rhythmic-metric period of a reiterating fragment (as an ostinato, generally a basso ostinato), against which other fragments will repeat according to "separate" or "independent" rhythmic-metric periods (as, for example, at Nos. 68–70 in the third tableau, Example 38).

Thus, too, however novel or exceptional we choose to consider the instrumentation or the "cantata-ballet" scheme of *Les Noces,* there can be little doubt that its musical substance is decisively "Russian." Indeed, without *Les Noces,* a "Russian" period becomes scarcely imaginable, in light of the supplementary harvest of suckers to which this piece, during the decade-long search for an appropriate instrumentation, so prodigiously gave rise.

SEVEN

HISTOIRE DU SOLDAT (1918)

Part I
"The Soldier's March" (Marching tunes)
Music to Scene I
Music to Scene II
Music to Scene III (reprise of Scene I)

Part II
"The Soldier's March" (Marching tunes)
"The Royal March"
"The Little Concert"
Three Dances: "Tango," "Waltz," "Ragtime"
"The Devil's Dance"
"The Little Choral"
"The Devil's Song"
"Great Choral"
"Triumphal March of the Devil"

> I received the idea of *Histoire du soldat* in the spring of 1917, but I could not
> develop it at the time as I was still occupied with *Les Noces* and with the task of
> preparing a symphonic poem from *The Nightingale*. The thought of compos-
> ing a dramatic spectacle for a *théâtre ambulant* had occurred to me more than
> once since the beginning of the war, however. The sort of work I envisaged
> would have to be small enough in the complement of its players to allow for
> performances on a circuit of Swiss villages, and simple enough in the outlines
> of its story to be easily understood. I discovered my subject in one of Afana-
> siev's tales of the soldier and the Devil. . . . Only the skeleton of the play is
> Afanasiev-Stravinsky, however, for the final form of the libretto must be
> credited to my friend and collaborator, C. F. Ramuz. I worked with Ramuz,
> translating my Russian text to him line by line. [*Expositions and Developments*,
> p. 101.]

PITCH RELATIONS

Now the question of pitch-class priority—of a "tone center," loosely
speaking—is problematic in many diatonic contexts of the "Russian" pe-

riod. For, obviously, just as with the two octatonic scales of Models A and B, the (0 2 3 5 7 9 10 (0)) D-scale and the (0 2 3 5 7 9 (0)) hexachord preclude tonally functional relations, the familiar harmonic progressions, and the definitions of key and cadence known to the tonal, C-scale (or major-scale) music of the seventeenth to nineteenth centuries. And while the (0 3 7/0 4 7) "minor" and "major" triads of these "Russian" diatonic contexts are naturally a part of the vocabulary of tonality and the C-scale, their confinement to these alternative references subjects them to behavior of a different sort, to a self-enclosed, repetitive, circular kind of activity which engenders the balance, "harmonic stasis," and deadlock of which we have spoken (although perhaps rather more persistently in connection with Stravinsky's octatonic contexts). These conditions relate to triadic superimposition, ostinatolike repetition, and abrupt block juxtaposition, where block juxtaposition, that peculiarly Stravinskian conception of form or architecture, is viewed as an abrupt shifting in the collectional reference (or in the partitioning thereof). Priority (or centricity) thus becomes a matter of stress or metric accentuation, occasionally of octave reinforcement or "fifth support," but perhaps most significantly of *survival*, a matter of the persistence or preservation of a given pitch class or grouping from one block or section to the next, a persistence we have been following in terms of shared, between-block (or between-reference) connecting links.

Of course, in addition to the (0 2 3 5) (7 9 0) tetrachordal and (0 3 7/0 4 7) triadic routine cited in connection with (0 2 3 5 7 9) hexachordal reference, the pairs of 2s or whole steps which encircle this diatonic segment, (0 2) (7 9), may exercise a critical role in the assertion of some form of pitch-class priority.[1] And in regard to the (D–E) (A–G) reiterations in the opening blocks of *Petroushka* (which encircle the (E D C♯ B A G) hexachord; see Example 21 in chapter 3), or indeed, the G–F–B♭–C contour of the opening tenor fragment in *Renard* (the encircling (G F) (C B♭) units of the (G F E D C B♭) hexachord; see Example 42), we may note, as before, that the relation expressed by these encircling (0 2) (7 9) units, the 2 or whole step, often acquires articulative cohesion. (In other words, (0 2) or (7 9) proximity, as defined by the (0 2 3 5 7 9) scalar ordering, is not merely "conceptual.") This *presented* (0 2) (7 9) whole-step articulation naturally relates to a (0 2 3 5) (7 9 (10) 0) tetrachordal partitioning of either the D-scale or the (0 2 3 5 7 9 (0)) hexachord, just as a (0 2) (6 8) tritone-related whole-step articulation would relate to Model B's (0 2 3 5) (6 8 9 11) tetrachordal partitioning of the octatonic scale. All of this 0–2 whole-step or (0 2 3 5) tetrachordal emphasis of the "Russian" period is conveniently mirrored by descending scales and pitch numberings.

But the decision as to which of these four encircling (0 2) (7 9) pitch elements is presiding varies from one (0 2 3 5 7 9) hexachordal context to the next. Thus, from within the diatonic G-scale-on-B framework of *The*

Example 42: *Renard*

Firebird's Finale at No. 1, we infer the (F♯ E D♯ C♯ B A) hexachord because of a harmonization of the borrowed folk melody in terms of this hexachord's (0,2) whole-step-related (0 4 7) "major" triads at B and A, (B D♯ F♯) and (A C♯ E). And since B and the B/F♯ "fifth" are sustained as points of departure and return in this (B D♯ F♯)–(A C♯ E) triadic oscillation, it is evidently these components which, as pitch numbers 7 and 7/0, assume priority. (See Example 25a in chapter 3.) In *Petroushka* at No. 0–2, we infer the (E D C♯ B A G) hexachord, in which, in contrast, the D, as pitch number 2, seems the most likely candidate for priority status. (See Example 21 in chapter 3.) In *Renard* at Nos. 0–9 (Example 42 above), we infer, from within the diatonic D-scale-on-G framework, an opening (G F E D C B♭) hexachordal foundation, in which G, as pitch number 0, acquires a degree of pitch-class centricity.[2] Consequently, quite apart from the ambiguity of pitch-class priority in many (0 2 3 5 7 9) contexts, there is also this variance with respect to those (0 2 3 5 7 9) contexts where a sense of pitch-class priority does seem to arise.

While the encircling (0 2) (7 9) units of the (0 2 3 5 7 9) hexachord are indeed frequently encountered as reiterating 2s or whole steps, it is perhaps ultimately to their definition as an 0–7–2–9 succession of three 7s or "fifths" (reading down; or as a 9–2–7–0 succession of three 5s or "fourths"), and then to the transposition and superimposition of (0 2 3 5 7 9) hexachords related by the interval of 7, a "fifth" apart, that we can best turn in order further to probe this ambiguity or variance. Moreover, all these factors respecting (0 2 3 5 7 9) hexachordal reference—the articulative routine, the question of fragmental enclosure, the encircling (0 2) (7 9) units and their role in the expression (or confounding non-expression) of pitch-class priority—take on a special urgency as we approach, finally, those interminable ostinati of "The Soldier's March" and the music to Scene I in *Histoire du soldat*. And pursuant to the 0–7–2–9 "fifth" articulation of these encircling (0 2) (7 9) units, we might briefly entertain, through Wilfrid Mellers, the tonal approach to the G–E/D ostinato of "The Soldier's March," an approach that Mellers evidently shares with Pierre Boulez in confronting Stravinsky's music (see chapter 2), but one that has also been advanced in countless publications:[3]

> Here, there is an unceasing ostinato in the bass consisting of the note G followed by D and E sounded together, a ninth apart. This seems to suggest the key of G. But the fragmentary tootling tune, nearly always out of step with the ostinato, is unambiguously in D. . . . This suggests that the D–E in the ostinato is really the tonic and dominant of D major elided together and that the G of the ostinato represents the subdominant. Traditional harmony revolves between the poles of tonic, dominant and subdominant. In telescoping two or even all three of these chords Stravinsky places in space, as it were, chords that would normally progress into one another. Instead of a resolved argument, we have a tension clinched, suspended in time.

For were we, in the presence here of a diatonicism but in the absence of anything remotely resembling C-scale (or major-scale) tonally functional behavior, to shun the specter of "keys," "chords," and the dominant-tonic-subdominant relation (to shun, especially, that reference to the opening "tootling tune" as being "unambiguously in D," since the concept of "D-major" is not inapplicable here—C-scale on D would do—but, even if applicable, hardly "unambiguously" so, since there is no cadential clarification, the "tootling tune" outlining and coming to rest on a (A C♯ E) triad or E–A "fifth"), and to replace this specter with the E–A–D–G series of three "fifths" defined by the encircling (E D) (A G) units of the (E D C♯ B A G) hexachord (the stability or balancing effect of these encircling "fifths" being sufficient cause for the "harmonic stasis" or "tension clinched"), the point Mellers raises would seem well taken: a fundamental ambiguity manifests itself with respect to pitch-class priority in the opening march, at least until No. 5, where the ostinato pattern is temporarily discarded and there arises, for the first time, a sense of priority on the part of D and the (D F♯ A) triad. Moreover, as Mellers notes, the elision of these "fifth"-related elements as a dominant-tonic-subdominant relation (referring to the E–A–D–G "fifth" succession between the G–E/D ostinato and the bassoon's reiterating A here, with the centrally positioned D and A–D components as the "tonic" and "tonic fifth," all of which we reinterpret in terms of the elision of these four encircling pitch elements of the (E D C♯ B

A G) hexachord) does constitute a kind of superimposition, with respect
to which the same kind of descriptive terminology might be invoked as
earlier in connection with Stravinsky's octatonic settings: balance, equilibrium, equal weight and independence, opposition, harmonic stasis, deadlock, etc.

   Indeed, prior to *Histoire*, pitches accounted for in terms of the encircling (0 2) (7 9) units of the (0 2 3 5 7 9) hexachord are on several occasions
conceived as ostinati. Apart from the (2–0) (7–9) whole-step reiterations
of *Petroushka*'s first tableau (which, presumably, are interpretable as ostinati), see, in Example 43a, "Tilimbom" from *Trois histoires pour enfants*
(1917). Here, a reiterating (D C A) fragment in the voice—once again, of
course, a (0 2 5) incomplete (0 2 3 5) tetrachord, the "basic cell" of the
"Russian" period—is joined by a (D F♯ A)–(C E G) triadic oscillation in the
piano, these two cohesive groupings yielding, in pitch content, the (A G F♯
E D C) hexachord. But this material is superimposed on a G–C–F–G basso

Example 43a: *Trois histoires pour enfants* ("Tilimbom")

ostinato whose pitches are among the encircling (D C) (G F) units of the (D C B A G F) hexachord, and therefore implicate the next "fifth"-related (0 2 3 5 7 9) hexachord "downward" from (A G F♯ E D C).[4] For another instance, see Stravinsky's *Berceuse* for voice and piano (1917), Example 43b.[5] The bass pattern of this (until 1962 unpublished) *Berceuse* is a C/G–G/F (2/7–7/9) articulation of the encircling (D C) (G F) units of the (D C B A G F) hexachord, and is therefore identical in pitch/interval content and order to the G–C–F–G basso ostinato of "Tilimbom." Also compare these (0 2 3 5 7 9) hexachordally conceived bass patterns in "Tilimbom" and the *Berceuse* to the ostinato of "The Soldier's March" and the music to Scene I in *Histoire,* Examples 43c and d. The correspondences here are striking.

Thus, as at Nos. 0–2 in *Petroushka*'s first tableau, we infer, straightaway, the (E D C♯ B A G) hexachord. (See Example 44.) *Petroushka*'s D–E reitera-

Example 43b: *Berceuse*

Example 43c: "The Soldier's March" (*Histoire*)

Example 43d: Scene I (*Histoire*)

Example 44: "The Soldier's March"

tion, (2-0) in this (E D C♯ B A G) hexachordal reference is here "sounded together" as E/D in the ostinato, alternating with a G, pitch number 9. A's (pitch number 7's) participation in this hexachordal (0 2) (7 9) encirclement in terms of (E D) (A G) is furnished by the "tootling tune"'s outlining of a (A C♯ E) triad and its coming to rest on the E/A "fifth" at No. 3, at which point the bassoon reiterates A over the continuing G–E/D (9–0/2) ostinato. Thus, from within the fully accredited diatonic framework, we infer the (E D C♯ B A G) hexachordal segment—or its articulative routine—as central to the activity; and from within this hexachordal segment, we infer E,D,A, and G as elements of priority, these elements constituting the encircling (0 2) (7 9) units of the (E D C♯ B A G) hexachord, an encirclement with an articulation very similar to that of the D–E and A–G (2–0 and 7–9) whole-step reiterations of *Petroushka*. And while it is undoubtedly the E–A–D–G "fifth" articulation of these units to which the ear is readily drawn, there is nonetheless exhibited, in the E/D (0/2) "sounding together" of the G–E/D ostinato, a degree of whole-step cohesion on the part of (E D) in this (E D) (A G) encirclement or partitioning.

Then, at No. 2+3, the sixteenth-note figure in the clarinet (which invariably follows the trumpet's opening "tootling tune" at subsequent repeats) outlines (0,2) whole-step-related (0 4 7) "major" triads at B and A,
(B D♯ F♯) and (A C♯ E). This cohesive (A C♯ E)–(B D♯ F♯) delineation
yields, in pitch content, the (F♯ E D♯ C♯ B A) hexachord, which is a transposition "upward," at the interval of 2, of the opening (E D C♯ B A G)
hexachord.[6] Consequently, with reference to the (0,7) "fifth"-related
overlapping of (0 2 3 5 7 9) hexachords already sketched in Example 22a
in connection with *Petroushka*, in Example 44 we outline another such format for Nos. 0–5 in *Histoire*, noting, however, that the "lower" (E D C♯ B A
G) hexachord presides, with respect to which the (0 2 3 5 7 9) hexachords
of the clarinet are extensions, and that pursuant to a more long-term or
global approach, the (0 2 3 5 7 9) hexachords of the clarinet would extend
"upward" yet another "fifth" to include the (C♯ B A♯ G♯ F♯ E) hexachord
as well. For although not shown in Example 44, the clarinet fragment is
transposed from A to E at Nos. 4 and 7, and hence from a (A C♯ E)–(B D♯
F♯) triadic delineation to a (E G♯ B)–(F♯ A♯ C♯) delineation.

Still, while the marching tunes of "The Soldier's March" and Scene I are
fragmentary (left "open") and repetitive in the same sense as the "tunes"
of *Le Sacre*, *Renard*, and *Les Noces* are, they are, as Mellers notes, "related to
clichés common to European art music." And it may also be indicative of
this "European art music" that, in place of the D-scale and the (0 2 3 5 7 9)
hexachord so often implicated by diatonic settings of the "Russian" period, the referential ordering of the fully accredited diatonic framework
at No. 5 appears to be that of the C-scale on D (or D-major scale, in tonal
terms), with D assuming a degree of pitch-class priority. (See Example
45.) The G–E/D ostinato is replaced by a reiterating D, while G's participation is curtailed, and the accentuation of F♯ in the bassoon fragment appears to expose a presiding (D F♯ A) triad at least through No. 7. Moreover, with respect to the E–A–D–G series of "fifths" defined by the
encircling (E D) (A G) units of the (E D C♯ B A G) hexachord, the A–D
"fifth" may be envisioned as centric without necessarily invoking Mellers's
specter of a dominant-tonic-subdominant relation.[7]

Example 45: "The Soldier's March"

But note the qualification that must accompany the "C-scale-on-D" ruling at No. 5: (1) the G–A–B–C♯–D–E hexachordal outline in the double bass over the reiterating D; (2) the sustained E (pitch number 0) in the clarinet and in the violin *jeté* interruptions which continues to accentuate E's (0 2) whole-step affiliation with D; (3) the (A C♯ E) triadic superimpositions outlined by the clarinet and violin *jeté* interruptions; (4) and then, at No. 10 (not shown in Example 45), the D/G (2/9) "fifth" in the violin accompaniment to the chromatic transformation of the "tootling tune." Thus ambiguity of (single) pitch-class priority persists. And we may wonder whether we are not ultimately better off accepting and defining it in terms of this (0 2) (7 9) encirclement of the (0 2 3 5 7 9) hexachord—or in terms of this encirclement's 0–7–2–9 "fifth" articulation—resigning ourselves, in other words, to an inability to establish a referential ordering (scale) for the "fully accredited diatonic framework." (That is to say: would it not make for a more accurate description of the opening march to conclude that pitch-class priority extends no "further" than (0 2) (7 9) encirclement of the (0 2 3 5 7 9) hexachord?)

Just prior to Scene I, the concluding simultaneity of the march, (A E G C) reading down, is a transposition, at the interval of 7, the "fifth," of the initial simultaneity at No. 1, (E B D G). This transposition signals a transposition of the march's presiding (E D C♯ B A G) hexachord "down" to the next (0,7) "fifth"-related (0 2 3 5 7 9) hexachord, (A G F♯ E D C). (See Example 46.) Accordingly, the (0 2) unit of the march's ostinato, the E/D "sounding together," becomes an A–G reiteration in Scene I's G–D–A–G ostinato; and pitch number 9, the G in the march, is replaced by a pitch number 7, the D in this new (A G F♯ E D C) hexachordal reference. But while the (A G F♯ E D C) hexachord presides at first, Scene I is ultimately more flexible with respect to (0 2 3 5 7 9) hexachordal reference. And this flexibility—or greater (0 2 3 5 7 9) maneuverability—may be attributed to Scene I's G–D–A–G (2–7–0–2) ostinato. In Scene I's ostinato it is pitch number 7 that alternates with pitch numbers 0 and 2 (of the (A G F♯ E D C) collection), not pitch number 9 that alternates with pitch numbers 0 and 2 (of the (E D C♯ B A G) collection of the March). These encircling pitch numbers 0, 2, and 7 of Scene I's (A G F♯ E D C) hexachordal ostinato (A, G, and D) are the encircling pitch numbers 7, 9, and 2 of the presiding (E D C♯ B A G) hexachord of the march. Consequently, Scene I's ostinato is really "open" or uncommitted with respect to (0 2) (7 9) encirclement of these two "fifth"-related (0 2 3 5 7 9) hexachordal collections, (E D C♯ B A G) and (A G F♯ E D C).[8] And this encircling (0 2) (7 9) neutrality of Scene I's G–D–A–G ostinato allows for a ready alternation between (A G F♯ E D C) contexts—such as that noted just before No. 3, where C replaces C♯, where (0 4 7) "major" triads are outlined at D and C, and where B, as pitch number 10, is either missing or peripheral—and (E D C♯ B A G)

Example 46: Scene I

contexts—such as that noted at No. 5 + 1, where C becomes C♯, where a (A C♯ E) triad merges with the ostinato's D–G "fifth," and where F♯, as pitch number 10, is either missing or peripheral. Moreover, this (A G F♯ E D C)–(E D C♯ B A G) alternation triggers an incessant (A C/A C♯) "minor-major third" play with respect to C/C♯, a "play" similar to that noted at No. 11 in *Petroushka* (see Examples 21 and 22a in chapter 3), and which can therefore similarly be attributed to (or can best be heard and interpreted as a manifestation of) "fifth"-related (0 2 3 5 7 9) adjacency or overlapping.

Further, the bassoon's F–G reiteration at No. 9, anticipated in the violin at Nos. 6–9, implicates an extension of "fifth"-related (0 2 3 5 7 9) overlapping "downward" to include the (D C B A G F) hexachord (F–G constituting the (7 9) unit of this (D C B A G F) hexachord), an extension that prompts additional "minor-major third" play involving F/F♯. Thus, as in Example 44 for the march, we may again compress (0 2 3 5 7 9) strategy by sketching the spread of engaged (0,7) "fifth"-related (0 2 3 5 7 9) hexachords. We need scarcely repeat how very handily this compression reflects the circumstances surveyed: the neutrality of the G–D–A–G ostinato pattern with respect to (0 2) (7 9) encirclement of the (E D C♯ B A G) and (A G F♯ E D C) hexachords; the various (E D C♯ B A G) and (A G F♯ E D C) contexts to which this neutrality lends itself; and the "minor-major third" play that this (0 2 3 5 7 9) alternation generates. Finally, note that the spread of "fifth"-related (0 2 3 5 7 9) hexachords extends "upward" in the march by means of the clarinet fragment's (0 2 3 5 7 9) hexachords, but "downward" in Scene I from the (E D C♯ B A G) hexachord. And it is, as always, the *presented* cohesion—the *presented* accentuation of the (0 2) and (7 9) overlapping defined by these spreads of (0 2 3 5 7 9) hexachords, the *presented* (0 2 3) (7 9 0) tetrachordal and (0 3 7/0 4 7) triadic articulation of the single (0 2 3 5 7 9) collections—that merits, as the most accommodating analytic-theoretical approach, the (0 2 3 5 7 9) perspective indicated.

The sigh of the dejected soldier in Scene II—surely one of Stravinsky's most poignant utterances—condenses the most pressing (0 2 3 5 7 9) relations of the preceding sections. (See Example 47.) The A♭–G♭ (or G♯–F♯) reiteration in the bassoon at No. 1 constitutes little more than a long, drawn-out continuation of the 0–2 whole-step reiterations of the preceding ostinati; then, in combination with the clarinet's E♭–G♭ figure above, it becomes a continuation, more determinately, of the G/A–E/G–G/A articulation in the solo violin at Nos. 3–5 in Scene I, now in terms of G♭/A♭–E♭/G♭–G♭/A♭. (See the bracketed material in the analytical sketches of Examples 46 and 47. The G♭/A♭–E♭/G♭–G♭/A♭ figuration in the clarinet and bassoon at No. 1 in Scene II, a (0 2 5) incomplete (0 2 3 5) tetrachordal articulation in terms of (A♭ G♭ E♭), is derived from the solo violin's G/A–E/G–G/A figuration at Nos. 0–3 in Scene I (a (A G E) (0 2 5) incomplete tetrachordal articulation), with which it thus identifies in interval content and registral spacing.)

But Scene II's "sigh"—never to be repeated, a circumstance which invests it with special significance—opens with a reference to both Collection II, (B A G♯ F♯) (F C), and the (B A G♯ F♯ E D) diatonic hexachord, an octatonic-diatonic interaction in which the initial B–A (0–2) whole-step reiteration, articulated jointly by the clarinet's triplet figure and the violin's sustained B, along with the clarinet's (B A G♯ F♯) tetrachordal articulation at m. 2, serve as shared, between-reference connecting links. The octa-

Example 47: Scene II

tonic (Collection II) contribution to this interpenetration is conspicuously marked by the "intrusion" of a "chromatic" pitch number 6, the F in the bassoon at m. 2, forming the tritone with the violin's sustained B, and by the presence, at the very outset, of a "chromatic" pitch number 11, the C of the violin's B/C simultaneity, which defines the "major seventh" in relation to the sustained B. (How familiar are these circumstances in Scene II. Indeed, how peculiarly "Russian" is the "sound" of this introductory "sigh," with its B–A (0–2) whole-step reiteration, its B–A–G#–F# (0 2 3 5) tetrachordal articulation, and the 0–11 or "major seventh" B–C interval span of the violin, a span which encloses Model B's (0,6) tritone-related (0 2 3 5) (6 8 9 11) tetrachords, (B A G# F#) (F C) here, Collection II.[9] With what remarkable consistency is the "chromatic" element in these "Rus-

Example 47 *continued*

sian" contexts heard, understood, and revealingly accounted for, in terms of the persistent "intrusion" of specific octatonic intervals. For these "intrusions" are invariably of the same order, referring, invariably from one context to the next, to these "chromatic" pitch numbers 6 and 11 of Model B's (0 2 3 5 6 8 9 11) octatonic scale, defining, in relation to a presiding pitch number 0, the tritone and the "major seventh." And so, too, how remarkably consistent does Stravinsky appear to have been in moving, during the "Russian" era, from one piece or context to the next.)

In the third measure of Example 47, the bassoon's F♯–C♯–G♯ fragment and the violin's B are the encircling (A♭ G♭) (D♭ C♭) units of the (A♭ G♭ F E♭ D♭ C♭) diatonic hexachord, with the initial (0–2) whole-step reiteration of the opening measure, B–A, replaced by A♭–G♭ (or G♯–F♯). Following this replacement, the bassoon lapses into that prolonged A♭–G♭ (or G♯–F♯) re-

Example 47 *continued*

iteration which, joined by the clarinet figure above, yields the (A♭ G♭ F E♭) (0 2 3 5) tetrachord. Then, with the "intrusion" of a "chromatic" D at No. 1 + 6 (pitch number 6, the tritone in relation to A♭ of the (A♭ G♭ F E♭) (0 2 3 5) tetrachord), the clarinet very gradually returns to the B–A reiteration of the opening triplet "sigh" by way of a D–C–B–A succession; by way, that is, of Collection II's (0,6) tritone-related (D C B A) tetrachord in relation to (A♭ G♭ F E♭). And so the lengthy clarinet-bassoon expanse at No. 1 refers initially to the (A♭ G♭ F E♭ D♭ C♭) diatonic hexachord, but then, with the "intrusion" of a "chromatic" D at No. 1+6, to Collection II's (0,6) tritone-related (A♭ G♭ F E♭) (D C B A) tetrachords, in which the "upper" (A♭ G♭ F E♭) tetrachord of these two interacting references serves as the shared, between-reference connecting link.

In the following episode at Nos. 3–5 (-2), the diatonic articulation refers to the (E♭ D♭ C B♭ A♭ G♭ (E♭)) hexachord: the trumpet and clarinet articulate first the "lower" incomplete (A♭ G♭ E♭) (7 9 0) tetrachordal unit of this hexachord, while the clarinet follows at No. 3+4 with the "upper" (E♭ D♭ C B♭) (0 2 3 5) unit. This diatonic (E♭ D♭ C B♭) (A♭ G♭ E♭) articulation is superimposed on B/C–A/D–B/D simultaneities in the violin which jointly yield the (D C A B) tetrachord. Accordingly, with the "lower" (A♭ G♭ E♭) (7 9 0) unit of the (E♭ D♭ C B♭) (A♭ G♭ E♭) hexachord as the shared, between-reference connecting link, Collection II may be inferred—as it was earlier at No. 1—in terms of its (0,6) tritone-related (A♭ G♭ F E♭) (D C B A) tetra-chords.

At No. 4 + 2 (or two measures before No. 5), the bassoon introduces a new fragment, a B♭–F–G–E♭–D♭–F contour which implicates the (B♭ A♭ G F E♭ D♭) hexachord. This fragment is superimposed over simultaneities in the violin and double bass that yield the (E D C♯ B) tetrachord. Hence, a (0 2 3 5 7 9) diatonic and (0 2 3 5 6 8 9 11) octatonic interaction may again be inferred, but here in terms of the (B♭ A♭ G F E♭ D♭) hexachord and Collection I's (0,6) tritone-related (B♭ A♭ G F) (E D C♯ B) tetrachords, in which the "upper" (B♭ A♭ G F) unit is the shared, between-reference con-necting link. Finally, this interaction is cut off at No. 5 + 2, as the clarinet and bassoon return in recapitulation to the material at No. 1. But the ma-terial is here transposed from the initial (A♭ G♭ F E♭) and (A♭ G♭ F E♭) (D C B A) articulation at No. 1 to a (B A G♯ F♯) or (B A G♯ F♯) (F E♭ D C) articu-lation; this is a transposition "up" by the interval of 3, a "minor third," which allows, on the octatonic side of the interaction, for continued refer-ence to Collection II. Scene II then concludes with this clarinet-bassoon material transposed back to its initial (A♭ G♭ F E♭) or (A♭ G♭ F E♭) (D C B A) articulation.

As with "The Soldier's March" and the music to Scene I in Examples 44 and 46, we can again compress the spread of (0,7) "fifth"-related (0 2 3 5 7 9) hexachords, four in all here in Scene II. Thus in Example 48 a "Rus-sian" summary is applied (as suggested by Example 22a in chapter 3, sketched for *Petroushka*'s first tableau), in which Scene II's spread of "fifth"-related (0 2 3 5 7 9) hexachords, confined to the left-hand side, im-plicate the octatonic Model B scales on the right-hand side (referring mostly to Collection II), with the two adjoining (0 2 3 5) (7 9 0) tetrachord-al units of these (0 2 3 5 7 9) hexachords positioned in the middle as con-necting links.

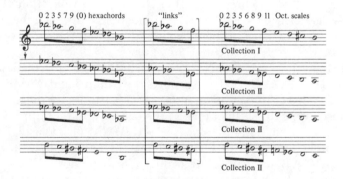

Example 48

And so, finally, the forlorn "sigh" of the weary and dejected soldier in Scene II seems in all these articulative and referential respects peculiarly "Russian." Indeed, conclusively so, the very essence of "Russian" musical thought. For there is first that fundamental 2 or 0–2 whole-step reiteration of "Russian" music (in terms here, for example, of A♭–G♭ (or G♯–F♯) in the bassoon at No. 1). This 2 or whole step aligns itself more articulatively to a (0 2 3 5) tetrachordal delineation (in terms, at No. 1, of (A♭ G♭ F E♭) in the clarinet and bassoon). And when referentially diatonic this (0 2 3 5) tetrachord may implicate the (0 2 3 5 7 9) hexachord (in terms of (A♭ G♭ F E♭ D♭ C♭) at No. 1), whose encircling (0 2) (7 9) units may accommodate the reiterating 2s (whole steps), or be articulated as an 0–7–2–9 series of "fifths" or "fourths." When referentially octatonic (or octatonic-diatonic), Model B's (0,6) tritone-related (0 2 3 5) (6 8 9 11) tetrachords may be inferred (in terms of (A♭ G♭ F E♭) (D C B A) at No. 1, for example), in which either the "upper" or "lower" of these tetrachords may serve as the shared, between-reference connecting link. And such—once again—is the nature of Stravinsky's "Russian" art. Or at least in matters pitch-relational, what are here judged critical aspects of that art.

LOOKING AHEAD:
TWO NEOCLASSICAL EXAMPLES

But as a final "finally" here, the reader's attention is drawn to a previously examined passage from *Les Noces* at Nos. 78–80 (Example 49a), and to two neoclassical passages (Examples 49b and 49c). For while the articulative routine of the diatonic (0 2 3 5 7 9) hexachord is characteristically "Russian," it may from time to time pertain to neoclassical and early serial contexts as well.

Thus, if we recognize G as the pitch class of priority at Nos. 78–80 in *Les Noces* (and disregard, momentarily, the harmonization of the G–F♯–

Example 49a: *Les Noces* (third tableau)

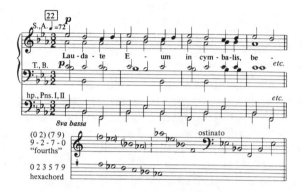

Example 49b: *Symphony of Psalms*

Example 49c: *Agon* ("Pas de quatre")

E–D–A–(G) fragment in terms of a (D F♯ A)–(C E G) reiteration at No. 80, articulative circumstances which, far more readily than those inferable at No. 22 in the final movement of the *Symphony of Psalms*, identify (0 2 3 5 7 9) hexachordal reference), the correspondence between this passage in *Les Noces* and that at No. 22 in the final movement of the *Symphony of Psalms* (Example 49b) becomes striking. Even if we, in Example 49b, interpret the A♭–E♭–B♭–F series of "fourths" defined by the encircling (F E♭) (B♭ A♭) units of the (F E♭ D C B♭ A♭) hexachord as a subdominant-tonic-dominant relation with the E♭–B♭ "fourth" centric in this interpretation or in a possible C-scale-on-E♭ or even "key-of-E♭-major" determination, this in no way qualifies the resemblance. For pitch organization remains fundamentally the same in these passages. Two melodic fragments, G–F♯–E–D–A–(G) in *Les Noces* and E♭–D–C–D–(E♭) in *Psalms*, are repeated (or move back and forth) ostinatolike. Pitch number 2, the G of the (A G F♯ E D C) hexachordal reference in *Les Noces*, the E♭ of the (F E♭ D C B♭ A♭) hexachord in *Psalms*, presides with a degree priority as the point of departure and return. These two reiterating fragments are superimposed over a basso ostinato in which the encircling (0 2) (7 9) units of the respective (0 2 3 5 7 9) hexachords are exposed as a 9–2–7–0 series of 5s or "fourths": a C–G–D–A succession with respect to the (A G F♯ E D C) hexachord of *Les Noces*, (A♭)–E♭–B♭–F with respect to the (F E♭ D C B♭ A♭) hexachord of *Psalms*. (Note the opening G/C (2/9) "fifth" of *Les Noces*, which corresponds to the opening E♭/A♭ (2/9) "fifth" of *Psalms*, although A♭, as pitch number 9, is not part of the ostinato pattern of *Psalms* but is merely sustained in the altos and cellos.) Upon successive repeats of these melodic fragments, the point of departure, the G in *Les Noces* and the E♭ in *Psalms*, takes on an altered harmonic complexion as a result of the variance in rhythmic-metric periods defined by these fragments and the ostinati below. The variance allows for a different "sounding together" on each occasion, although this inconstancy in vertical (or "harmonic") coincidence is local within the self-enclosed framework, in which each of the "fourth"-related elements stands in a fixed or polarized "opposition," and assumes a degree of "equal weight and independence."

(In other words, in *Psalms*, the rhythmic-metric period of the reiterating E♭–D–C–D–(E♭) fragment is three half-note beats, while that of the E♭–B♭–F–B♭–(E♭) basso ostinato is four. Hence the periods contradict each other; that is, they allow for a different (E♭/E♭), (E♭/B♭), or (E♭/F) "sounding together," a different harmonic complexion upon successive repeats. To quote again from Pierre Boulez in regard to the second of our two types of rhythmic-metric construction (as surveyed already in chapters 4, 5, and 6): "Stravinsky . . . utilized the system of superimposed rhythmic periods. . . . The linkings of these several superimpositions will not be reproduced at the same intervals, but so as to obtain a varied disposition."[10] But since, in these two conflicting periods in *Psalms*, 3 + 3 + 3 + 3 and $4+4+4$ equal 12, the "varied disposition" here, the inconstancy in vertical coincidence (or in harmonic complexion) is short-lived, sabotaged by the return of the first "sounding together," which assumes the role of a point of departure and return, and hence that of a norm in coincidence, both vertical and rhythmic-metric. Hence, too, local inconstancy or irregularity in vertical coincidence leads, in the the long run, to constancy, self-enclosure, deadlock, and stasis.)

That fundamental ambiguity of pitch-class priority in (0 2 3 5 7 9) hexachordal contexts manifested in regard to its encircling (0 2) (7 9) units or their 0–7–2–9 "fifth" or 9–2–7–0 "fourth" articulation, an ambiguity striking in *Histoire* but evident to a degree in all previously examined (0 2 3 5 7 9) contexts, seems again very much the point in the opening blocks of *Agon*'s "Pas de quatre." (See Example 49c.) Here again, as in the passages from *Les Noces* and the *Symphony of Psalms*, pitch number 2, the C of the (D C B A G F) hexachordal collection at mm. 1–5, presides in the trumpet as the reiterating point of departure; here again, an opening (2/9) "fifth," C/F of the (D C B A G F) hexachord, qualifies this priority of pitch number 2; here again, with signpost-like simultaneities at mm. 7 and 19, pitch numbers 0, 2, 7, and 9 of this (0 2 3 5 7 9) hexachordal reference, (D C) (G F) as the (0 2) (7 9) encircling units of the (D C B A G F) hexachord, are singled out for special emphasis; and here again, this special emphasis is conveyed by means of an 0–7–2–9 "fifth" articulation, but one that does not entirely deprive the (0 2) (7 9) units of a degree of whole-step cohesion. (Thus, the F/G (7/9) "sounding together" in the oboe and english horn at m. 7; or the D/C (0/2) and F/G (7/9) proximities in the concluding simultaneity at m. 60.)

Further, the opening blocks of *Agon* at mm. 1–7 are accounted for in terms of the two (0,7) "fifth"-related (0 2 3 5 7 9) hexachords (D C B A G F) and (A G F♯ E D C), accounted for, first, in terms of a "downward" transposition of the opening (D C B A G F) hexachord to (A G F♯ E D C) at mm. 5–7; and then, at m. 7, in terms of a transposition back to the initial (D C B A G F) hexachord. Thus, the opening C–B–A–B–C–D–B–A fragment in the trumpet is a (D C B A) tetrachord, the "upper" (0 2 3 5) tetrachord of the opening (D C B A G F) hexachordal collection; and this (D C B A) tetrachord is transposed "down" to (or is answered by) the F♯–E–G–A succession in the first horn at mm. 5 and 6, the "upper" (0 2 3 5) tetrachord of the adjacent (A G F♯ E D C) hexachord.

Moreover, it seems not the least whimsical to indicate (1) that the F♯–E–G–A–C and E–F♯–D–C successions in the horns at mm. 5–7 (accountable to the (A G F♯ E D C) hexachord) approach the octave C at m. 6 in a manner suggesting the II–I cadential formula so prevalent in Medieval and early Renaissance music of the fourteenth and fifteenth centuries; (2) and that this II–I formula, implicated by these F♯–E–G–A–C and

E–F♯–D–C successions in the horns, is further embellished, once again in relation to (D C B A G F) and its presiding C, by both the "double leading-tone" and "Landini" cadential inflections, the F♯ inflecting the "double leading tone," the terminating A/D–C/C approach to the octave C (or the A–C "gap" of the (A G F♯ E D C (A)) hexachord) inflecting (or accommodating) the "Landini cadence."[11]

In other words, a correspondence or accommodation manifests itself here—fairly obviously in this observer's judgment—between certain (0 2 3 5 7 9) hexachordal implications—specifically, "fifth"-related (0 2 3 5 7 9) hexachords and the A–C "gap" of the (A G F♯ E D C) hexachord—and certain cadential formulae of Medieval or early Renaissance music. And so these (0 2 3 5 7 9) referential implications, once peculiarly "Russian," are introduced in *Agon* to accommodate Renaissance voice-leading formulae, giving portions of that work a subtle neo-Renaissance quality. Indeed, the accommodation is not unlike so many others pursued rather more persistently on behalf of neoclassicism. We allude here, specifically, to pitch numbers 3 and 6, which, notwithstanding their potential envisioned in Model A as (0,3,6,9) symmetrically defined partitioning elements, are often Classically conceived as chromatic tendency tones or "melodic leading tones." This tendency-tone potential is available to each of the four triads of the octatonic collection, Model A.

Finally, we may note in Example 49c that the reiterating C–D–F–G–B–C fragment in the flutes and cellos of *Agon*'s Interlude continue to reflect—with that "missing" pitch number 10, the E—(0 2 3 5 7 9) hexachordal reference in terms of (D C B A G F). Thus, pitch number 2, the C in the trumpet, still presides as the point of departure and return, and the encircling (0 2) (7 9) units, (D C) (G F) here, are accorded a degree of whole-step cohesion. But the D–B span in the C–D–F–G–B–C fragment persists in the sections that lie ahead, and acquires, with respect to its registral spacing here, a certain *survival* priority. Joined by the B♭–D♭ reiteration in the timpani, this D–B unit prompts a form of octatonic Collection I (Model A) and diatonic (0 2 3 5 7 9) hexachordal or C-scale-on-C interaction. This is a form of octatonic-diatonic interpenetration, harboring certain C-scale tonally functional overtones (however parenthetical), which is peculiarly neoclassical. And so we can best address ourselves to subsequent sections of *Agon* within the context of either Stravinsky's neoclassicism or his early serialism, orientations whose special attributes we have yet to consider.

SOME GENERAL CONSIDERATIONS

The shoestring economics of the original *Histoire* production kept me to a handful of instruments, but this confinement did not act as a limitation, as my musical ideas were already directed toward a solo-instrumental style. My choice of instruments was influenced by a very important event in my life at that time, the discovery of American jazz. . . . The *Histoire* ensemble resembles the jazz band in that each instrumental category—strings, woodwinds, brass, percussion—is represented by both treble and bass components. The instruments themselves are jazz legitimates, too, except the bassoon, which is my substitution for the saxophone. . . . The percussion part must also be considered as a manifestation of my enthusiasm for jazz. I purchased the instruments from a music shop in Lausanne, learning to play them myself as I composed. . . . My knowledge of jazz was derived exclusively from copies of sheet music, and as I had never actually heard any of the music performed, I borrowed its rhythmic style not as played, but as written. I *could* imagine jazz sound, however, or so I liked to think. Jazz meant, in any case, a wholly new sound in my music, and *Histoire* marks my final break with the Russian orchestral school in which I had been fostered. [*Expositions and Developments*, pp. 102–03.]

Jazz—blanket term—has exerted a time-to-time influence on my music since 1918, and traces of blues and boogie-woogie can be found even in my most "serious" pieces, as, for example, in the *Bransle de Poitou* and *Bransle simple* from *Agon* [1957] and in the *pas d'action* and *pas de deux* (middle section) from *Orpheus* [1947]. In 1918 Ernest Ansermet, returning from an American tour, brought me a bundle of ragtime music in the form of piano reductions and instrumental parts, which I copied out in score. With these pieces before me, I composed the *Ragtime* in *Histoire du soldat*, and, after completing *Histoire*, the *Ragtime* for eleven instruments [1918]. The *Histoire* ragtime is a concert portrait, or snapshot of the genre—in the sense that Chopin's *Valses* are not dance waltzes, but portraits of waltzes. The snapshot has faded, I fear, and it must always have seemed to Americans like very alien corn. If my subsequent essays in jazz portraiture were more successful, that is because they showed awareness of the idea of improvisation, for by 1919 I had heard live bands and discovered that jazz performance is more interesting than jazz composition. I am referring to my non-metrical pieces for piano solo [Piano-Rag-Music, 1919] and clarinet solo [1919] which are not real improvisations, of course, but written-out portraits of improvisation. [*Dialogues and a Diary*, p. 87.]

The Eight Easy Pieces [for piano duet, 1915–17] were composed in Morges [Switzerland]—the Polka, March, and Valse just before *Renard*, in 1915, the others after the completion of that burlesque. I wrote the Polka first, as a caricature of Diaghilev, whom I saw as a circus animal-trainer cracking a long whip. . . . I played the Polka to Diaghilev and Alfredo Casella in a hotel room in Milan in 1915, and I remember how amazed both men were that the composer of *Le Sacre du printemps* should have produced such a piece of popcorn. For Casella a new path had been indicated, however, and he was not slow to follow it; so-called neoclassicism of a sort was born in that moment. But Casella was so genuinely enthusiastic about the Polka that I promised to write a little piece for him, too. This, the March, was composed immediately on my return to Morges. A little later I added the ice cream wagon Valse in

homage to Erik Satie, a souvenir of a visit with him in Paris. . . . The other five
pieces were composed as music lessons for my children Theodore and Mika.
[*Dialogues and a Diary*, pp. 72–73.]

While we have in this chapter seen fit to situate the diatonic and octatonic-
diatonic passages of *Histoire*'s "Soldier's March" and music to Scenes I and
II within the context of Stravinsky's "Russian" period, *Histoire* is still to be
acknowledged as a highly eclectic endeavor. As such, it partakes, in reality, of both "Russian" and neoclassical peculiarity. There is, to begin with,
the opening "tooling tune" of the "Soldier's March," with its suggestion
of a C-scale-on-D reference (or D-major-scale reference) at No. 5. The
"Soldier's March" and music to Scenes I and II, following condensed
(near) repeats, are succeeded by a C-scale-on-Bb (or pseudo-Bb-major)
reference in the "Royal March," with its "snippets of early nineteenth-
century Italian opera and corny Spanish figurations."[12] The "Royal
March" is followed by three stylized dance schemes (or dance "portraits"
as Stravinsky calls them; see the quotation above), the "Tango," "Waltz,"
and "Ragtime." These dances are in turn followed by two chorales, "Little" and "Great," but *pseudo* in that they, too, are stylized as ritual, being
"portraits" or "snapshots" of the authentic German-Protestant model.

And so *Histoire* is really a crossroads piece. While its initial sections are
distinctly "Russian" (with special reference to their (0 2 3 5 7 9)
hexachordally conceived ostinati, or to the (0 2 3 5) tetrachordal articulation in Scene II, both diatonic and octatonic-diatonic), later sections
clearly encompass peculiarities already a part of the neoclassical initiative.
Thus we detect a hint, in *Histoire* as a whole, of a Stravinsky increasingly
restless within the confines of his uniquely fashioned "Russian" musical
thought, increasingly eager to strike out from this terrain, increasingly
open to alternatives. This, in retrospect, need not be surprising. For he
had already composed somewhat similarly in 1915. Introducing the
"Polka" of his *Eight Easy Pieces* for piano duet (1915–17) to Diaghilev and
the Italian composer Alfredo Casella in February 1915, he was aware, as
he later recalled (see quotation above), that "a new path had been indicated"; that "neoclassicism of a sort" had been born. And "the suggestion
that was to lead to *Pulcinella*" (1920)—Stravinsky's first full-scale neoclassical ordeal, a recomposition of selections from the trio sonatas and operas
of the early eighteenth century Italian composer Giambattista Pergolesi,
later acknowledged as his "discovery of the past, the epiphany through
which the whole of my late work became possible"—lay just around the
corner. The "suggestion" here was Diaghilev's. It came on a spring afternoon in 1919, as the two strolled along the Place de la Concorde in Paris.
("Don't protest at what I am about to say," Diaghilev is reported to have
said. "I know you are much taken by your Alpine [Swiss] colleagues . . .
but I have an idea that I think will amuse you more than anything they can

propose. I want you to look at some delightful eighteenth-century music with the idea of orchestrating it for a ballet.")[13]

There is also the jazz element, an idiom with which Stravinsky had familiarized himself through sheet music provided by his "Alpine colleague" Ernest Ansermet, and whose impact, apart from the *Ragtime* itself, may be felt in *Histoire*'s jazzlike instrumental grouping of small ensemble and percussion. (Minus the saxophone, however. Stravinsky disliked its heavy, swelling vibrato, and opted for the bassoon instead.) This jazz element points, in turn, to an eclectic strain in Stravinsky's music, an eclecticism different in kind from the many "influences" or "backward looks" that characterize neoclassicism (as noted already in chapter 3), transcending, as well, the familiar distinctions that separate the "Russian," neoclassical, and serial orientation categories or "stylistic" trends. It points to the curious manner in which, so often in Stravinsky's music, a confrontation of opposites is posed, resulting in a melange or composite of (seemingly) conflicting or irreconcilable musical genres or "styles," an awkward, disjointed kind of disparity or incongruity.[14] For example: *Petroushka*'s blend of authentic Russian folk melodies and contemporary chansons; the insertion in the first tableau of a popular Russian "street song" (for which Stravinsky was reproached by his friend Andrei Rimsky-Korsakov, who questioned his right to use such "trash").[15] Or Diaghilev and Alfredo Casella, listening to Stravinsky's "Polka" in 1915, astonished that "the composer of *Le Sacre du printemps* should have produced such a piece of popcorn." Or that "traces of blues and boogie-woogie" should be found in some of Stravinsky's most "serious" ventures: in *Agon* (1953–57), and in the pas d'action and pas de deux of *Orpheus* (1947).[16] Or that, indeed, a piece like *Oedipus Rex* (1927), for so long judged the very pinnacle of neoclassical aspirations, "high neoclassicism at its highest" and most austere, should likewise partake of this freakish, eclectic strain. For while observers—to take but one example from *Oedipus*—have pointed to the grand, "triumphant," "monumental" effect of Creon's aria "Respondit Deus" at Nos. 27 and 40 in Act I, Stravinsky himself casually likened the passage to a Folies Bergères tune, venturing some stage directions: "The girls enter, kicking." His own description of the "raw material" of this pinnacle of neoclassical art reads as follows:

> Much of the music is a *Merzbild*, put together from whatever came to hand. I mean, for example, such little games as the offbeats at No. 50 and the Alberti-bass horn solo accompanying the Messenger. I also mean the fusion of such widely divergent types of music as the *Folies Bergères* tune at No. 40 ("The girls enter, kicking") and the Wagnerian 7th-chords at Nos. 58 and 74. I have made these bits and snatches my own, I think, and of them a unity. "Soule is form," Spenser says, "and doth the bodie make."[17]

This Merzbild quality, the merging of "widely divergent types of music," is as much a part of *Histoire* as it is of *Petroushka, Oedipus,* or *Agon.* The marching tunes of the opening "Soldier's March" are "related to clichés common to European art music," "clichés" followed, however, by a forlorn "sigh" in Scene II, among Stravinsky's most poignant utterances. But poignancy is followed, in turn, by a pompous "Royal March" composed of "snippets" of Italian opera and "corny Spanish figurations"; "snippets" and "figurations" are followed by the burlesque of the three contemporary dances; and the dances followed in turn by two stylized "snapshots" of a German-Protestant chorale. (And all transmitted by an ensemble with percussion closely resembling a jazz band from New Orleans.) Of course, as in *Oedipus,* a unity is forged. From this "raw material" a new reality emerges, something, again, peculiarly Stravinsky's own. But we are at the same time not unmindful of how strange this "unity" must have seemed in 1918; indeed, in the wake of the post-Romantic era, how outlandish a concoction to all "serious" musicians and audiences. For who had ever heard of such a thing? How was one to react to this music? Was it to be taken seriously? Was Stravinsky serious? And herein lies *Histoire's* endearing charm and fascination: deadly serious. Quite possibly because, as Wilfrid Mellers has so eloquently remarked, Stravinsky composed ritual, but ritual of a peculiar sort. Indeed, under both the "Russian" and neoclassical labels, often a kind of mock ritual; a cool, crisp, brittle mechanization of the musical manners or conventions—and hence, presumably, of the underlying beliefs, sanctities, and spiritualities—of bygone or nearly bygone eras. Cool, crisp, and brittle ("cold" and "heartless"; without sentiment), evidently as if to accentuate the circumstance of our removal, the fact that we the listeners—enlightened, self-conscious Modern Man—are painfully cut off, unable to partake as true believers. It is this felt removal from true participation—from true "letting go," as the theory has it—that somehow accounts for Stravinsky's pertinence, his contemporary guise. And while philosophical conjecture of this sort remains quite peripheral to our discussion, it may be that in our more descriptive lines an indication as to the meaning or relevance of these contentions is allowed.

Then, too, linked to *Histoire* as a crossroads piece—or as an eclectic excursion—is its instrumental compression. For *Histoire* marks Stravinsky's "final break" with the nineteenth-century Russian orchestral school in which he had been "fostered" (see the quotation at the outset of this subtitle), and seals, at the same time, the raw, "solo instrumental style" toward which his invention had been inclining since 1914. It was the "discovery of American jazz" (the "sound" of jazz, its small ensemble and percussion), along with the experience of *Histoire* (in which the effects of this "discovery" are initially felt), that ultimately sealed the instrumental fate of *Les Noces.* For the preoccupation with percussion here dramatically reduced the orchestral cloak in which *Les Noces* had first been conceived, leading in 1918–19 to that abandoned version for two cimbaloms, harmonium, pianola, and percussion (requiring five players), and then to the final "perfectly homogeneous, perfectly impersonal, and perfectly mechanical" settlement for four pianos and percussion in 1923.

But the "master orchestrator" who would seem with such certainty to lurk behind conceptions like *Petroushka* and *Histoire*, the composer who always "orchestrated while he composed" (whatever the preliminary sketch routine),[18] the inventor of novel instrumental blends or groupings with, at the same time, an uncanny feeling for the sound capabilities of individuals, the breathing of woodwinds, the bowing of strings, the hammering of the cimbalom, the bashing of a cymbal—this "master" has drawn unexpected criticism, and of a more fundamental type than that propagated by critics of revisions like the "new" *Petroushka* of 1947 (briefly alluded to in chapter 3). With particular reference to *Pribaoutki* and *Histoire*, this sensitivity has been viewed, by critics like Pierre Boulez, as a fetish, a perversity, a tyrannical "tic" flexed as an "end in itself," a "tic" flexed at the expense of musical substance (a substance which, while scintillating in instrumental garb, might alarm by its poverty when transcribed for piano); all of this revealingly to be compared to a composer like Anton Webern, for whom, on the contrary, "the idea of timbre is almost abstract," Webern having cared not at all about "the physical conditions of sound-emission."[19] No doubt Stravinsky would have responded as he had when questioned about his "manners" in *Oedipus*: that it was impossible for him to separate the manner of saying something from what was said, that "the manner of saying and the thing said are, for me, the same."[20] And, indeed, given the nature of this intimacy, this felt inseparability of substance from instrumental transmission, from "the physical conditions of sound-emission" (or, giving "substance" the edge, assuming that it rather than these "physical conditions" is more likely to prompt, direct, or guide), Boulez's argument seems fanciful, naive. For even if the naked substance of Stravinsky's music (whatever this can mean, given this intimacy) presupposed instrumental perception of a kind quite different from that experienced by Webern, can this legitimately constitute grounds for reproach? Assuming that Stravinsky was no mere predator of "effect"? Assuming that he did in fact have something to say (in pieces like *Pribaoutki* and *Histoire*)? (But can Webern have been all that indifferent to "timbre" or to "the physical conditions of sound-emission"? In a piece like the *Concerto for Nine Instruments*?) One is far more apt to marvel at the physical aspect of Stravinsky's musicality, the magnificent nonabstractness of his methods, the application of this extraordinary intimacy. "I am no mystic," he exclaimed; "I need to touch music as well as to think it, which is why I have always lived next to a piano."[21] And that is also why, after his "discovery of American jazz," he purchased the instruments at a store in Lausanne, and learned to play them as he composed. By the end of 1918 his studio bulged with a "cuisine" of percussion instruments, a cimbalom, a harmonium, and a pianola. "I had packed all of the instruments into my little musical pantry and learned to play all of them myself, spending as much time practicing them, in fact, and tinkering with and tuning the cymbalom, as I did composing. . . . Risky as my memory is, too, in matters of dates and places, I am certain of the position of each of the instruments of this little orchestra in my room, which must be because my acoustical reality . . . is part of my biological reality."[22]

What ultimately astonishes most about Stravinsky's "instrumental invention" (given his reputation as a "master orchestrator") are the stunning limitations imposed from one context to the next, the restraint pursued, the always apparent and enviable ability "to make do." Except perhaps for some early pieces like the *Scherzo fantastique* and *Fireworks*, this "invention" is distinguished not by a taste for the exotic, extravagant, or ostentatious, but by these limited courses of action; in addition to a truly remarkable diversity and ingenuity in instrumental grouping (so evident in a piece like *Agon*, for example), the persuasive manner in which selective ensembles persevere, and hence, again, this manifest ability "to make do" and the restrictions that seem always to have been a necessary preamble to composition. These are scarcely the symptoms of an orchestral playboy. Rather, they bespeak a profound fluency, a rare and miraculous faculty, a "sixth sense."

Still, some of the more specific idiosyncracies in orchestral or instrumental "touch" relate intricately to rhythmic-metric concerns, and to the necessity, imposed by these concerns, for a crisp, exact, and percussive articulation of the "musical substance." This brings us, quite fittingly, to the subject of the chapter which follows.

EIGHT
RHYTHMIC (OR METRIC) INVENTION

When I was nine my parents gave me a piano mistress. I very quickly learned to read music, and, as the result of reading, soon had a longing to improvise, a pursuit to which I devoted myself, and which for a long time was my favorite occupation. . . . I must say that my constant work at improvisation was not absolutely fruitless; for, on the one hand, it contributed to my better knowledge of the piano, and, on the other, it sowed the seed of musical ideas. Apropos of this, I should like to quote a remark of Rimsky-Korsakov's. . . . I asked him whether I was right in always composing at the piano. "Some compose at the piano," he replied, "and some without a piano. As for you, you will compose at the piano." As a matter of fact, I do compose at the piano and I do not regret it. I go further; I think it is a thousand times better to compose in direct contact with the physical medium of sound than to work in the abstract medium produced by one's imagination. [*An Autobiography*, p. 5.]

Often he came early to the theatre before a rehearsal began [*The Firebird*, 1910] in order to play for me over and over again some specially difficult passage. . . . It was interesting to watch him at the piano. His body seemed to vibrate with his own rhythm; punctuating staccatos with his head, he made the pattern of his music forcibly clear to me, more so than the counting of bars would have done. That rhythm lived in, at times took possession of, his body became evident to me as I watched him through the familiar intercourse of the following years. [Tamara Karsavina, "A Recollection of Stravinsky," p. 8.]

Instead of starting work on *Pulcinella* directly, I returned to Morges [June 1919], and finished a piano piece I had begun some time before with Artur Rubinstein and his strong, agile, clever fingers in mind. I dedicated this *Piano Rag Music* to him. I was inspired by the same ideas, and my aim was the same, as in *Ragtime* [1918], but in this case I stressed the percussion possibilities of the piano. What fascinated me most of all in the work was that the different rhythmic episodes were dictated by the fingers themselves. My own fingers seemed to enjoy it so much that I began to practice the piece; not that I wanted to play it in public—my pianistic repertoire even today [1935] is too limited to fill a recital program—but simply for my personal satisfaction. Fingers are not to be despised: they are great inspirers, and, in contact with a musical instrument, often give birth to subconscious ideas which might otherwise never come to life. [*An Autobiography*, p. 82.]

A real composer is not one who plays first on the piano and writes down what he has played. . . . A real composer conceives his ideas, his entire music, in his mind, in his imagination, and he does not need an instrument. [*Arnold Schoenberg Letters*, ed. Edwin Stein, trans. Eithne Wilkins and Ernst Kaiser (New York: St. Martin's Press, 1965), p. 218.]

[Apropos the *Violin Concerto in D*, 1931.] When he is working, Stravinsky is always in a hypersensitive state. Everything that occurs seems to be magnified. At first I was astonished at how slowly he worked. He often composes at the piano, intensely concentrated, grunting and struggling to find the notes and chords he seems to be hearing. I was amazed that so complex a score as *Le Sacre* was composed like this. [Samuel Dushkin, "Working with Stravinsky," p. 184.]

All my life I have tried out my music as I have composed it, orchestral as well as any other kind, four hands at one keyboard. That way I am able to test it as I cannot when the other player is seated at another piano. When I took up the Concerto again [*Concerto for Two Pianos*, 1935], after finishing the *Duo Concertante* [1932] and *Perséphone* [1934], I asked the Pleyel company to build me a double piano, in the form of a small box of two tightly-wedged triangles. I then completed the Concerto in my Pleyel studio, test-hearing it measure by measure with my son Soulima at the other keyboard. [*Dialogues and a Diary*, p. 74.]

I stood behind him [December 1947] and watched the short, nervous fingers scour the keyboard, searching and finding the correct intervals, the widely-spaced chords and the characteristically Stravinskyan broad melodic leaps. His neck, his head, his whole body accentuated the ingenious rhythmical design of the music by spasm-like bobs and jerks. He grunted, he hummed, and occasionally stopped to make an aside. . . .
  "See the fugue here," he would say, pointing to the beginning of the Epilogue [*Orpheus*, 1947]. "The two horns are working it out, while a trumpet and a violin in unison sing a long, drawn-out melody, a kind of *cantus firmus*. Doesn't this melody sound to you like a medieval *vièle* (a Viol)? Listen. . . ." And his fingers would start fidgeting again on the keyboard. [Nicolas Nabokoff, "Christmas with Stravinsky," p. 152.]

In July 1948, in Colorado where he had gone for concerts, Stravinsky unveiled the first *Rake* music he had composed. Then back in Hollywood he also played the movements of the *Mass* I did not know, the *Credo*, *Sanctus*, and *Agnus Dei* (these last three parts dated from the previous winter; the *Kyrie* and *Gloria* had been composed as long before as 1944). Though I have been similarly privileged a hundred times since with other preview auditions of new Stravinsky music, the impression of that first performance of his at the piano is the most memorable. The pages were unbound; the last ones were still ink-wet, in fact, and had to be held or clipped to a music rack above the keyboard. Stravinsky, as soon as he started to play, was aroused to a state of great excitement. The performance was anything but smooth. I was supposed to play treble parts, or vocal parts in treble octaves, but was unable to keep from getting ahead. Stravinsky sang the solo parts one, two and even three octaves below notation in a deep and tremulous non-voice. He also sang during the purely instrumental music, or groaned with impatience at his incapacity to realize the full score at the piano. [Robert Craft, "A Personal Preface," p. 8.]

R.C.: The musical idea: when do you recognize it as an idea?

I.S.: When something in my nature is satisfied by some aspect of an auditive shape. But long before ideas are born I begin work by relating intervals rhythmically. This exploration of possibilities is always conducted at the piano. Only after I have established my melodic or harmonic relationships do I pass to composition. Composition is a later expansion and organization of material. [*Conversations with Stravinsky*, p. 11.]

R.C.: What do you regard as the principal performance problems of your music?

I.S.: Tempo is the principal item. A piece of mine can survive almost anything but wrong or uncertain tempo. . . . The stylistic performance problem in my music is one of articulation and rhythmic diction. Nuance depends on these. Articulation is mainly separation. . . . I have also labored to teach [musicians] to accent syncopated notes and to phrase before them in order to do so. (German orchestras are as unable to do this, so far, as the Japanese are unable to pronounce "L.") In the performance of my music, simple questions like this consume half of my rehearsals: when will musicians learn to abandon the tied-into note, to lift from it, and not to rush the sixteenth notes afterwards? [*Conversations with Stravinsky*, p. 135.]

R.C.: Meters. Can the same effect be achieved by means of accents as by varying the meters? What are bar lines?

I.S.: To the first question my answer is, up to a point, yes, but that point is the degree of real regularity in the music. The bar line is much, much more than a mere accent, and I don't believe that it can be simulated by an accent, at least not in my music. [*Conversations with Stravinsky*, p. 21.]

New York Review of Books: And the other performances [at the New York Philharmonic Stravinsky Festival, Summer 1966]?

I.S.: The character of articulation in my music eluded most of the conductors, even in so simple a point as that the metrical lines are constituent to the rhythm, not mute, inglorious markers which the conductor is invited to ignore for the sake of something he calls the phrase. [*Retrospectives and Conclusions*, p. 43.]

Despite transient influences undergone, the rhythmic forms of Stravinsky are the product of our occidental musical evolution; they develop in realizing European metric concepts; they have become embodied thanks only to the fruitful convention of the bar. . . .

Nothing is fecund save the strife versus the obstacle, there is no creation save the action of overcoming resistance. . . . Stravinsky has never destroyed the measured bar; he struggles against it, he disarticulates it, he multiplies and hooks up the different metres, but he never permits himself once, and for good and all, to get rid of this bothersome fiction, for he needs the annoyance, the resistance, against which to leap and surge, for there is no rhythmic diversity without stability. [Boris de Schloezer, "An Abridged Analysis," p. 59.]

New York Review of Books: Debussy predicted that you would "tolerate no music as an old man," Mr. Stravinsky.

I.S.: But I love more music than ever before. . . . He [Debussy] also referred to me, I think in the same letter, as a "primitive" and "instinctual," rather than a "schooled," composer. And he was right. Like Ramanujan, who did his mathematics without formal mathematical education, I have had to depend on "natural" insight and instinct for all the learning I would have acquired if I had taken a Ph.D. in composition, except that I would have flunked the finals and never taken it. [*Retrospectives and Conclusions*, p. 75.]

New York Review of Books: But in your own mind, Mr. Stravinsky?

I.S.: My "mind" does not count. I am not mirror-struck by my mental functions. My interest passes entirely to the object, the thing made; it follows that I am more concerned with the concrete than the other thing, in which, as you see, I am easily muddled. And in the first place I do not regard composition as more of a mental function than a sensual pleasure. "Lascivious pleasing" is a famous description of the performance of a—very chaste, it would seem to us—lute song, and performances are but pale memories of creative acts. In music, as in love, pleasure is the waste product of creation. [*Retrospectives and Conclusions*, p. 48.]

New York Review of Books: Did you fly in from California, Mr. Stravinsky? How was it?

I.S.: Some "turbulence" interfered with the in-flight movie, and the pilot made an announcement that has stuck in my mind ever since. He said that the IBM flight plan had chosen 33,000 feet as the favored altitude, but that in his opinion we should be higher. This touchingly obsolete criticism of computer authority shocked me, I confess, and I sincerely hope that the relationships of men and their computerology (and, conversely, the computerology of men and their relationships) become more trusting. Part of my shock may also have come from the contrast of computerized flight control itself, and my memories of the Homeric air age of Saint-Exupéry and his contemporaries, who were guided at times by little more than their own apprehensions. But the principal part was due to the circumstance that in my own work I regard my feelings as more reliable than my calculations.

N.Y.R.: Would you explain the distinction, Mr. Stravinsky?

I.S.: It was probably an empty one, or, like the distinctions between analytical and empirical truths and learned and innate behavior, one not admitting of a very sharp line of separation. Our calculations and our feelings obviously overlap, or are congruent. I will persist, nevertheless, and say that I trust my musical glands above the foolproofing of my musical flight charts, although the flight charts are formed in part by the same glands; and add that I prefer to exercise the "free"option of my ear, rather than submit to a punch-card master plan. [*Retrospectives and Conclusions*, pp. 13–14.]

R.C.: Music an "abstraction," you say? "Music is powerless to express anything at all?"—what did you mean by that much-quoted remark? Don't you agree that music is a communicative art, in Cassirer's sense of the symbolic forms, and therefore *purely* expressive?

I.S.: That overpublicized bit about expression (or non-expression) was simply a way of saying that music is suprapersonal and superreal and as such beyond verbal meanings and verbal descriptions. It was aimed against the notion that a piece of music is in reality a transcendental idea "expressed in terms of" music, with the *reductio ad absurdum* implication that exact sets of correlatives must exist between a composer's feelings and his notation. . . . A composer's work *is* the embodiment of his feelings and, of course, it may be considered as expressing or symbolizing them—though consciousness of this step does not concern the composer. More important is the fact that the composition is something entirely new *beyond* what can be called the composer's feelings. And as you mention Cassirer, doesn't he say somewhere that art is not an imitation, but a discovery, of reality? Well, *my* objection to music criticism is that it usually directs itself to what it supposes to be the nature of the imitation—when it should be teaching us to learn and to love the new reality. A new piece of music *is* a new reality.

(On another level, of course, a piece of music may be "beautiful," "religious," "poetic," "sweet," or as many other expletives as listeners can be found to utter them. All right. But when someone asserts that a composer "seeks to express" an emotion for which the someone then provides a verbal description, that is to debase words *and* music.) . . .

R.C.: A question about forms and meanings. . . .

I.S.: Excuse me for interrupting, but I would like to remind you that composers and painters are not conceptual thinkers; what a Picasso or Stravinsky has to say about painting or music is of no value whatever from *that* side. (We do certainly love *talking* conceptually, though.) The composer works through a perceptual, not a conceptual, process. He perceives, he selects, he combines, and he is not in the least aware at what point meanings of a different sort and significance grow into his work. All he knows or cares about is his apprehension of the contour of the form, for the form is everything. He can say nothing whatever about meanings. What is it that Shakespeare's French Lord says in *All's Well That Ends Well*? "Is it possible he should know what he is. . . ." [*Expositions and Developments*, pp. 114–16.]

I.S.: If the real end of academicism is knowledge itself, as I think it is, then, academically speaking, I know very little. Though I have worked all my life in sound, from an academic point of view I do not even know what sound is. . . . My knowledge is activity. I discover it as I work, and I know it while I am discovering it, but only in a very different way before and after.

R.C.: How do you think the development of information theory in music might affect your art?

I.S.: I have always been interested in the theory of games (since a childhood reading of Cardano, in fact), but this has not meant anything to me as a composer or ever helped me at Las Vegas. I realize that choice is an exact mathematical concept, and that I ought to be looking beyond the particular example for the process that generated it (even though the particular example is all that matters to me). . . . But though I am confident these explanations would enlighten me, I am even more confident they would not help me to compose. My attitude is merely proof that I am not an intellectual, and therefore problems of explanation are of no very great interest to me. To borrow G. E. Moore's example—"I do not see how you can explain to anyone who does not already know it, what 'yellow' is"—I do not see any means of explaining why I have chosen a certain note if whoever hears it does not already know why when he hears it. [*Memories and Commentaries*, p. 108.]

R.C.: You say that you are a doer, not a thinker; that composing is not a department of conceptual thinking; that your nature is to compose music and you compose it naturally, not by acts of thought or will. A few hours of work on about one third of the days of the last fifty years have produced a catalogue which testifies that composing is indeed natural to you. But how is nature approached?

I.S.: When my main theme has been decided I know on general lines what kind of musical material it will require. I start to look for this material, sometimes playing old masters (to put myself in motion), sometimes starting directly to improvise rhythmic units on a provisional row of notes (which can become a final row). I thus form my building material. [*Conversations with Stravinsky*, p. 12.]

R.C.: What is theory in musical composition?

I.S.: Hindsight. It doesn't exist. There are compositions from which it is deduced. Or, if this isn't quite true it has a by-product existence that is powerless to create or even to justify. Nevertheless, composition involves a deep intuition of "theory." [*Conversations with Stravinsky*, p. 12.]

R.C.: Will you offer any cautions to young composers?

I.S.: I would warn young composers, Americans especially, against university teaching. . . . The numerous young people on university faculties who write music and who fail to develop into composers cannot blame their university careers, of course, and there is no pattern for the real composer, anyway. The point is, however, that teaching is academic (Webster: "Literary . . . rather than technical or professional. . . . Conforming to . . . rules. . . .) [*Conversations with Stravinsky*, p. 153.]

New York Review of Books: Have you any late-hour prescriptions for a young composer, Mr. Stravinsky?

I.S.: If he can turn an honest million outside music he might seriously consider neglecting his talents for a time and turn it. Otherwise, and untempted by all lesser sums, he should go directly underground and do nothing but compose: that is, not strive for Foundation awards, academic prizes, college presidencies, foreign fellowships; not attend culture congresses; not give interviews; not prattle on the radio about music appreciation; not review new scores (except his own, pseudonymously); and not push, prompt, maneuver, advertise, finagle, operate. [*Retrospectives and Conclusions*, p. 44.]

Intellectual man had become an explaining creature. Fathers to children, wives to husbands, lecturers to listeners, experts to laymen, colleagues to colleagues, doctors to patients, man to his own soul, explained. The roots of this, the causes of the other, the source of events, the history, the structure, the reasons why. For the most part, in one ear, out the other. The soul wanted what it wanted. It had its own natural knowledge. It sat unhappily on superstructures of explanation, poor bird, not knowing which way to fly. [Saul Bellow, *Mr. Sammler's Planet* (New York: The Viking Press, 1969), p. 3.]

One had to learn to distinguish. To distinguish and distinguish and distinguish. It was distinguishing, not explanation, that mattered. Explanation was for the mental masses. Adult education. The upswing of general consciousness. A mental level comparable with, say, that of the economic level of the proletariat in 1848. But distinguishing? A higher activity. [Bellow, *Mr. Sammler's Planet*, p. 63.]

If the speculative philosopher is at the same time a believer, as is also affirmed, he must long ago have perceived that philosophy can never acquire the same significance for him as faith. [Johannes Climacus, *Concluding Unscientific Postscript*, ed. S. Kierkegaard, trans. David F. Swenson and Walter Lowrie (Princeton: Princeton University Press, 1947), p. 53.]

After all, the denial of intentionality, however desirable in explication, is hardly a becoming social activity for the composer himself with respect to his own work, at least in the privacy of his own thoughts. But such is our music-conceptual world that, where popular "explainers" freely invoke as revelatory the "intentions" of inaccessible or incoherent composers, composers themselves sometimes plead "non-intentionality" in confronting discoveries or inquiries about their works, and refuse to take advantage of "privileged access" to reveal what they consider to be the crucial coherence-gambles taken by them. Indeed, there is even a tendency to criticize those who are willing so to articulate their motives as somehow—to take only the cogent aspect of such objections—likely to *overdetermine* the observer's ascriptions of coherence. But this is a worry whose implementation by reticence hardly bespeaks a decent respect for the critical or discriminative capacities of one's colleagues and auditors, a disrespect that would seem to make even more incomprehensible the apparently simultaneous confidence that, nevertheless, one's work will be appropriately received and understood—and even *more* appropriately received and understood—in the absence of "inside" conceptual or descriptive assistance. [Benjamin Boretz, "Meta-Variations, Part IV: Analytic Fallout (II)," pp. 190–91.]

We apprehend and acknowledge the *physical* nature and appearance of Stravinsky's musicality. "I am no mystic; I need to touch music as well as to think it, which is why I have always lived next to a piano."[1] Evidently, then, the piano was never really a pianist's piano (although it might occasionally be necessary to indulge, if not for financial compensation then in order that the percussive articulation of the musical structures be demonstrated). Nor, evidently, was its use restricted to a constant tuning of the ear, a constant testing "measure by measure." The piano appears, first and foremost, to have serviced an instinctual, biological need to be physically at one with music, to be physically engaged in the invention and expression of music, to articulate, always, physically. And so we see that, in contrast to Arnold Schoenberg's bleak proposal (cited above), improvisation was not to be belittled or discredited: "fingers . . . are great inspirers, and, in contact with a musical instrument, often give birth to subconscious ideas which might otherwise never come to life." Indeed, during and following Stravinsky's cautious adoption of serial techniques, composition continued at the piano (the reliance may have intensified), and was preceded, as always, by "relating intervals rhythmically," an "exploration of possibilities . . . always conducted at the piano."[2] The preference for a muted or "muffled" instrument, a kind of neutral or "uncommitted" medium, was no contradiction. Neutralizing the piano, the muting removed some of its (in most cases) irrelevant or distractive "pianism," helped keep the ear fastened to—or from straying from—an instrumental or orchestral hearing. (Or so we hypothesize. For Stravinsky orchestrated while he composed. And it is often the case, when dealing with a musical score away from the piano, that one's contextual and instrumental bearings are disrupted with any sudden injection of "pianism." But the muted piano might also have relieved Stravinsky's dread of eavesdropping—affronts, evidently, to the privacy of his "exploration of possibilities.")

And the "auditions" with Robert Craft: trancelike fumblings, murmurings, gruntings, groanings, gropings! Musical invention and expression appear for Stravinsky to have been uncompromisingly involuntary, "instinctual," impulsive—inward, spiritual, passionate, and utterly subjective inclinations. Hence, too, inscrutable. Stravinsky recoiled from systematic "explanation," felt ill at ease and often annoyed with conscious analytic-theoretical reckoning. The message forbade it: if not debased or defrauded by verbal (metaphorical) description, it was trivialized by formal, analytic-theoretical, explanatory hardware.

Of course, one might pursue analytic-theoretical study in response to—or on behalf of—immediate, urgently felt, creative needs. (A kind of *in the act* or "on-behalf-of" pursuit.) But a compulsion to regurgitate digested foodstuffs, to systematically retrace one's steps, to probe the mystery formally, to "push, promote, maneuver, advertise, finagle, operate," or publicize critical or explanatory, "conceptual" analytic-theoretical thought (a distilled, disembodied, disassociated, processed information) as a kind of semi-autonomous intellectual activity (on behalf of one's own or someone else's music)—all this appears to have been acutely alien to this mentality, perhaps a waste of time, a real bore, a drag. "I care less about my 'works' than about composing."[3]

But perhaps not even a drag, not even a simplification or a form of introspection that might ruinously confuse, distract, or numb the "innate" taste buds, the cherished inward certainty of the immediate, subjective response; perhaps, too often, misguidance, a misunderstanding of the artistic endeavor and its special appeal. Present-day thinkers to the contrary, the perceptual-conceptual, practice-theory, sensual-intellectual, innate-learned, doer-thinker dichotomies remained for Stravinsky meaningful distinctions. "I regard my feelings as more reliable than my calculations." And: while "our feelings and our calculations obviously overlap . . . I will persist, nevertheless, and say that I trust my musical glands above the foolproofing of my musical flight charts, although the flight charts are formed in part by the same glands; and add that I prefer to exercise the 'free' option of my ear, rather than submit to a punch-card master plan." Of course, "we certainly love *talking* conceptually." But: "The composer works through a perceptual, not a conceptual, process." And so Stravinsky fancied himself a "natural," an "innate," "instinctual," non-schooled, immensely *self*-disciplined composer; he imagined himself a "doer," never "mirror struck" by his "mental functions." (How divine a gift: "I am not mirror struck by my mental functions. My interest passes entirely to the object, the thing made.") And so it is to be supposed that he would not have sensed the urgency of Benjamin Boretz's plea for a continuing analytic-theoretical dialogue, for "inside conceptual or descriptive assistance"—a plea possibly directed at "indeterminacy" or "chance," but an eloquently reasoned rebuttal to Stravinsky's attitude (or "mentality") nonetheless. Stravinsky might have countered that such "assistance" is as apt to confuse, befuddle, or mislead as it is to illuminate, or have countered with his: "I do not see any means of explaining why I have chosen a certain note if whoever hears it does not already know why when he hears it." Even if the benefits or rewards of analytic-theoretical endeavor lay not so much in formal ("conceptual") "explanation" or "justification" (as he suggests), but, rather, in the process itself, in the seeking better to hear and understand, in the attempt to bring oneself closer to the music and to "take-possession-of" (a process in which the conceptual and perceptual boundaries cannot even be felt to overlap, but are, indeed, meshed and indistinguishable), then, just possibly, such pedagogical pursuits were the business of interested parties, certainly not of Stravinsky. Although he might occasionally intervene to avert or correct gross distortion (as an interpreter or observer), his works could not be salvaged, or rendered more credible or palatable, by analytic-theoretical reckoning, by "inside conceptual or descriptive assistance," however rigorous, ingenious, or well-intentioned.

Hence, too, the advice to young composers: shun the institutions, the foundations, the culture "supermarkets," the universities, the Ph.D. programs. Especially the universities: their propaganda, publicity, matters of standardized prestige; their institutional programming, crediting; their processed, packaged, sterile information; processed, sterile, systematized, conceptualized Systems, Methods, Rules, "academicism." What did they know? What *could* they know? For, here again, the mechanism was possibly not so much wasteful or distractive. It was, it seems, misguidance. It embodied a misconception of the true nature of the artistic plight, of inspiration, invention, and creation. (Then, too, Stravinsky found formal teaching awkward, possibly a bit comic. His contribution could come only in the form of how *he* would have done it. And intellectual gossip aside, just who, in his/her right mind, could—or would—benefit from this?[4] Nor was it possible for him, in his words, to be a "part-time composer" without compromise, without shirking the real obligation, or without a degree of artful deceit.)

Stravinsky might have found himself congenially at ease with Saul Bellow's Artur Sammler.[5] Mr. Sammler, too, is ever "alert to the peril and disgrace of explanations. . . . Arguments! Explanations! . . . All will explain everything to all, until the next, the new common version is ready. This version, a residue of what people for a century or so say to one another, will be, like the old, a fiction." Then, too, "so many false starts, blind alleys, postulates which decayed before the end of the argument. . . . A running out of certainties. . . . Explanation was for the mental masses. Adult education. . . . It was distinguishing, not explanation, that mattered. . . . A higher activity." There are surely few who could depart from Stravinsky's "conversations" and interviews, or from Robert Craft's diaries, unmindful that it was "distinguishing" that mattered to Stravinsky too, that this was "a higher [intellectual] activity," one pursued with relish, often with formidable insight and (apparent) ease. Like Sammler (or Saul Bellow), Stravinsky might have found Johannes Climacus arresting, urgent: that fundamental incommensurability so powerfully chiseled between the objective spirit of the speculative philosopher, of the intellectual inquirer or "explainer" (a spirit yielding only "approximation-knowledge," approximations and uncertainties leading only to further approximations and uncertainties), and the inward spirituality of the existing subject, a spirituality which properly defies direct communication (revealing itself through the "double reflection"), and to which adheres "all essential decisiveness" and ethical conduct (nondeception). "The more objective the contemplative inquirer, the less he bases an eternal happiness, i.e., his eternal happiness, upon his relationship to the inquiry; since there can be no question of an eternal happiness except for the passionately and infinitely interested subject."⁶

RHYTHMIC (OR METRIC) INVENTION (I)

But the physical imprint of Stravinsky's musicality harbors other implications. It harbors a rhythmic (or metric) invention—or inventiveness—which has seemed, above all else, to identify Stravinsky in the minds of the public. Indeed, in the wake of this century's heightened awareness of such invention, it represents the stamp of his originality, his unique contribution, his little "niche" in Music History.

Stravinsky manifested himself in these rhythmic (or metric) matters as a counterpuncher. That is to say, he sailed against the tide, moved against the grain. Or, as Hans Keller puts it, he swam "up-stream"⁷ His material encompassed—built-in, so to speak—a reference both to the progressive, developmental, forward-moving upbeat tendency or flow of our modern Western tradition (rhythm), *and* to this tradition's "background," down-beating "square metrical dance schemes" against which this upbeat flow was set in motion (meter). Stravinsky sadistically (or "sado-masochistically," as Keller puts it) contradicted or reversed the upbeat flow with-stressed, "unmitigated, unprepared and unresolved" *downbeats*. Hence the overall (in the long run) static, non-progressive effect of the invention. But hence, too, the tension: the stressed downbeating contradicted the upbeat grain, producing, again in Keller's words, *"retrograde tension,"* a "retrograde version of the upbeat."

Hence, too, the physicality of it all; the incentive for an active, physical engagement; the prompting of those "spasm-like bobs and jerks"; or that telling habit of beginning work by "relating intervals rhythmically." Or, correspondingly, the need for a crisp and exact articulation, for staccato unison doublings of legato lines, for the unprecedented stress signification, for all those indications of $sf>p$ and *ben marcarto*. There could be no confusion in matters of articulation. Confusion—flowing sluggishness or rubato—foretold certain death, a fiasco, a misapprehension of the musical structure. A stressed, downbeating $sf>p$ on an upbeat (e.g., a stress on an unaccented beat or pulse of the meter, assuming a degree of metric regularity) had to be discerned and forcefully articulated as such; one had to *feel* the downbeating upbeat, *feel* the contradiction, *feel* the friction, the sparks, and "lift from it." If not, the point was lost. The whole thing fell apart.

Still, there is more to it than this. The invention is possibly more subtle, more intricate, more ingenious. Stravinsky vented not only the "background," downbeating "square metrical dance schemes," but the suppressed, forward-moving upbeat tendency as well. He would in fact often introduce the latter as a point of departure, and then, impulsively (or sadistically) contradict or reverse. And so the rhythmic (or metric) invention of which we speak involved the subtle, intricate, ingenious (and often elaborately concealed) forging of a contradiction or reversal in the upbeat/downbeat identity of reiterating fragments, simultaneities, configurations. Or, more dramatically still, the forging of such displacement not in terms of the conventional upbeats and downbeats (the unaccented and accented or "weak" and "strong" beats of the meter), but in terms of off-the-beat/on-the-beat elements, in terms of a syncopation, a stressed off-the-beat element subsequently contradicted by a (felt) on-the-beat appearance (and regardless of metric irregularity, which, by accommodating the contradiction, might ultimately conceal it). So, too, the invention is as melodic, formal, or "harmonic," as it is rhythmic (or metric). For it has as much to do with a suppleness in the melodic invention—or in the melodic repetition—that lends itself to such upbeat/downbeat or off-the-beat/on-the-beat contradictions or reversals (a suppleness which nonenthusiasts have irreverently—or irrelevantly by missing the point—labeled "melodic poverty"); it has as much to do with abrupt block juxtaposition, a form or architecture brought into being by these contradictions or reversals (the effect of which is statically to arrest the forward-moving upbeat flow, these contradictions or reversals being in essence rhythmic-metric-identity *polarities*); and it has as much to do with a pitch organization which, referentially octatonic, diatonic, or octatonic-diatonic, in complementary fashion accommodates these contradictions or reversals, by way of all those examined nontonal conditions of balance, equilibrium, equal weight and independence, opposition, harmonic stasis, and deadlock. More specifically, it has as much to do with the confounding non-expression of—and consequent ambiguity with respect to—pitch-class priority.[8] Indeed, one could legitimately contend that our hearing and understanding of pitch organization, just as it encompasses or presupposes methods (or notions) of superimposition, abrupt block juxtaposition, and repetition, encompasses or presupposes the rhythmic (or metric) invention of which we now speak. Further, one could contend that any analytic-theoretical reckoning of its rhythmic-metric organization is, at the same time, a reckoning of its rhythmic-metric organization; or, correspondingly, that to invent new rhythmic-metric structures—as has here been alleged—is to invent new and different musical structures, new pitch organizations.[9]

Nonetheless, we shall here be endeavoring to find a perch between this exhilarating (and highly reassuring) conviction and Boulez's opposing view that the rhythmic-metric structure does assume a "life of its own" which can legitimately and usefully be isolated.[10] Thus, while we isolate and disengage, we shall not be tempted into supposing that the tactic can work to our advantage—or make any sense at all—if applied entirely in the abstract (i.e., without reference to pitch organization generally). Hence, in references to "separate" or "independent" rhythmic-metric periods we apply the quotation marks.

Indeed, we return briefly to some observations of Boulez cited earlier.

> Stravinsky also utilized the system of superimposed rhythmic pedals—that is to say, his polyphonic apparatus being made up to some degree of clearly characterized stages, he gives each of them an independent rhythmic period. The linkings of these several superimpositions will not be reproduced at the same intervals, but so as to obtain a varied disposition. There you have the chief lesson that [Olivier] Messiaen has helped us to learn from Stravinsky.[11]

True enough, of course. The rhythmic (or metric) invention may be approached—or may appear to manifest itself—in two dimensions: (1) the single (linear) dimension, the repetition of a rhythmic-metric period assigned to a single reiterating fragment, line, or part; (2) the multiple (linear *and* vertical) dimension, the registrally fixed repetition of fragments, lines, or parts which repeat according to *varying* and hence "separate" or "independent" rhythmic-metric periods, "the linkings" of which, given this variance, "will not be reproduced at the same intervals, but so as to obtain a varied disposition."

Thus, in the first of the *Three Pieces for String Quartet* (Example 31a in chapter 5), we may, apropos of the single dimension, examine the first violin part: a registrally fixed fragment repeats according to a stable period of twenty-three quarter-note beats, in which there is a smaller "rhythmic-cell" division of $11 + 6 + 6$. But apropos of the multiple dimension, this stable period of twenty-three quarter-note beats is superimposed on other reiterating fragments whose rhythmic-metric periods conflict "so as to obtain a varied disposition," an inconstancy in vertical (or "harmonic") coincidence. In the *Symphony of Psalms* at No. 22 in the final movement (Example 30c in chapter 4), the reiterating Eb–D–C–D–(Eb) fragment defines a stable period of three half-note beats to which the meter is adjusted. But this period is superimposed over an Eb–Bb–F–Bb–(Eb) basso ostinato with a "separate" or "independent" period of four half-note beats.

Still, the single dimension may apply to "whole structures" or configurations where the periods of the reiterating fragments do not vary but coincide unvaryingly. For example: the stretch of 7/4 measures in *The Firebird*'s Finale, Example 11 in chapter 1; "Jeu du rapt" at Nos. 46–48 in *Le Sacre*, as examined by Boulez; "Jeux des cités rivales" at No. 57 in *Le Sacre*, Example 30a in chapter 4; "Danse sacrale" in *Le Sacre*, as examined by Boulez;[12] the opening blocks at Nos. 0 and 1 in *Les Noces*, Example 33 in chapter 6; or the opening block at No. 0 in the *Symphonies of Wind Instruments*, Example 53a in this chapter. It is precisely in such cases—where the rhythmic (or metric) invention proceeds en masse, with the reiterating fragments sharing the same rhythmic-metric periods as defined by the meter (and hence synchronized unvaryingly in vertical (or "harmonic") coincidence)—that we are apt to encounter pronounced metric irregularity, the most abrupt and extensive changes in meter, the most overt kind of metric disruption. While, conversely, it is in cases where the invention proceeds by means of a superimposition of *varying* rhythmic-metric periods, which vary "separately from" or "independently of" one another (so as to effect a vertical coincidence which is inconstant, constantly changing), that Stravinsky is apt to hold fast to a steady meter, or perhaps to a steady varying meter (which will generally reflect one of the varying periods). For example: the accumulatively climactic Nos. 10–12 in the Introduction of *Le Sacre*, Example 27 in chapter 4; Nos. 64–71 in "Jeux des cités rivales" to the end of "Cortège du sage" in *Le Sacre*, where, as examined in Example 30b, chapter 4, the 4/4 and 6/4 meters persevere despite the conflicting and highly "mobile" periods of the horn and tuba fragments; the steady varying 3/4 + 2/4 + 2/4 meter in the first of the *Three Pieces* which corresponds to the stable period of the cello fragment, Example 31a in chapter 5; the block at Nos. 68–70 in *Les Noces*, Example 38 in chapter 6; No. 3 in the final movement of the *Symphony of Psalms*, Example 53e in this chapter; or, again, No. 22 in the final movement of *Psalms*, Example 30c in chapter 4.

This distinction embodies, as indicated already in chapters 4, 5, and 6, two usefully distinguishable types of rhythmic-metric construction, with respect to which the meter serves altered purposes. (This is not to suggest, of course, that the meter is any *less* significant in one case or the other, or that Stravinsky's insistence that his meters were always "much, much more" than "mere" accented beats is any less applicable to one case or the other. But only that, in the first of these rhythmic-metric types, we shall indeed be indicating that there are numerous instances where the irregular meter appears to conceal the "true" irregularity, the displacement, the contradiction or reversal in upbeat/downbeat or off-the-beat/on-the-beat accentuation, while it nonetheless—and, of course, not in the least paradoxically—intensifies the consequent ambiguity in rhythmic-metric identity.)

Still, it is to be noted that doubt, uncertainty, or confusion in the rhythmic-metric identity of a reiterating fragment may arise in contexts adhering to both of these rhythmic-metric types. And it is, of course, the rather subtle contention here that such doubt, uncertainty, or confusion is *necessarily* felt with reference to past rhythmic (or metric) invention, past rhythmic-metric habits and conventions, past regular metric periodicity; that, indeed, the reference is deliberate and is built into the structure irrespective of metric irregularity with respect to the first of these types, or of the varying, "separate" or "independent" rhythmic-metric periods with respect to the second; and that, furthermore, the reference pertains to "Russian" music as much as it does to neoclassicism—Boulez and *Le Sacre* (or portions of *Le Sacre, Three Pieces*, and *Les Noces*) notwithstanding.

In other words, it is here the contention that, in cases of metric irregularity (the first of our two rhythmic-metric types), a norm (or norms) in rhythmic-metric identity will sooner or later materialize with reference to some "background" regular metric periodicity; or, in cases reflecting the second of our two types, that while the "separate" or "independent" rhythmic-metric periods conflict so as to effect a degree of inconstancy in vertical coincidence, a norm (or norms) in this respect—and hence with respect to rhythmic-metric identity—will sooner or later materialize. Such norms reflect familiar upbeat/downbeat or off-the-beat/on-the-beat patterns of past, regular metric periodicity, the "square metrical dance schemes." Hence, doubt, uncertainty, or confusion in rhythmic-metric identity typically imposes itself in the form of (felt) upbeat/downbeat or off-the-beat/on-the-beat contradictions or reversals. And so metric irregularity with respect to the first of our two rhythmic-metric types (type 1), or inconstancy in vertical coincidence (the varying, "independent" rhythmic-metric periods) with respect to the second of these types (type 2), is often, in the long run, sabotaged (or reconciled). This is not to suggest, again, that Stravinsky's metric irregularity is "fake." Indeed, not to comply would be equally to miss the point. Only, the duty of such irregularity is often to intensify the contradiction or reversal in rhythmic-metric identity, a displacement which it thus conceals with a degree of deceit hinging on how acutely attuned the listener may be to the past, conventional rhythmic-metric patterns upon which apprehension of the concealment depends. All of this is again meant to suggest that, notwithstanding metric irregularity at mm. 5–20 in the opening "Soldier's March" of *Histoire*, $6+3+3$ and $4+4+4$ both equal 12; or, notwithstanding the two "separate" or "independent" rhythmic-metric periods at No. 22 in the final movement of the *Symphony of Psalms*, $3+3+3+3$ and $4+4+4$ both equal 12.

HISTOIRE DU SOLDAT (1918) AND RENARD (1916)

This brings us back to *Histoire du soldat*. For if, as Wilfrid Mellers contends, the material here consists of "clichés common to European art music," or, in the "Royal March," of "snippets of early nineteenth-century Italian opera and corny Spanish figurations," the question is posed: just what can the attraction be? And the answer must surely be that it rests with this subtle, intricate forging of an upbeat/downbeat contradiction or reversal in the rhythmic-metric identity of the material or ideas; with, naturally, a suppleness in the melodic invention in its response to this contradiction and consequent ambiguity; and in the further collaboration of pitch organization in the forging of this contradiction and ambiguity. (Perhaps little has been said here. Perhaps merely that the attraction rests with the "musical structure," or merely that contradictions or ambiguities are forged. This forging manifests itself, in the rhythmic-metric sphere, in terms of upbeat/downbeat or off-the-beat/on-the-beat contradictions or reversals; melodically in terms of a suppleness that yields to such contradictions or reversals; harmonically—or as regards pitch organization generally—in terms of a partitioning of the octatonic and diatonic collections that generates, in complementary fashion, conditions of equilibrium, equal weight and independence, opposition, polarity, and deadlock; and formally in terms of an abrupt juxtaposition of heterogeneous blocks of material. This form likewise implies a within-block static "downbeating," or implies that a contradiction or reversal is expressed in rhythmic-metric identity, in terms of the upbeat/downbeat or off-the-beat/on-the-beat implications of the material or ideas at hand. In other words, we may perceive the interaction as such, that to speak of symmetrically defined conditions of equilibrium, equal weight and independence, polarity, opposition, or deadlock—and hence conditions of contradiction and ambiguity—in pitch organization, is to suggest or imply that such conditions exist, or may be defined, with respect to other realms or dimensions of musical thought. Nonetheless, we persist.)

Thus, in Example 50a, we reexamine the trumpet's opening "tootling tune" of the "Soldier's March" at mm. 15–20.[13] This marching tune is su-

Example 50a: "The Soldier's March"

perimposed, appropriately enough, over a nearly unceasing basso ostinato, a marching beat or pulse with a stable rhythmic-metric period of two
quarter-note beats. This 2/4 marching period immediately guarantees the
listener a "square metrical dance scheme," a downbeating frame of reference or "pedal" against which the fragmentary "tootling tune" is set in motion. As for this setting in motion, we may spot the terminating
B–C♯–D–(E) upward sweep of the tune at mm. 16–17—or the first 3/8
measure at m. 16—as the troublemaker.

Or, rather, as the potential—or possibly projected—troublemaker. For
here at mm. 15–20 (Example 50a), the terminating upward sweep—the
first 3/8 measure—is followed by another 3/8 measure; and 3 + 3 equal 6.
Moreover, with the 3/4 measure at m. 14, 6 + 3 + 3 equal 12. Hence the two
successive 3/8 measures and the earlier 3/4 measure cancel each other out.
The coming-to-rest of the "tootling tune" on the E/A "fifth" on the first
beat at m. 17—the second 3/8 measure—may be felt as an *off*-the-beat
coming-to-rest, as a syncopation in relation to the ostinato's steady 2/4
period. (See the brackets in Example 50a, which refer to this "background" steady 2/4 periodicity of the ostinato pattern, and according to
which the passage is rebarred below.) Hence, despite metric irregularity,
the pattern is conventional: a guaranteed "square metrical dance
scheme"—the ostinato—and a flowing, upbeat "tootling tune." Hence, no
real metric disruption, no contradiction or reversal affecting the
rhythmic-metric identity, the upbeat/downbeat or off-the-beat/on-the-
beat implications, of the "tootling tune."[14]

The same is true of the reoccurrence of the marching tune's B–C♯–

Example 50b

D–(E) upward sweep at No. 7, mm. 45–46. (See Example 50b.) Despite the preserved 3/8 measure of the upward sweep at m. 45, the syncopated, *off*-the-beat identity of the E/A coming-to-rest on the first beat of the following measure—m. 46 here—holds fast.

But further on, at mm. 49–50, this identity is contradicted. (Example 50b.) For while the 3/8 measure of the upward sweep again perseveres (with reinforcing stress signification), the coming-to-rest on the E/A "fifth" at m. 50 may now be felt—in accord with the ostinato's steady 2/4 pulse (in accord with regular 2/4 metric periodicity, as bracketed and rebarred below)— as an *on*-the-beat coming-to-rest, not as a syncopated, *off*-the-beat coming-to-rest as at m. 17 and m. 46. Consequently, a contradiction is forged: the rhythmic-metric identity of the terminating B–C♯–D–(E) upward sweep—with reference, as always, to the ostinato's steady 2/4 pulse—is contradicted, reversed. Classically—for the maneuver assumes classic implications in Stravinsky's music—a felt syncopation is displaced, becoming a felt *on*-the-beat element. This reversal is preceded—and hence to a degree prepared and reinforced—by off-the-beat/on-the-beat reversals in the clarinet fragment at mm. 45–48. Indeed, the sixteenth-note clarinet fragment—a (E G♯ B)–(F♯ A♯ C♯) triadic reiteration—suffers far more insistently from off-the-beat/on-the-beat ambiguity, and poses for itself not even an "identity crisis"; it is in this respect wholly schizophrenic. For its on-the-beat takeoffs are invariably followed—and hence contradicted or reversed—by off-the-beat takeoffs. And so the clarinet fragment exhibits no discernible norm in rhythmic-metric identity in relation to the ostinato's steady 2/4 pulse. Its (exploited) suppleness yields multiple norms: an on-the-beat norm and an off-the-beat norm.[15]

Finally, at No. 8—or at mm. 50–57 (Example 50c), the two contradictory rhythmic-metric identities of the marching tune's upward sweep are fused, presented successively in a final tutti summation. In the first occurrence at mm. 52–53, the initial (and perhaps normal) off-the-beat identity is restored: despite the 3/8 measure, the coming-to-rest on the first beat at m. 53 may be felt, in accord with the ostinato's steady 2/4 pulse, as an off-the-beat coming-to-rest, a syncopation. But this off-the-beat identity is promptly followed by the contradiction or reversal at mm. 56–57, where, again in accord with the ostinato's steady 2/4 periodicity (as bracketed and then rebarred below), the E/A coming-to-rest assumes a felt on-the-beat identity.

Yet it may be prior to the contradiction—indeed, already at m. 54—that giddy doubt and confusion arise. Indeed, the on-the-beat contradiction at m. 57 may not even be felt as such. For we are—or at least this observer is—rhythmic-metrically "lost" at this point. The contradictions and reversals have become so persistent and the highly irregular stress in the per-

Example 50c

cussion (not shown in Example 50c) have wrought such additional havoc, that the steady 2/4 frame of reference of the ostinato itself is challenged.

Needless to say, remarkable. The "play": subtle, intricate, ingenious. And ultimately the stuff of which *Histoire* is made. For while we may always wish to respect, feel, and articulate the preserved "foreground" integrity of the 3/8 measure (or the 3/8 "metric cell") of the marching tune's upward sweep (indeed, not to comply would be equally to miss the point), it is, at the same time, all but impossible to remain oblivious to these "background" contradictions which this "foreground" irregularity accommodates—but ultimately *conceals*.

Similar circumstances are encountered in the opening passage of the "Royal March," mm. 1–10. (See Example 51a.) While Stravinsky begins with what is conventionally—and later actually materializes as—a stressed off-the-beat chord, here the impulse has been to "phrase" or measure it as a stressed *downbeat* in an opening 5/8 measure.[16] But the real "play" surfaces later at No. 1 (at m. 10). Here, this introductory passage is concluded *on* the stressed off-the-beat chords, which, by means of an irregular 5/8

Example 51a: "Royal March" (*Histoire du soldat*)

measure at m. 9, have been forced *on* the beat at m. 10. And so a stressed *off*-the-beat attack in mm. 1–9 becomes a stressed *on*-the-beat attack at m. 10, the classic contradiction or reversal. Of course, the stressed on-the-beat reversal at m. 10 is also a 5/8 measure. And so there is some cancelling-out here, some sabotage. The extra eighth-note beat of the second 5/8 measure enables the trumpet fragment to be felt as commencing quite conventionally off the beat. But the conclusion of this passage—or, in terms of its C-scale on B♭ or pseudo-B♭-major reference, its pseudo-cadence—comes nonetheless *on* the reversal, *on* the off-the-beat attacks which have been forced *onto* the beat.[17]

Finally, we reexamine the opening passage of *Renard* (Example 51b). Here, the irregular 5/8 measure at m. 5 is the troublemaker. But again, it may not be felt as such. Or it is not even really "the point." For the point is that it accommodates and reinforces, but also *conceals*, two potent contradictions. The first has to do with the over-the-barline, *off*-the-beat identity of the terminating G–B♭–C figure in the opening tenor fragment at mm. 3–4, which, when answered by the C–E♭–F figure in the bass at m. 6, is contradicted and reversed, becoming a (felt) *on*-the-beat figure (notwithstanding the preceding 5/8 troublemaker which, with its extra eighth-note beat, conceals this "background" contradiction or reversal by giving it the same barred off-the-beat identity as at mm. 3–4). The second contradiction, while of the same variety and pertaining to the first, is more subtle and far-reaching. The 5/8 measure at m. 5, with its extra eighth-note beat, generates titillating doubt and uncertainty as to the off-the-beat/on-the-beat identity of the clarinet's entrance at m. 7. Of course, this ambiguity has been prepared all along; it is built into the structure. For while we may

Example 51b: *Renard*

be unmindful of the fact, *Renard*'s basso ostinato begins with a crossing of the barline. Consequently, its "true" or stable rhythmic-metric identity is not revealed, and does not really fall into place, until *after* the 5/8 measure. Hence the rhythmic-metric displacement or "dislocation"—of which commentators have been prone to speak when addressing themselves to such matters—is, again, a form of off-the-beat/on-the-beat contradiction or reversal. And while we may always wish to feel and articulate the "foreground" 5/8 measure at m. 5, its immediate, metrically irregular 5/8 "phrasing" is not really the point. Rather, it accommodates and reinforces—but also harbors and conceals—the classic Stravinskian contradiction or reversal on two fronts: the *off*-the-beat G–B♭–C figure over the barline at mm. 3–4, which, in accord with regular 2/4 metric periodicity (bracketed in Example 51b and then rebarred accordingly below), is later at m. 6 contradicted or reversed as an *on*-the-beat C–E♭–F figure; and, more critically, the prompted uncertainty with respect to the off-the-beat/on-the-beat identity of the clarinet's entrance at No. 1 (m. 7). Without the "play"—without the (felt) rhythmic-metric ambiguity at No. 1 (m. 7)—this opening passage would be severely impoverished. And so the reader must allow him/herself to feel and articulate the clarinet fragment at No. 1 as an *on*-the-beat fragment (as barred), and then as a syncopated, *off*-the-beat fragment. Such an exercise can sharpen an awareness of concealed contradiction in rhythmic-metric identity, and of that suppleness in the melodic invention—or repetition—that so pliantly succumbs to the displacement, all of this constituting an invention tellingly Stravinskian.

RHYTHMIC (OR METRIC) INVENTION (II)

But there is still more to it than this. These contradictions or reversals in the upbeat/downbeat or off-the-beat/on-the-beat identity of reiterating fragments, simultaneities, or configurations cannot be the whole of it. Indeed, in this initial uncovering of what seemed immediately so potent—if concealed, and often elaborately so—an integral part of the invention has been overlooked: the nature and purpose of the concealment itself. For if the point of all this "play" were to reside solely with these (concealed) contradictions or reversals, the question would arise: what can be the purpose of respecting, however peripherally, Stravinsky's "foreground" metric irregularity? Why should *not* to comply with this irregularity be—as has here been insisted—"equally to miss the point"? Or, to rephrase the query: if concealed contradictions or reversals examined in the opening "Soldier's March" of *Histoire* are indeed "the stuff" of which this piece is made, why should Stravinsky have troubled himself with the shifting meter? With that irregular 3/8 measure of the marching tune's B–C♯–D–(E) upward sweep? Why not bar throughout according to the stable 2/4 period of the basso ostinato, and hence according to regular 2/4 metric periodicity, the "square metrical dance scheme" here (as defined by the brackets in Example 50a, b, and c), a barring or periodicity which would conveniently have exposed the very contradictions or reversals here deemed the heart of the matter? In other words: why bar, accentuate, "phrase" *against* these displacements? Why seek to run counter? Why *conceal*?

The answer would seem to be that Stravinsky—fiendishly, sadistically—wished it *both ways*. That he sought, on the one hand, to contradict or reverse the upbeat/downbeat or off-the-beat/on-the-beat consequences of his material (which naturally presupposes regular metric periodicity, even if of the "background" sort, as bracketed in Examples 50a, b, and c), and that he sought, on the other hand, to counter the effect of these contradictions or reversals by pressing—nonetheless—for a fixed rhythmic-metric identity in repetition. And so the rhythmic (or metric) invention of which we speak involved the forging of upbeat/downbeat or off-the-beat/on-the-beat contradictions or reversals. But subtle, intricate, and ingenious inasmuch as this forging entailed an element of counteraction, an effort to further confound the issue by pressing for a rhythmic-metric "sameness" in the repetition of a fragment, simultaneity, or configuration (often, in effect, a static, downbeating kind of "sameness"); to compose, indeed, as if the "repetition" were rhythmic-metrically genuine. Hence our determination to respect, feel, and articulate "foreground" metric irregularity (since by so doing we acknowledge this counteracting, opposite side of the invention's double edge). Hence our conclusion that not to comply would be "equally to miss the point." And hence Stravinsky's frequently voiced dissatisfaction with conductors or "interpreters" who, ignoring this "foreground" irregularity, fell prey "to something [they called] the phrase." This "phrase" doubtless encompassed "background" (concealed) regular metric periodicity, with respect to which the metrically irregular elements were interpreted as syncopations, an approach which naturally left the other side of the invention's double edge—static, downbeating "sameness"—unacknowledged.

Indeed: counteraction is applied—rhythmic-metric "sameness" preserved—by means which vary in accord with our two types of rhythmic-metric construction. Thus, in the opening "Soldier's March" of *Histoire*, Stravinsky opts in part for the first of these types. And with the consequence that "sameness," a fixed rhythmic-metric identity for the marching tune's B–C♯–D–(E) upward sweep, is preserved by metric irregularity, by holding fast to the same irregular 3/8 measure regardless of whether, in relation to the stable 2/4 rhythmic-metric "pedal" of the basso ostinato (and hence in relation to "foreground" or "background" regular metric periodicity as bracketed in Examples 50a, b, and c), the E/A coming-to-rest of this terminating upward sweep is heard and understood, on the opposite side of the invention's double edge, as a syncopated, *off*-the-beat element subsequently contradicted and reversed as an *on*-the-beat element.[18]

In the block at Nos. 64–71 in *Le Sacre* as examined earlier in chapter 4 (Example 30b), Stravinsky bars according to the second of our two rhythmic-metric types, according to steady 4/4 and 6/4 meters which persevere in spite of the varying, "independent" rhythmic-metric periods of the reiterating fragments in the horns and tubas. And so here with the consequence that "sameness" in repetition (a fixed rhythmic-metric identity for the horn's A–D–C–D fragment upon successive repeats) is preserved not by metric irregularity (not by shifting the meter, in other words), but by fixed stress and slur markings (the A being always stressed, the D–C–D unit always slurred), and regardless of whether, in relation to the "foreground" 4/4 meter, these A–D–C–D repeats are heard and understood as effecting a reversal in upbeat/downbeat accentuation. (See, in conjunction with Example 30b, our earlier commentary in chapter 4. Or the reader may consult Example 53e in this chapter for an analysis of the block at No. 3 in the final movement of the *Symphony of Psalms*, a block which also conforms to the second of our two rhythmic-metric types.) Consequently, while the means in these illustrations vary according to rhythmic-metric type, the ends—the nature of the "play" itself with its double edge or "both ways"—seem very much the same. Our conclusion might be that the distinctions embodied by these rhythmic-metric types are less pronounced than might at first be imagined, that the double edge or "both ways" endows each with fundamentals remarkably similar in overall effect.

So, too, in summary, that Stravinsky's rhythmic (or metric) invention may reflect, in outward appearance or application, one of the two types outlined here and in previous chapters: the first having to do with metric irregularity, the second with a steady meter. But that when these types are more closely examined from the standpoint of the repetition itself, an underlying double edge imposes itself: a contradiction or reversal in the accentual implications of a reiterating fragment, and then an element of counteraction which subverts this displacement by pressing for a rhythmic-metric "sameness" in fragmental repetition. So, too, in continued summary here, that despite marked differences in design, each of these types is to an extent implicated by the other. For the forging of upbeat/downbeat or off-the-beat/on-the-beat contradictions or reversals *always* implies regular metric periodicity, whether "background" (concealed) as with type 1, or "foreground" and hence barred as with type 2. The preservation of a rhythmic-metric "sameness" in repetition—often a static, downbeating "sameness"—suggests the reverse: metric irregularity, whether "foreground" as with type 1, or acknowledged merely by fixed stress and phrase (or slur) markings as with type 2. (In other words, the means by which the double edge is imposed reverses itself according to rhythmic-metric type.)

In the summary diagram of Example 52 these two types of rhythmic-metric construction are viewed as varying means by which the critical double edge is administered, demonstrated with reference once again to the "Soldier's March" of *Histoire* and the block at Nos. 64–71 in *Le Sacre*. Adhering to the first of our rhythmic-metric types (1), the contradiction or reversal affecting the off-the-beat/on-the-beat identity of the B–C♯–D–(E) termination in *Histoire*'s "Soldier's March" is concealed by metric irregularity, its apprehension thus being dependent on "background" regular metric periodicity as implied by the stable 2/4 period of the basso ostinato (and as bracketed in Examples 50a, b, and c); at the same time rhythmic-metric "sameness" in the repetition of the B–C♯–D–(E) upward sweep is preserved by "foreground" metric irregularity, by holding fast to the same irregular 3/8 measure upon successive B –C♯–D–(E) repeats. Adher-

	Type 1	Type 2
Contradiction or reversal in repetition	"background" (concealed) regular 2/4 metric periodicity as bracketed in Examples 50a, b, and c)	"foreground" regular 4/4 metric periodicity
"Sameness" in repetition	"foreground" metric irregularity	fixed stress and phrase (or slur) markings at successive A–D–C–D repeats (Example 30b)

Example 52

ing to the second of these rhythmic-metric types (2), the contradiction or reversal affecting the upbeat/downbeat identity of the horn's A–D–C–D fragment at Nos. 64–71 in *Le Sacre* is not concealed but is exposed by "foreground" regular 4/4 metric periodicity; at the same time "sameness" in the repetition of this A–D–C–D fragment is not metrically enforced but is imposed by fixed stress and phrase (slur) markings which accompany each A–D–C–D repeat.

In confronting these varying types of construction and the underlying double edge, we note the difficulty in coming to terms with traditional concepts of meter and rhythm, of attempting fixed distinctions between the two, and of then equating these terms and distinctions with the periodicity of tonal, C-scale (or major-scale) literature. (This difficulty is apparent not only when Stravinsky's music is "considered as a whole," but also in moving, within individual pieces, from one section or block to the next.) For our two rhythmic-metric types pose altered purposes for meter and rhythm. In the first type, meter and rhythm often coincide, their purposes or functions being virtually indistinguishable (at least insofar as an apprehension of rhythmic-metric "sameness" in repetition is concerned), whereas in the second type, meter may reflect the stable period of one of the reiterating fragments, in relation to which the varying, "separate," or "independent" periods of the other reiterating fragments could be construed as "rhythm." But even these neatly packaged "altered purposes" are subject to qualification once consideration is given the double edge of which both types partake. For an apprehension of this double edge is to a degree contingent on dual, concurrent meters: the one "foreground" and barred, the other "background" and unmarked (phantomlike). Thus, apropos the first of our rhythmic-metric types, the brackets in the examples of this chapter record "background" regular metric periodicity (upon which apprehension of the contradiction or reversal in upbeat/downbeat or off-the-beat/on-the-beat accentuation hinges), while "foreground" metric irregularity acknowledges and records rhythmic-metric "sameness" in repetition. And so despite this "foreground" metric irregularity in the first of our two types, the "square metrical dance schemes" of past (tonal, C-scale) literature still pertain. (Unless, of course, we choose to consider this "background" steady periodicity as "rhythm," a curious proposition in that it suggests for the first of our two rhythmic-metric types, a rhythm-meter relationship which is the opposite of that in music of the seventeenth to nineteenth centuries, rhythm becoming what is in effect meter in tonal, C-scale literature. But even if curious, awkward, or ironic, this idea is perhaps not entirely beside the point. For in numerous illustrations beginning with *The Firebird's* Finale in chapter 1 (see Example 11), contradictions or reversals in upbeat/downbeat or off-the-beat/on-the-beat accentuation were acknowledged as downbeatings of fragments, motives, simultaneities, or configurations which, in relation to tonal, C-scale literature, would most certainly have been conceived and barred as stressed upbeating or off-the-beat entities. Thus Stravinsky could in this respect quite legitimately be imagined as having relegated to meter purposes or functions which were formerly "rhythmic" in design. On the other hand, this metric downbeating, with its topsy-turvy inversion of the traditional rhythm-meter posture, conveys, as we continue to suggest, only one side of the invention's double edge. Thus while affording clues to the origin of Stravinsky's metric irregularity—the impulse from which much of it may have sprung—the inversion accounts for only part of what more comprehensively embodies the Stravinskian stamp.)[19]

Indeed, the reader will have noted that the "Soldier's March" of *Histoire* exemplifies both rhythmic-metric types. For while the stable 2/4 period of the basso ostinato is at times metric (indeed, initiates a steady 2/4 periodicity seemingly in accord with the second of our two rhythmic-metric types), the metric irregularity of the B–C♯–D–(E) termination disrupts this periodicity, and so inclines in overall intent toward the first type. (The crossings of the barline by the G–E/D basso ostinato reflect an attempt, on the one hand, to acknowledge an application of both rhythmic-metric types, and, on the other, to acknowledge the double edge of which both partake.) Hence, there is yet another difficulty here: the steady 2/4 period of the basso ostinato is at times metric and at times "rhythmic." Or it is simply "rhythmic-metric" (at times conforming to the meter and at times conflicting with it). Indeed, rhythmic-metric "sameness" in repetition is recorded by means which are at times metric and at times "rhythmic." It is metric—or rhythmic-metric—insofar as the first of our rhythmic-metric types is concerned, but "rhythmic"—as in the stress and phrase markings—with respect to the second. The result of this is the ambivalence of much of the terminology in this chapter, as exemplified by terms like rhythmic (or metric) invention, rhythmic-metric period, or rhythmic-metric sameness. It is all but impossible, in moving from one piece, section, or even block to the next, to identify a single, fixed purpose for meter, and to distinguish this purpose in some single, fixed, or meaningful fashion from some suitable conception of "rhythm." Indeed, to have approached rhythm and meter in Stravinsky's music from the character of their imposition in tonal, C-scale literature would not only have resulted in dwelling on what is often peripheral (or, with respect to the double edge, on what could represent only one "edge"), but also in forfeiting insights critical to the issue of fragmental repetition (an issue lying at the root of rhythmic-metric peculiarity). And so it is from the complex character of this repetition that our analysis of rhythm and meter takes its cue, and from which the more telling glimpses of subtlety, intricacy, and ingenuity are forthcoming. (Or, to rephrase this methodology: rhythm and meter are viewed as *means* by which crucial, underlying factors in the repetition are acknowledged and recorded in notation.)

Of course, Stravinsky himself would always in his casually conventional, casually tonal, C-scale frame of mind contend that his barline could not be "simulated by an accent," and that the means selected (barlines or stress markings, and related here to our two rhythmic-metric types) always reflected "the degree of real regularity in the music." There is little difficulty in accepting this contention, in respecting Stravinsky's barlines—*if it is heard and understood* that differing purposes may be at stake. These purposes may reflect the variety of rhythmic-metric types aluded to, and his barlines may in addition only reflect one side of the double edge toward which the rhythmic (or metric) invention, regardless of type, invariably aspires. On the other hand, such a contention as that the means selected (metric irregularity as opposed to regular metric periodicity with stress markings) always reflected "the degree of real regularity in the music" is scarcely plausible. For the conditions by which such a "degree" are assessed must necessarily vary from one context to the next; so that, in turn, the rationale which might conceivably have prompted an application of one of our rhythmic-metric types varies accordingly.

For example: "real [metric] regularity" is far more apparent in the "Soldier's March" of *Histoire* than it is at Nos. 64–71 in *Le Sacre* (owing, doubtless, to the stable 2/4 period of the basso ostinato, in comparison to which the steady 4/4 meter of *Le Sacre* is only vaguely discernible, obscured as it is by the varying and highly "mobile" rhythmic-metric periods of the reiterating horn and tuba fragments).[20] Yet it is in the "Soldier's March" that Stravinsky "jumps the fence." In place of sustaining the 2/4 design *throughout* and relying on identical stress and phrase (slur) markings to promote rhythmic-metric "sameness" in B–C♯–D–(E) repetition (and inclining therefore *throughout* toward the second of our two rhythmic-metric types), he disrupts this 2/4 periodicity to ensure counteracting "sameness" by shifting the meter, by preserving the same irregular 3/8 measure for each B–C♯–D–(E) repeat. And so his reasoning is manifestly contradicted. Indeed, evidence suggests the very opposite of what he contends: that it is in fact owing to the high degree of felt ("foreground" or "background") 2/4 periodicity in the "Soldier's March" that the need arises to ensure counteracting "sameness" in B–C♯–D–(E) repetition by means of metric irregularity (in place of fixed stress and phrase markings, as with the horn's A–D–C–D repeats at Nos. 64–71 in *Le Sacre*)—that, in other words, more radical means are harnessed for the preservation of downbeating "sameness" in repetition. In contrast, at Nos. 64–71 in *Le Sacre*, where the rhythmic-metric periods vary "separately from" one another and are highly "mobile," a steady meter is applied, and fixed stress and phrase (slur) markings prove sufficient for the promotion of rhythmic-metric "sameness" in A–D–C–D repetition. To this might be added that fixed stress and phrase markings, as applied to the reiterating A–D–C–D fragment in the horns at Nos. 64–71 in *Le Sacre*, create, in the interests of rhythmic-metric "sameness," a far more penetrating effect than would have been the case had they been applied to the reiterating B–C♯–D–(E) termination in the "Soldier's March" of *Histoire*. Thus, in addition to distinctions already drawn between our two rhythmic-metric types, the character of a reiterating fragment along with questions of tempo and instrumentation must all have figured—and far more persuasively than any absolute "degree of real regularity in the music"—as factors in determining the means—and hence the rhythmic-metric type— best suited in acknowledging the varied rhythmic-metric repetition of a particular fragment, simultaneity, or configuration.

Finally, from countless passages of the "Russian," neoclassical, and early serial periods which might enlighten our discussion at this point, we turn to several which demonstrate upbeat-downbeat or off-the-beat/on-the-beat contradictions or reversals of a more immediate and hence more readily discernible type. In Example 53a from the opening measures of the *Symphonies of Wind Instruments* (1920), the design conforms to the first of our two types: metric irregularity, with all the reiterating fragments, lines, or parts sharing the same irregular rhythmic-metric periods as defined by the shifting meter, and hence synchronized unvaryingly in vertical coincidence. Accordingly, this "foreground" irregularity exacts a downbeating "sameness" in the repetition of the (D)–D–D–B fragment in the clarinets, while it conceals a contradiction or reversal in the on-the-beat/off-the-beat accentuation of this reiterating (D)–D–D–B fragment, a

Example 53a: *Symphonies*

concealment whose apprehension hinges on "background" regular 2/4 metric periodicity (as recorded by the brackets in Example 53a and then rebarred accordingly below). And so in this opening, massed block of the *Symphonies*, "foreground" metric irregularity enforces a rhythmic-metric "sameness" in the (D)–D–D–B repetition. But a "background" 2/4 meter signals regular metric periodicity, with respect to which the reiterating (D)–D–D–B fragment may first be perceived as an *on*-the-beat D–D–D–B reiteration, contradicted or reversed at mm. 4–5 as a syncopated, *off*-the-beat D–D–B reiteration.

In the "Triple Pas de quatre" at m. 96 from *Agon* (1957) (Example 53b), a syncopated, off-the-beat D–A reiteration just before m. 97 in the flutes (punctuated by the strings, pizzicato) becomes an on-the-beat D–A reiteration at the fourth beat of m. 97. Here the off-the-beat/on-the-beat contradiction is concealed not by metric irregularity, but by a crossing of the barline, which effects a compromise between—or a notational acknowledgment of—both rhythmic-metric types, along with the double edge embedded in these constructions: the off-the-beat/on-the-beat contradiction in D–A accentuation is acknowledged by "foreground" 4/8 metric periodicity, while downbeating "fixity" or "sameness" is acknowledged by a crossing of the barline at mm. 96–97.[21] (Note, too, the pizzicato punctuation in the strings which underscores this downbeating "sameness" by percussively accentuating each A–D repeat.)

In the opening measures of *Threni* (1958) (Example 53c), an on-the-

Example 53b: *Agon*

Example 53c: *Threni*

beat F♯–F reiteration (*f>p*) is promptly contradicted by a stressed off-the-beat appearance; at No. 28 in *Orpheus* (1947) (Example 53d), a simultaneity intrudes on the beat, but is contradicted by an off-the-beat appearance at No. 28 + 2 (with the simultaneity slightly altered, however); and at No. 3 in the final movement of the *Symphony of Psalms* (1930) (Example 53e), an upbeating (C E G) triadic reiteration (on the second beat at No. 3) is

Example 53d: *Orpheus*

Example 53e: *Symphony of Psalms*

promptly contradicted by assuming, in relation to the regular 4/4 metric
periodicity here, a downbeating identity (on the first beat at No. 3+3).
Consequently, in these four passages from *Agon*, *Threni*, *Orpheus*, and
Psalms, the designs accord with the second of our two rhythmic-metric
types: "foreground" steady meters acknowledge contradictions or reversals in upbeat/downbeat or off-the-beat/on-the-beat accentuation; counteracting "sameness' is in one instance (*Agon*) signaled by a crossing of the
barline, and in the remaining three by fixed stress and phrase (or slur)
markings which accompany each repeat of the given fragment, motive,
simultaneity, or configuration.

Lastly, Example 53f from Act II of *Oedipus Rex* (1927) presents a rarity:
the single instance in the whole of Stravinsky's oeuvre where, instead of
pursuing the customary route of an either/or proposition with respect to
our two rhythmic-metric types, Stravinsky bars initially according to the
first of these types (at Nos. 139 and 140), and then according to the second
(at No. 144).[22] Thus, at No. 139, the block in question is sliced into small,
metrically irregular units, conceived and barred according to the first
rhythmic-metric type, metric irregularity. With the immediate (near) repeat of this block at No. 140, a contradiction or reversal materializes in
off-the-beat/on-the-beat accentuation. According to "background" regular 3/4 metric periodicity at Nos. 139–41 (as bracketed in Example 53f),
the block may first be perceived at No. 139 as commencing *off* the beat, but
contradicted or reversed at No. 140 by assuming an *on*-the-beat identity.[23]
But at No. 144, the true novelty appears: the "background" 3/4 meter of

Example 53f: *Oedipus Rex*

these successive (near) repeats at Nos. 139 and 140 (and upon which an apprehension of the aforementioned off-the-beat/on-the-beat contradiction or reversal hinges) is shifted to the "foreground," with the block now conceived and barred according to the second of our types, regular 3/4 metric periodicity. In this transformation from type (1) to type (2), the shifting meter of the (near) repeat at No. 140 is replaced at No. 144 by stress and slur markings. (This, of course, might have been expected. For as outlined earlier, the notational means by which the double edge is imposed reverses itself according to rhythmic-metric type: what is "foreground" in the first of these types (rhythmic-metric "sameness" in repetition preserved by means of metric irregularity) becomes "background" in the second ("sameness" preserved by means of fixed stress and slur markings); and what is "background" in the first (contradiction or reversal in accentuation, hinging on regular metric periodicity), becomes "foreground" in the second.) Accordingly, what was at first metric in design and outward appearance at No. 140 (or rhythmic-metric, since the purposes or functions of rhythm and meter tend to coincide in applications of the first of our rhythmic-metric types) becomes strictly rhythmic at No. 144 (with metric irregularity becoming a matter of stress and slur markings), while what was at first "background" at No. 140 becomes strictly metric at No. 144.

Consequently, Nos. 139–47 in Act II of *Oedipus* present a uniquely compelling context, one highly revealing insofar as all aspects of our present investigation are concerned. We shall be returning to it for further study (as transposed to a D-scale-on-D setting at Nos. 159–67; see Example 63 in chapter 10).

Perhaps the immediate and explicit nature of the contradiction or reversal in these final illustrations (from countless possible passages) affords an indication of how fundamentally this tactic must have figured in Stravinsky's inventive processes. For it occurs almost inevitably, from one context to the next, as a kind of reflex. It has the rebounding effect of the counterpunch, of a rhythmic-metric identity established and then contradicted and reversed. So, too, it appears—just as inevitably—concealed by counteraction, by the opposite, opposing side of the double edge or "both ways": by a stubborn intent to render the repetition—nonetheless—rhythmic-metrically "the same."

Finally, we acknowledge the constituent elements of this invention as being as melodic—or as formal or "harmonic"—as they are rhythmic-metric. Indeed, we have here been discussing not so much rhythmic (or metric) invention, or rhythmic-metric structure, as rhythmic-metric *identity(ies)*—how the accentual implications of a reiteration are displaced, yet accompanied by this counteracting effort to render each repeat—nonetheless—rhythmic-metrically "the same." (Perhaps it is the cross-purposes at which this double edge or "both ways" toils, the contradiction of its double-edged posture, to which is owing the manifest vitality of its imprint.) And scarcely, then, can Stravinsky be imagined as having conceived of this invention—or can his listeners be imagined as perceiving it—as any more "separate from" or "independent of" melodic, formal, or "harmonic" concerns than was—and remains—the conceptual or perceptual status of rhythm and/or meter in the tonal, C-scale literature of the seventeenth to nineteenth centuries. More accurately at stake in Stravinsky's music are changes in the relationship between the elusive rhythmic-metric factor and melody, form, and "harmony," the formation of different kinds of routines which presume, in relation to whatever tonal, C-scale envisioned concepts of rhythm and meter we care to entertain, new and altered purposes (however much an apprehension of these purposes may continue to hinge, to some degree, on regular metric periodicity, on the "square metrical dance schemes" of tonal, C-scale literature, whether "foreground" or "background" in conception). Hence, only in relation to this refined art—subtly, ingeniously pursued—of contradicting the upbeat/downbeat or off-the-beat/on-the-beat implications of his material (but insisting, nonetheless, on a counteracting "sameness" in repetition; composing, nonetheless, as if the "repetition" were designed as a carbon copy of the original), can Stravinsky be credited with having divorced melody or melodic repetition from fixed rhythmic-metric identity (or, as is here the case, from his own fiendishly imposed, counteracting "sameness" in rhythmic-metric identity), and only in this sense can we in turn speak of a kind of "dissociation" or "emancipation" of the rhythmic-metric presence.

Vertical coincidence—"harmony" or simultaneity—invites a similar evaluation. For while—to take the second of our rhythmic-metric types—changes in vertical coincidence are no longer governed by the system of harmonic progression known to the tonal, C-scale tradition, but arise as a consequence of this types's varying rhythmic-metric periods (which, varying "independently of" one another, effect a union or coincidence which is constantly changing); while it is possible to imagine, in comparison with the "traditional harmony" of tonality, a coincidence haphazard or accidental in character (effected without purpose or method), and hence indifferent to, or "dissociated" or "freed" from, melody, melodic repetition, and rhythmic-metric concerns; while these conditions are imaginable in some vague historical context, the reality is that these varying rhythmic-metric periods effect this seemingly random coincidence *within a general state of pitch-relational reference,* whose particulars of symmetry, far from dissociating "harmony" from melodic repetition and rhythmic-metric identity, bind all coordinates to a new and different interplay. Thus, for example, in the first of the *Three Pieces for String Quartet* as examined in chapter 5: the varying rhythmic-metric periods of the first violin, second violin, and cello fragments project a vertical coincidence which is absolutely irregular and variable. But the A–G, F♯–E–D♯–C♯, and E♭–D♭/ C fragments in this repetition are bound "harmonically" by their confinement to an A–G–F♯–E–D♯–C♯–C octatonic ordering and partitioning, Collection III; this symmetrical confinement binds—obviously— by delimiting coincidence. Moreover, norms in coincidence do subtly arise. And because these norms relate to the double edge in rhythmic-metric construction (and to that trace of regular metric periodicity upon which a hearing and understanding of one of these edges is contingent), they cannot be said to occur "at random" (with every applicable coincidence deemed an equal probability), but are, if this invention is to be judged meaningful, purposeful.

And so, once again, the question has not to do with true "dissociation" or "emancipation" (which can come, presumably, only from "pure chance"), but with a changed relationship or interplay between vertical coincidence and rhythm-meter, melody, and form. Much the same can be said about melody. For it has long been customary—perhaps fashionable—to cite Stravinsky for "poverty" in the pursuit of this age-old, seemingly indispensable commodity, and with scant consideration of what might have prompted the alleged neglect. Constant Lambert, in his keenly entertaining *Music Ho!*, commented as follows:

> The series of reactions by which Stravinsky has progressed have been imposed upon him not only by the exigencies of fashion, but by his complete lack of any melodic faculty. Even his greatest admirers, I think, would admit that from the pale Wagnerian reflections of the *Scherzo fantastique* (*La Vie des abeilles*) to the monotonous peasant fragments of *Les Noces* there is nothing in his music that can be described as a typical Stravinsky tune. We can recognize him immediately by his scoring, by his rhythm and by the setting he gives to his themes, but the themes themselves are either traditional or characterless. . . .
>
> To create even a synthetic melody—such as the one in the slow movement of Ravel's concerto—to any degree of satisfaction requires a power of sustained linear construction which it is only too clear Stravinsky does not possess. His melodic style has always been marked by extreme short-windedness and a curious inability to get away from the principal note of the tune. . . . But the essence of a classical melody is continuity of line, contrast and balance of phrases, and the ability to depart from the nodal point in order that the ultimate return to it should have significance and finality.[24]

But the question, as before, has not to do with "poverty" or neglect, but with a different kind of melodic invention and interplay. The citation may seem historically credible, but only in a crudely fashioned comparative vein. For if Brahms—to take but one example—characteristically required of his melodies that they submit, in repetition, to the most subtle gradation in harmonic hue (but all in accord with inherited tonal procedure), Stravinsky required of his that they pliantly succumb, in repetition, to the most subtle and intricate shifts in rhythmic-metric accentuation. And scarcely a fool would insist that the results could—or should—be of the same order. Curiously, however, this has been the point. Humphrey Searle, echoing the customary lament, dubs Stravinsky "a singularly poor melodist," but without denying the "melodist" his mastery of "orchestral" and "rhythmic effect."[25] As if, somehow, such "effect" could obtain without impinging on established rules of melodic formation. It shows naiveté of an unusual variety to acknowledge, on the one hand, the novelty of Stravinsky's rhythmic (or metric) invention with some depth of hearing and understanding, and then to insist, nonetheless, that his melodic or contrapuntal network toe the familiar lines, plough through the praiseworthy patterns, of his tonal, C-scale predecessors (or those emanating from the musical thought processes of his nontonal or quasi-tonal contemporaries).

Consequently, under these sets of coordinated conditions, the idea of Stravinsky's "dissociation" or "emancipation" of the rhythmic-metric factor, as well as the "harmonic" or melodic factors, is none too convincing. These components certainly did not become—in conception, perception, or analytic-theoretical review—autonomous entities, severed from one another in some formidably problematic sense—a sense that lets slip the at least peripheral awareness, which we try to preserve in our anatomizing, of the totality from which these components are momentarily dislodged as focal points in perception and analysis.

And so while we have here cautiously endeavored to isolate and disengage, it seems fitting to conclude our commentary with this—perhaps lasting—tribute by Benjamin Boretz:

> In Stravinsky's honor, then, the rhythmic genius may be exalted to the highest position in musical creation; but to honor his own special rhythmic genius requires necessarily—though also sufficiently—the recognition of his own special genius as a creator of whole new musical worlds: (consider it done.)[26]

REPERCUSSIONS

To what, then, is owing this renown of Stravinsky as a "rhythmic genius," this reputation as a composer who, instrumental wizardry aside, is preeminently engaged in the invention of ingenious rhythmic-metric display? It may have as much to do with the manner in which this invention manifests itself outwardly, with what Stravinsky himself termed "the character of articulation in my music," as with the underlying mechanics. It may involve matters like certainty in tempo and exactitude in punctuation. For some of Stravinsky's more idiosyncratic tastes in performance or general inclinations in instrumental layout are directly traceable to these "outward" matters of tempo and articulation.

Consider, as a point of departure, that angry, vexed contempt for "interpreters" and "interpretation" (running, as it does, like a continuo through the commentary and dialogues with Robert Craft). For "interpretation" can mean rubato or fluctuation in tempo or pulse, as in, say, the nineteenth century Romantic tradition. And Stravinsky's rhythmic-metric construction, the potent contradictions or reversals underlying so much of the metric irregularity or the stress and phrase signification, cannot tolerate such treatment. Nuance in tempo or pulsation (and often in dynamics as well) spells disaster, a collapse or crumbling of the musical structure, its "point."[27] (Of the many "performance problems" plaguing his music, Stravinsky acknowledged tempo as the principal one. "A piece of mine can survive almost anything," he averred, "but wrong or uncertain tempo.")[28]

Thus, the (C E G) triadic reiteration in the horns and bassoons at No. 3 in the final movement of the *Symphony of Psalms* (Example 53e) is first introduced on an unaccented or "weak" beat of the stable 4/4 metric design (as an upbeating reiteration), but this is subsequently contradicted or reversed by the assumption of an accented or "strong" identity two measures later (as a downbeating reiteration). The point of this subtle flexibility in upbeat/downbeat accentuation could be lost if subjected to uncertain sluggishness or any fluctuation in tempo or pulse. Moreover, if the tempo has to be exact, even metronomic, the articulation has equally to be crisp, clean, and percussive ("cold," "brittle," or "heartless," as Stravinsky so often observed). For if counteracting "sameness" in repetition is imposed by fixed stress markings (as is the case at No. 3 in the final movement of *Psalms*, where the steady 4/4 meter implicates the second of our rhythmic-metric types), the point of this downbeating "sameness" (or of these fixed stress markings intoned in opposition to the barred contradiction or reversal in upbeat/downbeat accentuation) would likewise be lost if the execution is not crisp, clean, and percussive. And so, not surprisingly, "articulation and rhythmic diction" rank, along with tempo, as critical "performance problems." The most perfunctory glance at any number of scores provides ample testimony to this. Apart from the stress and phrase signification cited in this chapter in conjunction with Examples 50–53f (which is aimed generally at the preservation of some rhythmic-metric "sameness" in repetition, in opposition to displacement), the additional markings—the $f>p$s, *ben marcatos* and staccato unison doublings of legato lines that typically abound—are designed to ensure the rhythmic-metric construction and its critical double edge the clean, crisp, incisive approach essential to their appreciation. (See, for example, the pizzicato punctuation in *Agon*, Example 53b, which percussively accentuates rhythmic-metric "sameness" in D–A repetition; the $f > p$ markings of the F#–F reiteration in *Threni*, Example 53c; the stress and slur signification in the oboe's legato lines at No. 144 in *Oedipus*, Example 53f, which is doubled in unison, staccato, by the clarinets; or the (D)–D–D–B reiteration in the clarinets at the outset of the *Symphonies of Wind Instruments*, which, although not shown in Example 53a, is doubled in unison, staccato, by the flutes.) These markings are the articulative outgrowth of all that is most profoundly a part of the invention here under review. And to such an extent, indeed, that reproaches directed against the "cold," "unfeeling," or "mechanical" quality of Stravinsky's music seem ultimately to reflect little else but an inability to apprehend the mechanism "below"; or, if apprehended, then a nostalgia for the lost tonal, C-scale circumstances which this invention logically forsakes. (Stravinsky himself countered this familiar rebuke by asking: "What is 'warm,' please? *Schmaltz*? And is the first canon in the 'Goldberg' Variations cold or warm?")[29]

But all of this, understandably, leaves little allowance for "interpretation." Conductors in particular need merely to initiate and sustain the beat, watch for cues, and acknowledge the metric irregularity and the stress and phrase (or slur) markings in as clean, crisp, and percussive a fashion as possible. Anything else would blunt or smother critical intent. Even the supposed difficulties of a score like *Le Sacre*, so immense and varied in instrumental layout, are largely imaginary in Stravinsky's view:

> I first conducted *Le Sacre* myself in 1928, for a recording by English Columbia. I was nervous about doing it at first, in view of its reputation as a difficult piece, but these famous difficulties, actually no more than the simple alternation of twos and threes, proved to be a conductor's myth; *Le Sacre* is arduous but not difficult, and the *chef d'orchestre* is hardly more than a mechanical agent, a time-beater who fires a pistol at the beginning of each section but lets the music run by itself. (Compare it, at the opposite extreme, to Berg's Three Pieces for Orchestra, which music depends to such a great extent on conductors' nuances.)[30]

While these strictures are doubtless taken for granted by a host of contemporary musicians (in the wake, possibly, of the Stravinsky-Craft recordings during the 1960s), we may still appreciate the problems encountered with conductors and orchestras accustomed to more flexible methods— with musicians unfamiliar with the novelty of this rhythmic-metric display and its special requirements in "articulation and rhythmic diction," requirements seemingly so fundamentally at odds—as the general interpretative case suggests—with those of the more familiar repertory of the eighteenth and nineteenth centuries. A brief account of a rehearsal of the *Capriccio* for piano and orchestra (1929) by the Concertgebouw orchestra of Amsterdam, under the direction of William Mengelberg during the early 1930s and with Stravinsky as soloist, tells the tale:

> My memories of Mengelberg are . . . not among the most deeply cherished. At our first rehearsal of the *Capriccio*, he began to conduct in an impossible tempo. I said I was unable to play at that speed, but I should have specified for he could not tell whether I had meant that he had been too fast or too slow. He was flustered, though, and instead of starting over, he embarked on a self-justifying oration: "Gentlemen, in my fifty years of conducting I think I have learned to recognize the proper tempo of a piece of music, but Mr. Stravinsky would like us to play like this—tick, tick, tick, tick; and he cocked his forefinger to mimic Herr Mälzel's very useful invention.
>
> Mengelberg was not wicked, of course, or ungenerous, or even totally devoid of musicianship. He was only morbidly dependent on flattery.[31]

If intolerant of departures from the strict tempo and articulative requirements of his own music, Stravinsky was no less so in respect to the classics of the eighteenth and nineteenth centuries. Here too, the books of "conversation" with Robert Craft provide memorable insights. A reaction to the Toscanini recording of Beethoven's First Symphony is typical. "The *Adagio molto* introduction was played not adagio but andante." The *Allegro* itself was "an absurdly fast Rossini-like tempo that obliterated phrase accents and articulations. . . . The ritardando . . . applied to the beginning of the recapitulation [second movement] was insufferably gross. . . . The whole minuet and trio were so absurdly fast as to make no sense at all."[32] Following a concert featuring a late symphony of Haydn's, Stravinsky complained that "the different lengths of its sentences" had been "stifled by tempi too fast and too slow—the *Andante* was played adagio and both allegros were played prestissimo: the natural respiration of the music was everywhere frustrated, and the performance was unreal—pulsation is the reality of music."[33] He professed himself unable to follow a recording of Brahms's First Symphony "because the second beats of the 6/8 movement were so delayed that the time signature might have been $6\frac{1}{2}/8$," and asserted that while the conductor might justify distortion of tempo as "emphasis" or "expressive freedom," the "natural rhythmic vitality is corrupted."[34]

Stravinsky's reasoning here cannot be difficult to follow. All this music was still essentially "dance music" (as Stravinsky viewed much of his own music, even when not expressly written for the ballet), and it was as "dance music" that the most precious and critical of links sprang to life. For if, as a "rhythmic genius," Stravinsky invented new forms of rhythmic-metric construction, much of the point of this construction continued to reside— as we continue to reiterate—with the regular metric periodicity and accentuation of this earlier "dance music" (or with the tonal, C-scale "square metrical dance schemes," along with the developmental upbeating sensibility, *against* which he can be imagined as having applied the mechanics of his own devices). Hence, to violate "the natural respiration" or pulse of the classics, to pervert their articulative circumstances, was to undermine the tradition, the rhythmic-metric foundation upon which rested a proper acknowledgment and apprehension of his own rhythmic-metric innovations. And so no more than his own music could such a foundation bear the mutilation of "interpretation" or "nuance." The sensitivity with which he reacted to all traces of interpretative "nuance," in his own music or in that of the classics, was ever acute. (Melodramatic gestures on the part of conductors were especially repugnant. He resented such display as deflecting from concentrated effort both in hearing and understanding and in musical transmission. And since expressivity was a *given*, part and parcel of the music itself, personality projections of this type deprived that given expressivity of its dignity. Performers had merely to abandon their pretensions as "interpreters" if music was to transcend its clownish preoccupation with personality and aspire to honest artistic endeavor. Ideally, the composers were the "interpreters." Performers were transmitters, conveyers, and little else.)[35]

Moreover, how intimately must the substance and articulative spirit of Stravinsky's rhythmic (or metric) invention have been bound up with his lifelong attraction to the ballet. (To a degree shared by no other composer, Stravinsky was aligned with the ballet, from the early "Russian" period to the late neoclassical, not only as a composer of original ballet music, but as a creator and coauthor of scenarios like *The Firebird, Petroushka, Le Sacre,* and *Les Noces*—the absence of formal credit notwithstanding.) The ballet could persuasively project this dance attribute and link; it could underscore the certainty in tempo and precision in punctuation that were so crucially a part of this attribute and link; and, more subtly, it might visually ignite some of the rhythmic-metric intricacies of his repetition. Small wonder, then, this affinity, his feeling of kinship and intimacy. It is also scarcely surprising that the neoclassical initiative, Stravinsky's "discovery" of the past, should have come by way of a ballet, *Pulcinella* (1920). Or that his studies of the Pergolesi texts for this first full-blown neoclassical venture should have led to a further discovery, revealing and prophetic: that rather than admitting to distinctions between operatic, concert, or dance music, between "rhythmic" and "melodic" music, these early texts were all "dance music." Indeed, all eighteenth century music, instrumental or vocal, sacred or secular, was in a wondrously enticing sense "dance music." (Why, he then asks, should "performance tradition" ignore this? Why does an eminent conductor, rehearsing Mozart's "Linz" Symphony, repeatedly urge the orchestra to "sing" when, as an appropriate gesture toward some fuller hearing and understanding, he should so obviously be reminding it to "dance," when, as a consequence, a "simple melodic content is burdened with a thick-throated late-nineteenth-century sentiment that it cannot bear, while the rhythmic movement remains turgid"?)[36] Original ballet scores from the "Russian" period are *The Firebird* (1910), *Petroushka* (1911), *Le Sacre* (1913), and the "cantata-ballet" *Les Noces* (1917). These were followed, during the neoclassical era, by *Pulcinella* (1920), *Apollo* (1928), *Le Baiser de la fée* (1928), *Jeu de cartes* (1936), *Scènes de ballet* (1944), *Orpheus* (1947), and *Agon* (1953–57). But these lists omit the many chamber and orchestral works for which ballets were subsequently staged by a host of choreographers, productions to which Stravinsky rarely if ever objected. (A single objection came in response to the 1917 ballet version of the early *Scherzo fantastique* (1908). But, as noted in chapter 2, the objection here focused not on the ballet itself—which Stravinsky failed to see—but on the apparently unauthorized use of Maeterlinck's *La Vie des abeilles* as a scenario and as a program note at performances.) In fact, the only original ballet music Stravinsky was later to prefer in the concert hall was *Le Sacre*. This was possibly because *Le Sacre* was too vehemently, too violently, "dance music," so that ballet productions tended to overwhelm, to be oppressively redundant, and to deteriorate into spectacle.)[37]

Then, too, the substance and articulative terms of the rhythmic-metric construction may be credited for distinct preferences in instrumental layout, ensemble, and blend, and even for the frequency or infrequency with which individual instruments mark their appearance. The heavy reliance on woodwind, brass, and percussion instruments, at the apparent expense of the string section, is often mentioned—with particular reference to the "Russian" category—as a "choir" balance in contradiction to that generally in use in the symphonic literature of the eighteenth and nineteenth centuries. (Besides the *Symphonies of Wind Instruments*—which uses no strings—and the *Symphony of Psalms*—which has no violin or viola sections—this reliance is striking in both *Petroushka* and *Le Sacre*, where the strings frequently have little more than accompanying "fill" operations, or punctuating or sustaining devices. Much of the rewriting in the revisions of *Le Sacre*'s "Danse sacrale" (1943) and *Petroushka* (1947) was undertaken to provide the string section with a greater sense of purpose.) This impulse may well have arisen as a reaction against the Romantic tradition of the late nineteenth century—specifically, against certain affective qualities for which the strings, with their finger-touch vibrato and scope in dynamic range and thrust, had proven so relentless and powerful a medium. (One need but glance at the first of the *Three Pieces for String Quartet* to see how at odds with this tradition the stiff, mechanical conception of Stravinsky's string writing is. Equally noteworthy in this respect is the fact that *Apollo* (1928), a ballet composed after nearly a decade of neoclassical experiments and with the intent—never entirely realized—

of supplanting all vestiges of "Russian" folklike melodicism with a broader and more extensive melodic line, should have been conceived for string orchestra alone.) But the details of this reliance are more significantly related to the light, airy bounce of Stravinsky's instrumental "touch." This "bounce" is linked in turn to "the character of articulation" in his music, an "articulation" whose implementation by the woodwind and brass instruments, with their potential for crisp, unaffected punctuality in phrasing and attack, must always have been tempting. (Stravinsky expressed a special fondness for what he termed "the breathing of woodwind instruments.") More specifically, the rich diversity in color or timbre offered by these woodwind and brass instruments was especially suited to applications of the second of our two rhythmic-metric types of construction, where a strong instrumental contrast could assist in enforcing the variance in rhythmic-metric periods defined by the superimposed, reiterating fragments. (*Le Sacre*'s Introduction comes to mind, as well as the block examined at Nos. 64–71, and we need but glance at the first of the *Three Pieces for String Quartet* to discover, in this instrumentally homogeneous setting, the lengths to which Stravinsky resorts—in bowing/plucking techniques and dynamics—in order to distinguish, instrumentally, between the rhythmic-metric periods defined by the first and second violin, viola, and cello fragments.)

Along with these instrumental blends solo preferences are equally revealing. Stravinsky disliked the saxophone because of its heavy, swelling vibrato (opting for the bassoon in the jazzlike ensemble of *Histoire du soldat*, for example). He abstained from the vibraphone until the *Requiem Canticles* (1966)—here too because of the swelling vibrato (and in spite of its widespread popularity during the 1950s and 1960s in the wake of Pierre Boulez's *Le Marteau sans maître*). With the exception of *Canticum Sacrum* (1955), he neglected the organ entirely (although he once considered it for the *Symphony of Psalms*, deciding against it, however, because of its *legato sostenuto*, its "mess of octaves," or, as he later quipped, because "the monster never *breathes*"). Among distinct preferences, a genuinely soloistic use of certain percussion instruments, dating from the "Swiss years" of World War I and his early familiarity with jazz, is noteworthy. From the "Danse infernale" of *The Firebird* (1910) to the opening "Pas de quatre" of *Agon* (1957), the use of the harp (*près de la table*) and piano as dry, percussive instruments, punctuating the articulation (or, more subtly, the duplicity in rhythmic-metric construction) is everywhere in evidence. (Stravinsky was pleased with this early, pioneering effort on behalf of the percussion section. He noted that before *Histoire* and his 1918–19 version of *Les Noces* for two cimbaloms, harmonium, pianola, and percussion, "the drums had never really been given their heads." Percussion sections had served merely as "arsenals or sound-prop departments," adding occasional color or weight. But after 1918 the section flourished as a "continuing and internally consistent element." He added, however, that the character of both *Histoire* and *Les Noces* is percussive, and that "that character is part of me, another of my biological facts.")[38] Among solo predilections the cimbalom should also be mentioned, Stravinsky's familiarity with this instrument dating, as with so many of the percussion instruments, from the earliest days of his " Swiss years." What seems to have attracted his attention was the cimbalom's approximation in sound of the ancient, string-plucked Russian guzla. For the guzla was soon to inspire much of the music and burlesque of *Renard*. But so soft and delicate was its plucked sonority (and so very nearly obsolete as well) that its replacement by the cimbalom soon proved necessary. An instrument was duly purchased and added to the expanding facilities of his "musical pantry." Indeed, both *Renard* and the *Ragtime* for eleven instruments (1918) were composed "on" the cimbalom, just as Stravinsky continued to compose the bulk of his music "on" the piano. And while its appearance is limited to these two works (along with the abandoned 1918–19 version of *Les Noces*), Stravinsky later found much of the piano writing in the *Capriccio* for piano and orchestra (1929) "cimbalomist in style." (See, especially, No. 37 in the second movement of the *Capriccio*; or the cadenza at No. 50.) Following the war, a cimbalom was installed in his Pleyel studio in Paris, where, until 1939, he continued to tinker with it on a daily basis. Much later he urged that "a society for the preservation of musical wildlife . . . be persuaded to endow one of the schools both with the instrument and with scholarships for its study." He was partial to wooden sticks which lit the glittering delicacy of the hammered sound like ice, the sound becoming "as compact as billiard balls."[39]

Still, of all these diverse ensembles and blends, likes and dislikes, none seems more eccentric—if "stylistically" consistent—than the early but little-known addiction to the pianola or player piano. Few known remnants remain of this prolonged encounter: apart from the 1918–19 version of the first and second tableaux of *Les Noces* for two cimbaloms, harmonium, pianola, and percussion (alluded to above in chapters 6 and 7), there is only the *Etude for Pianola* (1918). But the addiction proved not only insistent—beginning in 1914 and tapering off gradually toward 1930—but a real "influence," by Stravinsky's own admission, a compositional force. The reasons for this are again readily discernible. This "piano-player machine" could dutifully exact the ultimate in certainty of tempo and precision in punctuation; it could, by means of transcription (however arduous and time consuming), transmit in an absolutely mechanical fashion, without the slightest trace of "interpretation" or "nuance." A brief and insightful account of these "pianola years," encompassing what were ultimately to prove hours of wasteful drudgery, hours of "forgotten exercises to no purpose," reads as follows:

In Biarritz [France, 1921–24], I entered into a six-year contract with the Pleyel company in Paris, by which I agreed to transcribe my complete works for their player-piano machine, the Pleyela, in return for 3,000 francs a month and the use of one of their Paris studios. . . . (My transcriptions for the Pleyela, forgotten exercises to no purpose, represented hundreds of hours of work and were of great importance to me at the time. My interest in player-pianos dated from 1914, when I saw a demonstration of the pianola by the Aeolian Company in London. Aeolian wrote me during the war and offered me considerable "payola" for an original piece for pianola. The idea of being performed by rolls of perforated paper amused me, and I was attracted by the mechanics of the instrument. My *Etude* for pianola was composed in 1917, but I did not forget about the instrument afterwards. When I began my transcription work for Pleyel six years later, I borrowed one of their instruments for a study of the mechanism at first hand. . . . My experience with this schizoid instrument must have influenced the music I was composing then, at least where questions of tempo relationships and tempo nuances—the absence of tempo nuances, rather—are concerned. I should add that many of my Pleyela arrangements, especially of vocal works like *Les Noces* and the Russian songs, were virtually recomposed for the medium.)[40]

Finally, were we briefly to peruse the routine of Stravinsky's "setting words to music," we might find yet another confirmation of his rhythmic (or metric) invention and its articulative equations. For Stravinsky himself frequently remarked that his attention in these matters was drawn less to the poetic significance of a given text than to its sound and rhythmic quality; to a degree perhaps keener than his immediate predecessors or contemporaries, his imagination was stirred, his inspiration triggered, not so much by substance, tale, or imagery as by the phonetic sonority of the words and syllables; not so much by the "word sense" as by "sound sense."

> When I work with words in music, my musical saliva is set in motion by the sounds and rhythms of the syllables, and 'In the beginning was the word' is, for me, a literal, localized truth.[41]

This disposition took root comparatively early in his career, apparent as it is in his cantata *Zvezdoliki* (1912). Here, the Russian Symbolist movement, of which *Zvezdoliki*'s poet, Konstantin Balmont, was a leading exponent, seems scarcely to have mattered. Of consequence, rather, were the words in Balmont's poem, and their sonorous potential, not their meaning or meanings.

> His *Zvezdoliki* (The Star-Faced One) is obscure as poetry and as mysticism, but its words are good, and words were what I needed, not meanings. I couldn't tell you even now exactly what the poem means.[42]

This bent was to assume more startling consequences when, in Switzerland, severed from his homeland during the war, he turned to the two

anthologies of Russian popular verse compiled by Kireievsky and Afanasiev, and, with *Les Noces* as an ignition, commenced that stretch of "Russian" pieces beginning with *Pribaoutki* in 1914, culminating with a final
version of *Les Noces* itself in 1923.

> My profound emotion on reading the news of war, which aroused patriotic
> feelings and a sense of sadness at being so distant from my country, found
> some alleviation in the delight with which I steeped myself in Russian folk
> poems.
>   What fascinated me in this verse was not so much the stories, which were
> often crude, or the pictures and metaphors, always so deliciously unex-
> pected, as the cadence they create, which produces an effect on one's sensibil-
> ities very closely akin to that of music. . . .
>   I culled a bouquet from among them all, which I distributed in three
> different compositions that I wrote one after the other, elaborating my mate-
> rial for *Les Noces*. They were *Pribaoutki* (translated by Ramuz under the title
> *Chansons Plaisantes*), for voice, with the accompaniment of a small orchestra;
> then *Les Berceuses du Chat*, also for voice, accompanied by three clarinets; and,
> lastly, four little choruses for women's voices *a cappella* [*Four Russian Peasant
> Songs*, "Saucers"].[43]

And so his attention was drawn to the special musico-rhythmic qualities
of this Russian folk verse. Eager to exploit these qualities in a music of his
own, his sketches and notebooks for scores like *Pribaoutki* became infused
with bits of texts besmirched with a litter of prosody marks. Indeed, so
immersed was Stravinsky for a time in the sound, character, and rhythm
of this poetry that the librettos of both *Les Noces* and *Renard*, although
pieced together from texts derived from the Kireievsky and Afanasiev
collections, contain much that is doubtless his own. For he was soon in-
venting onomatopoeic nonsense words and interpolating these in response to that now fully charged "musical saliva." (*Les Noces* abounds with
word/syllable-play. As an example, Stravinsky cited "*lushenki*" in the final
tableau, a "rhythmic word" of his own having no real "sense" or meaning.)[44]

Momentous, however, was a discovery made during the early days of
these "Swiss years." While at work on *Renard*'s libretto in late 1914, he was
struck by a feature peculiar to Russian folk art: When sung, the accents or
stresses of the spoken verse are often ignored. His recollection of this discovery, one of the most "rejoicing" of his life, reads as follows:

> One important characteristic of Russian popular verse is that the accents of
> the spoken verse are ignored when the verse is sung. The recognition of the
> musical possibilities inherent in this fact was one of the most rejoicing discov-
> eries of my life; I was like a man who suddenly finds that his finger can be bent
> from the second joint as well as from the first. We all know parlor games in
> which the same sentence can be made to mean something different when

different words are emphasized. (*Cf.* Kierkegaard's demonstration of how "Thou shalt love thy neighbor" changes meaning depending whether "thou" or "shalt" or "neighbor" is the emphasized word. S.K.: *Works of Love*.) In *Renard*, the syllable-sounds within the word itself, as well as the emphasis of the word in the sentence, are so treated. *Renard* is phoneme music, and phonemes are untranslatable.[45]

A revelation, then, the discovery of this discrepancy in the pronunciation of Russian popular verse. The musical potential, as Stravinsky himself relates, was no less profound. For the idea must surely have dawned on him that here, in this quaint, "backwoods" oddity of Russian folk poetry, was a capability akin to that which he had already pursued in musical rhythm and meter; here, in this freeing of the syllabification from fixed practice by varying not only the emphasis of words within a repeated phrase or sentence but also the manner in which syllables were pronounced, was a flexible coordination which, put to his own musico-rhythmic ends, could complement the displacement of accents, already inextricably a part of his rhythmic (or metric) invention. Accordingly, free to apply the same flexibility to verbal syllabification that he had already applied to reiterating themes, fragments, configurations, and simultaneities, he could pursue a varied accentuation relatively "indifferent" to the musical component; he could counterpoint an accent or stress—however unorthodox—against some rhythmic-melodic "sameness" in musical repetition, or, in his repetition of a given syllable, word, or phrase (a repetition no less typical of his "setting words to music" than of his musical invention), vary an accent or stress in accord with some variance in the upbeat/downbeat, off-the-beat/on-the-beat implications of a musical reiteration. The possibilities must have seemed infinite. For no longer were the musical contradictions or reversals in upbeat/downbeat or off-the-beat/on-the-beat accentuation helplessly at the mercy of fixed practice in verbal accentuation. His fingers could be bent "from the second joint as well as from the first."

It is significant, too, that this capability realized in Russian popular verse was never abandoned during the neoclassical and serial eras. Exiled after the Revolution, his native tongue no longer of practical use, Stravinsky was not to relent as he turned first to Latin, then to French and English, and finally even to Hebrew in one of his late serial conceptions, *Abraham and Isaac* (1963). Thus, the choice of "Ciceronian Latin" for *Oedipus Rex* (1927) is known to have been influenced by the universal as well as monumental character of this language, its privileged exemption from common sentiment (*"un pur langage sans office,"* as Stravinsky later quoted St.-John Perse). These qualities were agreeably in accord with what seems quite early to have taken shape as an *Oedipus* ritual, a stage play of masks and rigid gesture, a "statuesque plasticity," as Stravinsky confided, "entirely in keeping with the majesty of the ancient legend." But no less influential was the opportunity to manipulate accents freely, to treat the text as "phonetic material," to " . . . dissect . . . at will."

> What a joy it is to compose music to a language of convention, almost of ritual, the very nature of which imposes a lofty dignity! One no longer feels dominated by the phrase, the literal meaning of the words. Cast in an immutable mold which adequately expresses their value, they do not require any further commentary. The text thus becomes purely phonetic material for the composer. He can dissect it at will and concentrate all his attention on its primary constituent element—that is to say, on the syllable. Was not this method of treating the text that of the old masters of austere style? This, too, has for centuries been the Church's attitude towards music, and has prevented it from falling into sentimentalism, and consequently into individualism.[46]

And while Latin was "a language of fixed accents," never does this fixity appear to have infringed on the powerful thrust of certain "musical dictates" (once these dictates had been "set in motion" by the text's sonorous potential):

> "Stravinsky's scansion of the Latin syllables is sometimes rather unorthodox." I quote a much quoted criticism. In fact, however, my scansion is entirely unorthodox. It must break every rule, if only because Latin is a language of fixed accents and I accentuate freely according to my musical dictates. Even the shift from "*OE*dipus" to "*OeDI*pus" (which must be pronounced "*OY*dipus" by the singers and "*EE*dipus" by the speaker) is unthinkable from the point of view of speech though that, of course, is *not* my point of view.[47]

A quite similar palate governs the conception of Latin in the *Symphony of Psalms* three years later. Here, too, it is the "*sounds* of the syllables" for which Stravinsky cares, the "*sounds*" which whet his appetite and activate his "musical saliva." Seeking to regulate his prosody accordingly, he grows indignant at experts forever counseling him on the consequent violence of his word-splitting, on the syllabification of *Dominum*, for example, in the famed "*Dominum* Cadence" which both introduces and concludes the allegro in the third and final movement:

> The final hymn of praise [No. 22] must be thought of as issuing from the skies, and agitation is followed by "the calm of praise," but such statements embarrass me. What I can say is that in setting the words of this final hymn, I cared above all for the *sounds* of the syllables, and I have indulged my besetting pleasure of regulating prosody in my own way. I really do tire of people pointing out that *Dominum* is one word and that its meaning is obscured the way I respirate it, like the Allelujah in the *Sermon* [1961], which has reminded everybody of the *Psalms*. Do such people know nothing about word-splitting in early polyphonic music? One hopes to worship God with a little art if one has any, and if one hasn't, and cannot recognize it in others, then one can at least burn a little incense.[48]

Nor was French an exception. Collaborating with André Gide on a text for *Perséphone* (1934), Stravinsky despaired of Gide's limited understanding of his methods, which he himself clearly recognizes as bound to tradition.

[Gide] had expected the *Perséphone* text to be sung with exactly the same stresses he would use to recite it. He believed my musical purpose should be to imitate or underline the verbal pattern: I would simply have to find pitches for the syllables, since he considered he had already composed the rhythm. The tradition of *poesia per musica* meant nothing to him. And, not understanding that a poet and a musician collaborate to produce *one* music, he was only horrified by the discrepancies between my music and his.

I turned to [Paul] Valéry for support, and no arbiter could have given me more. I do not know what he said to Gide. But to me he affirmed the musician's prerogative to treat loose and formless prosodies (such as Gide's) according to his musical ideas, even if the latter led to "distortion" of phrasing or to breaking up, for purposes of syllabification, of the words themselves.[49]

Even when turning to Hebrew in *Abraham and Isaac* during the later serial years (a language almost unknown to him), sections of a program note sound the familiar attitude:

No translation of the Hebrew should be attempted, the Hebrew syllables, both as accentuation and timbre, being a principal and a fixed element of the music. I did not try to follow Hebrew cantillation, of course, as that would have imposed crippling restrictions, but the verbal and the musical accentuation *are* identical in this score, which fact I mention because it is rare in my music. Repetitions of words occur—not a rare event with me—but never with exact musical repetition. . . .

Of the multiple origins of every work, the most important is the least easy to describe. I must say, however, that the initial stimulus came to me with the discovery of Hebrew as sound.[50]

The caution here that "no translation of the Hebrew should be attempted, the Hebrew syllables, both as accentuation and timbre, being a principal and fixed element of the music" is entirely apropos. For while Stravinsky, during the "Swiss years," had collaborated with C. F. Ramuz in the French translation of a host of "Russian" pieces (e.g., *Pribaoutki, Renard, Les Noces*), he quickly grew intolerant of wholesale linguistic transposition, to the point of preferring to hear these early pieces "in Russian or not at all." For the syllabification, "in accentuation and timbre," was too integral a part of the musical conception, too "principal" and "fixed" an element (as he reminds us in regard to *Abraham and Isaac*). Apart from a "cultural unity" summarily forfeited, translation too radically altered the character of his *music*.

Let librettos and texts be published in translation, let synopses and arguments of plots be distributed in advance, let imaginations be appealed to, but
do not change the sound and the stress of words that have been composed to
precisely certain music at precisely certain places. Anyway, the need to know
"what they are singing about" is not always satisfied by having it sung in one's
own language, especially if that language happens to be English. There is a
great lack of school for singing English, in America at any rate; the casts of
some American productions of opera in English do not all seem to be singing
the same language. And "meaning," the translator's *argument d'être*, is only
one item. Translation changes the character of a work and destroys its cultural unity.

An example of translation destroying text and music occurs in the latter
part of my *Renard*. The passage I am referring to—I called it a *pribaoutki*—
exploits a speed and an accentuation that are natural to Russian (each language has characteristic tempi which partly determine musical tempo and
character). No translation of this passage can translate what I have done musically with the language. But there are many such instances in all of my Russian vocal music; I am so disturbed by them I prefer to hear those pieces in
Russian or not at all. Fortunately Latin is still permitted to cross borders—at
least no one has yet proposed to translate my *Oedipus*, my *Psalms*, my *Canticum*, and my *Mass*.

The presentation of works in original language is a sign of a rich culture in
my opinion. And, musically speaking, Babel is a blessing.[51]

All of this final item is further testimony to an immensely resourceful
spirit, a composer who, taking as cue an obscure trait pervading the pronunciation of Russian popular verse, managed his syllabification in such a
way as to accommodate the most profoundly personal of impulses made
manifest in the rhythmic (or metric) invention—but equally in the other
realms of melody, form, and vertical (or "harmonic") coincidence. With
respect to this we again find it tempting to invoke the parting tribute of
Benjamin Boretz. For the "whole new musical worlds" fondly envisioned
by Boretz on behalf of this "rhythmic genius" are not only whole musical
structures, whole pitch organizations with all dimensions, realms, or domains of musical thought, or categories of inference, subsumed, but encompass, as inseparable matter, the "outward" repercussions of certainty
in tempo, precision in articulation, predilection in instrumental layout,
and flexibility in verbal/syllable stress to which our attention has in the
final section of this chapter directed itself.

NINE
THE NEOCLASSICAL INITIATIVE

CHANGE OF LIFE

I have had to survive two crises as a composer, though as I continued to move from work to work I was not aware of either of them as such, or, indeed, of any momentous change. The first—the loss of Russia and its language of words as well as of music—affected every circumstance of my personal no less than my artistic life, which made recovery more difficult. Only after a decade of samplings, experiments, amalgamations did I find the path to *Oedipus Rex* [1927] and the *Symphony of Psalms* [1930]. Crisis number two was brought on by the natural outgrowing of the special incubator in which I wrote *The Rake's Progress* [1948–51]. . . . The period of adjustment [i.e., with serial techniques] was only half as long this time, but as I look back on it I am surprised at how long I continued to straddle my "styles." [*Themes and Episodes,* p. 23.]

My instinct is to recompose, and not only students' works, but old masters' as well. When composers show me their music for criticism, all I can say is that I would have written it quite differently. Whatever interests me, whatever I love, I wish to make my own (I am probably describing a rare form of kleptomania). [*Memories and Commentaries,* p. 104.]

The suggestion that was to lead to *Pulcinella* [1920] came from Diaghilev one spring afternoon while we were walking together in the Place de la Concorde: "Don't protest at what I am about to say. I know you are much taken by your Alpine colleagues"—this was said with withering contempt—"but I have an idea that I think will amuse you more than anything they can propose. I want you to look at some delightful eighteenth-century music with the idea of orchestrating it for a ballet." . . .

I looked, and I fell in love. My ultimate selection of pieces derived only partly from Diaghilev's examples, however, and partly from published editions, but I played through the whole of the available Pergolesi before making my choices. . . .

Pulcinella was the swan song of my Swiss years. It was composed in a small attic room of the Maison Bornand in Morges, a room crowded by a cimbalom, a piano, a harmonium, and a whole *cuisine* of percussion instruments. I began by composing on the Pergolesi manuscripts themselves, as though I were cor-

252

recting an old work of my own. I began without preconceptions or aesthetic attitudes, and I could not have predicted anything about the result. I knew that I could not produce a "forgery" of Pergolesi because my motor habits are so different; at best, I could repeat him in my own accent. That the result was to some extent a satire was probably inevitable—who could have treated *that* material in 1919 without satire?—but even this observation is hindsight; I did not set out to compose a satire and, of course, Diaghilev hadn't even considered the possibility of such a thing. A stylish orchestration was what Diaghilev wanted, and nothing more, and my music so shocked him that he went about for a long time with a look that suggested The Offended Eighteenth Century. In fact, however, the remarkable thing about *Pulcinella* is not how much but how little has been added or changed. . . .

Pulcinella was my discovery of the past, the epiphany through which the whole of my late work became possible. It was a backward look, of course— the first of many love affairs in that direction—but it was a look in the mirror, too. No critic understood this at the time, and I was therefore attacked for being a *pasticheur*, chided for composing "simple" music, blamed for deserting "modernism," accused of renouncing my "true Russian heritage." [*Expositions and Developments*, pp. 126–29.]

[Apropos *Oedipus Rex* (1927).] Although I have been concerned with questions of musical manners all my life, I am unable to say precisely what these manners are. That, I think, is because they are not precompositional, but of the essence of the musical act: the manner of saying and the thing said are, for me, the same. But am I not unusually conscious of the manner question, nevertheless? All I can say is that my manners are my personal relations with my material. *Je me rends compte* in them. Through them I discover my laws. The direction of the next melodic interval is involved with the musical manners of the whole work. Thus, the clarinet trill at *"lux facta est"* is a manifestation of my *Oedipus* manners: the trill is not just a trill but an indispensable mannerism. I have been told that such things merely indicate the culture-consciousness found in all *émigrés*, but I know that the explanation is deeper than that, as I worked and thought in exactly the same way in Russia. My manners are the birthmark of my art.

. . . . I do not now recall any predatory attractions to other composers at the time, though, if another composer is suggested in my score, he is Verdi. Much of the music is a *Merzbild*, put together from whatever came to hand. I mean, for example, such little games as the offbeats at No. 50 and the Alberti-bass horn solo accompanying the Messenger. I also mean the fusion of such widely divergent types of music as the *Folies Bergères* tune at No. 40 ("The girls enter, kicking") and the Wagnerian 7th-chords at Nos. 58 and 74. I have made these bits and snatches my own, I think, and of them a unity. "Soule is form," Spenser says, "and doth the bodie make." . . .

The music? I love it, all of it, even the Messenger's fanfares, which remind me of the now badly tarnished trumpets of early 20th Century-Fox. Neoclassicism? A husk of style? Cultured pearls? Well, which of us today is not a highly conditioned oyster? I know that the *Oedipus* music is valued at about zero by present progressive-evolutionary standards, but I think it may last awhile in spite of that. I know, too, that I relate only from an angle to the German stem (Bach—Haydn—Mozart—Beethoven—Schubert—Brahms—Wagner—Mahler—Schoenberg), which evaluates solely in terms of where a thing comes from and where it is going. But an angle may be an advantage. [*Dialogues and a Diary*, pp. 10-11.]

In *Apollo* [1928] I tried to discover a melodism free of folk-lore. . . .

Apollo was my largest single step toward a long-line polyphonic style, and though it has a harmonic and melodic, above all an intervallic, character of its own, it nourished many later works as well. [*Dialogues and a Diary*, pp. 17–19.]

R.C. In your Greek-subject pieces *Apollo, Oedipus, Orpheus, Perséphone,* dotted rhythms are of great importance. . . . Is the use of these rhythms a conscious stylistic reference to the eighteenth century?

I.S. Dotted rhythms are characteristic eighteenth-century rhythms. My uses of them in these and other works of that period, such as the introduction to my Piano Concerto, are conscious stylistic references. I attempted to build a new music on eighteenth-century classicism, using the constructive principles of that classicism (which I cannot define here) and even evoking it stylistically by such means as dotted rhythms. [*Conversations with Stravinsky*, pp. 17–18.]

[Apropos the *Capriccio* for piano and orchestra (1929).] Mendelssohn's elegance attracted me early in my career as my *Scherzo fantastique* indicates, but my appreciation of Weber did not come until the 1920's with a performance of *Der Freischütz* in Prague conducted by Alexander von Zemlinsky. I acquainted myself with all of Weber's music after that *Freischütz*, with the result that his piano sonatas may have exercised a spell over me at the time I composed my *Capriccio;* a specific rhythmic device in the *Capriccio* may be traced to Weber, at any rate. [*Dialogues and a Diary*, pp. 17–18.]

[Apropos the *Concerto for Two Pianos* (1935).] I had steeped myself in the variations of Beethoven and Brahms while composing the Concerto, and in Beethoven's fugues. I am very fond of my fugue, and especially of the after-fugue or fugue consequent, but then, the Concerto is perhaps my "favorite" among my purely instrumental pieces. The second movement, the *Notturno,* is not so much night music as after-dinner music, in fact, a digestive to the larger movements. [*Dialogues and a Diary*, p. 75.]

[Apropos the "Dumbarton Oaks" *Concerto in E♭* (1938).] I studied and played Bach regularly during the composition, and I was greatly attracted to the Brandenburg Concertos, especially the third, which I have also conducted. The first theme of my Concerto is, of course, very like Bach's in that work, and so is my instrumentation—the three violins and three violas, both frequently *divisi a tré,* though not chordally as in Bach. I do not think, however, that Bach would have begrudged me the loan of these ideas and materials, as borrowing in this way was something he liked to do himself. [*Themes and Episodes,* p. 40.]

Apropos the *Symphony in C* (1940).] [Pierre] Suvchinsky reported in Paris that he had seen the score of Tchaikovsky's First Symphony on my piano. This information, together with the discovery of a similarity in our first themes, is responsible for the rumor of relationship between my Symphony and Tchaikovsky's which was soon claiming model status for the latter. . . . What, however, if Suvchinsky had told of the Haydn and Beethoven scores on my desk? No one would have paid him any attention, yet those two celestial powers stand behind the first, and even the pastoral second, movement far more significantly than my lonely, self-pitying compatriot. . . .

But enough of autobiography! And enough of musical biography, too— for what can one say about a score that is so unmysterious and so easy to follow at all levels and in all of its relationships? The answer is that critics (who must also earn their livelihood) will find a great deal of nothing to say, finding factitious comparisons with other music, then drawing attention to the severity of the diatonicism while tracing the development of the motive in the first movement and accusing me, in it, of consistency (which I dislike because only mediocre composers are consistent, as only good ones are capable of being very bad). They will also uncover my supposed use of Italianate song-and-accompaniment in the second movement, and of *fugato* in the last two movements, and discover the existence of a suite-of-dances in the third movement and of flirtations with ballet in other movements, but anyone who had failed to notice this much would require a different sort of commentary in any case. [*Themes and Episodes*, pp. 42–44.]

Having chosen a period-piece subject, I decided—naturally, as it seemed to me—to assume the conventions of the period as well. *The Rake's Progress* [1948–51] is a conventional opera, therefore, but with the difference that these particular conventions were abjudged by all respectable (i.e., progressive) circles to be long since dead. My plan of revival did not include updating or modernizing, however—which would have been self-contradictory, in any case—and it follows that I had no ambitions as a reformer, at least not in the line of a Gluck, a Wagner, or a Berg. In fact, these great progressivists sought to abolish or transform the very clichés I had tried to re-establish, though my restitutions were by no means intended to supersede their now conventionalized reforms (i.e., the leitmotif systems of Wagner and Berg.)

Can a composer re-use the past and at the same time move in a forward direction? Regardless of the answer (which is "yes"), this academic question did not trouble me during the composition, nor will I argue it now, though the supposed backward step of *The Rake* has taken on a radically forward-looking complexion where I have compared it with some more recent progressive operas. Instead, I ask the listener to suspend the question as I did while composing, and, difficult as the request may be, to try to discover the opera's own qualities. For a long time *The Rake* seemed to have been created for no other purpose than journalistic debates concerning: (a) the historical validity of the approach; and (b) the question of pastiche. If the opera contains imitations, however—especially of Mozart, as has been said—I will gladly allow the charge if I may thereby release people from the argument and bring them to the music. [*Themes and Episodes*, pp. 49–50.]

Stravinsky, in 1924, began a concert career as conductor and pianist, much busier and more lucrative than Bartók's or Schoenberg's, though still obscure compared with a Toscanini or Rachmaninov, and less than satisfying in the light of Stravinsky's early success. He provided himself with new pieces: the Piano Concerto, Piano Sonata, and Serenade in A. Each was a different kind of embodiment of the "traditionalist" policy that he had established in *The Soldier's Tale*, made firm in *Pulcinella*, deliberately proclaimed in *Mavra*, and epitomized in the Octet. But audiences and managers wanted to hear the early "revolutionary" ballets more than any of these strange new-old pieces, thus betraying their shallow understanding of the ballets, disappointing the composer, and perhaps inducing him to exaggerate his reactionary, counter-revolutionary stand. The new works, to be sure, won him fresh admiration from an élite larger than Schoenberg's close-knit circle or Bartók's interna-tional group of friends, and they gradually made their way almost as far as the audience that appreciated the *Rite*. But works like the Piano Concerto would never spread so far as *Firebird*. They presumed sophistication. They alluded not simply to Bach and Beethoven, but to separate traits of the classic styles. They treated these traits with such dry irony, such jerky stiffness, and such evident distortion that even a sympathetic listener needed several hear-ings to penetrate beneath the wit and skill to the glowing warmth of the melo-dies and the subtle continuity of the forms. [William W. Austin, *Music in the 20th Century*, p. 330.]

CHANGE OF LIFE

So there *is* a dividing line then, something tangible separating and distin-guishing the neoclassical initiative from "Russian"thought. Stravinsky tired of Russian folk versification. Or he tired of those reiterating (0 2 3 5) tetrachordal fragments and their referential implications. Or else, as he says, he "fell in love," determined to seek an accommodation and "make his own" certain practices, conventions, or idiosyncracies of certain hitherto neglected musical traditions. (We are prone to forget that Stra-vinsky's "love affairs"—Pergolesi, Bach, Mozart, Beethoven, Mendel-ssohn, Tchaikovsky, Weber, etc.—were directed not so much at the material at hand as at the always sought-after, the always to-be-realized *accommodation*, at reinterpretation and recomposition. These "love affairs," "backward looks," or "raids on the past" were predicated on the consciousness of a potential, on the stirring of the ear toward a potent merger between the consistency, identity, and distinction of his own music and certain practices, conventions, or idiosyncracies of those neglected musical traditions. The object of his affection lay not, strictly speaking, in the music of the above-noted composers but in accommodation and ap-propriation, the "making his own" (his "rare form of kleptomania"); it lay not in his "models," but in his recomposition, his "accent," his own music—and then not even in his own music, but in the *composing* of his own music.)

But what may seem peculiar or even unprecedented from an analytical-theoretical or historical perspective is the *non-immediacy* of all these transient "influences," the distance that now separates Stravinsky from his past, his "models." (Compare, in this respect, Schoenberg's historically more "natural" preoccupation with his immediate past in the music of his immediate predecessor, Mahler, and his teacher-pupil relationship with contemporaries like Webern, Berg, and Krenek.)[1] It is this non-immediacy which gives neoclassicism its most distinctive, yet unexpected and ironic, twist: notwithstanding these studied encounters with the past, the impression gained of Stravinsky is that of a loner, of a composer severed, set apart, sidetracked. Stravinsky seems as obsessively preoccupied with his newly found, uniquely fashioned forms of accommodation with Baroque and Classical C-scale (or major-scale) literature as he was earlier with his uniquely fashioned "fabrication" of Russian folk-like material. In other words, notwithstanding these many and varied "love affairs"; these studied accommodations or appropriations; the extraordinary "reach" in historical scope; the "widely divergent types of music" ultimately subsumed (for the neoclassical label has as much to do with Baroque, Romantic, and even Renaissance conventions as it does with eighteenth-century Classicism); the numerous and lengthy concert tours undertaken as a conductor and pianist (principally of his own music); the truly international, cosmopolitan, worldly air assumed by Stravinsky as a consequence of all this traffic, the impression gained is one of personal and artistic isolation. From *Petroushka* onward, during both the "Russian" and neoclassical eras, Stravinsky remained aloof, strangely unaffected by the music of his immediate predecessors and contemporaries.[2] Even the early jazz influence—certainly contemporary—seems almost incidental when supposedly most conspicuous (e.g., in *Histoire du soldat* (1918), *Ragtime* (1918), and the *Piano Rag-Music* (1919), or in the later *Ebony Concerto* (1945)), so distorted, so completely enveloped is this "influence" by accommodation. (Stravinsky later confessed that his early knowledge of jazz was derived from sheet music; its appeal was thus naturally subject to his own efforts at "simulation.")[3]

And there is that curious indifference toward—or ignorance of—the music of his immediate predecessors and contemporaries. Apart from some early borrowings from Debussy (noted in chapter 5), the only truly contemporary piece of music which seems to have left an impression was Schoenberg's *Pierrot lunaire* (1912), which Stravinsky heard with Diaghilev on a visit to Berlin in December 1912 (when he also met Schoenberg). Indeed, so impressed was Stravinsky that, on returning to France, he relayed his enthusiasm to Debussy and Ravel, and set about composing the

Three Japanese Lyrics (1913). But this influence of Schoenberg (through *Pierrot*) was to prove not only superficial (*Pierrot* was understood "instrumentally" in the *Three Japanese Lyrics;* or *d'un façon impressioniste*, as Pierre Boulez has remarked, an estimate with which this observer agrees), but also short-lived.[4] For while Stravinsky later insisted that *Pierrot* constituted "the great event of my life" and that he was aware of its being "the most prescient confrontation in my life," even though its "real wealth" lay beyond him (as it lay beyond most others), there is no evidence of a follow-through (after *Lyrics*).[5] Indeed, incredible as it now seems, not until after Schoenberg's death in 1951 did Stravinsky, in the early 1950s, make any studied attempt (despite frequent opportunities) to rekindle his early enthusiasm and familiarize himself with the music of Schoenberg and his two disciples, Webern and Berg.[6] Of course, there was doubtless an element of self-protection in this. We can well imagine Stravinsky echoing in reference to Schoenberg what he would later cite Rimsky-Korsakov as having said about Debussy: "Better not listen to him; one runs the risk of getting accustomed to him and one would end by liking him."[7] But whatever the reasons, personal or professional, conscious or unconscious, this neoclassical impression of a loner, and its curious irony in light of all the many and varied "love affairs," "backward looks," or "raids on the past," remains indelible: Stravinsky was a tough, determined, defiant, and guarded composer (immensely guarded, as Robert Craft has commented, perhaps precisely because so "radically susceptible to personal influence").[8]

(It is noteworthy, too, that apart from Arthur Lourié in the 1920s and Robert Craft from 1948 to 1971, Stravinsky's closest friends and associates were rarely composers or even musicians, but most often writers, philosophers, ballet impresarios, and choreographers: Stepan Mitusov, Sergei Diaghilev, C. F. Ramuz, Charles-Albert Cingria, Pierre Suvchinsky, Paul Valéry, George Balanchine, Lincoln Kirstein, Franz Werfel, Christopher Isherwood, Aldous Huxley, among others. Of these, Diaghilev appears to have been the only one whose artistic advice and opinions Stravinsky heeded. As for Craft, this comparative latecomer earned the "dubious distinction" of being the only one directly to disagree with Stravinsky and "survive.")[9]

SOME GENERAL CONSIDERATIONS

But turning now to the musical implications of the non-immediacy, relative isolation, and self-inflicted "change of life" of the critical "Russian"-noeclassical juncture, we could make some general observations about neoclassicism:

1. A new—but ultimately merely additional—interest in "absolute music," in instrumental invention divorced from the theater or from extra-musical implications. This interest is apparent at the outset in the *Concertino* for string quartet (1929), the *Symphonies of Wind Instruments* (1920), the *Octet* (1923), the *Piano Concerto* (1924), and the *Piano Sonata* (1924). (This interest is merely additional because the attraction to the ballet continues—albeit now to the so-called classical ballet—with *Pulcinella* (1920), *Apollo* (1928), *Le Baiser de la fée* (1928), *Jeu de cartes* (1936), *Scènes de ballet* (1944), *Orpheus* (1947), and *Agon* (1953–57). These ballets are complemented by some hybrid theater works, most notably the opera/oratorio (with speaker) *Oedipus Rex* (1927), and the "melodrama" *Perséphone* (1934).)

2. A frequently to be inferred—and naturally corresponding—preoccupation with the formal attire of Baroque and Classical C-scale (or major-scale) literature. Some preliminary examples: sonata-form accommodation in the first movements of the *Concerto for Two Pianos* (1935), the *Symphony in C* (1940), and the *Symphony in Three Movements* (1945); variation-form accommodation in the second movement of the *Octet* (1923), the third movement of the *Concerto for Two Pianos* (1935), the second movement—or second "Deal"—of *Jeu de cartes* (1936), and the third movement of *Danses concertantes* (1942); fugue or fugato at No. 51 in the variation movement of the *Octet* (1923), in the second movement of the *Symphony of Psalms* (1930), at No. 13 in the first movement of the "Dumbarton Oaks" *Concerto in E♭* (1938), at No. 23 in *Babel* (1944), or in the concluding third tableau—Apotheosis—at No. 143 in *Orpheus* (1947).

3. A frequently to be inferred—and naturally corresponding—breakdown of the rigid block structure of "Russian" works; or, more generally, a tendency, in the juxtaposition of heterogeneous blocks of material, to become less abrupt, rigid, or "heterogeneous" in an effort to accommodate the Baroque and Classical forms alluded to above. One preliminary example of this is sonata-form accommodation in the first movement of the *Symphony in C*. Here, the traditional scheme may be apprehended (as well as its classicism: regular metric periodicity, classical "surface gesture" of "theme and accompaniment," etc.). But Stravinsky fails to exploit the familiar C-scale tonally functional conceptions of harmonic progression, modulation, dominant-tonic relationships, applied dominant functioning, definitions of key and cadence (all of this constituting, obviously, the origin or rationale of the sonata form), so that the traditional key areas are ambiguous and are as apt to resemble Stravinsky's abruptly juxtaposed blocks (with their harmonically static ostinati) as they are the key areas or points of arrival and departure in the Classical C-scale conception. A further consequence of this is that much of the dynamic, progressive, developmental "style" of the Classical sonata is forfeited.

Thus, in reference to the I–II–III C–D–E sequence of "shifts" or blocks beginning at No. 5 in the first movement (i.e., the "shifts" from a "tonic" area to a "supertonic" area and to a "mediant" area), Edward T. Cone compares Stravinsky's I–II–III accommodation to the unambiguous I–II–V progression with applied dominants at the beginning of the Allegro con brio in the first movement of Beethoven's First Symphony (in C-major):

> Another example of the new perspective on older procedures is the presentation of the first theme, recalling as it does the corresponding passage in Beethoven's First Symphony with its I–II–V sequence. With Beethoven the movement from each degree to the next is a clearly functional harmonic step, with Stravinsky these movements sound less like true progressions than like his characteristic harmonic shifts. There are several reasons for this effect. In the first place, the C–E ambiguity casts doubt even on the solidity of the tonic. This doubt extends to the dominant, which is also suspiciously tinged with the E coloring. Then there is the peculiar phrase-structure: extended, repetitive developments over an *ostinato* so nearly static that harmonic inflections within each phrase sound like incidents in the part-writing. Owing to the consequent absence of unambiguous harmonic cadences, clear phrase-divisions must be achieved by interruption and even by interpolation, as in mm. 39–42. As a result the function of the supertonic statement thus prepared is obscured, in contrast to the corresponding harmony in the Beethoven, unequivocally established by an applied dominant. When Stravinsky's dominant arrives (m. 48) it is heavily colored by the previously noted E. What we hear then, suggests the stepwise shift of I–II–III as an alternate and even more persuasive interpretation of an ostensibly functional I–II–V.[10]

Correspondingly, in regard to fugal design, we cite Stravinsky's description of accommodation between the Baroque conception and his own "method" of abrupt juxtaposition, a description of the third tableau in *Orpheus* but applicable, in one way or another, to all instances of abrupt block juxtaposition:

> "See the fugue here," he would say, pointing to the beginning of the Epilogue. "The two horns are working it out, while a trumpet and a violin in unison sing a long, drawn-out melody, a kind of *cantus firmus*. Doesn't this melody sound to you like a medieval *vièle* (a viol)? Listen . . ." And his fingers would start fidgeting again on the keyboard. Then coming to a passage in the Epilogue where a harp solo interrupts the slow progress of the fugue, he would stop and say: "Here, you see, I cut off the fugue with a pair of scissors." He clipped the air with his fingers. "I introduced this short harp phrase, like two bars of an accompaniment. Then the horns go on with their fugue as if nothing had happened. I repeat it at regular intervals, here and here again." Stravinsky added, with his habitual grin, "You can eliminate these harp-solo interruptions, paste the parts of the fugue together and it will be one whole piece."[11]

4. A frequently to be inferred—and naturally corresponding—pre-occupation with Baroque and Classical C-scale "surface gesture," including, as we have suggested, typically Baroque patterns of toccata-like figuration, typically Classical formulations of "theme and accompaniment," and typically eighteenth-century dotted rhythm patterns. Some preliminary examples: apropos Baroque figuration, the opening material in the piano in the second movement of the *Capriccio* for piano and orchestra (1929); apropos Classical "theme and accompaniment," the variation theme at No. 24 in the second movement of the *Octet* (1923), or the second movements of the *Symphony in C* (1940) and the *Symphony in Three Movements* (1945); apropos dotted rhythms, the opening measures of *Apollo* (1928).

PITCH RELATIONS

On the other hand, while it is possible to take refuge in a documentation of this "Russian"-neoclassical divide merely in terms of form or "surface gesture," we shall be endeavoring to draw the distinction as it pertains more substantively to matters of pitch organization; or, to reverse the sequence, as pitch organization is linked to formal design, melody, and rhythm-meter. This is not to suggest, of course, that "surface gesture" is an inconsequential aspect of the accommodation, but only that its typicality, its Baroque or Classical imprint, is naturally heard and understood as it relates to the critical question of *reference*. Then, too, we shall naturally be wanting to know the fate of all those general methods of procedure (triadic superimposition, block juxtaposition, ostinatolike repetition) and all those predilections, peculiarities, or regularities compounded on behalf of "Russian" thought. In this respect we could acknowledge neoclassicism in the following manner:

1. The demise of that earlier "Russian" preoccupation with Model B's (0 2 3 5) tetrachordal partitioning of the octatonic collection, this partitioning implicating the 2, 1 whole-step–half-step descending interval ordering of the scale in terms of (0 2 3 5 6 8 9 11).[12]

2. In octatonic or octatonic-diatonic material (0 3 7/0 4 7/0 4 7 10 (1)) triadic, (0 1 3 4) tetrachordal, or (0 3 4/3 4 7/3 6 7) "minor-major third" partitioning of the octatonic collection is nearly always to be inferred. This partitioning implicates Model A's 1, 2 half-step–whole-step ascending interval ordering of the scale in terms of (0 1 3 4 6 7 9 10 (0)), and is evident in blocks or passages of unimpaired, explicit reference (see List 1 in chapter 2) and in blocks or passages exhibiting forms of octatonic-diatonic interaction and interpenetration (List 2 in chapter 2).

3. A diatonic articulation, while at times implicating the interval order-

ing of the E-scale and the A-scale (the descending minor scale, to use tonal terms), now rather persistently—and revealingly in relation to neo-classicism—implicates the interval ordering of the C-scale (the major scale in tonal terms). This C-scale reference was almost nonexistent in lengthy "Russian" works like *Le Sacre, Renard,* and *Les Noces.*

4. A persistent preoccupation with certain chromatic inflections of Baroque and Classical C-scale literature, this preoccupation often imposing itself in the form of an octatonic (Model A) and diatonic C-scale interpenetration.

5. An occasional yielding, in however parenthetical or "impure" a fashion, to certain tonally functional relations of C-scale literature, most notably the dominant-tonic relation, which often surfaces as a kind of terminating convenience (a kind of "cadence").

6. Accommodations between abrupt "block" juxtaposition and the tonally conceived forms of Baroque and Classical C-scale literature are frequently to be inferred. (The modes of this accommodation have been briefly surveyed above.)

And so our interests rest largely with these specific developments. Chapter 10 will examine (0 3 7/0 4 7/0 4 7 10) triadic, (0 1 3 4) tetrachordal, and (0 3 4/3 4 7/3 6 7) "minor-major third" partitionings of the octatonic collection (Model A; 1, 2 ascending interval ordering of the scale). These partitionings interact with the chromatic-tendency-tone or "melodic-leading-tone" convention of Classical C-scale literature, this interaction prompting a form of octatonic (Model A) and diatonic C-scale interpenetration. Chapter 11 will examine typically Stravinskian "progressions" involving the (0,3,6,9) symmetrically defined (0 3 7/0 4 7/0 4 7 10) triads and "dominant sevenths" of the octatonic collection (Model A; 1, 2 interval ordering), which may at times suggest past C-scale harmonic maneuvers even where reference to the collection is unimpaired and explicit. Chapter 12 will examine neoclassical passages, sections, or pieces in which an octatonic partitioning element, generally with (0 4 7 10 (1)) "dominant-seventh" or "dominant-minor-ninth" supplementation, acquires, retroactively, the characteristic "feel" of a dominant by virtue of a kind of tonic resolution concluded on its behalf for purposes of terminating such passages, sections, or pieces.[13]

In regard to the first of the concerns of chapter 10—(0 1 3 4) tetrachordal or (0 3 4/3 4 7/3 6 7) "minor-major third" partitioning of the octatonic collection (Model A) and the interaction of this partitioning with Classical tendency-tone inflections—the reader will find this typically neoclassical form of octatonic (Model A) and diatonic C-scale interaction summarized (in a preliminary *reference* fashion) in Examples 54, 55, and 56 of this chapter. In all three examples, Collection II has been selected from the three octatonic collections of distinguishable pitch content. In Example

54, Collection II is partitioned at three successive levels (as it was earlier in Model A, chapter 2): the first level records its "background" (0,3,6,9) symmetrically defined partitioning elements, D, F, A♭, and B; the second level records its (0,3,6,9) symmetrically defined (0 3 7/0 4 7/0 4 7 10 (1)) triads, "dominant sevenths," and "minor ninths" at D, F, A♭, and B; and the third level records its (0,3,6,9) symmetrically defined (0 1 3 4) tetrachords at D, F, A♭, and B (each with its embedded "minor-major thirds"). Example 55 records, on the octatonic side of the dotted line, the possibility of presiding D (D having been selected at random from the four (D, F, A♭, B) partitioning elements of Collection II); Collection II's symmetrically defined (0 3 4/3 4 7/3 6 7) "minor-major third" units in terms of (D F F♯/F F♯ A/F G♯ A); the (D F♯ A) "major" triad; these groupings jointly yielding, with a total (0 3 4 6 7) pitch content of (D F F♯ G♯ A), the (D E♭ F F♯ G♯ A B C (D)) reference collection, Collection II. On the interacting diatonic C-scale-on-D side of the dotted line, D is reinterpreted as a "tonic"; pitch numbers 3 and 6 of the "minor-major third" complexes, E♯ [F] and G♯ here, become Classical chromatic tendency tones or "melodic leading tones" to pitch numbers 4 and 7, F♯ and A as the "major third" and "fifth" of the (D F♯ A)

Example 54

Example 55

"tonic" triad; these groupings again yielding a (D F F♯ G♯ A) pitch content, but implicating the diatonic D-scale on C (the D-major scale in tonal terms, with E♯ [F] and G♯ as "outside" chromatic tendency tones). Finally, Example 56 allows for an alternative reading of this octatonic-diatonic interaction from the standpoint of the diatonic C-scale-on-D reference: pitch numbers 3 and 6, E♯ [F] and G♯, are conceived as Classical C-scale chromatic tendency tones to pitch numbers 4 and 7, the F♯ and A of the (D F♯ A) "tonic" triad, but also, but virtue of any cohesive affiliation with Collection II's (D E♭ F F♯/F F♯ G♯ A) tetrachordal or (D F F♯/F F♯ A/F G♯A) "minor-major third" complexes (coming generally in the form of a "clash"), as intruding "impurities," as octatonic (Collection II) pitches or intervals infiltrating and subverting the "purity" of the diatonic C-scale (on D) reference.[14]

Hence, as here interpreted, neoclassical manifestations of (0 3 4/3 4 7/3 6 7)—or even of (0 1 3 4/3 4 6 7)—"minor-major third" emphasis typically project a duplicity in function. They are conceived, on the one hand, as cohesive units, groupings, or partitionings within an octatonic system, and, on the other, with reference to the chromatic tendency-tone convention, derived from the Classical C-scale. Neoclassicism here reveals itself in the form of an interaction between symmetrically defined octatonic groupings and Classical C-scale tendency-tone inflections, that is, as a form of octatonic (Model A) and diatonic C-scale interpenetration.[15]

But the question arises: why not interpret these neoclassical manifestations of (0 1 3 4/3 4 6 7) or (0 3 4/3 4 7/3 6 7) "minor-major third" emphasis merely in terms of the "minor" and "major thirds"? Or why not interpret them solely in terms of the tendency-tone inflection? Or if articulated unconventionally—as is invariably the case with the (0 3 4/3 4 7/3 6 7) conceived "clash"—why not interpret such emphasis merely in terms of *superimposition*, in terms of a static "clashing" of the chromatic tendency tones with the chord tones (the "major thirds" and "fifths" of the (0 4 7) "major" triads) to which they traditionally tended *in succession* (notwithstanding appoggiaturas, suspensions, pedals, and the like)? In other words, why not hear and understand solely in terms of "impurity"? Indeed, the "minor-major third" phenomenon bears a striking resemblance in this respect to that earlier elision or superimposition of the dominant-tonic-

Example 56

subdominant relation (noted in chapter 7 in connection with the ostinati of *Histoire,* which we reinterpreted in terms of the superimposition of the four (0 2) (7 9) encircling elements of the (0 2 3 5 7 9) diatonic hexachord, not only because of the absence of C-scale tonally functional relations, but also because the articulation seemed conspicuously to warrant such an interpretation, especially in view of the persistence of the (0 2 3 5 7 9) hexachord in diatonic material of the "Russian" period). In light of all the static, symmetrically defined superimpositions, polarities, oppositions, and deadlocks encountered in these pages, this present (0 3 4/3 4 7/3 6 7) "minor-major third" phenomenon—especially the "clash" or "impurity"—might revealingly be apprehended as just another static super-imposition, polarity, or deadlock, indeed, as *just what might have been expected* from the neoclassical initiative, from Stravinsky's "raids on the [C-scale] past."

The answer to this is twofold. First, it is only with reference to earlier octatonic invention of the "Russian" period that this present neoclassical (0 1 3 4/3 4 6 7) or (0 3 4/3 4 7/3 6 7) "minor-major third" emphasis—or the special manner of its articulation in Stravinsky's neoclassical music—is revealingly heard and understood as just another characteristic superimposition, as "just what might have been expected." In other words, it is the symmetrically defined octatonic implications of the emphasis that tellingly reflect its typicality (i.e., its peculiarly Stravinskian imprint), and that enable us to pursue a hearing and understanding of identity and distinction with respect to both neoclassicism and Stravinsky's work "considered as a whole." Thus, all neoclassical manifestations of (0 1 3 4/3 4 6 7) or (0 3 4/3 4 7/3 6 7) "minor-major third" emphasis, whether found in passages explicitly octatonic or not, are here viewed as having their origin in the octatonic pitch collection. Evidence suggests that Stravinsky was drawn to the emphasis by way of his earlier invention with referentially octatonic material.

Second, it is persistently the case that these (0 1 3 4/3 4 6 7) or (0 3 4/3 4 7/3 6 7) "minor-major third" groupings are conceived as cohesive units in Stravinsky's music. Indeed, as complexes of pitches they often exercise a constructive or referential role as critical as the (0 4 7) "major" triads they are apt to encircle or surround (which are very often incomplete precisely in order that this constructive or referential integrity be ensured).[16] And so we prefer to speak positively of these complexes rather than negatively—or somewhat disrespectfully—in terms of "wrong notes" or "impurities." So, too, apart from any convenient comprehensive hearing and understanding of consistency, identity, and distinction, it is by acknowledging their octatonic credentials that we interpretatively confirm this constructive or referential integrity.

In other words, to interpret these "minor-major third" complexes—or

the pitches they encompass—merely in terms of Classical chromatic tendency tones or, when they are articulated unconventionally (cohesively,
usually as a form of "clash"), merely in terms of "wrong notes," "impurities," "clashes," or "minor-major third" superimpositions, is to acknowledge only one side of the coin: the C-scale side, the Classical major-scale
derivation. This denies these groupings the special manner of their articulation, their cohesive, symmetrically defined octatonic implications—
indeed, the typically Stravinskian "basic-cell" status they often achieve.

Hence, we shall here be interpreting the neoclassical (0 1 3 4/3 4 6 7) or
(0 3 4/3 4 7/3 6 7) "minor-major third" phenomenon as a form of octatonic
(Model A) and diatonic C-scale interaction or interpenetration. This will
mean that we may occasionally acknowledge the manner in which diatonic
C-scale settings are subverted by "intrusions" of cohesively articulated,
symmetrically defined, octatonic (0 1 3 4/3 4 6 7) or (0 3 4/3 4 7/3 6 7)
"minor-major third" groupings, or—perhaps a bit more frequently—the
manner in which Model A's symmetrically defined partitioning of the octatonic collection is modified or undermined in identity by a neoclassical
preoccupation with Classical C-scale conventions or chromatic tendency-
tone inflections. For while the pitch content of any (0 3 4/3 4 7/3 6 7)
"minor-major third" grouping is as octatonic as it is diatonic C-scale (the
latter, of course, only by virtue of the chromatic tendency-tone interpretation of pitch numbers 3 and 6), it is persistently the case that a (0 3 4/3 4 7/3
6 7) partitioning merely encircles or surrounds the (0 4 7) "tonic" triad (as
indicated in Example 55 in regard to Collection II's (D F♯ A) triad). Consequently, without some further transposition of this (0 3 4/3 4 7/3 6 7) partitioning to pitch numbers 3 and 6 (or without some additional (0 3 7/0 4 7/0
4 7 10 (1)) triadic or (0 1 3 4) tetrachordal "support" at pitch numbers 3
and 6—the E♯ [F] and G♯ in relation to the (D F♯ A) triad in Example 55),
these pitch numbers 3 and 6 are denied much of their potential (as envisioned in Model A) as (0,3,6,9) symmetrically defined partitioning elements. This is particularly true of pitch number 6, the tritone.[17] While
asserting a degree of independence, it cannot demonstrate that previously noted (0,6) tritone-defined "equal weight" and stand in a static, polarized "opposition" to pitch number 0 without some further transposition or additional (0 1 3 4) or (0 3 7/0 4 7/0 4 7 10 1) triadic "support."
Typically, then, *neoclassical manifestations of (0 1 3 4/3 4 6 7) or (0 3 4/3 4 7/3
6 7) "minor-major third" emphasis limit (0,3,6,9) symmetrically defined partitioning of the octatonic collection to pitch numbers 0 and 3*. Even under these conditions, this partitioning denies pitch number 3 the (0 3 7/0 4 7) triadic "support" accorded pitch number 0, that is, the partitioning merely encircles
or surrounds the (0 4 7) "tonic" triad. And so, perhaps rather persistently
in cases of (0 3 4/3 4 7/3 6 7) "minor-major third" emphasis, we shall be
acknowledging the manner in which the identity of the octatonic contri-

bution is undermined and placed at a disadvantage in relation to its inter-penetrating diatonic C-scale counterpart.

Still, rarely does Stravinsky deny the units of a (0 3 4/3 4 7/3 6 7) partitioning *some* integrity, *some* articulative cohesion (very often by means of the "clash"). Indeed, so crucial is this integrity in countless neoclassical settings that to imagine any such denial is often to banish Stravinsky from the scene, to imagine or envision just another Baroque or Classical C-scale (or major-scale) piece (but, as often as not, one without tonally functional relations, without the familiar harmonic progressions, modulations, definitions of key, cadence, and the like. Thus, the more cohesively articulated these complexes are, the firmer their octatonic implications become, and the less likely we are to encounter such tonally functional relations or progressions. And it is, of course, precisely the frequent absence of such relations or progressions in neoclassical passages exhibiting (0 1 3 4/3 4 6 7) or (0 3 4/3 4 7/3 6 7) "minor-major third" emphasis that has prompted us to restrict our reckoning of the C-scale side of this neoclassical octatonic (Model A) and diatonic C-scale interaction to chromatic tendency-tone inflections—instead, that is, of inferring a more committed applied- or secondary-dominant functioning for these inflections, for which rarely, if ever, is there sufficient evidence.)[18]

In chapter 11 we shall be examining "progressions" involving the (0,3,6,9) symmetrically defined (0 3 7/0 4 7/0 4 7 10) triads and "dominant sevenths" of the octatonic collection—more specifically, the extent to which, from one passage or piece to the next, correspondences with the "traditional harmony" of tonal, C-scale literature might legitimately constitute a basis for interpretation. (For the question has not to do with the actual presence of such correspondences, but with their relevance to our hearing and understanding of these octatonically conceived "progressions.")

Finally, in chapter 12, we turn to neoclassical substantiations, however parenthetical or "impure," of the dominant-tonic relation of tonal, C-scale literature. We shall here be confining our analysis to passages, sections, or pieces where a partitioning of the octatonic collection figures prominently, that is, where it is an octatonic partitioning element, generally with (0 4 7 10) "dominant-seventh" supplementation, that acquires, retroactively, the "feel" of a dominant by virtue of a toniclike resolution (toniclike because the "resolution" is invariably riddled with a peculiarity or "impurity" that tellingly reflects the specifics of the accommodation). Accordingly, this final neoclassical accommodation is to be reckoned as yet another form of octatonic (Model A) and diatonic C-scale interaction.

Nonetheless, the terms of this interaction differ markedly from those of the (0 1 3 4/3 4 6 7) or (0 3 4/3 4 7/3 6 7) "minor-major third" phenomenon. For while the chromatic tendency tones of Classical C-scale literature are referentially octatonic and thus available to each of the collection's (0,3,6,9) symmetrically defined (0 4 7) "major" triads, the dominant-tonic relation is not available to the octatonic collection and is therefore not in the same respect "referentially octatonic." Consequently, the toniclike resolution materializes outside the collection, and the "tonic" of the transaction is inevitably one of the four pitch elements not accountable to the collection to which the "dominant," as an octatonic partitioning element, is accountable.

Thus, in Collection I the four (0,3,6,9) symmetrically defined (0 4 7) "major" triads are rooted on E, G, B♭, and D♭. As potential "dominants," these (0 4 7) triads implicate A, C, E♭, and G♭ respectively as "tonics," all pitches lying outside Collection I (in fact they are the (0,3,6,9) symmetrically defined partitioning elements of Collection III).

In the first movement of the *Symphony of Psalms* (Example 68 in chapter 12), octatonic blocks accountable to Collection I (Model A's (0 3 7/0 4 7 10) triads and (0 1 3 4) tetrachords at E, G, and B♭) interact with, or are juxtaposed with, diatonic blocks or passages implicating the E-scale on E. And E or the (E G B) triad (the *"Psalms chord"*) crisply punctuates this interaction as the principal connecting link, articulatively shared between these interacting or interpenetrating collections of reference. Nonetheless, G, as a Collection I symmetrically defined partitioning element, steadily asserts itself with (G B D F) "dominant-seventh" supplementation. The "half cadence" on G which concludes the first movement suddenly prepares, in dominant-toniclike fashion, for the (quasi) C-minor fugal exposition which follows in the second movement, as well as for the (C E) simultaneities at Nos. 0–3 in the third and final movement, and the concluding (C E) simultaneity of the piece.

By the same token, B♭, as a Collection I partitioning element with "dominant-seventh" supplementation in the first movement, anticipates the C-scale-on-E♭ reference at Nos. 22 and 26 in the final movement. The (A C♯ E) triads at No. 5 + 4 in the final movement—and the (A C E/A C♯ E) triads at No. 8 with their (0 3 4/3 4 7) "minor-major third" emphasis—are in like manner anticipated or prepared by the E of the first movement; this long-range E anticipation is reinforced by the octatonic Collection I passage beginning at No. 4 + 8 with reiterating (E G♯ B) triads in the horns (explicit reference, List 1). Consequently, in regard to these long-term dominant-tonic transactions, we can imagine four options available to the octatonic collection: its four (0,3,6,9) symmetrically defined (0 4 7) triads, (0 4 7 10 (1)) "dominant sevenths" or "dominant minor ninths" may, as "dominants," anticipate four possible "tonic resolutions." (Further regularities are also to be detected in the transaction, or in each of the three collections. Thus, in Collection I, Stravinsky seems to have favored a form of C-scale-on-C (C-major scale) or A-scale-on-C (descending A-minor

scale) diatonic interaction as well as certain forms of (C E G) "tonic" conclusions.)

Finally, while we shall in chapter 12 be confining our discussion of the
dominant-tonic transaction to certain octatonic or octatonic-diatonic passages, sections, or pieces (circumventing much neoclassical material which
might, in this tonally functional respect, be considered highly relevant),
this confinement is no mere convenient yielding to the analytic-theoretical
prejudices of this inquiry. For it can just in this referentially octatonic respect be deemed a matter of consequence that Stravinsky should have singled out the *Symphony of Psalms* as a point of arrival, as an ultimate in neoclassical accommodation and synthesis.[19] In *Psalms* (and especially in the
first movement) we encounter as thorough a realization of Model A's (0 3
7/0 4 7/0 4 7 10) triadic and (0 1 3 4) tetrachordal partitioning of the octatonic collection (Collection I) as any in the literature. Coming after works
like *Apollo* (1928), *Le Baiser de la fée* (1928), and the *Capriccio* (1929) where
the collection figures peripherally if at all, portions of *Psalms*'s first and
final movements reclaim that earlier "Russian" commitment to octatonic
partitioning on an unimpaired, explicit basis. This referential commitment coincides with a highly abrupt from of block juxtaposition (especially in the first movement), so that, revealingly, the more abrupt and incisive formulations of this "architectural curiosity" may now seem to
reflect just such a commitment to (0,3,6,9) partitioning of the octatonic
collection (and hence to the static, non-progressive implications of this
partitioning).

To demonstrate this tellingly Stravinskian interplay between pitch organization and formal design, we briefly compare the first movement of
Psalms (Example 68 in chapter 12) with the first movement of the *Symphony in C* (1940), which was cited earlier in this chapter in connection with
sonata-form accommodation. Although the static ostinati of the *Symphony
in C* tend to undermine the Classical design and to forge a compromise or
accommodation with abrupt block juxtaposition, these blocks, however
static internally, project a recognizable sonata-form model, and even
reflect specific areas (e.g., "exposition," "recapitulation") of such a model.
But a design or model of this type is irrelevant in *Psalms*, so distinct are the
octatonic (Collection I) and diatonic E-scale-on-E blocks in instrumental,
dynamic, registral, and (above all) referential character, so incisively,
upon successive (near) repeats, are these blocks placed in abrupt juxtaposition, cut off and detached by the punctuating (E G B) *"Psalms* chord"
(which acts like a spacer, a signpost), and then by brief quarter-note
pauses (pauses of digestion).[20] The same stability in block identity and
abruptness in juxtaposition is found in the first movement of the *Symphony
in Three Movements* (1945), a movement which, like the first in *Psalms*, re-
claims that earlier "Russian" commitment to octatonic partitioning on an

unimpaired, explicit basis, and in which, as a consequence, the sonata form is so strictly formal as to be scarcely discernible at all. (See Lists 1 and 2 in chapter 2, and Example 75a in chapter 12.) And so, to repeat: symmetrically defined octatonic relations invariably—indeed, necessarily—prompt, provoke, or induce more abrupt forms of block juxtaposition, while passages or pieces in which such relations figure peripherally if at all reflect a greater consciousness of the traditional forms of Baroque and Classical C-scale (or major-scale)—literature.

Still, it is in *Psalms* that we encounter octatonic (Model A) and diatonic C-scale interaction in which the C-scale contribution imposes itself by way of these long-range dominant-tonic transactions. This is not to suggest that the transaction—or this form of octatonic (Model A) and diatonic C-scale interaction—is not already present in the concluding measures of the *Symphonies of Wind Instruments* (Example 67 in chapter 12), or in the variation movement of the *Octet* at Nos. 24–26 (Example 66 in chapter 12). However, its decisive formulation does appear to have been concluded in *Psalms* (Stravinsky's acknowledged summit, his point of arrival vis-à-vis neoclassical processes of accommodation).

TEN
(0 3 4/3 4 7/3 6 7) "MINOR-MAJOR THIRD" EMPHASIS

Such tendencies as have in the preceding chapter been ascribed to neoclassicism are by no means cut and dry or invariably apropos. Conceivably, neoclassicism might be traced to the Joseph Lanner tunes in *Petroushka*, to the *Eight Easy Pieces* for piano duet (1915), to the "snippets of early nineteenth-century Italian opera" in the "Royal March" of *Histoire*, or to the "Tango," "Waltz," "Ragtime," and chorales ("Little" and "Great") which conclude this eclectic affair—notwithstanding the "Soldier's March" and the music to Scenes I and II, which, as examined in chapter 7, do seem quite "Russian." Moreover, the *Symphonies of Wind Instruments* (1920) follows *Pulcinella* (1920). And the material here—or pitch organization generally—reflects "Russian" thought more readily than it does peculiarities of neoclassicism. And so there is some overlapping here, some "straddling," very much to be expected, best not overlooked.

More specifically, Model A's (0,3,6,9) symmetrically defined (0 3 7/0 4 7/0 4 7 10) triadic and "dominant-seventh" partitioning of the octatonic collection is as "Russian" as it is neoclassical. What gives Model A its "Russian" imprint are the links forged with Model B's (0 2 3 5) tetrachordal partitioning of the collection. For Model B's (0 2 3 5) partitioning of the octatonic collection *is* peculiarly "Russian," indeed, very nearly exclusively so. And the implications here are that this "Russian" (0 2 3 5) tetrachordal emphasis prompts the nearly always to be inferred (0 4 7 10) "dominant-seventh" partitioning of the collection with respect to Model A: pitch numbers 0, 2, and 5 of the (0 2 3 5) tetrachord (reading down) merely become, in the process of transformation, pitch numbers 0, 10, and 7 (the root, seventh, and fifth respectively) of Model A's (0 4 7 10) "dominant-seventh" complex. Hence the frequently to be inferred (0 2 5) incomplete articulation of the (0 2 3 5) tetrachord in "Russian" music. And hence our hearing and understanding of Model A's "dominant sevenths" in "Russian" music, summarized in chapters 4, 5, 6, and 7 in regard to *Le Sacre, Les Noces,* and *Histoire,* as a surfacing appendagelike to a prevailing (0 2 3 5) tetrachordal articulation.

But then, too, Model A's (0 1 3 4) tetrachordal and (0 3 4/3 4 7/3 6 7) "minor-major third" partitioning of the octatonic collection, surveyed in Examples 54, 55, and 56 of the preceding chapter, is likewise as "Russian" as it is neoclassical. To demonstrate this, three "Russian" passages examined earlier are here reassembled for inspection. Each of these passages is reinterpreted in terms of (0 1 3 4) or (0 3 4/3 4 7/3 6 7) emphasis, implicating the 1, 2 half-step–whole-step ascending interval ordering of the scale, Model A. In Example 57a (the opening measures of "Jeu du rapt" at No. 37 in *Le Sacre*), Collection III's (0 4 7 10) "dominant sevenths" at C and E♭ are reinterpreted with reference to the (0 1 3 4) and (0 3 4/3 4 7) units embedded in the configuration: (C D♭ E♭ E) and (C E♭ E/E♭ E G). In Example 57b (the block at No. 57 + 4 from "Jeux des cités rivales" in *Le Sacre*), the octatonic Collection II (F A C) triad, standing "in opposition" to the "lower" G♯–F♯ reiteration, is reinterpreted in terms of the (0 1 3 4) tetrachordal complex, (F F♯ G♯ A). Finally, in Example 57c, the Collection III (C–A–A/B♭/C♯–A) ostinato at Nos. 59–65 in *Les Noces* is reinterpreted in terms of the embedded (0 1 3 4) and (0 3 4) complexes, (A B♭ C C♯) and (A C C♯). Accordingly, without reference to a hearing and understanding of identity and distinction in "Russian" thought—and ignoring a more global attitude with respect to these contexts—the listener now hears, un-

Example 57a: *Le Sacre* ("Jeu du rapt")

Example 57b: *Le Sacre* ("Jeux des cités rivales")

Example 57c: *Les Noces* (second tableau)

derstands, and interprets these passages in terms of Model A's (0 1 3 4) and (0 3 4/3 4 7/3 6 7) "minor-major third" units.

Conveniently, however, a distinction arises. In these "Russian" pieces the interacting diatonic reference is decidedly not that of the C-scale (or major scale). These "Russian" manifestations of (0 1 3 4) or (0 3 4/3 4 7/3 6 7) emphasis surface without a trace of Classical C-scale conventionality, chromatic tendency-tone inflections, or any Classical C-scale "minor-major third" ambiguity upon which apprehension of the Stravinskian C-scale reference—or this present neoclassical form of octatonic (Model A) and diatonic C-scale interaction—hinges. A neoclassical accommodation is here scarcely in evidence.

Thus, at No. 37 in "Jeu du rapt" (Example 57a), the diatonic fragment in the flutes appears to implicate the D-scale on A with (0 2 3 5) tetrachordal emphasis in terms of (A G F♯ E) (D C B A)—reading down, as always in our analysis of Stravinsky's (0 2 3 5) tetrachordally oriented music, whether octatonic (Model B) or diatonic in conception. And E♭, far from exhibiting Classical C-scale tendency-tone behavior in relation to E of the (C E G) triad, is more readily heard and understood with reference to that persistent, globally defined 0–11 vertical interval span already registrally fixed in terms of E♭-E at No. 13 in "Danses des adolescentes." Articulatively, E♭ identifies more readily with Collection III's (E♭ D♭ B♭ G) "dominant seventh" than it does with Collection III's (C D♭ E♭ E) tetrachord. Consequently, while a (0 1 3 4) or (0 3 4/3 4 7) partitioning *may* be inferred, there is no interaction with Classical C-scale conventionality.

And so neoclassical manifestations of (0 1 3 4/3 4 6 7) or (0 3 4/3 4 7/3 6 7) "minor-major third" emphasis have not merely to do with a (0 1 3 4) or (0 3 4/3 4 7/3 6 7) partitioning of the octatonic collection, Model A. For such a (0 1 3 4) or (0 3 4/3 4 7/3 6 7) partitioning may always be inferred, with varying degrees of emphasis, where there is a Model A (0,3,6,9) symmetrically defined (0 3 7/0 4 7/0 4 7 10) triadic partitioning of the collection. Rather, manifestations of (0 1 3 4/3 4 6 7) or (0 3 4/3 4 7/3 6 7) "minor-major third" emphasis are neoclassical only by virtue of a shared, intersecting relationship with Classical C-scale conventions and inflections, and hence only when this relationship surfaces in the form of an octatonic (Model A) and diatonic C-scale interaction or interpenetration. Thus, as indicated from the vantage point of Classical C-scale conventionality in chapter 9: there must, apropos neoclassicism, be a yielding to both sides of the coin. A duplicity in the functional behavior of pitch numbers 3 and/or 6 of the "minor-major third" units must somehow impose itself. We must, on the one hand, be cognizant of a symmetrically defined, cohesive articulation of these units (Model A), and, on the other, of a reference to C-scale conventionality, with pitch numbers 3 and 6 as Classically conceived chromatic tendency tones. Moreover, being referentially as octatonic (Model A) as they are Classical C-scale, these (0 3 4/3 4 7/3 6 7) "minor-major third" groupings (along with the (0 4 7) "tonic" triad they are apt to encircle or surround) will constitute the principal connecting links in octatonic (Model A) and diatonic C-scale interaction, functioning in this pivoting, connecting-link capacity much as did the (0 2 3 5) tetrachord in "Russian" pieces. (See, again, Examples 54, 55, and 56 in chapter 9, and compare these to the connecting-link summaries sketched for *Petroushka, Le Sacre, Renard, Les Noces, Histoire du soldat,* and a host of subsidiary works in chapters 3, 4, 6, and 7.) Indeed, apart from their role as (between-reference) octatonic-diatonic connecting links, these (0 3 4/3 4 7/3 6 7) "minor-major third" groupings acquire the kind of germinal "basic-cell" status in neoclassical contexts that the (0 2 3 5) tetrachord—generally (0 2 5) incomplete—did in "Russian" contexts.

These, then, are the circumstances that permit a hearing and understanding of this neoclassical (0 1 3 4/3 4 6 7) or (0 3 4/3 4 7/3 6 7) "minor-major third" phenomenon in terms of an interaction between a partitioning of the octatonic collection, Model A, and certain conventions and inflections of Baroque and Classical C-scale (or major-scale) literature.

"BASLE" CONCERTO IN D (1946)

First Movement

Introduction (*Vivace)*	Nos. 0–5
Section A (*Vivace)*	Nos. 5–27
Section B (*Moderato)*	Nos. 27–38
Section C (*Con moto)*	Nos. 38–48
Section A' (*Vivace)*	Nos. 48–55
Section B' (*Moderato)*	Nos. 55–57
Coda	Nos. 57–End

The situation is for our purposes ideal some thirty years later in the "Basle" *Concerto in D.*[1] In contrast to Examples 57a, b, and c from *Le Sacre* and *Les Noces,* the introductory passage of the *Concerto* at Nos. 0–5 seems not only diatonic but neoclassical. (See Example 58a.) For this is a diatonicism conspicuously tinged with the conventions of Classical C-scale literature. Indeed, octatonic-diatonic interaction appears tipped in its favor, the C-scale on D here (the D-major scale in tonal terms).

And with what a vengeance does (0 3 4/3 4 7) "minor-major third" partitioning of the octatonic collection here impose itself in the form of a double functioning! With what insistence is neoclassicism revealed in the form of an octatonic (Model A) and diatonic C-scale interaction between Collection II's (0 3 4/3 4 7) "minor-major third" complexes, (D F F♯/F F♯ A), and Classical C-scale (on D) conventionality! Manifestly, the point of this introductory passage at Nos. 0–5 rests precisely with the dual, pivoting behavior of pitch number 3, the E♯ [F]. This E♯ [F] is conceived, first, as a member of Collection II's symmetrically defined, cohesively articulated (D F F♯/F F♯ A) "minor-major third" units, owing primarily to the (F F♯ A) simultaneity or "clash" at Nos. 0 + 2 and 1 + 1, but also to the (D F F♯) *spiccato* figuration in the upper strings at No. 3 + 2 (superimposed here over an F–F♯ reiteration in the cello). Second, it is also conceived as a Classical C-scale-on-D chromatic tendency tone to pitch number 4, the F♯ of the (D F♯ A) "tonic" triad, by virtue of the E♯–F♯ reiteration in the F♯–E♯–F♯–B–A theme at No. 1. Thus, octatonic (D F F♯/F F♯ A) affiliation

Example 58a: "Basle" *Concerto in D*

and Classical intent exist side by side. This duplicity in the functional behavior of pitch number 3 is acknowledged notationally whenever possible
with an E♯ when its function is clearly that of a chromatic tendency tone to
F♯, and with an F when the intention is more clearly Collection II's (D F
F♯/F F♯ A) conceived "clash"—with consequent elevation of pitch number 3 from a mere chromatic tendency tone to an element on a par with its
neighbors, warranting accountability at the collectional level, an accreditation which the C-scale on D cannot properly confer. Consequently, in
recognition of this duplicity we opt for an interaction between Collection
II and the C-scale on D. (See the dotted line in Example 58a, which, as
always in the analytical sketches of this volume, reflects octatonic-diatonic

interaction. The left-hand side refers to the octatonic Collection II contribution, while the pitches and groupings held in common are reinterpreted on the right-hand side in terms of the diatonic C-scale on D, the D-major scale.)

However, this hearing and understanding may be contingent on the fully accredited (accounted-for) C-scale-on-D reference introduced at No. 5 (not shown in Example 58a). For the (0 3 4 7 9) pitch content in terms of (D F F♯ A B) at Nos. 0–5 is as octatonic (Collection II) as it is diatonic C-scale on D. Indeed, inasmuch as this referential neutrality hinges on the chromatic tendency-tone behavior of E♯ [F] as pitch number 3—behavior only occasionally in evidence—Collection II's contribution may seem to outweigh or overshadow that of the C-scale on D. (The referential neutrality here at Nos. 0–5 is analogous to that of the opening block of *Les Noces*, where the incomplete (0 2 3 5) tetrachord in terms of (E D B) is similarly neutral or uncommitted. However, this (E D B) unit is assimilated by Collection I at No. 1, and this No. 1 block yields a Collection I pitch content of (E D B B♭ F). See Example 33 in chapter 6.)

But the irony at Nos. 0–5 in the "Basle" *Concerto* is that such an octatonic (Collection II) determination seems unreal. Despite the impeccable octatonic credentials of this passage (though incomplete, not fully accredited); despite the unimpaired, explicit reference to Collection II (List 1 in chapter 2); and despite the absence of tonally functional relations (harmonic progressions, definitions of key, cadence, and the like), the ear is still likely to opt for a hearing and understanding primarily in terms of the C-scale on D—with possible "minor-major third" emphasis. This preference for the C-scale on D is not only a result of the setting, of the forceful articulation of E♯ as a chromatic tendency tone in the F♯–E♯–F♯–B–A thematic outline at No. 1, or of the fully accredited and fully committed C-scale-on-D reference at No. 5. For unlike the Collection I (E D B B♭ F) pitch content at No. 1 in *Les Noces* (which likewise totals five referentially octatonic pitch elements), there is no pitch number 6 here, no tritone in relation to pitch number 0 (no G♯ for the "tonic" D, not even as a V–of–V chromatic tendency tone to A of the (D F♯ A) "tonic" triad.) And while the (3 4 7) unit in terms of (F F♯ A) is naturally a (0,3) symmetrically defined transposition—and transformation—of the (0 3 4) unit in terms of (D F F♯), this Collection II (D,F) partitioning denies pitch number 3, the E♯ [F], the (F A C) triadic "support" rendered pitch number 0, the "tonic" D, in the form of (D F♯ A). Consequently, while the listener is conscious of the integrity of Collection II's (D F F♯/F F♯ A) "minor-major third" units, the identity of the contribution suffers, and Collection II is placed at a disadvantage vis-à-vis its interacting, interpenetrating diatonic counterpart, the C-scale on D. Indeed, a more telling demonstration of the effects of the neoclassical accommodation on Stravinsky's octatonic routine(s) could scarcely be envisioned. Interacting now with the conventions, inflections, and gestures of Classical C-scale literature, (0 4 7) triadic and (0 3 4/3 4 7) "minor-major third" partitioning of the octatonic collection is "classicized." A good comparison would be with Nos. 68–70 in *Les Noces* (Example 38, chapter 6), where reference is similarly to Collection II, but where each of Collection II's (0,3,6,9) symmetrically defined partitioning elements, B, F, G♯, and D, is accorded (0 4 7 10) "dominant-seventh" supplementation.

And so, perhaps inevitably, we are led to this and similar neoclassical material with a diatonic C-scale (or major-scale) reference in mind, a reference hinging on certain conventions of Classical C-scale literature (since, as often as not, the tonally functional relations of this reference fail to materialize). Instead of an octatonic routine being affected by Classical C-scale conventionality, we are more apt in these cases to speak of a C-scale context being affected, contaminated, subverted, intruded upon, rendered pseudo or "impure"—in a word, Stravinskian—by peculiarities or "impurities" originating from a somewhat weakened, less forcefully asserted, but nonetheless still coalescing and interacting octatonic reference.

Indeed, we are here reminded that not once did Stravinsky admit to the octatonic implications of his invention; not once, in reference to neoclassicism, did he acknowledge the octatonic implications of his successive reinterpretations, "backward looks," or "raids on the past." (Never in his "composing with intervals" did he acknowledge the frequent confinement of these "intervals" to the octatonic collection.) Like so many early observers who, without recourse to the octatonic collection, interpreted his "dissonance" rather simplistically in terms of "unresolved appoggiaturas" (unresolved chromatic tendency tones?),[2] Stravinsky seems likewise to have viewed his neoclassicism—indeed, much of his "Russian" music as well—primarily in terms of past (tonal) C-scale conventions, inflections, and gestures. His only concession in regard to neoclassicism was to label certain pieces "in D," "in E♭," or "in C," leaving the minor-major implications of these key references in doubt. Even this awareness of (0 3 7/0 4 7) ambiguity is essentially anachronistic, predicated, as it is, on the (tonal) formulation or definition of keys.[3] Consequently, that the "Basle" *Concerto* at Nos. 0–5 could just as legitimately have been labeled "in Collection II" as "in D" would doubtless have struck Stravinsky as a bizarre proposition.

But however past observers (including Stravinsky) may have heard, understood, and interpreted, what remains for us of consequence is that we can now revealingly account for the articulation of all sorts of neoclassical peculiarities, "wrong notes," and "impurities"—a descriptive terminology obviously predicated on the Classical C-scale perspective—account, indeed, for the most frequently encountered of such "impurities," the (0 3 4/3 4 7/3 6 7) "minor-major third" phenomenon, in terms of the interacting octatonic collection. We do so through a continuing application of the notion of octatonic-diatonic interaction, whatever the changes in orientation from the *Scherzo fantastique* (1908) to *Agon* (1953–57), and however much these changes affect the specifics of the interaction.

We can well imagine how this interaction might have surfaced *in the act*, how ideas might have been conceived and nurtured with an ear keenly alert to their interacting octatonic and diatonic C-scale potential. We could even speculate that a not inconsiderable part of the delight in that "discovery" of Baroque and Classical C-scale literature might well have come by way of just such a sensitivity, from an awareness of the shared, intersecting status of the octatonic collection's symmetrically defined (0 3 4/3 4 7/3 6 7) "minor-major third" groupings and C-scale conventionality, and of how, by means of this intersection, a cherished heritage might be transformed.

There are subsequent passages in the "Basle" *Concerto*, first movement, that can further illuminate this perspective. In the Moderato section at No. 27, the pitch number 3–4 reiteration of the opening theme, E♯–F♯ in relation to the (D F♯ A) "tonic" triad, is transposed, becoming an E–F reiteration in relation to a (D♭ F A♭) "tonic" triad. (See Example 58b.) In this transposition from the octatonic (Collection II) and diatonic C-scale-on-D

Example 58b

interaction at Nos. 0–5 to the octatonic (Collection I) and diatonic C-scale-on-Db interaction at No. 27, the 3–4 reiteration is joined by a pitch number 6–7 reiteration in terms of G–Ab. Or, to revise this terminology in accord with Classical C-scale conventionality, the chromatic tendency tone to the "third" of the (D F♯ A) "tonic" triad at Nos. 0–5, the E♯, becomes an E in relation to the new (Db F Ab) "tonic" triad at No. 27, where it is joined by the chromatic V–of–V tendency tone to the "fifth" of this (Db F Ab) "tonic" triad, the G. (See the E–F and G–Ab or E/G–F/Ab reiterations, divisi in the first and second violins, Example 58b.)[4] Then, in the return of the Moderato section at No. 55 (see Example 58c), this material is transposed into the original mixed octatonic (Collection II) and diatonic C-scale-on-D conception: pitch numbers 3 and 6, the E♯ [F] and the G♯ here, may be heard and understood as intruding "impurities," statically "clashing" with pitch numbers 4 and 7, the F♯ and A of the (D F♯ A) "tonic" triad, effecting (0 3 4/3 4 7/3 6 7) "minor-major third" emphasis in terms of Collection II's (D F F♯/F F♯ A/F G♯ A) units; but on the Classical C-scale (on D) side of the interaction, they also function as chromatic tendency tones to these same pitch numbers 4 and 7, the F♯ and A of the (D F♯ A) "tonic" triad, holding this second identity by virtue of the E♯ [F]–F♯ and G♯–A or E♯[F]/G♯–F♯/A reiterations in the violins.

On a more broadly defined, literaturewide basis (with reference to

Example 58c

some of the distinctions already drawn between "Russian" and neoclassical thought), these pitch number (3–4) (6–7) reiterations in the "Basle" *Concerto* at Nos. 0–5, 27, and 55, all defining the interval of 1 or 13 (the half step or the "minor ninth"), are to be compared with the octatonically conceived (0–2) (6–8) or diatonically conceived (0–2) (7–9) reiterations (the 2s or whole-step reiterations) that litter "Russian"-period material (principally as ostinati; see, among the numerous passages examined in this light, Examples 32a, b, and c in chapter 5). For the change here from a 2 to a 1 (from a whole step to a half step) underscores the previously noted switch from the Model B emphasis of the "Russian" era (with each of the (0,3,6,9) symmetrically defined partitioning elements succeeded by the interval of 2) to the neoclassical Model A orientation (with each of these same (0,3,6,9) symmetrically defined partitioning elements succeeded by the interval of 1). This switch in turn reflects the neoclassical preoccupation with Classical C-scale tendency-tone inflections for pitch numbers 4 and 7 of the (0 4 7) "tonic" triad, or the interaction of this conventionality with a partitioning of the octatonic collection, Model A. More subtly, though, Model B's "chromatic" 0–11 or "major-seventh" interval span of the "Russian" era (see our analysis of *Le Sacre*, Example 27 in chapter 4; of *Les Noces*, Examples 33, 38, and 41 in chapter 6; or of Scene II in *Histoire du soldat*, Example 46 in chapter 7) is here replaced by a Model-A–conceived 0–13 or "minor-ninth" interval span (see the F–F♯ span of the (F F♯ A) "clash" at Nos. 0+2 and 1+1, or the G–A♭ stretch in the opening measures of the *Symphony in Three Movements*, Example 75a in chapter 12). With pitch number 0 of this 0–13 span accorded varying degrees of (0 4 7/0 4 7 10) triadic "support," the 13—or "minor ninth"—often carries "dominant-minor-ninth" implications, the variety of tonic-like resolutions concluded on its behalf constituting the focus of our concern in chapter 12.

On the other hand, rhythmic-metric implications in this concerto do seem as pertinent to "Russian" discourse as to neoclassicism. The rhythmic-metric scheme at Nos. 0–2, for example, adheres to the first of our two rhythmic-metric types: barred metric irregularity, with all the reiterating fragments, lines, or parts sharing the same rhythmic-metric periods as defined by the shifting meter. (Again, see Example 58a.) But note the concealed upbeat/downbeat contradiction or reversal in the successive repeats of the (F F♯ A) "minor-major third" simultaneity at Nos. 0+2 and 1+1. For Stravinsky's 6/8 upbeating at Nos. 0–2 (with the three F♯s commencing on the second beat of the 6/8 measure) obscures what, in relation to (tonal) C-scale literature, would most certainly have been conceived and barred as a downbeating 6/8 scheme (with the three F♯s commencing on the first beat of the 6/8 measure, as bracketed in Example 58a and rebarred accordingly below). Hence the (F F♯ A) simultaneity or "clash," while placed on the upbeat at No. 0 + 2, may actually be felt as a downbeat simultaneity. Then, with the irregular 9/8 measure at No. 1, the extra beat here enables the conventional (concealed) downbeating to fall into place. But not—and this is the point—without (felt) displacement: in accord with the conventional downbeating (and, of course, regular 6/8 metric periodicity), the (felt) downbeat identity of the (F F♯ A) simultaneity at No. 0 + 2 is at No. 1 + 1 contradicted or reversed, becoming a (felt and barred) upbeat simultaneity. Consequently, as is so often the case in applications of the first of our two rhythmic-metric types, metric irregularity—the irregular 9/8 measure at No. 1 here—is not really the point. Rather, it merely reinforces—but conceals—upbeat/downbeat ambiguity, the classic Stravinskian reversal, the sadistic "twitch."

Still, the opposing side of this invention's double edge is here equally in evidence. For while the (F F♯ A) simultaneity may, in accord with regular 6/8 periodicity, be heard and understood as effecting a contradiction or reversal in upbeat/downbeat identity, the irregular 9/8 measure at No. 1 allows it to assume the same upbeat identity at each repeat. Hence in direct opposition to the concealed contradiction or reversal (hinging, for its apprehension, on "background" regular 6/8 periodicity), this "foreground" irregular measure produces a counteracting "sameness" in (F F♯ A) repetition, which is in turn reinforced by fixed stress and dynamic markings accompanying the (F F♯ A) repeats. (In other words: the purpose of the shifting meter at No. 1 is to preserve, in opposition to the (concealed) upbeat/downbeat displacement, a fixed rhythmic-metric identity for (F F♯ A) and its subsequent repeat.)

Then, too, we may note the static character of the rhythmic-metric "play." The concealed contradiction or reversal, however titillating by provoking doubt and uncertainty as to the "true" (stable) rhythmic-metric identity of the (F F♯ A) simultaneity, has an arresting, halting tendency. This is because upbeat/downbeat or off-the-beat/on-the-beat displacements, pursued by means of the first or second of our two rhythmic-metric types, form in essence *polarities* of rhythmic-metric identity. A rhythmic-metric identity, once established, is subsequently—and very often immediately and abruptly—negated. And so the rhythmic (or metric) invention becomes self-enclosed, plagued by the same sense of stasis, "polarity," and deadlock (brought about by the confrontation of forces somehow of "equal weight and independence") that has seemed so much a part of pitch organization generally, and (0,3,6,9) symmetrically defined relations in particular. To the extent that these conditions manifest themselves in the formal realm (as they do in the "Basle" *Concerto* at Nos. 0–2, following the upbeat/downbeat contradiction or reversal of the (F F♯ A) simultaneity at No. 1 + 1), there is, strictly speaking, "nothing more to say" here, or perhaps "nowhere to go" (to simulate the composer's plight for a moment). Except, of course, to cut, to juxtapose, and to repeat the block and its built-in upbeat/downbeat contradiction or reversal by means of successive block repetitions. This is precisely what Stravinsky does in the majority of cases (although not in the "Basle" *Concerto*, whose opening block at Nos. 0–2 is never repeated), and particularly in those to which the first of our two rhythmic-metric types applies. In the opening block of the *Symphonies of Wind Instruments* (1920) as surveyed in chapter 8, Example 53a, the on-the-beat D–D–D–B reiteration in the clarinets is immediately contradicted or reversed at m. 4 by an off-the-beat D–D–B appearance (despite metric irregularity, which, in opposition to this concealed contradiction or reversal, imposes a rhythmic-metric "sameness" in (D)–D–D–B repetition). By this immediate contradiction or reversal, Stravinsky may be imagined as having afforded himself few options (to continue with his imagined plight), few options other than once again to break off, to abruptly juxtapose, and then to repeat this opening block via a succession of (near) repeats—as happens in the *Symphonies* at Nos. 2, 9, 26, 37, and 39.

Hence abrupt block juxtaposition. Or, we apprehend the interplay between rhythmic (or metric) invention and form. Stravinsky's abruptly disposed blocks seem necessarily the result not only of the static, polarized, deadlocked implications of (0,3,6,9) symmetrically defined relations (not only of pitch relations *tout court*), but equally (and at the same time) of the static, polarized, deadlocked implications of these upbeat/downbeat or off-the-beat/on-the-beat polarities.

The crisp, percussive punctuation essential to an apprehension of this rhythmic-metric "play" is underscored in the "Basle" *Concerto* not only by stress markings, but in the instrumentation as well. Once again, staccato lines double legato lines: the arco reiteration of F♯ in the first violins and violas at Nos. 0–2, spaced two octaves apart with accent markings and *fp*s, is reinforced, percussively, by pizzicato unison doublings in the second violins and cellos. In general summation: how utterly Stravinskian is the introductory setting at Nos. 0–5—in every conceivable respect, and notwithstanding the fact that features peculiar to the neoclassical stamp are here tellingly brought to bear.

Finally, in the C-scale-on-B♭ (or pseudo-B♭-major) framework of the second movement, "Arioso" (see Example 58d), the half-step reiterations of the first movement are converted into a bel canto A–B♭ reiteration, this reiteration defining, in relation to the C-scale-on-B♭ framework, a "leading-tone"–"tonic" succession. But since A, the C-scale-on-B♭ "leading tone," lies outside the octatonic collection in which B♭, the "tonic," figures as a (0,3,6,9) symmetrically defined partitioning element (Collection I), the octatonic implications of this final transposition (and transformation) are dropped altogether. (In other words, the leading-tone–tonic succession of tonally functional C-scale literature is not available to the single octatonic collection with the collection's (0,3,6,9) symmetrically defined partitioning elements envisioned as "tonics," and hence is not ref-

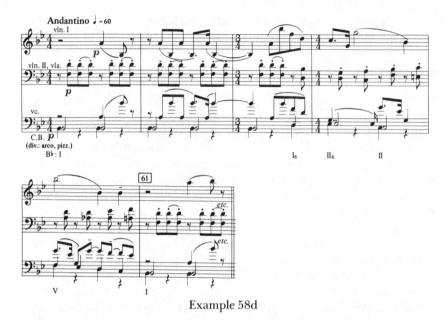

Example 58d

erentially octatonic in the sense in which this designation has been heard and understood.) Only the so-called melodic leading tones, the Classical C-scale chromatic tendency tones to pitch numbers 4 and 7, the third and fifth of the (0 4 7) "major" triad, are referentially octatonic—hence neither *the* leading tone nor the triadically disposed dominant-tonic progression or cadence. [See Examples 54, 55, and 56 in chapter 9; or consult Model A in chapter 2. We shall be discussing the dominant-tonic "imperative," its non-octatonic implications and the specifics of its accommodation in neoclassical works, in chapter 12.]

In its non-octatonicism, this pseudo-Bb-major framework of the second movement may be judged one of the most serenely Classical of neoclassical settings, one of Stravinsky's least ambiguously Classical—or at least ambiguously tonal/major-scale—accommodations. One discerns, with almost no octatonically conceived "spice" or "impurity," a I-ii₆–V *progression* in the first five measures, the first "phrase." To it we therefore apply, with little hesitation, the familiar codification of C-scale tonally functional behavior, the symbols of "traditional harmony."[5]

SYMPHONY IN THREE MOVEMENTS (1945): NOS. 112–18

Circumstances here at Nos. 112–18 in the second movement of the *Symphony in Three Movements* are remarkably similar to those surveyed in the

"Basle" *Concerto*. (See Example 59.)[6] Again we find the Classical setting, the typically Classical enunciation of theme and accompaniment. Again, the C-scale on D, the D-major scale in tonal terms; this reference is with us unmistakably at the outset, however, and fully accredited, fully accounted for. And again, "impurity" imposes itself in the form of pitch number 3, the F in the pizzicato accompaniment, this pitch number "intruding" or "clashing" with pitch number 4—its Collection II (D F F♯/F F♯ A) affiliation—but occasionally betraying conventional tendency-tone behavior with respect to this pitch number 4, the F♯ of the (D F♯ A) "tonic" triad. Pitch number 6, the G♯, is also with us here at the outset in the accompaniment, although it surfaces at No. 112+2 rather more as a Classical C-scale-on-D, V–of–V chromatic tendency tone to the A than as a member of Collection II's (F G♯ A) "minor-major third" unit.

Then, further along in the flutes and clarinets at No. 117, the (0 3 4 6 7 9) figuration in terms of (D F F♯ G♯ A B), as octatonic (Collection II) as it is Classical C-scale on D, continues to unfold with conspicuous reference to Collection II's (0 3 4/3 4 7/3 6 7) "minor-major third" complexes in terms of (D F F♯/F F♯ A/F G♯ A) and the duplicity in function: pitch numbers 3 and 6, F and G♯, may occasionally be heard and understood as independent elements, referentially octatonic (Collection II), and occasionally as chromatic tendency tones to pitch numbers 4 and 7, F♯ and A of the (D F♯ A) "tonic" triad, their Classical C-scale-on-D derivation. Moreover, the transposition of the Collection II and C-scale-on-D interaction from D to F (from pitch number 0 to 3) at No. 118 is revealing, for it reflects the prior (octatonically conceived) "intruding" and independent behavior of F, to an extent that Collection II, to which this behavior refers, may be credited with having prompted the harmonic direction at this point. Indeed, viewed as an extension or further elaboration of Collection II's interacting (D F F♯/F F♯ A/F G♯ A) "minor-major third" emphasis, this (0,3)-defined transposition from D to F emerges as a conciliatory gesture to Classical C-scale literature, an act of accommodation. For in place of a more fully committed octatonic framework at Nos. 112–18, in place of a (0,3) symmetrically defined triadic partitioning with Collection II's (D F♯ A) (F A C) triads placed in direct juxtaposition or superimposition (with pitch number 3, in other words, accorded its (F A C) triadic "support"), neoclassicism opts for this (0,3)-defined *transposition* of the whole octatonic (Collection II) and diatonic C-scale-on-D interaction from D to F—a (0,3)-defined pseudo-modulation. A very revealing—and highly incriminating—act of accommodation. For the surroundings come as close to the Classical C-scale on D (or C-scale on F at No. 118) as neoclassicism gets. Or *can* get, without relinquishing Collection II's side of the accommodation, without ceding the "neo" of neoclassicism, banishing Stravinsky from the scene—which, as we have seen, *almost* happens in the

Example 59: *Symphony in Three Movements*, second movement. Used by permission of European American Music Distributors Corporation.

opening "phrase" of the "Basle" *Concerto*'s second movement, Example 58d above. Yet, behind the pseudo-modulation, Collection II does wield its influence, and we shall in forthcoming neoclassical passages be witnessing similar (0,3)-defined transpositions or pseudo-modulations. The maneuver became a neoclassical habit.

But there are short-term "progressions," too. The (D F G♯) "diminished" triad at No. 113 is interpretable in traditional (tonal) terms as the (0 3 6) "raised supertonic," a verticalization of pitch numbers 3 and 6, the chromatic tendency tones. Traditionally, this verticalization has resolved to the (0 4 7) "tonic" triad, as, indeed, is here the case. But here, too, we might credit octatonic penetration for the harmonic direction, noting that this (0 3 6)–(0 4 7) "progression" in terms of (D F G♯)–(D F♯ A) is as octatonic (Collection II) as it is Classical C-scale on D. Hence, like the (0,3)-defined pseudo-modulation at No. 118, this (D F G♯)–(D F♯ A) "progression" is prompted as much by Collection II's (D F F♯/F F♯ A/F G♯ A) interaction as it is by Classical C-scale conventionality. (In the first movement of the "Basle" *Concerto in D*, it is this same (0 3 6) "diminished" outline in terms of (D F G♯) which at No. 18 anticipates a return to the opening C-scale-on-D material of No. 5; in the first movement of the "Dumbarton Oaks" *Concerto in E♭* (1938), it is this same (0 3 6) outline— but in terms of (E♭ F♯ A)—which at No. 2 + 2 breaks up and scatters the opening C-scale-on-E♭ figuration; in *Oedipus Rex* (1927), it is this same (0 3 6) outline—but (0 3 6 9) in terms of (C E♭ F♯ A)—which anticipates a return to the C-scale-on-C or (C E G) figuration at No. 28; and, again in *Oedipus*, this same (0 3 6 9) outline—but in terms of (F A♭ B D)—abruptly terminates the C-scale-on-F setting at No. 158, prompting a succeeding Collection I passage.) And so, revealingly, this (0 3 6 (9))–(0 4 7) succession—or its reverse—appears to have been one "progression"—or one Classical C-scale harmonic maneuver—that Stravinsky seems to have admitted rather freely. And its admittance is manifestly owing to octatonic (Model A) and diatonic C-scale interaction, to the fact that the "progression" is accountable to both interacting or interpenetrating references (or systems).[7]

Thus, as in the "Basle" *Concerto in D* at Nos. 0–5, we interpret in terms of an interpenetration between Collection II (Model A: 0= D) and the C-scale on D. Of course, this determination is predicated on the dual functioning of pitch numbers 3 and 6, the F and the G♯; their status as "impurities," independent pitches accountable to Collection II; and their state of dependency as conventional C-scale on D chromatic tendency tones to F♯ and A of the (D F♯ A) "tonic" triad. F and G♯ are without the (0 3 7/0 4 7) triadic "support" accorded pitch number 0, the "tonic" D, for, as indicated, the referentially octatonic (0 3 4/3 4 7/3 6 7) "minor-major third" units merely surround the (0 4 7) "tonic" triad. Consequently, while asserting a measure of independence, F and G♯ are denied much of the potential envisioned in Model A (and Collection II) as (0,3,6,9) symmetrically defined partitioning elements. A good comparison would be to Nos. 68–70 in *Les Noces*, Example 38 in chapter 6; or to Nos. 88–94 in the first movement of this *Symphony* (although not shown here), where D and F are accorded (F A C E♭) and (D F♯ A C) "dominant-seventh" supplementation, and are superimposed over a B–D–B basso ostinato (explicit octatonic reference, List 1 in chapter 2).

DANSES CONCERTANTES (1942)

Still, we need not venture that far afield, certainly not back to the Collection II block at Nos. 68–70 in *Les Noces* (1917), to consider in terms that are specifically neoclassical how very precariously, in both the first movement of the "Basle" *Concerto in D* and at Nos. 112–18 in the second movement of the *Symphony in Three Movements*, the referential balance is tipped in favor of Classical C-scale (on D) conventionality. Conveniently confining ourselves to yet another C-scale-on-D setting (or another octatonic (Collection II) and diatonic C-scale-on-D interaction), a lengthy passage at Nos. 30–34 in *Danses concertantes* seems a worthy antidote. (See Example 60.)[8]

Here, pitch-relational matters are at first glance markedly similar. The E♯–F♯–B–A theme itself, in general contour and pitch content, is equivalent to that of the "Basle" *Concerto*. And with the D in the accompaniment of the first few measures, the between-reference Collection II and C-scale-on-D (0 3 4 7 9) pitch content in terms of (D E♯ [F] F♯ A B) matches that at Nos. 0–5 in the "Basle" *Concerto*. (With the addition of pitch number 6, the G♯ at No. 30 + 3, the pitch content becomes the same as that at No. 117 in the *Symphony*.) Moreover, the notational fluctuation of pitch number 3 seems again to reflect, as in the "Basle" *Concerto*, a duplicity in function: as an F (as at No. 33), it may be heard and understood as an independent element, aligned with Collection II's (D F F♯/F F♯ A/F G♯ A) "minor-major third" complexes; but as an E♯ (as at No. 30), it functions as a Classical C-scale-on-D chromatic tendency tone to the F♯ of the (D F♯ A) "tonic" triad. Pitch numbers 3 and 6, the E♯ and the G♯, are introduced simultaneously at No. 30 as part of a (3 6 9)–(4 7) "progression" in terms of (E♯ G♯ B)–(F♯ A), a "progression" similar to that at Nos. 27 and 55 in the "Basle" *Concerto*, and to that at No. 113 in the *Symphony* (along with the supplementary examples cited in this connection).

But however marked these coincidences, the octatonic contribution is at Nos. 30–34 in *Danses concertantes* far more persuasively in evidence. Underneath the theme at No. 30 + 3 and No. 33, the inclusion of a pitch number 10, the C, boosts the cohesive octatonic count to seven pitch elements,

Example 60: *Danses concertantes*

(0 3 4 6 7 9 10) in terms of (D F F♯ G♯ A B C). This pitch number 10, the C, identifies articulatively with an (F A C) triadic accompaniment in the bass, an articulation with which pitch number 3, the E♯ [F], likewise identifies (and above which the (D F♯ A) triadic outline of the theme is crisply superimposed). Consequently, this latter pitch number 3, the E♯ [F], acquires precisely the kind of (F A C) triadic "support" absent from the mixed octatonic (Collection II) and diatonic C-scale-on-D passages examined in the "Basle" *Concerto* and in the *Symphony*. (Indeed, this music embodies the kind of Model A potential replaced in the *Symphony* by that "conciliatory gesture" in the form of a (0,3)-defined transposition or pseudomodulation from D to F.) And so here at Nos. 30–34 in *Danses concertantes*,

a hearing and understanding more readily octatonic are possible, the referential balance being possibly complete. For while the articulative partitioning limits itself to pitch numbers 0 and 3—as is typical of neoclassicism—E♯ [F], as a member of Collection II's (D F F♯/F F♯A/F G♯ A) "minor-major third" complexes or as a Classical C-scale on D chromatic tendency tone, no longer merely surrounds and confines itself to the (D F♯ A) "tonic" triad. Its articulative alignment with (F A C) boosts its credentials as a Collection II (D,F,G♯,B) symmetrically defined partitioning element. Our structural-level format is therefore apt to approximate those proposed earlier for the more fully developed octatonic settings of the "Russian" period.

(Another *Danses* context favorably heard and understood in these terms of a more equitable octatonic (Model A) and diatonic C-scale referential balance may be found at Nos. 125–27: a (G B D) "tonic" triad is superimposed over its (0,3) related (B♭ D F) triad, outlined in the bass as an accompaniment. Or see the (0,3) partitioning of Collection I in terms of the superimposed (G B D) and (E G♯ B) triads at Nos. 53–55; or, directly following this passage, the (0,6) partitioning of Collection III in terms of its (C E G (B♭)) and (F♯ A♯ C♯) triads, cited earlier in connection with *Petroushka*'s second tableau, Example 16a in chapter 2.)

BABEL (1944)

And all that has been detailed on behalf of the "Basle" *Concerto in D*, the second movement of the *Symphony in Three Movements* and *Danses concertantes*, also pertains to *Babel*.[9] (See Examples 61a, b, and c.) Except that we have here at the outset to do with Collection I rather than Collection II. This means that our referentially octatonic (0 1 3 4/3 4 6 7) or (0 3 4/3 4 7/3 6 7) "minor-major third" partitioning will at Nos. 0–8 and 16–21 (Examples 61a and b) be surrounding the (E G♯ B) and (G B D) triads—both E and G being among Collection I's (0,3,6,9) symmetrically defined partitioning elements, (E,G,B♭,D♭). Then, with the transposition of this material into Collection II at Nos. 21–27 (see Nos. 23 and 25 in Example 61c), this partitioning will be surrounding the (B D♯ F♯) triad—B being among Collection II's (0,3,6,9) symmetrically defined partitioning elements, (B,D,F,G♯).

But the commitment to a partitioning of the octatonic collection is in *Babel* more decisive than in either the "Basle" *Concerto* or the *Symphony in Three Movements* at Nos. 112–18 (indeed, more decisive—and certainly more persistent, more global—than at Nos. 30–34 in *Danses concertantes*). *Babel* opens with a basso ostinato (explicit octatonic reference, List 1) yielding a Collection I (0 1 3 4 6 7) pitch content of (E F G G♯ A♯ B). This

Example 61a: *Babel*. Used by permission of European American Music
Distributors Corporation.

material registers six octatonic pitch elements, not five as in the "Basle"
Concerto at Nos. 0–5. And so we are at the outset entrusted with pitch numbers 1 and 6, the F and the A♯, in addition to pitch numbers 0, 3, 4, and 7 in
terms of E, G, G♯, and B. Moreover, interrupted by a diatonic block at
Nos. 8–16, this commitment perseveres at Nos. 0–8 and 16–21: Collection
I's contribution overshadows interacting diatonic implications. Thus, *Babel* may be one neoclassical venture where the octatonic (Model A) and
diatonic C-scale interaction is tipped in favor of octatonicism. (Other such
ventures include the first and third movements of both the *Symphony of
Psalms* (1930) and the *Symphony in Three Movements* (1945); some of this
material is to be examined in chapter 12.)

A (G B D F) "dominant seventh" surfaces at No. 1+1. In addition to
extending Collection I's count to seven pitch elements in terms of (E F G
G♯ A♯ B D), this (G B D F) "dominant seventh" is *superimposed* over the low

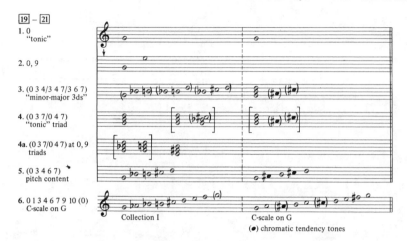

Example 61b. Used by permission of European American Music
Distributors Corporation.

E of the ostinato pattern. And so G, as pitch number 3, quickly acquires (G
B♭ D/G B D) articulative "support." This "support" is subsequently reinforced by the (G B D) figuration in the oboe at Nos. 1–8, by the reiterating
(G B♭ D) triads at No. 16, which are superimposed over the (E (F) G G♯ A♯
B) ostinato material,[10] and by a (0,3)-defined transposition of the (E (F) G
G♯ A♯ B) ostinato patterns to G at No. 19—minus pitch number 1, however, a Collection I (0 3 4 6 7) stipulation in terms of (G B♭ B C♯ D). Consequently, apart from the assertion of "independence," pitch number 3
asserts itself as a Collection I (E,G,B♭,D♭) symmetrically defined partitioning element in relation to Model A, assumes a degree of "equal
weight and independence," and stands "in a certain (fixed or polarized)
opposition" to pitch number 0, the E. So that in representing Collection I's
contribution at Nos. 0–8 and 16–21, the structural-level format in Example 61a, like that sketched for Nos. 30–34 in *Danses concertantes*, will more
closely resemble those for the referentially octatonic material in *Petroushka, Le Sacre,* and *Les Noces.* Omitting the somewhat problematic (single) pitch-class priority stipulation at Level 1, the successive levels of this
format record: (2) "background" (0,3) symmetrically defined partitioning
of Collection I in terms of E and G; (3) (0 3 4/3 4 7/3 6 7) "minor-major
third" partitioning of Collection I at E and G; (4) (0 1 3 4/3 4 6 7)
tetrachordal partitioning of the collection at E and G; (5) (0 3 7/0 4 7/0 4 7
10) triadic partitioning of the collection at G and E; (6) more articulative
partitioning in terms of the (0 (1) 3 4 6 7) ostinato and its (0,3)-defined
transposition—minus pitch number 1—from E to G at No. 19; (7) the (E F
G G♯ A♯ B C♯ D (E)) reference collection, Collection I, with brackets indicating the "background" (0,3) relation in terms of E and G.

Example 61c. Used by permission of European American Music
Distributors Corporation.

On the other hand, the possibility that pitch numbers 3 and 6, G and A♯,
might serve as Classical C-scale-on-E chromatic tendency tones to pitch
numbers 4 and 7, the G♯ and B of the (E G♯ B) "tonic" triad, is at least
suggested at Nos. 0–8 and 16–19. (Compare, in this connection, the A♯
notation of pitch number 6 with the B♭ notation in the first movement of
the *Symphony of Psalms*, where this pitch number 6, entrusted with (B♭ D F
A♭) "dominant-seventh" supplementation, asserts itself more forcefully
as a (0,3,6,9) symmetrically defined partitioning element, Collection I.) In
what ultimately materializes as a concession to this chromatic tendency-
tone potential, pitch number 1, the F, is dropped from the (E (F) G G♯ A♯
B) ostinato material at Nos. 16–19. And in the subsequent (0,3)-defined
transposition of this pattern to G at No. 19, (0 3 4 6 7) in terms of (G B♭ B
C♯ D) similarly lacks a pitch number 1, the A♭ here. Consequently, in recognition of this potential, we simply reinterpret the transposition to (G B♭
B C♯ D) at Nos. 19–21 in terms of a Collection I and C-scale-on-G interaction (see Example 61b).

In the final transposition of the opening (0 (1) 3 4 6 7) ostinato material
to Collection II at Nos. 23 and 25 (Example 61c), pitch number 1 is again
omitted, producing (0 3 4 6 7) in terms of (B D D♯ F F♯). In the contrapun-

tal network that unfolds in the horns, trumpets, and trombones at Nos. 23 and 25, the duplicity in the functional behavior of pitch numbers 3 and 6, the D and the F here, is now more apparent. Thus, in surrounding the (B D♯ F♯) triad, these pitch numbers 3 and 6 may be heard and understood both as independent elements, as members of Collection II's symmetrically defined (0 3 4/3 4 7/3 6 7) "minor-major third" complexes in terms of (B D D♯/D D♯ F♯/D F F♯), *and* as Classical C-scale-on-B chromatic tendency tones to pitch numbers 4 and 7, the D♯ and the F♯of the (B D♯ F♯) "tonic" triad. The (0 3 4 6 7) figuration here at Nos. 23 and 25 is remarkably similar to the (0 3 4 7 9) figuration at Nos. 0–5 in the "Basle" *Concerto*, and to the (0 3 4 6 7 9) figuration at No. 117 in the second movement of the *Symphony in Three Movements* and at Nos. 30–34 in *Danses concertantes*. And so Nos. 23 and 25 are in Example 61c interpreted in terms of an interaction between Collection II's (0 3 4/3 4 7/3 6 7) "minor-major third" complexes and Classical C-scale (on B) conventionality.

Then, too, the (0,3)-defined transposition of *Babel*'s (E (F) G G♯ A♯ B) ostinato material to G in terms of (G B♭ B C♯ D) at No. 19 may be compared with the (0,3)-defined pseudo-modulation at No. 118 in the second movement of the *Symphony in Three Movements*. For while *Babel* is decisively octatonic, both of these (0,3)-defined transpositions are prompted by the same kind of referentially octatonic (0 3 4/3 4 7/3 6 7) penetration. Both reflect the neoclassical predilection for (0,3)-defined partitioning, a limiting of (0,3,6,9) symmetrically defined partitioning to (0,3) partitioning, with pitch number 3 accorded varying degrees of articulative "support." In regard to these typically neoclassical (0,3)-defined transpositions—or (0,3)-defined pseudo-modulations where the diatonic C-scale reference may prevail—we acknowledge the following: (1) in the *Symphonies of Wind Instruments* (1920), the within–Collection I (0,3)-defined transposition of the opening No. 0 block from G to E at No. 26 (see Example 73b in chapter 12); (2) in piece No. 6 of *The Five Fingers* for piano (1921), the (0,3)-defined transposition of the reiterating, five-note (D E F♯ G A) figure to (F G A B♭ C);[11] (3) in the variation movement of the *Octet* (1923), the (0,3)-defined transposition of the Collection III (A B♭ C C♯) tetrachordal unit of the variation theme at No. 24 to (C C♯ D♯ E) at No. 25 (see Example 72 in chapter 12); (4) in the third and final movement of the "Dumbarton Oaks" *Concerto in E♭* (1938), the (0,3)-defined transposition of the opening (G A♭ B♭ C D E♭ F (G)) material centered on G to (B♭ C♭ D♭ E♭ F G♭ A♭ (B♭)) at No. 57; (5) in the "Eclogue" or second movement of the *Ode* (1943), the (0,3)-defined transposition of the opening octatonic (Collection I) and diatonic C-scale-on-B♭ interaction to the octatonic (Collection I) and C-scale-on-G interaction at Nos. 20–26 (with special reference here to Collection I's interaction at Nos. 24–26). These are but a few of the more conspicuous examples of (0,3)-defined transpositions—or pseudo-modulations—in neoclassical contexts.

SYMPHONY OF PSALMS (1930): THIRD MOVEMENT, NOS. 0–3

In the final movement of the *Symphony of Psalms* at Nos. 0–3 an interaction between Collection III and the A-scale on C (the descending C-minor scale in tonal terms) materializes with scarcely a trace of chromatic tendency-tone behavior. (See Example 62.) This is because the diatonic side of the interaction appears to implicate the A-scale on C (more readily than, say, the C-scale on E♭). C establishes itself as the pitch class of priority through, among other things, the G–C reiteration at No. 1 (*Laudate*), the G–C–G ostinato-like accompaniment beginning at No. 2, and the (C E♭ G B♭), (C E), and (C E B♭) concluding simultaneities all rooted on C at No. 1 (the "*Alleluia* cadence"), at No. 1 + 3, and just before No. 3 (the "*Dominum* cadence"). Interacting with this A-scale-on-C reference are Collection III's (0 3 4/3 4 7) "minor-major third" complexes in terms of (C E♭ E/E♭ E G), and its triads and "dominant sevenths" in terms of (C E♭ G/C E/C E B♭) and (E♭ G B♭), and its pitch number 4, this E alternating with E♭ at No. 1 + 6—effecting (C E♭ E/E♭ E G) "minor-major third" emphasis— but ultimately most conspicuous in the (C E) and (C E B♭) concluding simultaneities at No. 1 + 3 and just before No. 3 (the "*Dominum* cadence").

And so what distinguishes this excerpt from previous examples is the A-scale (or pseudo-C-minor) reference, the implication being that pitch number 3, not 4, is directly accountable to—or is critical to the identity of—the diatonic side of the interaction (the "minor third" rather than the "major third"), while pitch number 4, not 3, directly implicates Collection III in terms of its (C E♭ E♭ E G) "minor-major third" complexes or its (C E♭ G/C E/C E B♭) and (E♭ G B♭) triadic complexes. Thus, apprehension of the A-scale-on-C reference will not (or cannot as readily) hinge on C-scale chromatic tendency-tone behavior on the part of pitch number 3, the E♭. And so we interpret in terms of a merger between Collection III and the A-scale on C.

Still, on behalf of pitch number 4, the E in the (C E) and (C E B♭) concluding simultaneities at No. 1 + 3 and just before No. 3 (the "*Dominum* cadence"), observers more traditionally inclined could put in a claim for the *tierce de Picardie* inflection. And a supplementary reference to this effect might well be in order. For the convention neatly complements Classical chromatic tendency-tone behavior on the part of pitch number 3 in interacting octatonic (Model A) and diatonic C-scale contexts. Thus, with respect to its Classical C-scale (or A-scale) implications, the neoclassical (0 3 4/3 4 7) "minor-major third" emphasis takes on a new "twist": a *tierce de Picardie* inflection on the part of pitch number 4 (the "major third") in mixed octatonic (Model A) and diatonic *A-scale* (or minor-scale) contexts, and a chromatic tendency-tone inflection on the part of pitch number 3 (the "minor third") in mixed octatonic (Model A) and diatonic C-scale (or major-scale) contexts.

Example 62: *Symphony of Psalms*, third movement

Care must be taken, however, not to exaggerate these claims. They represent, as we have indicated, only one side of the coin, only part of the accommodation. Even in contexts where the diatonic C-scale or A-scale prevails, it is only with reference to octatonic-diatonic interaction, to an interacting partitioning of the octatonic collection (Model A), that we can begin to account for peculiarity in the exhibition of these Baroque and/or Classical conventions, inflections, and gestures.

But from yet another diatonic vantage point, it could be argued that our octatonic (Collection III) and diatonic A-scale-on-C interaction fails to consider the centricity of C and E♭, or the centricity of the (C E♭ G) and (E♭ G B♭) triads they root, as a specifically *diatonic* phenomenon; that while these (0,3)-related "minor" and "major" triads at C and E♭ are referentially octatonic (Collection III), they could be heard and understood diatonically in terms of an elision or fusion of what would formerly, in tonal A-scale literature, have defined the tonic-mediant relation (or the reverse for the C-scale, the tonic-submediant relation; or, with respect to the interval orderings defined in relation to the diatonic collection, "relative keys"); and that, therefore, the peculiarity or ambiguous nature of Stravinsky's A-scale reference (or his pseudo-C-minor reference here) rests not only with Collection III's interaction (however conspicuous in terms of (C E♭ E/E♭ E G) "minor-major third" emphasis at No. 1+6), but also with this assimilation, along lines typical of Stravinsky, of this harmonic or "key" relationship of Baroque and Classical C-scale (or A-scale) literature.

There are two aspects of this alternative that bear on our discussion: (1) this present elision or fusion is not unlike many other unions or superimpositions encountered in these pages, most particularly the (0 3 4/3 4 7/3 6 7) "minor-major third" phenomenon, in which pitch numbers 3 and 6, the Classical chromatic tendency tones, collide or "clash" in static simultaneity with the chord tones, pitch numbers 4 and 7 of the (0 4 7) "major" triad, to which they formerly tended in succession; (2) it is by acknowledging the Baroque or Classical C-scale (or A-scale) derivation that this elision emerges as yet another *act of accommodation*, an accommodation between Model A's (0,3,6,9) symmetrically defined partitioning of the octatonic collection and the conventional harmonic or "relative-key" relationship. And from countless neoclassical settings that apply in this respect, there are at least two to which we shall be directing our attention: (1) the block at Nos. 167–70 in *Oedipus Rex*, where a (D F♯) reiteration alternates with a (B D F♯) triadic outline, these units defining a (0,3) relation identical to that in *Psalms* (in *Oedipus* in terms of (B,D)), but a (0,3) relation whose ambiguity is heightened by the omission of the "fifth" of the (D F♯ (A)) "major" triad (critical to (D F♯ (A))'s identity in relation to the (B D F♯) "minor" triad), an ambiguity which beclouds the referential status of the famous—or per-

haps by now infamous—"*Lux facta est* cadence" at the close of this block;
(2) the block at No. 5 in *Orpheus*'s "Air de danse," in which the elision of the
(Bb Db F) and (Db F Ab) "tonic" triads—or of the interval orderings these
triads define in relation to the diatonic collection—likewise defines a (0,3)
relation corresponding to that in *Psalms* (but in *Orpheus* in terms of
(Bb,Db)).

Caution is again advised, however, not to exaggerate these Baroque or
Classical C-scale (or A-scale) claims. They represent, as we again insist,
only part of the accommodation. Indeed, as with the neoclassical (0 3 4/3 4
7/3 6 7) "minor-major third" emphasis, Stravinsky is likely to have been
drawn to this additional elision because of its octatonicism, because the
(0,3)-related (0 3 7) "minor" and (0 4 7) "major" triads are as octatonic
(Model A) as they are Classical C-scale (or A-scale). The reader will have
noted in the diverse octatonic (Model A) and diatonic C-scale interactions
surveyed in this chapter a cohesive octatonic-diatonic (0 3 4 6 7 9) articulation, arising by way of all manner of themes, fragments, motives, accompaniment figures, and the like. Pitch number 9 in these articulations lies a
"minor third" below the (0 4 7) "tonic" triad. (In *Psalms*, C is pitch number
9 in relation to the Eb.) Consequently, this pitch number 9 may occasionally distinguish itself as root of the (0 3 7) "minor" triad lying a "minor
third" below the (0 4 7) "tonic" triad rather than as part of some cohesive
(0 3 4 6 7 9) articulation (possibly tilting the diatonic side of the interaction
toward the A-scale or some form of C-scale/A-scale integration). (This is
not to sidestep the Classical C-scale or A-scale issue, but merely to suggest
that the alternative is part and parcel of the neoclassical octatonic-diatonic
interacting circumstances to which the discussion in this chapter has been
drawn.) Moreover, this static fusion or "coming together" of these (0,3)-
related "minor" and "major" triads occurs without the tonally functional
relations of Baroque or Classical C-scale (or A-scale) literature: there is
scarcely a trace, in the examples cited, of harmonic progression, or of any
tonally functional definition of the "relative keys," still less of any nonsen-
sical simultaneous unfolding of "separate keys" ("bitonality"). And so it is
to octatonic-diatonic interaction, to an interacting partitioning of the octatonic collection (Model A) that we turn in order to acknowledge peculiarity in the exhibition of these Baroque or Classical formulae and their evident transformation by the assumption of a second referential identity.

OEDIPUS REX (1927): NOS. 166–70

Although I have been concerned with questions of musical manners all my
life, I am unable to say precisely what these manners are. That, I think, is
because they are not precompositional, but of the essence of the musical act:
the manner of saying and the thing said are, for me, the same. But am I not

unusually conscious of the manner question, nevertheless? All I can say is that my manners are my personal relations with my material. *Je me rends compte* in them. Through them I discover my laws. The direction of the next melodic interval is involved with the musical manners of the whole work. Thus, the clarinet trill at "*lux facta est*" is a manifestation of my *Oedipus* manners: the trill is not just a trill but an indispensable mannerism. I have been told that such things merely indicate the culture-consciousness found in all *émigrés*, but I know that the explanation is deeper than that, as I worked and thought in exactly the same way in Russia. My manners are the birthmark of my art. [*Dialogues and a Diary*, p. 10.]

In *Oedipus Rex*, Nos. 166–70 in Act II shed additional light on these diatonic A-scale (or minor-scale) complications, conveniently encompassing, as well, the aforementioned "*Lux facta est* cadence." (See Example 63.) We are here confronted, in typically Stravinskian fashion, with two juxtaposed blocks of distinct referential character: a diatonic block at No. 166, and a mixed octatonic (Collection II) and diatonic C-scale-on-D/A-scale-on-B block at Nos. 167–70. The diatonic block at No. 166 is both harmonically and melodically static. By this is meant that, harmonically, the block consists merely of a static (D F A) reiteration in the strings, and melodically of a repetitive, incantatory, circular motion around D. But the referential ordering is in doubt, for there is no B♭ here to identify the neoclassical A-scale (or descending minor scale) on D. In fact, in the preceding and more extensive (near) repeats of this block at Nos. 159–62 and 164–66 (not shown here), B identifies the D-scale on D, a referential complexion confirmed even earlier in the first (near) repeats of this block at Nos. 139–47, where the D-scale is centered on G. And so the diatonicism of this block, with its D-scale-on-D reference and its repetitive, incantatory sequence, may seem peculiarly "Russian," as may also its rhythmic-metric guise, which reflects the first of our two rhythmic-metric types: barred metric irregularity, with all the reiterating fragments, lines, or parts sharing the same irregular rhythmic-metric periods as defined by the shifting meter, and hence synchronized unvaryingly in vertical (or "harmonic") coincidence. Indeed, the particulars of this type are in evidence. For while the barring of the four-bar melody or "phrase" at No. 166 perseveres at No. 166 + 4, the repeat at No. 166 + 4 harbors a concealed off-the-beat/on-the-beat contradiction or reversal. In accord with regular 3/4 metric periodicity (as bracketed in Example 63), the initial D–C–D figure may first be perceived as an on-the-beat inflection, contradicted or reversed at No. 166 + 4 as an off-the-beat inflection. (From this results the double edge of the "play": in opposition to the concealed off-the-beat/on-the-beat displacement (hinging, for its apprehension, on "background" regular metric periodicity), the shifting meter does not alter but *preserves* a fixed rhythmic-metric identity, exacting a counteracting "sameness" in the repetition of the four-bar "phrase".)[12]

Example 63: *Oedipus Rex*

Further, the rhythmic-metric "play" is dramatically apropos. For the curtly drawn, metrically irregular "phrases" mirror the breathless hesitancy with which a shepherd and messenger jointly intone the fateful news of the king's murderous, incestuous relationship with the wife/mother, Jocasta. It is Oedipus the king who has caused the plague at Thebes.

(While our present analysis focuses on Nos. 166–70, it encompasses the preceding (near) repeats of this No. 166 block as well. And inasmuch as the (F A C) "tonic" triad of the diatonic C-scale-on-F block at Nos. 152–58

Example 63 *continued*

(Oedipus's aria "Nonne monstrum") is, like the (D F A) triad of the D-scale-on-D block, accountable to Collection II, the entire section at Nos. 139–70 may be considered as under mixed octatonic (Collection II) and diatonic review.[13] Moreover, between-block or between-section relations in *Oedipus* are conceived with as much reference to the octatonic collection's (0,3,6,9) symmetrically defined partitioning elements and the (0 3

7/0 4 7) triads they root as to C-scale (or A-scale) tonally functional schemes of modulation or transposition ("dominant keys," "relative minor" or "relative major keys," etc.). Thus, apart from Nos. 139–70 here in Act II, the (B♭ D♭) unit of the pulsating B♭–B♭–B♭–D♭–D♭–D♭ basso ostinato at Nos. 2–7 in Act I unites the opening diatonic A-scale-on-B♭ block (with its B♭–minor key signature) with both Collections III and I, (B♭ D♭ E G) constituting the shared "diminished-seventh" chord between these collections: Collection III interacts with its cohesive (A B♭ C D♭) tetrachord, its (A C E) triads, and descending (D♭ B♭ G E) and (C A F♯ E♭) "diminished-seventh" chords at Nos. 3–5, and then with its (C C♯ D♯ E) tetrachord and (A C E/A C♯ E) triads at No. 9, while Collection I interacts with its (B♭ D F A♭) and (E G B♭ D♭) triadic complexes at No. 7, and its (G B D) triads at Nos. 25–27. Collection I's interaction with the C-scale-on-C framework at Nos. 40–45 will be examined in chapter 12.)

Then, with (D F A) retained in the strings as the pivoting between-block or between-reference connecting link, the diatonic D-scale-on-D block at No. 166 is in turn succeeded by the mixed octatonic (Collection II) and diatonic C-scale-on-D/A-scale-on-B block at Nos. 167–70. Collection II's contribution to this interaction at Nos. 167–70 encompasses virtually all reiterating fragments: the (D F A) reiteration in the strings, the (D F) unit of the clarinets, (D F♯) in the flutes, the F♯–B succession in the timpani, and finally the (B D F♯) triadic outline of Oedipus's B–C♯–D–B–F♯ versification, all of these triadic or semi-triadic groupings jointly yielding a "background" (0,3) partitioning of Collection II in terms of (D, B). Moreover, the (D F F♯) "minor-major third" simultaneity or "clash" between the clarinet's (D F) unit and the F♯ of the timpani's F♯–B succession also refers to Collection II—it forms a (0 3 4) grouping in relation to the (D F♯ (A)) triad, and (3 6 7) in relation to (B D F♯).

But it is perhaps more conspicuously on the diatonic C-scale-on-D or A-scale-on-B side of this referential coin at Nos. 167–70 that a pronounced ambiguity insinuates itself, by means of three principal items. The first of these has to do with a possible merging or fusion of (D F♯ (A)) and (B D F♯) as conflicting "tonic" triads, (0,3)-related "major" and "minor" triads which would formerly, in relation to (D F♯ (A)), have defined the tonic-submediant relation (or, with respect to the interval orderings defined in relation to the diatonic collection, "relative keys"); but this fusion is exceedingly ambiguous here owing to the incompleteness of the (D F♯ (A)) component, which consists of (D F♯) in the flutes, without the fifth, critical to (D F♯ (A))'s identity in relation to (B D F♯).[14] The second item entails the very slight suggestion of a *tierce de Picardie* inflection on the part of (D F♯) in the flutes in relation to (D F A) in the strings, but this is also highly ambiguous, since the (D F A) triad, on whose behalf the *tierce* is inferred, is not accounted for in terms of the possible C-scale-on-D or A-scale-on-B references at Nos. 167–70, nor, as indicated, in terms of the neoclassical A-scale on D at No. 166, but only in terms of the "Russian"-like D-scale on D (or, octatonically, in terms of Collection II).[15] Finally, the third item entails a trace of chromatic tendency-tone behavior on the part of F [E♯], which, although initially the third of the (D F A) triad and effecting "minor-major third" emphasis by "clashing" with F♯ in the (D F F♯) simultaneity between the clarinet's (D F) reiteration and the timpani's F♯, tends chromatically to F♯ in the clarinet's F [E♯]–F♯ trill in the concluding *"Lux facta est* cadence," this second identity defining a pitch number 3–4 succession in relation to the (D F♯) unit and a 6–7 succession in relation to (B D F♯). (Hence, with respect to this final item, Stravinsky's reference to the clarinet's F [E♯]–F♯ trill in the *"Lux facta est* cadence" as somehow aping the musical "manners" of *Oedipus* (see the quotation above) has not merely to do with the trill *tout court*, but also with the typically neoclassical "manner" in which, through the trill here, a duplicity in the functional behavior of F [E♯] is revealed. F [E♯] is at Nos. 167–69 referentially octatonic, cohesively a member of Collection II's (D F A), (D F) and (D F F♯) complexes; but it may in the "cadence" be heard and understood as a chromatic tendency tone to F♯, the "major third" of the incomplete (D F♯ (A)) triad, the fifth of the (B D F♯) triad.)

And of special note here is the static character of all this juxtaposed reiteration, the absence of a true sense of harmonic progress. Collection II's (D F A/D A/D F♯/B D F♯) triadic and (D F F♯) "minor-major third" complexes are stiffly set apart, placed in static juxtaposition or superimposition; they remain registrally and instrumentally fixed in repetition, with no developmental exchange or "dialogue" among parts. The strings merely reiterate their (D F A) triad in the same register throughout; the flutes, their (D F♯) unit; the clarinets, their (D F) unit (and effect (D F F♯) "minor-major third" emphasis with the timpani's F♯); the timpani, its B–F♯ succession; and Oedipus, his B–C♯–D–B–F♯ versification—all until No. 169, the *"Lux facta est* cadence." Rhythmic-metric implications are similarly disposed. For while the diatonic D-scale-on-D block at No. 166 is metrically irregular, and adheres to the first of our two rhythmic-metric types, it is very nearly the only such block in *Oedipus*. And while the succeeding octatonic-diatonic block at Nos. 167–70 might, with its steady 3/4 meter, appear to reflect the second rhythmic-metric type, this is only superficially the case. For unlike all schemes conforming to this second rhythmic-metric type (with its regular metric periodicity), the rhythmic-metric periods defined by the reiterating fragments do not vary "separately from" or "independently of" one another and effect, as a consequence, a vertical (or "harmonic") coincidence which is irregular and variable. On the contrary, the reiterations in the strings, flutes, timpani, and voice (Oedipus) all share the same rhythmic-metric period of six quarter-note beats. (The clarinet's (D F) unit has a cycle of three quarter-note beats, however, and a touch of "mobility" or irregular spacing at No. 168 + 2, where it enters on the second beat of the 3/4 measure rather than, as in preceding measures, on the third beat.) Indeed, Stravinsky would later contend that the "rhythms" in *Oedipus* were "more static and regular" than any of his music to that date (1927), and that if he had "succeeded in freezing the drama in this music, that was accomplished largely by rhythmic means."

And so all this pitch-relational, registral, instrumental, and rhythmic-metric staticity at Nos. 167–70 invests the passage with a chill austerity. For which, as might be expected, there are dramatic purposes. For we have now come, following the final departure of the shepherd and messenger at No. 166, to the high point of the opera/oratorio: Nos. 167–69 coincide with Oedipus's recognition of guilt, fate, and doom; No. 169, the *"Lux facta est* cadence," with his final resignation. Hence, both musically and dramatically Nos. 167–70 represent a period of waiting and anticipation, a pause to consider, reflect, and digest. (Stravinsky's "Ciceronian Latin," an impersonal, detached medium unsullied by conventional sentimentality, tends naturally to enhance this austerity, indeed the solemnity or "distance" of much of *Oedipus*—as do his uniquely designed stage directions for the opera, which leave the actors/singers behind masks, moving only with their heads and arms, addressing the audience in an icy, "still-life" confrontation with fate.)[16]

But what, then, can we here expect in the way of accommodation? In light of the reputation of this piece as a model of Baroque and Classical virtue, a "husk of style" (in Stravinsky's words), a kind of "high neoclassicism" at its "highest," the answer is disconcerting: *precious little.* For we are here left, on the Baroque or Classical C-scale or A-scale side of the accommodation, with little more than this (D F♯ (A)) (B D F♯) ambiguity, two potential "tonic" triads which formerly might have defined the "relative key" relationship (but here, as indicated, the (D F♯ (A)) contingent lacks its fifth, and in place of a C-scale tonally functional sense of harmonic progress or a definition of the "relative keys" of D-major and B-minor, there is merely this static reiteration, oscillation, or superimposition of the two triads). Besides this there is only the slight suggestion of a *tierce de Picardie* on the part of (D F♯) in relation to (D F A)—the ambiguous nature of which has already been noted—and F [E♯] as a chromatic tendency tone to F♯ in the clarinet's F [E♯]–F♯ trill of the *"Lux facta est* cadence." In other words, we find here the same conventions, the same inflections, gestures, and harmonic maneuvers, and the same interaction of this surface conventionality with a (0 3 4/3 4 7/3 6 7) "minor-major third" and (0 3 7/0 4 7) triadic partitioning of the octatonic collection, Model A, that has characterized the Baroque or Classical C-scale (or A-scale) side of the accommodation in all previously examined pieces or passages of pieces. Indeed, as is evident, the obscurity of the Classical C-scale or A-scale claim is heightened. The hint of a *tierce de Picardie* inflection is very nearly camouflaged beyond the possibility of apprehension. For not only does (D F♯) in the flutes lack the (D F♯ A)'s fifth; not only does this incompleteness project ambiguity in relation to (B D F♯) as, just possibly, *the* "tonic" triad; but, as indicated, the (D F A) reiteration, in relation to which the *tierce* is inferred, is not accounted for, diatonically, in terms of the C-scale on D or A-scale on B at Nos. 167–70, nor in terms of the neoclassical A-scale (or descending minor scale) on D, but only in terms of the D-scale on D, most familiar from "Russian" contexts.

And so we are left, finally, with the seeming irrelevance of C-scale tonally functional relations, without, at the very least, some peripheral recognition of the cohesive, symmetrical confinement of *all* reiterating fragments to the octatonic Collection II. Indeed, the subtlety, the techniques of triadic reiteration, of oscillation and superimposition, all the pitch-relational identity and distinction that must inevitably be set aside or ignored when squeezing, in bulk, whole contexts like *Oedipus Rex* into the Baroque or Classical C-scale tonally functional compound. And if not set aside, the chaotic depths into which this compound plunges in the process.

Still, the reader wishing an alternative to our perspective may consult Wilfrid Mellers's "Stravinsky's *Oedipus* as 20th-Century Hero" for a C-scale tonally functional reading in terms of "key sequences" or "changes of key" ("dominants," "tonics," "relative minors," etc.), although, for the reasons cited (and despite some thoughtful philosophical conclusions reached on its behalf), the approach cannot work.[17]

ORPHEUS (1947)

First tableau

Introduction	Nos. 0–4
"Air de danse"	Nos. 4–28
"L'Ange de la mort et sa danse"	Nos. 28–41
Interlude	Nos. 41–47

Second tableau

"Pas des furies"	Nos. 47–77
"Air de danse"	Nos. 77–89
Interlude	Nos. 89–90
"Air de danse"	Nos. 90–92
"Pas d'action"	Nos. 92–101
"Pas de deux"	Nos. 101–22

Interlude	Nos. 122–25
"Pas d'action"	Nos. 125–43
Third tableau	
Apotheosis	Nos. 143–End

Finally, while exemplification is likely to prove repetitious at this point, the neoclassical ballet *Orpheus* offers a consummate demonstration of all these examined conventions, inflections, gestures, and harmonic maneuvers of Baroque and Classical C-scale (or A-scale) literature, and their neoclassical interaction with a (0 3 4/3 4 7/3 6 7) "minor-major third" and (0 3 7/0 4 7) triadic partitioning of the octatonic collection, Model A.

Thus, from the opening measures of the "Air de danse" at No. 4 to the close of "Pas des furies" at No. 77 in the second tableau, a (B♭ D♭) dyad— or a (B♭ D♭ E G) "diminished-seventh" chord—serves as the principal connecting link between the blocks, passages, and sections of varied octatonic and diatonic implications, asserting itself in the following manner:

"Air de danse," No. 4: At No. 4, "Air de danse," and at subsequent (near) repeats of this introductory block at Nos. 8 and 21–23, (B♭ D♭) is referentially octatonic (Collection III). (See Example 64a.) Although set apart and sustained as a cohesive unit (which underscores its pivoting role as a between-block or between-reference connecting link), it identifies articulatively with the upsweeping (C E G B♭ (D♭)) "dominant seventh" or

Example 64a: *Orpheus* ("Air de danse")

"ninth" in the bassoon at No. 4 + 1, and with the (A C♯ E) triadic figuration in the clarinet; and then with Collection III's (A B♭ C D♭) tetrachord, in relation to which its members effect "minor-major third" emphasis. Then, on the final beat at No. 4 + 4, this commitment breaks off, (B♭ D♭) suddenly aligning itself with a (B♭ D♭ F) triad in anticipation of its mixed octatonic (Collection I) and diatonic A-scale-on-B♭/C-scale-on-D♭ credentials at No. 5.

No. 5: At No. 5, "Air de danse," along with (near) repeats and extensions of this material at Nos. 9, 23, and 25, (B♭ D♭) and (B♭ D♭ E G) are wedded to an octatonic (Collection I) and diatonic A-scale-on-B♭/C-scale-on-D♭ interaction, in which B♭ and D♭ are roots of the (B♭ D♭ F) and (D♭ F A♭) "tonic" triads shared by these interacting collections of reference, and in which E and G may serve as intruding "impurities," "clashing" with F and A♭ and effecting (0 3 4/3 4 7/3 6 7) "minor-major third" emphasis in terms of Collection I's (D♭ E F/E F A♭/E G A♭) groupings, or as Classical A-scale-on-B♭ or C-scale-on-D♭ chromatic tendency tones to the "major thirds" and "fifths" of these (B♭ D♭ F) and (D♭ F A♭) "tonic" triads. (See Example 64b.) Collection I's contribution is subsequently enhanced by a (E G♯ B) triadic outline at No. 11, an articulation which, with (E G G♯/G G♯ B) "minor-major third" emphasis, momentarily boosts its (0,3) triadic partitioning to (0,3,6) in terms of (B♭,D♭,E).

Accordingly, on the diatonic side of the interaction, a fusion or "coming together" of the (0,3)-related "minor" and "major" triads at B♭ and D♭ may be inferred (or of the interval orderings these triads define in relation to the diatonic collection, orderings interpretable in tonal C-scale (or A-scale) literature as "relative keys"). This "coming together" is similar to that at Nos. 0–3 in the final movement of *Psalms*, but there in terms of (C,E♭), or to that at Nos. 167–70 in *Oedipus*, but there in terms of (B,D).

Note, in this connection, the first-inversion articulation of the (B♭ D♭ F) triad in the pizzicato accompaniment (an articulation Stravinsky seems so frequently to have favored over—in his words—"the flat-footed tonic"). The articulation has here to do with the ambiguity of these (B♭ D♭ F) and (D♭ F A♭) "tonic" triads, with D♭ (shared as the "third" of the "minor" and the root of the "major") rather than B♭ (not shared) statically positioned in the bass.[18]

Then, too, compare the E–F reiteration in the solo violin—a pitch number 6–7 reiteration in relation to (B♭ D♭ F), 3–4 in relation to (D♭ F A♭)—with the (E–F) (G–A♭) reiterations which encircle the (D♭ F A♭) "tonic" triad at No. 27 in the "Basle" *Concerto* (Example 58b). Or compare the (0 3 4 6 7 9) figuration here in terms of (D♭ E F G A♭ B♭)—with the first violin's (E F A♭ B♭) figure subsequently doubled by the flute at No. 6, and with a further extension at No. 24—with the (D♭ E F G A♭) figuration at No. 27 in the "Basle" *Concerto*.[19]

Example 64b: "Air de danse"

Indeed, to the (0 3 4 (6) 7 9) figuration in terms of (D F F♯ (G♯) A B) at Nos. 0–5 and No. 55 in the "Basle" *Concerto* (Examples 58a and c); at No. 117 in the *Symphony in Three Movements* (Example 59); at No. 30 in *Danses concertantes* (Example 60); or, in terms of (B D D♯ F F♯), at No. 23 in *Babel* (Example 61c). The correspondences here, in articulation and in the processes of octatonic-diatonic interaction exhibited, are remarkable.

No. 27: At No. 27, "Air de danse," the octatonic (Collection I) and A-scale-on-B♭/C-scale-on-D♭ interaction is concluded with a (D♭ B♭/F/D♭ F/A♭) simultaneity (reading down), in which the (B♭ D♭ F) and (D♭ F A♭) "tonic" triads are superimposed and fused into one. (See Example 64c.) Prior to the simultaneity, however, (B♭ D♭)'s earlier referential commitment to Collection III (in the introductory block at No. 4) suddenly reappears: up-sweeping (A C♯ E G) and (C E G B♭) "dominant sevenths," superimposed in the flutes, are followed by a (B♭ D♭)–(A C)–(B♭ D♭) reiteration. Then, with (B♭ D♭) sustained in the flutes as the pivoting between-block and between-reference connecting link, the octatonic (Collection I) and

Example 64c: "Air de danse" (conclusion)

diatonic A-scale-on-B♭/C-scale-on-D♭ interaction concludes with (D♭ B♭/ F/D♭ F/A♭).

Note the appropriateness of this "chord," the conviction of this "impurity" as a verticalized summation of prior circumstance. For this conviction has not merely to do with the static fusion or superimposition of these (B♭ D♭ F) and (D♭ F A♭) "tonic" triads (thus, its interval content in terms of (B♭ D♭ F A♭) is equivalent to that of the (C E♭ G B♭) simultaneity in the "*Allelulia* cadence" at Nos. 0–3 in the final movement of *Psalms*), nor with the fact that the triadic relationship is as octatonic (Collection I) as it is A-scale on B♭/C-scale-on-D♭. It is, rather, in the spacing or registral distribution of the components that its effect is revealed (as a verticalized summation of prior circumstance). Thus, from top to bottom, the high D♭ in the flute reflects the earlier D♭ of the introductory block at No. 4 (which, joined by the B♭, continues to isolate (B♭ D♭) instrumentally and registrally here as the pivoting, connecting link); the registral positioning of the following F in the first violins reflects the solo violin's E–F reiterations; the registral positioning of the following D♭ or D♭–F interval span in the second violins and violas reflects the clarinet's F–B♭–D♭ reiterations (which reappear in the lower strings to introduce the following section at No. 28); while the final A♭ in the cellos, the only pitch *not* held in common, and critical to the identity of (D♭ F A♭) in relation to (B♭ D♭ F), is placed in the lowest position in the bass.

    "L'Ange de la mort et sa danse," No. 28: At No. 28, "L'Ange de la mort et sa danse," (B♭ D♭) and (B♭ D♭ E G) momentarily resume their affiliation with the octatonic (Collection I) and diatonic A-scale-on-B♭/C-scale-on-D♭ interaction of the "Air de danse." (See Example 64d.) Thus, following the reiterating F–B♭–D♭ figure (now in the violas and cellos), the (B♭–D♭) unit in the flutes and the F–A♭ span (now in the bassoons) reintroduce the Air's concluding simultaneity, but with a distinction: E and G, the chromatic tendency tones to the "major thirds" and "fifths" of the (B♭ D♭ F) and (D♭ F A♭) "tonic" triads, are now fused as part of the finality. Consequently, to the initial "impurity" of the superimposed (B♭ D♭ F) and (D♭ F A♭) "tonic"

Example 64d: "L'Ange de la mort et sa danse"

triads *is now added this most characteristic of all neoclassical "impurities"* (as anticipated in the preceding "Air de danse," of course), *where pitch numbers 3 and 6, the Classical chromatic tendency tones, "clash" in static simultaneity with the chord tones, the "major thirds" and "fifths," to which they would formerly have tended in succession*; and effect "minor-major third" emphasis in terms of the octatonic collection's interacting and symmetrically defined (0 3 4/3 4 7/3 6 7) groupings, a duplicity or ambiguity in function, intent, derivation, or referential status.

Still, the C in the simultaneity at No. 28+2 points to octatonic-diatonic interacting circumstances different in kind from those examined in this chapter, interactions in which the (0,3,6,9) symmetrically defined octatonic partitioning elements and the (0 3 7/0 4 7) "minor" and "major" triads they root serve not as between-reference "tonics" or "tonic" triads but as "dominants" or "dominant" triads in relation to the interacting diatonic C-scale or A-scale reference. This is a species of interaction to be considered in chapter 12.

"Interlude," No. 41: At No. 41, "Interlude," B♭, D♭ [C♯], and E introduce the opening octatonic (Collection III) B♭–D♭–E–C–B♭ "subject" of a solemn, fuguelike exposition. But a bargain is struck with the conventional scheme in that the succeeding "entrance" occurs a "fourth" below in terms of F–A♭–B–G–F; this "entrance" is followed at No. 43 by a return to the original Collection III statement (all in imitation, of course, of the traditional tonic-dominant fugal dialogue). Of interest, however, is Stravinsky's "octave displacement": the contour of the initial statement is subtly altered by means of interval complementation.

The "Interlude" concludes at No. 46 with an octatonic (Collection II) block: a (D F A) triad, first inversion, is sustained in the horns and lower strings, while the second and fourth horns reiterate F♯–G♯, effecting (0 3 4/3 4 7/3 6 7) or (3 4 6 7) "minor-major third" emphasis in terms of Collection II's (D F F♯/F F♯ A/F G♯ A) or (F F♯ G♯ A) units.

"Pas des furies," Nos. 47–53: At Nos. 47–77, "Pas des furies," the alignment of (B♭ D♭) or (B♭ D♭ E G) with the octatonic Collections I and III, together with the assortment of diatonic C-scale and A-scale references these contingencies implicate, brings to octatonic (Model A) and diatonic interaction a pace and a richness in variety and detail possibly without equal in neoclassical contexts.

In the opening simultaneity at No. 47, (B♭ D♭ E G) is superimposed in the strings, pizzicato, over an F in the bass. This simultaneity is followed by a (A C♯ E G) "dominant seventh" in the horns, superimposed over a B♭ in the bassoon, possibly an allusion to (B♭ D♭ E G)'s earlier affiliation with Collection III. But the superimposed F, the (B♭–A) (F–E) reiterations in the rapid, *spiccato* string figuration, and the sustained (B♭ D♭ E G) in the woodwinds at Nos. 48(+3)–50 obscure interacting diatonic consequences. There is, first, the suggestion of an interacting C-scale-on-B♭ reference (which the key signature implies), but this reference is obscured by a D♭ just prior to No. 49. The possibility arises of an interacting (D F A) "tonic" triad at Nos. 47–50 with respect to which the (B♭ D♭ E G) unit could be construed as a "dominant." But so fleeting are these implications at Nos. 47–53 as to render them very nearly beyond proper apprehension and definition.

Nos. 53–57: At Nos. 53–57, "Pas des furies," the octatonic pendulum, as it concerns (B♭ D♭) or (B♭ D♭ E G), swings toward Collection III. (See Example 64e.) Here, a Collection III (F)–F♯–G–A–B♭–C–D♭ ascending scale in the bassoon is repeated in the violas at No. 54, in the first violins at No. 54 + 2, and again in the bassoon at No. 55. Underneath this ascending scale is a Collection III E♭–D♭–E♭–(A♭)–C–D♭ succession in the second violins at No. 53; a Collection III (A♭)–B♭–D♭–G♭–B♭–C–D♭–B♭–G♭ succession in the cellos, which suggests a (G♭ B♭ D♭) or (F♯ A♯ C♯) triadic outline; and a Collection III (C E♭ G) triad outlined in the cellos and bassoons at

Example 64e: "Pas des furies"

No. 54 (+ 3)–56. Then, above the successive repeats of the ascending scale are upsweeping (C E G) triads in the flutes at Nos. 53 and 55; these, joined by the (G♭ B♭ D♭) and (C E♭ G) triadic outlines in the cellos and bassoons, suggest a (0,6) tritone partitioning of Collection III in terms of (G♭ B♭ D♭) and (C E♭ G/C E G). But this triadic delineation is obscured by the stepwise unfolding of the (F)–F♯–G–A–B♭–C–D♭ scale pattern, and these octatonic implications are in turn obscured by the persistence of the non-octatonic (non-Collection III) pitch elements F and A♭, and often by the rapid, *spiccato* accompaniment figuration as well (largely ignored in Example 64e).

No. 58: At No. 58, "Pas des furies," C♯ [D♭] and E partake of an octatonic (Collection I) and diatonic C-scale-on-C♯ [D♭] interaction, in which C♯ is the root of the between-reference (C♯ E♯ G♯) "tonic" triad, and in which E, as pitch number 3, effects (0 3 4/3 4 7) "minor-major third" emphasis in terms of Collection I's (C♯ E E♯/E E♯ G♯) units, or is alternatively a chromatic tendency tone to E♯ [F], the "major third" of the (C♯ E♯ G♯) "tonic" triad. (See Example 64f.) (Note that while pitch numbers 3 and 4, the E and the E♯ here, are sustained statically as part of the (C♯ E E♯ G♯) simultaneity, it is pitch number 4, the E♯, that gains the advantage as the chord tone. This is owing not only to the reiterating Fs [E♯s] in the second

Example 64f: "Pas des furies"

trumpet (which punctuate this chord tone at Nos. 58 and 59), but also to the duplicity—and hence instability—in the functional behavior of pitch number 3, the E (a duplicity to which, of course, the ear has by now accustomed itself):[20] pitch number 3, the E, "clashing" with pitch number 4, the E#, may be perceived as a cohesive member of Collection I's symmetrically defined (C# E E#/E E# G) "minor-major third" complexes, but also as a Classical C-scale-on-C# chromatic tendency tone to pitch number 4, the E#. The result is that most persistent of neoclassical "impurities" or "clashes": by means of (C# E E# G#), pitch number 3 "clashes" in static, symmetrically defined simultaneity with the element to which, in tonal, C-scale literature, it would have tended in succession.)[21]

The opening mixed octatonic (Collection I) and diatonic C-scale-on-C# block alternates in rapid succession with a (C D♭ E) simultaneity in the woodwinds and first trumpet, joined in turn by a (C E G) triadic outline in the first violins (and later in the first trumpet). This second block suggests C#'s (or D♭'s) and E's affiliation with Collection III in terms of its (C D♭ E) "minor-major third" complex and its (C E G) triad, in which E is now the chord tone, the "major third." Indeed, there is at Nos. 58-60 not so much a rapid exchange of two abruptly juxtaposed blocks of distinct referential implications as an overlapping of these blocks and these implications. (Thus, for example, the anticipatory C in the first trumpet at No. 58+1, which "belongs to" the (C E G) triad of the succeeding Collection III block at No. 58+3.) This overlapping prompts new and ever more varied and subtle gradations of duplicity, ambiguity, and flexibility with respect to the functional behavior of C# [D♭] and E, the elements of between-block or between-reference intersection.

No. 63: At No. 63, "Pas des furies," C# [D♭], E, and G are part of an octatonic (Collection I) and diatonic A-scale-on-C# interaction, in which C# is the root of the (C# E G#) "tonic" triad shared by these interacting references, and E is a chord tone as the "minor third." (See Example 64g.) While Stravinsky fancifully adds a conflicting "C-major" key signature in the violas (such a conflicting signature constitutes a rare occurrence in his music, and here, significantly, the violas merely reiterate a (C E G) triad, not the collection stipulated by the C-scale on C), it is not really the separateness or superimposed quality of (C E G) that is of immediate consequence, but E as the "minor third" of the (C# E G#) "tonic" triad and G as pitch number 6. This G effects (3 6 7) "minor-major third" emphasis in terms of Collection I's (E G G#) unit, or, on the Classical A-scale-on-C# side of the equation, tends to pitch number 7, the G# or fifth of the (C# E G#) "tonic" triad, as a V–of–V chromatic tendency tone. (In other words, it is E and G as elements of intersection in this octatonic (Collection I) and diatonic A-scale-on-C# interaction to which the ear is drawn.) Indeed, the priority of E and G over, say, C (the root of the (C E G) triad) is apparent at

Example 64g: "Pas des furies"

the close of this section at Nos. 75–77 (which concludes the "Pas des furies"): C is omitted altogether, while E and G are sustained in the violas and first violins. The lengthy suspension of G here, first in the violas and then in the first violins, seems in contradiction to Classical procedure, a contradiction whose consequence is the accentuation of (3 6 7) "minor-major third" emphasis in terms of (E G G♯). For in place of sustaining the chord tone G♯ (which, in Classical procedure might perhaps have been expected), it is G, the nonchord tone as pitch number 6, the V–of–V chromatic tendency tone to G♯, which is sustained (as if, somehow, *it* were the chord tone), while G♯ and its (C♯ E G♯) "tonic" triad merely "intrude" as part of the accompanying figuration in the second violins, cellos, and double basses.

But duplicity in the functional behavior of G is very much in evidence. For the scoring is such (especially on the final occasion of the "intruding" accompaniment at No. 76+4) that while the sustained G "clashes" in simultaneity with the G♯ and effects (3 6 7) "minor-major third" emphasis in terms of (E G G♯), its Classical derivation as a V–of–V chromatic tendency tone to the G♯ may yet be discerned.

Thus, octatonically at Nos. 4–77 in *Orpheus*, a bond is forged between Collections I and III via (B♭ D♭) or (B♭ D♭ E G), with (B♭ D♭ E G) as the shared "diminished-seventh" chord between these two octatonic collections (although B♭, D♭, E, and G do not constitute, for Collection III, the (0,3,6,9) symmetrically defined partitioning elements that they do for Collection I. This is why Collection I figures so much more persistently than Collection III.) Then, alongside these octatonic implications are the interacting diatonic C-scale (or major-scale) and A-scale (or descending minor-scale) references, in which (B♭ D♭) and (B♭ D♭ E G) likewise serve as pivoting, between-block, and/or between-reference connecting links. For example, the octatonic (Collection I) and diatonic A-scale-on-B♭/C-scale-on-D♭ interaction at No. 5 in the "Air de danse," in which B♭ and D♭ are roots of the (B♭ D♭ F) and (D♭ F A♭) "tonic" triads shared by these interacting collections of reference, and in which E and G may foment "impurity" as members of Collection I's (D♭ E F/E F A♭/E G A♭) "minor-major third" units, or, on the Classical A-scale-on-B♭/C-scale-on-D♭ side of the coin, tend chromatically to the chord tones F and A♭, the "major thirds" and/or "fifths" of these (B♭ D♭ F) and (D♭ F A♭) "tonic" triads. Then, too, long-range planning in block or sectional transposition is as octatonic as it is Classical C-scale or A-scale, having as much to do with the collection's (0,3,6,9) symmetrically defined succession of (0 3 7/0 4 7) triads as with the transpositions or modulatory procedures of tonal C-scale (or A-scale) literature. The relationship of the introductory block at No. 4, with (near) repeats at Nos. 8 and 21–23, to the succeeding block at No. 5, with (near) repeats at Nos. 9, 23, and 25, is *octatonic*: through the shared (B♭ D♭) and (B♭ D♭ E G) units, (C E G B (D♭)) and (A C♯ E G (B♭)) relate to the octatonic (Collection I) and diatonic A-scale-on-B♭/C-scale-on-D♭ interaction as Collection III relates to Collection I. The transposition of the octatonic (Collection I) and diatonic A-scale-on-B♭/C-scale-on-D♭ interaction at No. 5 to the suggestion of a Collection I and C-scale-on-B♭ interaction at No. 49, and then to the Collection-I/C-scale-on-C♯[D♭] and Collection-I/A-scale-on-C♯[D♭] interactions at Nos. 58 and 63, unfolds with unmistakable reference to Collection I.

And so (B♭ D♭) or (B♭ D♭ E G) twists and turns in its referential alle-

giance, implicating the octatonic Collections I and III and a host of interacting diatonic C-scales and A-scales. While immediate and explicit connections of this sort between two of the three possible octatonic collections
may be found elsewhere in Stravinsky's music, it is to the pace of this twisting and turning and to the subtlety of the diatonic interaction that *Orpheus*
owes its special quality, its special hue.[22]

CONCLUSIONS

Indeed, in Example 65 we attempt a summary of this referential twisting
and turning in *Orpheus*. And on the octatonic side is, first, Collection I with
its (0 3 7/0 4 7) triads and its (0 3 4/3 4 7/3 6 7) "minor-major third" groupings positioned at B♭ and D♭ [C♯]; second, Collection III with its (0 3 7/0 4
7/0 4 7 10 (1)) triadic complexes at A, C, and G♭ as implicated at No. 4 in
the "Air de danse" and at Nos. 53–56 in the "Pas des furies." Then, on the

Example 65: *Orpheus*, Nos. 4–77

diatonic side, balancing Collection I, is the interacting C-scale-on-B♭ reference at Nos. 48–50 in the "Pas des furies"; the interacting A-scale-on-B♭/
C-scale-on-D♭ reference of the "Air de danse"; and the interacting C-
scale-on-C♯[D♭] and A-scale-on-C♯[D♭] references at Nos. 58 and 63 in the
"Pas des furies." With respect to these B♭ and D♭ are roots of the (0 3 7/0 4
7) "tonic" triads, and E and G are chromatic tendency tones to the "major
thirds" and "fifths" of these "tonic" triads.[23]

Similar formats may be composed for any of the several contexts examined in this chapter. Transposing the *Orpheus* summary into Collection II,
we derive a summary of the block examined at Nos. 167–70 in *Oedipus*
(Example 66a); or if into Collection II, a summary of the passage surveyed
at Nos. 30–34 in *Danses concertantes* (Example 66b). And were we to ex-
pand these designs to incorporate the stipulated potential available to Col-

Example 66a: *Oedipus Rex*, Nos. 166–70

Example 66b: *Danses concertantes*

lection I, the sketch of Example 67 might apply, where, reading down on the octatonic side, the (B♭, D♭, E, G) symmetrically defined partitioning elements are roots of the overlapping succession of (0 3 7/0 4 7) triads as well as members of the overlapping (0 3 4/3 4 7/3 6 7) "minor-major third"—or possibly (0 1 3 4) tetrachordal—complexes; on the interacting diatonic side, these same (B♭, D♭, E, G) elements are roots of the same succession of triads (implicating the diatonic C-scale or A-scale orderings indicated), as well as Classical C-scale (or A-scale) chromatic tendency tones to the "major thirds" and "fifths" of this triadic succession.

Further, on the most elementary and comprehensive of levels, it is quite possibly not so much the (0 3 4/3 4 7/3 6 7) "minor-major third" groupings that serve as the principal between-block or between-reference connecting links in octatonic-diatonic interaction (or serve neoclassicism as its governing "basic cells") as it is the centricity of some (0 3 7/0 4 7) "tonic"

Example 67

triad and the variety of functions, octatonic or diatonic, assumed by pitch numbers 3, 6, and 9 in their encirclement of this (0 3 7/0 4 7) "tonic" centricity. (In other words, a (0 3 7/0 4 7)/(0 3 6 9) relationship would seem to insinuate itself, in which one of the deepest of neoclassical "secrets" resides with the (0,3,6,9) symmetrically defined partitioning elements of the octatonic collection, Model A, conceived with reference to the collection or—in the exhibition of duplicity—to conventions, inflections, and harmonic maneuvers of Baroque and Classical C-scale (or A-scale) literature.) Accordingly, we envision the centricity of some (0 4 7) "tonic" triad shared by interacting octatonic (Model A) and diatonic C-scale references;[24] with respect to which pitch number 0 is the root, pitch numbers 4 and 7 the "major third" and "fifth"; with respect to which pitch numbers 3 and 6 are, octatonically, members of the encircling (0 3 4/3 4 7/3 6 7) or (0 1 3 4) "minor-major third" groupings; with respect to which pitch numbers 3 and 6 are, on the Classical C-scale side of the accommodation, chromatic tendency tones to pitch numbers 4 and 7, the "major third" and "fifth" of the (0 4 7) "tonic" triad; with respect to which pitch number 9 might partake, octatonically and diatonically, of some cohesive between-reference (0 3 4 6 7 9) articulation, or possibly of some cohesive (0 3 6 9) "diminished-seventh" articulation in an (0 4 7)–(0 3 6 (9)) exchange, "clash," or superimposition; with respect to which this same pitch number 9 might, octatonically and diatonically, constitute the root of the (9 0 4) "minor" triad, this alternative possibly signaling the fusion or "coming together" of triads which would formerly have defined a tonic-submediant relation (or, with respect to the interval orderings defined in relation to the diatonic collection, "relative keys"); and with respect to which these same pitch numbers 3, 6, and 9 might constitute roots of additional (0 3 7/0 4 7/0 4 7 10) triadic articulation, or signal long-range block or sectional transpositions. Such, truly, is the nature of neoclassical thought, or, if not of neoclassical thought as a whole, then of some very sizable chunk thereof. For these are the principal points of intersection that distinguish the mode of octatonic-diatonic interaction which this chapter has sought to confront: an accommodation between Model A's (0,3,6,9) symmetrically defined partitioning of the octatonic collection and certain idiosyncracies of Baroque and Classical C-scale (or A-scale) literature. It is from the particulars of this integration that neoclassicism derives much of its typicality, identity, and distinction, as well as its startling variety from one context to the next.

ELEVEN
OCTATONIC "PROGRESSIONS"

It is evidently not possible to pass from the "Russian" period to pieces exhibiting a neoclassical bent without at some point having to confront the
elusive presence of C-scale (or major-scale) tonally functional relations. A
"strict constructionist" may claim that none of Stravinsky's neoclassical
material submits to interpretation along these lines and that attempts to
investigate his methods by employing tonality and its terminology as a
norm from which to gauge critical departures are all ill-conceived. And
this has quite definitely been our analytic-theoretical perspective. Apart
from the many and varied accommodations forged between abrupt block
juxtaposition and the formal practice of Baroque and Classical C-scale literature, as well as that very special neoclassical dominant-tonic transaction which surfaces as a kind of long-range terminating convenience (to
which we shall be devoting our attention in chapter 12), the Classical C-
scale side of the bargain has seemed to manifest itself in terms of "surface
gesture" (the "gesture" of "theme and accompaniment," for example); in
terms of the centricity of some (0 4 7) "major"—or possibly (0 3 7)
"minor"—"tonic" triad (shared, however, by the interacting octatonic collection); in terms of chromatic tendency tones (which, interacting with a (0
3 4/3 4 7/3 6 7) "minor-major third" and (0 3 7/0 4 7) triadic partitioning of
the octatonic collection, Model A, take on "impurity," their peculiarly
Stravinskian stance); in terms of a few (0,3)-defined transpositions or
pseudo-modulations of octatonic (Model A) and diatonic C-scale interactions (prompted, however, as much by octatonic penetration in the form
of an "intruding" or "clashing" pitch number 3 as by Classical C-scale harmonic or modulatory procedure); and in terms of the superimposition,
fusion, or "coming together" of the (0,3)-related "minor" and "major"
triads, which, in relation to the diatonic collection, might have defined a
submediant-tonic or "relative-key" relationship, but, as Stravinsky uses
them, suggest the octatonic scale, Model A, as clearly as the Classical C-
scale or A-scale. In other words, there is no appearance of any substantive
formulation of the harmonic progressions, the transpositions and modu-

321

lations, the definitions of key or cadence associated with C-scale (or A-scale) music of the seventeenth to nineteenth centuries.

Yet the neoclassical label may often wield a legitimacy transcending not only superficial gesture but also the conventions to which we have thus far been addressing ourselves. Even Arthur Berger, an observer who very persuasively skirts the tonal issue in search of a "self-contained theory," finds himself faced with a tonal presence or "residue" in the *Symphony of Psalms* (1930), acknowledging "the tonal bias that obviously governed its conception," and Stravinsky's "congenital orientation" toward "traditional harmony." He suggests, nonetheless, that this presence or "residue" constitutes a mere "semblance" of past authenticity, an "appearance or outward seeming of" a tonal functionality divested of imperatives like "resolution," and thus "distinctly parenthetical" to the principal forces at work, whether octatonic, diatonic, or octatonic-diatonic.[1]

As noted earlier in chapter 9, the first movement of *Psalms* affords a stunning demonstration of octatonic partitioning (Model A) and octatonic-diatonic interaction: blocks accountable to Collection I ((0,3,6) "background" partitioning in terms of (E,G,Bb)) are abruptly juxtaposed with—and interpenetrate with—blocks accountable to the diatonic E-scale, with respect to which E and the (E G B) "*Psalms* chord" act as punctuation, constituting the principal between-block (or between-reference) connecting links. But this first movement concludes with a "half cadence" on G that is all but unmistakable. And while the G of this "half cadence" is a Collection I (G,Bb,Db,E) partitioning element—and functions as such throughout the first movement—it prepares, in dominant-toniclike fashion, for the quasi-C-minor fugal exposition of the second movement, and for the (C Eb G Bb), (C E), and (C E Bb) concluding simultaneities at Nos. 0–3 in the third and final movement which reappear to conclude the symphony.

Still, questions may linger about the effect of such a presence—or about the effect of all these Baroque or Classical C-scale conventions, inflections, and gestures—on our senses, and the extent to which traditional terminology might still prove reliable as a means of communication—reliable in the sense of not requiring a crippling degree of qualification. The answer here, of course, is that barring stupefying linguistic impasses, all will naturally depend on the perspective or approach we deem most useful (most compelling, revealing, or instructive) in relation to our experiences, preoccupations, and ambitions as listeners, performers, or composers, and the results in interpretation or analysis may not so much conflict as supplement each other.

To take but one example: while Nos. 0–5 in the "Basle" *Concerto in D* (Example 58a in chapter 10) may be heard and interpreted as referentially octatonic—and while this determination is useful and revealing in that it can account for C-scale (or major-scale) "impurity" in a way that relates to Stravinsky's lifelong predilections in pitch organization (octatonic partitioning)—the E♯–F♯ reiteration and the full C-scale-on-D setting introduced at No. 5 render the tendency-tone inflection on the part of pitch number 3, the E♯ [F], unmistakable. It would be difficult for this observer to so divorce himself from past experience, from past Baroque or Classical C-scale literature, as not to recognize the significance of the implication (neoclassicism), not to recognize that, by such means, past C-scale conventions and a partitioning of the octatonic collection interrelate, invoking traditional terminology in order to account for traditional or quasi-traditional behavior (i.e., the Classical C-scale side of the bargain). Then, too, while it is possible to settle for octatonic hegemony in the first movements of *Psalms* and the *Symphony in Three Movements* (1945), certain tonally functional "imperatives' (the dominant-tonic "resolution," specifically) do materialize toward the conclusion of these movements as a result of that suggestive potential in Model A's (0 4 7 10) "dominant sevenths" of the octatonic collection, a partitioning to which the octatonic construction in both these works relates. So with this in mind, we shall in this chapter be discussing Stravinskian "progressions" involving the octatonic succession of (0 4 7 10) "dominant-seventh" complexes; these "progressions," like those briefly surveyed in the preceding chapter, may carry the suggestion of a C-scale tonally functional harmonic maneuver. We can then move on to materializing "imperatives" in chapter 12, to the dominant-tonic transaction or "resolution" which unfolds on a more global scale, and on whose behalf we shall quite definitely have to acknowledge the presence of a (non-octatonic) C-scale tonally functional *progression* (notwithstanding "impurities" which often mar its authenticity, and which may reflect the specifics of the accommodation, and notwithstanding its seeming irrelevance to pitch organization generally, resulting from the incidental or "distinctly parenthetical" manner in which it surfaces as a terminating convenience).

THE (0 4 7 10) "DOMINANT-SEVENTH" COMPLEXES

It will be remembered that the principal articulative unit in *The Firebird* Introduction was a four-note figure introduced as part of the opening ostinato pattern, Derivative I. Derivative I consisted of two intervals, one defined by four semitones and the other by three, these "major and minor thirds" jointly spanning a tritone (not four semitones, a "major third," as with the (0 3 4) and (0 1 3 4) complexes). The interval content of the ostinato pattern and its derivative was referentially octatonic, and subsequent transpositions and transformations were "pursued with unmistakable reference to the octatonic collection." The tritone relation was fundamental to the identity of these patterns, this (0,6) partitioning being defined at mm. 1–10 in terms of A♭ and D, Collection I.

Critical, however, was the implication that the roots of the (0,6) tritone-related (E G♯ B) (B♭ D F) triads outlined by the configuration at mm. 5–7, E and B♭, did not assume priority, which was determined by the ostinato and its derivative, which assert A♭ and D. Indeed, this non-correlation between the elements of priority and the roots of the triads implicated by the configuration at mm. 5–7 seemed the principal condition of confinement, and a revealing one in view of the distinctions unveiled when the configuration was compared with the "*Petroushka* chord."

Still, should the original interval order defined by Derivative I be inverted, the elements asserting priority would coincide with the roots of the (0 4 7) "major" triads implicated by the configuration, a circumstance that would naturally enhance the potential for (0 3 7/0 4 7) triadic exposure (Model A). And this is precisely what happens over the barlines at mm. 13–14 and 20–21. (See Example 68.) On each of these occasions, the inverted form in terms of (A♭ C) (B D)—reading up—spans the tritone A♭–D, the elements of this (0,6) relation asserting priority. But the pitch content of these (A♭ C) (B D) inversions refers to Collection II, not Collection I. Consequently, A♭ and D are at mm. 13–14 and 20–21 (0,3,6,9) symmetrically defined partitioning elements as roots of Collection II's succession of triads at A♭, B, D, and F (Model A). And, revealingly, it is on these occasions that the listener is relieved of that back-and-forth oscillation initiated by the ostinato pattern, a true sense of over-the-barline "progress" emerging in the form of two highly conventional harmonic progressions.

Now these "progressions" at mm. 13–14 and 20–21 feature (0 4 7 10) "dominant sevenths" at A♭ and D and at A♭ and F. They are preceded, on

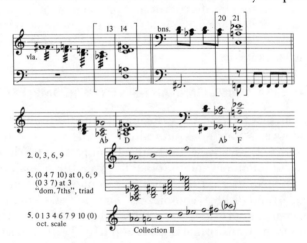

Example 68: *The Firebird* (Introduction)

each occasion, by a (B D F♯) triad, also accountable to Collection II. And their surroundings suggest that these triads and "progressions" undoubtedly arose from a commitment in this (octatonic) direction. But no less are they a part of traditional harmonic practice, a circumstance that could scarcely have escaped the composer's notice (being "congenitally oriented" in this sense, as Berger has suggested). For the conventional effect of a tonally functional transaction presses itself on the listener acquainted, as Stravinsky must have been, with nearly two centuries of such maneuvers.

Over the barline at mm. 20–21 the traditional (tonal) effect is pronounced. Here, with conventional voice-leading intact, an incomplete (0 4 7 10) dominant seventh at A♭ is succeeded by an incomplete (0 4 7 10) dominant seventh at F. This (0,3)-defined progression constitutes, in tonal C-scale literature, one of the familiar irregular resolutions of a dominant seventh, one in which the resolution to its tonic is forsaken, deceptively replaced by yet another dominant seventh whose root lies three semitones (a "minor third") below.

Tonally, the progression may occur in the form of V2–V7-of-vi–vi, or, indeed, with any number of variations in function and voice distribution. It has as its origin the familiar ascending sequence in which the second of the dominant sevenths fulfills its dominant-tonic obligation. (See Examples 69a and 69b.)

But there are more sophisticated tonal versions in circulation. The sequence shown in Example 69c was widely used during the latter half of the nineteenth century, and was a favorite of Brahms. But rarely was the cycle of four dominant sevenths (at A♭, F, D, and B here, Collection II) actually completed; rarely were the symmetrical implications, by such completion, allowed to destroy the tonal orientation. Thus, at mm. 27–31 in the first movement of Brahms's Fourth Symphony (Example 70), this sequence unfolds in its typical (tonal) transitory and incomplete fashion.

On the other hand, if we now view these "progressions" as octatonic rather than as part of a tonal environment, we need only continue the descent by the interval of 3 ("root movement" by "minor thirds") until the (0,3,6,9) partitioning cycle of the octatonic collection is complete and its succession of (0 4 7) triads, each separated from its neighbor by the interval of 3 and each with (0 4 7 10 (1)) "dominant-seventh" and "dominant-

Example 69a   Example 69b   Example 69c

Example 70: Brahms, Fourth Symphony

Ab   F   D   B

Example 71

minor-ninth" supplementation, accounted for. (See Example 71; or Model A, Collection II.)

Confined to the octatonic collection, these "progressions" are now "stuck," enclosed within a symmetrical or circular order that subjects them to pulls and attractions of a sort different from those of the tonal system and the asymmetrical C-scale reference. Thus, as potential "dominants," the (0 4 7 10) complexes in these "progressions" are, octatonically, incapable of realizing the traditional (tonal) escape route: there can be no "resolution" to a "tonic." Nor, for that matter, can these triadic complexes, as "tonalities" or "tonic" triads, elicit "leading-tone" support: there can be no "leading-tone" function in support of the partitioning elements, the "accented tones," the potential priorities (or the triads they root) of the octatonic collection with interval order 1, 2 (Model A). (In other words, at mm. 20–21 in *The Firebird* Introduction, the partitioning elements Ab and F, and the (0 4 7 10) "dominant-seventh" complexes they root, can neither, as "dominants," "resolve" to their respective "tonics"—there being no Db or Bb in Collection II—nor, as "tonics," elicit "leading-tone" support—there being no G or E.) Hence Berger's reference to a "semblance" of functionality. The tonally functional relation is little more than an effect, little more than "an appearance or outward seeming," a "residue," something "distinctly parenthetical," and, in *The Firebird* Introduction, transient in nature. The (0 4 7 10) "progression" at mm. 20–21 might, as a purely local affair, be accountable to both "systems," retaining in the new some sense of the old (which, of course, is where the difficulty— or the duplicity—arises). But once an octatonic framework is brought more securely into play, the authenticity of the tonal reference fades. It becomes a "semblance," a side effect; the triads or "progressions" acquiring a different "feel," a different identity, owing to the symmetry of which they are now felt to be a part.

And the whole question of "progress" becomes problematic. The tonal, irregular resolution in Examples 69b and 69c harbors its own brand of deception, of course, as the ultimate progress—the tonic resolution—is delayed with the advance of another dominant seventh. And because the "progression" at mm. 20–21 in *The Firebird* Introduction is an unmitigated over-the-barline succession—uncontested, so to speak—a "residue" of this tonal deceptive play may yet be sensed in it. But what happens to these (0,3)-related (0 4 7 10) "dominant-seventh" complexes in Examples 10b and 10c from the *Symphony of Psalms* (No. 0) and the *Symphony in Three Movements* (Nos. 7–13), and in Example 57a from *Le Sacre* (No. 37)?[2] In the midst now of superimposition, of abrupt block juxtaposition and repetition, octatonic partitioning, and the symmetrical pulls and attractions this reference triggers in association with these procedures, is brought more fully to bear, and the old feeling of a deceptive tonal progression is scarcely evident.

Thus, in the first two of these passages (Examples 10b and 10c), the (0,3)-related (0 4 7 10) "dominant-seventh" complexes oscillate in a manner similar to the (0,6) tritone-related triads at mm. 5–7 in *The Firebird* Introduction (or at No. 51 in *Petroushka*; or at No. 68–70 in *Les Noces*), with the consequence that the succession they reiterate is deprived of "progression." Fixed registrally, they are also fixed configurally as a unit; their separateness is diminished, with no hint of a local, short-term (tonal) "escape" for either. Moreover, these configurations are uncompromisingly octatonic, because of the introduction of a third partitioning element, the E or (E G B) "*Psalms* chord" in *Psalms*, the A or A–C–A basso ostinato in the *Symphony in Three Movements* (this third element stipulating the same relation in each case, by juxtaposition in *Psalms*, by superimposition in the latter). This third element extends (0,3) partitioning to (0,3,6), an extension which further "grounds" or immobilizes the oscillating (0 4 7 10) complexes above. We are in the midst, then, of equal weight and independence, of opposition, and locked confrontation (a kind of non-progression)—octatonically induced symmetry brought about by the simultaneous assertion of priority on the part of two or three of the collection's (0,3,6,9) symmetrically defined partitioning elements, each with (0 3 7) or (0 4 7 10) articulative "support."

The passage at No. 37 in *Le Sacre* (Example 57a in chapter 10) is exemplary: the (0,3)-related (0 4 7 10) "dominant sevenths" at E♭ and C, fixed registrally and configurally, locked in superimposition, define no progression at all. (Nor, as we have indicated, is there any hint of the chromatic tendency-tone inflection to which the (0 3 4) "minor-major third" complex embedded in this configuration, (C E♭ E), would later, as part of the neoclassical orientation, lend itself.) And note again the logic or rationale behind block juxtaposition: as here defined (and illustrated by these examples), symmetrical construction within blocks defies internally motivated "development" along traditional tonal lines. Change, progress, renewal, or "development" is possible only by abruptly cutting off the deadlock and juxtaposing it with something new in the collectional reference—or in the partitioning thereof—through which some relation, possibly continuously operative, may be left "hanging" as a connecting link. Thus, as we have maintained, octatonically induced symmetry interrelates with these procedures of superimposition, block juxtaposition, and repetition, forging the conditions (immobility, equilibrium, opposition, deadlock) invariably associated with this symmetry.

Still, even with the symmetry in the passages just cited so uncompromising, the sense of a symmetrically defined deadlock so impressive, we are perhaps not entirely free of past reference, the suggestion of a conventional (tonal) harmonic transaction in the form of a (0 4 7 10) dominant seventh irregularly resolved. Indeed, we venture to suggest that tonal implications of this sort, while less conspicuous in Examples 10b and 10c from *Psalms* and the *Symphony in Three Movements* than in *The Firebird*'s Introduction (and certainly more remote or less easily discernible than the Classical C-scale chromatic tendency tones examined in the previous chapter), are precisely what prompted Boulez to label the vocabulary of *Le Sacre*—a work whose octatonic credentials are as unsullied by tonal implications as any in the literature—a mere "surcharge of an existent [tonal] language." For we are dealing with (0 3 7/0 4 7) triads (Model A); triads, after all, with (0 4 7 10) "dominant-seventh" supplementation.

Moreover, a critical associative factor linking Stravinsky's (0,3)-defined (0 4 7 10) "dominant-seventh" partitioning of the octatonic collection to its tonal conception as a dominant seventh irregularly resolved has thus far eluded our attention: while the oscillating (0,3)-related (0 4 7 10) "dominant sevenths" in Examples 10b and 10c from *Psalms* and the *Symphony in Three Movements* are registrally and configurally fixed, *tonally conceived voice-leading remains intact.* In other words, in the (B♭ D F A♭)–(B D F G) oscillation in Example 10b from *Psalms*, the B♭ "progresses" (ascends) to the B, and the A♭, the "dominant seventh," "progresses" or "resolves" (descends) to the G (and, of course, *vice versa*). It is this kind of associative factor that allows us to move quite smoothly from Boulez on Stravinsky to Stravinsky on Rimsky-Korsakov. Some remarks of Stravinsky regarding the methods of his teacher revealingly parallel the concerns of Boulez in regard to Stravinsky.[3] For it is probable that when Stravinsky dismissed Rimsky's "modernism" as having consisted of little more than a few "flimsy enharmonic devices," the tonal (enharmonic) conception of (0,3,6,9) symmetrically defined partitioning of the octatonic collection (Model A) lay somewhere in the back of his mind.[4] Rimsky (according to his own testimony) was conscious of the octatonic collection as a cohesive frame of reference;[5] he followed through with its full (0,3,6,9) symmetrically defined potential *unimpaired.* (See, for example, the opening measures of the second tableau in *Sadko,* Example 15a in chapter 2.) But Rimsky did not *superimpose;* nor did he *juxtapose* or oscillate back and forth accordianlike *à la Stravinsky.* Consequently, owing to *succession*—or even to *progression*—and to conventional voice-leading, tonally conceived enharmony may have been—and may still be—as apparent as "octatonic accountability" in Rimsky's application. Thus, Stravinsky may have been unaware of the nature and scope of his "debt." (This, however, need not concern us overly, for we remain convinced of his "complicity," the evidence being too substantial, too overwhelming that he, like his predecessor, was conscious of the octatonic collection as a cohesive frame of reference—notwithstanding the absence of an acknowledgment of this effect in his six books of "conversation" with Robert Craft.)

We are reminded, once again, that the extent to which these suggestions of C-scale tonally functional harmonic maneuvers are heeded (for there can be no mistaking their actual presence) will depend on the approach or perspective we find most suited to our experiences, preoccupations, and ambitions as listeners, performers, or composers. This observer finds the suggestions difficult to ignore, although their potency varies from one context to the next. In Examples 10b, 10c, and 57a, the (0,3)-defined (0 4 7 10) "progression," as conventionally defined in Examples 69b and 69c, is scarcely evident. But at other times, the conventional (tonal) effect of this octatonic "progression" seems as unmistakable as the chromatic tendency-tone inflection, which, as we have seen in chapter 10, Model A is equally capable of implicating (and, like this present maneuver, without interpenetrating assistance from the diatonic C-scale in the form of non-octatonic pitch elements).

TWELVE
THE DOMINANT-TONIC
RELATION

Most incriminating with respect to an actual C-scale (or major-scale) tonally functional presence in Stravinsky's neoclassical material are passages, sections, or pieces where an octatonic partitioning element—generally with (0 4 7 10) "dominant-seventh" supplementation, Model A partitioning—acquires the "feel" of a dominant by virtue of a kind of tonic resolution concluded on its behalf.

Now up to this point, Stravinsky's neoclassical C-scale reference has seemed not substantively to partake of the tonally functional relations, the harmonic progressions, the modulations or definitions of key and cadence known to the Baroque, Classical, and Romantic traditions. The Baroque or Classical C-scale imprint has seemed rather to impose itself by way of "surface gesture," by way of the centricity of some (0 3 7/0 4 7) "tonic" triad, by way of chromatic tendency-tone inflections to the "major thirds" and "fifths" of this "tonic" centricity, by way of blends or juxtapositions of the (0,3)-related "minor" and "major" triads (or of the interval orderings these triads define in relation to the diatonic collection, orderings which would formerly have distinguished themselves as "relative keys"); or by way of a few harmonic maneuvers like the (0 3 6 (9))–(0 4 7) exchange or "clash" (a verticalization of the chromatic tendency tones, pitch numbers 3 and 6 conceived as part of a "raised supertonic"–"tonic" succession), or the (0,3)-related (0 4 7 10) "dominant-seventh" chords (which, as surveyed in the previous chapter, might occasionally invoke the authentic "feel" of a dominant seventh irregularly resolved). The preoccupation with these phenomena seemed owing to the fact that, referentially, they were as octatonic (Model A) as they were Baroque or Classical C-scale; in the exhibition of this duplicity in derivation or referential status, they sealed an octatonic (Model A) and diatonic C-scale interaction crucial to the Stravinskian stamp and to a hearing and understanding of the neoclassical accommodation within the broader context of Stravinsky's music "considered as a whole." Then, too, general methods of procedure seemed at odds with tonal C-scale processes. The symmetrically defined octatonic implications of these conventions, inflections, gestures, and harmonic maneuvers seemed underscored by techniques of superimposition (forms of "clashes"), by the ritual of chordal reiteration or back-and-forth oscillation, and by abrupt block juxtaposition and the contradictions or reversals so intimately a part of the rhythmic-metric "play."

And so the following condition prevailed in neoclassical passages exhibiting octatonic (Model A) and diatonic C-scale interaction: a single presiding pitch, (0 3 7/0 4 7) triad, or (0 3 4/3 4 7/3 6 7) "minor-major third" unit, asserted itself on behalf of both references. These assertions of priority served to unite these references as connecting links, as pivoting points of intersection. For example, in passages from the "Basle" *Concerto in D*, the *Symphony in Three Movements* and *Danses concertantes* (Examples 58a, 58c, 59, and 60 in chapter 10), the (D F♯ A) "tonic" triad and pitch numbers 3 and 6, the E♯ [F] and G♯, asserted themselves on behalf of both Collection II and the C-scale on D; E♯ [F], and G♯ "clashed" in static simultaneity with F♯ and A and effected "minor-major third" emphasis in terms of Collection II's (D F F♯/F F♯ A/F G♯ A) symmetrically defined units, but also tended to these "thirds" and "fifths" as chromatic tendency tones (exhibiting, through this duplicity, their Classical C-scale derivation).

But, obviously, where a long-range tonic "resolution" manifests itself, the "tonic" cannot, as we have observed, be accountable to the octatonic collection to which the "dominant," as a Model A partitioning element, is accountable. Or to rephrase this: *the* leading tone is not available to the (0,3,6,9) symmetrically defined partitioning elements of the octatonic collection(s), Model A, envisioned as "tonics"; nor, with these same elements envisioned as "dominants," can they "resolve" to their respective "tonics." (To reiterate: only the so-called chromatic tendency tones or "melodic leading tones" are octatonic, and are thus available to the "major thirds" and "fifths" of each of the (0,3,6,9) symmetrically defined (0 4 7) "major" triads of the octatonic collection. See Examples 54, 55, and 56 in chapter 9; or consult Model A in chapter 2.) Hence the triadically conceived dominant-tonic transaction (with leading tone) is not "referentially octatonic" as are the Classical C-scale chromatic tendency tones or any of the conventions or harmonic maneuvers examined thus far. The dominant-tonic relation materializes outside the octatonic collection, and not only represents Baroque or Classical C-scale behavior quite different from these previously examined formulae—all of which can materialize where reference to the octatonic collection is unimpaired—but also defines, as a consequence, conditions of octatonic (Model A) and diatonic C-scale interaction different from those recorded above.

Significantly, however, it is often an octatonic partitioning element that acquires, retroactively as it were, the characteristic "feel" of a dominant by virtue of a toniclike resolution concluded on its behalf. By this is meant that the "tonic resolution" often surfaces as a kind of terminating convenience in contexts either octatonic or octatonic-diatonic in conception, so that, apart from qualifying "impurities" in the concluding simultaneity itself (which may reflect the specifics of the accommodation), the "resolution" may seem incidental to pitch organization generally, and hence assume the "distinctly parenthetical" character alluded to in the preceding chapter. Consequently, notwithstanding its blatant non-octatonicism, its origin as a C-scale tonally functional *progression*, the Stravinskian dominant-tonic transaction in neoclassical contexts is reckoned as instantiating yet another form of octatonic (Model A) and diatonic C-scale interaction. The peculiarity of the "dominant" in this transaction rests nonetheless with a duplicity in function: the "dominant" is conceived with reference to the octatonic collection, as a (0,3,6,9) symmetrically defined partitioning element, its triad placed in conjunction with (superimposed over or oscillating with) other (0 3 7/0 4 7/0 4 7 10) triads and "dominant sevenths" of that particular collection to which it adheres; *and* it is conceived as something like a true dominant, preparing, in however parenthetical or "impure" a fashion, for an eventual, terminating "tonic resolution."

In a broad frame of reference, the specifics of the transaction are as follows: the (0,3,6,9) symmetrically defined partitioning elements of Collection I are G, B♭, D♭, and E. As potential "dominants" with (0 4 7 10 (1)) "dominant-seventh" or "dominant-minor-ninth" supplementation, they may implicate, as potential "tonics," C, E♭, G♭, and A respectively (all of which lie outside Collection I, being the (0,3,6,9) symmetrically defined partitioning elements of Collection III). Still, regularities may be inferred. Apropos Collection I Stravinsky seems rather consistently to have favored the C-scale-on-C (or A-scale-on-C) interaction, and hence forms of (C E G) or (C E♭ G) concluding conveniences. And so in general summation: it is to the (0,3,6,9) symmetrically defined partitioning elements as potential "dominants" rather than as "tonics" (along with the fresh assortment of diatonic C-scale or A-scale references that this contingency implicates) that our discussion is now drawn. And while the pieces or passages of pieces to be examined will continue to exhibit the diverse neoclassical formulae described in earlier chapters, it is this second octatonic-diatonic interaction that now constitutes the focus of our concern.

OCTET (1923)

Second Movement ("Tema con variazioni")
Theme   Nos. 24–26
Variation A ("ribbons of scales")   Nos. 26–28

Variation B	Nos. 28–31
Variation A ("ribbons of scales")	Nos. 31–33
Variation C (waltz)	Nos. 33–38
Variation D	Nos. 38–49
Variation A ("ribbons of scales")	Nos. 49–51
Variation E (fugato)	Nos. 51–56

The *Octuor* was quickly composed (in 1922). The first movement came first and was followed immediately by the waltz in the second movement. I derived the *tema* of the second movement from the waltz, which is to say that only after I had written the waltz did I discover it as a good subject for variations. I then wrote the "ribbons of scales" variation as a prelude to each of the other variations.

The final, culminating variation, the *fugato*, is my favorite episode in the *Octuor*. The plan of it was to present the theme in rotation by the instrumental pairs—flute-clarinet, bassoons, trumpets, trombones—which is the idea of instrumental combination at the root of the *Octuor*. . . . The third movement grew out of the *fugato*, and was intended as a contrast to that high point of harmonic tension. Bach's two-part Inventions were somewhere in the remote back of my mind while composing this movement, as they were during the composition of the last movement of the Piano Sonata [1924]. The terseness and lucidity of the inventions were an ideal of mine at that time, in any case, and I sought to keep those qualities uppermost in my own composition. What could be more terse than the punctuation of the final chord, in which the first inversion suffices to indicate *finis* and at the same time gives more flavor than the flat-footed tonic?

My appetite was whetted by my rediscovery of sonata form and by my pleasure in working with new instrumental combinations. [*Dialogues and a Diary*, p. 71.]

In Examples 72–76 the reader will find assembled, in abridged form, five passages exemplifying this tonally incriminating behavior.[1] In the first from the *Octet* (1952 version; see Example 72a), the complete (A B♭ C C♯ E F♯ G) variation theme introduced by the flute and clarinet at No. 24 is wholly octatonic, Collection III, and stresses A as the pitch class of priority. Moreover, the initial contour of the theme is (0 1 3 4) tetrachordal in conception, articulated at A (pitch number 0) in terms of (A B♭ C C♯) at No. 24, at C (pitch number 3) in terms of (C C♯ D♯ E) in the trumpet at No. 25, and then back to A again three measures before No. 26. And so pitch number 3, the C, is unconventional (octatonic) at No. 24, given its cohesive affiliation with Collection III's (A B♭ C C♯) tetrachord and the (A B♭ C C♯ E F♯ G) theme. But in view of the (0,3)-defined transposition of the (A B♭ C C♯ E F♯ G) theme to (C C♯ D♯ E A) at No. 25, C also asserts itself as a Collection III (A,C,E♭, F♯) symmetrically defined partitioning element, assuming a degree of "equal weight and independence" vis-à-vis pitch number 0, the A. Consequently, with respect to the variation theme's un-

Example 72a: *Octet* (Variation theme)

impaired, explicit reference to Collection III and its subsequent within-Collection III transposition to (C C♯ D♯ E A) at No. 25, we acknowledge: (1) A as asserting pitch-class priority; (2) (0,3) partitioning in terms of (A,C); (3) (A B♭ C C♯) (C C♯ D♯ E) tetrachordal articulation at A and C; (4) the (A B♭ C C♯ E F♯ G) complete variation theme and its transposition to (C C♯ D♯ E A) at No. 25; (5) these groupings jointly yielding Collection III in terms of (A B♭ C C♯ D♯ E F♯ G (A)).

However, beneath the (A B♭ C C♯ E F♯ G) theme at No. 24 there is an accompaniment that implicates an interpenetrating diatonic reference. This diatonic reference stresses D, implicating, given the pitch content, the A-scale on D (or a kind of pseudo-D-minor reference). But neither D nor the (D F A) "tonic" triad is accountable to Collection III, the octatonic reference collection of the variation theme above. Consequently, among other tonally derived ambiguities (such as the (A B♭ C C♯) tetrachord's B♭ as the sixth degree of the A-scale on D), a bond or connection is here forged between the variation theme and its accompaniment in the form of a dominant-tonic relation, a kind of superimposition of Collection III's A or (A B♭ C C♯) tetrachord over the A-scale on D's "tonic" D or (D F A) "tonic" triad. This relation is consummated in the final measure by a "tonic resolution" on D, in which the variation theme's terminal—and shared, between-reference—F♯ neatly unites Collection III with the accompaniment's A-scale on D in a *tierce de Picardie* "twist." (This "twist" is to be compared with the behavior of Collection III's E or its (C E) concluding simultaneity at Nos. 0–3 in the final movement of the *Symphony of Psalms*, or possibly with Collection II's F♯ or (D F♯) reiteration at Nos. 166–70 in *Oedipus*. See Examples 62 and 63 in chapter 10.)

Hence, apart from the Classical framework of "theme and accompaniment," neoclassicism imposes itself in the form of an octatonic (Collection III) and diatonic A-scale-on-D interpenetration in which Collection III's cohesively articulated (A B♭ C C♯) tetrachord, or its complete (A B♭ C C♯ E F♯ G) variation theme, is superimposed over the diatonic A-scale-on-D reference. The bond or connection between these collections of reference is thus loosely that of a dominant-tonic relation, a relation consummated or "brought together" in the final measure by a "tonic resolution" on D (with the shared, between-reference or intersecting F♯ delineating the *tierce de Picardie* inflection).

Still, the bond or connection is scarcely that of an authentic Baroque or Classical C-scale tonally functional progression. Not only does the cohesively articulated (A B♭ C C♯) (C C♯ D♯ E) tetrachordal partitioning of Collection III wield its interacting influence (or exert its "impurity" or, perhaps more accurately, its confounding duplicity by way of the between-reference, intersecting status of the theme's (A B♭ C C♯ E F♯ G) pitch content), but also, prior to the final, terminating "tonic resolution" on D, the "dominant" element in the theme (Collection III's A, or its (A B♭ C C♯) tetrachord) is merely *superimposed* over the "tonic" element in the accompaniment (the (D F A) triad and its A-scale-on-D or pseudo-D-minor reference).

Hence, too, the peculiarity (or the duplicity in function) of the neoclassical "dominant" here. On the one hand, the A is a Collection III (A,C,E♭,F♯) symmetrically defined partitioning element, cohesively aligned with Collection III's (A B♭ C C♯) tetrachord and (A B♭ C C♯ E F♯ G) variation theme; and, on the other, it functions, in relation to the (D F A) "tonic" triad of the accompaniment, as a parenthetical dominant, statically superimposed over this interacting diatonic reference until the final toniclike resolution on D with its F♯ *tierce de Picardie* "twist." And while the (A B♭ C C♯ E F♯ G) content of the variation theme intersects with the A-scale on D (the descending D-minor scale) and tonality's hybrid ascending D-minor scale (with B♭ and C as the sixth and seventh degrees of the former; C♯ as the seventh, leading-tone degree of the latter), it is not really to these tonal, diatonic minor scales that the articulation of the encompassed pitches relates, but rather to the symmetrically defined Collection III groupings alluded to.

Although not shown in Example 72a, the "ribbons of scales" Variation A at Nos. 26–28 (with near repeats at Nos. 31 and 49 preceding each variation in the form of a prelude; see Stravinsky's remarks above) transposes Collection III's (A B♭ C C♯) tetrachord into Collection I: a (B♭ [A♯] B D♭ [C♯] D) tetrachordal delineation. This Collection I delineation of the variation theme interpenetrates with diatonic A-scale-on-D and A-scale-on-B scale passages (Stravinsky's "ribbons of scales"), the between-reference, interpenetrating circumstances of which are reflected by the alternatives in pitch notation (e.g., the B♭ for the interpenetrating A-scale on D, the A♯ as the C-scale, tonally conceived leading tone to the B of the interpenetrating A-scale-on-B reference).

But the final, "culminating variation," the fugato at No. 51 (Stravinsky's favorite episode, a very stately and moving culmination indeed), restores the variation theme's earlier referential allegiance to Collection III: the fugato's "subject," a C♯–A–C♯–B♭–C, C–A–C♯–C–A–C♯, and A–B♭–E–G contour, stresses Collection III's (A B♭ C C♯) tetrachord. (See Example 72b.) A bargain is struck with the traditional tonic-dominant dialogue of fugal design, however, in that Collection III's (A B♭ C C♯) tetrachordal statement in the first bassoon is "answered" at the "fifth" by a (E F G G♯) tetrachordal delineation in the clarinet. Hence, octatonically (or (0 1 3 4) tetrachordally) speaking, Collection III's (A B♭ C C♯) "tonic" contribution at No. 51 is "answered" by Collection I's (E F G G♯) "dominant" contribution at No. 51 + 4. The connecting link in this fugal, tonic-dominantlike "questioning" and "answering" is neatly sealed at the juncture at No. 51 + 4 by an emphasis on those Collection-III–Collection-I pitches held in common: as members of the (B♭ C♯ E G) "diminished-seventh" chord shared by Collections III and I, C♯ is sustained in the second bassoon, while B♭, E, and G of the first bassoon's third and concluding A–B♭–E–G

Example 72b: Variation E (fugato)

contour smoothly anticipate the initial G♯–E–G♯–F–G–E–G♯ contour of the clarinet's "dominant answer." (C♯ serves as "root" of a (C♯ E G♯) triadic outline at No. 54 + 4—scarcely an authentic "dominant answer," then, but appropriate, and revealing, insofar as the octatonic implications of the bargain are concerned.) Furthermore, on the Baroque or Classical C-scale side of the accommodation, chromatic tendency-tone behavior on the part of pitch number 3 in these (A B♭ C C♯) (E F G G♯) tetrachordal delineations, while scarcely evident in the initial thematic statements at Nos. 24–26, may occasionally be inferred. That is to say: C tends occasionally to the C♯ of Collection III's (A B♭ C C♯) "tonic" contribution at No. 51; G tends occasionally to the G♯ of Collection I's (E F G G♯) "dominant" contribution at No. 51 + 4.

SYMPHONIES OF WIND INSTRUMENTS (1920)

The chorale which concludes the *Symphonies* was composed June 20, 1920, in Carantec, a fishing village in Finistère; I had rented a cottage there for the summer, but had to have a piano carted in from a neighboring town. The complete work was composed by July 2, though I returned to it a few days later to add the two adumbrative bits of chorale in the body of the piece. My sketch score contains few indications of instrumentation, but that is because I was certain of the sound and knew I would remember its components; I had merely to copy my sketch score into full score form. [*Themes and Episodes*, p. 29.]

In the next three examples from the *Symphonies of Wind Instruments*,[2] the *Symphony of Psalms*, and the *Symphony in Three Movements*, a toniclike resolution materializes to conclude the piece or movement, behavior made possible, as we have suggested, by prolonged stress on an octatonic partitioning element. In all three examples it is G, as a Collection I (G,B♭,D♭,E) symmetrically defined partitioning element with (G B D F (A♭)) "dominant-seventh" or "dominant-minor-ninth" supplementation, that prepares for the "tonic resolution" on C, the G thus acquiring, retroactively, the characteristic "feel" of a dominant.

In the *Symphonies of Wind Instruments* (1947 version here; see Examples 73a and b), the (C E G) triad that concludes this work (with a D and B left "hanging" from the preceding chorale blocks) relates in this fashion to the opening octatonic blocks at Nos. 0–6, which, wholly accountable to Collection I, stress G as the principal element of priority. And while this octatonic Collection I G at Nos. 0–6 (with (G B D F) "dominant-seventh" articulation) is placed "in opposition" to a B♭—with *its* (B♭ D F A♭) "dominant-seventh" articulative "support," thus again defining (0,3) partitioning of the octatonic collection, Model A, but here in terms of (G,B♭)—the persistent intrusion of the chorale block toward the close of

Example 73a: *Symphonies*

the work, also stressing G (see Nos. 56 and 65 in Example 73b), reinforces
the long-term doninant-tonic effect (which, admittedly, would have been
only remotely discernible without these chorale-block intrusions). Moreover, while subsequent (near) repeats of the opening Collection I block at
No. 0 fail to reiterate (0,3) partitioning in terms of (G,B♭), (near) repeats at
Nos. 26, 37, and 39 *are* transpositions *within* Collection I. At No. 26, 27,
and 39, (near) repeats are transpositions from G to E: Collection I's E,
with (E G♯ B D) "dominant-seventh" articulative "support," stands in a
(0,3) symmetrically defined "opposition" to G with its (D G) "support."
(These transpositions are foreshadowed earlier in the piece at No. 5,
where the tutti (B♭ D F A♭/F B A♭ D) chordal reiteration at Nos. 1 and 4 is
momentarily replaced by (B♭ D F A♭/E B A♭ [G♯] D), a superimposition of
(B♭ D F A♭) over its (0,6) tritone-related "dominant seventh," (E G♯ B D).
Aside from this foreshadowing, the E or (E G♯ B D) contingent solidifies

Example 73a *continued*

Collection I's presence at Nos. 0–6 by intensifying the pulls and attractions of its locked symmetry.) And so these conditions would seem to indicate, with reference to the many (C E G) endings in Stravinsky's neoclassical works, a kind of global framework with the thrust toward the terminating (C E G) "tonic" triad conceived not only in terms of G, but also in terms of the entire Collection I (G,B♭,D♭,E) symmetrically defined network which G implicates in the course of its confinement as a partitioning element.

Although the *Symphonies* follows *Pulcinella*, the first of Stravinsky's full-blown neoclassical ventures, it is ultimately more reflective of "Russian" idiosyncrasy than it is of neoclassicism. Apart from its melodicism (which is very "Russian," with circular, reiterating fragments exceedingly limited in range and content, often (0 2 3 5) tetrachordal or (0 2 3 5 7 9) hexachordal in conception), a highly incisive form of abrupt block juxtaposition manifests itself throughout. Indeed, the blocks, upon successive (near) repeats, attain a self-enclosed stability, a distinction and insulation possibly without equal in Stravinsky's oeuvre. This highly incisive form of abrupt block juxtaposition is defined, as always, through its content, with each of the blocks, in addition to whatever distinctions they derive from tempo, register, dynamics, and instrumentation, acquiring a "collectional

Example 73b: *Symphonies*

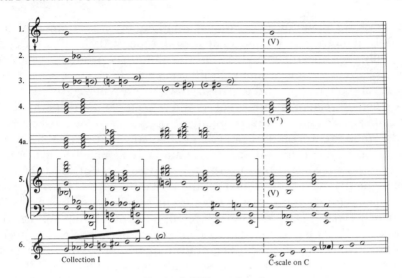

Example 73b *continued*

identity" and once again coincides (perhaps *necessarily* coincides, as has
been suggested) with an unimpaired, explicit reference to the octatonic
collection. There is an unimpaired, explicit reference to Collection I in
the opening blocks at Nos. 0–6, and the first of these at No. 0 is repeated
very nearly verbatim at Nos. 2, 9, 26, 37, and 39 (although transposed at
Nos. 9, 26, 37, and 39).[3] (Not until the first movement of the *Symphony of
Psalms* (1930), which comes after what Stravinsky termed "a decade of
[neoclassical] samplings, experiments, amalgamations," do we again confront a block juxtaposition as rigid, incisive, or abrupt as that in the *Symphonies*, or, as a seemingly inseparable coordinate, relations so unconditionally committed to a (0,3,6,9) symmetrically defined partitioning of the
octatonic collection, Model A.) Linked to the static implications of this
formal/pitch-relational interplay are contradictions or reversals in the
rhythmic-metric design. Thus, the opening block at No. 0 conforms to the
first of our two rhythmic-metric types: barred metric irregularity, with all
the reiterating fragments, lines, or parts synchronized unvaryingly in vertical (or "harmonic") coincidence, and hence all sharing the same
rhythmic-metric periods as defined by the shifting meter. But while this
2/8 + 3/8 + 2/8 + 3/8 + 2/8 + 3/8 metric irregularity exacts a rhythmic-
metric "sameness" in the repetition of the (D)–D–D–B bell-like motive (in
the first and second clarinets), it harbors, at the same time, the concealed
contradiction or reversal. For in accord with regular 2/4 metric periodicity
(as bracketed in Example 73a), the reiterating (D)–D–D–B fragment may
first be perceived as an on-the-beat reiteration, but is immediately contradicted or reversed at m. 4 as an off-the-beat reiteration. ((Near) repeats of

this block do allow for an occasional lengthening or shortening of the D–D–D–B motive and its immediate D–D–B repeat. At No. 37, for example, only the repeat is included. This juggling may prompt a renewed sense of rhythmic-metric identity with regard to (D)–D–D–B or, at Nos. 26, 37, and 39, with regard to ((B)–B–B–G♯), or a renewed sense of displacement in relation to prior repeats and regular 2/4 metric periodicity. At both Nos. 26 and 37 the accompanying fragments in the third clarinet and trombone enter off the beat rather than on the beat, so that the initial on-the-beat synchronization at Nos. 0 and 2 is reversed in a manner reflecting the second of our two rhythmic-metric types of construction.) Consequently, with these added off-the-beat/on-the-beat contradictions or reversals (or rhythmic-metric *polarities*, in essence), Stravinsky may be imagined as having afforded himself few options, other than to break off Collection I's (G,B♭) symmetrically defined deadlock at No. 0 (with its built-in off-the-beat/on-the-beat contradiction or reversal in (D)–D–D–B repetition), and to abruptly juxtapose it with something new and different (which at Nos. 1 and 4 takes the form of a massive, tutti (B♭ D F A♭/F B A♭ D) chordal reiteration, referentially aligned, however, with Collection I). And then few options, following this initial juxtaposition, other than to return to the opening block of No. 0, with its (G,B♭)-conceived deadlock and its off-the-beat/on-the-beat "play," through a series of (near) repeats, as at Nos. 2, 9, 26, 37, and 39.

But perhaps more to the point, these formal, pitch-relational, and rhythmic-metric conditions, fundamentally Stravinskian in conception, invest the final, culminating toniclike resolution on C with the curiously incidental, "distinctly parenthetical" quality alluded to earlier. (See Example 73b.) In other words, notwithstanding "impurities" in the concluding (C E G B D) simultaneity at No. 75 + 2 (where B and D of the chorale's (G B D) and (E G B) triads are left hanging, in order to reflect the specifics of the accommodation—of this tonally incriminating transaction and the octatonic (Collection I) and diatonic C-scale-on-C interaction it initiates), the C-scale-on-C "resolution" has little to do with pitch organization generally, with respect to both local, within-block activity and the more global or between-block perspective. The "resolution" surfaces, rather, as a *terminating convenience*, an expedient, a "device." (Baroque or Classical C-scale tonally functional schemes of modulation or definitions of key are as irrelevant here in the *Symphonies* as they are in the pieces or passages of pieces examined in chapters 10 and 11.)

Thus, even the two "adumbrative bits" of chorale introduced "in the body of the work" (see Stravinsky's remarks above), which, with their dominantlike (G B D F/D A♭ F D) articulation foreshadow the final "tonic resolution" on C, are in reality without dominant pretensions.[4] The first of these "bits," introduced at Nos. 42, 56, and 65, defines no internal, within-block progression at all, only oscillation, a back-and-forth motion between (G B D) and (G A♭ C) statically positioned over a reiterating (D A♭ F B) simultaneity in the bass. Indeed, the presiding (G B D F/D A♭ F D) simultaneity in this oscillation is, in interval content and spacing, very nearly identical to the tutti (B♭ D F A♭/F B A♭ D) chordal reiteration at Nos. 1 and 4: it is actually a within-Collection I transposition from B♭ back to G. And inasmuch as the second "bit" or consequent of the chorale, the answering D–C–E–F–C–D contour at No. 66, is likewise present in these earlier blocks at Nos. 1 and 4 (tacked on in the oboes as an appendage to the (B♭ D F A♭/F B A♭ F) chordal reiteration), the concluding chorale is in fact fully accounted for at Nos. 0–6. And so its concluding appearances at Nos. 42, 56, and 65 are likely to be heard and understood with reference to these prior contexts (and to the self-enclosed nature of these contexts as blocks), not as a sustained "dominant" awaiting an impending "resolution" to the "tonic" C. (Note the remarkable constancy in chordal disposition that marks off the successive blocks plotted in Example 73b. It is to the inert, self-enclosed, and largely symmetrically devised compound nature of this constancy that the concluding chorale relates and to which by adhering it refers—not to some truly informed dominant which, in tonal, C-scale fashion, anticipates a gradual and terminating progression to a tonic.) Hence, only in the final measures—and only *retroactively*, strictly speaking—does the chorale's (G B D F/D A♭ F D) articulation acquire the characteristic "feel" of a "dominant seventh" (or of a "dominant minor ninth" if the A♭ is included) "resolving" to its "tonic," the (C E G) triad.

(Consider, in other words, the spacing or chordal disposition of the concluding chorale—the first music to be composed—and how this spacing conditions the opening blocks at Nos. 0–6. The chorale, with its two phrases, antecedent and consequent, is fully present at Nos. 1 and 4, so that one discerns, apart from the effect of "continuity," how the opening material, diverse in outward appearance, might readily have sprung from the original conception. Further, this closely guarded conditioning of a piece (or of a section or movement) by some uniquely designed spacing of a "chord" or configuration—the manner in which, to rephrase, "musical worlds" are capsulized and summed up by such a spacing (however familiar some orthodox version—or the interval content thereof—might be to the vocabulary of "traditional harmony")—is a pronounced feature in Stravinsky's music, one to which reference has been made in these pages, most particularly in connection with registral fixity in fragmental repetition, but also, as in our analysis of *Orpheus* at Nos. 4–28, with respect to the verticalization or chordal "freezing" of certain key elements at registrally fixed points. While it undoubtedly serves as a unifying device (in terms of "continuity," "coherence," and the like), it is linked to the effect of "harmonic stasis," to the symmetrically imposed "polarities," "oppositions," deadlocks, and confrontations so intimately a part of pitch organization generally.)

SYMPHONY OF PSALMS (1930): FIRST MOVEMENT

The commissioning of the Symphony of Psalms began with the publisher's routine suggestion that I write something popular. I took the word, not in the publisher's meaning of "adapting to the understanding of the people," but in the sense of "something universally admired," and I even chose Psalm 150 in part for its popularity, though another and equally compelling reason was my eagerness to counter the many composers who had abused these magisterial verses as pegs for their own lyrico-sentimental "feelings." . . . I began with Psalm 150 [third and final movement] and my first notation was the figure

that bears such a close family resemblance to Jocasta's *"Oracula, oracula."* After finishing the fast-tempo sections of the Psalm, I went back to compose the first and second movements. The Allelujah and the slow music at the beginning of Psalm 150 [Nos. 0–3, third and final movement], which is an answer to the question in Psalm 40, were written last. . . .

The first movement, "Hear my prayer, O Lord," was composed in a state of religious and musical ebullience. The sequences of two minor thirds joined by a major third [the (0 1 3 4) tetrachords of Model A], the root idea of the whole work, were derived from the trumpet-harp motive at the beginning of the *allegro* in Psalm 150. I was not aware of Phrygian modes [E-scales], Gregorian chants, Byzantinisms, or anything of the sort, while composing this music, though, of course, influences said to be denoted by such scriptwriters' baggage-stickers may very well have been operative. . . .

The "Waiting for the Lord" Psalm [second movement] makes the most overt use of musical symbolism in any of my music before *The Flood* [1962]. An upside-down pyramid of fugues, it begins with a purely instrumental fugue of limited compass and employs only solo instruments. The restriction to treble range was the novelty of this initial fugue, but the limitation to flutes and oboes proved its most difficult compositional problem. The [C–E♭–B–D] subject was developed from the sequence of thirds used as an ostinato in the first movement. . . .

Though I chose Psalm 150 first, and though my first musical idea was the already-quoted rhythmic figure in that movement, I could not compose the beginning of it [Nos. 0–3] until I had written the second movement. Psalm 40 is a prayer that a new canticle may be put into our mouths. The Allelujah is that canticle. . . . The rest of the slow-tempo introduction [Nos. 0–3], the *Laudate Dominum*, was originally composed to the words of the *Gospodi Pomiluy*. This section is a prayer to the Russian image of the infant Christ with orb and scepter. I decided to end the work with this music, too, as an apotheosis of the sort that had become a pattern in my music since the epithalamium at the end of *Les Noces*. [*Dialogues and a Diary*, pp. 76–78.]

This brings us once again to the *Symphony of Psalms* (Example 74), already so persistently the focus of our attention in these pages that we can only summarize and elaborate a bit on the role of C-scale tonally functional relations in the first movement. (See, especially, our brief survey in chapter 8 of the rhythmic-metric design at No. 3 in the third and final movement, the allegro sections of Psalm 150 that begin with the rhythmic figure cited by Stravinsky above, evidently the first of his musical notations; our gen-

Example 74: *Symphony of Psalms*

Example 74 *continued*

eral outline in chapter 9 of pitch organization in the first movement and
its relationship to abrupt block juxtaposition; our analysis in chapter 10 of
the octatonic (Collection III) and diatonic A-scale-on-C interaction at
Nos. 0–3 in the third and final movement, the *Alleluia* and *Laudate
Dominum* sections of Psalm 150, which, as Stravinsky notes above, were the
last sections to be composed; and our mention in chapter 11 of the "half-
cadence" on G that concludes the first movement and leads, in dominant-
toniclike fashion, to the quasi-C-minor fugal exposition of the second.)

Very briefly, blocks accountable to Collection I—(0 4 7 10) "dominant-
seventh" complexes oscillating at G and B♭)—are juxtaposed with diatonic
blocks accountable to the E-scale on E, while E and the (E G B) "*Psalms*
chord" act as punctuating between-block or between-reference connecting links, as the principal intersecting element and complex of fusion between these interacting and interpenetrating collections of reference.

Example 74 *continued*

The octatonic contribution to this mixed Collection I and E-scale-on-E framework surfaces in the form of a cohesive (0 1 3 4) tetrachordal articulation at E, G, B♭, and C♯ (but mostly at E and B♭ [A♯]), Stravinsky's "sequences of two minor thirds joined by a major third," constituting, as he suggests, "the root idea of the whole work"),[3] but a (E G B), (G B D F), and (B♭ D F A♭) triadic partitioning with respect to E, G, and B♭ manifests itself with equal persistence. (The juxtaposition of the (E G B) "*Psalms* chord" with the (B♭ D F A♭)–(B D F G) "dominant-seventh" oscillation at the commencement of this movement is abrupt, while subsequent (near) repeats of the Collection I block at Nos. 4–6, 7, and 12 + 3 unfold with the (B♭ D (B) F A♭)–(B D F G) oscillation in prolongation (as an accompaniment in the bassoons), the initial sixteenth notes being superseded by eighth notes. This formula also applies to the diatonic E-scale-on-E block, with its rapid, sixteenth-note figuration at No. 2: at subsequent (near) repeats at Nos. 9 and 12, the first piano, joined by four flutes and four horns at No. 12, superimpose an eighth-note delineation of this figuration over its original sixteenth-note conception. Then, spaced between these blocks of distinct referential implications is the shared, intersecting (E G B) "*Psalms* chord," which is like a punctuation mark, a cracking of the whip that crisply silences the back-and-forth motion of Collection I's ostinati, and by so doing cements a self-enclosure which by its nature—the confinement here of relations to the octatonic Collection I—cannot emit that familiar sense of "development," progress, or resolution known to the "traditional harmony" of tonal C-scale music. Nor can it submit, on any but the most superficial level, to the formal handiwork of this "harmony." The result is, as we continue to reiterate in matters of formal, pitch-relational rhythmic-metric, and instrumental interplay, Stravinsky's twin options of abrupt block juxtaposition and block repetition.)

In Example 74 we acknowledge with regard to Collection I this octatonic (Collection I) and diatonic E-scale-on-E block interaction in the first movement. (Level 1) E as the shared, between-reference, intersecting pitch class of priority; (Level 2) (0,3,6) "background" partitioning in terms of (E,G,Bb); (Level 3) (0 1 3 4) tetrachordal articulation at E, G, Bb, and C♯ in terms of (E F G Ab), (G Ab Bb B), (Bb B C♯ D), and (C♯ D E F); (Level 4) (0 3 7/0 4 7/0 4 7 10) triadic articulation in terms of the punctuating (E G B) "*Psalms* chord" and the oscillating "dominant sevenths" (G B D F) and (Bb D F Ab) (these articulative groupings assembled more or less as presented); (Level 5) the (E F G Ab Bb B C♯ D (E)) octatonic reference collection, Collection I with brackets stipulating the principal elements of priority.

A methodological conflict of interest presents itself here in our attempts to accommodate Stravinsky's application of abrupt block juxtaposition with the underlying rationale of this application, pitch organization generally with its two distinct collections of reference, Collection I and the diatonic E-scale on E (together, of course, with all the shared, intersecting complications that subtly accrue.) Thus, the first movement encompasses three distinct blocks (with some crucial overlapping yet to be considered): the punctuating (E G B) "*Psalms* chord" with (near) repeats just prior to Nos. 1, 2, 9, and 10; the octatonic Collection I block with (near) repeats at Nos. 4–6, 7, and 12 + 3; and the diatonic E-scale-on-E block with (near) repeats at Nos. 2, 9, and 12. Our approach in graphic design has thus far been to expose such blocks by treating them individually and marking off points of intersection by means of brackets and the like. However, while the punctuating (E G B) "*Psalms* chord" is a block unto itself, its shared, between-block, between-reference, intersecting status with respect to Collection I and the E-scale on E is crucial. And so we forfeit a strict block-by-block disclosure in Example 74 in favor of a more global survey, bearing in mind, however, that a series of charts, formal, pitch-relational, rhythmic-metric, and/or instrumental in emphasis, might have complemented this effort. Thus our present endeavor is but a shortcut, with matters pertaining to form or architecture—the separate and abruptly juxtaposed blocks of distinct referential implications—largely reserved for comment in the text.

Nevertheless, through this Collection I (E,G,B♭) symmetry and the diatonic E-scale on E, G, as the "third" of the punctuating (E G B) "*Psalms* chord," as the third degree of the diatonic E-scale on E, and as a Collection I symmetrically defined partitioning element with (G B D F (A♭)) "dominant-seventh" and "dominant-minor-ninth" supplementation, steadily gains the advantage, unmistakably acquiring the "feel" of a dominant at the conclusion of the first movement by means of a "half cadence" on G which, in dominant-toniclike fashion, anticipates the quasi-C-minor fugal exposition of the second movement. This final, tonally incriminating transaction has been foreshadowed earlier in the piece. For in addition to block juxtaposition of Collection I and the diatonic E-scale on E, there are areas where these references interpenetrate by virtue of the coming together of pitches or complexes of pitches not held in common. Thus, for example, the passage at Nos. 2–4, with its non-octatonic, non-Collection I "diatonic C." Here, the diatonic E-scale-on-E block at No. 2 begins with its unimpaired E-scale-on-E reference: the figuration in the second horn and piano descends from E to B through an E–D–C–B succession over a sustained E in the bass. However, upon reaching the B prior to No. 3, the piano figuration reverts to the (B♭ D (B) F A♭)–(B D F G) "dominant-seventh" oscillation of the Collection I block, while the first horn and a solo cello ascend from B to E, reversing the initial E–D–C–B descent.[6] Hence, Collection I and the diatonic E-scale on E interpenetrate at No. 3: the C is not accountable to Collection I; it is in fact the only non-Collection I pitch element at No. 3, and is subsequently replaced by Collection I's C♯ in the fully accredited, fully committed Collection I block which follows at Nos. 4–6.

Further, before this final ascent from B to E, the B–C unit in this diatonic B–C–D–E succession is repeated; this repeat, which is superimposed over the (B♭ (B) D F A♭)–(B D F G) oscillation in the piano, gives it the suggestion of a C-scale-on-C leading-tone–tonic succession. More significantly, the phrasing of the B–C reiteration at No. 2 + 3 is identical to that of the E–F reiteration in the oboes and altos of the Collection I block at Nos. 4–6, which it thus anticipates, and with respect to which it serves as the diatonic counterpart (although, of course, the E–F unit, while referentially octatonic at Nos. 4–6, intersects with the E-scale on E; and these (B–C) (E–F) units constitute but a fraction of the many octatonic and/or diatonic 0–1 half-step reiterations which associate, on a more articulative level, with the various groupings assembled in Example 74. Note, too, that B–C, as the "diatonic counterpart" to Collection I's E–F reiteration, is also conspicuously a part of the diatonic E-scale-on-E figuration at Nos. 2, 9, and 12.) Consequently, while the final dominant-toniclike transaction (Collection I's dominantlike association with C) may yet be felt as a terminating convenience and thus as incidental to pitch organization generally (as in the *Symphonies of Wind Instruments*), the transaction may nonetheless also be felt as having been anticipated in *Psalms* by an earlier suggestive "feel" in this direction (certainly at No. 3, and, although not shown in Example 74, possibly also at No. 5, where the non-octatonic (non-Collection I) "diatonic C" reappears in an otherwise securely fastened octatonic context.)

Then, too, with respect to these tonally functional overtones, the (Bb D (B) F Ab)–(B D F G) "dominant-seventh" oscillation of the Collection I blocks could alternatively (however peripherally) be heard and understood as a dominant seventh (Bb D F Ab) irregularly resolved to another dominant seventh (B D F G), and hence in terms of the "distinctly parenthetical" suggestion of a conventional tonal, C-scale harmonic maneuver alluded to in the preceding chapter on octatonic "progressions." This is to say that notwithstanding the securely fastened octatonic Collection I framework of the oscillation (and the absence of progression, the two "dominant sevenths" merely oscillating back and forth as an ostinato, a self-enclosed configuration), *tonally conceived voice-leading remains intact*: the Bb "progresses" (ascends) to the B; D and F are sustained as "common tones"; and Ab, as the "dominant seventh," "progresses" (descends or "resolves") to the G. And then in conjunction with the "half cadence" on G and its dominant-toniclike association with the fugal exposition of the second movement, (Bb D F Ab)–(B D F G) becomes again (however peripherally) part of a long-range V-of-III-V$_5^6$–1 arrangement in terms of (Bb D F Ab)–(B D F G)–(C Eb G).

But perhaps more significantly, the extraordinary regimentation of the (E G B) "*Psalms* chord" exposes G to such an extent that the "chord," too, becomes implicated in the eventual priority assumed by G. Indeed, the spacing of the "chord," with its two (E G B) triads posted four octaves apart and G doubled in the middle, assumes something of a determinacy of its own. The oboe-bassoon doubling of the sixteenth-note (Bb D F Ab)–(B D F G) oscillation at Nos. 0–2 is spaced by two octaves; the first oboe's doubling of the E–F reiteration at No. 7 is a double-octave doubling, as is also the doubling of the diatonic E-scale-on-E figuration in the first piano at No. 9.

Finally, there are rhythmic-metric implications that merit consideration. The design at Nos. 0–2 conforms to the first of our two rhythmic-metric types: while the initiating 2/4 + 3/4 + 2/4 + 2/4 metric irregularity exacts a rhythmic-metric "sameness" in the repetition of the punctuating (E G B) "*Psalms* chord," it harbors a concealed contradiction or reversal.

In accord with regular 4/4 metric periodicity (as bracketed in Example 74), the "chord" may first be perceived as a downbeat punctuation, subsequently contradicted or reversed at No. 0 + 3 as an upbeat punctuation. (These displacements effect the juxtaposed (B♭ D F A♭)–(B D F G) oscillation as well.) Were we to pursue this "background" periodicity through the entirety of Nos. 0–4, we would find that the regular 4/4 meter introduced by the Collection I block at Nos. 4–6 enters "on target." The 4/4 meter, coinciding quite logically at Nos. 4–6 with the prolongation of Collection I's (B♭ D (B) F A♭)–(B D F G) oscillation, has been anticipated; it is built into the structure. (The reader should consult the score for verification at this point because of Example 74's condensation.)[7] Moreover, *Psalms* abounds with that most characteristic of all articulative means, staccato unison doublings of legato lines. This procedure grows out of efforts to ensure the rhythmic (or metric) invention, the neat, crisp articulation so essential to its grasp. Indeed, apart from his partiality for "the breathing of wind instruments" (noted earlier in chapter 8), these efforts seem largely responsible for the peculiarity of the symphony's orchestra (with its omission of violins, violas, and clarinets, its two pianos and quadrupling of flutes and oboes). Thus, with the opening oboe-bassoon sound firmly entrenched through Collection I's (B♭ D F A♭)–(B D F G) oscillation, clarinets may gradually have seemed irrelevant, while the additional oboes could assist in subsequent staccato unison doublings, allowing for a preservation of the initial blend (i.e., staccato unison doublings in the same instrument). See, especially, such doublings of Collection I's ostinati in the oboes and bassoons at Nos. 4–6, 7, and 12 + 3, or those in the (near) repeats of the diatonic E-scale-on-E block at Nos. 9 and 12.

SYMPHONY IN THREE MOVEMENTS (1945)

First Movement

Introduction	Nos. 0–5
Transition	Nos. 5–7
Section A	Nos. 7–38
Section B	Nos. 38–88
Section A¹	Nos. 88–97
Section B¹	Nos. 97–105
Coda (Introduction material)	Nos. 105–End

In 1944, while composing the Kyrie and Gloria [of the *Mass* (1948], I was often in company with Franz Werfel. As early as the spring of 1943, the distinguished poet and dramatist tried to encourage me to write music for his *Song of Bernadette* film. I was attracted by the idea and by his script, and if the conditions, business and artistic, had not been so entirely in favor of the film producer, I might have accepted. I actually did compose music for the "Apparition of the Virgin" scene, however, and this music became the second movement of my *Symphony in Three Movements*. (The first movement of the symphony was composed in 1942; I thought of the work then as a concerto for orchestra.) [*Expositions and Developments*, pp. 65–66.]

R.C.: You have at times referred to your Symphony in Three Movements as a "war symphony." In what way is the music marked by the impression of world events?

I.S.: I can say little more than that it was written under the sign of them. It both does and does not "express my feelings" about them but I prefer to say only that, without participation of what I think of as my will, they excited my musical imagination. . . .

The third movement actually contains the genesis of a war plot, though I recognized it as such only after completing the composition. The beginning of that movement is partly, and in some—to me wholly inexplicable—way, a musical reaction to the newsreels and documentaries that I had seen of goosestepping soldiers. The square march-beat, the brass-band instrumentation, the grotesque *crescendo*, in the tuba—these are all related to those repellent pictures. . . .

But let us return to the plot of the movement. In spite of contrasting episodes, such as the canon for bassoons, the march music is predominant until the fugue, which is the stasis and the turning point. The immobility at the beginning of the fugue is comic, I think—and so, to me, was the overturned arrogance of the Germans when their machine failed. The exposition of the fugue and the end of the Symphony are associated in my plot with the rise of the Allies, and perhaps the final, albeit rather too commercial, D-flat sixth chord—instead of the expected C— tokens my extra exuberance in the Allied triumph. The figure

$$\flat \gamma \quad \gamma \quad \flat \gamma \quad \flat \flat \gamma$$

was developed from the rumba in the timpani part in the introduction to the first movement. It was somehow associated in my imagination with the movements of war machines.

The first movement was likewise inspired by a war film, this time a documentary of scorched-earth tactics in China. . . .

The formal substance of the Symphony—perhaps Three Symphonic Movements would be a more exact title—exploits the idea of counterplay among several types of contrasting elements. One such contrast, the most obvious, is that of harp and piano, the principal instrumental protagonists. Each has a large *obbligato* role and a whole movement to itself and only at the turning-point fugue, the *queue de poisson* of the Nazi machine, are the two heard together and alone.

But enough of this. In spite of what I have said, the Symphony is not programmatic. Composers combine notes. That is all. How and in what form the things of this world are impressed upon their music is not for them to say. [*Dialogues and a Diary*, pp. 83–85.]

Jazz Commercials

R.C.: What were the origins of your pieces for so-called jazz and other popular band ensembles—the *Circus Polka, Scherzo à la russe, Ebony Concerto, Ragtime* for eleven instruments—and how do you regard this music today?

I.S: With the exception of the *Ragtime*, these were all journeyman jobs, commissions I was forced to accept because the war in Europe had so drastically reduced the income from my compositions. The idea of the *Circus Polka* was George Balanchine's. He wanted a short piece for a ballet of elephants, one of whom was to carry Vera Zorina, who was at that time Balanchine's wife. . . . The music was first performed in someone else's arrangement for the Ringling Brothers' Circus Band. . . .

The *Scherzo à la russe* was commissioned by Paul Whiteman for a special radio broadcast. I wrote it originally to exact specifications of his ensemble, then rewrote it for standard orchestra.

The *Ebony Concerto* was also written for a prescribed instrumentation, to which I added a French horn. Mr. Woody Herman wanted the piece for a concert that already was scheduled, and I had to compose it in a hurry. [*Dialogues and a Diary*, pp. 85–86.]

"The war in Europe," as Stravinsky remarks above, "drastically reduced" his income. Having settled in Hollywood in August 1940 (following the delivery of his Charles Eliot Norton lectures at Harvard the previous winter), he was forced to take on "journeyman jobs," composing a series of "jazz commercials" like the *Circus Polka* (1942), the *Scherzo à la russe* (1944), and the *Ebony Concerto* (1945). These commissions, which, as he says, he would not have accepted under ordinary, peacetime conditions, did in fact boost his wartime yield, which also included the third and fourth movements of the *Symphony in C* (1940), *Danses concertantes* (1942), the *Four Norwegian Moods* (1942), the *Ode* (1943), *Babel* (1944), *Scènes de ballet* (1944), the *Sonata for Two Pianos* (1944), the Kyrie and Gloria sections of the *Mass* (1944), the *Elegy* for solo viola or violin (1944), and the *Symphony in Three Movements* (1945). Wartime conditions were responsible for the fractured, checkered conception of much of this music.[8] The first and second movements of the *Symphony in C* were composed in France, the third and fourth in the United States. The second movement of the *Ode*, "Eclogue," was conceived as incidental music for a hunting scene in Orson Welles's production of *Jane Eyre*, a project which never materialized. The Kyrie and Gloria of the *Mass* were composed in 1944; the Credo, Sanctus, and Agnus Dei remained incomplete until March 1948. The first movement of the *Symphony in Three Movements* was composed in 1942, at which time it was envisioned as part of a "concerto for orchestra" (see the quotation above), while the second movement was designed to accompany the "Apparition of the Virgin" in Franz Werfel's *Song of Bernadette*, yet another abortive film project.

But however fractured, or however enveloped in the imagery of "scorched-earth tactics," "war plots," or war "machines" the initial conception of this present "war symphony" may have been, its substance remains true to the accommodation of neoclassicism, to the C-scale conventions, inflections, gestures, and tonally incriminating behavior to which our discussion of this accommodation has been drawn, and to the uniquely Stravinskian interaction of this conventionality with a (0,3,6,9) symmetrically defined partitioning of the octatonic collection, Model A (in addition, of course, to those more general presuppositions of this pitch-relational network: superimposition, oscillation, abrupt block juxtaposition, and repetition). Stravinsky himself suggests as much, of course: The third movement contains "the genesis of a war plot," but was recognized as such "only after completing the composition." And he quickly recoils from these extramusical associations: "But enough of this. In spite of what I have said, the Symphony is not programmatic. Composers combine notes. That is all."

Indeed, global conditions in the first movement are markedly similar to those surveyed in the *Symphonies of Wind Instruments* and in the first movement of *Psalms*, notwithstanding the distance of some twenty-five years from the former and fifteen from the latter. (See Example 75a.) Thus, if we momentarily sidestep diatonic penetration in the form of "white-note" scale passages in the trombones and tuba at No. 1 and in the violins and violas at No. 4, the symphony opens with an explicit reference to Collection I at Nos. 0–5, unmistakable in the successive repeats of the principal theme's G–Ab/G–F–Db–Ab contour at Nos. 0–4, and in the Ab/F/Ab–G/Bb/G–F/Ab/F–G/E/G–Ab/F/Ab–Ab/F/Ab–E/Db/E figuration that follows these repeats in the woodwinds and trumpets at Nos. 1 and 4. But in place of E and the punctuating (E G B) triad in *Psalms*, it is Collection I's G which, as a (G,Bb,Db,E) symmetrically defined partitioning element with (G B D F (Ab))"dominant-seventh" and "dominant-minor-ninth" supplementation, immediately asserts itself as the principal element of priority. And in place of the (E,G,Bb) symmetry of *Psalms*, it is Collection I's Db which, as a symmetrically defined partitioning element with (Db F Ab) triadic "support," assumes a degree of "equal weight and independence" in relation to G, and defines a "background" (0,6) tritone partitioning of the collection in terms of (G,Db). (See, very generally, the opening (G) (Db F Ab) tritone "opposition" of the G–Ab/G–F–Db–Ab theme, an "opposition" underscored registrally by the upsweeping 0–13 or "minor-ninth" G–Ab stretch, a spacing which already gives this (G,Db) tritone "opposition" a superimposed quality. See also the superimposition of the (Db F Ab) triad over the G–B–D ostinato in the strings at Nos. 22–24; or, in the final movement (Example 75b), the rumba block at Nos. 152–54 with (near) repeats at Nos. 161 and 169, where the rumba theme's (Db F Ab) triadic

Example 75a. Used by permission of European American Music
Distributors Corporation.

outline is superimposed over a (G B D/G B♭ D) ostinato in the strings.)
Still, a climactic E/G/E incomplete (E G B) triad surfaces at Nos. 29–32 as a
concluding simultaneity to the figuration at Nos. 26–29, where a (D♭ F
A♭)–(E♭ G B♭)–(E G♯ B)–(G B D) triadic succession in the woodwinds and
horns—of which only the (E♭ G B♭) triad lies outside Collection I as a passing entity—is superimposed over (0 4 7 10) "dominant sevenths" at G and
B♭ in the strings. And so the (G,B♭,D♭,E) partitioning of Collection I at
Nos. 26–32 is highly reminiscent of the "sound" of *Psalms*. And as in both
the *Symphonies* and *Psalms*, this Collection I material eventually submits to

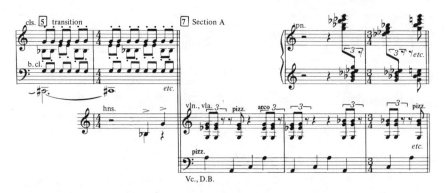

Example 75a *continued*

a toniclike resolution on C, a "C-ending" in the final measures of the Coda at Nos. 105–12.

But the *Symphony in Three Movements* is in mood and general layout far more expansive than these earlier works, its separate and juxtaposed blocks lengthier and more varied in referential implications. In the first movement of *Psalms*, only Collection I, of the three octatonic collections, was present. And while this collection predominates in the first movement of this work, all three collections are nonetheless present on an unimpaired, explicit basis. (The same is true of the third movement. While Col-

Example 75a *continued*

lection I predominates in the rumba block at Nos. 152–54 and at subsequent (near) repeats at Nos. 161 and 169, the block at Nos. 156–59 refers to Collection II.) Indeed, the blocks which comprise the Introduction, Transition, and Section A at Nos. 0–38 are best heard and understood as a succession of transpositions or shifts from one octatonic collection to another, shifts which are in turn marked by sudden and pronounced changes in instrumental, melodic, registral, dynamic, and rhythmic-metric design. And so we might simply complement the block-by-block disclosure of this scheme in Example 75a with some additional remarks.

Example 75a *continued*

The blocks of the Introduction at Nos. 0–5 consist of an interaction between Collection I and the diatonic C-scale on C: a (G,D♭) tritone partitioning of Collection I is superimposed over diatonic "white-note" passages in the trombones and tuba at No. 1, and in the strings at No. 4. Then,
at Nos. 5–7, the (G,B♭,D♭,E) symmetrically defined partitioning elements
of Collection I are isolated in a brief passage of transition. (G,B♭,D♭ [C♯],
and E are the only pitches at Nos. 5–7, except for an upsweeping scale
passage in the flutes just prior to No. 6.) The logic behind this transition

Example 75a *continued*

may readily be discerned in relation to the block which follows at Nos.
7–13, the first block of Section A. This block refers to Collection III on an
unimpaired, explicit basis. And the "diminished-seventh" chord shared
between Collections I and III is (G B♭ D♭ E)—although, of course, G, B♭,
D♭, and E do not constitute for Collection III the (0,3,6,9) symmetrically
defined partitioning elements they do for Collection I. Hence the transition is a buffer, a neutral bridge placed neatly between the Collection I
blocks of the Introduction at Nos. 0–5 and the initial Collection III block
of the A section at Nos. 7–13. With (G B♭ D♭ E) as the pivoting connecting
link, Collection I thus moves very smoothly into Collection III. This

Example 75a *continued*

results in a shift "upward" by the interval of 2, a whole step, from a G priority to a (possible) A priority, or, more determinately, a shift "upward" from the (G,D♭) tritone partitioning of Collection I at Nos. 0–5 to a (A,E♭) or (A,C,E♭) tritone partitioning of Collection III at Nos. 7–13, with (E♭ G B♭) in the upper strings statically positioned over an A in the bass, and with oscillating (E♭ G B♭ D♭) (C E G B♭) "dominant sevenths" introduced by the piano at No. 7 + 1. Or, from yet another angle, a shift "upward" from the G–B♭–G punctuation in the horns and trumpets at Nos. 5–7 to the A–C–A basso ostinato in the lower strings at Nos. 7–13. Through this succession of transpositions, through the Introduction at Nos. 0–5, the

Example 75a *continued*

transition at Nos. 5–7, and the initial block of Section A at Nos. 7–13, it is G, B♭, D♭ [C♯], and E which persevere as the pitches of intersection shared between Collections I and III, and which assume, at Nos. 7–13, a new identity because of their new referential affiliation with Collection III. (The smoothness of the transaction is underscored by registral fixity: the clarinet's reiterating Gs in the transition at Nos. 5–7, along with the horn's G–B♭–G punctuation, are registrally retained by the (E♭ G B♭) string reiteration at Nos. 7–13. On the other hand, this preserved registral identity of those pitches held in common tends, at the same time, to heighten the effect of the collectional shift. By this is meant that it is precisely by retain-

ing the registral identity of those elements or complexes of elements held
in common that elements not held in common are more readily exposed
to the ear.)

In the block which follows at Nos. 13–16 (Section A), another transposition may be detected, but this time from Collection III to Collection II.
Here the shift is "upward" from a (possible) A priority to a (possible) B
priority, or, more determinately, from the (A,E♭) or (A,C,E♭) tritone partitioning of Collection III at Nos. 7–13 to a (B,F) or (B,D,A♭) tritone partitioning of Collection II at Nos. 13–16. The transposition materializes by
the same means as at Nos. 0–13: the "diminished-seventh" chord shared
between Collections III and II, (A C E♭ G♭), perseveres at Nos. 13–16 (although, as before, the elements of this chord do not constitute for Collection II the (0,3,6,9) symmetrically defined partitioning elements they do
for Collection III). Note the preserved A–C–A punctuation in the strings
at Nos. 13–16, a preservation once again underscored by registral fixity,
and the persistence, too, of the (0,6) tritone "opposition" or "polarity"
throughout these successive block transpositions from the Introduction
to Nos. 13–16: the initial (G) (D♭ F A♭) tritone "opposition" of the principal theme at Nos. 0–5; Collection III's "opposition" between the basso
ostinato's A and the (E♭ G B♭) string reiteration at Nos. 7–13; and Collection II's (B) (F A C) "opposition" between the lower strings and the
woodwind-horn figuration at Nos. 13–16.

Finally, Nos. 16–19 signal a return to the initial octatonic (Collection I)
and diatonic C-scale-on-C interaction of the introductory blocks at Nos.
0–5: a (G,B♭) partitioning of Collection I is superimposed over ascending
"white-note" scale passages in the strings and timpani. With a gradual expansion in Collection I's contribution—the (C♯ E♯ G♯)–(E G♯ B) triadic reiteration at Nos. 19–21 and the (D♭ F A♭)–(E G♯ B)–(G B D) triadic succession at Nos. 26–29—this interaction persists to the close of this A section at
No. 38.[9]

Nevertheless, by means of the mixed octatonic (Collection I) and
diatonic C-scale-on-C passages in the Introduction at Nos. 0–5 and in the
A section at 16–38, G, as a Collection I (G,B♭,D♭,E) symmetrically defined
partitioning element with (G B D F (A♭)) "dominant-seventh" and
"dominant-minor-ninth" supplementation, subtly acquires the "feel" of a
dominant in the Coda at Nos. 105–12, and does so here, as in the Symphonies and the first movement of Psalms, retroactively by virtue of a toniclike concluding simultaneity on C. As a concession to this tonally incriminating turn of events, the Coda's lengthy prolongation of the woodwind
figuration at Nos. 109–12, following the repeat of the principal theme's
G–A♭/G–F–D♭–A♭ contour at No. 108, is revised: the terminating E/D♭/E
simultaneity in the initial statement of this A♭/F/A♭ – G/B♭/G – F/A♭/F –
G/E/G – A♭/F/A♭ – A♭/F/A♭ – E/D♭/E figuration at Nos. 0–5 is superseded

by an E/C/E simultaneity at No. 110 + 1, with the non-octatonic, non-Collection I "diatonic C" thus replacing Collection I's D♭. This replacement neatly tilts octatonic-diatonic interaction toward the C-scale on C, intensifying G's "feel" as a dominant, along with the "feel" of A♭ as a "dominant minor ninth" in support of G (rather than as the "fifth" of Collection I's (0,6) tritone-related (D♭ F A♭) triad). Indeed, on the diatonic C-scale-on-C side of the coin, the principal theme's (D♭ F A♭) outline could be construed as the "Neapolitan-sixth chord," with its F and A♭ sustained over the barline at No. 109—as earlier at No. 1—as the "seventh" and "minor ninth" of the shared, intersecting (G B F A♭) incomplete "dominant minor ninth" which follows. Moreover, as in *Psalms*, the final "resolution" on C is anticipated at an earlier stage: by the ascending "white-note" passages in the trombones and tuba at No. 1, and in the strings at No. 4, and by the ascending and descending "white-note" scale passages in the lower strings at Nos. 16–22 (punctuated at Nos. 16–19 by a (C E G) triadic outline in the timpani)—these articulations jointly implicating diatonic interaction or interpenetration in terms of the C-scale on C.

Still, the concluding "C-ending" is not without its "impurity." Reflecting the specifics of the accommodation, B is left "hanging" from the preceding Collection I blocks, and positioned so as to reflect the earlier assertions of priority on the part of both Collection I's G and E. The spacing of the final (C E G B) "chord," particularly with respect to the embedded G/B/G incomplete (G B D) triad, is indicative of what Stravinsky might justly have termed the "root idea" of the first movement. For if a "root idea" could be envisioned in *Psalms* as "sequences of two minor thirds joined by a major third" (Model A's (0 1 3 4) tetrachords), or in the *Symphonies* as a complete (0 4 7) "major" triad in "closed position" superimposed over its "dominant seventh" and/or "dominant minor ninth," then much of the articulation here seems conditioned by sequences of octaves to which, internally on one side or the other, a "minor" or a "major third" is attached—in other words, a not unfamiliar version of the incomplete triad so prevalent in Stravinsky's music: an incomplete "minor" or "major" triad with its root doubled and its fifth missing. (See, especially, the woodwind figuration at Nos. 0–5; the G–B♭–G punctuation in the horns and trumpet at Nos. 5–7, which is succeeded by the A–C–A basso ostinato at Nos. 7–13; the F/A♭/F and F/A/F figuration in the woodwinds and brass at Nos. 13–16; the E/G/E concluding simultaneity at No. 29; the D/B/D or D–B–D articulation in the horns and piano at the beginning of the B or middle section of this movement at No. 38 (not shown in Example 75a); or, finally, the concluding simultaneity itself, where G/B/G is superimposed over the (C E G) "tonic" triad).[10] Accordingly, if the concluding simultaneity of the *Symphonies*, a superimposition of the shared, intersecting (G B D) "dominant" triad over the (C E B) "tonic" triad, reflects not only Collection I's continuing presence but, in registral spacing, the articulative circumstances of that presence as well, then this present simultaneity, with G/B/G positioned over the (C E G) "tonic" triad, equally reflects Collection I's presence, but in a manner befitting *its* articulative circumstances. (Both concluding simultaneities may be heard and understood as a superimposition of (G B (D)) over (C E G), but distinctions in interval content or spacing reflect differing patterns of articulation.) As before, however, Stravinsky fails to inform as to the referential implications of these sequences of octaves in the first movement and their confinement, particularly when flanked internally by the "minor third," to the octatonic collection.

In regard to the third movement, a casual remark by Stravinsky that the material here might just as suitably have concluded with a "C-ending" as with the (D♭ F A♭ B♭) complex ultimately selected—indeed, that such a "C-ending" was the more "expected" of the two—is entirely apropos. For such an alternative between D♭ and C could have suggested itself only by virtue of (0,6) tritone partitioning of Collection I in terms of (G,D♭), and only by virtue of the dominant-toniclike association of Collection I with the C-scale (or A-scale) on C, an association that by 1945 was habitual in neoclassical contexts. Moreover, critical remarks to the effect that the symphony constitutes a return to the earlier "vitality" of some of the "Russian" works are best understood not merely in terms of orchestral resources or an "absence of melody" (in comparison, say, with the *Symphony in C*), but in terms of pitch organization generally.[11] For the *Symphony in Three Movements* figures among Stravinsky's most octatonically inspired creations, matched or excelled in the explicitness and persistence of that reference only by the *Scherzo fantastique, Le Sacre, Les Noces*, the *Symphony of Psalms*, and—although a much shorter work—*Babel*. Specifics, too, relate rather conspicuously to earlier works. The oscillating (0,3)-related (E♭ G B♭ D♭) (C E G B♭) "dominant sevenths" in the piano at Nos. 7–13 recall, in regimentation and overall treatment, Collection II's articulation in Pianos I and III at Nos. 68–70 in *Les Noces*. (See Example 38 in chapter 6.) But the *Symphony in Three Movements* also teems with C-scale inflections and tonal implications of a type not to be found in *Le Sacre* or *Les Noces*, inflections and implications more extensive and varied (and more incriminating) than those of *Psalms* (where construction is on the whole more concise and tightly knit). Indeed, this present symphony *sprawls* in comparison with *Psalms*, in the abundance and diversity of material and in the referential implications thereof. And perhaps for these reasons—the persistence of octatonic or octatonic-diatonic invention and the profusion of neoclassical C-scale conventions and inflections—it provides observers with an excellent summary of some of the most persistent of peculiarities of both neoclassicism and Stravinsky's music "considered as a whole."

In the third movement there occurs what in this observer's estimate rates as one of the most exhilarating octatonic passages in the literature: the return of the rumba block at Nos. 161–63. (See Example 75b.) Here, with startling effect, Collection I's (G B D) and (E G♯ B) triads in the piano, trumpet, and violas are superimposed over the rumba theme's (D♭ F A♭) triadic outline, which, earlier at Nos. 152–54, had been accompanied by a much milder (G B D/G B♭ D) ostinato in the strings. The (0,3,6) octatonically conceived "clash" in terms of (D♭,E,G), Collection I, is truly stunning here, another triumph of the octatonic imagination. And it is therefore with this and similar passages that observers can best initiate a study of Stravinsky's octatonic routine(s): with passages that exhibit an extensive and conspicuous (0,3,6,9) symmetrically defined partitioning of the collection, Models A or B. Following this, the subtleties of octatonic-diatonic interaction, along with the C-scale conventions, inflections, and tonally in-

Example 75b: Third movement (rumba block). Used by permission of European American Music Distributors Corporation.

Example 75b *continued*

criminating behavior that this interaction imposes neoclassically, should gradually become apparent.

OEDIPUS REX (1927): ACT I, NOS. 27–45

Finally, a last glance at *Oedipus Rex* seems in order. (See Example 76.) At Nos. 27–45 in Act I the general global situation is essentially the reverse of that encountered in *Symphonies of Wind Instruments*, or in the first movement of *Psalms* and the *Symphony in Three Movements*. In these pieces or passages of pieces, a partitioning of the octatonic collection, Collection I, imposed itself at the outset on an unimpaired, explicit basis. And so G, as a Collection I (G,Bb,Db,E) symmetrically defined partitioning element with (G B D F (Ab)) "dominant-seventh" or "dominant-minor-ninth" supplementation, was referentially octatonic to begin with—as were Bb, Db, and

Example 76: *Oedipus Rex*

E with their varying degrees of triadic and "dominant-seventh" supplementation. Hence only suddenly—and only toward the close of these
passages—did G assume the characteristic "feel" of a dominant by means
of a variety of toniclike "C-endings" concluded on its behalf ("C-endings"
riddled, to be sure, with varieties of "impurity"). So, too, the dominant-
toniclike association between Collection I and the C-scale (or A-scale) on C
surfaced as a terminating convenience. For even when anticipated at an
earlier stage by C-scale intervention, the characteristic "feel" of a dominant on the part of G seemed retroactive, because more or less incidental
to pitch organization generally.

But in *Oedipus* at Nos. 27–45 it is the diatonic C-scale on C which, with its

Example 76 *continued*

(C E G) "tonic" triad, imposes itself at the outset on an unimpaired, explicit basis.[12] And with the consequence that the climactic octatonic (Collection I) and diatonic C-scale-on-C interpenetration reached at No. 42—with (B♭ D F A♭) and (G B D F) "dominant sevenths" superimposed over a

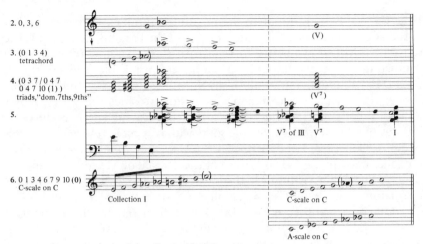

Example 76 continued

(E G B) triadic outline in the bass, a cohesive (E,G,B♭) symmetrically
defined partitioning of Collection I similar to that in the first movement of
Psalms and at Nos. 26–32 in the first movement of the *Symphony in Three
Movements*—constitutes an "intrusion" into an already established, fully
accredited or fully accounted-for C-scale-on-C reference.

Hence the reversal. Collection I's (E,G,B♭) contribution at No. 42 *intrudes* on a securely fastened diatonic C-scale-on-C setting.[13] Hence, too, G
and its (G B D F) articulation at No. 42 + 1 may, with respect to Collection
I's dominant-toniclike association with C and the C-scale on C, more
readily be perceived as a "dominant" in relation to its "tonic," the (C E G)
triad. Moreover, Collection I's (F B♭ A♭ F)–(F B G F) succession at No. 42
(the triplet figuration in the woodwinds, horns, and piano), while statically
superimposed over E and its (E G B) triadic outline in the bass, is an actual
progression rather than a mere oscillation as in *Psalms*. Predictably too,
tonally conceived voice-leading remains intact. As noted with regard to
this same (B♭,G) symmetrically defined "dominant-seventh" succession in
Psalms, the B♭ "progresses" (ascends) to the B, F is sustained as the "common tone," while the A♭ or "dominant seventh" "progresses" (descends or
"resolves") to the G. Consequently, the tonally conceived "feel" of a dominant seventh irregularly resolved—the (F B♭ A♭ F) dominant seventh progressing deceptively to the (F B G F) dominant seventh in a V⁷-of-III–V⁷
type framework in relation to the C-scale on C—may be considered, especially in view of the initial C-scale-on-C framework, as exerting a credible
presence.

Nonetheless, directly following this tonally conceivable (F B♭ A♭ G)–(F
B G F) progression (sandwiched between the progression and its eventual
C-scale-on-C (or A-scale-on-C) destination at Nos. 44 and 45) is Collection

I's (E G♯ [A♭] B D F) "dominant-minor-ninth" complex, which somewhat paradoxically here seals Collection I's side of the bargain; it augments the sense of a locked symmetry in regard to (E,G,B♭), and renders these conflicting referential implications all but unmistakable. Indeed, the (E G♯ B D F) "dominant minor ninth" at No. 42 + 3, with its shrill E/F "clash" between the trumpets, trombones, and horns coinciding with Creon's final sound of alarm (*peste infikit Thebas*), is a musical high point in the Oedipus drama. For it is here that ambiguity with respect to reference reaches a climax. Collection I and the C-scale on C are here intertwined, with the outcome perceptible only by virtue of the C-scale on C's initial predominance. (The (C F A♭) outline in the bass, alternating with (E G B), ensures the diatonic C-scale-on-C's (or A-scale-on-C's) continuing presence at No. 42.) Of course, the E at No. 42 + 3 is anticipated by the prolonged A♭–G–F–E–D–C whole-note descent in the trumpets and trombones. But in place of a "diatonic E," which might well have been expected in view of the preceding (F B♭ A♭ F)–(F B G F) progression and its tonal implications in relation to the C-scale on C, the E at No. 42 + 3 is octatonic, aligned with (E G♯ B D F); so that Collection I's cycle from B♭ to G is here extended another notch to include E and its (E G♯ B D F) articulation within its cohesive (B♭,G,E) grip. A stirring and climactic passage, needless to say, but also a very telling one insofar as the peculiarity of Stravinsky's "dominant" is concerned. (G B D) refers to the C-scale on C, but also to Collection I and the (E,G,B♭,(D♭)) symmetrically defined succession of triads this second referential identity imposes.

But as should by now be equally apparent, there are marked similarities with all previously examined pieces or passages of pieces. Not only do Nos. 27–45 exemplify the dominant-toniclike association between Collection I and the C-scale (or A-scale) on C (traced in these pages to global conditions in the *Symphonies*), but specifics correspond conspicuously to earlier works (or to the later *Psalms* and *Symphony in Three Movements*). The superimposition of Collection I's (B♭ D F A♭) (G B D F) "dominant-seventh" complexes over the (E G B) triadic outline in the tuba and lower strings is very nearly identical in articulation to Collection I's (E,G,B♭) contribution in the first movement of *Psalms* (perhaps not surprisingly, since *Oedipus* predates *Psalms* by less than three years). The B–C reiteration in the vocal line and strings, with its non-Collection I "diatonic C" constituting the only non-octatonic pitch element at No. 42, is reminiscent of the B–C reiteration in the first horn and solo cello at No. 3 in *Psalms*, where C is likewise the only non-octatonic pitch element. Then, too, the Collection I material at No. 42 submits in dominant-toniclike fashion to the (C E G) triadic "resolution" at No. 44 (Creon's cadence: *Apollo dixit deus*); or "resolves" to the A-scale-on-C (or pseudo-C-minor reference) at No. 45, where Oedipus reacts to the alarm in a calm, confident, somewhat lordly manner: *Non, non; non reperias vetus skelus*. The pseudo-C-minor reference at No. 45 may be compared with the quasi-C-minor fugal exposition in the second movement of *Psalms*, which likewise comes in response to a (E,G,B♭) symmetrically defined partitioning of Collection I, and with respect to which G likewise acquires the characteristic "feel" of a dominant in preparation for its (by now) habitual "C-ending."

THIRTEEN
THE SERIAL PERIOD (I)

CHANGE OF LIFE

I have had to survive two crises as a composer, though as I continued to move from work to work I was not aware of either of them as such, or, indeed, of any momentous change. The first—the loss of Russia and its language of words as well as of music—affected every circumstance of my personal no less than my artistic life, which made recovery more difficult. Only after a decade of samplings, experiments, amalgamations did I find the path to *Oedipus Rex* [1927] and the *Symphony of Psalms* [1930]. Crisis number two was brought on by the natural outgrowing of the special incubator in which I wrote *The Rake's Progress* [1948–51] (which is why I did not use Auden's beautiful *Delia* libretto; I could not continue in the same strain, could not compose a sequel to *The Rake*, as I would have had to do). The period of adjustment [i.e., with serial techniques] was only half as long this time, but as I look back on it I am surprised at how long I continued to straddle my "styles." Was it because one has to unlearn as well as to learn, and at seventy the unlearning is more difficult? However that may be, the slow climb through the 1950's eventually brought me to the *Movements* [1959], which I now see as the cornerstone of my later work. And the future? I know only that in the *coronat opus* of my later years, the Princeton Requiem [*Requiem Canticles*, 1966] (I say that now because I am working on it), I continue to believe in my taste buds and to follow the logic of my ear, quaint expressions which will seem even quainter when I add that I require as much hearing at the piano as ever before; and this, I am certain, is not because of age, is not a sign of dotage. I know, too, that I will never cross the gulf from well-tempered pitches to "sounds" and "noises," and will never abdicate the rule of my ears. But predictions are dangerous. *Basta!* [*Themes and Episodes*, pp. 23–24.]

I had heard Schoenberg's name as early as 1907, but *Pierrot lunaire* was my first contact with his music. I had not seen any score by him either, and to my recollection nothing by him was played in St. Petersburg while I lived there. I do not know how the Berlin meeting with him came about, but the initiative for it must have been Diaghilev's; Diaghilev wanted to commission Schoenberg. I remember sitting with Schoenberg, his wife Mathilde, and Diaghilev at a performance of *Petroushka*, and I have a clear memory of Schoenberg in his green room after he had conducted the fourth performance of *Pierrot lunaire* in the Choralion-saal, 4 Bellevuestrasse, Sunday, December 8, 1912, at twelve o'clock noon; I still have my canceled ticket. . . .

The real wealth of *Pierrot*—sound and substance, for *Pierrot* is the solar plexus as well as the mind of early twentieth-century music—was beyond me as it was beyond all of us at that time, and when Boulez wrote that I had understood it *d'un façon impressioniste*, he was not kind but correct. I *was* aware, nevertheless, that this was the most prescient confrontation in my life, though "the future" is never an idea in one's mind, is never part of one's speculations at such moments. Time does not pass but only *we* pass and I do not know *more* now than I did then, for the quality of my knowledge is different, but I did know and recognize the power of the man and his music at that meeting half a century ago.

Shortly after the performance of *Pierrot*, Schoenberg left for St. Petersburg to conduct his *Pelleas und Melisande*. We were on good terms at parting, but we never met again. In Morges, in 1919, I received a very cordial letter from him asking for pieces of my chamber music to include in his Vienna concerts "The Society for Private Performances." I wrote and he wrote again. Then, in 1920 or 1921, I heard *Pierrot* in Paris, conducted by Darius Milhaud, and performed by Marya Freund. After that, incredibly, I did not hear another note by Schoenberg until the *Prelude to Genesis*, in Hollywood in November 1945, at which time we might well have met, for we were in the recording studios on the same day and we sat on opposite sides of the Wilshire Ebell Theater at the premiere of the *Genesis Suite*. . . .When I came to Los Angeles in 1935, Klemperer and other mutual friends tried to bring us together, but only after 1948 did a meeting seem possible. I saw Schoenberg for the last time in 1949 when he appeared onstage at a concert and read a delicately ironic speech acknowledging the honor of the freedom of the city of Vienna just conferred on him, a half-century too late, by the Austrian consul. [*Dialogues and a Diary*, pp. 53–55.]

When I first moved there [1948] Los Angeles was divided, like the rest of the musical world, into twin hegemonies of Stravinsky and Schoenberg. The dividing was Los Angeles' and the world's doing, of course, not the two masters': divisions meant little to them in their search for that humility which, to adapt St. Bernard's 'perfectio humilitatis, cognitio veritatis,' is the perfect knowledge of one's art. Perhaps they even meant the same thing when Stravinsky said, characteristically: 'Music is powerless to express anything at all'; and Schoenberg: 'Music seeks to express all that dwells in the subconscious like a dream.' The fact remains: they were kept separate and isolated. Paris and Vienna had crossed the world with them, re-establishing small and exceedingly provincial Viennas and Parises separated by only ten miles of Hollywood no-man's land, but as far apart as ever. Musicians came from all over the world to visit them, not mentioning to one composer their meetings with the other one. . . .

Though he had already been exposed to a considerable amount of serial music Stravinsky was not at that time really familiar with a single example of it—a fact which will shock the 'hypocrite lecteur' who, most likely, had not even heard of Webern before about 1947. Stravinsky's first deep impression of such music came from the *Quartet* opus 22 by Webern which he heard several times in January and February, 1952. Shortly afterwards he used a kind of series (it is really only a melodic phrase turned four ways and used in canons) in the *Sacred History* [Ricercar II] of the *Cantata*.

Throughout the rest of 1952 he took advantage of a number of opportunities to study the music of Schoenberg. He was probably influenced in the choice of a Gigue for his *Septet* by the Gigue in Schoenberg's Suite op. 29 (and perhaps led by it also to those turned-around fugues). But in all his study of Schoenberg he did not seem to be attracted by any of the music except *Pierrot* and the *Serenade*; elsewhere he found much to admire: everything, in fact, but the music itself. Referring to the *Violin Concerto* he would say: 'The pathos is last century's and since pathos is created by language, the language in essence must be last century's too; harmonize the second movement in a purely Brahmsian manner—you have only to move a few notes over a bit—and the theme is happily restored to its true habitat; Schoenberg is the evolutionary centre but only up to a period many years before this *Concerto*.'

In the years between 1952 and 1955 no composer can have lived in closer contact with the music of Webern. Stravinsky was familiar with the sound of the Webern *Cantatas* and of the instrumental songs at a time when some of these works had not yet been performed in Europe. The challenge of Webern has been the strongest in his entire life. It has gradually brought him to the belief that serial technique is a possible means of musical composition. So far he himself has employed series horizontally only, though parts of the *Canticum* (the chords in "Surge, aquilo") and *Agon* show that he has understood the time dimension idea of series applied strictly in every direction. [Robert Craft, "A Personal Preface," pp. 7–13.]

Schoenberg's work has too many inequalities for us to embrace it as a whole. For example, nearly all of his texts are appallingly bad, some of them so bad as to discourage performance of the music. Then, too, his orchestrations of Bach, Handel, Monn, Loewe, Brahms differ from the type of commercial orchestration only in the superiority of craftsmanship: his intentions are no better. Indeed, it is evident from his Handel arrangement that he was unable to appreciate music of "limited" harmonic range, and I have been told that he considered the English virginalists and in fact, any music that did not show a "developing harmony," primitive. His expressionism is of the naivest sort, as, for example, in the directions for lighting the *Glückliche Hand*; his late tonal works are as dull as the Reger they resemble or the César Franck, for the four-note motive in the *Ode to Napoleon* is like César Franck; and his distinction between "inspired melody" and mere "technique" ("heart" vs. "brain") would be factitious if it weren't simply naive, while the example he offers of the former, the unison Adagio in his fourth Quartet, makes me squirm. We—and I mean the generation who are now saying "Webern and me"—must remember only the perfect works, the *Five Pieces for Orchestra* (except for which I could bear the loss of the first nineteen opus numbers), *Herzgewächse*, *Pierrot*, the *Serenade*, the *Variations* for orchestra, and, for its orchestra, the "Seraphita" song from op. 22. [*Conversations with Stravinsky*, pp. 78–79.]

R.C.: How do you esteem Berg's music?

I.S.: If I were able to penetrate the barrier of style (Berg's radically alien emotional climate) I suspect he would appear to me as the most gifted constructor in form of the composers of this century. He transcends even his own most overt modeling. In fact, he is the only one to have achieved large-scale development-type forms without a suggestion of "neoclassic" dissimulation. His legacy contains very little on which to build however. He is at the end of a development (and form and style are not such independent growths that we can pretend to use the one and discard the other), whereas Webern, the Sphinx, has bequeathed a whole foundation, as well as a contemporary sensibility and style. . . . [*Conversations with Stravinsky*, p. 79.]

R.C.: What music delights you most today?

I.S.: I play the English virginalists with never-failing delight. I also play Couperin, Bach Cantatas too numerous to distinguish, Italian madrigals even more numerous, Schutz *sinfoniae sacrae* pieces, and masses by Josquin, Ockeghem, Obrecht, and others. Haydn quartets and symphonies, Beethoven quartets, sonatas, and especially symphonies like the Second, Fourth, and Eighth, are sometimes wholly fresh and delightful to me. Of the music of this century I am still most attracted by two periods of Webern: the later instrumental works, and the songs he wrote after the first twelve opus numbers and before the *Trio*-music which escaped the danger of the too great preciosity of the earlier pieces and which is perhaps the richest Webern ever wrote. [*Conversations with Stravinsky*, pp. 145–46.]

R.C.: Have you changed your mind in any particular way about Webern?

I.S.: No; he is the discoverer of a new distance between the musical object and ourselves and, therefore, of a new measure of musical time; as such he is supremely important. . . .

Webern the man has now begun to emerge, too, with the publication of his letters to Berg, Humplik, and Jone. The Webern of the letters is, first of all, profoundly religious, and not only institutionally . . ., but in the simple holiness of his feeling toward each of God's *essents* (a flower, a mountain, "silence") as well. Music is a mystery to him, a mystery he does not seek to explain. At the same time, no other meaning exists for him but music. He stands before the Parthenon friezes and marvels at the sculptor's "conception," which he compares to his own "composition method . . . always the same thing in a thousand different ways" (in another letter: ". . . the meaning is always the same, however different the means"). He never explains beyond that, and he even admits, in one letter, to being severely tried by the necessity of explanation: "I am sometimes . . . tortured by teaching." [*Memories and Commentaries*, pp. 97–98.]

A DECADE LATER

University of Washington Interviewer: To go back to the question of scope, Mr. Stravinsky, do you consider Webern's to be too narrow?

I.S. Not for Webern—which is no answer, of course, but I cannot understand the word in musical terms. Webern's timescale is tiny, his quantity is minute, the variety of his forms is small, but whether these are measurements of scope I am unable to say. If, for example, scope is also a question of depth and not merely of width and expanse, then Webern's can be very great, and it is in any case perfectly circumscribed, which I say to remind you that we can only judge what the composer has done, not what he did not set out to do. But can we be certain, to begin with, that the scope we are looking for is really Webern's and not your own Beethovenesque idea of what it should be? Admittedly, Webern often seems to have put a low premium on his listener's sense of involvement. His music is wholly unrhetorical and in that sense unpersuasive. There is no movement from simple to complex, no development of subsidiary parts or integration of counterthemes, second subjects, fugal episodes, and the like. The listener is definitely not invited to participate in the argument of the creation as he is in the symphonies of Beethoven. On the contrary, each opus offers itself only as a whole, a unity to be contemplated. Now obviously such an artwork is essentially static, and obviously, too, the cost in subjectivity is high. Naturally I concede that it is possible to feel constricted when listening to a succession of, especially, the very short pieces, and to attribute this feeling to lack of scope, but I consider the very attempt to follow a chain of, as I say, unities, to be a quantitative mistake; I mean, just because they are clock-time short. For a test you must try the single opus and in the neighborhood of other music. Thus, in Venice a few years ago I heard the Parennin Quartet struggle through some forty minutes of Boulez's *Livre pour quatuor*, then play the four minutes of Webern's *Bagatelles*. I assure you that since then scope has never seemed to be a matter of size.

U.W.I.: What are your present criticisms of the music, Mr. Stravinsky?

I.S.: They are mere differences of palate, mostly, and doubtless more revealing of myself than of Webern. Those *molto ritenuto, molto espressivo*, and "dying away" phrase endings weary me now, and there is a touch of cuteness in the vocal music which I dislike. . . .

U.W.I.: As you have noted some of your criticism, Mr. Stravinsky, would you also evaluate the high points?

I.S.: After the *Five Movements* and the *Six Pieces*, the next peaks come a decade later, with the Trakl songs, the Canons, the *Volkstexte*, the clarinet and guitar songs. But for me, the *Trio*, the *Symphony*, and the orchestra *Variations* are Webern's greatest achievements.

U.W.I: Has your estimation of Webern's position changed appreciably in the last decade, Mr. Stravinsky?

I.S.: Not mine, but certainly that of many others. "With it" composers have now turned away, or developed away, from his influence, though their music often continues to be a *catalogue raisonné* of derivations from his. But all of us owe something to him, if not in rhythmic vocabulary, then in our sensibility to musical time, for I think Webern has raised everyone's sense of refinement in this regard (well, *nearly* everyone's). [Hans Moldenhaur, comp., and Demar Irvine, ed., *Anton von Webern: Perspectives*, pp. xxi–xxvi.]

R.C: Of your works, the young *avant-garde* admire *Le Sacre du Printemps*, the *Three Japanese Lyrics*, various of the Russian songs, *Renard*, and the *Symphonies of Wind Instruments*. They react strongly against your so-called neoclassic music, however (*Apollo*, the Piano Concerto, *Jeu des Cartes*, etc.), and though they affirm your more recent music they complain that triadic harmonies and tonic cadences are solecisms in the backward direction of the tonal system. What do you say to all this?

I.S.: Let me answer the latter complaint first: my recent works *are* composed in the—my—tonal system. These composers are more concerned with direction than with realistic judgements of music. This is as it should be. But in any case they could not have followed the twenty years of their immediate forebears, they had to find new antecedents. A change in direction does not mean that the out-of-influence is worthless, however. In science, where each new scientific truth corrects some prior truth, it does sometimes mean that. But in music advance is only in the sense of developing the instrument of the language—we are able to do new things in rhythm, in sound, in structure. We claim greater concentration in certain ways and therefore contend that we have evolved, in this one sense, progressively. But a step in this evolution does not cancel the one before. . . . If my music from *Apollo* and *Oedipus* to *The Rake's Progress* did not continue to explore in the direction that interests the younger generation today, these pieces will nonetheless continue to exist.

Every age is an historical unity. It may never appear as anything but either/ or to its partisan contemporaries, of course, but semblance is gradual, and in time either and or come to be components of the same thing. For instance, "neoclassical" now begins to apply to all of the between-the-war composers (not that notion of the neoclassic composer as someone who rifles his predecessors and each other and then arranges the theft in a new "style"). The music of Schoenberg, Berg, and Webern in the twenties was considered extremely iconoclastic at that time but the composers now appear to have used musical form as I did, "historically." My use of it was overt, however, and theirs elaborately disguised. (Take, for example, the Rondo of Webern's *Trio*; the music is wonderfully interesting but no one hears it as a Rondo.) We all explored and discovered new music in the twenties, of course, but we attached it to the very tradition we were so busily outgrowing a decade before. [*Conversations with Stravinsky*, pp. 144–45.]

I was born to causality and determinism, and I have survived to probability theory and chance. . . . But I was also born to a non-progressivist notion of the practice of my art, and on this point, though I have survived into a musical society that pursues the opposite idea, I have not been able to change. I do not understand the composer who says we must analyze and determine the evolutionary tendency of the whole musical situation and proceed from there. I have never consciously analyzed any musical situation, and I can follow only where my musical appetites lead me. [*Dialogues and a Diary*, p. 28.]

CHANGE OF LIFE

And so we arrive at the juncture of yet another "change of life," a change in disposition and general musical orientation: the adoption of twentieth-century serial techniques. Coming on the heels of *The Rake's Progress* (1948–51), the first signs of a move in this direction, in the Ricercar II of the *Cantata* (1952) and the Passacaglia and Gigue of the *Septet* (1953), seem to have taken nearly everyone by surprise. And well might this have been the case, for the eighteenth-century Classical credentials of *The Rake* are truly formidable. Inspired initially by the series of Hogarth engravings (on exhibit at the Chicago Art Institute in 1947), graced by an exquisite libretto authored jointly by W. H. Auden and Chester Kallman, *The Rake* is in fact closely modeled after Mozart. (We have it from both Stravinsky and Craft that recordings of *Cosi fan tutte* were a daily routine at the time of its inception and composition. And Craft revealingly adds that Stravinsky habitually limited his "musical intake" when occupied with composition, "listening only to those pieces which he regards as directional to his work."[1]) Dramatically the scenario adjusts itself to the familiar sequence of recitatives, arias, duets, trios, choruses, and instrumental interludes; musically one finds a severely tried diatonicism, a Classical C-scale (or major-scale) reference with themes, counterthemes, accompaniment figures, chromatic inflections, and harmonic transactions resurrected on a scale virtually unprecedented in this oeuvre. Stravinsky is there, of course; the "neo" is still legitimate, if at times just barely. Very conspicuous are varieties of (0 3 4/3 4 7/3 6 7) "minor-major third" emphasis, that most ubiquitous of neoclassical predispositions, occurring with a persistence that suggests—Stravinsky's denials notwithstanding—the formality of a *leitmotiv*. On the very first page, the first vocal entry (Anne: "The woods are green") is a C–C♯–A–F♯ succession, introduced within a securely fastened C-scale-on-A or psuedo-A-major setting in the string accompaniment. This constitutes a typical neoclassical (0 3 4 9) homogeneity, with C as pitch number 3 tending chromatically to the C♯, pitch number 4 or the "major third" of the (A C♯ E) "tonic" triad, and with F♯ as pitch number 9 injecting additional ambiguity as part of a (F♯ A C♯) triadic outline. The result is a blurring or "coming together" of triads which might formerly in harmonic succession have defined the tonic-submediant relation   (or, with respect to the two interval orderings defined in relation to the diatonic collection, the "relative keys" of "A-major" and "F♯-minor"). This emphasis is pointedly underscored at No. 3, where Anne's C–C♯ succession is accompanied by an E–C–A–C♯ "minor-major third" triadic outline in the flutes and bassoon. But seldom are the (0,3,6,9) symmetrically defined octatonic implications of the emphasis—that side of the bargain which has seemed so crucially to seal the

Stravinskian stamp—brought to the fore. Witness, in this respect, the C-scale-on-C setting of Scene II of Act I, where D♯ and F♯, pitch numbers 3 and 6 in relation to the (0 4 7) "tonic" triad in terms of (C E G), merely encircle and surround E and G as chromatic tendency tones, their Classical C-scale (on C) derivation. Small wonder, then, the puzzled reception to this most extraordinary turn of events. *The Rake* seemed reactionary; indeed, it seemed to have positioned Stravinsky ever more dependably within the confines of his neoclassical modes of thought.

But at the same time, there existed the Schoenberg-Stravinsky rift to which the musical world had long accustomed itself. This bore, however problematic the undertow, the earmarks of a rivalry of opposing camps, the one aligned to the music and ideas of Schoenberg and his disciples Webern and Berg, the other still seeking and finding in Stravinsky's neoclassical modes of accommodation an alternative to "the method of composing with twelve tones." (To which Milton Babbitt has added a third category: those with no particular ties to either.[2]) It is Craft's contention that these "hegemonies" were in large part the creation of the Musical Establishment, and that as the Vienna-Paris split shrank to a ten-mile radius of Hollywood, California, the division meant little to the trapped "protagonists" themselves. "They were kept separate and isolated." But surely there is more to it than this. Stravinsky listened enthusiastically to *Pierrot lunaire* while on a visit to Berlin with Diaghilev in December 1912. But although in his later recollection, "the most prescient confrontation in my life," this early encounter was quickly forgotten as he turned to the stimulus of Russian popular verse and his own uniquely fashioned "Russian" musical thought, and then, circa 1919, to his "discovery of the past" in *Pulcinella*, "the epiphany through which the whole of my late work became possible." He is reported to have taken offense at Schoenberg's *Drei Satiren* (1925), the second of which taunted "der kleine Modernsky," and according to the recollections of his friend Pierre Suvchinsky (reported by Craft), the mood toward Schoenberg and his "school" was one of hostility during the 1920s and 1930s. Those favorably inclined were disowned as "traitors," Berg's *Wozzeck* dismissed as "*une musique boche*," and Mahler ignominiously mispronounced as "Malheur."[3] He was present at the 1925 I.S.C.M. Festival in Venice to perform his *Piano Sonata*, but missed Schoenberg's *Serenade*. He also missed the Paris premiere of the *Five Pieces for Orchestra* in 1922, and the world premiere of the *Suite*, opus 29, in Paris in 1927.[4] Indeed, as he himself relates, he failed after 1921 to absorb another note of Schoenberg's until the premiere of the *Genesis Suite* in Hollywood, 1945, an event which he might also have ignored had not his own *Babel* been a part of that bizarre concoction. True, there was in all this doubtless an element of self-protection. Convinced of the validity of his claim, of its continuing potential, he may not have wished to be disturbed, distracted, diverted. (Each of these composers had such longstanding musical investments; each in their separate ways was so deeply entrenched.)

But how can one explain the eleven years of proximity in "The City and County of Los Angeles"? Why should these composers, approaching or within the twilight of their careers, so stubbornly have kept their distance, shunning even the most perfunctory acquaintance? (Stravinsky might well have acquiesced. Professionally and artistically the more secure, he was the less lonely, the less neglected or abused of the two.) But such questioning may on the other hand be out of order. Curious and unnatural in retrospect, the separate but equal status might at the time have seemed very natural, eminently sensible. And who knows but that, given the climate of the times, the condition of these separate commitments, the two might, after all, have had very little to say to one another?

And so by what might Stravinsky's final "change of life" have been caused? An about-face so unforeseen, so improbable—if nonetheless, as it happened, carefully negotiated? Was it perhaps—as some have suggested—that Stravinksy stirred, his "rare form of kleptomania" became active, only when tempted by the music of dead composers? Did Schoenberg's death on 13 July 1951 suddenly bracket the serial advance with a historical legitimacy, a sense of tradition which it could not have had with its founding father still alive? (Removing, at the same time, the potentially crippling handicap of an all-too-knowing, watchful ear?) Or were its origins of a more direct, more practical, and specifically musical nature? Could *The Rake*, three years in the making, have exhausted the neoclassical palate, leaving Stravinsky restless and increasingly eager to strike out from this terrain? He suggests as much. "Crisis number two was brought on by the natural outgrowing of the special incubator in which I wrote *The Rake's Progress*." And a second Auden libretto is declined on grounds that it would have required him to continue as before, to compose a sequel to *The Rake*. To this might be added, however, that the serial pretensions of the *Rake*-like *Cantata* (1952), Stravinsky's succeeding opus, do not exactly overwhelm. The tenor of the Ricercar II is wholly serial, and reference is made to the standard four set-variants, orders, or forms (indeed, in a rather stiff, mechanical fashion, with all set-factors registrally fixed throughout).[5] But the set itself is a succession of eleven factors with duplications of three of these (C, D, and E; this produces a content of six pitch elements in all). "Chromaticism" stems, perhaps not unpredictably at this stage, from the (0 3 4) "minor-major third" unit in terms of (C E♭ E), of which the (C E) unit acquires a centric position owing, among other variables, to the selection of I–8 as the "untransposed" I form, which preserves the centric (C E) unit and intersects with all set-factors of the Prime except E♭, for which the C♯ is substituted. (See Example 77.)[6]

Stravinsky's pronouncements at this time scarcely project the image of a

Example 77

full-fledged convert. In an interview dated May 1952, he willingly grants the serialists their "discipline," their "pure music," but then imagines them imprisoned by "the figure twelve," while he himself still finds "quite enough to do with the seven notes of the scale."[7] The "figure twelve" was, of course, cautiously approached, and then in *Canticum Sacrum* (1955),

Canticum Sacrum (1955): "Surge, Aquilo"

Threni (1958)

Example 77 *continued*

Agon (1953–57), and *Threni* (1958) couched in a canonic framework highly reminiscent of Renaissance polyphony.

Or could Stravinsky have been stirred, as Craft suggests, by a chance hearing of Webern's *Quartet* opus 22, which in 1952 left him deeply impressed? And what might Craft's role have been in this miraculous flip-flop? Perhaps something other than a mere guide? (The confidant has steadfastly denied all responsibility. "As if anyone," he later mused, "could lead *that* horse to water if he didn't want to go, let alone make it drink."[8])

Perhaps with all said and done, a web of such entries. Each may have figured in one way or another. But why Webern? Why should Stravinsky have turned from the very start to "the Sphinx?" To that member of the Viennese "hypostatic trinity of twentieth-century music" who had so completely divested himself of the rhetoric which neoclassicism had variously sought to reclaim, and who by so doing had bequeathed to the opposing camp, serialism and the younger generation of "post-Webernists," a whole new sense of musical timing and space (which Stravinsky himself acknowledges, but which would not really affect his own work until the later stage of his development, which begins with *Movements* in 1959)? One may grant the cleansing, antidotal incitement to which this Webern encounter might have given rise, and that the cool, detached manner of Webern's intensity, his mosaics of an "immediately given," of a "sufficiency unto itself" would perhaps in any event have met with a sympathetic ear, but especially in juxtaposition with the "radically alien emotional climate" of Berg or the melodramatic, *fin-de-siècle* pathos of so much of Schoenberg. Was it the leanness of utterance, the transparency of texture that attracted Stravinsky? A transparency which, apart from its own virtue, might readily have lent itself to an apprenticeship, to an initiation into the then wholly unfamiliar mechanics of the serial operation? Or was it perhaps the coincidence of this discipline and a highly overt, almost archaically imposed canonic edifice? (For Stravinsky's appetite during the early stage extends with as much zeal to the polyphonic masters of the Renaissance as to the twentieth-century serialists. In *Canticum Sacrum, Agon,* and *Threni* the serial presence, twelve-tone or other, is closely linked to a very traditional Renaissance-like canonic part-writing.) And then later, after the publication of Webern's letters, Stravinsky admired "Webern the man": simple, pure, honest and direct; a nontheorist, nonteacher; "a village priest" seeking not to explain but to behold—indeed, "severely tried by the necessity of explanation," as Stravinsky saw him, "sometimes tortured . . . by teaching."

But there is occasion for greater specificity here. Could Stravinsky have been attracted by the symmetry of the sets, the segmental patterning by which this symmetry exposed itself, and the mobilelike back-and-forth (or forwards-and-backwards) motion to which these patterns in application gave rise? Perhaps he found in the segmentation itself, in the (0 1 4/0 3 4) and (0 1 3 4) "minor-major third" units, familiar grounds from which to depart. And then in the subordination of this segmental articulation to the higher-order hexachordal and twelve-tone determinacies, a means of accommodation, a means of entry. A means of imposing pitch/interval order-determinacy on a familiar articulative routine (but without necessarily severing all ties with its referential past). So that, in effect, just as neoclassicism is heard and understood as a form of accommodation between Classical C-scale (or major-scale) conventionality and a (0,3,6,9) symmetrically defined partitioning of the octatonic collection, so might the early serial stage be reckoned an imposition of a formalized order-logic on an existent articulative mold; and just as the hazards of a potential runaway or paralytic symmetry (with respect to the symmetrically defined octatonic implications of this mold) are averted by diatonic interaction, so might the larger unit order-determinacies be viewed. (For never in this oeuvre are octatonic relations encountered on an unimpaired, explicit basis for any considerable duration. Such relations are confined to blocks of material, juxtaposed in turn with blocks of varied referential implications; or they intersect or "clash" with elements attributable to the diatonic collection. It is by way of block juxtaposition that symmetrically defined, self-enclosed deadlocks are broken, and that a sense of release, of movement or progress, is effected.) All of this stands quite apart from the outward appearance of Webern's music—its *molto ritenutos, molto expressivos,* and "dying away phrase-endings" (which appear not to have influenced Stravinsky at all, and of whose presence in Webern's music he steadily grew weary), and its pointillism, its graphics of a quite precise and restricted intervallic typicality (which does occasionally appear to have had an effect, as in the "Pas de deux" of *Agon* at mm. 411–51, but scarcely at all in *In Memoriam Dylan Thomas* (1954), *Canticum Sacrum,* and *Threni*).

Examining the sets in Example 77, without, for the moment, probing too deeply into the pieces themselves, we conclude that such would indeed seem to be the case. In the three sets of Webern's *Concerto, Variations,* and *Cantata II,* successions of (0 1 4/0 3 4) and (0 1 3 4) "minor-major third" units abound, and with the sets so deployed as to afford these groupings a quite unmistakable measure of articulative cohesion. In the *Concerto,* the three concluding (0 1 4/0 3 4) units in terms of Eb–G–F♯, G♯–E–F, and C–C♯–A are, respectively, the transposed retrograde inversion, retrograde, and inversion of the initial (0 1 4) unit, B–Bb–D; in the *Variations* the segmentation is more readily tripartite, with the initial (0 1 3 4) unit in terms of A–Bb–Db–C having as its (transposed) retrograde inversion the concluding F–E–G–Ab segment. (Additional symmetries might be noted: the second hexachord of the *Variations* set is the inverted retrograde of the first hexachord; the concluding seven set-factors of this set are a transposition, with the two pivoting "common tones," D and D♯, of its first seven factors; and the inversion of the entire set is in interval order equivalent to the retrograde.) It is precisely these (0 1 4/0 3 4) and (0 1 3 4) "minor-major third" groupings which are significantly a part of the serial mechanism of both *In Memoriam Dylan Thomas* and *Agon.* The five-tone row of *In Memoriam* has as its first four factors the (0 1 3 4) unit with a Prime ordering of 4–3–0–1 in terms of E–Eb–C–C♯. (Note the symmetry of the (0 1 3 4) unit, and of its embedded three-note (0 1 4) and (0 3 4) units as well.) All the sets in *Agon* commence with the (0 1 3 4) tetrachord, except those of the Coda at mm. 185–253 and the "Bransle simple" and "Bransle gay" (which, however, are not without their (0 1 3 4) implications, or, indeed, without (0 2 3 5) implications, an articulative unit equally familiar to Stravinsky, and whose serial implementation is not unlike that realized on behalf of the (0 1 4/0 3 4) and (0 1 3 4) groupings). The set or "basic cell" of the entire "Pas de deux" at mm. 411–519 is, in fact, the single (0 1 3 4) unit, and with a Prime ordering of 0–1–4–3 in terms of Bb–B–D–Db at mm. 411–51.

More critical, however, is the serial identification of this segmentation—not merely the subjection of these units to the standard operations of transformation (retrograde, inversion, and retrograde inversion) and transposition, but also their subordination to more extended pitch/interval successions of five, six, seven, and twelve factors. Thus the fifth set-factor of the Webern *Variations* set curls inward, "chromatically" sealing off the (0 1 3 4) gap with pitch number 2, the B, and, with the fourth set-factor, C, as a pivoting "common tone," initiates a sequence of interlocking (0 1 3 4) units in terms of A–Bb–Db–C/C–B–D–D♯ and D–D♯–F♯–F/F–E–G–G♯. (See the brackets in Example 77.) From this formula much of the serial manipulation in the aforementioned Stravinsky pieces is derived. The Prime of the *In Memoriam* set inverts Webern's initial 0–1–4–3 ordering to 4–3–0–1 in terms of E–E♭–C–D♭, but is in like manner "chromatically" (or serially) sealed off by a concluding fifth set-factor, the D. (This factor tends naturally to inhibit (C D♭ E♭ E)'s octatonic potential with respect to Collection III, but without necessarily depriving it of a measure of articulative cohesion.) The first words of Thomas's poem ("Do not go gentle into that good night") are accompanied by a sequence of overlapping (0 1 3 4) units identical in interval order to that defined by the first seven factors of the Webern set: B♭–B–D–D♭/ D♭–C–E♭–E here. (Octatonically, the first of these (0 1 3 4) units refers to Collection I, the second to Collection III.) From beginning to end, this "chromatic" curling with the fifth set-factor, or (0 1 3 4) overlapping with the third and fourth set-factors, is a prominent feature in set-form linkage or association.[9] Similar, too, are the (0 1 3 4) extensions in *Agon*. Beginning with the single (0 1 3 4) unit of the "Pas de deux" at mm. 411–51 (where, graphically, Webern makes his most conspicuous appearance), subsequent sets all derive from the Webern example. With respect to their first seven set-factors, the thirteen-tone extension at m. 452 is a replica, as is the seven-tone row of the Coda at m. 495, and the twelve-tone set of the "Four Duos" and "Four Trios" at mm. 520 and 539. (Stravinsky ranked the orchestral *Variations* among Webern's "greatest achievements" and later, in *Themes and Conclusions*, called them "the tallest of them all."[10] Moreover, the (0 1 3 4) tetrachord, "chromatically" sealed off by a fifth set-factor, appears in several pieces of the later stage, conspicuously in the brief *Double Canon* (1959) and then in *A Sermon, A Narrative and A Prayer* (1962). See Example 86 in chapter 14.)

It is perchance to such correspondences that Webern's special fortunes in the matter of accommodation may be ascribed. Still, we cannot admit to an overriding concern with this question of outside influence. If we probe a bit further, a great number and variety of contemporary influences suggest themselves, by no means exclusively serial in origin, and of which the most consequential are often the least open to systematic analysis. Thus the twelve-tone sets of *Canticum Sacrum* and *Threni* are not at all like Webern's. They encompass, to be sure, a segmental content with a (0 1 3 4) or (0 2 3 5) articulative potential; and there are successions of octatonic intervals that appear to have significantly influenced the handling of the series, operations of transformation and transposition, and set-form selection with respect to both succession and vertical alignment. (See, in Example 77, the brackets applied to the set of *Canticum Sacrum*'s second movement, "Surge, Aquilo." These refer to an uninterrupted Collection III succession of six set-factors, duplicated by all untransposed forms, and then extended by a select group of transpositions.) And while, perhaps like Webern's, the approach is linear, with two or more set-forms superimposed as lines or parts in a contrapuntal or canonic framework, the expansive effect of the polyphony, above all its rhythmic-metric guise, seems closer to the traditional part-writing of the Renaissance or Baroque.

Nor, for that matter, do our concerns extend with great fervor to the sheer mechanics of set manipulation, to the—in Stravinsky's words—"spelling of the note order," or, drearier still, to a listing of those practices, methods, or procedures that might be deemed typical or characteristic. We are for the moment far from pressed by the formality itself, taxed by such information as that a particular transposition has, to follow Milton Babbitt, "a singular hexachordal relation to P in that it preserves the greatest number of pitches (four) between corresponding hexachords of any set not in the initial complex"; or by such insights into set-structure as that "the (unordered) content of the two disjunct hexachords are inversionally equivalent, so that there will be associated with every set-form an inversionally related form whose corresponding hexachords have no pitch-classes in common." (This may be eventful in the music of Schoenberg, and later, of course, in that of Milton Babbitt (among others), but the exhibition of "hexachordal combinatoriality," inversional (virginal) or otherwise, is of no great consequence in Stravinsky's. His first twelve-tone set, that of "Surge, Aquilo" of *Canticum Sacrum*, is so endowed, with P's first hexachord having as its complement, its equivalent in pitch/interval content, I–1's first hexachord. But only toward the close of this (second) movement at mm. 86–93 can this condition be heard and understood as having been taken into account. Similarly, too, the Prime of the *Introitus* (1965) set has a first hexachord that yields its complement at I–7, but this circumstance, to the hearing and understanding of this observer, is virtually ignored.) For here, as in the question of outside influence, Stravinsky's methodology suggests a great number and variety of practices (which, indeed, might with ease be left at the doorstep of any number of composers). And were we to confine our scrutiny solely to the "Bransle simple," Bransle gay," and "Bransle double" of *Agon* (a stretch of some one hundred measures), we would find exemplified nearly all of the so-called classical techniques commonly inferred from the music of Schoenberg, Webern, and Berg—the very stock in trade itemized, say, in a compendium such as George Perle's *Serial Composition and Atonality*: "Nondodecaphonic Serial Composition," "The Set as a Thematic Formation," "The Set as a 'Melodic Prototype,' " "Segmentation," "The Verticalization of Adjacencies," "The Verticalization of Nonadjacent Linear Elements," "Invariant Formations," "The Simultaneous Statement of Different Set-forms," etc. Rather, our immediate concerns rest with assimilation and accommodation—with the fate of an articulative routine, referential bonds, rhythmic-metric schemes, and general methods of procedure compounded on behalf of "Russian" and neoclassical thought. We are interested in the fate, once again, of an acknowledged identity and distinction in pitch organization, formal layout, and rhythmic-metric construction. And so while by no means indifferent to the process, to the serial derivative, we survey the scene not so much from the standpoint of its literature and theoretical haunts as from that of Stravinsky's past, confronting the at times elusive but nonetheless unmistakable circumstance that somehow Stravinsky remains Stravinsky.

For example, in music of both the "Russian" and neoclassical periods two distinct categories of reference imposed themselves, the octatonic and the diatonic. In "Russian" pieces this imposition took the form of an interaction between what was termed a Model B (0,3,6,9) symmetrically defined (0 2 3 5) tetrachordal partitioning of the octatonic collection (with Model A's (0 3 7/0 4 7/0 4 7 10) triadic partitioning often becoming apparent as an offshoot or appendage) and a (0 2 3 5) tetrachordal or (0 3 7/0 4 7) triadic partitioning of the diatonic collection, often implicating its (0 2 3 5 7 9 10 (0)) D-scale or (0 2 3 5 7 9) hexachordal ordering. In neoclassical works the form was that of an interaction between Model A's (0,3,6,9) symmetrically defined (0 3 7/0 4 7/0 4 7 10) triadic, (0 3 4/3 4 7/3 6 7) "minor-major third," or (0 1 3 4) tetrachordal partitioning of the octatonic collection and a variety of conventions, inflections, and harmonic transactions associated with the Classical C-scale (or major-scale) ordering of the diatonic collection. Now it is quite true that none of the sets examined in Example 77 are reasonably described as octatonic or diatonic, least of all, obviously, the twelve-tone sets. And while it is also true that set deployment often stresses a (0 1 4/0 3 4) "minor-major third" or (0 1 3 4) or (0 2 3 5) tetrachordal segmental content (Stravinsky thus turning, at the outset of the serial excursion, to an accustomed articulative habitat), the octatonic or octatonic-diatonic referential complexions with which these groupings might earlier have been identified are often, as has been indicated, blocked *à la* Webern by a fifth set-factor, which, "chromatically" (or serially) sealing off the gaps, secures that particular advantage to which the serial side of the bargain evidently lays claim. But if blocked *à la* Webern, where do we stand with respect to identity and distinction in pitch organization—given, that is, the extent to which this identity and distinction is conditioned by referential premises? In this connection a second question is posed: might conditions of transformation and transposition—set-form selection with respect to succession and vertical alignment—ensure the articulation some residual measure of its former referential self? Might, in other words, such conditions, by duplicating and/or extending such segmental content, potentialize that former referential self? And might, therefore, identity and distinction continue to reside with referential character, preserved by pockets of concentration?

For example, the twelve-tone set of *Agon*'s "Bransle double" cannot reasonably be described as octatonic. But the second hexachord of its Prime contains a Collection I pitch succession of G–A♭–B♭–B–D♭. And this succession is followed at mm. 340–43 by RI, whose first hexachord contains a Collection I succession of B–D♭–D–E–F. The passage as a whole exhibits a P–RI linkage superimposed over reiterations of P–3's second hexachord with a Collection I succession of B♭–B–D♭–D–E. This renders, at least to the hearing and understanding of this observer, a cohesive, symmetrically defined referential commitment to Collection I virtually unmistakable. (See Example 82. Transpositions of a given set-form at 3, 6, and 9 naturally duplicate and/or extend the octatonic implications of a segment thereof.)

Questioned about his motives in *Conversations* (1959), Stravinsky conceded that the rules and restrictions widened and enriched "harmonic scope," and that "one starts to hear more and differently than before," and is compelled "to greater discipline than ever before" (a discipline likened to "the great contrapuntal schools of old"). But he quickly adds that he composes "vertically," and that he continues to hear "harmonically" and to compose "in the same way I always have." Nor are his working habits noticeably affected. He still begins "by relating intervals rhythmically," an "exploration of possibilities always conducted at the piano." With the birth of some "auditive shape," a musical idea or "main theme," he sets himself in motion "by playing old masters," or "by starting directly to improvise rhythmic units on a provisional row of notes (which can become a final row)." We gather, then, one not prone to belabor the serial routine. Speaking later of the *Epitaphium* (1959), he affirmed that "in the manner . . . described in our previous conversations, I heard and composed a melodic-harmonic phrase." Indeed: "I certainly did not (and never do) begin with a purely serial idea, and, in fact, when I began I did not know, or care, whether all twelve notes would be used. After I had written about half the first phrase I saw its serial pattern, however, and then perhaps I began to work toward that pattern."[11] Later, in regard to the *Elegy for J.F.K.* (1964), he questions the usefulness of a "serial autopsy," since he had already joined "the various melodic fragments before finding the possibilities of serial composition in them," there thus being "virtually no element of predetermination in such a procedure."[12] But to compose "vertically"? To hear "harmonically"? To compose "in the same way I always have"? One might, from one so disposed, have expected a pronounced verticalization of adjacent and nonadjacent elements, a vertically imposed serialism with the set's members distributed among several lines or parts, or possibly a vigorous "combinatorial" policy along the lines initiated by Schoenberg. But such, decidedly, is not the case. Stravinsky's most common approach is linear, with several set-forms employed simultaneously in a contrapuntal and often canonic framework. These associations do not tend to form twelve-tone "aggregates"; he combines, rather, to duplicate, to reinstate, to reinforce. Hence to compose "vertically," to hear "harmonically" (or to compose "in the same way I always have") must necessarily have to do (1) with pitch/interval succession (with segments presumably heard and understood in some vertically or "harmonically" cohesive fashion), but perhaps most significantly (2) with vertical alignment, with a superimposition of set-forms which, rhythmic-metrically engaged, will bring about a vertical or "harmonic" compliance of some sort. Of this compliance we infer the preservation of an articulative routine along with referential ties not entirely severed; of the "greater discipline than ever before" we suspect difficulties at the threshold—difficulties in coordinating the old with the new, of coping with what must necessarily have had to be disposed of and with what might still have seemed apropos; in short, the difficulties of an apprenticeship, an initiation, of assimilation and accommodation.

Nonetheless, before turning to more detailed analysis (and notwithstanding this rather restrictive analytic-theoretical slant), it may be useful as a point of departure and frame of reference to underline certain assumptions regarding set usage in the early serial works.

1. The set, series, or row characteristically imposes itself in the form of a linearization. Two or more set-forms are superimposed as lines or parts in a more or less traditional part-writing fashion, and then keep to their respective lines or parts with little or no transference of set-members. The conception is therefore thematic or "melodic" in general appearance, the texture contrapuntal and often canonic. There are exceptions, of course, quite apart from "chords" or simultaneities in the strictest sense of "simultaneous attack-durations" (such as, for example, the concluding simultaneity of *Agon*'s "Bransle simple," a verticalization of its hexachordal set). In the first measure of "Surge, Aquilo" of *Canticum Sacrum*, set-factors of a single order are distributed among several lines or parts (see Example 85b); while in the opening setting of *Agon*'s "Bransle gay," the flute, bassoon, and harp parts all derive from a single hexachordal unit. (See Example 81. In contradiction to linearization, this approach has been termed "vertical serialism.")

2. It follows from item 1 that "harmony" or simultaneity is most commonly a circumstance of the vertical alignment of set-forms, and that, therefore, to compose "vertically" encompasses the selection of set-forms which, vertically aligned and rhythmic-metrically engaged, will induce a vertical or "harmonic" cohesion of some sort.

3. The four untransposed orders of the set—Prime (P) and its standard affiliates, Retrograde (R), Inversion (I), and Retrograde Inversion (RI)—are apt to acquire a privileged status, if only by virtue of their predominance, and may therefore assume the character of a "home base," with respect to which transpositions are perceived as departures or auxiliaries.

In the second movement of *Canticum Sacrum*, "Surge, Aquilo," there are twenty-three statements of the twelve-tone set (excluding independent hexachordal delineations), fourteen of which refer to the untransposed orders, eleven of these fourteen to the (untransposed) P and R forms. This preferential treatment is all the more pronounced in the later works (beginning with *Movements*, 1959), where complete, ordered twelve-tone sets are rarely stated other than in their untransposed forms, and where conventional operations of transposition are superseded by a uniquely devised scheme of hexachordal transposition-rotation.

4. There is a tendency to double back on an initial set-statement (presumably P) through its retrograde (presumably R), with P's concluding (and R's initiating) set-factor as the pivoting "common tone"; and then to return, obviously, to P's initial set-factor. (The scheme might be reversed with respect to P and R.) These conditions of set linkage and "common-tone" overlap are occasionally met by RI and even I (succeeding P), as in the opening canon for trumpets in *Agon*'s "Bransle simple" (see Example 80a), or the P–RI doubling back of the violins at mm. 336–43 in the "Bransle double" (see Example 82). And here too, there is a foreshadowing of later developments: in Stravinsky's hexachordal transposition-rotation scheme, the rotations of a given hexachordal group commence with a common set-factor.

5. It follows from items 3 and 4 that the initial and concluding set-factors of the untransposed orders are apt to accumulate stress; indeed, they frequently acquire a privileged status analogous to that assumed by the untransposed orders as a whole, one often underscored by duplications, octave doublings, "fifth support," and the like.

6. In the earliest of Stravinsky's twelve-tone pieces, the hexachordal bar of the set is fundamental, and hexachords are often treated as independent serial entities to which operations of transformation and transposition apply without regard to complementation on the opposite side of the hexachordal bar. In "Surge, Aquilo" of *Canticum Sacrum* (Stravinsky's first completely twelve-tone movement), RI–8's first hexachord is employed independently of its second (see Example 85b), and in the opening A section of *Agon*'s "Bransle double" at mm. 336–51, the trumpet-trombone line confines itself to transformations and transpositions of P's second hexachord: P–3 (7–12), RI–3 (1–6), I–5 (7–12), and R–3 (1–6). (See Example 82.)

AGON (1953–1957)

R.C. You say that you are a doer, not a thinker; that composing is not a department of conceptual thinking; that your nature is to compose music and you compose it naturally, not by acts of thought or will. A few hours of work on about one third of the days of the last fifty years have produced a catalogue which testifies that composing is indeed natural to you. But how is nature approached?

I.S. When my main theme has been decided I know on general lines what kind of musical material it will require. I start to look for this material, sometimes playing old masters (to put myself in motion), sometimes starting directly to improvise rhythmic units on a provisional row of notes (which can become a final row). I thus form my building material. [*Conversations with Stravinsky*, p. 12.]

The Series

R.C. Do you think of the intervals in your series as tonal intervals; that is, do your intervals always exert tonal pull?

I.S. The intervals of my series are attracted by tonality; I compose vertically and this is, in one sense at least, to compose tonally.

R.C. How has composing with a series affected your own harmonic thinking? Do you work in the same way—that is, hear relationships and then compose them?

I.S. I hear certain possibilities and I choose. I can create my choice in serial composition just as I can in any tonal contrapuntal form. I hear harmonically, of course, and I compose in the same way I always have.

R.C. Nevertheless, the Gigue from your *Septet* [1953] and the choral canons in the *Canticum Sacrum* [1955] are much more difficult to hear harmonically than any earlier music of yours. Hasn't composing with a series therefore affected your harmonic scope?

I.S. It is certainly more difficult to hear harmonically the music you speak of than my earlier music; but any serial music intended to be heard vertically is more difficult to hear. The rules and restrictions of serial writing differ little from the rigidity of the great contrapuntal schools of old. At the same time they widen and enrich harmonic scope; one starts to hear more things and differently than before. The serial technique I use impels me to greater discipline than ever before.

R.C. Do you think your time world is the same for the kind of music you are now composing and for your music of thirty-five years ago (*Mavra*, piano Sonata, piano Concerto, *Apollo*)?

I.S. My past and present time worlds cannot be the same. I know that portions of *Agon* contain three times as much music for the same clock length as some other pieces of mine. Naturally, a new demand for greater in-depth listening changes time perspective. Perhaps also the operations of memory in a nontonally developed work (tonal, but not eighteenth-century-tonal system) is different. We are located in time constantly in a polyphonic work, whether Josquin's *Duke Hercules Mass* or a serially composed non-tonal-system work. [*Conversations with Stravinsky*, pp. 22–23.]

R.C. You have often remarked that the period of harmonic discovery is over, that harmony is no longer open to exploration and exploitation. Would you explain?

I.S. Harmony, a doctrine dealing with chords and chord relations, has had a brilliant but short history. This history shows that chords gradually abandoned their direct function of harmonic guidance and began to seduce with the individual splendors of their harmonic effects. Today harmonic novelty is at an end. . . . Rhythm, rhythmic polyphony, melodic or intervallic construction are the elements of musical building to be explored today. When I say that I still compose "harmonically" I mean to use the word in a special sense and without reference to chord relations. [*Conversations with Stravinsky*, p. 121.]

The last of the intentional ballets (if we except the choreographic scenes of *The Flood*), prefaced—appropriately enough—by a dedication to Lincoln Kirstein and George Balanchine (the commissioners for the New York City Ballet), *Agon* is a crossroads piece, and perhaps in much the same fashion as *Histoire du soldat* is with respect to the earlier "Russian" and neoclassical eras. It is also, with its Renaissance-like cadential formulae, its traces of jazz (as in the "Bransle gay" or at mm. 352–64 in the "Bransle double"), conspicuously eclectic, a trait likewise shared by its predecessor of some forty years (although it is, of course, eclectic in a special Stravinskian sense; it is not a collage but a true assimilation, the making of Stravinskian identity out of bits and pieces of otherwise vastly disparate idioms, "styles," or musical routines).

Begun in December 1953, the opening "Pas de quatre" was the first music to be composed. (The "Pas de quatre" returns to conclude the ballet as a final Coda at mm. 561–620. The introductory fanfare for trumpets, harp, piano, and strings was originally conceived with trombones; and the mandolin part in the block at mm. 10–13, with its near repeat at mm. 23–25, was first composed for the guitar.) There then followed, in February and March, a brief intermission for *In Memoriam Dylan Thomas*. Craft estimates that before embarking on *Canticum Sacrum* in June 1955 Stravinsky had completed two-fifths of the ballet—in rough approximation, it appears, to what now stands as the nonserial portions from the "Pas de quatre" to the close of the "Gailliarde" at m. 184.[13] Following *Canticum*, however, there was another interruption: the instrumentation of Bach's Chorale Variations on "Vom Himmel Hoch," begun in December 1955 and completed in February of the following year. But work was resumed in Spring 1956, and the final product is dated 27 April 1957. This final resumption is reported to have caused considerable difficulty, inasmuch as the second, third, and fourth movements of *Canticum Sacrum* are Stravinsky's first twelve-tone pieces (or movements), and these experiences must greatly have altered his sense of direction, compounding the problems already posed by interruption and delay. The effects of these difficulties are felt in the general format: a division, at least on paper, into four large sections, each separated by the Prelude with subsequent near repeats as an Interlude. However, *Agon* is most readily perceived as a string of compacted miniatures, as diverse within sections as they are from one section to the next. And so as buffers or "spacers" in the delineation of its large four-part framework, subsequent appearances of the Prelude (as Interlude) are not altogether convincing (or may appear, with the addition of each miniature, increasingly irrelevant). Nonetheless, the specifics of this general outline are as follows:

I. 1. Pas de quatre: mm. 1–60
    2. Double Pas de quatre: mm. 61–95
    3. Triple Pas de quatre: mm. 96–121

    Prelude
II. 1. Saraband: mm. 146–63
    2. Gailliarde: mm. 164–84
    3. Coda: mm. 185–253

    Interlude
III. 1. Bransle simple: mm. 278–309
     2. Bransle gay: mm. 310–35
     3. Bransle double: mm. 336–86

    Interlude
IV. 1. Pas de deux: mm. 411–519
    2. Four Duos: mm. 520–38
    3. Four Trios: mm. 539–60
    4. Coda (Pas de quatre): mm. 561–620

As a work of transition, stretching through the initial serial period, with the nonserial confronting the serial, the non-twelve-tone serial the twelve-tone serial, *Agon* seems ideally suited to our purposes. Curiously, however, the nonserial (and predominately diatonic) sections are not especially reflective of neoclassical thought. The "Pas de quatre," for example, is devoid of accommodation as detailed in previous chapters. One does not find in it the Classical C-scale (or major-scale) conventions, inflections, and harmonic transactions, and the interaction of this idiosyncrasy with Model A's (0, 3, 6, 9) symmetrically defined partitioning of the octatonic collection (on whose behalf, obviously, the transformed Stravinskian or neoclassical C-scale reference is inferred). The formal outline is routine; blocks of material are placed in abrupt juxtaposition, each of these blocks, upon successive (near) repeats, acquiring a marked and stable distinction in melodic content, dynamics, register, instrumentation, and collectional identity. (Thus, in Example 78, the block at mm. 7–9 with its (near) re-

Example 78: "Pas de quatre"

peats at mm. 19–22 and 35–38; or the mandolin block at mm. 10–13 with
its (near) repeat at mm. 23–25.) This is a routine prevalent from the beginnings of the "Russian" period to the end of the serial (with *Requiem
Canticles* in 1966), and in no way peculiar to any one of the three general
orientation categories or "stylistic" trends.

In fact, pitch organization in the "Pas de quatre" is "Russian" in origin.
The principal articulative unit is the (0 2 3 5) tetrachord, which imposed
itself with such regularity by way of all manner of reiterating, folkish fragments in the "Russian" period. And although referentially neutral with
respect to the octatonic and diatonic pitch collections (having served, by
means of this duplicity, so conveniently as a pivoting go-between or connecting link), it is here conspicuously diatonic; indeed, it aligns itself with
the (0 2 3 5 7 9) diatonic hexachordal segment, a grouping which imposed
itself with equal persistence in diatonic and octatonic-diatonic settings of
the "Russian" period, from the opening blocks of *Petroushka*'s first tableau,
through the octatonic-diatonic passages of *Le Sacre*, *Renard*, and *Les Noces*,

Example 78 *continued*

to the opening "Soldier's March" and Music to Scenes I and II of *Histoire
du soldat* (with their (0 2 3 5 7 9) hexachordally conceived ostinati). With
this in mind we might supplement the analytical chart of Example 78 by
noting: (1) that the referential profile is ostensibly (0 2 3 5 7 9) hexachordal, realized locally in terms of (D C B A G F) at mm. 1–4, 7–9, and 19–22,
(A G F♯ E D C) at mm. 5–6, and then centrally in terms of (E D C♯ B A G) at
mm. 10–13 and 23–25; (2) that the pairs of 2s or whole steps which encircle this (0 2 3 5 7 9) hexachord, (0 2) and (7 9), are frequently exposed as
"fourths" or "fifths," an exposure from which they derive a degree of
pitch-class priority, especially pitch number 2, the C from the initial (D C
B A G F) hexachord at mm. 1–4, 7–9, and 19–22, the D from the (E D C♯ B
A G) hexachord at mm. 10–13 and 23–25 (see, especially, the simultaneities at mm. 1–3, 7, 13, and 19; or, in the analytical chart below, the boxed-
off and bracketed material); (3) that the principal melodic fragment is the
(0 2 3 5) tetrachord, realized locally in terms of (D C B A) in the trumpet at
mm. 1–4, in terms of F♯–E–G–A in the first horn at mm. 5–6, and then in

Example 78 *continued*

terms of D–E–C♯–B in the mandolin at mm. 10–13; (4) and that chromaticism in this ostensibly diatonic setting has often to do with the transposition and superimposition of (0 2 3 5 7 9) hexachords related by the interval of 7, a "fifth," with the encircling pairs of 2s constituting the points of overlap or intersection.

But if not especially reflective of neoclassical thought, neither are these articulative conditions all that "Russian"-sounding. This is principally because, in the "Pas de quatre," these groupings are assembled in collaboration with an assortment of Medieval or early-Renaissance cadential formulae, which invest the piece—indeed, whole portions of *Agon*—with a subtle "neo-Renaissance" quality. (See Example 78 in continuation.) In this connection we might observe, as we did in chapter 7, that the F♯–E–G–A–C and E–F♯–D–C successions in the first and second horns at mm. 5–6 (accounted for in terms of the (A G F♯ E D C) hexachordal collection) approach the octave C in a manner suggesting, in relation to (D C B A G F) and its presiding pitch number 2, the C, the II–I formula so prevalent in music of the fourteenth and fifteenth centuries; and, further, that this II–I formula is embellished by both the "double leading tone" and Landini inflections, the F♯ effecting or accommodating the "double leading tone," the terminating D/A–C/C succession between the first and second horns effecting the so-called Landini cadence. See also the mandolin block at mm. 10–13, where the superimposed "fifth"-related (0 2 3 5 7 9) hexachords (B A G♯ F♯ E D) and (E D C♯ B A G), similarly accommodate both the "double leading tone" and "Landini" conventions, but here in relation to (E D C♯ B A G)'s presiding D; G♯ effects the "double leading tone," while the terminating B–D succession of the mandolin's D–E–C♯–B–(D) tetrachordal outline accommodates the "Landini" convention. These formulae also apply to the close of the Prelude (as Interlude) at mm. 275–77 (Example 79), where the II–I cadence in terms of D–C is embellished with F♯ as the "double leading tone."

All the same, it is to the serial miniatures of *Agon* that our eyes and ears are drawn. These begin with the Coda at mm. 185–253, and then, following a (near) repeat of the Prelude (as Interlude) at mm. 254–77, stretch from the "Bransle simple" to the close of the "Four Trios" at m. 560 (at which point the "Pas de quatre" reappears as a concluding Coda). And while, as we have observed, the conviction with which subsequent appearances of the Prelude (as Interlude) delineate *Agon*'s large-scale structure may ultimately be open to question, there is little doubt that the Interlude at mm. 254–77 figures as an effective bridge between the nonserial diatonicism of, say, the opening "Pas de quatre," and the serial octatonic-diatonicism of the miniatures which follow.

The construction is here at the outset familiar enough. (See Example 79.) In compliance with the second of our two rhythmic-metric types, four fragments, registrally and instrumentally fixed, repeat according to periods, spans, or cycles which vary "independently of" one another, and effect a variable rhythmic-metric or vertical (or "harmonic") coincidence. There are a few idiosyncrasies: *All* fragments are rhythmic-metrically

Example 79: Interlude

"mobile" in that the periods defined by their successive repeats or entrances are irregularly spaced; and the meter, possibly as a consequence
of this all-inclusive "mobility," is irregular (which is not ordinarily the case

with schemes of this type), alternating between 3/4 and 3/8 periodicities in apparent conformity with the irregularly spaced repeats of the timpani's B♭–D♭ fragment. But underlying these complications is a rhythmic-metric "play," consisting of the contradictions or reversals in upbeat/downbeat or off-the-beat/on-the-beat accentuation, common to all such rhythmic-metric types. For in accord with regular 3/4 metric periodicity (see the brackets in Example 79), the on-the-beat identity of the opening B♭–D♭ reiteration of the timpani fragment is promptly contradicted or reversed at m. 256 as an off-the-beat identity. (Stravinsky's dotted lines suggest a "concealed" 3/8 meter within the 3/4 measures, but in reality confirm "background" 3/4 periodicity, upon which apprehension of these contradictions or reversals is naturally contingent.) And indeed all reiterating fragments, except the trumpet's C reiterations (which, although "mobile" or irregularly spaced, assume the same identity with respect to regular 3/4 or 2/4 metric periodicity), effect off-the-beat/on-the-beat contradictions or reversals with increasing intensity at mm. 254–60. (A steady 2/4 meter seems almost equally appropriate as a "background" frame of reference throughout the Interlude. See, especially, the *Meno mosso* passage at mm. 268–77, where, despite the perseverence of the 3/4 design, the material is more readily duple in conception.)

But more to the point: the upsweeping C–D–F–G–B–C articulation of the flute-cello and cello (pizzicato) fragments, with its missing seventh pitch element, the E, implicates the (D C B A G F) diatonic hexachordal segment of the opening "Pas de quatre," and then, with the trumpet's reiterating C (pitch number 2 in relation to this hexachordal reference), the pitch-class priority circumstances of the opening fanfare. But this diatonic C–D–F–G–B–C articulation now interacts with a B♭–D♭ dyadic or (B♭ D♭ F) triadic outline in the timpani fragment, and seals an octatonic-diatonic interaction with respect to Collection I and the (D C B A G F) hexachord at mm. 354–60, and then in terms of Collection I and the C-scale on G at mm. 264–76, the specifics of which are of special significance to the serial miniatures which lie ahead. For not only do succeeding sets exhibit a (0 2 3 5) or (0 1 3 4) segmental content that rather consistently implicates Collection I; not only is this referential profile reinforced by conditions of set transformation and transposition; but the (B♭ D♭)/D–B component of this interaction, Collection I's (0 1 3 4) tetrachord in terms of (B♭ B D♭ D) as outlined jointly by the upsweeping C–D–F–G–B–C fragments, the sustained (D G B) triad at mm. 263–71, and the timpani's B♭–D♭ reiteration, also steadily acquires, with the registral spacing defined by the Interlude's fragments often preserved (see the brackets in Example 79), a fixed intersectional pitch-identity determinacy, globally transcending local serial identification from one miniature to the next. Thus, looking ahead, see the D–B span of the trumpet's hexachordal delineations at mm. 278–82 in the "Bransle simple" (Example 80a); the B♭/D–B span in the concluding simultaneity at m. 314 in the "Bransle gay" (Example 81); the B♭–B–D♭–D segment of the trombone-trumpet tetrachordal delineations at mm. 336–39 in the "Bransle double" (Example 82); the D♭–B♭/D–B span of the opening string figuration at mm. 411–12 in the "Pas de deux" (Example 83a); or the concluding C♯–A♯/D–B simultaneity at m. 462 in the "Pas de deux" (Example 83b). These are but a few of the more conspicuous instances in which this (B♭ B D♭ D) tetrachord, marked in registral distribution, binds material of an otherwise pronounced diversity in melodic, "harmonic," dynamic, instrumental, and serial content.

Thus, in the opening canon for trumpets of the "Bransle simple," the D–E–F–G–F♯–B and B–A–G♯–F♯–G–D delineations of the hexachordal set are confined to the D–B span, with D and B as the initial or concluding set-factors of these alternating P and I–9 forms. (See Example 80a.)[14] While Collection I's (B♭ D♭) unit is missing, there is an additional association here, Collection I's (0 2 3 5) tetrachord in terms of (D E F G), but this Collection I potential is temporarily inhibited—as is so frequently the case with the serially conceived (0 1 3 4) tetrachordal unit in *Agon*—by an "intruding," non-octatonic (non-Collection I) fifth set-factor, the F♯ here. This factor, curling inward and "chromatically" sealing off one of (D E F G)'s gaps—thereby securing that advantage to which the serial side of the bargain evidently lays claim—skips up a "fourth" to P's concluding factor, the B. The P-statement is in turn followed by I–9, which (0 2 3 5) tetrachordally completes P's F♯–B "fourth" in terms of (B A G♯ F♯). In fact, this critically "intruding," "chromatic" fifth set-factor suggests a division of the six-tone row into four and two set-factors (or two and four factors with respect to the R and RI forms), the first of these with its "fourth" (0 2 3 5) tetrachordally complete, the second (0 2 3 5) tetrachordally incomplete (as a "fourth"). Although the symmetrical implications of this P–I–9 exchange are demonstrated in Example 80a, we supplement them as follows:

1. I–9 allows for a doubling back on the initial P-statement, with P's concluding and I–9's initiating set-factor, the B, as the pivoting "common tone"; and then for a return to P's initiating (and I–9's concluding) set-factor, the D, which is thus also a pivoting "common tone."

2. I–9 preserves, with its concluding and initial set-factors, the D–B span of the P-statement, the span inherited from, or referring back to, the preceding Interlude.

3. I–9 completes P's F♯–B "fourth" with its (0 2 3 5) tetrachord in terms of (B A G♯ F♯), and then encircles P's complete (D E F G) tetrachordal segment with a G–D "fourth," just as, in reverse order, I–9's (B A G♯ F♯) tetrachordal segment is encircled by P's F♯–B "fourth."

Example 80a: "Bransle simple"

4. Most significantly, this P–I–9 exchange seals, in terms of its inter-locking (D G) (F♯ B) "fourths" or (D E F G) (F♯ G♯ A B) tetrachords, an interaction between Collection I, represented here by (D E F G), and Col-lection II, represented by (F♯ G♯ A B), that governs the process of serial

extension not only in the "Bransle simple" at mm. 278–87 but also in the succeeding "Bransle gay" and throughout the "Pas de deux" at mm. 411–519 as well.

In other words, with respect to this final item, five factors of the set's Prime refer to Collection I: D, E, F, G, and B. Of the remaining two octatonic collections, Collection II is closest with four pitch elements: D, F, F♯, and B. In the A section of the "Bransle simple" at mm. 278–87 (which returns at mm. 298–309 to define, broadly speaking, an ABA formality), all complete (0 2 3 5) tetrachords refer either to Collection I or Collection II. (See Examples 80b and c. With repeats there are a total of seventeen setstatements in the A section, eleven of whose (0 2 3 5) tetrachordal delineations refer to Collection I, six to Collection II.)

The back-and-forth articulation of this (0 2 3 5) tetrachordally conceived Collection-I–Collection-II interaction harbors wider implications. For P in terms of D–E–F–G–F♯–B at mm. 278–82 is transposed "up" by the interval of 7, a "fifth," to P–7 in terms of A–B–C–D–C♯–F♯ at mm. 283–87, a transposition whose (0 2 3 5) tetrachord in terms of (A B C D) refers to Collection II. But this transposition is answered in turn by R–6 in terms of F–C–C♯–B–A♯–G♯, whose (0 2 3 5) tetrachord in terms of (C♯ B A♯ G♯) is (0,6) tritone-related to Collection I's opening (D E F G). Hence, the (0 2 3 5) tetrachordally conceived Collection-I–Collection-II interaction in terms of (D E F G)–(B A G♯ F♯) at mm. 278–82 (serially in terms of P–I–9) shifts to a Collection-II–Collection-I interaction in terms of (A B C D)–(C♯ B A♯ G♯) at mm. 283–87 (serially in terms of P–7–R–6); and with the terms of this transaction punctuated by the (A D F♯) concluding simultaneity at m. 287, which, with its embedded A–F♯ span, relates to the D–B span or (D G B) triadic outline of the opening D–E–F–G–F♯–B P-delineations by the interval of 7, the "fifth." (Although, of course, unlike

Example 80b

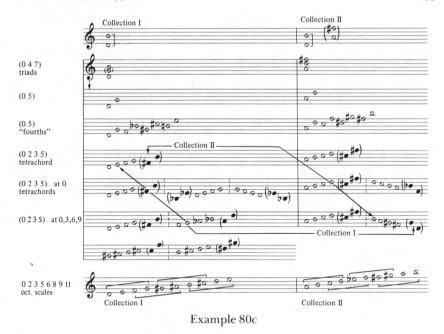

Example 80c

the A–F♯ span, which refers only to Collection II, the D–B span is accountable to both Collections I and II, a critical condition of intersection with
respect to these Collection-I–Collection-II (0 2 3 5) tetrachordal linkages.)
Finally, in the closing measures of the piece (the reprise of the A section at
mm. 298–309), the (A D F♯) simultaneity is abruptly followed by a verticalization of the untransposed Prime, and with the registral spacing of P's
D–B span preserved in simultaneity. (Indeed, this concluding simultaneity's general disposition might bring any number of previously examined
nonserial contexts to mind, especially, in view of its Collection I implications, that at Nos. 71–75 in the *Symphonies of Wind Instruments*; the first
movement of the *Symphony of Psalms*; or Nos. 29–34 in the first movement
of the *Symphony in Three Movements*.)

There is in the preceding "Bransle simple" a quite deliberately con-
trolled fluctuation between a "tight" and a "loose" positioning of the set's
intervals. This fluctuation coincides with its ABA structure, the canonic
trumpeting of the A section giving near-exclusive vent to tighter arrangements (indeed, the tightest possible), the contrasting B or middle section
to looser or more widely spaced interval-delineations. In the "Bransle
gay" this scheme is reversed. (See Example 81.) Here it is the contrasting B
or middle section to which, beginning with the flute solo at m. 321, the
tighter arrangements apply; while the flanking A sections introduce a
configuration of considerable expanse, extending from the widely spaced

Example 81: "Bransle gay"

C–B♭ fragment of the first bassoon (P's third and sixth set-factors) to the high D–F reiteration of the first flute (P's second and fourth set-factors). (See, in Example 81, the centrally positioned C–B span between the first bassoon and second flute, a span subsequently "plugged" at m. 321 by the tightly positioned RI-delineations in terms of C–G–F–B♭–A♭–B in the

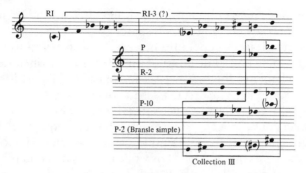

Example 81 *continued*

solo flute.) Such programmed fluctuations are common elsewhere in Stravinsky's serial works, with tighter delineations often identified with vocal or choral settings, looser ones often with a strictly instrumental vocabulary; or the tighter possibly appear in conjunction with a straightforward rhythmic-metric display, the looser at times with "polyrhythmic combinations" of extraordinary complexity. Significantly, however, the fluctuation is as formal as it is melodic or "harmonic," having as much to do with long-range design, with the delineation of a block structure, as with melody or vertical ("harmonic") coincidence.

But the "Bransle gay" distinguishes itself by means more varied and intricate than these. In marked contrast to the A section of the "Bransle simple" (where eight set-forms surface within a stretch of less than ten measures, seventeen set-statements in all), the A section of the "Bransle gay" confines itself to but one set-form, the untransposed P in terms of B–D–C–F–Eb–Bb. And again in contrast, the P-statements of this A section are not exclusively linear in conception (as is typically the case with Stravinsky) but vertical, with P's members distributed among several reiterating fragments in the flutes, bassoons, and harp. Indeed, the repetition here proceeds in accord with the first of our two rhythmic-metric types: barred metric irregularity, with the reiterating fragments, lines, or parts synchronized unvaryingly in vertical (or "harmonic") coincidence, and hence all sharing the same rhythmic-metric periods defined by the shifting meter. The novelty, however, is that "background" regular metric periodicity is imposed in the form of a *notated* (barred) second meter: from start to finish, a regular 3/8 metric pulse in the castanet. And there is subtlety, too, in the near repeat of the opening configuration at mm. 316–19, where the initial sequence of block measures is reshuffled. Thus, with these block measures labeled A B C D at mm. 311–14, the distribution at mm. 316–19 reads C D A B. This reshuffling allows the B or middle section at m. 321 to commence not after the cadencelike finality of the D block at mm. 314 and 317, but after the open effect of the B block at m. 319, with its centrally positioned C–B span.

In pitch organization generally, however, the two bransles are not greatly distant. The hexachordal set of the "Bransle gay" includes five octatonic pitch elements, the first five set-factors of the P and I forms, the last five from R and RI. The first five set-factors of the set's Prime in terms of B–D–C–F–E♭–B♭ refer to Collection II; while, of the remaining two octatonic collections, Collection I is closer with four elements, B, D, F, and B♭. And here, as in the "Bransle simple," this Collection-II–Collection-I link is of immediate consequence. For while there is no D♭ in the Prime to complete Collection I's (B♭ D♭)/D–B global component, B♭, D, and B as P's sixth, second, and first set-factors (D–B also intersecting with Collection II) allow for a B♭/D–B concluding simultaneity at mm. 314 and 317 (a verticalization of nonadjacent elements, as it is commonly called), with the registral spacing of the preceding Interlude and "Bransle simple" conspicuously preserved.

At m. 321, the contrasting B or middle section is introduced with two tightly positioned delineations of the untransposed RI form in the first flute; and an immediate link with P of the A section is sealed in terms of the C–B span defined by RI's initial and concluding set-factors (with RI thus "plugging" the centrally positioned C–B gap of the A section, as defined by P's third and first set-factors in the first bassoon and second flute). These RI delineations, with their five-factor Collection I segments in terms of (C)–G–F–B♭–A♭–B, initiate a Collection I pocket of concentration of unmistakable bearing at mm. 321–25. (See, in Example 81, the boxed-off area.) For of the RI form only C is foreign to Collection I; and while the five-factor octatonic segments of the R–1 and P set-forms subsequently introduced by the second flute and first clarinet at mm. 324 and 325 are not Collection I segments, the deployment of these set-forms is such that this cohesive "feel" of a Collection I pocket is enhanced. In other words, the positioning of R–1's C♯ above RI's A♭ at m. 325, and the entrance of P's B–D unit above R–1's sustained C♯ (with R–1's concluding, non-Collection I set-factors held back until after this B–D entrance) both prompt a hearing and understanding not so much in terms of R–1 and P as in terms of RI–3—in terms, that is, of a (0,3) symmetrically defined transposition of RI, with RI's Collection I (C)–G–F–B♭–A♭–B content duplicated and extended in terms of RI–3's (E♭)–B♭–A♭–C♯–B–D succession. (See, again in Example 81, the bracketed RI and RI–3 forms at mm. 321–25.) Then, after Collection I at mm. 321–25, there follows a Collection III pocket of concentration at mm. 326–31 (to the close of the B section), introduced by P–10 in the flutes, a set-form with a Collection III segmental content of A–C–B♭–E♭–D♭–(A♭). Here P–10's first and second set-actors, A and C, are introduced below the briefly sustained D♭ and B♭

of the completed P and R–2 forms in the clarinets, and yield a Collection III (0 1 3 4) tetrachord in terms of (A B♭ C D♭) which in registral spacing closely approximates that of Collection I's (B♭ D♭)/D–B global component. Although not shown in Example 81, this commitment is further underscored at mm. 328–31 by a return to the hexachordal set of the "Bransle simple" in terms of E–F♯–G–A–G♯–C♯, a set-form whose Collection III elements in terms of E–F♯–G–A–C♯ (excluding the non-Collection III G♯) are used as a simultaneity at mm. 330–31, but tightly positioned, and thus in contrast to the widely spaced arrangement of the concluding simultaneity of the "Bransle simple."

Through such groupings or pockets of referential cohesion a vertical (or "harmonic") distinction is revealed, one that relates to Stravinsky's music "considered as a whole," but perhaps more critically here to the process of accommodation, the imposition of an order-determinacy on an established articulative and referential routine.

The "Bransle double" concludes *Agon*'s magical batch of bransles appropriately with a twelve-tone set whose first and second hexachords are, respectively, the hexachordal sets of the "Bransle simple" (with interval order intact) and the "Bransle gay" (with interval order slightly revised). The format is predictably ABA, but with a coda tacked on at the close. In Example 82, however, reference is to the first half of the A section at mm.

Example 82: "Bransle double"

336–51, the second half being a near repeat with fortification in the lower strings. And we confine our remarks accordingly by noting: (1) that there is here exhibited the habitual doubling back on an initial P-statement, with the first and concluding set-factors of P and RI in this P–RI exchange, C and G♭, serving as pivoting "common tones"; (2) that the first five set-factors of P's second hexachord refer to Collection I in terms of G–A♭–B♭–B–D♭(G♭), and RI's first hexachord completes this referential commitment in terms of (G♭)–B–D♭–D–E–F; (3) that this Collection I commitment is further underscored in the trombone-trumpet line by R–3's second hexachord in terms of B♭–B–D♭–D–E–(A), and then by RI–3's first hexachord in terms of (A)–D–E–F–G–A♭ (see the boxed-off area in Example 82); (4) that the non-Collection I E–A "fourth" of P's first hexachord relates, as an added link, to the E–A "fourths" of these R–3 and RI–3 independent hexachordal delineations; (5) and that hexachords—as should be apparent—are treated as independent serial entities, to which operations of transformation and transposition apply irrespective of their twelve-tone complements on the other side of the hexachordal bars. R–3's first hexachord (1–6) includes as its first four set-factors Collection I's (0 1 3 4) global unit in terms of B♭–B–D♭–D, marking an additional link in set-form selection or determination.

In the "Pas de deux" at mm. 411–519, following a near repeat of the Prelude (as Interlude), matters are seemingly brought to a head. Here, from the opening Adagio for strings to the concluding Coda, *Agon*'s (0 2 3 5) or (0 1 3 4) tetrachordal articulation, serial in the three bransles (but with referential links to the past never entirely severed), secures an expression of truly remarkable eloquence and sophistication. Indeed, as the lengthiest of the miniatures, the "Pas de deux" is itself a string of compacted miniatures, each marked by subtle shifts in tempo, dynamics, and instrumental ensemble: the Adagio for strings at mm. 411–62; the *Più mosso* section for horns and piano at mm. 463–72 (with a near repeat at mm. 484–94); the *L'istesso tempo* section for flutes and strings at mm. 473–83; and the concluding Coda at mm. 495–519. And while each of these gems might handily have serviced analytic-theoretical needs, it is to the Adagio (Examples 83a–b) and the Coda (Example 83c) that our immediate attention is drawn.

The serial unit of the entire "Pas de deux" (indeed, of the "Four Duos" and "Trios" as well) is the (0 1 3 4) tetrachord. And as "basic cell" or common denominator, it is in the opening measures of the Adagio first introduced in terms of (B♭ B D♭ D); that is, in terms of Collection I's global unit, and with a (D♭ B♭)/B–D vertical disposition very close to that of the Prelude (along with its subsequent near repeats as Interlude). Indeed, so persistent is this (B♭ B D♭ D) realization, through the stretches of violin solo at mm. 417–22, 427–29, and 437–46 (see the boxed-off material in Example 83a) and then as a boundary or concluding sonority of repose at mm. 411–12, 427–29, and 458–62 (nearly the only instances in which all four members of the (0 1 3 4) unit are sustained in simultaneity), that it acquires the character of a "home base" in the Adagio, a point of departure and return, and serially the character of a Prime with an initial 0–1–4–3 ordering in terms of B♭–B–D–D♭. It is from this primal B♭–B–D–D♭ unit that the serial excursion is launched, that routine in set-form selection is gauged, and that, by such routine, the delineation of larger serial units in the form of (0 1 3 4) extensions are apprehended.

Of these modes of (0 1 3 4) tetrachordal linkage, two are standard. The first is wholly octatonic in conception, having to do with (0 1 3 4) successions and vertical alignments spaced by the intervals of 3, 6, or 9. Thus, for example, at mm. 423–24, Collection I's (0,6) tritone-related (0 1 3 4) tetrachords in terms of B–B♭–C♯–D and F–E–G–A♭, or at mm. 426–29 its (0,3)-related (0 1 3 4) tetrachords in terms of A♭–G–B♭–B and B♭–B–D–D♭; Collection II's (0,6) tritone-related (0 1 3 4) tetrachords in terms of F–G♭–A–A♭ and C–B–D–E♭ at mm. 414–15, or later in terms of D–E♭–F♯–F and G♯–A–C–B at mm. 455–56; or, indeed, Collection III's (0,6) tritone-related (0 1 3 4) tetrachords in terms of A–B♭–C♯–C and E♭–E–G–F♯ in the violas at mm. 452–66. These are (0 1 3 4) extensions of explicit octatonic intent, forming pockets of cohesion in which transformations and transpositions of the 0–1–4–3 unit are pursued with unmistakable reference to the octatonic collection.[15]

The second of these approaches is serially of greater consequence, however. It consists, in contrast to the disjunct (0,6) tritone-related (0 1 3 4) tetrachords of the octatonic collection, of conjunct or interlocking (0 1 3 4) tetrachords, with a potential fifth set-factor curling inward and "chromatically" sealing off the (0 1 3 4) tetrachord's gap with a pitch number 2 (securing, once again, that advantage to which the serial process lays claim). The fourth factor acts as a pivoting "common tone" of a seven-tone row in the form of a P–RI or RI–P interlock. Collection I's B♭–B–D–D♭ tetrachordal emphasis in the first two measures of the Adagio is at mm. 414–15 followed by Collection II's (0,6) tritone-related (0 1 3 4), tetrachords, F–G♭–A–A♭ and C–B–D–E♭, and, although not shown in Example 83a, Collection I's (D♭ B♭)/D–B boundary sonority at mm. 427–29 is in the *prima volta* section followed by a Collection II pocket of concentration. It is through this Collection-I–Collection-II exchange—as foreshadowed earlier in the "Bransle simple" and "Bransle gay"—that the mechanics of this seven-tone extension unfold, with a Collection I (0 1 3 4) tetrachord followed by a Collection II (0 1 3 4) for the RI–P interlock, and the reverse for P–RI.

Most explicit in this regard is the concluding string passage at mm.

Example 83a: "Pas de deux" (Adagio)

Example 83a *continued*

452–62, where the pace in (0 1 3 4) tetrachordal delineation quickens markedly. (See Example 83b.) Here, in the first violins, Collection II's D–E♭–G♭–F unit is followed by Collection I's F–E–G–G♯ unit, with F, the fourth set-factor, as the pivoting "common tone"; this seven-tone P–RI interlock in terms of D–E♭–G♭–F–E–G–A♭ is subsequently extended to a thirteen-tone interlock with the transposition to A♭ at m. 454 in terms of A♭–A–C–B–B♭–C♯–D. (In order for this interlock to effect Collection I and Collection II (0 1 3 4) tetrachords, the Collection I tetrachords must be RI-orderings, those of Collection II P-orderings; or the reverse, with the Collection I tetrachords I-orderings, those of Collection II R-orderings.)[16] At the conclusion of the Adagio at mm. 458–62, the identical sequence of four overlapping (0 1 3 4) tetrachords, but introduced by an RI–P rather than a P–RI, interlock, with Collection I's B–B♭–D♭–D unit followed by Collection II's D–E♭–G♭–F unit. This adjustment very conveniently allows, owing to the doubling back on the sequence at m. 460,

Example 83b

for the use of Collection I's (D♭ B♭)/D–B global unit as a punctuating
boundary sonority. Still, the first clue to these (0 1 3 4) interlocks surfaces
much earlier in the Adagio, at m. 423, where Collection II's D–E♭–C–B
unit overlaps with Collection I's B–B♭–D♭–D unit in an R–RI formulation
of this Collection-I–Collection-II (0 1 3 4) tetrachordal exchange, which is
subsequently exploited in the *L'istesso tempo* section for flutes and strings at
mm. 473–83.

All succeeding sections are serially derived from these methods of (0 1 3

4) tetrachordal linkage. Thus, for example, the G–A♭–B–B♭–A–C–D♭ seven-tone set of the Coda at mm. 495–519 (with a doubling back on the initial P-statement; see Example 83c); or the twelve-tone set of the "Duos" and "Trios," whose first seven set-factors are equivalent in interval order to the seven-tone (0 1 3 4) extensions of the "Pas de deux's" Adagio at mm. 452–62.[17]

Agon has frequently been depicted as a misfit, an untidy hodgepodge of "irreconcilable tendencies," a contradiction in musical discipline. But the piece may thrive because of these alleged "irreconcilable tendencies" rather than in spite of them: the novelty in formal layout; the inventiveness in instrumental detail; the exquisite delicacy and sophistication of the neoclassical (or "neo-Renaissance") effort, especially in the Prelude and in the "Gailliarde," but also in the opening "Pas de quatre," where the (0 2 3 5) and (0 2 3 5 7 9) groupings so typical of the "Russian" period are introduced in surroundings now as much "neo-Renaissance" as they are "Russian" or neoclassical (this "neo-Renaissance" quality being suggested not only by the instrumentation (mandolin) but by voice-leading procedures at cadence points, with the II–I formula embellished with inflections which recall the "double leading-tone" and "Landini cadences" of the fourteenth and fifteenth centuries). However, the most extraordinary aspect of the work is the imposition of an order-determinacy defined by four, five, six, seven, or twelve pitch elements on a "system" which still seems fundamentally content-oriented, an orientation richly endowed with octatonic articulative habits and with the conventions and tonal implications of the neoclassical octatonic (Model A) and diatonic C-scale forms of interaction. Apparent attempts by Stravinsky and Craft to shortchange this heritage by referring rather persistently to the *Doppio lento* section at mm. 504–11 as the *crème de la crème* of *Agon* appear to reflect: (1) a temporary preoccupation with Webern's methods, and (2) a curiously apologetic attitude toward the neoclassical past, as if serialism, construed as some grievously overlooked Final Solution, could in some ultimate sense threaten the legitimacy of all other processes of musical invention.

Example 83c: "Pas de deux" (Coda)

(Stravinsky would soon repent and become, with an anti-evolutionary, anti-progressivist stance ever more insistent during the later years, increasingly suspicious of all those seemingly led by historical calculation rather than by their "musical appetites.") For it is *the whole of Agon*, the whole of its vast, pluralistic reach in historical reference, that is bold, unique, and—because the synthesis "works"—breathtakingly—well-nigh miraculous.

CANTICUM SACRUM (1955)

Dedicatio	mm. 1–9
First movement	"Euntes in Mundum," mm. 10–45
Second movement	"Surge, Aquilo," mm. 46–93
Third movement	"Ad Tres Virtutes Hortationes: Caritas, Spes, Fides," mm. 94–249
Fourth movement	"Brevis Motus Cantilenae," mm. 250–306
Fifth movement	"Ille Autem Profecti," mm. 307–End

R.C.: Your Mass [1948] *Canticum Sacrum*, and *Threni* [1958] are the strongest challenges in two hundred years to the decline of the Church as a musical institution.

I.S.: I wish they were effective challenges. I had hoped my *Mass* would be used liturgically, but I have no such aspiration for the *Threni*, which is why I call it, not *Tenebrae Service* but *Lamentations*. Whether or not the Church was the wisest patron—though I think it was; we commit fewer musical sins in Church—it was rich in musical forms. How much poorer we are without the sacred musical services, without the Masses, the Passions, the round-the-calendar cantatas of the Protestants, the motets and sacred concerts, and vespers and so many others. These are not merely defunct forms but parts of the musical spirit in disuse.

The Church knew what the psalmist knew; music praises God. Music is as well or better able to praise Him than the building of the church and all its decoration; it is the Church's greatest ornament. Glory, glory, glory; the music of Orlando Lasso's motet praises God, and this particular "glory" does not exist in secular music. And not only glory—though I think of it first because the glory of the Laudate, the joy of the Doxology, are all but extinct—but prayer and penitence and many others cannot be secularized. The spirit disappears with the form. I am not comparing "emotional range" or "variety" in sacred and secular music. The music of the nineteenth and twentieth centuries—it is all secular—is "expressively" and "emotionally" beyond anything in the music of the earlier centuries: the *Angst* in *Lulu*, for instance—gory, gory, gory—or the tension, the perpetuation of the moment of epitasis, in Schoenberg's music. I say simply that, without the Church, "left to our own devices," we are poorer by many musical forms. . . .

R.C.: Must one be a believer to compose in these forms?

I.S.: Certainly, and not merely a believer in "symbolic figures," but in the Person of the Lord, the Person of the Devil, and the Miracles of the Church. [*Conversations with Stravinsky*, pp. 141–42.]

Bleak and stern, without cheer and very nearly without "play" (without "compromise" as some would have it), *Canticum Sacrum* is of a world far removed from the sophisticated dazzle, the sheer secular exuberance of *Agon*. A few clues do suggest its position sandwiched between the nonserial beginnings and the serial completion of the ballet. The B♭–D♭ reiteration in the bass pattern of the first movement, joined by a D–B span and occasional (G B D) triad in the chorus and brass at mm. 10–16, brings *Agon*'s Prelude to mind (especially the timpani and sustained (G B D) triad; see, in Example 79, mm. 264–67 of the Interlude); while the rapid, sixteenth-note motion of the brass recalls some of the trumpeting of *Agon*'s opening three sections. And there is unmistakably a touch of the Stravinskian dance in the first movement, if only by virtue of a fiendishly tricky dotted quarter-note at mm. 10, 12, and 41: although placed off the beat, this dotted quarter is more readily heard and understood on the beat, with succeeding measures encumbered by an uncertain (concealed) off-the-beat stagger, as if by some inadvertence (the dots) the entire block had been misconceived, scarred by a horrendous oversight. But the overwhelming impression of the work as a whole is one of distance, of a widening gap separating secular from sacred interests, or purely instrumental from vocal-instrumental invention.

This gravity in mood has ultimately to do with belief, and belief evidently profoundly institutional in spirit. Stressed above all is the issue of faith and the trials of the fallen, themes which would also find subsequent expression in a host of biblical and liturgical texts, the lamentations of Jeremiah, the stoning of Stephen, the saga of Noah, the sacrifice of Abraham. The *Symphony of Psalms* and the *Mass* may be cited as forerunners. But the general climate is nonetheless increasingly characteristic of the serial period. *Agon* would be followed by *Movements* (1959) and the *Variations* for orchestra (1964). But *Canticum* would host a more plentiful lot: *Threni, Id Est Lamentationes Jeremiae Prophetae* (1958) during the early stage; *A Sermon, a Narrative, and a Prayer* (1961), *The Flood* (1962), *Abraham and Isaac* (1963), *Introitus* (1965), and the *Requiem Canticles* (1966) among the latest of the late.

Commissioned by the Venice Biennial Festival of Contemporary Music, *Canticum* is dedicated to Venice and its Patron Saint "the Blessed Mark, Apostle": *Canticum Sacrum ad Honorem Sancti Marci Nominis*. The premiere was in fact held at St. Mark's (13 September 1955), a circumstance which is now widely felt to have influenced features of the score. The five domes of the cathedral may have inspired the five movements, with the lengthy middle movement in three parts symbolic of the cathedral's central dome.

And according to Craft, the cathedral's "anti-Stravinskian" acoustics prompted the composer to follow the example of his Renaissance predecessors in interrupting busy *forte* passages with pauses of rest, allowing for a general sound-dispersal.[18] (On the other hand, given the rigid "block" structure of the opening movement, the abruptness in juxtaposition between the massive tutti block and the quiet interlude for organ and bassoons, the need for these interruptions could not have hampered the composer unduly. See, in this connection, the low bass tone sustained during these pauses (a B♭ in the bassoons at mm. 16 and 31), which, as Craft suggests, assists in absorbing the murky aftereffect.) Then, too, following tradition, an organ is included in the ensemble, a most un-Stravinskian instrument, but fulfilling a structural role in the first movement which is nonetheless a characteristic one. The orchestra is quasi-Venetian, with its four trumpets (including bass trumpet), four trombones (including bass and contrabass), and its scattering of oboes and bassoons. There are no violins or cellos, only violas and double basses.

The first and last movements are nonserial. They are true flanking movements, and bound as such in a most unusual fashion: the last is a nearly literal retrograde of the first. This may not be immediately discernible, the listener merely sensing in the final movement something of a continuation and conclusion. (Pointing to the "mechanical ugliness" of retrograde rhythms in general, Craft finds the invention of "rhythms that work so fluently both ways" a notable achievement. However, the awkwardness of such "rhythms" (or of the literal retrograde as a whole) may very well be a part of their peculiar fascination. When they are combined with a sense of intimacy, logic, and purpose, there is evident method—or magic—in the "mechanical ugliness.")[19] And as might be expected, it is in these nonserial boundary movements that the Stravinsky of the past, of whatever "stylistic" persuasion, is most readily apparent.

Two blocks are placed in abrupt juxtaposition, yielding an overall A B A B A structure. The first of these is densely scored for full orchestra and chorus, the second merely for organ with bassoons doubling the bass line—a juxtaposition reinforced by changes in tempo and in dynamic and rhythmic-metric design. The referential implications of the scheme are of special note: the initial tutti block is octatonic-diatonic in conception (Collection I interacting with the D-scale and/or A-scale on D), while the organ block is wholly diatonic, implicating the D-scale on D and then on G. (See Example 84. The octatonic Collection I contribution is conspicuous in the opening statement of the tutti block at mm. 10–16. In subsequent near repeats of this block at mm. 26–31 and 41–45, the diatonic side prevails, with these repeats becoming less "near" than is generally the case with such incisive applications of abrupt block juxtaposition.) Moreover the

Example 84

deployment of Collection I is routine. Spaced between the soprano's D and the low B♭ is the (B♭ B D) "minor-major third" unit, which here assumes the role of a "home-base" sonority, owing primarily to the stressed D–B♭–(B D) succession of the chorus, which is in turn verticalized as simultaneity in the sixteenth-note brass figuration (a typical neoclassical "minor-major third" clash, in other words), and then used as such by the organ. Collection I's triads at E, G, and B♭ are in evidence: superimposed at mm. 10–12, an E–G♯–B outline in the second trumpet; a D–B♭–G outline in the third trumpet; G–B–D in the bass trumpet, and then B♭–F–F in the trombones. Of these triads, too, (G B D) or (G B♭ D/G B D) appears to take precedence: the B♭–G–B♭ unit of the bass pattern; the (G B♭ D/G B D) triadic complex on the second and fourth quarter-note beats at mm. 11

Example 84 *continued*

and 12 respectively (with an added F in the trombones, however); and the pronounced exposure of (G B D) in the chorus at mm. 10–16. (G would thus serve as root of presiding (G B♭ D/G B D) triads. The centric (B♭ B D) "minor-major third" unit is in turn complemented by (G B♭ B), yielding the typical neoclassical (0 3 4/3 4 7) grouping, here in terms of (G B♭ B/B♭ B D).)

Still, difficulties arise in assessing priority beyond the (B♭ B D) "home-base" unit. For in contradiction to the common neoclassical condition where a centric (0 3 7/0 4 7) "tonic" triad is encircled by its (0 3 4/3 4 7/3 6 7) "minor-major thirds," the true constancy in "Euntes in Mundum" is the (B♭ B D) "minor-major third" unit itself, in relation to which the triads assume an encircling role. Indeed, Collection I's (E G♯ B) (G B♭ D/G B D) (B♭ D F) triads are obscured by the tightness of the superimposition, and by the irregular shifting of the (G B♭ D♭) bass pattern; and it is G's *absence* from (B♭ B D) that is of consequence, overshadowing, as it were, its occasional and elusive articulation as root of the presiding (G B♭ D/G B D) triads. (G, then, is scarcely the—or possibly even a—pitch class of priority.) And so the (B♭ B D) unit is thrust to the foreground, with its triadic affiliation(s) obscured, and this massive block may be counted among those special circumstances where the implications of that incomplete triad so prevalent in neoclassical works, (D B D) in relation to (G B D) here, with the root missing and the "fifth" doubled, are fully brought to bear.

Other complications follow. For as indicated, G, as root of the presiding (G B♭ D/G B D) triads, is not the pitch class of priority. Rather, of the three pitches of the (B♭ B D) unit, D seems the most likely candidate for priority status. This is principally because of the diatonic side of the interaction (in the chorus particularly), where D, often doubled, is repeatedly stressed as the point of departure and return. (B♭ is also in contention here, although perhaps on a secondary level, owing to the B♭/B ambiguity in relation to the (G B♭ D/G B D) triads.) But as the principal point of octatonic (Collection I) and diatonic intersection, D, unlike G or B♭, is not among Collection I's (G B♭ D♭ E) symmetrically defined partitioning elements. Consequently, while the articulation of Collection I is routine (Model A), the interaction itself is from the neoclassical standpoint unusual: on the diatonic side not only might the D-scale on D be inferred (as much as, say, the neoclassical A-scale on D, with B♭ intersecting as the "flatted sixth degree"), but the D priority refers not to Collection I as a (0,3,6,9) octatonic partitioning element but to Collection II. (This may be in fact the origin of the (B D F♯) triad, whose superimposition over (B♭ D) yields the (B♭ D F♯) "augmented triad," which is not among the triadic superimpositions especially characteristic of Stravinsky. See the context at Nos. 166–70 in *Oedipus*, Example 63 in chapter 10, where the (0 3 7/0 4 7) triads and (0 3 4/3 4 7) "minor-major third" units which interact with the diatonic D-scale on D and its presiding (D F A) triad refer not to Collection I but to Collection II.) Moreover, as an added complication, the (G B♭ D♭) bass pattern includes a D♭. And D♭, in conjunction with (B♭ B D), yields a cohesive Collection I (B♭ B D♭ D) tetrachordal articulation. And it is precisely this (B♭ B D♭ D) tetrachord which, with the (B♭ D♭)/D–B registral spacing here between the bass line, organ, brass, and chorus very nearly intact, figures so prominently in *Agon's* Prelude (along with subsequent near repeats as Interlude); and which, following the completion of *Canticum*, would serve as the principal serial unit of *Agon's* "Bransle double" and Adagio section of the "Pas de deux" (again with *Canticum's* registral spacing very nearly intact). (Compare the (B♭ D♭)/D–B spacing of this (B♭ B D♭ D) tetrachord in *Canticum* with that at m. 264 in the Interlude (Example 79); at m. 314 in the "Bransle gay" (Example 81); or at mm. 411–13 in the string Adagio (Example 83a). With (B♭ B D♭ D) as a constancy, these correspondences

highlight not only the similarities between these contexts but also the sub-
tler distinctions that may be drawn in pitch organization generally.[20])

Finally, the opening tutti block is composed of four principal superimpositions: reading from top to bottom, the chorus, the brass, the organ
(punctuating the centric (B♭ B D) unit of the chorus and brass), and the (G
B♭ D♭) bass pattern. Given the steady 6/4 meter, the second of our two
rhythmic-metric types seems indicated. Thus, successive entrances of the
chorus, marked by pauses and sustained Ds at mm. 10–16, define irregularly spaced intervals of 8, 11½, and 18 quarter-note beats, intervals with
which the brass layer is in bulk synchronized. (Chorus and brass move together, in other words, en masse.) But there are complications here as
well. For while each of the four superimpositions assumes a fixed registral, instrumental, and—to an extent—rhythmic character (the fixed, lay-
ered structure so typical of settings conforming to either one of the two
rhythmic-metric types), the repetition is modified extensively in content
and when not in content, then, to a degree, rhythmically.

For example, while the sixteenth-note brass figuration is distinguished
by the reiterating (B♭ B D) unit and the (B♭ B D)–(D F♯ B) succession at
pauses or sustained Ds of the chorus, the repetition of this layer is far from
exact at mm. 10–16, and even less so at near repeats of the tutti block at
mm. 26–31 and 41–45. And while the bass pattern confines itself merely
to G, B♭, and D♭ (and to a pace not exceeding the quarter-note beat), it is
not an ostinato, and, apart from the first three measures, exhibits no cohesive grouping in relation to which successive entrances or rhythmic-
metric periods are defined. Only the punctuating (B♭ B D) simultaneity of
the organ, omitted at subsequent near repeats of the block, exhibits the
familiar stability. With successive entrances at mm. 11, 13, and 15 defining
an irregular spacing of 11½, 12, and 9½ quarter-note beats, some of the
familiar "play" might even be inferred: introduced on the beat at m. 11 (in
accord with Stravinsky's steady 6/4 periodicity), the simultaneity assumes,
in contradiction or reversal, an off-the-beat identity at m. 13.

But the "play" of the tutti block, its Stravinskian dancelike substance,
derives more readily from the dotted quarter-note beats at mm. 10 and
12. And while the means of this "play" vary, the effect is not unlike that
found in earlier contexts. An illustration of this is the opening passage of
Renard, Example 51b in chapter 8. Here the point of the irregular 5/8
measure (within an established 2/4 framework) seemed to reside not with
the irregular 5/8 "phrasing" as such, but rather with the implications of
this irregularity with respect to the clarinet entrance just ahead at No. 1:
placed on the beat, this entrance assumed, by virtue of the extra eighth-
note beat two measures earlier, an off-the-beat quality. (The extra eighth-
note beat is not subsequently resolved or "cancelled." The off-the-beat/
on-the-beat doubt lingers for a time.) The same is true of the dotted

quarter-note beats of *Canticum*'s opening tutti block. For while the dotted attacks at m. 10 are introduced off the beat, they are as such unprepared—without context, so to speak. Hence the implied off-the-beat "syncopation" will not at first rest with these dotted quarters (which more readily assume an on-the-beat character), but with what follows immediately of the massive tutti entrance at mm. 11–12. Barred on the beat, the massive quarter-note motion of this entrance will take on a fierce, disjointed off-the-beat quality, in turn reinforced by an additional dotted quarter at m. 12. Indeed, as on-the-beats (in contradiction to Stravinsky's barring), the dotted quarters at mm. 10 and 12 conspicuously suggest a steady 4/4 periodicity. (See the brackets in Example 84, which, along with the dotted lines, mark off this concealed, "background" 4/4 meter. And notice how readily the irregularly spaced entrances of the chorus and brass underscore, at least initially, this 4/4 alternative.) Thus, too, the organ's punctuating (B♭ B D) simultaneity, introduced on the beat at m. 11, may actually assume an off-the-beat identity, subsequently contradicted or reversed by an on-the-beat appearance at m. 13—the opposite, in other words, of what Stravinsky's barring suggests.

And as in the opening passage of *Renard*, the doubt or uncertainty in rhythmic-metric intent is not subsequently resolved or "cancelled." It lingers for a time, quite possibly up to the entrance of the organ interlude at m. 17.[21]

Canticum's second movement, "Surge, Aquilo" for tenor, flute, english horn, harp, and three double basses, is Stravinsky's first completely twelve-tone movement (or piece, inasmuch as the third and fourth movements are derived from a different set). But the set of "Surge, Aquilo" is quite unlike the non-twelve-tone conceptions examined earlier in *In Memoriam* and the serial miniatures of *Agon*, where the symmetrically linked (0 1 3 4) tetrachords and (0 3 4/3 4 7) "minor-major third" units seemed so reflective of an articulative past and Stravinsky's early studies of Webern. Indeed, while the lyricism is at times graphically Webernesque (suggestive of that refined, intervallic typicality), the reiterating 1s and 2s (half and whole steps) are obviously unlike Webern, and lend the piece an ornate, almost Baroque quality (or Stravinsky-Baroque, *à la Symphony of Psalms*, second movement); indeed, it is "Italianate," as one composer-critic has commented, just where Webern, in contrast, is "almost puritanically non-ornate."[22]

On the other hand, features of set manipulation are in accord with premises outlined in this chapter. The set is approached linearly, with vertical coincidence a function of the superimposition of separate set-forms (which, keeping to their respective paths, unfold in an almost conventional part-writing fashion);[23] the untransposed forms of the four orders acquire an advantage, there being, of the twenty-three complete set-statements (excluding eight independent hexachordal delineations), fourteen which refer to P, R, I, and RI, and eleven of these latter to P and R; the tenor's initial P-statement at mm. 47–49 is followed by R at mm. 52–55 (with, however, R (1–6) and RI-8 (1–6) sandwiched between them), thus conforming to the habitual doubling back on such initial set-presentations; and the hexachordal bar is of consequence, with, for example, R (1–6) and RI-8 (1–6) deployed independent of twelve-tone complementation (i.e., independently of R (7–12) and RI-8 (7–12)).

In the unfolding of the privileged, untransposed P, R, I, and RI forms, initial and concluding set-factors acquire stress. This is especially true of A♭ and A, since, of the four untransposed orders, P and R predominate. (See Example 85a. Apart from the untransposed variants, only those forms actually engaged are given.) But by far the most exposed of these boundary set-factors are E♭ and A, with E♭ initiating or concluding the P (7–12) and R (1–6) hexachords. This exposure of E♭ and A (along with the tritone they define) is owing in part to their role as embellished points of departure and return (the E♭–D♭ reiteration in the tenor at mm. 48–49, 51, and 53–54, for example); in part to the preponderance, in the tenor,

Example 85a

of hexachords flanked by E♭ and A; and in part to the use of R (1–6) and RI–8 (1–6) as independently deployed hexachords, both of which are framed by E♭ and A as initiating/concluding set-factors. (Only the R (1–6) and RI–8 (1–6) hexachords are treated independent of twelve-tone complementation. As shown in Example 85a, the E♭–A (or A–E♭) hexachords are P(7–12), R (1–6), I–2 (7–12), RI–2 (1–6), I–8 (7–12), and RI–8 (1–6). P–6 (7–12) and R–6 (1–6) are naturally also E♭–A hexachords (being transpositions at the tritone), but are ignored.) Accordingly, all E♭–A (or A–E♭) hexachords, whether treated independently or not, are of special significance in "Surge, Aquilo," and the E♭–A relationship as a hexachordal boundary unit inevitably assumes a decisive role in set-form relations with respect to both linear succession and the vertical aspect.[24]

The opening measures both introduce and underscore this highly privileged E♭–A condition: joining the tenor's E♭–D♭ whole-step ornamentation at mm. 48–49, RI–2 is introduced in the English horn. (See Example 85b.) RI–2's first two set-factors, A and G, are in tritone imitation of the E♭–D♭ unit. Moreover, since both P (7–12) and RI–2 (1–6) are E♭–A hexachords, relations are governed not only by this immediate (E♭–D♭) (A–G) tritone imitation, but by the E♭–A hexachordal bond as well. (Pointing to a similar back-and-forth configuration in the *Elegy to J.F.K.* (1964), Stravinsky would later make reference to this whole-step "stutter" as "a lifelong affliction," evident from *Les Noces* to the string *Concerto in D*. These remarks will seem especially apropos in connection with a prolonged D♯–C♯ reiteration in the Te Deum music of *The Flood*, to be discussed in chapter 14. But the horn's A–G tritone imitation of the tenor's E♭–D♭ motion is symptomatic, far more tellingly, of relations fundamental to octatonic thought of the "Russian" period, suggesting in this respect a host of contexts examined earlier. See, especially, the first of the *Three Pieces for String Quartet*, chapter 5, along with the supplementary Examples 32a, b, and c.)

In fact, the octatonic implications of the set are equally critical to the issue of set-form selection, or to vertical coincidence (or "harmony") as a function of superimposed set-forms. For while, as we have indicated, the set is without obvious (0 1 3 4) or "minor-major third" linkages, there are (0 2 3 5) tetrachords: the interrupted (G F E D) unit of P (1–6), and the (E♭ D♭ C B♭) unit of P (7–12). Furthermore, straddling the hexachord bar is an uninterrupted octatonic Collection III succession of six factors, beginning with P's fifth member: F♯–E–E♭–D♭–B♭–C. (See the brackets applied to the various set-forms in Examples 85a and b. P's concluding A would naturally extend this Collection III span to a succession of seven pitches, with the B excluded.) And since P's first four factors in terms of A♭–G–F–D refer to Collection I, a Collection-I–Collection-III bond may in addition be inferred. Indeed, the E♭–D♭ reiterations and manifold

Example 85b

Eb–A hexachords of the tenor are usually associated with set-forms which
duplicate and/or extend Collection III implications; while the D–F–G–Ab
succession at the conclusion of R is often accompanied by segments of set-
forms which are in turn suggestive of Collection I. In this fashion a

Example 85b *continued*

Stravinskian sheen, a symmetrically cohesive "harmonic" character, is at
times conspicuously brought to the fore.

Thus, to begin with, the passage at mm. 50–52. The tenor's initial P-
statement is here succeeded by the E♭–A hexachords R (1–6) and RI–8
(1–6), with E♭ and E♭–D♭ embellished at midpoint as the common, overlapping initiating/concluding set-factors. And as an accompaniment in
the flute, R–3, with a Collection III succession of C–(D)–E♭–D♭–E–F♯–
G–A, is introduced in scalelike formation. The resultant "feel" here of a
symmetrically cohesive octatonic pocket, Collection III, is unmistakable.
Significant, too, are R–3's concluding factors, G and A, which are once
again in tritone imitation of the tenor's E♭–D♭ reiteration, and are briefly
retained and embellished as such in the flute at mm. 51–52.

With respect to P's and R's Collection I affiliation, the passages at mm. 55–56 and 71–75 are unequivocal. In both instances, R, with its concluding D–F–G–Ab Collection I succession, is brought to a close in the tenor, and in both the embellished G–Ab close is accompanied by set-forms whose first four members intensify the Collection I effect. At mm. 55–56, I–11 in the english horn seems favored owing not only to its G–Ab overlap with R's G–Ab close, but to its initial G–Ab–Bb–Db Collection I segment as well; while at m. 73, I–2 in the flute is similarly favored, with R's D–F–G–Ab Collection I segment extended in uninterrupted fashion to D–F–G–Ab–Bb–B–Db–E (Collection I fully accounted for). At m. 72, the (E F G) simultaneity, composed of I's concluding three factors, also refers to Collection I. The "vertical serialism" at mm. 69–71, referring at first to RI and then to I, is remarkably sympathetic to these overtones, the punctuating (C C♯ Eb F♯) units referring to Collection III, the (E F G) unit to Collection I.

And so it would seem that, quite apart from the question of a serial order, of privileged, untransposed set-forms, of Eb–A hexachords and stressed initiating/concluding set-factors, an octatonic sensitivity is here made manifest through the Eb–A relationship and segments of six and four factors within the set itself, particularly at terminating points of the privileged orders (twelve-tone or hexachordal), which are in turn often marked off by half-step or whole-step embellishment in the tenor.

As a final illustration, we turn briefly to the context at mm. 58–61. Here, the Eb–A tritone is formed more intricately by the joining, at the hexachordal bar, of I–8 in the tenor and RI–2 in the flute. But Eb–A is in turn joined by D–Ab. This means that, octatonically, Eb–A will refer not to Collection III (as the set's untransposed orders readily suggest), but to Collection II. And as is abundantly clear, the six-factor octatonic successions of both I–8 and RI–2 confirm this orientation. Especially conspicuous is the Collection II Gb–Ab–A–B–D–C succession of the tenor, where the embedded (A B C D) tetrachord is modestly cohesive, set apart slightly by the triplets at m. 61.[25]

FOURTEEN
THE SERIAL PERIOD (II)

I *have* discovered new (to me) serial combinations in the *Movements for Piano and Orchestra* [1959], however, (and I have discovered in the process, too, that I am becoming not less but more of a serial composer; those younger colleagues who already regard "serial" as an indecent word, in their claim to have exhausted all that is meant by it and to have gone far beyond, are, I think, greatly in error), and the *Movements* are the most advanced music from the point of view of construction of anything I have composed. No theorist could determine the spelling of the note order in, for example, the flute solo near the beginning, or the derivation of the three Fs announcing the last movement simply by knowing the original order, no matter how unique the combinatorial properties of this particular series. Every aspect of the composition was guided by serial forms, the sixes, quadrilaterals, triangles, etc. . . . The fifth movement, for instance (which I had to rewrite twice), uses a construction of twelve verticals. The *gamma* and *delta* hexachords in this movement are more important than the A and B, too. Five orders are rotated instead of four, with six alternates for each of the five, while, at the same time, the six work in all directions, as though through a crystal.

Now that I have mentioned my new work, I should add that its rhythmic language is also the most advanced I have so far employed; perhaps some listeners might even detect a hint of serialism in this too. *My* polyrhythmic combinations are meant to be heard vertically, however, unlike those of some of my younger colleagues. . . .

Each section of the piece is confined to a certain range of instrumental timbre (another suggestion of serialism?), but the five movements are related more by tempo than by contrasts of such things as timbre, "mood," "character"; in a span of only twelve minutes, the contrast of an *andante* with an *allegro* would make little sense; construction must replace contrast. Perhaps the most significant development in the *Movements*, however, is the tendency toward anti-tonality—in spite of long pedal point passages such as the clarinet trill at the end of the third movement, and the sustained string harmonics in the fourth movement. I am amazed at this myself, in view of the fact that in *Threni* [1958] simple triadic references occur in every bar. [*Memories and Commentaries*, pp. 100–01.]

I began the *Epitaphium* [1959] with the flute-clarinet duet (which I had originally thought of as a duet for two flutes and which can be played by two flutes;

the piece was written to be performed in a program with Webern's songs, op. 15, which use the flute-clarinet combination). In the manner I have described in our previous conversations, I heard and composed a melodic-harmonic phrase. I certainly did not (and never do) begin with a purely serial idea, and, in fact, when I began I did not know, or care, whether all twelve notes would be used. After I had written about half the first phrase I saw its serial pattern, however, and then perhaps I began to work toward that pattern. . . .

Only after I had written this little twelve-note duet did I conceive the idea of a series of funeral responses between bass and treble instruments, and, as I wanted the whole piece to be very muffled, I decided that the bass instrument should be a harp. . . . There are four short antiphonal strophes for the harp, and four for the wind duet, and each strophe is a complete order of the series—harp: O, I, R, RI; winds: 0, RI, R, I. [*Memories and Commentaries*, p. 99–100.]

[Apropos *Orpheus*, 1947.] But how different are my time scales, today and in 1947! I could never compose such a motionless measure now as the one before number [4]; or allow the flutes and clarinets to run on at such dilatory length at [100], or the strings, *ditto*, in the measure after [98]. . . . And the time scale is the vital question. It must work for every age. Miscalculation is death. [*Themes and Episodes*, p. 46.]

And isn't the fugal exposition in the second movement of the *Symphony of Psalms* altogether too obvious, too regular, and too long? [*Expositions and Developments*, p. 124.]

But what are we to make of the latest of the late? A period which begins with *Movements* for piano and orchestra (1959)—"the cornerstone of my later work," as Stravinsky called it—and stretches through *A Sermon, a Narrative and a Prayer* (1961), *The Flood* (1962), *Abraham and Isaac* (1963), the *Variations* for orchestra (1964), and the *Requiem Canticles* (1966), including as well seven miniatures or pieces of short duration—*Epitaphium* (1959), *Double Canon* (1959), *Anthem: The Dove Descending* (1962), *Elegy for J.F.K.* (1964), *Fanfare for a New Theater* (1964), *Introitus* (1965), and *The Owl and the Pussycat* (1966)? When, with few exceptions, there is so little of the articulative routine and its referential foundations, and so little of the element of repetition (with its embedded rhythmic-metric "play") on which so much of the identity and distinction of Stravinsky's music has seemed to hinge? When it is the serial process itself—with its presumed "total chromatic"—that gains in intensity ("I have discovered . . . that I am becoming not less but more of a serial composer"), and, pursued in conjunction with a uniquely devised scheme of independent hexachordal transposition-rotation ("I have discovered new (to me) serial combinations"), yields a species of pitch/interval order ever more pressing to the musical imagination? And when, in coincidence with these developments, new "polyrhythmic combinations" emerge, fives and sevens which, metrically mobile, supplement the threes (triplets) which had characterized the "polyrhythm" of the earlier stage? And in further coincidence a radically new sense of musical timing which, first acknowledged on behalf of *Agon*, now attains a level of unprecedented compression and thrift? (All this, we should add, when Stravinsky was in his seventies, even an octogenarian at the time of the *Variations, Introitus,* and *Requiem Canticles*. And although reassured by Stravinsky about the nature of "historical unities"—that with the passing of time either/or partisanships yield to categories of semblance—we cannot but gasp at the enormity of the gulf that separates—in less than one decade—the neoclassical *Rake's Progress* from *Movements*.) What are we to make of it?

The threads are fewer and farther between, intimations of the past increasingly rare (and then fleeting), with all former inclinations, predispositions, preoccupations, and routines either obscured beyond meaningful apprehension or—in the face of all that is indeed quite "new"—reduced to seeming irrelevance. There are exceptions, of course, perhaps most notably in formal layout: excluding *Abraham and Isaac* (whose seams are blurred by a music very nearly continuous throughout), block juxtaposition is prominent in all of Stravinsky's late work, a permanent and evidently indispensable part of his musical thought (of whatever orientation or "stylistic" persuasion). Such structure is evident, for example, in the fourth movement of *Movements*, spectacularly so in the *Variations* and again in the *Introitus* and certain sections of the *Requiem Canticles*. In the *Variations* (which, incidentally, bear not the slightest resemblance to anything this title might conventionally connote, there being, among other notable discrepancies, no "theme" upon whose melodic, rhythmic-metric, or harmonic character subsequent "variations" may be observed to depend), the opening section has as its near repeat or varied recapitulation the twelfth and final "variation," although recognizable as such chiefly on rhythmic grounds; while in the seventh section or "variation" at mm. 73–85, three blocks with successive near repeats are placed in rigid juxtaposition, the first of these consisting of two verticals scored *forte* and then *piano* for harp and strings and then for oboes, horns, and piano (framed within a 4/8 measure), the second of a counterpoint scored *piano* for three trombones, and the third of a single measure of silence (a 2/8 measure on each occasion). (The construction in this "variation" is therefore incontestably Stravinskian, in accord with the first of our two rhythmic-metric types, a rapid block development in fact, with a delicate balancing in degrees of fixity, the first block mechanically confined to one 4/8 measure, the second extended a bit upon its successive near repeat. But it is the extreme brevity in application that bespeaks the new economy, the new condensed sense of musical pace.) And the remarkable block or "variation" of "twelve-part polyphony" at m. 23 (with which Stravinsky expressed such satisfaction at the time of its first hearing, it sounding, in his words, "like a sprinkling of very fine broken glass"), unfolds with near repeats at mm. 47 and 118, the fifth and eleventh "variations": the separate rhythmic identities of the twelve "parts," along with a fixed tempo, dynamic level, and metric scheme, remain intact (being sufficient to guarantee recognition as near repeats), while the instrumentation and serial ordering are altered, and the vertical alignment of the "parts" reshuffled. (The "isorhythm" that may be inferred in these reshuffled rhythmic identities upon successive near repeats at mm. 47 and 118 has a conspicuous precedent in the fourth movement of *Movements*, where the piano block, roving through a succession of untransposed set-forms, similarly retains its identity by means of a fixed rhythmic guise. But the origin of this much discussed technique is in all probability neither the ancient variety of isorhythm nor the contemporary—isorhythm being, after all, as "old," in modern terms, as serialism itself (if one examines the works of Schoenberg with not too strict an interpretation). It seems to have sprung more readily from the canonic invention (rhythmic and intervallic, applied to superimposed set-forms) prevalent at the very outset of Stravinsky's serialism, and which seems always to have been closely identified with the serial mentality itself.) The "Dies irae," Interlude, "Rex tremendae," and "Lacrimosa" sections of the *Requiem Canticles* are among Stravinsky's most eloquent expositions of this by now well-documented "architectural curiosity."

Before entering into greater detail we may wish, as before, to confront certain assumptions underlying set usage:

1. Complete, ordered twelve-tone sets invariably appear in their untransposed forms. A few exceptions may be noted: the brief *Double Canon*, where the P, R, and IR forms are transposed once; or the 12/4 measure at mm. 6, 179, 496, and 582 in *The Flood*, where the "Jacob's Ladder" music (as Stravinsky dubbed it) is entrusted with transpositions of P and R (P–5 and R–5). These transpositions, however, remain confined to this single 12/4 measure and its subsequent near repeats.

2. To the four standard, untransposed P, R, I, and RI serial orders a "fifth order" is now added (to which Stravinsky makes reference in his remarks regarding *Movements*), *the inversion of the retrograde*, or IR form. (See the selection of sets in Example 86.) While this inverted retrograde or IR form is inevitably a transposition of RI (in *Movements*, for example, RI–4), it seems preferable to make a distinction in signification at this point by including it among the now *five* untransposed orders, if only because it figures so much more persistently than the traditional untransposed RI arrangement. In pieces like the *Epitaphium, Double Canon, Anthem,* and *Introitus*, RI is ignored altogether; while in *Movements, The Flood, Abraham and Isaac,* and the *Variations*, its role is exceedingly limited, with IR the very heavy favorite. (See, for example, the fourth movement of *Move-*

Example 86

ments, along with its introductory prelude at m. 92; or mm. 40–45 in the first movement. Among the manifold complete set-statements in *The Flood*, RI appears only once: in the second of the voices of God at m. 190.) Some confusion may result from Stravinsky's own inconsistencies, however. Referring to the *Epitaphium*, he lists the untransposed RI form—which in reality is the untransposed IR; while in the labeling of his serial charts, IR is frequently labeled RI.

3. Conventional operations of set-transposition are replaced by an independent hexachordal transposition-rotation scheme, applied systematically to all five orders. This mechanism is ignored in the seven miniatures or works of small dimension (which are confined, with the exception of the *Double Canon*, to the untransposed forms). But it appears with increasing frequency in all the larger works, reaching its most intricate and extensive elaboration in *Abraham and Isaac* and the *Requiem Canticles*. With the serial charts for *The Flood* and *Abraham and Isaac* as a point of reference (see Examples 89 and 92), the mechanics of this uniquely designed rotation-scramble are as follows: being hexachordally independent in conception, the scheme generates, for each half or hexachordal division of the five untransposed orders, five rotations (or "six alternates" as Stravinsky calls them, if the initial untransposed unit is included). And since, in each of the resultant hexachordal groups, the scheme is triggered by a common set-factor, rotation proceeds *by way of interval order alone* (in the manner indicated by the diagonal lines as applied to the Pa hexachords for *The Flood* and *Abraham and Isaac* in Examples 89 and 92). The first rotation begins with the second interval of the original untransposed hexachord, and completes its cycle upon reaching the original's first interval; the second rotation then begins with the original's third interval, completing its cycle with the original's second interval; and so forth. Of paramount concern, obviously, are the pitch-duplications of the initiating set-factors. For while, in the application of this scheme, rotations may frequently be found scattered about, there is a noticeable tendency to group them according to hexachordal group-affiliation; and hence with little regard for their "complements" on the other side of the hexachordal bar. (The term "alternates" is therefore a trifle misleading, since the rotations are more readily found in group formation than as isolated, alternative representatives of hexachordal rotation groups in the formation of a systematic, interhexachordal design. Such interhexachordal designs exist, of course, but they involve hexachordal *groups* more often than isolated individuals.) The delineation of these hexachordal rotations may be unpatterned (without regard to systematic ordering), or, more characteristically, patterned in one of two ways: either the music proceeds up or down a hexachordal ladder, reading from right to left or from left to right (or, less systematically, through a combination of these readings); or it proceeds up or down a hexachordal ladder by means of a spiral or zigzag course, alternating with each successive rotation between a right-to-left and a left-to-right reading. (See the charts of passages in *The Flood* and *Abraham and Isaac*, Examples 91 and 94.) Finally, the scheme harbors a special preserve for simultaneity or verticalization. Read from top to bottom, the six six-factor vertical alignments of each hexachordal group (with the first of these "verticals" constituting the single, shared initiating

set-factor) are a source of chord formation. These vertical alignments are called "serial verticals" by Stravinsky, and invariably occur as simultaneities or "chords" in the strictest sense of "simultaneous attack-durations," invariably patterned in group formation from "vertical" 1 to 6 or the reverse. (See, again from *The Flood* and *Abraham and Isaac*, Examples 90, 95, and 96.)

4. The serial apparatus of the orchestral *Variations* is an exception to the hexachordal transposition-rotation scheme. Here, rotation is applied to the untransposed forms of the complete twelve-tone set. But the system of rotation remains the same. Under each order-heading there are five rotations (but of five complete twelve-tone sets, not two distinct groups of five hexachords); and the patterns referred to earlier with respect to hexachordal rotation are also applied to these twelve-tone rotation groups. (See Examples 97 and 98.)

All the same, in spite of a serial artistry as deliberate and determined as this (and quite apart from renewed applications of abrupt block juxtaposition), we need not divest ourselves altogether of the hearing and understanding achieved in regard to Stravinsky's earlier music. Scanning the sampling of sets in Example 86, we find inheritances that are striking and, to a remarkable degree, reliable. In the terse little *Epitaphium* for flute, clarinet, and harp (an extraordinarily compressed seven measures of music in honor of Prince Max Egon zu Fürstenberg, patron of the Donaueschingen Festival), octatonic implications abound: in the set's Prime, a succession of five octatonic pitch elements (Collection III) is followed, with an overlapping C, by a Collection II C–B–F♯–F–D–(G)–G♯–A pitch succession (as bracketed). (Following publication of the *Epitaphium*, the composer was repeatedly advised of the identity in interval content between this set's initial hexachord and the six-note ostinato pattern of *The Firebird*'s Introduction.[1] Stravinsky's remarks, as recorded above, fail to suggest direct or conscious borrowing. But since he had toiled for nearly half a century under the referential cloak implicated by this material, neither can the circumstance of this identity be dismissed as wholly coincidental.) These octatonic successions appear to have influenced the handling of the series significantly, even with the set confined to the compass of four untransposed orders (without benefit, that is, of transpositions which might have intensified the effect): P, R, I, and IR (IR in place of RI). For as in previous works, pockets of octatonic concentration are unmistakable; and the *Epitaphium* is perhaps in just this respect not significantly hexachordal in conception, its seams being more reflective of these alluded-to successions of five and seven set-factors. (See Example 87.) In m. 3, the first five set-factors of I (Collection I) are separated from the remaining seven by an eighth-note rest; while in the concluding seventh

Example 87: *Epitaphium*

measure, IR's first seven set-factors (Collection III, except for the B) are in like fashion separated from its remaining five, which form a Collection II concluding simultaneity in the harp. Most incriminating, however, is the passage over the barline at mm. 4–5 (boxed-off and bracketed in Example 87). Here, IR in the second flute-clarinet "strophe" is followed by R in the third harp "strophe"; this occasions, with pitch duplications of D, F, F♯, and G♯, a Collection II succession in terms of F♯–D–D♯–G♯–F–A–G♯–(G)–D–F–F♯–B–C. (All forms, by units of five or seven, retain by duplication and/or extension the Collection II segment of the Prime.) The articulation here is also highly suggestive: a (D F A/D F♯ A) "minor-major third" triadic outline; a (0 3 4) "clash" conceived in terms of (D F F♯) at m. 5; and, at m. 4, F and G♯, pitch numbers 3 and 6 in relation to this (0 3 7/0 4 7) triadic outline, jointly encircling or surrounding the "major third" (F♯) and the "fifth" (A) as grace notes. Then too, G, as the third set-factor of R and the only non-Collection II element in the succession, is in m. 5 pointedly "out of order" as a grace note, precisely, it would seem, in order not to deflect from the symmetrically defined, cohesive nature of the articulation. (The G in m. 5 is the only such infraction in this otherwise highly regulated *Epitaphium*. And as, at the same time, the only non-Collection II set-factor at mm. 4–5, its disorder cannot—at least in the hearing and understanding of this observer—be judged incidental to these articulative/ referential implications.)

Pertinent, too, is the vertical or "harmonic" treatment of the series throughout, which is contrary to Stravinsky's usual manner of exposing the set-forms as "melodies" or "linear constructs." And all of this is in marked contrast to the *Double Canon* for string quartet, where the canonic initiatives follow the usual course in a very strict, traditional sense: after a twelve-tone linearization as "subject," there are no octave transpositions whatever, and the original rhythmic-metric guise is preserved throughout. But the series is nonetheless a characteristic one: its first five pitch elements are equivalent in interval content to the five-tone set of *In Memoriam Dylan Thomas*; to the initial five set-factors of the (0 1 3 4) tetrachordal extensions in the "Pas de deux," "Four Duos" and "Trios" of *Agon*; and to the first and final five set-factors that frame the series of *A Sermon, a Narrative and a Prayer*. (In "older" terms, of course, this is a (0 1 3 4) tetrachord which spans the interval of 4 or "major third"; but now the fifth set-factor, curling inward and "chromatically" sealing off the gap with a pitch number 2, secures that advantage to which the serial process lays claim, effectively curtailing the tetrachord's octatonic potential.) While the octatonic implications that may in application be inferred from this set and its initial (0 1 3 4) tetrachord are not very conspicuous, the concluding canonic initiative in the first and second violins refers to IR, whose terminating C–B–D♯–D succession is a transposition, at the tritone, of the Prime's initiating F♯–F–A–G♯ succession—extending, in other words, Collection II's original, and much repeated, (F F♯ G♯ A) tetrachordal unit with a terminating (0,6) tritone-related transposition to (B C D D♯).

But it is the set of the *Anthem* which, with its stretch of six consecutive octatonic pitch elements (bracketed in Example 86), appears octatonically the most sensitive; but ironically this sensitivity remains unproductive. For nowhere, in this brief a cappella piece composed to T. S. Eliot's "The dove descending breaks the air," are the Collection III implications of the six consecutive pitch elements, preserved and extended by all forms, brought to bear. The principal cause of this is the prominence of the non-Collection III D. D's exposed position as the initiating set-factor of the P-statements tends to give succeeding intervals—indeed, whole stretches of the piece—a decidedly diatonic complexion, tinged with a (D F♯ A) triadic centricity with D as root. There are a few inflections worthy of note, however: at terminal points at mm. 25 and 43, the concluding two set-factors of P and IR (G–F and E–G♯ respectively) unite in a (0 3 4) "minor-major third" clash in terms of (E F G♯).

THE FLOOD (1962)

Prelude
   "Chaos" episode   mm. 1–6
   Te Deum, Sanctus (Chorus)   mm. 7–61
   Instrumental-speech (Narrator)   mm. 62–82
   Voices of God (2 Basses)   mm. 83–126
   Lucifer/Satan (Tenor)   mm. 127–67
   Melodrama (Narrator)   mm. 168–79
   Voices of God, Noah   mm. 180–247
"The Building of the Ark"   mm. 248–334
"The Catalogue of the Animals"   mm. 335–70
"The Comedy"   mm. 371–98
"The Flood"   mm. 399–456
"The Covenant of the Rainbow"
   Voices of God, Noah   mm. 457–89
   "Chaos" episode   mm. 490–96
   Satan (Tenor)   mm. 497–525
   Sanctus, Te Deum (Chorus)   mm. 526–End

My first idea for *The Flood*—that the celestials should sing while the terrestrials should merely talk—was a theatrical conception. My next preliminary notion was that *The Flood* should be a dance piece in character, a story told by dance as well as by narration. And, in fact, I have followed this idea: even the Te Deum is a dance piece, a fast-tempo dance chorale. The first difficulty I experienced was in trying to imagine the musical characterization of God— until I forgot about "profundities" and became a theater composer doing a theater job. Then I saw that God must always sing in the same manner, in the same tempo, and I decided to accompany Him by only bass instruments at first, until I saw that this could become monotonous. . . . The notion that God should be sung by two basses, and Satan by a high, slightly pederastic tenor (at any rate, Satan is sexually less "sure" than God) came to me somewhat later. Satan walks on a carpet of complex and sophisticated music, incidentally— unlike God—and his vanities are expressed, to a certain extent, by syncopation. . . .

My "Representation of Chaos" is not so different from Haydn's. But what does "Chaos" mean? "Things without forms"? "The negation of reality"? This is phraseomania—and suggests something beyond the limits of my poor imagination. How, please, does one represent chaos in music? I took certain elements, intervals, and chords made up of fourths. My "material of Chaos" is limited, however, and I couldn't make my Chaos last very long. At the beginning of the Te Deum—a piece that sounds "Byzantine" (to me) and that, to some extent, but purely by coincidence, suggests a well-known 5-tone Byzantine chant—I begin my serial construction. (Thus "chaos" may also be thought of as the antithesis of "serial.") [*Expositions and Developments*, pp. 140–42.]

Turning to some of the lengthier works, we find it is *The Flood* where an element of accommodation is most conspicuous, where intimations of the past, occasional but unmistakable, coalesce with a serial edifice now fully equipped with the system of independent hexachordal transposition-rotation. Subtitled *A Musical Play*, the piece is scored for large orchestra (whose forces, surprisingly at this late date, are occasionally in evidence); for chorus, tenor (Lucifer/Satan), and two basses (the voices of God); with "speaking parts" (speech or rhythmic, pitchless declamation) for Noah, Noah's wife, Noah's sons, a Narrator, and a Caller. The texts were "chosen and arranged" by Robert Craft from the Book of Genesis and medieval miracle plays, the dance episodes planned and arranged in collaboration with George Balanchine. A large enterprise, then. But concluded, as is widely known, under unfortunate auspices. Commissioned by CBS Television, *The Flood* seems even now not to have escaped the onus of its crippling debut. (In the recollection of this viewer, an unqualified disaster. The telecast was marred above all by the screen itself, whose projection proved incapable of accommodating the delicately poised interplay of narration, music, stage play, and choreography. In retrospect it is difficult to imagine Stravinsky, with his well-known distaste for the hustled, over-promoted exhibits of the culture "supermarkets," acceding to the project; entrusting his toil, with all its imaginative potential in such fond collaboration with Robert Craft and George Balanchine, to the realities of the American tube. And notwithstanding financial compensation; or his quite understandable attraction to the "musical economy" of the medium, its instantaneous "visualisations" sparing him "the afflatus of overtures, connecting episodes, curtain music.")[2]

Of intimations of the past, these are most apparent in the Te Deum music at mm. 7–45, which follows the opening "Chaos" episode, and then returns to conclude the play at mm. 552–82. (See Example 88.) Of course, from a strictly serial point of view, such intimations could hardly be presumed to exist. Quite simply, the (untransposed) IR form unfolds with its first hexachord, IRa, assigned to the chorus (sopranos, altos, and tenors), and its second hexachord, IRb, to the accompanying bassoon part. Crucial, however, is the simultaneous deployment of these complementary hexachords, which allows for the exposure of certain inter-hexachordal octatonic implications. At mm. 18–22, C♯ and D♯ as the first two set-factors of IRa are superimposed, as a reiterating unit, over a B♭–C–E ostinatolike pattern in the bassoon, IRb's first three set-factors. This results in a cohesive Collection III (B♭ C C♯ D♯ E) framework for these measures, whose "minor-major third" consequences with respect to the embedded

Example 88: *The Flood* (Te Deum)

(0 1 3 4) tetrachord in terms of (C C♯ D♯ E) are clearly in evidence. Then, at m. 23, these C♯–D♯ and B♭–C–E reiterating fragments are cut off in the completion of their respective IRa and IRb delineations; but *jointly* cut off so that, except for IRa's terminal A, a cohesive Collection I pitch count results in terms of (C♯ D E F G G♯), whose, in this instance, (0 3 4) "minor-major third" consequences in terms of (C♯ E F) are brought to bear. (See the IR set prefacing Example 88. The boxes refer to Collection III, the loops to Collection I. And note, in addition, the serial disorder at m. 23, where IRa's second set-factor, the non-Collection I (Collection III) D♯, is

Example 88 *continued*

dropped so as—evidently—not to disrupt the very firm sense of an over-the-barline Collection-III–Collection-I shift at this point.) Finally, the simultaneity at mm. 24, 35, and 44, punctuating successive (near) repeats of the chorale block, refers to IRb. And except for F, IRb is wholly octatonic, accountable to Collection III.

In his "Working Notes for *The Flood*" Stravinsky termed the Te Deum music "*Noces*-like," a species not of Gregorian but, in his words, "Igorian chant."[3] And while referring perhaps generally to the fast-tempo choral settings in *Les Noces*, he may nonetheless have been tempted a bit more specifically by the passages at Nos. 35–40 and 82–87 in the second and third tableaux, with their identical 0–2 whole-step reiterations in terms of Eb–Db or D#–C#. (A brief extract from *Les Noces* at No. 83 is included in Example 88. See, also in this connection, Example 38 in chapter 6.) True, *Les Noces* at Nos. 35–40 or 82–87 is securely octatonic, with a local and global partitioning of the collection (Collection III) more deliberate than anything we might care to infer in *The Flood* at mm. 7–45. But the spelling of this *Noces-Flood* (Te Deum) relationship acquires an added dimension in the *Elegy for J. F. K.*, when reference is made to still another 0–2 whole-step reiteration, described by Stravinsky as "two reiterated notes [which] are a melodic-rhythmic stutter characteristic of my speech from *Les Noces* to the *Concerto in D,* and earlier and later as well—a lifelong affliction, in fact."[4] In the *Concerto in D* the reiteration is, of course, an 0–1 reiteration, two "notes" related by the interval of 1, a half step, not, as in *Les Noces, The*

Flood, or the *Elegy,* by the interval of 2, a whole step (see Examples 58a, b, c, and d in chapter 10); it embodies, as we have frequently remarked in earlier chapters, a distinction critical to "Russian," and neoclassical thought (signaling a change in octatonic perspective from the "Russian" Model B emphasis to the neoclassical Model A emphasis), with the interval of 1 neoclassically interacting (or referentially intersecting) with the chromatic tendency-tone inflections of Classical C-scale (or major-scale) literature. But the 0–2 whole-step reiterations of *The Flood* and *Elegy are* chronically "Russian;" and in this connection the reader need hardly be reminded of the profusion of 2s that litter "Russian" material from the opening measures of *Petroushka* to the ostinati of *Histoire,* all with their referential allegiance to the octatonic collection (Model B) and/or the diatonic (the D-scale or the (0 2 3 5 7 9) hexachordal segment). But broader implications than these may reasonably be inferred. For the "two reiterated notes" are ultimately a form of back-and-forth oscillation; and in this respect they may indeed be found reaching into every crevice of melodic, rhythmic, formal, or pitch-relational matter.

But such intimations of the past are not confined to matters strictly pitch-relational (if indeed such confinement were possible), but extend as well to elements of form and rhythmic-metric construction. There are two distinct blocks of fixed intent at mm. 18–45, in which successive near repeats of the chorale block at mm. 18–24, 26–29, 30–35, and 37–44 are placed in abrupt juxtaposition with—or are punctuated by—near repeats of the IRb simultaneity at mm. 24, 35, and 44.[5] The near repeats of the chorale block are partially in accord with the first of our two rhythmic-metric types: a shifting meter, with the registrally and instrumentally fixed reiterating fragments (in the chorus and bassoon here) synchronized unvaryingly in vertical (or "harmonic") coincidence. But while the metric irregularity exacts a rhythmic-metric "sameness" in the repetition of the chorus's C♯–D♯ reiteration and terminating C♯–D–G♯–B–A succession upon successive near repeats of the chorale "block" (the terminating C♯–D–G♯–B–A succession thus always barred on the beat through two successive 3/8 measures), these repeats harbor—as is habitual in settings of this type—the potent contradiction or reversal. For in accord with "background" regular 2/4 metric periodicity (all but unmistakable here, given the steady quarter-note pulse of the bassoon fragment), the C♯–D♯ reiteration and its terminating C♯–D–G♯–B–A succession may at mm. 18–24 be perceived as an on-the-beat reiteration and terminating succession, contradicted or reversed at mm. 26–29 as an off-the-beat reiteration and terminating succession. (See the brackets in Example 88 which record this "background" regular 2/4 meter. Except for initial entrances, the C♯s at mm. 18–24 are thus on-the-beat C♯s, while those at mm. 26–29 are off-the-beat C♯s. The accentuation of the terminating C♯–D–G♯–B–A succession is in like manner displaced, its on-the-beat entrance at m. 24 being contradicted or reversed at m. 28 by an off-the-beat entrance.) Still, were this passage at mm. 18–45 to be more readily heard and understood in relation to the preceding measures at mm. 7–17, the bassoon's initial B♭ could then be perceived as an off-the-beat element (since, in accord with regular 2/4 metric periodicity, these preceding measures, if one disregards the metric irregularity, are concluded on the offbeat); this need not affect the underlying "play" itself, of course, but merely reverses the specifics with regard to contradiction or reversal in off-the-beat/on-the-beat accentuation (although perhaps further confusing the issue nonetheless).[6] Accordingly, we acknowledge the by now predictable manner in which a pitch organization, endowed with a pronounced inheritance factor (serial credentials notwithstanding), at the same time exhibits formal and rhythmic-metric conditions no less reflective of the past. It is in this respect enlightening that Stravinsky should so readily have identified the Te Deum as "a dance piece," a "fast-tempo dance chorale."

The concluding Sanctus at mm. 46–61 encompasses a serial oddity: set-factors of different untransposed forms, IR and RIR (retrograde of the IR form), are transferred between discrete, concurrently running parts, transference of this sort being exceedingly rare with Stravinsky. But the most remarkable serial feature of *The Flood* at mm. 1–400 (before a flash of lightning in the piccolo, xylophone, and piano signals the beginning of the flood itself, a choreographic setting with a massive, literal retrograde or "turn-about" at m. 427) is its steadfast fidelity to the untransposed forms of the complete, ordered twelve-tone set. Such allegiance—with pronounced linear exposure—is of course characteristic of Stravinsky. But *The Flood* was composed with the system of hexachordal transposition-rotation in full gear, so it is a circumstance of some note that, except for a handful of passages which branch off into transposition-rotation (along with the conventional set transpositions of the "Jacob's Ladder" music at mm. 6 and 179, or of the two solo double basses which accompany the voices of God as at mm. 116–25), Stravinsky is content to traverse the Te Deum and Sanctus at mm. 7–61, the instrumental-speech episode at mm. 62–82, the voices of God at mm. 83–247 (including the Lucifer/Satan episode at mm. 127–67), "The Building of the Ark" at mm. 248–334, "The Catalogue of the Animals" at mm. 335–70, and "The Comedy" between Noah and his wife at mm. 371–98 with *eighty*-odd complete statements of the set's untransposed orders—clearly, no mean feat.

Still, it is to the scattered passages of independent hexachordal transposition-rotation that our attention is drawn, and for whose acquaintance the reader is referred as a point of departure to the serial charts in Example 89. These scattered passages occur in the more purely instrumental sections such as "The Building of the Ark" and at mm.

Example 89: *The Flood*

387–98 in the "Comedy," in conjunction with some of the "polyrhythmic" elaboration which first appeared with such prominence in *Movements*. (In much of Stravinsky's late work, instrumental and vocal writing are distinguished in rhythmic-metric design. "Polyrhythmic combinations," like those found in *Movements* or *The Flood*'s "Building of the Ark," are generally instrumental in conception, while the vocal writing is far simpler in rhythmic-metric organization.) In "The Building of the Ark," whose instrumentation and "polyrhythm" are suggestive of an energetic carpentry (with "random" hammering sounds and the like), a chain of Pa rotations is introduced at m. 268. (See Example 90.) The initial Pa–4 rotation is out of formation, however, precluding a strictly patterned sequence. (The variance may be owing to Pa–4's embedded D–C♯–D♯ unit, which relates to the initial C♯–D♯–D unit of IR, whose complete, ordered succession has appeared three times at the outset of "The Building of the Ark.") But at mm. 275–83, the hectic "polyrhythm" of the carpentry approaches a unified climax with a strictly patterned chain of Ia rotations (down Ia's

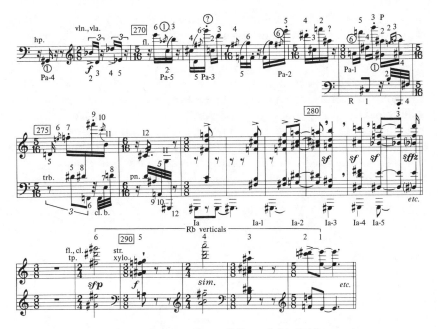

Example 90: "The Building of the Ark"

hexachordal ladder, from the untransposed Ia to the Ia–5 unit). Here the rotational chain is grouped as a succession of six five-factor simultaneities, with the shared initiating set-factor, G♯, as punctuation in the bass. (Similar chains of verticalized rotations—but of the Ra group, with C♯ as the shared, initiating factor—frame the Lucifer/Satan scene at mm. 127–30 and 146–49. Lucifer is introduced with Ra's verticalized rotation chain at mm. 127–30, and with each chordal punctuation—interrupted by speech-phrases such as "But Lucifer was vain / Lucifer was proud / Lucifer was ambitious"—he gradually "takes shape." In his "Working Notes," Stravinsky envisioned Lucifer "jumping to a higher rock with each chord, but missing the last one," until, with the arioso at m. 130, "he is at floor level dancing a lithe, athletic 'twist.' ")[7] Finally, in a scintillating instrumental exchange at mm. 289–94, the vertical alignments or "serial verticals" of the Rb group are introduced. And here, as earlier at mm. 275–83, this verticalization climactically offsets the "random," "polyrhythmic" array of the surrounding context. (The pitch duplications in these Rb "serial verticals" are frequently written as octaves—the doubled G♯ in vertical 6, for example; and Stravinsky's patterned chain (reading from left to right on the serial chart) includes, as its final "vertical," Rb's single, initiating set-factor, E.)

Patterned chains of hexachordal rotation groups are also found in the final measures of "The Catalogue" (the Rb group) and at mm. 387–98 in "The Comedy" between Noah and his wife. (See Example 91.) The first of these in "The Comedy" is, except for the initial untransposed Pb hexachord, a spiral pattern up Pb's hexachordal ladder (reading alternatively from left to right and from right to left from Pb–5 to Pb–1) which accompanies Noah's reluctant wife as she enters the Ark. (This has been a trying experience, requiring the combined persuasive powers of Noah and his sons throughout "The Comedy." The sustained *p subito* pauses at m. 387 with the sixth and final set-factors of Pb and Pb–5, D♭ and E♭ respectively, may reflect continued hesitation on the part of Noah's wife, or consternation and renewed effort on the part of Noah and his sons—but only until the final, frenzied plunge at m. 388. In "Working Notes," Stravinsky pictured Noah's wife as "a Xantippe with a bottle. . . . She has disregarded

Example 91: "The Comedy"

the Ark when it was building, and she is on her way to a pub when the flood begins. At the last minute her sons . . . hoist their kicking mother and carry her into the Ark.")[8] Finally, the Lento section which concludes "The Comedy" at mm. 395–98 (doubtless representing a settling-in period; "the earth is overflowed with flood") consists of a patterned descent down Pa's hexachordal ladder (reading from left to right from the untransposed Pa to the Pa–5 unit), with the shared, initiating set-factor, G♯, sustained in the strings along with G and A.

Finally, the reader is referred to the rotations of the Rb group with initial F at mm. 387–89, and then to IR's initial C♯–D♯ or C♯–D♯–D unit. For these reveal "gravitations," "centers," or points of departure which, enclosed within a different serial edifice, are of paramount concern in Stravinsky's next venture, *Abraham and Isaac.*

ABRAHAM AND ISAAC (1963) et al.

Abraham and Isaac is a sacred ballad for high baritone voice (*baryton martin*) and small orchestra composed on the Hebrew (Masoretic) text of Genesis (B're-shit) chapter XXII.

The six parts, including one purely orchestral movement, are performed without interruption, but they are distinguished by changes to successively slower pulsations. Nineteen verses are used, and they are comprised in ten musical units. Though the verses are sometimes expressed in dialogue form in the Bible, my setting does not impersonate the protagonists, but tells the whole story through the baritone-narrator. The change of speaker is indicated by, among more interesting devices, changes in dynamics.

No translation of the Hebrew should be attempted, the Hebrew syllables, both as accentuation and timbre, being a principal and a fixed element of the music. . . .

A twelve-note series is employed, but hexachordal and smaller units are stressed rather than full orders. Octaves occur frequently, fifths and doubled intervals are everywhere, and I suppose that "key" gravitations will be found to exist. None of these is in contradiction to the serial basis of the composition, but the result of concordances from the several serial forms, or what I call serial verticals.

Of the multiple origins of every work, the most important is the least easy to describe. I must say, however, that the initial stimulus came to me with the discovery of Hebrew as sound. [*Themes and Episodes*, pp. 55–56.]

My Variations [1964] were composed on the following pitch series, a succession of notes that came to my mind as a melody. . . . After writing it out, I gradually discovered the possibilities in it as material for variations. The bipartite division is basic, six-note formations being as integral components as the classical four orders. The halves, moreover, are unities as well as fragments, and are therefore divisible in turn, and invertible, reversible, mirror-invertible, mirror-reversible. The vocabulary of the composition (at least) was very abundant.

Veränderungen—alternates or mutations, Bach's word for *The "Goldberg" Variations*—could be used to describe my Variations as well, except that I have altered or diversified a series, instead of a theme or subject. In fact, I do not have a theme, in the textbook sense, whereas Bach's theme (for comparison) is a complete aria. . . .

The density of the twelve-part variations ["twelve-part polyphony"] is the main innovation in the work. One might think of these constructions as musical mobiles, in that the patterns within them will seem to change perspective with repeated hearings. They are relieved and offset by music of a contrasting starkness and even, notably in the first variation, by *Klangfarben* monody—which is also variation. [*Themes and Episodes*, pp. 60–62.]

In ways that are varied and numerous, *Abraham and Isaac* differs markedly from its predecessor. The text is biblical, of course, and in Hebrew, a language unknown to Stravinsky at the time, for whose translation, accentuation, and inflection he enlisted the assistance of several notables, including most prominently, Sir Isaiah Berlin. While there is predictably an element of theater or drama in the pacing of its delivery, *Abraham and Isaac* is not like *The Flood, A Musical Play*, with musically drawn personalities and choreographic settings, but an oratorio for the concert hall, *A Sacred Ballad for Baritone and Chamber Orchestra* to be exact, in which the text's narrative and spoken parts are entrusted to a single vocal line. Significantly, too, the instrumentation is lean in contrast to that of *The Flood*, and very much an accompaniment. Still, it is an accompaniment that shoulders the burden of formalizing this near-seamless music: nineteen verses of the text are confined to ten sections—or "ten musical units," as Stravinsky calls them in his program notes. These sections are buffered by fermatas, measured pauses, and short instrumental breaks (the lengthiest of these breaks occurring at the end of Section III at mm. 89–105), and then distinguished from one another in instrumentation and changes in tempo. The sections are as follows:[9]

    I.   verses 1, 2; mm. 1–50; eighth-note = 132
   II.   verse 3; mm. 51–72
  III. verses 4, 5; mm. 73–104; quarter-note = 120
  IV. verses 6, 7; mm. 105–35; quarter-note = 92–96
   V. verses 8, 9, 10; mm. 136–62
  VI. verses 11, 12; mm. 163–81; quarter-note = 76
 VII. verse 13; mm. 182–96; quarter-note = 72
VIII. verse 14; mm. 197–206
  IX. verses 15, 16, 17, 18; mm. 207–39
   X. verse 19; mm. 240–54; quarter-note = 60

Underlying this format are distinctions no less marked in set manipulation. In *The Flood*, the untransposed orders of the complete twelve-tone set were ever-present, a constant serial reminder, so much so at mm. 6–400 that the hexachordal rotation patterns of the instrumental sections were clearly diversionary, an appendage to a rather straitlaced, down-to-earth twelve-tone system. But *Abraham and Isaac* is, on the contrary, nearly exclusively hexachordal in design. Reference is made to all ten hexachordal rotation groups of the basic five orders, and to the vertical alignments or "serial verticals" of Pb, Rb, IRa, and IRb. Only once—at the beginning of the piece in the violas and bassoon—is there an ordered rendition of the complete twelve-tone set. (See Example 93.) Indeed, of all Stravinsky's late works (except the Interlude and "Lacrimosa" of the *Requiem Canticles*), *Abraham and Isaac* is in its hexachordal transposition-rotation routine the most insistent and elaborate.

Yet within this hexachordal deliria a hierarchy of sorts takes shape. There are two distinct—but interrelated—areas of pitch-relational concern, the first centered around F (given F's frequent octave doublings, pitch duplications, repetitions, and insistent use as a point of departure), the second centered around C♯. The F area encompasses, first, the initial F–E–F♯ or F–F♯—E trichordal units of IRa and Ra (as boxed off in Examples 92–96). Sections I (baritone entrance at m. 12), III, VI, VII, and VIII all depart with this seemingly privileged F identification; and there are clusters of F–E–F♯s or F–F♯–Es with notable octave doublings and repetitions of F at mm. 12, 73, 182, and 197. (Of the RIa and RIb hexachordal rotation groups only RIa–5 and RIb–4 are employed, and these either begin or end with the F–E–F♯ or F–F♯–E unit. These RI rotations occur in the first section at mm. 23–25 and 30–31, amidst a host of IRa rotations initiated, significantly, by F. See examples 92 and 93.) F's second identity is as the shared, initial set-factor of IRa's five rotations (and, to a somewhat lesser extent, of Ra's five rotations). There are several illustrations of this: the quasi-patterned chain of IRa rotations in the first section at mm. 17–30, interrupted only by RIa–5 and RIb–4 with their embedded F–F♯–E units, Example 93; the patterned spiral of IRa rotations in Section III, Example 94; the heavy concentration of IRa rotations in the ornate clarinet-bassoon exchange at mm. 185–95 in Section VII (only partially recorded in Example 95; there is a total of thirteen rotation-statements, all referring to the IRa group except Pb–1, whose concluding set-factor, G, is in fact replaced by F, as it also had been in the opening Pb–1 statement of the baritone part at m. 184); and the patterned chain of Ra rotations at mm. 211–19 in Section IX, Example 96. (All of this might with some justification lead to the impression of an *Abraham and Isaac* "all about IRa," its rotations, and the relationship of these rotations to all other rotations initiated or concluded by F, of whatever hexachordal group-

Example 92

denomination.) Finally, F's third identity is as the just-noted initial or concluding set-factor of rotations with hexachordal group-affiliations other
than IRa or Ra. The RIa–5 and RIb–4 rotations in Section I might be included here, but the most significant is IRb–1.

In fact, it is this peripheral fringe of rotations initiated by F (with hexa-

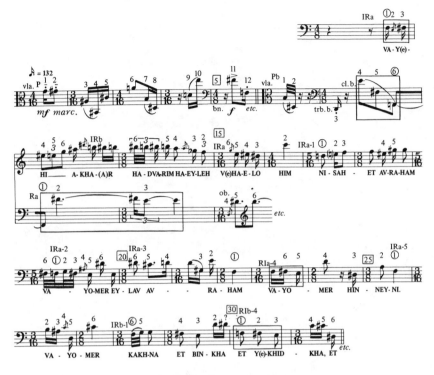

Example 93: (Section I)

chordal affiliations *not necessarily those of IRa or Ra*) that links F's sphere of influence (or IRa's sphere of influence) to the somewhat less assertive C♯ area; the C♯ of this secondary area is closely identified with D♯, and then with the rotations with initial C♯ of the IRb group and the rotations with initial D♯ of the Ib group (some of these Ib rotations are duplicated in the IRa group—Ib–3 and Ib–4, for example, being the same as IRa–3 and IRa–2—but in reverse order, reading from left to right). Especially active in this linking are IRa–5 and IRb–1, both of which are flanked by F and C♯. (See the arrows on the serial chart of Example 92.) An example of this can be seen in the passage at mm. 73–85 in Section III: a succession of IRb rotations with initial C♯ succeeds the opening patterned chain of IRa rotations with initial F, with IRa–5 positioned at the juncture (m. 79) as the pivoting unit. A similar intergroup linkage may be inferred in Section I, where the initial IRa emphasis is followed by a succession of IRb rotations at m. 31. Then, turning to C♯'s or C♯–D♯'s individual sphere of influence, we find that the baritone part in Section II (not shown here) consists, from m. 57 onward, of a patterned spiral of IRb rotations with initial C♯ (down IRb's hexachordal ladder), which is followed by a patterned spiral of Ib

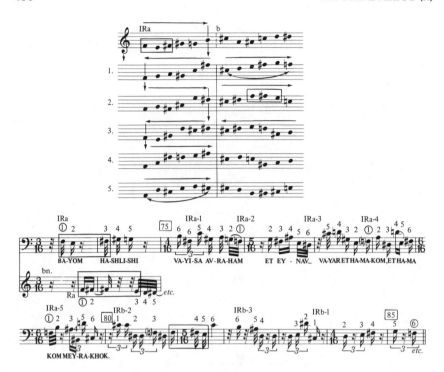

Example 94: (Section III)

rotations with initial D♯ (up Ib's hexachordal ladder). Yet even these elaborate IRa, Ra, IRb, and Ib displays fail to exhaust the supply of patterned hexachordal rotation chains in *Abraham and Isaac*. Following an initial succession of rotations beginning or ending with F in Section VI, the baritone part is composed entirely of a patterned spiral of Pb rotations (down Pb's hexachordal ladder from the untransposed Pb to the Pb–5 unit).

The Interlude and "Lacrimosa" sections of the *Requiem Canticles* are similarly endowed with elaborately patterned chains of hexachordal transposition-rotation groups. But in the orchestral *Variations*, transposition-rotation is applied on a twelve-tone as well as on a hexachordal basis. Still, the scheme itself remains the same. Under each order-heading there is a common initiating set-factor which yields five rotations (or five complete twelve-tone sets; see Example 97). In the first section at mm. 6–22 (termed "*Klangfarben* monody" by Stravinsky, and which, as he suggests, "is also variation"), there is a patterned chain of P rotations up P's ladder from P–5 to the untransposed set in the final measures. (See Example 98.) The remarkable "twelve-part polyphony"—or "twelve-part variations"—which follows in stunning contrast at mm. 23–33 (with, as

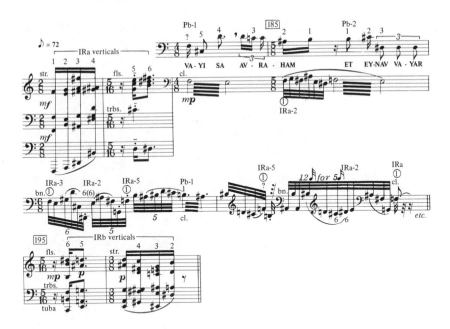

Example 95: (Section VII)

indicated earlier, its near repeats at mm. 47 and 118), includes twelve-
tone rotations from all five orders except RI (of which only the untransposed form appears), with the rotations of each "part" usually confined
to one group-denomination. (See Example 99.) Also see, although not
shown here, the patterned chain of R rotations in the sixth "variation" at
mm. 59–72; the concentration of IR rotations in the eighth "variation" at
mm. 86–94; and, in the tenth "variation" at mm. 101–17, the rhythmic
("isorhythmic") fugato with its patterned chain of R rotations in the violins and violas (up R's ladder with R–5 as "subject"), superimposed over a
similarly patterned chain of I rotations in the violas (with I–5 as the second fugal entry at m. 104), and then over a chain of IR rotations in the
lower strings (with IR–5 as the third entry at m. 109).

But the most remarkable feature of the *Variations* is doubtless its breathless compression, its mercurial shifts within a framework still here and
there imbued with the strongest of ties to both the distant and immediate
past (or perhaps, as ever with Stravinsky, a multiplicity of "pasts"). Thus,
quite apart from the archaic formalism of the fugal exposition itself at
mm. 101–17 (whose conventional rhythmic-metric guise offers such striking relief to the "polyrhythmic" glitter of its surroundings), the end of the
fugato's "subject" has as its rhythmic precedent the Coda of *Agon*'s "Pas de
deux" at mm. 495–503.[10] (See Example 83c in chapter 13.)

Example 96: (Sections VIII and IX)

A CONCLUSION

I do not understand the composer who says we must analyze and determine
the evolutionary tendency of the whole musical situation and proceed from
there. I have never consciously analyzed any musical situation, and I can follow only where my musical appetites lead me. . . . Whether I am a forefront
or rear-guard or road-hog composer is beside the point, which is the disparity
between the doer and the explainer. . . . My agenbite of inwit is that I do not
know while composing, am not aware of, the value question. I love whatever I

Example 97: *Variations*

am now doing, and with each new work I feel that I have at last found the way,
have just begun to compose. I love all of my children, of course, and like my
father, I am inclined to favor the backward and imperfectly formed ones. . . .
[*Dialogues and a Diary*, pp. 28–30.]

We arrive then at the close of a discourse on questions of identity and distinction in the music of Igor Fedorovich Stravinsky. More specifically, our
subject has been how this identity is linked to a Russian heritage and to
conventions of the Baroque and Classical C-scale (or major-scale) traditions, and how it imposes itself, with adjustments, modifications, and accommodations, in the three familiar orientations or general "stylistic"
trends, the early "Russian" period, the neoclassical, and the serial.

Needless to say, the task has not been easy. But it seems doubtful that
there can be an "easy" approach to this music, given the prolific yield of
this most extraordinary inventor of "whole new musical worlds" and the
pronounced changes in orientation evidenced by those "worlds." True,
an octatonic routine is both persistent and fundamental; as are applications of the two rhythmic-metric types detailed at length in these pages; as

Example 98: *Variations*

is abrupt block juxtaposition, that peculiarly Stravinskian conception of form; as are more general techniques of triadic superimposition, back-and-forth oscillation, and ostinato-like repetition. But Stravinsky's octatonicism, together with its (0,3,6,9) symmetrically defined interaction with diatonic material, underwent changes of a critical sort from the early *Scherzo fantastique* and *Firebird* to the serial works. And there is then that

12 vln. solo

1.   R-1 (1-12); R-2 (1-12); R-3 (12-1); R-5 (12-1)
2.   I-1 (12-1); I-3 (1-12); I-5 (12-1)
3.   RI (1-12); I-2 (1-12); I-4 (12-1)
4.   I-1 (1-12); I-3 (12-1); I-5 (1-12)
5.   IR (12-1); IR-3 (1-12); IR-3 (12-1)
6.   IR-2 (1-12); IR-2 (12-1); IR-5 (1-12)
7.   IR (1-12); IR (12-1); IR-1 (1-12)
8.   IR-5 (12-1); IR-4 (1-12); IR-4 (12-1); IR-1 (12-1)
9.   R-5 (1-12); R-4 (12-1); R-4 (1-12)
10. P (1-12); R (1-12); R-1 (12-1)
11. R-3 (1-12); R-2 (12-1)
12. I (1-12); I-2 (12-1); I-4 (1-12)

Example 99: *Variations*, Section II ("12-part polyphony")

curious link between his neoclassical C-scale diatonicism and C-scale (or major-scale) tonally functional relations, a link that remains, to say the least, elusive, perplexing, and highly problematic.

But can there be an "easy" approach to any music or any "literature"? Are we not—as listeners, musicians, or composers—always seeking to hear and understand, altering or modifying our perspective(s) accordingly? And for anyone attempting formally to organize and transmit a hearing and understanding, can, therefore, the situation ever be "easy"? All that tidy or accommodating? Probably not. Because every "explanation," every analytic-theoretical assertion breeds counterexplanations, counterassertions, counterintelligence. And this is neither to be decried nor to be met with fits of *angst*. It is inevitable; it is the very nature of the analytic-theoretical pursuit, of attempts to interpret, to reckon, to come to terms.

And so we are again reminded that the rewards or benefits of such undertakings lie not so much in "explanation," in interpretative results or conclusions, as they do in the process itself, in the actual *seeking* to hear and understand, in the taking-possession-of. Analytic-theoretical assertions are always to be "laid against the data." This means not only that they derive their meaning and significance from the contexts from which they arise, but also, crucially, that they can be of assistance only if we, as listeners, musicians, or composers, are willing to undertake the excursion for ourselves. Consequently, while we welcome any perspective or approach that might assist in our seeking to hear and understand, we recognize that the quest must be of our own making, and that every "explanation" is but a beginning, a commencement.

NOTES

INTRODUCTION

1. Roy Travis, "Toward a New Concept of Tonality?" p. 257; Allen Forte, *Contemporary Tone Structures*. For an example of the model approach, see Edward T. Cone, "The Uses of Convention: Stravinsky and His Models."

2. Paul Collaer, *A History of Modern Music.*

3. Alexandre Tansman, *Igor Stravinsky: The Man and His Music*; Roman Vlad, *Stravinsky*; Eric Walter White, *Stravinsky: The Composer and His Works*. These comprehensive surveys are not without merit. Tansman and Vlad are occasionally perceptive in regard to the general "stylistic" appearance of some of Stravinsky's music, and White's book is useful as a catalogue of chronology, general outlines, ballet scenarios, manuscript material, etc.

4. See, for example, Forte, *Contemporary Tone Structures*, p. 137; or, Benjamin Boretz, "Meta-Variations, Part IV: Analytic Fallout (I)," p. 150.

5. Stravinsky later acknowledged these three categories or "stylistic" periods as "changes of life." See the quotation from his *Themes and Episodes* at the outset of this Introduction.

6. Arthur Berger, "Problems of Pitch Organization in Stravinsky," p. 123.

7. The reader will find nearly all of Stravinsky's works cited in one way or another in this volume. We are beginning with *The Firebird* rather than a still earlier work (such as *Fireworks* or the *Scherzo fantastique*, both from 1908) because of the widespread popularity of this early ballet, not because of an analytical-theoretical prejudice. (Indeed, we could as easily have chosen the *Scherzo fantastique*, which, while devoid of some practices or general methods of procedure readily identified with Stravinsky's music of all "stylistic" persuasions, nonetheless ranks among his most thoroughly octatonic creations.) It seemed advantageous to begin our quest—which will be difficult at times—with music familiar to the general reader.

8. This phrase is borrowed from Mario Bunge, *Causality* p. 272.

9. Arnold Isenberg, "Critical Communication," in *Aesthetics and Language*, ed. William Elton (Oxford: Basil and Blackwell, 1959), p. 139. Quoted in Arthur Berger's "New Linguistic Modes and the New Theory," p. 28.

10. See, by the present author, "Some Characteristics of Stravinsky's Diatonic Music."

11. For additional biographical detail and insights into Stravinsky's musical personality or mentality, the reader can best consult these six books authored jointly by Stravinsky and Robert Craft (to which, as indicated, reference is frequently made in these pages), or Craft's own later compilation, *Stravinsky: Chronicle of a Friendship, 1948–1971*. (From 1948 to Stravinsky's death on 6 April 1971, Craft was Stravinsky's closest associate, in both a personal and professional sense.) But C. F. Ramuz's *Souvenirs sur Igor Stravinsky* and Paul Horgan's *Encounters with Stravinsky* are also immensely informative. Lillian Libman's sober account of the last twelve years of Stravinsky's life, *And Music at the Close: Stravinsky's Last Years*, is likewise informative and highly readable. (As for the controversy raised by Libman's book over the extent of Stravinsky's participation in some of the Stravinsky-Craft books and the later

interviews—in which the octogenarian was ever witty, enviably clever, and keen—this is a matter on which this observer can unfortunately offer no first-hand, authoritative opinion. But since the truth is rarely pure or simple, and since Craft and Libman must necessarily have benefited from personal and professional relationships with Stravinsky of quite different sorts—Libman was his personal secretary for a time, and not a musician—it seems reasonable to suppose that the contradictions in their separate accounts are not all hopelessly at odds, and that they offer "slices of reality" perhaps not entirely irreconcilable.) On the other hand, a truly informed, insightful, compelling—and, of course well-written—account of "The Life and Times of Igor Stravinsky" has yet to appear. This may be owing to Stravinsky's lifelong insistence on personal privacy (a steadfast refusal to cultivate a "public image" of himself beyond that as a composer), as well as to Craft's many and varied contributions. For Craft is so knowledgeable, so sensitive to nuance, so skillfully "true" to his subject (his portrayal is confirmed in a variety of ways by C. F. Ramuz, Samuel Dushkin, Nicolas Nabokov, Paul Horgan, and other friends and associates) that such a project seems not only unnecessary, but scarcely conceivable—at least for the time being.

CHAPTER 1

1. *Expositions and Developments*, p. 146.

2. Stravinsky's private lessons with Rimsky-Korsakov began in 1903 and continued for about three years. Conducted twice a week, these lessons consisted primarily of assignments in orchestration. Soon, however, a close friendship transcended the teacher-pupil formality, and Stravinsky later recalled becoming a member of the Rimsky-Korsakov household and enjoying the friendship of Rimsky's two sons, Vladimir an Andrei (at least until *The Firebird*, when the Rimsky-Korsakov "clan" apparently "turned against" him—or his music). Rimsky-Korsakov died in June 1908. The score of Stravinsky's *Chant funèbre* (1908), dedicated to Rimsky and, in Stravinsky's words, "the best of my works before *The Firebird*," was lost during the Russian Revolution. See Igor Stravinsky and Robert Craft, *Memories and Commentaries*, p. 57.

3. Stravinsky's music is customarily divided (with much overlapping or "straddling") into three general orientation categories or "stylistic" periods: the "Russian" period from the beginning to the *Symphonies of Wind Instruments* (1920); the neoclassical period from *Pulcinella* (1920) to *Agon* (1953–57); and the serial period from the *Cantata* (1952) to the *Requiem Canticles* (1966). Stravinsky himself acknowledged these "changes of life," as he called them, as indicated already in the preceding Introduction.

4. "Pitch class" as opposed to "pitch" entails the by now common and useful distinction drawn between, say *any* C (the class of C) and a *given* C (e.g., the pitch of "middle C" on the keyboard). Also, since the term "chromatic," as applied to tonality and the major scale, refers to pitch elements that are outside the diatonic collection ("altered" elements) but nevertheless a part of the tonal system (e.g., the familiar tendency or leading tones, or the augmented-sixth chords), it becomes somewhat inaccurate or misleading to speak of music that is referentially whole tone or octatonic (music accountable, in other words, to collections with an interval content different from that of the diatonic collection, and thus a part of systems different from that of tonality) as "chromatic." Hence the quotation marks.

5. See the quotation above from *Expositions and Developments*. In a letter to Stravinsky in May 1913, Pierre Monteux, who conducted the first rehearsals and performance of *Le Sacre*, referred to the music as an "explosion." The letter (or a portion thereof) appears in Robert Craft's "*Le Sacre* and Pierre Monteux: An Unknown Debt," p. 33.

6. Tamara Karsavina, "A Recollection of Stravinsky," p. 7.

7. S. L. Grigoriev, *The Diaghilev Ballet, 1909–1929*, p. 31.

8. Ibid., p. 32.

9. Ibid., p. 37.

10. *Expositions and Developments*, p. 151. See the full quotation at the outset of this chapter.

11. Such stripping is customary when focusing on pitch relations, but it should be obvious that as a representational device seeking to enhance the aural and visual participation of the reader, stripping does not mean that analysis is undertaken without reference to the rhythmic scheme. All matters of context—meter, rhythm, register, instrumentation—are implicated in the grouping and weighing of pitch elements that constitute both perception and a formal analysis of this type, even though certain details of the implication—or of the interplay—may at times be taken for granted. Nor can these "contextual" matters be neglected by the reader. Such neglect may not block communication altogether; the logic of the reckoning or of the conceptualization may run its course, and if the reader is adept at deciphering notation, whatever is gained may not entirely lack musical (aural) consequence. However, if unable to summon the presence of a musical context (for which the illustrations can only occasionally be of service as reminders), the reader will have no means—beyond that of extra musical logic—to judge the validity or significance of what is being demonstrated, or to engage in that continuing give-and-take between conceptualization and perception that alone renders analysis or theory a musically useful endeavor. These concerns become critical in the final stages of this and subsequent analyses, where, through an ever increasing refinement in reduction, highly abstract patterns evolve in the form of scales and configurations which are carried over to assist in the analysis of subsequent works precisely because they have been made to embody the peculiarities or consistencies in pitch organization which this inquiry seeks to define. This embodiment cannot obtain—the formulations will be found lifeless and without meaning—unless anchored to a consciousness of the contexts from which they arose.

12. Together with the familiar "minor-major" vocabulary of tonality, the reader will note a concurrent use of pitch numbering here, the numerical quantification of intervals or relations by counting the semitones they contain. The advantage of pitch numbering arises from the following: (1) it conveniently circumvents the tonal implications of a tonally conceived vocabulary, a vocabulary often exceedingly awkward where the implications no longer apply (e.g., the "dominant-seventh" complex in Stravinsky's octatonic settings, which, being accountable to a different collection of reference than the diatonic—and hence also a part of a different "system" than that of tonality—rarely behaves in the manner of a tonally functional dominant); (2) it conveniently bypasses, de-emphasizes, or only indirectly implicates pitch-class identity, so that, in moving from one piece or "stylistic" orientation to the next, relations are handily identified with respect not only to intervals but also to (more) articulative groupings (e.g., reoccurring "themes," "fragments," "motives," or "chords"). Thus, apart from its noncommittal nature with respect to "theories," "literatures," "styles," or "systems," pitch numbering is particularly useful when dealing with matters of consistency, identity, and distinction for a body of works. Accordingly, a "major third" becomes a 4, the interval of 4, the interval defined by 4 semitones; the "minor" and "major" triads and the "dominant seventh" of tonality become (0 3 7), (0 4 7), and (0 4 7 10); and a favorite articulative grouping of the "Russian" period becomes the (0 2 3 5) tetrachord with interval order 2,1,2, this tetrachord generally spanning the interval of 5, the "fourth." This latter (0 2 3 5) complex identification, like much of the vocabulary associated with tonality (e.g. "tonic triad," "dominant"), not only de-emphasizes pitch-class identity but also disregards the interval complementation and order stipulated by a given (0 2 3 5) fragment in its convenient emphasis on relations (or on the codification of these relations) in moving from one context or piece to the next. When a pitch numbering of intervals and fragments is made to correspond to a pitch numbering of the appropriate reference collections (e.g., scales), the whole process becomes doubly advantageous.

13. The term "partitioning" derives from a consciousness of the reference collection, in

the sense that one interprets or conceives of intervals, themes, fragments, motives, chords, or simultaneities (a more general and noncommittal term than chord) as partitionings of the reference collection. Thus, we speak here of the articulative Derivative I as an articulative partitioning of the octatonic (reference) collection, a partitioning available at A♭ and D (with inversions at B♭ and E) with respect to the (A♭ B♭ B C♯ D E F G (A♭)) collection; and we speak of this Derivative I partitioning perhaps in much the same way as one might refer to the (0 3 7/0 4 7) "minor" and "major" triads of the diatonic collection as partitionings of that collection in terms of this (0 3 7/0 4 7) triadic grouping.

14. Tonality is here viewed in its more restricted and Western, historically oriented sense as a hierarchical system of pitch relations based on the diatonic major scale (the C-scale), a system encompassing an intricate yet fairly distinct set of harmonic—(0 3 7/0 4 7) triadic— and contrapuntal (voice-leading) procedures commonly known as *tonal functionality*, the historical development of which can be traced from roughly the beginning of the seventeenth century to the end of the nineteenth. We quote from Arthur Berger: "Tonality . . . is defined by those functional relations postulated by the structure of the major scale. A consequence of the fulfillment of such functional relations is, directly or indirectly, the assertion of the priority of one pitch class over the others within a given context—it being understood that context may be interpreted either locally or with respect to the totality, so that a hierarchy is thus established, determined in each case by what is taken as the context in terms of which priority is assessed. It is important to bear in mind, however, that there are other means besides functional ones for asserting pitch-class priority; from which it follows that pitch-class priority per se: (1) is not a sufficient condition of that music which is tonal, and (2) is compatible with music that is not tonally functional." ("Problems of Pitch Organization in Stravinsky," p. 123.) Thus terms like "tonal practice," "tonal functionality," and "triadic tonality" are all, within the context of this inquiry, synonymous with "tonality." In accord with this restricted interpretation of tonality as a relatively stable, self-contained, and autonomous system of pitch relations, the reader will note, as in Berger's brief definition, the use in this inquiry of the noncommittal "priority" in place of "tonic" or "tone center." For it is imperative that the assertion of priority (on behalf of a pitch class or an articulative grouping) by tonally functional means be properly distinguished from this assertion by means other than tonally functional (e.g., by octave reinforcement, metric accentuation, persistence, etc.). The use here of "home base" instead of "key" or "tonic triad" is also to avoid tonal implications where they are clearly irrelevant.

15. Another distinction here (indeed, one to which attention has already been drawn in these pages): Taking the piano's "white notes" as representing the diatonic pitch collection, we adopt Arthur Berger's method of identifying the various interval orderings (or scales) available to this collection by a C-scale/D-scale type of labeling in place of the traditional "major scale"/"Dorian mode" type of designation. ("Pitch Organization in Stravinsky," p. 129.) The rationale for this is similar to that for the use of pitch numbering in place of tonality's vocabulary: the identification aims at greater generality in musical thought, freeing the analysis from irrelevant theoretical, historical, or "stylistic" considerations, freeing it from modal (archaic and modern) and tonal implications were these implications no longer apply. Moreover, this method entails another useful distinction, also mentioned earlier, namely, that between the *reference collection* (the total pitch-class and/or interval *content* stipulated by a given passage) and the *referential ordering of intervals* (or scale) that the collection will assume on the basis of the pitch class to which priority is assigned. Thus in Nos. 28–30 in *Le Sacre*, the total pitch-class and/or interval content stipulates the diatonic collection; and since E♭ assumes a measure of pitch-class priority (by means other than tonally functional ones), the interval ordering or scale for the collection will be that of the D-scale at E♭ (formerly "Dorian mode" at E♭). While all this may now seem a bit fussy, a recognition of these distinctions is essential if we are to arrive at a useful definition of consistency, identity, and distinction in pitch organi-

zation. Thus, much of Stravinsky's "Russian"-period music (e.g., *Petroushka, Renard, Les Noces*) is diatonic, accountable to the diatonic pitch collection. But the assertion of priority with respect to pitch class or articulative groupings more often than not implicates the interval ordering of the D-scale, the G-scale, or a diatonic hexachordal segment, rather than that of the C-scale (the major scale). This assertion unfolds by means of processes bearing little resemblance to past modal practices, but this more general vocabulary can also be applied equally to cases where modal or, particularly, tonal considerations do arise: the C-scale (formerly, major-scale) determination *may* implicate tonally functional relations, but not *necessarily*. For a more detailed discussion of these matters, see Benjamin Boretz, "Meta-Variations: Studies in the Foundations of Musical Thought (I)."

16. Still, it is to be noted that the added bass line in the recapitulation of the mm. 5–7 configuration at mm. 18–20 (see Example 3) renders the (0,6) tritone-related (E G♯ B) (B♭ D F) triadic implications of the configuration more explicit.

17. The reader will have noted that our analysis in Examples 3–7 ignores the awkward (and irrelevant) notational implications of this A♭-minor key signature and retains the A♭ merely to ensure a degree of contact. Stravinsky's notation at mm. 18–20 is far more comprehensible, and the change here may have been prompted by the added bass line, which tends more readily to expose the (E G♯ B) (B♭ D F) triadic implications of the mm. 5–7 configuration. Moreover, while we have in Examples 3–7 chosen to represent the octatonic reference collection as a descending scale from A♭, the question of a descending or ascending scale is of no real consequence here in the Introduction. (The articulation could equally have suggested an ascending scale on A♭, although this would have reversed the scalar interval ordering of whole and half steps.) However, this ascending/descending choice, and the implications it poses with respect to pitch-class priority, articulative routine, and scalar interval ordering, does become critical to our hearing and understanding of octatonic relations beginning with *Petroushka* in chapters 2 and 3.

18. The octatonic collection is limited to three transpositions; or, to put it another way, there are only three octatonic collections of distinguishable pitch content. All three of these are, as we have seen, implicated in the Introduction. Again, these considerations will be discussed more thoroughly in chapter 2.

19. *Expositions and Developments*, p. 89. See, also, *Memories and Commentaries*, p. 57. In connection with *Sadko* (the symphonic poem), there is a brief reference to the octatonic collection in Rimsky-Korsakov's autobiography, *My Musical Life*, p. 72.

20. Apart from the Introduction, the octatonic succession of (0 3 7/0 4 7/0 4 7 10) triadic complexes related by the interval of 3 (a "minor third" apart)—a symmetrical or "equal" partitioning of the octave by (0 3 7/0 4 7/0 4 7 10) triadic complexes at pitch numbers 0,3,6, and 9 (these pitch numbers constituting the roots of these triadic complexes)—appears already in Stravinsky's *Fireworks* (1908) at Nos. 16–21, and in his *Scherzo fantastique* (1908) at Nos. 7–10, 25, 32–35, 47, 54–56, 60, 74–76, and 93 (see Example 15b in chapter 2); indeed, it is to be found even earlier in the opening measures of the second tableau of Rimsky's opera *Sadko* (see Example 15a in chapter 2).

21. All the same, few of Stravinsky's works exhibit a more persistent and conspicuous referential commitment to the octatonic collection than the early *Scherzo fantastique*. Completed in March 1908, the *Scherzo* was apparently composed under Rimsky-Korsakov's supervision, although not to an extent approaching that of the earlier—and rather severely academic— *Symphony in E♭* (1905–07). At the time of its first performance in 1909, a program was attached to the score with a reference to Maeterlinck's *La Vie des abeilles*; in 1917, following Stravinsky's success in Paris with *The Firebird, Petroushka*, and *Le Sacre*, the work was performed as a ballet, *Les Abeilles*. Stravinsky later insisted that the *Scherzo* had been written "as a piece of 'pure' symphonic music"; that the reference to Maeterlinck had originated with his publisher, "who thought a 'story' would help sell the music"; and that he—Stravinsky—had

never been consulted on the 1917 ballet production, which was unauthorized. See Igor Stravinsky and Robert Craft, *Conversations with Stravinsky*, p. 40.

22. The staccato doubling of legato lines becomes a persistent feature of Stravinsky's scoring. A logical instrumental consequence of this dry, crisp, percussive impulse, it extends to all branches or "choirs" of the orchestra: woodwinds, brass, strings, and percussion. In even so slow, quiet, and nearly motionless a setting as *The Firebird*'s Introduction its effects are felt: in the opening measures, two double basses double the legato ostinato pattern, playing pizzicato.

23. *Expositions and Developments*, p. 168.

24. Specifically, the two 7/4 measures or "phrases" of the Finale's theme at No. 17 define an alternation or oscillation between the two (0 4 7) "major" triads related by the interval of 2 (a whole step apart), (B D♯ F♯) and (A C♯ E) here, a triadic alternation that implicates, referentially, the (F♯ E D♯ C♯ B A) hexachordal segment of the diatonic collection. This alternation or oscillation between (0,2) related (0 4 7) "major" triads—and the (0 2 3 5 7 9) diatonic hexachordal segment implicated by it—is characteristic of Stravinsky's "Russian" musical thought.

25. The first of these "Khorovod" melodies appears as No. 79 in Rimsky-Korsakov's *100 Russian National Songs*, opus 24, while the borrowed melody of the Finale appears as No. 21 in the same collection. In 1960 Stravinsky could no longer recall which of the folksong collections available to him at the time (those by Tchaikovsky, Liadov, and Rimsky) served as his immediate source (*Memories and Commentaries*, p. 92).

26. Gerald Abraham, *Studies in Russian Music*, p. 56.

CHAPTER 2

1. *Expositions and Developments*, p. 156. For a vivid account of the scenario—and one that appears to encompass Stravinsky's "vision" or stated objectives—see Alexandre Besnois, *Reminiscences of the Russian Ballet*. Besnois was responsible for the decor.

2. The number and variety of works known to have been conceived with material or ideas of octatonic or octatonic-diatonic reference (*The Firebird*, *Petroushka*, the *Octet*), or that in finished form commence with material or ideas exhibiting such reference (*Fireworks*, *The Firebird*, *Zvezdoliki*, *Le Sacre*, *Symphonies of Wind Instruments*, *Capriccio*, *Symphony of Psalms*, *Babel*, *Scènes de ballet*, *Symphony in Three Movements*, "Basle" *Concerto in D*) are astonishing. The reader is referred—somewhat prematurely—to Lists 1 and 2 in this chapter.

3. Note that in more general references to intervals, relations, or complexes of pitch elements, the number 0 need not entail the assertion of pitch-class priority. Thus, in contrast to the analysis of *The Firebird* Introduction in Example 3, the text may refer more generally to a (0 4 7) "major" triad in which the number 0 merely signifies the root of the (0 4 7) complex without necessarily encompassing priority with respect to a given context. This distinction should always be evident from the analytic-theoretical context within which these references occur. However, note the difference between a 6 and a (0,6) designation (or between a 3 and a (0,3) designation): the former refers merely to the interval defined by the numbering, while the latter does indeed signal the assertion of some degree of priority on the part of the designated pitch classes in that attention is drawn, by means of the comma, to (more) articulative complexes with respect to which these classes have respectively been recognized as exercising a degree of priority (e.g., (0,6) tritone partitioning in *The Firebird* Introduction, which implicates the articulative Derivative I, with respect to which 0 and 6, as A♭ and D, are recognized as exercising priority). The term "complex" naturally refers to an internally unordered grouping, association, or composite of pitch elements in which interval complementation and order with respect to a specific, presented design are disregarded (e.g., the (0 4 7)

"major"-triad designation, or the (0 2 3 5) tetrachordal complex in Stravinsky's "Russian" period material).

4. This Collection III sequence at No. 75 in the *Scherzo fantastique* is preceded by a similar pattern at No. 74, accountable only to a different octatonic collection: (0 4 7/0 4 7 10) triadic complexes at D, F, A♭, and B instead of at C,E♭,F♯, and A. But, as noted already in the preceding chapter, the octatonic credentials of this early scherzo are among the most impressive in the whole of Stravinsky's music. Like a whirlwind, the piece swirls from one (0,3,6,9) octatonically conceived sequence to the next, often on an explicit basis (unimpaired by outside interference), with extensive reference to all three of the octatonic collections. For a list of these passages the reader is again referred to Lists 1 and 2 of this chapter.

5. Obviously, the *"Petroushka* chord" at Nos. 49, 50, and 51, numbering six distinct pitches not eight, fails to exhaust the octatonic collection inferable (Collection III). However, in the introductory measures at No. 48, there is a G–C–G–F♯–E–E♭ contour in the woodwinds and piano, followed, just prior to the "chord" at No. 49, by a (E♭ G B♭ D♭)–(C E G) succession in the piano. (See Example 14.) This figuration boosts Collection III's presence with an E♭. Moreover, the reappearance of the *"Petroushka* chord" at No. 77 in the third tableau features the (0,6) tritone-related (0 4 7) triadic subcomplexes not at C and F♯ but at the remaining two (0,3,6,9) symmetrically defined partitioning elements of Collection III, E♭ and A. Apart from exhausting Collection III, this transposition of the "chord" in the third tableau tends naturally also to suggest an *in-the-act* awareness of these referential implications on Stravinsky's part.

6. The reader is encouraged, both here and elsewhere in this volume, to improvise (mentally and/or at the keyboard) as a means of "getting into" the material. Thus, in regard to Example 16b, he/she might run through this sequence, inverting or altering the given registration, applying the same formula to the remaining two (0,6) tritone-related (0 4 7) triads of Collection III (the (0 4 7) triads at E♭ and A: see No. 77 in the third tableau), and then transposing the improvisation to the remaining two octatonic collections (see Model A in this chapter). Such improvisation will, of course, temporarily divert attention from the relations immediately at hand. But correspondences with other known works (of this or other "literatures") will present themselves. Improvisation of this kind thus serves dual purposes: (1) it ("synthetically") accustoms the reader to that more general "sound universe" which this inquiry seeks to define (a "universe" from which it gradually—with the addition of each new work—becomes possible to imagine Stravinsky picking and choosing the more specific relations that obtain from one context to the next); and (2) it ("analytically") allows at the same time for a sharper hearing and understanding of those more specific relations that obtain from one context to the next (e.g., the slight variances in articulation that distinguish the configuration at mm. 5–7 and m. 12 in *The Firebird* Introduction from the *"Petroushka"* chord").

7. Olivier Messiaen, who classified the octatonic scale as the second among "modes of limited transposition," appears to have been the first—at least in print—to associate Stravinsky (among others) with its use, in his *Technique de mon langage musical*. Since then, Roman Vlad has referred briefly to the scale in his discussion of Stravinsky's early works (*Stravinsky*, pp. 7–8), as has Eric Walter White (*Stravinsky*, p. 161). But these references by Vlad and White are perfunctory, and introduced in reference to only two or three works. The first to examine octatonic construction in Stravinsky's music systematically was Arthur Berger in "Problems of Pitch Organization in Stravinsky," to which this author is indebted for some of the background information encompassed by this chapter. See also, Nicholas Slonimsky, *Thesaurus of Scales and Melodic Patterns* (New York: Coleman-Ross, 1947).

8. *Memories and Commentaries*, p. 108. See, also, *Expositions and Developments*, pp. 114-17.

9. The following comment on the first movement of the *Symphony of Psalms* (1930) is revealing: "The sequences of two minor-major thirds joined by a major third, the root idea of

the whole work, were derived from the trumpet-harp motive at the beginning of the *allegro* in Psalm 150." (Igor Stravinsky and Robert Craft, *Dialoques and a Diary*, p. 77). Stravinsky fails to mention in these reflections that the first movement of *Psalms*—"composed," as he says, "in a state of religious and musical ebullience"—is one of the most thoroughly octatonic of his creations, and exemplifies not only (0 1 3 4) partitioning at E, G, and B♭ (i.e., "the sequences of two minor thirds joined by a major third"), but (0 3 7/0 4 7/0 4 7 10) triadic partitioning at these pitches (as demonstrated already in   Example 10b), partitioning schemes with which, by 1930, he had been dealing for years (and with which he would continue to deal for years thereafter).

10. That Stravinsky consciously inherited the octatonic collection from his teacher, Rimsky-Korsakov, and that his early (unimpaired) deployment of it in lengthy passages in the *Scherzo fantastique*, *The Firebird*, *Petroushka*, *Le Sacre*, and *Les Noces* was also conscious, seems beyond reasonable doubt. However, apart from the sizable sections of explicit octatonic reference to be found later in such works as the *Symphony of Psalms*, *Babel*, and the *Symphony in Three Movements*, subsequent use during the lengthy neoclassical era may have become increasingly unconscious or "instinctual," perhaps in much the same way that much of codified tonal practice must always have been, for every tonal practitioner, a vast, nonimmediate, instinctual "given." But a composer's acknowledged concerns or intentions need not constitute the only (nor necessarily the most reliable) indication of what might ultimately qualify as a useful analytic-theoretical review (as all musicians—but perhaps especially composer-musicians—must surely be aware). So while this inquiry cautiously subscribes to an "it-may-be-inferred" attitude, it will from time to time point to circumstances that could be construed as evidence of "complicity" (e.g., the within-Collection III transposition of the "*Petroushka* chord" at No. 77 in the third tableau).

11. Apart from Rimsky-Korsakov, Scriabin, and Messiaen, the Dutch composer Willem Pijper (1894–1947) occupied himself rather persistently with octatonic ideas. Indeed, his Piano Sonatina no. 2, a striking work, is wholly octatonic and reflects a preoccupation with (0,3,6,9) symmetrically defined (0 3 7/0 4 7) triadic partitioning similar to Stravinsky's (as defined in Model A of this chapter). As an early admirer of *Le Sacre* (and ardent opponent of neoclassicism long before Pierre Boulez & Co.), Pijper may have initially inferred the collection from *Le Sacre*.

12. "Pitch Organization in Stravinsky," p. 141. Berger concludes: "With sufficient confidence, therefore, it may be said that what passes for one of the most peculiarly Stravinskian 'sounds,' rises out of the octatonic scale."

13. Difficulties are likely to persist with regard to the classification and selection of Lists 1 and 2. Specifically, if octatonic-diatonic interaction is to encompass not only instances of octatonic-diatonic interpenetration but instances of octatonc-diatonic block juxtaposition as well, there is virtually no limit to the extent to which octatonic relations "might reasonably be inferred" in Stravinsky's music. Thus, for example, the whole first movement of the *Symphony of Psalms* (1930) is octatonic-diatonic in this latter sense (and is so regarded in List 2); octatonic blocks are placed in abrupt and repeated juxtaposition with blocks accountable to the diatonic collection, principally the E-scale on E. But the same might apply to works which, like *Oedipus Rex* (1927), are fundamentally—or may at first glance appear—more diatonic than octatonic; since this diatonicism interacts with blocks or sections of octatonic or octatonic-diatonic reference (and since this interaction is critical to a hearing and understanding of the totality of relations), these works might also, on a global scale, be deemed "octatonic-diatonic." Octatonic and diatonic relations thus interact (and so interrelate or "influence each other") not only by means of shared connecting links (elements or groupings held in common), but also through critical points of interpenetration. Indeed, to the extent to which certain diatonic partitioning processes might be considered typical of Stravinsky, they are often so by virtue of the links forged with certain octatonic partitioning processes

(i.e., the specific manner of the interaction, "Russian," neoclassical, or early serial). And so, once again: the lists in this chapter are handy guides to octatonic penetration in Stravinsky's music, by no means limiting the extent to which such penetration might ultimately be inferred, but merely acknowledging the most obvious or readily detectable instances of such penetration.

14. Hence Messiaen's classification of the scale among the "modes of limited transposition" (*Technique*, p. 52).

15. See "Pitch Organization in Stravinsky," p. 133. In addition to quoting directly from Berger in these preliminary remarks, we are also paraphrasing liberally, seeing, on the one hand, no reason to alter what has already been presented in a thoroughly efficient manner, but on the other, an occasional need to revise in accordance with the findings of this inquiry. In this connection it should be noted that Berger ignores the 2,1 interval ordering of the scale and (0 2 3 5) tetrachordal partitioning (Model B).

16. Ibid., p. 133.

17. This will not necessarily mean, however, that in juxtaposition or interpenetration with non-octatonic material (or even in passages where octatonic reference is unimpaired), C-scale tonally functional relations, even if judged parenthetical, may not somehow impose themselves. We shall be discussing the nature of this imposition, principally a neoclassical phenomenon, in chapters 11 and 12.

18. "Pitch Organization in Stravinsky," p. 137. "Polarity" emerges from Berger's translation of a passage from Stravinsky's *Poétique musicale*, p. 26.

19. Exceptions may be found in the *Scherzo fantastique* at Nos. 7–9, 25, 32–34, 48, 54, 74–76, and 93; in *Le Sacre* at No. 42 ("Jeu du Rapt"); in *Renard* at No. 24; and in *Les Noces* at Nos. 35–40, 68–72, and 82–87. But with regard to "equal footing," a strong case can be made for an Eb pitch-class priority (or a (0 4 7 10) "dominant-seventh" complex at Eb) in *Le Sacre* as a result of its prominence "in and about," while in *Renard* a G priority is unmistakable despite the "harmonization" of a melody with all (0 4 7) triads of Collection I (at G, Bb, Db, and E) present in succession.

20. "Musical Syntax (II)," p. 233.

21. Benjamin Boretz, "Meta-Variations, Part II," p. 68.

22. Boretz, "Musical Syntax (II)," p. 236.

23. The term "complex" refers to a presumably cohesive grouping of pitches, without regard to interval complementation and order. Thus, for example, the (C E G) "major" triad is always a (C E G) "major" triad whatever the specifics in registral spacing and order. With (C E G) omitted (or with pitch numbering substituting for the pitch letters), pitch-class identity can also be ignored and only interval content taken into account (i.e., the (0 4 7) "major" triad).

24. The (0 4 7 10) "dominant seventh," most particularly as *simultaneity* (of attack and duration), is in Stravinsky's music very nearly exclusively octatonic (Model A) in conception. And while, in his neoclassical works, where, on the diatonic side of the referential coin, the familiar C-scale (or major scale) may often be inferred, certain correspondences may indeed be drawn with the "irregular resolutions" of tonal, C-scale practice (briefly to be noted in chapter 11), and while, too, it may occasionally take on the "feel" of a dominant owing to a variety of dominant-tonic-like resolutions concluded on its behalf (to be discussed in chapter 12), still it is invariably introduced within a securely octatonic or at least octatonic-diatonic framework, and hence superimposed on or oscillating with other triads and "dominant sevenths" of the particular octatonic collection to which it adheres.

25. As indicated in chapter 1, the numbering runs as follows: the half step or semitone is a 1, the interval defined by one half step; the whole step is a 2; the minor third, a 3; the major third, a 4; the fourth, a 5; the tritone, a 6; the fifth, a 7; and so forth. Then, of the groupings or complexes of pitches, the numbering will refer to the (0 3 7/0 4 7) "minor" and "major"

triads, to the (0 4 7 10) "dominant seventh," and occasionally to the (0 3 6 9) "diminished-seventh" chord; and then to Model A's four-note (0 1 3 4) tetrachord, and Model B's (0 2 3 5) tetrachord. Then of the scales, to the two octatonic scales of Models A and B, 0 1 3 4 6 7 9 10 (0) for Model A, 0 2 3 5 6 8 9 11 (0) for Model B; and, beginning in chapter 3, to the D-scale of the diatonic collection, 0 2 3 5 7 9 10 (0), and the (0 2 3 5 7 9) hexachordal segment. We might also note, as in chapter 1, the labeling of the diatonic scales: taking the keyboard's "white notes" as representing the diatonic collection, we identify these interval orderings or scales by a C-scale/D-scale type of labeling in place of the traditional "major-scale"/"Dorian-mode" type of designation. The rationale here is similar to that which underlies pitch numbering. The identification aims at a greater generality in musical thought, freeing the analysis from irrelevant theoretical, historical, or "stylistic" considerations, from tonal and model (archaic and modern) implications where these implications no longer apply.

26. Apart from the writings of Pierre Boulez cited below, the reader is referred to Robert Craft's brief mention of the "chorus of ghosts" episode in Act III of *The Nightingale* (List 1) as "typical" of Stravinsky, in "Music and Words," p. 86; to Henry Boys's documentation of "immobility," "harmonic mass," "harmonic stasis," and "polarity" in Nos. 125 + 1–130 of the second movement of the *Symphony in Three Movements* (Lists 1 and 2), in "Stravinsky: The Musical Materials," p. 15; and to Edward T. Cone's revealing discussion of Stravinsky's "method" of abrupt juxtaposition, in "Stravinsky: The Progress of a Method," a discussion advanced largely with reference to the *Symphonies of Wind Instruments* and the *Symphony of Psalms*, but in which, as in the above instances, accountability to the octatonic collection (the root of the typicality) is ignored or overlooked.

27. *Notes of an Apprenticeship*, p. 74.

28. Ibid., p. 249.

29. Ibid., pp. 74, 250.

30. For an illuminating discussion of this "method" of abrupt block juxtaposition, see Edward T. Cone's "Progress of a Method," even though Cone ignores (or overlooks) the symmetrically defined referential implications of the "method."

31. The terms "deadlock" or "locked confrontation" are suggested by the sense of an internal "pulling and tugging" or "opposition" always to be felt among the superimposed, registrally fixed (0,3,6,9) symmetrically defined partitioning elements or articulative fragments (a felt "opposition" in which the variance in rhythmic-metric periods defined by the reiterating fragments naturally plays a role), so that the balance is seldom passive or frictionless, but surges with an inner, self-contained tension. The following analogy, introduced by Rudolf Arnheim in regard to visual perception, is instructive: " 'Dead center' is not dead; no pull in any one direction is felt, because at middle point pulls from all directions balance each other. To the sensitive eye, the balance of the middle point is alive with tension. Think of a rope that is motionless while two men of equal strength are pulling it in opposite directions. It is still, but it is loaded with energy" (*Art and Visual Perception*, p. 6).

32. A term borrowed from Benjamin Boretz, "Meta-Variations, Part IV: Analytic Fallout (II)," p. 169.

33. *Notes of an Apprenticeship*, p. 7.

34. See Allen Forte, *Contemporary Tone Structures*, p. 137; or, more recently, Boretz, "Meta-Variations, Part IV: Analytic Fallout (I)," p. 150.

35. "Pitch Organization in Stravinsky," pp. 134–35.

36. *Expositions and Developments*, p. 156.

37. We allude, particularly, to varying applications of tonally inspired reckoning: e.g., Roy Travis's analysis of the opening blocks of *Le Sacre*'s Introduction in "Toward a New Concept of Tonality?"; or, Allen Forte's analysis of *Petroushka* in *Contemporary Tone Structures*. Again, it is not that these studies lack insight, only that in regard to abrupt juxtaposition and its implications for the critical question of reference, much of Stravinsky's music seems fun-

damentally at odds with these tonally conceived schemes of "coherence" or "continuity," so that: (1) they are ultimately of little assistance in matters pertaining to the consistency, identity, and distinction of Stravinsky's music; (2) the at-times elaborate transfer of terms and concepts intimately associated with the tonality of C-scale literature to a body of works which is surely problematic in this respect tends more to confuse than to illuminate; (3) the improper or confusing transfer undermines, as suggested already, any binding or particularizing hearing and understanding that these terms and concepts afford the (tonal) C-scale literature for which they were intended.

38. "Pitch Organization in Stravinsky," p. 148.

39. Berger's interpretation of pitch number 6 as a possible Classical "tendency tone" in the 2,1 interval ordering of the scale (Model B) seems grossly abstract (or completely irrelevant) with respect to (0 2 3 5) tetrachordal partitioning in Stravinsky's music, there being, to this observer's knowledge, no instances of such partitioning where pitch number 6, reading "up" or "down," is not readily identified with the (6 8 9 11) tetrachordal unit, standing thus in a (0,6) symmetrically defined (fixed or polarized) "opposition" to pitch number 0 of the (0 2 3 5) tetrachord.

CHAPTER 3

1. Benjamin Boretz has referred to the (0 2 3 5 7 9) diatonic hexachord in his analysis of *Petroushka*, first tableau, in "Meta-Variations, Part IV: Analytic Fallout (II)," p. 167. Boretz infers the (0 2 3 5 7 9) hexachord in terms of the (E D C♯ B A G) collection at No. 1, and discusses *Petroushka*'s diatonicism independent of tonal considerations. But some noncorrespondences with the present analysis are noteworthy. While Boretz, as here above, equates abrupt block juxtaposition with "pitch-collection change," he interprets the juxtaposed blocks as "time spans"; and his reference to the symmetry that obtains from the pattern of these "spans" is a facet largely ignored here (at least for the time being). More significantly, Boretz's "referential" diatonic hexachord is the (D E)(A G)(B♭ C) collection first introduced by the oscillating (B♭ D A)–(C E G) simultaneities at No. 2(-2), from which he subsequently at No. 3 (m. 27) derives an "extension" in the form of a "superimposition of *two* hexachords inversionally related . . . producing the 'diatonic collection' *as their union*," with respect to which succeeding blocks are interpreted. Moreover, Boretz does not subscribe to any assertion of (single) pitch-class priority (the "inversionally related" hexachords merely produce the diatonic collection "as their union"), while the present study's D-scale-on-G determination at Nos. 3–6 obviously does (according to the criteria indicated in the preceding chapter: persistence, octave reinforcement, metric accentuation, etc.). Thus, a certain significance is here attached to the (0 2 3 5 7 9) hexachord, to the nature of its "incompleteness" and its affiliation with the D-scale, the pairs of 2s that encircle it, and (0,7) "fifth"-defined adjacency or overlapping. These concerns relate ultimately to the interaction, intervention, or "intrusion" of referentially octatonic material, a matter alluded to only briefly in Boretz's discussion. These special (0 2 3 5 7 9) hexachordal considerations may have been prompted by a hearing and understanding of consistency, identity, and distinction for this particular body of "Russian"-period works.

2. Hence, too, the first tableau's "D-minor" (or possibly "F-major") key signature is ignored in Example 21, the articulation having little or nothing to do with any of the tonally functional transactions associated with this signature. Clearly, the absence of an F in the opening block at Nos. 0–2 is too critical, too fundamental (or referential) an omission for one to assume its hypothetical presence on behalf of the A-scale on D (or, in tonal terms, on behalf of the "descending" or "ascending minor scale" on D), or to assume, indeed, that it *is* an omitted F rather than an omitted F♯; and the C♯ at No. 1, far from functioning as a "leading

tone" to the "tonic" D in tonality's "ascending minor scale" on D, identifies articulatively with the (E D C♯ B) tetrachord, and referentially with the (E D C♯ B A G) diatonic hexachord, not with a dominant "leading" to its "tonic" D. It will be remembered in this connection that, in chapter 1, an A♭-minor signature in *The Firebird* Introduction was dismissed on grounds that the context was ostensibly octatonic. Here in *Petroushka* the context is clearly diatonic, but nonetheless exhibits an articulation (or a partitioning of the diatonic collection) that fails to implicate the familiar C-scale or "D-minor scale" interval orderings of the diatonic collection, and hence any of the tonally functional relations associated with these interval orderings. But the signature in *Petroushka* is convenient, since the B♭ figures in the (E D C B♭ A G) block at No. 2, in the passage using the D-scale on G at Nos. 3–6, and in the octatonic-diatonic block at No. 7. For this reason we can well understand how earlier observers might have been misled, following their eyes rather than their ears, into accepting, unconditionally, the tonal implications of the "D-minor" signature.

3. The folk melody at No. 5, foreshadowed by the blocks at Nos. 2 and 3, is a Russian Easter song, and appears as No. 47 in Rimsky-Korsakov's 1876 collection of *100 Russian National Songs*. For an excerpt from Rimsky's arrangement of it for voice and piano, see Example 26 in this chapter.

4. For a realization of this IV(ii)–V "half cadence" or progression "in F," or of this vi–IV–V–vi–(I₆)–ii–V tonally functional harmonization of the borrowed Russian folk melody at No. 5 "in the key of F-major," see, again, Rimsky-Korsakov's arrangement in Example 26 of this chapter. We shall presently be discussing Rimsky's version and comparing it to Stravinsky's adaptation in greater detail.

5. How close we are, indeed, to the "sound" of *Le Sacre*, where the static "vertical chromaticism" becomes interpretable in terms of Model B's 0–11 or "major-seventh" interval span, with its "upper" (0 2 3 5) tetrachordal fragment standing "in opposition" to the "lower" pitch number 11.

6. For further comment on these borrowings, and for some English translations of the Russian lyrics, see Frederick W. Sternfeld, "Some Russian Folk Songs in Stravinsky's *Petroushka*," in *Petroushka*, ed. Charles Hamm. The two attributions here to the Istomin-Diutsch and Swerkoff collections are derived from Sternfeld. Moreover, while unable to cite any immediate sources, Stravinsky did acknowledge an early familiarity with the collections by Tchaikovsky, Liadov, and Rimsky-Korsakov (*Memories and Commentaries*, p. 91). On the other hand, some of this folk material may have been so well known at the time that immediate borrowing may not always have been necessary.

7. An earlier adaptation of this tune appears in Balakirev's *Overture on Three Russian Themes* (1858).

8. Thus, in regard to *Les Noces*, Stravinsky writes as follows in his *Autobiography*, p. 106: "It was not my intention to reproduce the ritual of peasant weddings, and I paid little heed to ethnographical considerations. My idea was to compose a sort of scenic ceremony, using as I liked those ritualistic elements so abundantly provided by village customs which had been established for centuries in the celebration of Russian marriages. I took my inspirations from those customs, but reserved to myself the right to use them with absolute freedom." The same attitude prevailed with respect to Russian folk music, whether authentic or of the nineteenth century westernized variety. As has so frequently been suggested in this connection, Stravinsky often mimicked, borrowed, or "stole," but made of this "raw material" something new and different, something peculiarly his own. The same attitude pertained to the many "influences" or "backward looks" of Stravinsky's neoclassicism. From these too, something was to emerge that remained peculiarly his own.

9. For a general discussion of this subject, see Alfred J. Swan, "The Nature of The Russian Folk-Song"; and Viktor Beliaiev, "Kastalsky and Russian Folk Polyphony."

10. *Memories and Commentaries*, p. 92. We should note, however, that contrary to

Stravinsky's insistence on "fabrication" and the strictly unconscious nature of his "folk memory" after *Petroushka*, recent study has suggested a far from tenuous link to genuine samples of Russian folk material throughout the "Russian" period generally. With reference to *Le Sacre* and its clutter of (0 2 3 5) folklike fragments, see Richard Taruskin, "Russian Folk Melodies in *The Rite of Spring*."

11. For further comment on *Petroushka*'s 1947 revision, see Henry Boys, "Note on the New *Petroushka*." On Stravinsky's revisions generally, see David Drew, "Stravinsky's Revisions."

12. In Stravinsky's 1943 revision of the "Danse sacrale" in *Le Sacre*, the string parts were also rewritten. On the whole, however, this revision, along with the earlier and more extensive revison of *Le Sacre* for a Diaghilev revival in 1921, was directed at adjustments in notation, designed "to facilitate performance by means of an easier-to-read unit of beat," or by means of shortening the measure lengths in some of the sections. (See *Expositions and Developments*, p. 168.)

13. *Memories and Commentaries*, p. 37.

14. *Expositions and Developments*, p. 156.

CHAPTER 4

1. Pierre Boulez has described *Le Sacre* as a work in which a "vertical chromaticism" coincides with a "horizontal diatonicism" (*Notes of an Apprenticeship*, p. 74). The present analysis is an interpretation of this "vertical chromaticism" in terms of a nearly globally determinate 0–11 or (0–5,11) partitioning of the octatonic collection (Model B), and of the coinciding "horizontal [presumably, linear or fragmental] diatonicism" in terms of the (0 2 3 5) tetrachord. On the other hand, it is to be noted (as it was in chapter 3 in regard to *Petroushka*, especially in conjunction with Examples 20, 24a, and 24b) that the single (0 2 3 5) tetrachord, as the principal melodic fragment of the "Russian" period (and certainly here in *Le Sacre*), may in its referential implications be either octatonic (Model B), diatonic, or octatonic (Model B) and diatonic, serving, by means of this neutrality, as the principal between-reference link connecting successive blocks of distinct referential character. And so the description Boulez gives of its "diatonicism" is ultimately misleading.

2. The persistence of this 0–11 or "major-seventh" vertical interval span (the persistence of the "vertical chromaticism," in other words, sustained statically and very nearly continuously from one block or section to the next), accounts for the pronounced harshness of the "dissonance" in *Le Sacre*, a harshness which, apart from certain rhythmic-metric intricacies, may still be *Le Sacre*'s most striking attribute (indeed, may continue to stun, shock or overwhelm as it so scandalously did in 1913; see Stravinsky's brief recollection of the 1913 premiere in the above quotation). Our intent is first to trace the articulation of this persistent and nearly globally determinate 0–11 vertical interval span, to trace its articulation and the referential implications thereof from one block or section to the next, and to situate this hearing and understanding within the general framework of Stravinsky's "Russian" musical thought. We can then move on to some of the formal, melodic, instrumental, or rhythmic-metric consequences of this organization in the third and fourth sections of this chapter, "Some General Considerations" and "Rhythmic-Metric Implications."

3. See, in the Introduction at No. 6 (Example 27), the reiterating "upper" (B♭ G F) incomplete tetrachordal fragment in the english horn "in opposition" to the "lower" B sustained in the bassoon; in "Danses des adolescentes" at No. 13, the "upper" (E♭ D♭ B♭) incomplete tetrachord of the (E♭ D♭ B♭ G) "dominant seventh" "in opposition" to the "lower" E in the bass; in "Jeux des cités rivales" at No. 64, the "upper" (G F E D) complete tetrachordal fragment in the strings "in opposition" to the "lower" G♯ in the tubas; or in "Action rituelle

des ancêtres" at No. 131–35 (Part II), the "upper" (C♯ B A♯ G♯) complete tetrachordal fragment in the trumpets and horns "in opposition" to the "lower" D of the bassoon's D–B♭ ostinato. These are only a few of the more conspicuous examples of this global (0–5,11) partitioning. Our reasons for citing the 0–11 interval span as globally more basic or fundamental
than, say, the tritone relation defined by pitch numbers 5 and 11 in the (0–5,11) format, are
primarily based on the metric accentuation invariably accorded this 0–11 span, an accentuation which, apart from its persistence, renders the unit highly conspicuous from one block or
section to the next.

4. Although rivaled by the *Scherzo fantastique*, *Petroushka*'s second tableau, the *Symphony
of Psalms* (1930), and the *Symphony in Three Movements* (1945), *Le Sacre* is without question the
most thoroughly octatonic of all Stravinsky's works, in respect both to the use of Models A
and B and the persistence and explicit nature of this reference. Thus, as one can see from the
analysis of Example 27, successive blocks often entail only a moving from one octatonic collection to another, with occasional patches of diatonic interpenetration or blocks of unimpaired D-scale diatonicism. As the most thoroughly octatonic of Stravinsky's works, *Le Sacre*
may very well be the most extensive piece of octatonic music ever written.

5. This (E♭ D♭ B♭) incomplete tetrachord—with the C omitted—is first introduced as
part of a (E♭ D♭ B♭ G) "dominant seventh" in the strings at No. 13, from which it detaches
itself at No. 14 as a D♭–B♭–E♭–B♭ ostinato figure in the english horn, becoming *the* principal
melodic fragment of "Danses des adolescentes." (E♭ D♭ B♭)'s identification with both the (E♭
D♭ B♭ G) "dominant seventh" and the D♭–B♭–E♭–B♭ ostinato is anticipated by the concluding block of the Introduction at No. 12 + 3, where the (E♭ D♭ B♭ G) "dominant seventh"
appears in the horns and the D♭–B♭–E♭–B♭ ostinato pizzicato in the first violins. However,
Stravinsky began *Le Sacre* with "Danses des adolescentes," completing Part I in its entirety
before returning to compose the Introduction. (See the quotation from *Expositions and Developments* prefacing this chapter.)

6. The reasons prompting us to dismiss the customary ascending approach in scale formation and pitch numbering in cases of (0 2 3 5) articulative partitioning were discussed in
chapter 2. Accordingly, references to (0 2 3 5) tetrachordal activity in music referentially
octatonic (Model B), diatonic, or octatonic (Model B) and diatonic, will always entail a descending approach in scale formation and pitch numbering, while references to the (0 3 7/0 4
7/0 4 7 10) triadic complexes will entail the customary ascending approach. On the other
hand, as noted earlier, the symmetry underlying (0 2 3 5) partitioning of the octatonic collection (Model B) extends to the (0 2 3 5) tetrachord itself, making the switch—or even a constant switching—from the descending formula for Model B to the ascending formula for
Model A far less burdensome than might be expected. (In other words: the 2,1,2 interval
ordering and consequent pitch numbering for the (0 2 3 5) tetrachord is the same, whether
descending or ascending. The same holds for the diatonic—and symmetrical—(0 2 3 5) (7 9
10 0) D-scale: its pitch numbering/interval-ordering is the same, whether descending or ascending.)

7. In *Pribaoutki* (1914), see, especially, the second song and, above all, the fourth, "Le
Vieux et le lièvre," where the (0 2 3 5) tetrachord in terms of (D C B A) in the voice and
clarinet, superimposed in static "opposition" over its (0,6) tritone-related pitch number 6,
the G♯ in the violin, yields an incomplete (0 2 3 5) (6 8 9 11) tetrachordal formation in terms
of (D C B A)(G♯ F♯ F E♭), accountable to Collection II. (See Example 17c in chapter 2.) In
Renard (1916), see, among numerous passages, the (A G F♯ E) (E♭ D♭ C B♭) articulation at
Nos. 9 + 1, 41 + 1, 44, and 48 + 2. In chapters 5, 6, and 7 we shall be discussing additional
instances of Model B partitioning in *Three Pieces for String Quartet* (1914), *Les Noces* (1917),
and *Histoire du soldat* (1918).

8. *Notes of an Apprenticeship*, p. 73.

9. Still, we may have overlooked at least one "true descendant." Quite apart from pitch

relations and the rhythmic-metric factor, Stravinsky's "method" of abrupt block juxtaposition, particularly the kind of within-block registral and instrumental "fixity" this "method" poses with respect to reiterating fragments or simultaneities (all so conspicuously evident in *Le Sacre*), does appear to have had a marked and lasting effect on Edgard Varèse (1885–1965), particularly in pieces like *Offrandes* (1922), *Octandres* (1923), and *Intégrales* (1925).

10. Igor Stravinsky and Robert Craft, *Retrospectives and Conclusions*, p. 76.

11. *Expositions and Developments*, p. 163.

12. Hence our insistence on the notion of *presupposition* here, since our analysis of pitch organization entails a hearing and understanding of form or architecture (abrupt block juxtaposition), melodic content or melodic repetition, and instrumental and rhythmic-metric procedure. Hence, too, continued discussion at this point constitutes little more than a rephrasing of this analysis and commentary, but a rephrasing from the vantage points of these several components or coordinates.

13. Mention was made of Boulez's account of pitch organization in *Le Sacre* in our general survey of octatonic relations in chapter 2. In a highly descriptive vein—but a revealing one nonetheless—Boulez interprets *Le Sacre*—or the question of superimposition generally—in terms of a "coagulation" which creates for the reiterating, superimposed fragments a "false counterpoint," all of this "eminently static in the sense that it coagulates the space-sound into a series of unvarying stages . . . and in the sense that it annuls the entire logic of the development" (*Notes of an Apprenticeship*, p. 249). Less revealing, however, are references to the makeup of this superimposition, to the specifics of pitch organization. Overlooking—evidently—the critical question of reference and its symmetrical implications with respect to both the octatonic and diatonic (D-scale) collections, Boulez interprets superimposition, "coagulation," or "polarity" in terms of a subdominant-tonic-dominant relation, the "language" of *Le Sacre* thus constituting little more than a "surcharge of an existent [tonal] language" (*Notes of an Apprenticeship*, p. 250). While this terminology can doubtless be reinterpreted to accord with *Le Sacre*'s occasional diatonic D-scale fragments (complete or incomplete), or with pitch numbers 0, 2, 5, and 7 of this D-scale rearranged as a series of "fifths" or "fourths," the account is hopelessly inadequate insofar as the bulk of relations are concerned, these being, as should by now be apparent, octatonic or octatonic-diatonic, and lying not only at the heart of *Le Sacre* but at the heart of typicality in Stravinsky's music generally, "Russian," neoclassical, or (at least early) serial. Moreover, no piece of the "Russian" or neoclassical categories seems so conspicuously devoid of C-scale tonally functional relations—and hence of some subdominant-tonic-dominant formulation—as *Le Sacre*.

14. All the same, see the (0,6) tritone-related "dominant-seventh" complexes at E♭ and A, (E♭ D♭ B♭ G)(A G E C♯), superimposed in the pizzicato accompaniment at Nos. 190–240 in the second movement of Bartók's *Music for String Instruments, Percussion and Celesta* (1936). But here again, the infusion of chromatic detail above in the piano and xylophone (a variation of the fugal statement of the first movement) might deter us from inferring the octatonic collection (Collection III) as a cohesive, referential factor.

15. *Notes of an Apprenticeship*, pp. 72–145.

16. Boulez gives the second of these rhythmic-metric types this description: "Stravinsky . . . utilized the system of superimposed rhythmic pedals—that is to say, his polyphonic apparatus being made up to some degree of clearly characterized stages, he give each of them an independent rhythmic period. The linkings of these several superimpositions will not be reproduced at the same intervals, but so as to obtain a varied disposition" (*Notes of an Apprenticeship*, p. 62).

17. Strictly speaking, in the first of these rhythmic-metric types (as exemplified by "Jeux des cités rivales" at Nos. 57–64, Example 30a), rhythm becomes meter and meter becomes rhythm (with the two thus interchangeable), while in the second (to be examined at Nos. 64–71, Example 30b), meter projects the stable rhythmic-metric period(s) of one of the reit-

erating fragments, with respect to which the conflicting rhythmic-metric periods of the other superimposed, reiterating fragments could be construed as "rhythm." It is noteworthy in this connection, however, that Stravinsky made the distinction between a shifting meter (1) and a steady meter (2) contingent on what he termed "the degree of real regularity in the music," and insisted that his barline was always "much, much more than a mere accent" and could not be "simulated by an accent," thus insisting, in some sense, on the continuing validity or relevance of rhythm and its separation from meter (*Conversations with Stravinsky*, p. 21). Thus, in the second of our two rhythmic-metric types, the conflicting, superimposed rhythmic-metric periods of the reiterating fragments are evidently not to be construed as conflicting, superimposed meters, but as "rhythm" in relation to the stable metric design. On the other hand, the implications of Stravinsky's rhythmic-metric schemes are from one context or piece to the next diverse and complex, and by no means as consistent or as straightforward as our two rhythmic-metric types (or as Stravinsky's comments) seem to suggest. We shall be endeavoring to expose some of these wider implications both in our present analysis and in chapter 8 when we deal with rhythmic (or metric) invention.

18. There is an additional reiterating fragment omitted in Example 30b, a bass-drum punctuation with a conflicting (but nonetheless stable, non-"mobile") rhythmic-metric period of three quarter-note beats. Together with a timpani fragment introduced at No. 67, this conflicting period foreshadows the eventual shift to the 6/4 meter at No. 70. Also, as shown by the brackets, pauses or rests that *follow* a reiterating fragment are always counted as part of the rhythmic-metric period. This procedure is also followed by Boulez.

19. With the conventional 4/4 meter, the first and third quarter-note beats are, of course, the downbeats (the accented or "strong" beats of the measure), while the second and fourth quarter-note beats are the upbeats (the unaccented or "weak" beats). And so it is here our contention that, notwithstanding the "mobility" or irregular spacing of the horn fragment's rhythmic-metric periods (bracketed in Example 30b), the ear is likely to hear and understand this irregularity in terms of displacement, in terms, that is, of a contradiction or reversal of the upbeat/downbeat identity of this reiterating A–D–C–D fragment.

20. *Conversations with Stravinsky*, p. 21.

21. Indeed, our contention is equally that, even in cases where Stravinsky "jumps the fence" by opting for the first of our two rhythmic-metric types (where, in other words, he shifts the meter in order metrically to *preserve* rhythmic-metric "sameness"), even in such cases the listener is often likely to hear and feel this duplicity, and hence some regular metric periodicity in the "background," regardless of the shifting meter, which, while concealing the duplicity, ultimately renders it more acute. And so we are not entirely in agreement with all of Stravinsky's pronouncements on the function of rhythm and meter in his music. Notwithstanding his claim that the means reflected "the degree of real regularity in the music" (presumably, the persistence or intensity of some felt, regular metric periodicity and accentuation), the distinction between the two types of rhythmic-metric construction examined above (metric irregularity as opposed to regular metric periodicity) is frequently, in actual effect, obscured, and the rationale which might conceivably have prompted an application of one of these types seems also to vary from one context or piece to the next.

CHAPTER 5

1. Debussy seems to have been under the delusion that Stravinsky was being influenced by the music of Arnold Schoenberg. There is a famous letter (to his Swiss friend Robert Goudet, dated October 14, 1916) in which he expressed the conviction that "Stravinsky is inclining dangerously *du côté de Schoenberg*." Stravinsky later speculated that this attitude may have been prompted by his—Stravinsky's—enthusiasm for Schoenberg's *Pierrot lunaire*,

which he heard while on a visit to Berlin in December 1912. (See *Expositions and Developments*, p. 78.) But, as we shall presently be indicating in chapter 9, this early enthusiasm was short-lived. After the *Three Japanese Lyrics* (1913), *Pierrot* was soon forgotten, and Stravinsky's interest in Schoenberg's music lay dormant for some forty years, not to be rekindled until the early 1950s.

2. In *Expositions and Developments*, p. 149, Stravinsky recalled a night at the opera with Debussy: "I was not so honest about the work we were then hearing. I thought *Pelléas* [*et Mélisande*] a great bore as a whole, and in spite of many wonderful pages." (He remembered, too, that at intermissions "people in the foyer were making fun of the *récit* style and intoning little sentences *à la Pelléas* to each other.") When asked by Robert Craft, over fifty years later in 1968, when he had last heard *Pelléas*, Stravinsky replied, curtly, "with Debussy." (*Retrospectives and Conclusions*, p. 289.) And so we detect a degree of indifference on Stravinsky's part as well, at least after *Petroushka* and *Le Sacre*, when his own "language" had taken shape.

3. In addition to the *Symphonies of Wind Instruments* (1920; see the quotation above), Stravinsky dedicated to Debussy his early cantata *Zvezdoliki* (*Le Roi des étoiles*), composed at Ustilug in 1911–12, after *Petroushka* and just before *Le Sacre*. Although honored, Debussy replied, in a letter dated August 18, 1913, that he could foresee no performances of this "cantata for planets" on "our modest Earth" (*Conversations with Stravinsky*, p. 51). The harmonic complexity of this work—which frequently leaves the vocal writing without instrumental support—posed major problems in intonation, and the piece was not performed until 1939. However, the "complexity" that has always been ascribed to its harmonic layout (which is certainly no more complex that that of *Le Sacre*) is eased considerably (as it is in *Le Sacre*) once the octatonic implications are fully taken into account. If one ignores the opening "motto," *Zvezdoliki* opens with an explicit (unimpaired) reference to Collection III at Nos. 0–2 (−2) (List 1, chapter 2). An A–G–E♭ succession in the strings is followed by a (E F♯ G) "cluster" simultaneity, which is sustained "above" reiterating (C E G) and (A C/C♯ E) triads in the chorus, all accountable to Collection III. At No. 9 (among other octatonic and octatonic-diatonic blocks), the dense, intricate contrapuntal network is, except for a single F♯ before the concluding (G B D) simultaneity, wholly octatonic, accountable to Collection I. And so the (0 3 7/0 4 7) or (0 3 4/3 4 7) "minor-major third" superimpositions, introduced earlier in the opening "motto" chords and characteristic of *Zvezdoliki* generally, are conceived, by and large, as partitionings of the octatonic collection, with an extensive—and often rapidly shifting—reference to all three collections of distinguishable pitch content. (See Lists 1 and 2 in chapter 2.)

4. *Expositions and Developments*, p. 154.

5. Stravinsky had, to say the least, mixed feelings about his childhood, his early family life, and his studies in St. Petersburg. In answer to some of Robert Craft's questions about his St. Petersburg years—and with particular reference to his piano lessons with Mlle Kashperova—Stravinsky put it bluntly: "I am most in Kashperova's debt, however, for something she would not have appreciated. Her narrowness and her formulae greatly encouraged the supply of bitterness that accumulated in my soul, until, in my mid-twenties, I broke loose and revolted from her and from every stultification in my studies, my schools, and my family. The real answer to your questions about my childhood is that it was a period of waiting for the moment when I could send everyone and everything connected with it to hell" (*Memories and Commentaries*, p. 25). Stravinsky's talent went unnoticed by his parents; and he seems not to have been taken seriously as a composer.

6. This move to the United States had been anticipated before the outbreak of war, however. Stravinsky had accepted an invitation to deliver the Charles Eliot Norton lectures at Harvard University during the 1939–40 academic year. These lectures were subsequently published "in the form of six lessons," his *Poétique musicale*, or, in English translation, *Poetics of Music*.

7. See the final chapter in Robert Craft's *Stravinsky: Chronicle of a Friendship*.

8. "Mobility," a term borrowed from Boulez (see chapter 4), refers to a reiterating fragment whose entrances or rhythmic-metric periods are irregularly spaced and of unequal duration. Thus, while the successive entrances or rhythmic-metric periods of the viola, cello, and first violin fragments vary "separately from" or "independently of" one another (these durations totaling seven and twenty-three quarter-note beats respectively; see the brackets in Example 31a), they remain stable within themselves; the entrances of the second violin's F♯–E–D♯–C♯ fragment are irregularly spaced, and are hence termed "mobile."

9. As noted earlier, rhythmic-metric or "harmonic" coincidence in Stravinsky's music is not generally as ambiguous as it is here in the first of *Three Pieces*, or in certain passages in *Le Sacre* and *Les Noces*. Usually, "independent" rhythmic-metric periods assigned to reiterating fragments remain stable within themselves, and hence will sooner or later project a detectable norm (or norms) in coincidence, often subtly linked to a kind of upbeat/downbeat ambiguity. And so the "development" defined by the second of our two types of rhythmic-metric construction is usually "sabotaged" by a materializing norm (or norms) in vertical alignment.

10. To recapitulate here: while the "separate" or "independent" rhythmic-metric periods of the cello, viola, and first violin fragments remain stable within themselves, they effect a union or coincidence from both a rhythmic-metric and a vertical (or "harmonic") standpoint, which is constantly changing. But there is in the reiterating (G A B C) fragment of the first violin a slight trace of regular 2/4 metric periodicity, owing to its possible G-major reference, and to the construing of A–G as a cadential figure with A as an appoggiatura. Hence our contention is that the doubt or uncertainty as to the "true" (stable) rhythmic-metric identities of these reiterating fragments (in combination) is felt in relation to this trace of regular 2/4 periodicity, or, more subtly, that this doubt or uncertainty is necessarily prompted by at least the suggestion of some "background" periodicity of a regular metric kind.

CHAPTER 6

1. Robert Craft and William Harkins, "Stravinsky's *Svadebka* (*Les Noces*)."

2. *Music Ho! A Study of Music in Decline*, p. 91.

3. Hence the 1917 listing here for *Les Noces*, although a final scoring was not finished until 1923.

4. Stravinsky himself suggested as much on several occasions. In *An Autobiography*, pp. 53–55, he writes: "My profound emotion on reading the news of the war. . . found some alleviation in the delight with which I steeped myself in Russian folk poems. . . . I culled a bouquet from among them all, which I distributed in three different compositions that I wrote one after the other, elaborating my material for *Les Noces*. They were *Pribaoutki*, for voice, with the accompaniment of a small orchestra; then *Les Berceuses du chat*, also for voice, accompanied by three clarinets; and, lastly, four little choruses for women's voices *a cappella* ['Saucers']." About *Pribaoutki*, he later wrote: "After *The Nightingale* [1914], my sketchbooks began to fill with melodic-rhythmic and chordal ideas, any one of which might have become part of *Renard, Les Noces*, or even *Histoire du soldat*, almost equally well; or so it would appear at a glance, though a composer soon separates his materials or, rather, fits them together when he begins to work" (*Themes and Episodes*, p. 27).

5. *Expositions and Developments*, p. 104. Or, see the quotation at the outset of chapter 7 on *Histoire*.

6. For further comment on this particular version of *Les Noces*, see *Retrospectives and Conclusions*, pp. 117–21. The arrangement was abandoned, Stravinsky writes, because of the difficulties in synchronizing the mechanical pianola with the "live" component, or because of "the near impossibility of finding competent cymbalomists." There is in Stravinsky's manu-

script collection seven pages of a still earlier version for chamber ensemble, approximating the size and composition of *Renard*'s mini-orchestra. (See *Themes and Episodes*, p. 27.)

7. In the octatonic-diatonic connecting-link summaries sketched in chapters 3 and 4 for *Petroushka* and *Le Sacre*, the (0 2 5) incomplete (0 2 3 5) tetrachord has already been envisioned as a kind of "basic cell" for the "Russian" period generally. This grouping, apart from its articulation in the form of all manner of (0 2 3 5) folkish fragments, systematically attaches itself to a (0 2 3 5)(7 9 (10) 0) tetrachordal partitioning of the diatonic collection (implicating the D-scale or the (0 2 3 5 7 9) hexachord), or to a (0 2 3 5) tetrachordal partitioning of the octatonic collection (implicating the (0 2 3 5 6 8 9 11) ordering, Model B, reading down as always in Stravinsky's (0 2 3 5) tetrachordally-oriented music); or it defines the link between Model B's (0 2 3 5) partitioning of the octatonic collection and Model A's (0 4 7 10) "dominant-seventh" partitioning. Still, less decisively (or less determinately), the (0 2) whole-step unit of this (0 2 (3) 5) tetrachord might similarly be posited: apart from the "Russian" litter of articulative 0–2 reiterations, this 2 would attach itself referentially in the manner indicated by our analysis of No. 1 of *Three Pieces* in chapter 5. (Indeed: that fundamental 2 of "Russian" music; those (0–2) whole-step reiterations duplicated by the (7–9) unit of the diatonic (0 2 3 5 7 9 (10) 0) hexachord or D-scale, or duplicated in turn by the (6–8) unit of the octatonic collection, where pitch number 6, or the (0,6) tritone relation it defines with pitch number 0, signals the imposition of octatonic relations (Model B). Again, see Examples 20 and 24a in chapter 3.)

8. *Les Noces* is in fact often cited as the antithesis of *Le Sacre*, *Le Sacre* being "all chromatic," *Les Noces* "all diatonic." But this diatonicism is deceptive, for, as we continue to reiterate, the principal melodic fragment or "basic cell," the (0 2 5) incomplete (0 2 3 5) tetrachord, may in its referential implications be either octatonic (Model B) or diatonic from one block or context to the next. And so while the diatonic contribution may occasionally seem to predominate or assume a central role, the bulk of *Les Noces* is octatonic-diatonic, with the blocks of explicit octatonic reference (List 1 in chapter 2) sizable and intricate. So, too, while *Les Noces* is not primarily octatonic as is *Le Sacre*, it nonetheless exhibits a fairly even distribution of these two collections of reference.

9. The articulative conditions (partitioning formulae) of the six-note (0 2 3 5 7 9) hexachord, so prevalent as a cohesive frame of reference in diatonic contexts of the "Russian" period, were introduced earlier in regard to *Petroushka*'s first tableau, Examples 19, 20, 21, 22a, and 22b in chapter 3. Of concern here in *Les Noces* are the adjoining (0 2 3 5)(7 9 0) tetrachords (with the "lower" of these incomplete owing to the 9–0 "gap," the "missing" seventh pitch element), and the three triads, two of which are (0 4 7) "major" and related by the interval of 2 (a whole step), and the third (0 3 7) "minor." Thus, with (F♯ E D♯ C♯ B A) as an example, the two tetrachords are (F♯ E D♯ C♯) (B A F♯), while the two (0 4 7) "major" triads are (B D♯ F♯) and (A C♯ E), the (0 3 7) "minor" triad (F♯ A C♯). These groupings jointly yield, in content, the (F♯ E D♯ C♯ B A) hexachord.

10. It is, of course, this diatonic framework or block at Nos. 9, 14, 20, and 65 that directly precedes each (near) repeat of the transition at Nos. 10, 16–18, 20 + 3, and 67. Thus, in Examples 35, 36, and 38, there is first this diatonic block at Nos. 9, 20, and 65 (with F♯ E C♯) as the "basic cell"); then, the octatonic (Collection II) and diatonic-hexachordal transition itself at Nos. 10, 20 + 3, and 67; and, finally, the octatonic (Collection II) blocks at Nos. 11, 21, and 68. Thus, too, in the successive blocks at Nos. 0–12 in the first tableau, the (0 2 5) articulative unit or "basic cell" is first diatonic—or referentially "open"—in terms of (E D B) at No. 0; second, referentially octatonic (Collection I) in terms of (E D B) at No. 1; third diatonic again in terms of (F♯ E C♯) at No. 9; and, finally, at No. 11 (following the transition at No. 10), octatonic (Collection II) in terms of (B A G♯ F♯) (F E♭ (D) C), Collection II's (0,6) tritone-related (0 2 3 5) (6 8 (9) 11) tetrachords, Model B.

11. In moving in blocks from one octatonic collection to another, the shared "diminished-

seventh" chord is often exposed (quite explicitly, as here in Piano IV at Nos. 68–72 in *Les Noces*), as the between-reference connecting link. In the first movement of the *Symphony in Three Movements* (Example 75a in chapter 12), the opening Collection I blocks at Nos. 0–5 are succeeded by a Collection III block at No. 7, in which (G B♭ D♭ E), as the shared "diminished-seventh" chord between Collections I and III, is isolated in a transitional passage at No. 5. In *Orpheus* at Nos. 4–77 (Examples 64a, b, and c in chapter 11), (G B♭ D♭ E) is again exposed as the shared "diminished-seventh" chord between the interacting Collections I and III.

12. Because of Example 38's condensation, these "mobile" or irregularly spaced periods of the reiterating "dominant sevenths" in Pianos I and III are not shown. However, the "dominant sevenths" enter for a duration of ten quarter-note beats at No. 68 + 3, for seven quarter-note beats at No. 69 + 2, and then for a concluding eight quarter-note beats at No. 69 + 5. Hence the "mobility" here, the successive periods of ten, seven, and eight quarter-note beats being of unequal duration. (Pauses or rests that follow a reiterating fragment are always counted as part of its rhythmic-metric period. Thus, the two measures of four quarter-note beats of reiterating "dominant sevenths" at No. 68 + 3 are followed by three measures of six quarter-note beats of rest. This makes a period of five measures or ten quarter-note beats.) But much of the subtlety in rhythmic-metric construction at Nos. 68–70 rests, curiously, not so much with this exquisitely placed "mobility" of the "dominant-seventh" entrances in Pianos I and III, as with the stable "pedal" of Piano IV's G♯–F–B–D basso ostinato. For while this ostinato defines a stable rhythmic-metric period of four quarter-note beats (to which the meter is adjusted), it encompasses a melodic repetition which lasts five quarter-note beats. In other words, because of the tied quarter-note beat, the melodic period totals five quarter-note beats, and thus overlaps—by one beat—the rhythmic-metric period of four quarter-note beats. Hence it is only after sixteen quarter-note beats (on the second beat at No. 69 + 3, not shown in Example 38) that these two overlapping cycles are synchronized in accord with their initial appearance at No. 68.

CHAPTER 7

1. The articulative routine (partitioning strategy) of the six-note (0 2 3 5 7 9) hexachord, prevalent as a cohesive frame of reference in diatonic material of the "Russian" category, was first examined in *Petroushka*'s first tableau, Examples 19, 20, 21, 22a, and 22b in chapter 3. (But see, also, the blocks at Nos. 58–65 and 80–82 in the second and third tableaux of *Les Noces*, Examples 41 and 38 in chapter 6.) Of significance are the hexachord's (0 2) (7 9) encircling units, articulated either as 2s (whole steps) or as an 0–7–2–9 series of 7s or "fifths"; its (0 2 3 5)(7 9 0) tetrachords (the "lower" of these being incomplete owing to the 9–0 "gap," the critically "missing" seventh pitch element); and its three triads, two of which are (0 4 7) "major" (related by the interval of 2, a whole step), the other (0 3 7) "minor." Thus, taking (E D C♯ B A G (E)) as an example, the (0 2) (7 9) encircling units are (E D) (A G), with an 0–7–2–9 "fifth" articulation of E–A–D–G; the (0 2 3 5) (7 9 0) tetrachords are (E D C♯ B) (A G E); and the two (0 4 7) "major" triads are (A C♯ E) (G B D), the (0 3 7) "minor" triad (E G B). Then, too, transpositions are habitually pursued at the interval of 7, the "fifth," with the (0 2) (7 9) encircling units constituting the points of overlap on either side. (See, in this latter connection, Example 22a in chapter 3, or, in this chapter, Examples 42, 43a, 44, 46, and 48a.)

2. Apart from these diatonic D-scale-on-G and (G F E D C B♭) hexachordal implications in *Renard* at Nos. 0–9 (Example 42), note the A♭ in the basso ostinato, a "chromatic" pitch number 11 in relation to the presiding G. These relations do prompt a fully octatonic Collection I setting at Nos. 24–26 in terms of (G F E D C♯ B B♭ A♭), explicit octatonic reference, List 1 in chapter 2; and hence with the seeds of this Collection I context embedded in this open-

ing block at Nos. 0–9 by means of the ostinato's A♭ or Collection I's (and Model B's) 0–11 or "major-seventh" interval span, G–A♭. But a more immediate octatonic connection materializes earlier. The clarinet's A–G–E succession at No. 1 becomes octatonic at No. 9 + 1 with an F♯ and (E♭ D♭ C B♭) tetrachordal articulation in the bassoon: (A G F♯ E E♭ D♭ C B♭), Collection III.

3. Wilfrid Mellers, *Romanticism and the 20th Century*, p. 202. Or, see Henry Boys, "Stravinsky: The Musical Materials," pp. 12–17; Roman Vlad, *Stravinsky*, p. 51; G. W. Hopkins, "Stravinsky's Chords," p. 6; or Pierre Boulez, *Notes of an Apprenticeship*, pp. 74, 250.

4. The peculiar radiance of "Tilimbom"—possibly the best known of Stravinsky's songs for voice and piano—is in large part owing to this widely spaced (and statically positioned) superimposition of these two "fifth"-related (0 2 3 5 7 9) hexachords, (A G F♯ E D C) and (D C B A G F), and then, in turn, to their overlapping (A G) (D C) and (D C) (G F) encircling units conceived as an A–D–G–C–F succession of "fifths." (See the analytical sketches to Example 43a.) The chromaticism between the F♯ of the piano's reiterating (D F♯ A) triad and the F of the G–C–F–G basso ostinato is not octatonically conceived (as is generally the case with Stravinsky), but is a specifically diatonic, "Russian" phenomenon having to do with the superimposition of these two "fifth"-related (0 2 3 5 7 9) hexachords and their embedded and overlapping A–D–G–C and D–G–C–F "fifth" successions. The sound of "Tilimbom," with these superimposed "fifth"-related (0 2 3 5 7 9) hexachords, the (D F♯ A) (C E G) triadic articulation of the (A G F♯ E D C) hexachord, and this special chromaticism posed by "fifth"-related (0 2 3 5 7 9) adjacency, is close to "The Soldier's March" and the music to Scene I in *Histoire*.

5. First published in *Expositions and Developments* (London: Faber & Faber, 1962). (It does not appear in the American edition.)

6. The close oscillation or rapid back-and-forth movement between (0 4 7) "major" triads related by the interval of 2 figures prominently as a cohesive triadic configuration in diatonic contexts of the "Russian" period. The six pitches of these two (0 4 7) "major" triads yield—as indicated already—the six-note (0 2 3 5 7 9) hexachord as a frame of reference, with their roots and "fifths" constituting the hexachord's (0 2) (7 9) encircling units. The configuration is (1) specifically diatonic, and (2) peculiarly "Russian." In addition to the (A C♯ E)–(B D♯ F♯) fragment of the clarinet here in *Histoire*'s "Soldier's March," see *The Firebird*'s Finale at No. 17 (Example 25a in chapter 3), where the folk melody is harmonized in terms of a (B D♯ F♯)–(A C♯ E) triadic alternation, implicating the (F♯ E D♯ C♯ B A) hexachord; *Les Noces* at No. 80 (Example 38 in chapter 6), where a reiterating G–F♯–E–D–A–(G) fragment is harmonized in terms of a rapid (D F♯ A)–(C E G) triadic oscillation in the piano, implicating the (A G F♯ E D C) hexachord. Then, too, although not shown here, see "On Saints' Days," the first of the *Four Russian Peasant Songs* ("Saucers"), 1917. While Stravinsky's 1954 addition of fanfarelike flourishes (with four horns) implicates the D-scale on D, this song outlines an alternation of (0 4 7) triads at G and F; this (G B D)–(F A C) alternation naturally yields the (D C B A G F) hexachord, which is inferable from within the fully accredited diatonic D-scale-on-D framework.

7. The problem with Mellers's account is that, without a traditional (tonal, C-scale) sense of harmonic progression, of cadential clarification, and hence of some reasonably unambiguous definition of key (the key of D-major here), there can really be no question in "The Soldier's March" of a hearing and understanding in terms of dominants, tonics, and subdominants (still less of an elision of this functioning), but only of an elision or superimposition of these E–A–D–G "fifth"-related elements which, in tonal C-scale (on D) music, *might formerly* have defined the dominant-tonic-subdominant relation. Indeed, were we actually to pursue the question of a key and a dominant-tonic-subdominant relation for D and the E–A–D–G "fifth" succession (with the meaning and significance that both key and this relation embody in tonal, C-scale-on-D music of the seventeenth to nineteenth centuries), the

whole articulative fabric would invite such a crippling degree of qualification as to render the pursuit virtually meaningless. There is in the articulative and referential makeup far too much that seems fundamentally at odds with tonal C-scale practice and theory. And so while modestly insightful as analogy, the cue Mellers offers becomes abstract insofar as our perceptual experience is concerned, and ultimately misleading in our analytic-theoretic attempts to deal with that experience. We are confronted, far more directly, with a pronounced diatonicism (most often with two sharps, F♯ and C♯); with the exposure of E, A, D, and G as elements of priority, these elements, articulated either as whole steps or "fifths," constituting the (E D) (A G) encircling units of the (E D C♯ B A G) hexachord; with a (0 3 7/0 4 7) triadic and—especially in Scene II—a (0 2 3 5) (7 9 0) tetrachordal articulation of this hexachordal reference; and then with extensions, transpositions, and superimpositions of this hexachord at the interval of 7, the "fifth." Should these interpretative conclusions be found meager, compared with what is generally expected from the analysis of a tonal C-scale piece, we might caution that both the trumpet's "tootling tune" and the clarinet fragment are subjected to contradictions or reversals in off-the-beat/on-the-beat identity, and that the consequent ambiguity in rhythmic-metric identity tends further to obscure the issue of (single) pitch-class priority or centricity (of a "tone center" or "tonic"), and hence of some reasonably unambiguous definition of key. We shall be discussing these rhythmic-metric implications of "The Soldier's March" in chapter 8 on "Rhythmic (or Metric) Invention."

8. In other words, pitch number 9, along with pitch numbers 0 and 2, identifies or "fixes" a given (0 2 3 5 7 9) hexachord, as E, D, and G do (as pitch numbers 0, 2, and 9) for the (E D C♯ B A G) hexachord of the march. Thus, had Stravinsky opted for a literal transposition of the march's ostinato, C, as pitch number 9, along with A and G, as pitch numbers 0 and 2, would immediately have identified or "fixed" the (A G F♯ E D C) hexachord in Scene I.

9. It is, of course, precisely this 0–11 or "major-seventh" interval span, articulated by Model B's (0,6) tritone-related (0 2 3 5)(6 8 9 11) tetrachords, that accounts for so much of the static "vertical chromaticism" in *Le Sacre*, and toward which our analysis in chapter 4 was so persistently directed. But see the octatonic Collection II block at No. 11 in *Les Noces*, where Collection II's tritone-related (B A G♯ F♯) (F E♭ (D) C) tetrachordal articulation, in Piano I and the bass solo, is very nearly identical in pitch content to that in these opening measures of Scene II.

10. *Notes of an Apprenticeship*, p. 62. The rhythmic-metric implications of this passage from *Psalms* were noted briefly in chapter 4, Example 30c, and the passage quoted here from the third tableau of *Les Noces* appeared earlier as part of Example 38 in chapter 6.

11. Stravinsky acquainted himself with much Renaissance music during the 1950s, the motets and masses of Josquin des Pres, collections of Elizabethan keyboard music, and the madrigals of Gesualdo and Monteverdi. Feelings of kinship with Gesualdo's music led him, in 1956–59, to supply the missing sextus and bassus parts to three of Gesualdo's *Sacrae Cantiones* (a book of twenty sacred motets for six and seven voices), published as *Tres Sacrae Cantiones*, and, at the same time, to commit to instrumentation three of Gesualdo's madrigals, published as *Monumentum Pro Gesualdo*. Stravinsky was less than satisfied with the last of these endeavors, however. In May 1963, he told Craft that "the harmonic tension is shortchanged in transferring the music from voices to instruments, and the most radical progressions to sing sound tame and archaic when played" (*Themes and Episodes*, p. 244). For some reflections on *Monumentum Pro Gesualdo* see *Expositions and Developments*, p. 119; on Gesualdo himself, see *Retrospectives and Conclusions*, pp. 107–16; on Monteverdi's madrigals, see *Retrospectives and Conclusions*, pp. 58–60.

12. Mellers, *Romanticism and the 20th Century*, p. 202.

13. Stravinsky's recollection of this fateful stroll appears in *Expositions and Developments*, p. 126. For a more extensive extract, see the quotation at the outset of chapter 9.

14. This "cultivation of incongruity" is the subject of Lawrence Morton's brief study, "In-

congruity and Faith." A certain contrariness may often seem fundamental, a kind of daring in which conventional or orthodox procedure—or accompanying sentiment—is inverted, and acquires a curious, ironic twist. The tactic may be "deflationary," as Morton suggests, embodying a reaction against the pretensions of Romantic or post-Romantic sensibility.

15. *Expositions and Developments*, p. 154.

16. *Agon* occupies a somewhat similar position as a crossroads piece in relation to the neoclassical and serial stages as *Histoire* does in relation to the "Russian" and neoclassical ones, even though *Agon*, while begun in 1953, was not completed until April 1957, and hence after such serial or partially serial conceptions as *In Memoriam Dylan Thomas* (1954) and *Canticum Sacrum* (1955). Thus, *Agon*'s initial sections are distinctly neoclassical, while serial techniques infiltrate the Coda at m. 185, and are present from this Coda to the reintroduction of the opening fanfare or "Pas de quatre" at mm. 561–620. Like *Histoire*, too, *Agon* is highly eclectic. Apart from this crossroads aspect, there is the subtle neo-Renaissance flavor alluded to earlier in this chapter, surfacing with the suggestion of early Renaissance cadential formulae. Then, too, the jazz element, acknowledged by Stravinsky, is apparent in *Agon*'s "Bransle simple" and "Bransle gay."

17. *Dialogues and a Diary*, p. 11.

18. Thus, in regard to *Le Sacre*, Stravinsky recalled that its orchestration was "a mechanical job, largely, as I always compose the instrumentation when I compose" (*Expositions and Developments*, p. 162). And, in connection with the *Symphonies of Wind Instruments* (1920): "My sketch score contains few indications of instrumentation, but that is because I was certain of the sound and knew I would remember its components; I had only to copy my sketch score into full-score form" (*Themes and Episodes*, p. 29). Still, when questioned by Robert Craft as to whether the inception of a musical idea was always accompanied by its instrumental sound, Stravinsky cautioned that this was not always the case. "Sound (timbre)," he said, will not "always be present." However: "If the musical idea is merely a group of notes, a motive coming suddenly to your mind, it very often comes together with its sound" (*Conversations with Stravinsky*, p. 12).

19. Boulez, *Notes of an Apprenticeship*, pp. 251–52.

20. *Dialogues and a Diary*, p. 10.

21. *Retrospectives and Conclusions*, p. 119.

22. *Retrospectives and Conclusions*, p. 118. Stravinsky always rejoiced that his early musical training and experiences in St. Petersburg, although limited in scope, had at least been "live" rather than synthetic, having consisted regularly of live performances and active music making, instead of recordings and remote, physically inactive listening.

CHAPTER 8

1. *Retrospectives and Conclusions*, p. 119.

2. In acknowledging this third and final, serial stage of his three orientation categories or "changes of life," Stravinsky drew attention to his continuing, unrepentant reliance on the piano. "I know only that in the *coronat opus* of my later years, the Princeton Requiem [*Requiem Canticles*, 1966] . . . I continue to believe in my taste buds and to follow the logic of my ear, quaint expressions which will seem even quainter when I add that I require as much hearing at the piano as ever before; and this, I am certain, is not because of age, is not a sign of dotage." See the quotation at the outset of chapter 13; or, in context, *Themes and Episodes*, pp. 23–24.

3. *Retrospectives and Conclusions*, p. 82.

4. Brief mention is made in *Memories and Commentaries*, p. 93, of a single pupil—or, as

Stravinsky sarcastically puts it, "a composer, rather, who visited me twice a week to have his works recomposed." Elsewhere, in *Themes and Episodes*, p. 7, he comments as follows: "Speaking of my own experience, I know that I have learned throughout my life as a composer chiefly through my mistakes and pursuits of false assumptions, not by my exposures to founts of wisdom and knowledge."

5. Indeed, some of Stravinsky's last interviews in New York with the *New York Review of Books* and *Harper's* (most of these reprinted in *Retrospectives and Conclusions*, pp. 14–101) vividly bring Saul Bellow's *Mr. Sammler's Planet* to mind. Thus: "Sammler did feel somewhat separated from the rest of his species if not in some fashion severed—severed not so much by age as by preoccupations too different and remote, disproportionate on the side of the spiritual, Platonic, Augustinian, thirteenth-century" (*Mr. Sammler's Planet*, p. 43).

6. Climacus, *Concluding Unscientific Postscript*, p. 33.

7. "Rhythm: Gershwin and Stravinsky," p. 19. Keller demonstrates what he calls Stravinsky's "retrograde version of the upbeat" by an analysis of the rhythmic-metric implications of the reiterating (C E G) triad in the horns and bassoons at No. 3 in the final movement of the *Symphony of Psalms*. The demonstration of this "strictly retrograde tension"—or of Stravinsky's rhythmic (or metric) invention generally—is revealing. Indeed, it is as instructive vis-à-vis the bulk of Stravinsky's oeuvre as Pierre Boulez's much publicized observations on *Le Sacre*.

8. In other words, if a contradiction or reversal develops with respect to the rhythmic-metric identity of a reiterating fragment (its upbeat/downbeat or off-the-beat/on-the-beat implications), then this ambiguity will manifest itself in terms of pitch organization generally, that is, in terms of the equilibrium, equal weight and independence, opposition, polarity, harmonic stasis, or deadlock of which we have spoken. Or, to reverse this sequence, if the (0,3,6,9) symmetrically defined partitioning elements of the octatonic collection, Models A or B, generate ambiguity with respect to priority, then this ambiguity will manifest itself as a contradiction or reversal affecting the upbeat/downbeat or off-the-beat/on-the-beat implications of a reiteration of which these pitch numbers are a part.

9. This is the point of Benjamin Boretz in "In Quest of the Rhythmic Genius." Boretz argues that a "rhythm"—a "rhythmic identity" or a "pattern-of-attack-duration complex"—is always "a rhythm *of* something"; that it is impossible to determine which "rhythm," or which "rhythmic identity" or "pattern of attack-durations," might be relevant (beyond the trivial "one-attack-at-a-time level") prior to "an identification of the things of which they are durations" (or "rhythms"); that such "things depend for *their* identification on observed functional activity in dimensions other than that of duration" (e.g., in the pitch-structural or timbre-structural dimensions); that such "other dimensional functional things" (i.e., "pitch things, timbre things, registral things, etc., and their complexes"). . ."create those rhythms by virtue of the times they take to occur and to be succeeded"; and that, hence, a "rhythmic structure" cannot be "determinately isolated" and is in this respect not analogous to "pitch structure" or "timbral structure." Nonetheless: "But equally it follows that to speak of a structure formed within any musical dimension(s) is to speak solely of a rhythmic structure, a structure unfolded in time. . . . *Thus, in the denial of the independence of rhythm, its transcendence is affirmed:* (the *rhythmic* structure of a piece is, in the current view, simply all of its musical structure, subsuming every dimensional and inter-dimensional substructure, *including* as a more or less significant aspect the foreground structure of attack durations). The theory of rhythm, then, is nothing more or less than the theory of musical structure in its most comprehensive form." For a less embellished version of this approach, see William W. Austin, *Music in the 20th Century*, p. 261: "Some students have claimed that the *Rite* represents a sort of emancipation of rhythm, comparable to Schoenberg's emancipation of dissonance, and that rhythm works independently of melody and harmony in this music, or subordinates melody and harmony to its elemental power. This is a mistake. There is a value in analyzing

the rhythm separately, to be sure, but to appreciate the *Rite* it is essential to restore the distinctive rhythm to it place and to see something of how it is actually coordinated with other elements to compose a unique form. The new and old rhythms together are in fact closely coordinated with the melodies and polychords. . . . If rhythm were actually independent, or supreme, the *Rite* could never have brought its distinctive kind of rhythm into the tradition of world music, but would have been merely an individual's experiment."

10. See, for example, Boulez's analysis of the No. 13 block of "Danses des adolescentes" in *Le Sacre*, a block described as a "rhythmic theme" whose constituent "rhythmic cells," echoed variably at Nos. 15 and 16 + 4, achieve "real existence inside a moveless sound-verticalization" (*Notes of an Apprenticeship*, p. 89). Thus, in Boulez's musical imagination it is the harbored rhythmic (or metric) invention that is the treasure of *Le Sacre* (and possibly *Les Noces* and *Renard* too), with respect to which pitch organization is "archaic," devoid of a "sense of development" or of "renewal." Indeed: "Because these horizontal or vertical coagulations are simple, easily manageable materials, one can attempt much sharper rhythmic experiences" (*Notes of an Apprenticeship*, p. 75). And so, the "archaism . . . doubtless permitted . . . the most daring research into rhythmic structures" (p. 140). Compare this approach with Boretz's in the above-cited "In Quest of the Rhythmic Genius" (which, incidentally, begins with a reference to the No. 13 block of *Le Sacre*), or with Austin's in *Music in the 20th Century*. The analyses or attitudes of these musicians are not wholly dissimilar or incommensurable, but they do persuasively reflect different trains of thought about the highly elusive rhythmic-metric factor, evidently prompted by different inclinations or concerns. For example, Boulez's ideas about rhythmic (or metric) "independence" in *Le Sacre* are reminiscent of the twelve-tone ordering procedures in his own compositions, where an "independent" serial mechanism is applied to the rhythmic-meter component; so that Stravinsky could be imagined as having foreshadowed an "emancipation" of rhythm-meter analogous to the "emancipation of dissonance" proclaimed by Schoenberg with reference to pitch organization.

11. *Notes of an Apprenticeship*, p. 62.

12. For the block at Nos. 46–48 in *Le Sacre*, see *Notes of an Apprenticeship*, pp. 96–99. For the "Danse sacrale," see p. 62 and pp. 124–35.

13. Readers familiar with Leonard B. Meyer's *Emotion and Meaning of Music* will find the illustrations here (specifically, Example 50c) similar to that introduced on p. 119 of Meyer's book. But the present analysis varies in its emphasis. The question of displacement in the rhythmic-metric identities of the reiterating fragments is ignored in Meyer's discussion. And while Meyer rebars a passage in accord with the steady 2/4 periodicity of the G–E/D basso ostinato (as here in Examples 50a, b, and c), the question as to *why* Stravinsky might have opted for the shifting meter (in place of the conventional 2/4 design) is not broached.

14. Note, however, that what in relation to past regular metric periodicity (the stable 2/4 rhythmic-metric "pedal" here) would have been conceived and barred as a syncopated, off-the-beat element coming-to-rest on E/A at m. 17 has here already been contradicted and reversed, owing to the irregular 3/8 measure at m. 16, which forces this conventional off-the-beat coming-to-rest *onto* the beat. But our contention is nonetheless that this (barred) on-the-beat coming-to-rest at m. 17 will more readily be felt and heard as a syncopated, off-the-beat element in relation to the established 2/4 rhythmic-metric period of the basso ostinato, so that, notwithstanding the immediate contradiction or reversal of conventional (tonal, C-scale) rhythmic-metric procedure, a felt contradiction or reversal in off-the-beat/on-the-beat accentuation has as yet not taken place, and *will* in fact not take place until this "background," syncopated, off-the-beat accentuation is itself contradicted and reversed, becoming a barred *and* felt on-the-beat accentuation at mm. 49–50 and 56–57 (see Examples 50b and c).

15. A reminder here: in conventional 2/4 meter the first quarter-note beat is, of course,

the downbeat (the accented or "strong" beat of the measure), while the second quarter-note beat is the upbeat (the unaccented or "weak" beat). In a further subdivision into four eighth-note beats, the downbeat and upbeat are, of course, *on* the beats, while the second and fourth eighth-note beats are *off* the beats. Thus, in accord with the regular 2/4 periodicity of the basso ostinato (bracketed in Examples 50a, b, and c and rebarred accordingly), the E/A coming-to-rest of the marching tune's B–C♯–D–(E) termination appears on the second and fourth eighth-note beats at mm. 17 and 46 (Examples 50a and b), and assumes therefore a syncopated, *off*-the-beat identity, while later at m. 50 it appears on the first eighth-note beat, and hence assumes, in contradiction or reversal, an *on*-the-beat identity. Thus, too, the sixteenth-note clarinet fragment is introduced on the third eighth-note beat at m. 45, assuming (in accord with regular 2/4 metric periodicity) an *on*-the-beat identity, but then enters on the fourth eighth-note beat at m. 47, contradicted and reversed by an *off*-the-beat appearance. And so both the opening marching tune and the clarinet fragment exhibit displacements of the off-the-beat/on-the-beat variety, while elsewhere in Stravinsky's music this displacement may take the form of upbeat/downbeat contradictions or reversals.

16. The same principle applies here as noted earlier at m. 17 in the opening "Soldier's March": what would in relation to past (tonal, C-scale) regular metric periodicity have been conceived and barred as an off-the-beat element is immediately contradicted or reversed, becoming an on-the-beat element by means—in the "Royal March"—of an opening, irregular 5/8 measure. This metric downbeating of a conventionally conceived upbeating or off-the-beat element is a rhythmic-metric "play" noted already in connection with the 7/4 measures at No. 17 in *The Firebird*'s Finale: an upsweeping horn glissando, certainly an upbeat figure in relation to the melody's first F♯, is accommodated as a downbeating glissando by means of the irregular 7/4 measures. (See Example 11 in chapter 1.)

17. Note, too, the subtle harmonic contradiction in this introductory passage. In relation to its C-scale-on-B♭ or pseudo-B♭-major reference, the chords or "harmonies" of the off-the-beat attacks suggest a "tonic-dominant" alternation (with a sustained, low D as pedal). But this alternation is not synchronized with the harmonic or "tonic-dominant" implications of the marching tune in the trombone, and the contradiction or non-synchronization arises at m. 6. Here, the off-the-beat chords return to a (B♭ D F) "tonic" emphasis, while the harmonic implications of the trombone tune continue to suggest the (F A C) "dominant." The effect of this non-synchronization is thus to isolate or set apart the off-the-beat attacks from the tune, providing them with a rhythmic-metric period of four off-the-beat attacks (if one disregards the opening 5/8 measure), a period whose "independence from" the marching tune is thus guaranteed—or is thus defined—"harmonically." This is subtle, intricate, and ingenious—and reminds us, too, that this invention is as fundamentally melodic, formal, and "harmonic" as it is rhythmic (or metric) in conception.

18. In other words, in accord with Stravinsky's "foreground" metric irregularity, this B–C♯–D–(E) termination is always barred as an irregular 3/8 measure, and hence has always the same rhythmic-metric identity. Hence the purpose of the irregularity would seem to be to preserve a fixed identity for this termination and its E/A coming-to-rest, in opposition to the concealed off-the-beat/on-the-beat displacements which hinge, for their apprehension, on the "background" regular 2/4 periodicity defined by the basso ostinato.

19. It has frequently been remarked that in passages of metric irregularity (passages reflecting the first of our rhythmic-metric types), Stravinsky's rhythm disintegrates into meter, with rhythm becoming meter and vice versa. As noted, there is an element of truth in the contention. Thus, in "The Soldier's March" of *Histoire*, the conventional (tonal C-scale) approach would most certainly have been to bar the material according to the regular 2/4 metric periodicity indicated by the brackets in Examples 50a, b, and c. On the other hand, this criticism ignores the potent double edge of the invention. The "absence of melody" in Stravinsky's music is also frequently bewailed. But here the question has not really to do with

melodic neglect, but with a different kind of melody, which, often of limited range and content and subjected to ostinatolike repetition, can pliantly succumb to the rhythmic-metric "play," to the displacements in upbeat/downbeat or off-the-beat/on-the-beat accentuation here under discussion.

20. By regular metric periodicity or "real [metric] regularity" is implied *regular metric accentuation* rather than pulse, the latter merely suggesting a regular beating (but one unordered metrically as to accentuation). Also, with reference to the present comparison, another auditor might claim that, on the contrary, the rhythmic-metric periods defined by the tuba fragment at Nos. 64–71 in *Le Sacre* unmistakably acknowledge regular 4/4 metric periodicity. But this inferred 4/4 periodicity is challenged by the persistent "mobility" of the horn's rhythmic-metric periods, and, although not shown in Example 30b (chapter 4), by the stable 3/4 rhythmic-metric period in the percussion. And so regular periodicity seems at the very least as ambiguous at Nos. 64–71 in *Le Sacre* as it is in the opening "Soldier's March" in *Histoire.*

21. As here heard and understood, this crossing of the barline is a compromise, a hybrid formulation, of the two rhythmic-metric types. But since both types partake of the same double edge (although by the differing notational means outlined in this chapter), the crossing is equally an attempt to acknowledge and record the fundamentals of this latter tactic.

22. It is at this point in *Oedipus Rex* that a messenger contrives, hesitantly, to broach the fateful news of Oedipus's murderous, incestuous relationship with the wife/mother, Jocasta. The curtly drawn, metrically irregular units here, in such contrast to the regular metric periodicity which predominates in *Oedipus*, mirror the breathless as well as fateful nature of the occasion. These and other implications of the *Oedipus* plot—and its bond to Stravinsky's music—will be subject to brief comment in the more extended musical analysis introduced in chapters 10 and 11.

23. Later at Nos. 159–67 (where the D-scale on G is transposed to the D-scale on D), the second of these two rhythmic-metric identities, the on-the-beat identity at No. 140, predominates and assumes the character of a "norm." The persistent E here gives the setting its D-scale (on G) referential complexion.

24. *Music Ho! A Study of Music in Decline*, pp. 94–99. The "lack of thematic distinction" in Stravinsky's music is painfully evident to Lambert in *Histoire du soldat*, where the "rhythmical dissection" is wholly abstract, a mere "objective juggling with rhythm, or rather metre, for there can be no true rhythm where there is no melodic life." Lambert also finds rhythm and orchestration "dissociated" from the "melodic and harmonic components" in *Le Sacre*, although, unlike Boulez, he finds the condition perverse and devoid of consequence.

25. *Twentieth Century Counterpoint* (London: Williams and Norgate, 1954), pp. 29–30.

26. "In Quest of the Rhythmic Genius," p. 155.

27. Although less rare than accelerando or ritardando markings, crescendos, decrescendos, or "swells" are infrequently encountered in Stravinsky's scores. Fixed dynamic levels more often identify individual blocks and their successive (near) repeats, with respect to which "swelling" could obscure the stress and phrase (or slur) signification, a proper intonation of which is essential to a hearing and understanding of the rhythmic-metric "play."

28. For a more extended extract, see the quotation at the outset of this chapter; or, in context, *Conversations with Stravinsky*, p. 135.

29. *Dialogues and a Diary*, p. 12.

30. *Expositions and Developments*, pp. 165–66.

31. *Themes and Episodes*, p. 150.

32. *Memories and Commentaries*, pp. 105–06.

33. Ibid., p. 107.

34. *Themes and Episodes*, p. 145.

35. Conductors appear always to have borne the brunt of heavy and insistent attack. Of-

ten they were little more than charlatans, clowns, matinee idols. They were unduly susceptible to ego disease, which "grew like a tropical weed under the sun of a pandering public." Or,
more to the point, "great" conductors, unable to adapt themselves to a work, "adapted the
work to themselves, to their 'style,' their mannerisms," with the consequence that the authority they wielded was "purely egotistical, false, and arbitrary." Conductors themselves were
accorded a position "out of all proportion to [their] real value in the musical, as opposed to
the music-business, community" (*Themes and Episodes*, pp. 145–56).

36. *Expositions and Developments*, p. 126.

37. Ibid., p. 165.

38. *Retrospectives and Conclusions*, p. 121.

39. Ibid., p. 120.

40. *Expositions and Developments*, p. 80–81. Apart from the *Etude* commissioned by the Aeolian company, Stravinsky's transcriptions for the pianola include *The Firebird, Le Sacre*, and
the first movement of the *Concerto for Piano*. The list for the Pleyel company in Paris is more
extensive: *Petroushka*, the *Histoires pour enfants, Le Chant du rossignol*, the *Four Russian Peasant
Songs* ("Saucers"), *Les Noces, Piano-Rag-Music, Pulcinella*, the *Concertino*, and *The Five Fingers*.
For brief comment see Eric Walter White, *Stravinsky*, pp. 573–74.

41. *Dialogues and a Diary*, p. 4. Obviously, "setting words to music" is a simplistic notion,
scarcely indicative of the rather complex process to which reference is made. Stravinsky reasoned that words, when combined with music, lose the initial "rhythmic and sonorous relationships that obtained when they were words only"; and that these relationships are ex-
changed for new ones, hence for a new "magic" (*Memories and Commentaries*, pp. 70–71). His
own reflections suggest a give-and-take in which neither words nor music seem to have prevailed with respect to the process as a whole. The rhythms or sonorous potential of a text may
have sparked the musical component and set the "musical saliva" in motion, while, as he
suggests in regard to *Oedipus Rex*, once sparked, the musical train of thought subsequently
dictated verbal stress or accentuation.

42. *Memories and Commentaries*, p. 78.

43. *An Autobiography*, pp. 53–55.

44. *Expositions and Developments*, p. 132.

45. Ibid., p. 138.

46. *An Autobiography*, p. 108.

47. *Dialogues and a Diary*, p. 15.

48. Ibid., pp. 78–79.

49. *Memories and Commentaries*, p. 71

50. *Themes and Episodes*, pp. 55–56.

51. Ibid., p. 57.

CHAPTER 9

1. Schoenberg and Stravinsky have in many respects, and on many different occasions,
been posited as "opposites." For Stravinsky's own reflections on this "thesis-antithesis" notion, see *Dialogues and a Diary*, pp. 56–58. And for further comment on the non-immediacy
of Stravinsky's (neoclassical) "influences" or "love affairs," see Donald Mitchell, *The Language
of Modern Music*, p. 95.

2. Some observers have blamed Stravinsky's émigré status for this isolation and "perverse" preoccupation with the conventions of the remote past. But Stravinsky countered that
his "love affairs" would have "happened" with or without Russia. See the quotation above
from *Dialogues and a Diary*, pp. 10–11.

3. What appealed to Stravinsky was the "sound" of jazz, its instrumental grouping of percussion and small ensemble. (See the lengthy quotation from *Expositions and Developments* prefacing "Some General Considerations" in chapter 7.) Still, the characteristic manner in which jazz percussively accentuates the unaccented beats or off-the-beat attacks of a stable metric pulse must also have whetted Stravinsky's appetite, although he does not mention these implications (and although, of course, this downbeating on the upbeat constitutes, as indicated in chapter 8, only part—perhaps an insignificant part in itself—of Stravinsky's rhythmic (or metric) invention).

4. See *Dialogues and a Diary*, p. 54. Boulez, *Notes of an Apprenticeship*, pp. 242–53.

5. *Expositions and Developments*, p. 78; *Dialogues and a Diary*, p. 54.

6. Both Schoenberg and Stravinsky attended the I.S.C.M. Festival at Venice in September 1925, Schoenberg to conduct his *Serenade*, Stravinsky to perform his *Piano Sonata* (1924). "But neither of us heard the other's music," Stravinsky later confessed in *Dialogues and a Diary*, p. 55. (Nor, obviously, did they bother to renew that earlier acquaintance of December 1912 in Berlin.) Stravinsky again heard *Pierrot lunaire* in Paris during the early 1920s, but then, "incredibly, I did not hear another note by Schoenberg until the *Prelude to Genesis*, in Hollywood in November 1945, at which time we might well have met, for we were in the recording studios on the same day and we sat on opposite sides of the Wilshire Ebell Theater at the premiere of the *Genesis Suite*." Indeed, his attitude toward Schoenberg and his music seems to have been one of outright hostility—with ill-concealed ignorance—rather than of mere indifference, especially during the lengthy neoclassical era. For his part, Schoenberg is alleged to have had Stravinsky—or Stravinsky's neoclassicism—in mind when he wrote the lyrics to the second of his *Drei Satiren* (op. 28): *Das ist ja der kleine Modernsky! / Hat sich ein Bubikopf Schneiden Lassen / . . . Wie echt falsches Haar! . . . ganz der Papa Bach!* In Robert Craft's recollection of a meeting in Paris with Pierre Suvchinsky (one of Stravinsky's oldest and closest friends) in November 1956, Suvchinsky is quoted as saying that musicians favorably inclined toward Schoenberg or Berg were branded as "traitors," while Stravinsky went about "dismissing *Wozzeck*, which he had not heard, as *une musique boche*, and Mahler, of whom he knew nothing, as *Malheur*" (*Retrospectives and Conclusions*, p. 193). Indifference seems quite definitely to have been his attitude toward Bartok and Hindemith (although he was always on friendly terms with Hindemith, their concert tours frequently intersecting during the 1930s). After Schoenberg's death in 1951 and the gradual adoption of serial methods in his own music, Stravinsky's attitude changed (his intolerance of criticism directed at his own music never abated). Apart from Schoenberg, Berg, and Webern (and his studies of Renaissance music), he grew to respect and appreciate much music by Varèse, Boulez, Stockhausen, Ives, Carter, and many others. This was music which, earlier in the century, would have been dismissed on principle. Indeed, in answer to a reporter's question in 1968, Stravinsky could truthfully reply, "But I love more music than ever before." (See *Retrospectives and Conclusions*, p. 75.)

7. *An Autobiography*, p. 18.

8. *Retrospectives and Conclusions*, p. 157.

9. Ibid., p. 157. Craft quotes a comment by Vera de Bosset, Stravinsky's second wife (they were married in 1939), that certain of Stravinsky's aesthetic attitudes were "virtually parroted" from Diaghilev, and that "before age and America changed Stravinsky's character, he opened his heart only to Diaghilev, and Diaghilev's criticisms were the only ones he ever heeded." But the Diaghilev-Stravinsky partnership became strained after Stravinsky accepted a commission for *Apollo* (1928) from Mrs. Elizabeth Sprague Coolidge—his first American commission (with choreography by George Balanchine), and the first ballet not to be commissioned by Diaghilev. Diaghilev taunted him: *"Cette Americaine est complètement sourde—Elle est sourde, mais elle paie—Tu penses toujours à l'argent."* (See *Dialogues and a Diary*, p. 16; also, *Expositions and Developments*, p. 75.) The final breakdown came with the acceptance,

later in 1928, of a commission from Mme Ida Rubinstein for *Le Baiser de la fée*. Diaghilev died in August 1929. He was buried in Venice, on the island of San Michele, where his grave now lies but a few yards from that of his early protégé.

10. Edward T. Cone, "The Uses of Convention: Stravinsky and His Models," p. 26.

11. Nicolas Nabokoff, "Christmas with Stravinsky," p. 146.

12. As suggested in chapter 2, Model B's (0 2 3 5) tetrachordal partitioning of the octatonic collection is confined largely to "Russian" works, surfacing only rarely—and then fleetingly—in neoclassical material. Stravinsky's partiality for Model A's (0 3 7/0 4 7/0 4 7 10 (1)) triadic, (0 1 3 4) tetrachordal, and (0 3 4/3 4 7/3 6 7) "minor-major third" partitioning of the collection is manifested throughout the neoclassical period, thus encompassing the bulk of his oeuvre, with respect to which Model A's complexes appear to have afforded a better foundation for accommodation than the (0 2 3 5) tetrachords of Model B.

13. In pitch-relational matters, we continue to regard the consistency, identity, or distinction of Stravinsky's music as linked inextricably to a partitioning of the octatonic collection, and to the manner in which this partitioning interacts or interpenetrates with diatonic material, even though neoclassicism involves this switch from the Model B emphasis of the "Russian" period to a Model A emphasis, and even though this Model A partitioning will now interact or interpenetrate with the conventionality of C-scale (or major-scale) literature rather than with the D-scale or (0 2 3 5 7 9) hexachord so prevalent in "Russian" material.

14. The chromatic tendency tones or "melodic leading tones" of tonally functional C-scale literature, the E♯ and G♯ in relation to the (D F♯ A) triad in Examples 55 and 56, are commonly termed "melodic" when the harmonic implications of their chromaticism, the (C♯ E♯ G♯) and (E G♯ B) triads as applied or secondary dominants in relation to the C-scale on D in Examples 55 and 56, are missing. So pervasive are these chromatic inflections in tonally functional C-scale literature, from Haydn and Mozart to Wagner, Mahler, and Richard Strauss, that they scarcely require exemplification. However, as a well-known sample, we cite the theme in the slow movement of Mozart's D-minor Piano Concerto, K466: in B♭-major, an F/D–G/E♭–F/D–E♭/C–D/B♭ contour is embellished by the chromatic tendency tones C♯ and E. These elements chromatically tend to the D and F of the (B♭ D F) tonic triad (pitch numbers 3 and 6 tending to 4 and 7 of the (0 4 7) tonic triad), the contour thus becoming F/D–E/C♯–F/D–E/C♯–F/D–G/E♭–F/D–E♭/C–D/B♭–D/B♭. This chromatic tendency-tone convention is available octatonically to each of the four (0,3,6,9) symmetrically defined (0 4 7) "major" triads of the octatonic collection (Model A). This availability seems readily to have lent itself to accommodation to the neoclassical initiative (given that prior preoccupation with octatonic partitioning, Models A and B, in "Russian" works). This accommodation takes shape in the form of an octatonic (Model A) and diatonic C-scale interpenetration, since, in its characteristically neoclassical guise, pitch numbers 3 and 6 are not only octatonically exploited as symmetrically defined, cohesively articulated (0 3 4/3 4 7/3 6 7) "minor-major third" partitionings, but their original C-scale derivation as chromatic tendency tones is also made manifest. This duplicity or ambiguity in functioning persists as one of the most characteristic "sounds" in neoclassical works.

15. The "minor-major third" phenomenon in neoclassical works has frequently (and often exclusively) been heard and understood as effecting an ambiguity in the "minor" or "major" status of the (0 4 7) "tonic" triad. In fact such status is seldom in doubt, because pitch number 3, the "minor third," is, on the Classical C-scale (or major-scale) side of the interaction, far more readily heard and understood as an "outside" chromatic tendency tone to pitch number 4, the "major third" of the (0 4 7) "tonic" triad, than as the "minor third" of a potentially conflicting (0 3 7) "tonic" triad. Only in neoclassical settings where the "tonic" triad is (0 3 7) "minor" does an ambiguity occasionally arise. In such cases the ambiguity has to do not with (0 3 7/0 4 7) "minor" and "major" triads sharing the same root, but with triads whose roots are related by the interval of 3, a "minor third" ("tonic" triads, in other words,

which would formerly, by tonally functional means, have defined the relative-key relationship). We shall be discussing this neoclassical A-scale (or descending minor-scale) complication in passages from the *Symphony of Psalms, Oedipus,* and *Orpheus,* Examples 62, 63, and 64b in chapter 10.

16. For example, at Nos. 0–5 in the "Basle" *Concerto in D* (Example 58a in chapter 10), the articulation of the (D F♯ A) "tonic" triad is invariably incomplete, most often (D F♯) or (F♯ A). This incompleteness manifestly ensures the constructive or referential integrity of the (0 3 4/3 4 7) "minor-major third" units in terms of (D F F♯/F F♯ A)—an integrity, to repeat, as critical to a hearing and understanding of this passage as the (D F♯ A) "tonic" triad these units encircle and surround.

17. Compare Example 56 with Example 20 in chapter 3, the latter sketched in reference to Stravinsky's "Russian" thought. In both summaries pitch number 6 is viewed as a referentially octatonic ("chromatic") "intrusion," signaling the intervention of octatonic relations. But in Example 20 of chapter 3, no Classical C-scale tendency-tone behavior is inferred for this "intrusion." As demonstrated at No. 1 in *Les Noces* (Example 33 in chapter 5), pitch number 6, the B♭ in *Les Noces,* "intrudes" into a diatonic (0 2 3 5) partitioning framework; and since it is articulatively affiliated with the referentially octatonic pitch number 11, the F, it immediately assumes those symmetrically defined conditions of "equal weight and independence" and stands in a (0,6) tritone-defined "opposition" to pitch number 0, the E. On the other hand, in the neoclassical summary of Example 56, this pitch-number-6 "intrusion" interrelates with the Classical C-scale chromatic V-of-V tendency-tone convention. And since, more often than not, it is denied the (0 3 7/0 4 7) triadic "support" that a (0 3 4/3 4 7/3 6 7) "minor-major third" partitioning renders pitch number 0, it cannot as readily assume "equal weight and independence" or stand in a (0,6) tritone-defined "opposition" to pitch number 0, the D in Example 56.

18. All the same, not all neoclassical pieces exhibiting (0 3 4/3 4 7/3 6 7) "minor-major third" emphasis are most advantageously heard, understood, or interpreted with even partial, interpenetrating reference to the octatonic collection, Model A. Lengthy passages of such emphasis in *Perséphone* (1934) and *Jeu de cartes* (1936) were excluded from consideration in List 2 in chapter 2. (See, for example, No. 22 or Nos. 23–28 in Act I of *Perséphone;* or the variation movement in *Jeu de cartes,* especially Variations I and IV.) The same is true of *The Rake's Progress* (1948–51), one of the most Classical of Stravinsky's neoclassical endeavors (with its frequent and obvious Mozartean overtones), and in which this (0 3 4/3 4 7/3 6 7) "minor-major third" emphasis figures so prominently as to assume the character of a leitmotiv or "basic cell." (See, for example, the first page of Act I, where Anne's vocal entrance commences with a pitch number 3 chromatic tendency tone in relation to the (A C♯ E) "tonic" triad: C–C♯–A–F♯, with the C–C♯ inflection subsequently elaborated in the flutes and clarinets at No. 3. Or see Act I, Scene II, where, in the lengthy "C-major" passages, pitch numbers 3 and 6, the D♯ and F♯, and their function as chromatic tendency tones in relation to the (C E G) "tonic" triad are nearly all this music can be said "to be about.") But the problem with these passages is that the original, Classical C-scale derivation of the (0 3 4/3 4 7/3 6 7) "minor-major third" emphasis—pitch numbers 3 and 6 as chromatic tendency tones to 4 and 7 of the (0 4 7) "tonic" triad—is all too persistently or conspicuously in evidence. With no additional octatonic intervals (apart from 0, 3, 4, 6, and 7), and thus no form of (034/347/367) "clash" (only *succession*), and no additional (0 3 4/3 4 7/3 6 7) or (0 3 7/0 4 7) triadic "support" involving transpositions and superimpositions at pitch numbers 3 and 6, the symmetrically defined octatonic implications of the emphasis are obscured, being completely overshadowed by the Classical C-scale intent.

19. See the first quotation, "Change of Life," from *Retrospectives and Conclusions* at the beginning of this chapter.

20. But these silences or quarter-note pauses are loaded with a kind of breathless, pent-

up tension, for the symmetrically defined relations of these juxtaposed blocks seem never to progress. By means of configurations which merely oscillate or move back and forth (as ostinati), these relations turn and churn like gears, so that there is in reality no release from this symmetrical confinement until the concluding (G B D) simultaneity which prepares, in dominant-toniclike fashion, for the C-minor (or quasi- C-minor) fugal exposition of the second movement. Even this terminating dominant-tonic transaction is retroactive, having little or nothing to do with pitch organization generally in the first movement. It surfaces parenthetically as a concluding convenience.

CHAPTER 10

1. The "Basle" *Concerto* for string orchestra was commissioned by the Basler Kammerorchester under the direction of Paul Sacher in 1946. We forfeit chronological order here primarily because the *Concerto* immediately offers such strikingly typical illustrations of the (0 3 4/3 4 7/3 6 7) "minor-major third" phenomenon and its neoclassical link to Classical C-scale conventionality. Conveniently, too, pitch-relational matters, as well as instrumental and rhythmic-metric features, relate conspicuously—and not in the least paradoxically, as should by now be clear—to our discussion in earlier chapters, and hence revealingly to the literature as a whole. But we shall be turning to earlier works, most notably the *Symphony of Psalms* (1930) and *Oedipus Rex* (1927). And in chapter 12 we more or less resume proper chronology, commencing our discussion with the *Symphonies of Wind Instruments* (1920) and the *Octet* (1923) and concluding it with the first and third movements of the *Symphony in Three Movements* (1945), along with a final glimpse of Act I of *Oedipus*.

2. See, for example, Wilfrid Mellers, *Caliban Reborn*, p. 91.

3. This practice is not only anachronistic but most often irrelevant. For at Nos. 0–5 in the "Basle" *Concerto* (and elsewhere in neoclassical contexts where the C-scale reference prevails), the (0 4 7) "major" status of the "tonic" triad, (D F♯ A) here, is never really in doubt. Apart from the cohesive exposure of the (D F F♯/F F♯ A) "minor-major third" units (which may overshadow the (D F♯ A) "tonic" triad itself), this is principally because pitch number 3, E♯ [F] as the "minor third," is, on the Classical C-scale-on-D (or D-major scale) side of the interaction, far more readily perceived as an "outside" chromatic tendency tone to pitch number 4, the F♯ of the (D F♯ A) "tonic" triad, than as the true "minor third" of a conflicting (D F A) "tonic" triad. (Or, to rephrase this, E♯ [F] and F♯ are not really "equals" with respect to this alleged ambiguity. For E♯ [F], as the "minor third," can readily effect a conventional state of chromatic dependency, a state of being chromatically "outside" the diatonic reference collection as a tendency tone, while F♯, as the "major third," cannot. And while in A-scale (or descending minor-scale) settings, where the "tonic" triad is (0 3 7) "minor," the "major third" may produce the *tierce de Picardie*, this is far less pervasive a phenomenon than is the chromatic tendency tone in octatonic-diatonic C-scale contexts.) And so the true ambiguity of this context has not really to do with these "minor-major" implications of the "tonic" triad, but far more subtly (as we here continue to insist) with this duplicity in the functional behavior of E♯ [F] as "minor third."

4. Although not shown in Example 58b, a (G B D) triad in the violins at No. 35, superimposed over an F/A♭ contingent and in direct anticipation of a return to the (D♭ F A♭) "tonic" triad at No. 36, reinforces Collection I's contribution in this Moderato section at Nos. 27–38. In the Con moto section which follows at Nos. 38–48, this (0,6) tritone-related (G B D (F)) triad reappears (superimposed over an E), with respect to which an encircling D♭ [C♯]–B♭ articulation may suggest either (G B♭ B/B♭ B D/B♭ C♯ D) "minor-major third" emphasis or chromatic tendency-tone behavior.

5. All the same, note the exquisite details in the octave doubling of the A–B♭ reiteration between the first violins and cellos (Example 58d). The first violins descend to the low B♭ (on their G-strings), while the cellos stretch upward to the high B♭ (on their A-strings) through the interval of 13, a "minor ninth." The effect of this exchange is to lend the reiteration—and the serenely Classical setting as a whole—an intensity that would not have been forthcoming had this doubling been scored with the first violins and cellos merely reiterating the interval of 1, the B–A♭ half step. Note, too, the pizzicato doubling (*divisi* in the double basses) of the *arco* B♭–D–E♭–C–F bass line in the cellos (also *divisi*).

6. The *Symphony in Three Movements*, dedicated to the New York Philharmonic Symphony Society, was completed late in 1945. Its inception was episodic. Portions of the first movement were composed in 1942, at which time they were envisioned as part of a concerto for orchestra, while the second movement (which opens with the section here under review) was completed in 1943 as part of an abortive film project. Some of Stravinsky's recollections of these details are recorded as we resume our analysis of this *Symphony*, its first and third movements, in chapter 12.

7. This particular version of the diminished triad or seventh, (D F G♯ (B)) in relation to the (D F♯ A) "tonic" triad here in Example 59, has two possibilities for resolution in Classical literature. In the first it functions as an applied or secondary dominant (incomplete dominant minor ninth), very often of the V-of-V variety, and thus progresses to the dominant; in the second it functions as a "raised supertonic" in which the root and third of the supertonic triad are sharped (a verticalization of the chromatic tendency tones) in progressing to the tonic triad—and very often, in Mozart for example, as part of a ii 6/5–ii 6♯/5–I6/4–V–I (VI) cadential sequence, with the tonic triad in second inversion as the cadential six-four chord. Hence it is to the second of these two possibilities that the Classical D-scale side of Stravinsky's accommodation refers. Indeed, note in Examples 58b and c that this (0 3 6 (9))–(0 4 7) "progression" might similarly have been inferred: in Example 58c, the (D F G♯) "diminished" triad succeeded by the (D F♯ A) "tonic" triad. On these occasions the "progression" might even invoke the characteristic "feel" of a dominant-tonic transaction, although without the finality of the authentic version, since it lacks—perhaps conveniently—the Classical C-scale-on-D (and non-octatonic, non-Collection II) leading tone, (C♯) to the "tonic" D here. On the other hand, in the Moderato sections of the "Basle" *Concerto*, note how subtly these (0 3 6 (9))–(0 4 7) "progressions" take on the more tellingly Stravinskian ritual of chordal reiteration, of static, oscillating back-and-forth motion, the often-cited "accordian effect," which, traced in these pages to the ostinato pattern of *The Firebird*'s Introduction and *Petroushka*'s second tableau (where it characteristically reflects a (0,3,6,9) symmetrically defined partitioning of the octatonic collection along with the superimpositions and "clashes" this partitioning invariably engenders), now becomes as neoclassical as, earlier, it was "Russian" in conception.

8. Despite its title (and those accompanying its five movements), *Danses concertantes* was not conceived as a ballet. Commissioned by the Werner Janssen Orchestra of Los Angeles (and first performed by that orchestra in February 1942, with Stravinsky conducting), it was an abstract, concert-hall conception for chamber orchestra. In 1944, however, George Balanchine composed the choreography for a stage production, mounted in New York by the Ballet Russe de Monte Carlo.

9. A cantata based on a few sections from *Genesis*, *Babel* was commissioned by Nathaniel Shilkret, a music publisher. Its conception was curious. The commission was part of a collective effort in which several composers (including the diverse likes of Alexandre Tansman, Milhaud, Schoenberg, and Shilkret himself) were to contribute individual sections, each based on different episodes from the early chapters of *Genesis*. The premiere of this bizarre project, the *Genesis Suite*, at the Wilshire Ebell Theater in Los Angeles in November 1945, is worth noting, however, in that it afforded Stravinsky his first opportunity, after an absten-

tion of nearly twenty years, of listening to music by Schoenberg (who contributed the opening Prelude). (See *Dialogues and a Diary*, p. 55.)

10. The sequences of reiterating (G Bb D) triads at No. 16 relate rather conspicuously, with respect to the grouping exhibited, to the reiterating (C E G) triads introduced at No. 3 in the final movement of the *Symphony of Psalms*. (See Example 53e in chapter 8.) But the relation is more than just rhythmic, extending to pitch organization. For while No. 3 in *Psalms* is not explicitly octatonic (exhibiting only a possible interpenetrating Collection I), the context at No. 4 + 8 (two measures before No. 5), where the reiterating (0 4 7) triads are transposed to E in terms of (E G♯ B) and accompanied by a G–F figure below, is wholly octatonic (unimpaired), referable to Collection I, the collection of *Babel* at Nos. 0–8 and 16–21. And so the conception of this reiteration, while only partially octatonic earlier in *Psalms* (1930), became unequivocatingly so in *Babel* (1944). More fundamentally though, *Babel*'s (0,3) "background" partitioning of Collection I in terms of (E,G) is reminiscent of the (0,3,6) partitioning in terms of (E,G,Bb) in the first movement of *Psalms*.

11. This transposition is "hatched" in much the same fashion as in the passages surveyed in this chapter: pitch number 3, an F in the bass as part of (D F A) triadic outline, "clashes" with pitch number 4, the F♯ of the reiterating (D E F♯ G A) figure above, and effects (0 3 4/3 4 7) "minor-major third" emphasis in terms of (D F F♯/F F♯ A), precipitating the eventual transposition from D to F. *The Five Fingers* (*Les Cinq Doigts*) was orchestrated in 1962 in the form of *Eight Instrumental Miniatures*. The original order was revised, however, with this sixth piece, "Lento," appearing as the third of the *Miniatures*.

12. While we superimpose regular 3/4 metric periodicity here, a 2/4 or even a 4/4 meter might have seemed equally appropriate in this respect, and would in fact have yielded like circumstances with respect to the concealed contradiction or reversal. But it is regular 3/4 periodicity which figures conspicuously in the more elaborate (near) repeats of this block at Nos. 159–62 and 164–66, and especially at Nos. 139–47, where as illustrated by Example 53f in chapter 8, a switch does occur to this "background" 3/4 formulation at No. 144 (and where the metric irregularity is replaced by stress and slur markings).

13. However, Collection II does not exhaust interacting octatonic implications at Nos. 139–70. The (D B F Ab) "diminished-seventh" chord which abruptly terminates Oedipus's aria "Nonne monstrum" at No. 157 leads to a brief Collection I block at Nos. 158–59, which is in turn followed by (near) repeats of the diatonic D-scale block at Nos. 159–62.

14. It is the persistence of the (D F A) reiteration in the strings (with *its* fifth), along with D stationed as the lowest pitch in the bass, that sustains the (D F♯ (A)) component of this (D F♯ (A)) (B D F♯) ambiguity to the very last (managing to keep (D F♯ (A)) "in business," so to speak). In the concluding "*Lux facta est* cadence" itself, (D F♯ (A)) is still without its fifth, while the final B–F♯ descent of Oedipus's F♯–D–B–F♯ succession echoes the B–F♯ descent of the timpani, thus managing to sustain the (B D F♯) component. Consequently, while (D F A) in the strings is not accounted for in terms of the possible C-scale-on-D or A-scale-on-B references at Nos. 167–70 (only in terms of the D-scale on D or the octatonic Collection II), its presence is crucial to the preservation of the (D F♯ (A)) (B D F♯) ambiguity.

15. Note the resemblance in "sound," registral spacing, instrumentation, and *tierce-de-Picardie* implications between this (D F♯) reiteration in the flutes and the (C E) concluding simultaneity of the "*Dominum* cadence" in *Psalms*, final movement at Nos. 0–3. (See Example 62 above.)

16. Jean Cocteau collaborated with Stravinsky on the general condensation of Sophocles' play; Jean Danielou translated the French into Latin. What seems to have hampered *Oedipus* at the start, however, was its schizoid opera/oratorio status. *Oedipus* was originally conceived as an opera, and only gradually did Stravinsky—perhaps because of the near-motionless, "still-life" conception of his stage directions—switch to the dual approach. While this strategy seems also to have been designed to promote frequent performances, it had, until fairly recently, the opposite effect. Even Diaghilev (to whom the music was presented as a gift to

commemorate the twentieth anniversary of the Russian Ballet, but who seems not to have been overly impressed; "*un cadeau trés macabre*," was his response) first intended to mount *Oedipus* as an opera but switched to the concert version, evidently because of financial difficulties. This was a grave error, for *Oedipus* is best heard and understood as opera, with Stravinsky's stage directions scrupulously observed. Difficulties remain, however. Stravinsky would later detest the use of speaker or narrator in both *Oedipus* and *Perséphone* (1934)—a "disturbing series of interruptions" whose substance might well have seemed, with the passing of time, grossly pretentious. "But, alas," Stravinsky sighed, "the music was composed with the speeches, and is paced by them" (*Dialogues and a Diary*, pp. 13–14).

17. Or see, along the same lines, Wilfrid Mellers, "1930: *Symphony of Psalms*," *Tempo*, no. 96 (1971), where, in the first movement of *Psalms*, Mellers hears progressions and keys (and presumably C-scale tonally functional definitions of keys) where, apart from some discreetly parenthetical nods in this direction, there are in reality only statically superimposed or oscillating triads, "dominant sevenths," and (0 1 3 4) tetrachords, referentially octatonic (Collection I) and placed in juxtaposition with a diatonicism referring not to the Classical C or A-scale, but (most often) unambiguously to the E-scale on E. More disturbing in this regard, however, is Eric Walter White's analysis of *Oedipus* in *Stravinsky: The Composer and His Works*, where the Mellers account in "*Oedipus* as 20th-Century Hero" seems to have been paraphrased, and with the predictable—but apparently unintended—consequence that *Oedipus* emerges as just another Baroque or Classical tonally functional C-scale (or A-scale) piece—which, as should be apparent, it most assuredly is not. Worse, in an attempt to lend some coherence to the maze of "tonalities" ("major" and "minor keys," "dominant keys," etc.) that ensues, White ponders some startling absurdities: "As for Oedipus, he strives continuously towards the affirmation of major keys; but generally they prove elusive and evade his grasp" (p. 295). Or, further along: "Generally speaking, the flat keys, both major and minor, are geared closely to the Oedipus complex, while the sharp keys relate to the world of normality." Or: "Oedipus' keys are flat keys. His final and vain attempt to escape his doom is made in the F major 'Nonne monstrum rescituri' aria; but with the final revelation and realization, he emerges at last out of his flat keys and minor modes into a blindingly clear D major close [the "*Lux facta est* cadence"]. "The blindingly clear D major close" here, as ambiguous a "close" as any in the neoclassical repertoire, seems a final and unpardonable insult to musical literacy. For how is it possible to ignore the ambiguity of this passage, so tellingly Stravinskian? Or the symmetrically defined octatonic implications (Collection II)? See Lawrence Morton's review of White's book in *Musical Quarterly* 53 (1967), p. 589, for a succinct rebuttal of the remarks on *Oedipus*.

18. Elsewhere in mixed octatonic (Model A) and diatonic *C*-scale contexts, the preference for the first-inversion articulation—especially insofar as the between-reference (0 4 7) "tonic" triad is concerned—seems linked to (0 3 4/3 4 7/3 6 7) "minor-major third" emphasis. Thus, with the inflexible root positioned elsewhere, the bass is free (so to speak) to engage in the variety of pitch number (3–4) (6–7) reiterations, fluctuations, or "clashes" typifying the emphasis. See, for example, in the introductory passage of the "Basle" *Concerto in D*, Example 58a, the (F F♯ A) simultaneities at Nos. 0 + 2 and 1 + 1 (with F, pitch number 3, in the bass), or the F–F♯ reiteration in the bass at Nos. 2–5.

19. Inasmuch as *Orpheus* (1947) directly follows the "Basle" *Concerto* (1946), the *Concerto*'s Moderato section at No. 27, with its mixed octatonic (Collection I) and diatonic C-scale-on-D♭ reference, its D♭-major key signature, and its pitch number 3–4 reiteration in terms of E–F (not to mention, of course, its string texture) is likely to have spawned the mixed octatonic (Collection I) and diatonic A-scale-on-B♭/C-scale-on-D♭ material at No. 5 in *Orpheus*.

20. See, for example, the E–F reiterations in the "Air de danse" (Examples 64b and c), which are pitch number 6–7 reiterations in relation to the (B♭ D♭ F) "tonic" triad, 3–4 in relation to (D♭ F A♭).

21. Observers (including Stravinsky) have oversimplified apprehension of the (0 3 4/3 4

7/3 6 7) "minor-major third" phenomenon in neoclassical contexts by calling attention merely to an ambiguity with respect to the "minor" or "major" status of the (0 3 7/0 4 7) "tonic" triad. In this manner much of the subtlety of the "play" is overlooked; not only the integrity of the (0 3 4/3 4 7/3 6 7) units as constructive or referential factors (or their symmetrically defined octatonic implications), but also the duplicity in function of pitch numbers 3 and 6 as Classical C-scale chromatic tendency tones (crucial to neoclassicism, of course, because crucial to a hearing and understanding of the Classical C-scale side of the interaction).

22. As detailed in chapter 6, each of the three octatonic collections contains, in addition to the triads and tetrachords of Models A and B, two "diminished-seventh" chords, one of these constituting, in each case, the (0,3,6,9) symmetrically defined partitioning elements. And since the two "diminished sevenths" of Collection I are (B♭ D♭ E G) and (B D F A♭), while those of Collection III are (B♭ D♭ E G) and (C E♭ F♯ A), (B♭ D♭ E G) is shared by these two collections. See, as examined earlier in this connection, Nos. 68–72 in the third tableau of *Les Noces* (Example 38 in chapter 6), where Collection II at Nos. 68–70 relates to Collection I at Nos. 70–72 through (B D F G♯), the shared "diminished-seventh" chord, which is articulated throughout as a G♯–F–B–D basso ostinato in Piano IV; or, Nos. 0–13 in the first movement of the *Symphony in Three Movements* (Example 75a in chapter 12), where Collection I at Nos. 0–5 relates to Collection III at Nos. 7–13 through (G B♭ C♯ E), which is isolated in a passage of transition at Nos. 5–7.

23. Although ignored in our discussion, *Orpheus*'s introductory section at Nos. 0–4 might have figured in this summary, with E and the (E G B) triad of its diatonic E-scale-on-E framework linked to Collection I. (Indeed, the reiterating E in the harp's E-scale-on-E scale passages is registrally the "same" E as that of the solo violin's E–F reiterations in the Collection I A-scale-on-B♭/C-scale-on-D♭ interaction at No. 5). Then, too, E, along with the (A C♯ E G) "dominant seventh" which concludes this section, is accountable to Collection III; with (A C♯ E G) thus in direct anticipation of the succeeding Collection III block at No. 4 (with its (C E G B♭ (D♭)) and (A C♯ E) triadic figuration.)

24. With (0 3 7) envisioned as the "tonic" "minor" triad in interacting octatonic (Model A) and diatonic A-scale circumstances, pitch number 3 is naturally a chord tone as the "minor third" of the triad, and cannot effect, on the Classical A-scale side of the coin, chromatic tendency-tone behavior in relation to pitch number 4, the "major third." Still, apart from its octatonic implications, pitch number 4 might acquire Classical A-scale (or minor-scale) credentials in a *tierce de Picardie* inflection (of which, as we have seen, there is at least a suggestion at Nos. 0–3 in the final movement of *Psalms* and at Nos. 167–70 in *Oedipus*). Moreover, in settings where this (0 3 7) "minor" triad presides, the fusion or "coming together" of the (0,3)-related "minor" and "major" triads will entail pitch numbers 0 and 3 as roots, these triads formerly interpretable as a tonic-mediant relation; in octatonic (Model A) and diatonic C-scale interactions, it is pitch numbers 0 and 9 which define this relationship, one formerly interpretable as a tonic-submediant relation. Hence, either way, the interval orderings defined by these (0,3)-related "minor" and "major" triads in relation to the diatonic collection would have distinguished themselves, in the tonality of Baroque and Classical literature, as "relative keys" (although, as we have observed, there is in Stravinsky's music generally no functional activity to legitimatize any C-scale tonally functional definition of these separate "keys").

CHAPTER 11

1. "Problems of Pitch Organization in Stravinsky," p. 154.
2. The reader may also consult Examples 74 and 75a in chapter 12.
3. It is precisely the preservation of tonally conceived voice-leading (pursued in con-

junction here with this (0,3) symmetrically defined (0 4 7 10) "dominant-seventh" partition-ing of the octatonic collection) that has led so many observers to view the (B♭ D F A♭)–(B D F G) oscillation in the first movement of *Psalms* exclusively in terms of a "dominant seventh" "irregularly resolved," and hence in terms of the "distinctly parenthetical," the mere sugges-tion of a C-scale tonally functional harmonic maneuver, which this discussion has sought to unravel. This "irregular resolution"—if the second movement is included forms part of a global V-of-III–V 6/5–i strategy in terms of (B♭ D F A♭)–(B D F G)–(C E♭ G). (Compare this (B♭ D F A♭)–(B D F G)–(C E♭ G) strategy with the tonal formulation of Example 69b.) The problem is that until the final measures of this movement there is scarcely a trace of *progres-sion*, only of static oscillation and ostinati, and that such a tonal reading neglects the symmet-rically defined octatonic implications of (B♭ D F A♭)–(B D F G) in relation to the punctuating (E G B) "*Psalms* chord," as well as the (0 1 3 4) tetrachordal partitioning of the collection (Collection I) so persistently and articulatively in evidence throughout. As a result, any such exclusive reliance on the C-scale, tonal processes to which these remnants of past authentic-ity are linked is obliged to overlook or disregard the principal forces at work, whether octa-tonic, diatonic, or octatonic-diatonic in conception. See, as noted already in chapter 10, Wilfrid Mellers, "1930: *Symphony of Psalms*," *Tempo*, no. 96 (1971).

4. *Memories and Commentaries*, p. 57.

5. *My Musical Life*, p. 72.

CHAPTER 12

1. Seven, actually, if we include the Credo of Stravinsky's *Mass* (1947) and our discussion of *Agon* in chapter 13. But neoclassicism abounds with (non-octatonic) toniclike resolutions conceived as terminating conveniences to octatonic or octatonic-diatonic material, and espe-cially with reference to Collection I. The persistent dominant-toniclike association of this collection with the C-scale (or A-scale) on C, initiating forms of (C E G/C E♭ G) terminating conveniences (or "C-endings" as Stravinsky called them), became a neoclassical routine.

2. The solemn, processional chorale which concludes the *Symphonies* at Nos. 65–75 (with "adumbrative bits," as Stravinsky notes above, introduced "in the body of the piece") was first conceived separately as a contribution to the special *hommage à Debussy* issue of *La Revue musi-cale* (December 1920). But possibilities for a work of near-symphonic proportions were rec-ognized immediately. Stravinsky's expansion of his initial *hommage*, completed in July 1920, bears the following inscription: "*Symphonies pour instruments à vent à la memoire de Claude Achille Debussy.*"

3. Nos. 0–6 (Example 73a) encompass two separate blocks. The first of these is intro-duced at No. 0, with a (near) repeat and extension at No. 2, the second at No. 1, with a (near) repeat at No. 4. Our approach in graphic design has thus far been to acknowledge these abruptly disposed blocks by treating them individually (especially where octatonic blocks are placed in juxtaposition with diatonic or octatonic-diatonic blocks). But since the blocks in question are of brief duration, and since both refer to Collection I, jointly articulating (0,3) partitioning in terms of (G,B♭) or (G B D F) (B♭ D F A♭), it seemed advantageous to group them as a whole (as part of a more global or long-range perspective), and to draw our conclu-sions accordingly. Example 73b then plots subsequent appearances of these initial blocks in relation to the concluding chorale at Nos. 65–75.

4. As Stravinsky relates, the chorale at Nos. 65–75 is composed of two "bits" or "phrases" which are joined in the form of an antecedent and consequent. The antecedent "bit" consists of a (G B D)–(G A♭ C) oscillation over a (D A♭ F B) simultaneity in the bass, and is introduced by the trumpets, trombones, and tuba at Nos. 42, 56, and 65; the second or consequent one, defining a quarter-note D–C–E–F–C–D contour at No. 66, is introduced by the oboes as an

appendage to the (B♭ D F A♭/F B A♭ F) chordal reiteration Nos. 1 and 4, and subsequently reappears in like manner following (near) repeats of the No. 0 block at Nos. 9 and 26.

5. See, at Nos. 4–6, the oscillating B–D–A♯–C♯ ostinato in the oboes and english horn, a (B♭ [A♯] B C♯ D) tetrachordal delineation; at No. 7, the superimposition of the (B♭ [A♯] B C♯ D) tetrachord over its (0,6) tritone-related F–A♭–E–G tetrachord in the cellos and double basses; and at Nos. 5 and 13, the descending F–A♭–E–G/D–F–C♯–E/B–D–B♭C♯/ A♭–B–G–B♭/F–A♭ sequential line in the oboes (where the octatonic implications of these (0 1 3 4) tetrachordal delineations from Collection I are as conspicuous as anywhere in the literature). See, too, the C–E♭–B–D "subject" of the second movement's fugal exposition, a (0 1 3 4) tetrachord in terms of (B C D E♭). Stravinsky fails to mention the referential status of these cohesively articulated (0 1 3 4) tetrachords—the confinement of his "sequences of two minor thirds joined by a major third" to Collection I.

6. Note the oscillating, back-and-forth motion inherent in this reversal, apparent here on a long-term basis as well as in the form of short-term ostinati. This procedure is fundamental to the "musical world" of *Psalms* as it is to the musical thought processes of Stravinsky generally.

7. This "targeting" of "background" regular metric periodicity in blocks, passages, or sections adhering to the first of our two rhythmic-metric types ("foreground" metric irregularity) is typical of Stravinsky. As these blocks, passages, or sections draw to a close, the "background" regular periodicity is invariably brought into synchronization with the shifting meter of the "foreground" level. This "targeting" or eventual synchronization naturally intensifies the felt presence of the "background" steady meter, along with the upbeat/ downbeat or off-the-beat/on-the-beat contradictions or reversals that hinge, for their apprehension, on this presence. (See, among the countless contexts that apply in this respect, the opening two blocks of *Les Noces*, Example 33 in chapter 6; "The Soldier's March" of *Histoire*, Examples 50a, b, and c in chapter 8; or the opening blocks at No. 0—or indeed the whole succession of opening blocks at Nos. 0–6 in the *Symphonies of Wind Instruments*, Example 53a in chapter 8 or Example 73a in this chapter.) Moreover, here in *Psalms* at Nos. 0–2, the punctuating (E G B) "*Psalms* chord" occurs four times. And in accord with the "background" regular 4/4 periodicity (as bracketed in Example 74), these punctuations occur on the first, fourth, third, and second beats respectively. Hence the upbeat/downbeat contradictions or reversals assume a patterned cycle of displacement, and this, too, is characteristic of Stravinsky. (See our discussion of the opening blocks of *Les Noces*, Example 33 in chapter 6.)

8. Cases of fracture are uncharacteristic of Stravinsky. Once assured of a "find" (and being so attentive to his instincts, so trusting in his immediate impressions), he preferred to stick it out from start to finish without interruptions or postponements, particularly after having begun composition. The decadelong struggle with *Les Noces* is an exception, and *Agon* was interrupted for *In Memoriam Dylan Thomas* (1954) and *Canticum Sacrum* (1955). But the problem with *Les Noces* was very nearly exclusively instrumental, and *Agon* may in part be excused because of difficulties arising from the neoclassical-serial juncture. Stravinsky later confessed that the future seemed never to furnish the certainty of the present, that ideas, once spawned, were best encouraged when new and fresh, and that delays made it difficult to recapture his initial enthusiasm. (Perhaps, too, it was difficult to resurrect the unspecified peripheral framework upon which the freshness of whatever lay concrete must to some degree have been dependent.) Stravinsky was also a "clean" composer. There are few pages that remained incomplete or unused in some fashion.

9. In the second A section at Nos. 88–97, the Collection III block at Nos. 7–13 is transposed into Collection II: (0 4 7 10) "dominant-seventh" complexes oscillating at D and F over a B–D–B basso ostinato. And in conforming to the transpositional sequence initiated by the original A section, the block which follows at No. 96, corresponding to that at Nos. 13–16, refers to Collection I.

10. The incompleteness in (0 3 7/0 4 7) triadic articulation is closely linked to the collectional mobility traced in Example 75a and described above; it is to be compared, perhaps, with the first movement of *Psalms*, where the triadic articulation is invariably complete and the referential implications toward Collection I quite stable. Thus, all complete (0 3 7/0 4 7) triads are "fixed" referentially with respect to one of the three possible octatonic collections. But the incomplete (0 3 7) "minor" triad without "fifth" may refer to two of these three collections. Hence the increased mobility or flexibility of this particular version of the incomplete triad. See the G–B♭–G punctuation in the transition at Nos. 5–7, which persists as part of a (E♭ G B♭) triad in the Collection III block which follows at Nos. 7–13; the preserved A–C–A punctuation in moving from the Collection III block at Nos. 7–13 to the Collection II block at Nos. 13–16; or the F/A♭/F figuration in the woodwinds at Nos. 13–16, retained by the Collection I block at Nos. 16–19.

11. See, in this connection, Donald C. Mitchell, *The Language of Modern Music*, pp. 114–16.

12. Some observers have termed this stormy C-scale-on-C passage at No. 27, Creon's aria "Respondit deus" (the passage returns at No. 40), "magnificent," "triumphant," "scintillating," etc. But Stravinsky was less extravagant, more "in tune." Alert to the incongruity of much of *Oedipus*, its mélange of what he called "widely divergent types of music," he characterized it as a "*Merzbild*, put together from whatever came to hand." Thus, the "magnificent" C-scale-on-C setting was likened to a "*Folies Bergères* tune . . . ('The girls enter, kicking')," while the Messenger fanfares reminded him of the "now badly tarnished trumpets of early 20th-Century Fox." Still, "I have made these bits and snatches my own, I think, and of these a unity." And he loved it, "all of it." (See the quotation from *Dialogues and a Diary* prefacing chapter 9.)

13. The reversal is not, however, unique to *Oedipus* at Nos. 27–45. In the third movement of the *Symphony in Three Movements*, the initial block at No. 142, with (near) repeats at Nos. 144 and 146, suggests the C-scale on C with (0 3 4/3 4 7) "minor-major third" emphasis in terms of (C E♭ E/E♭ E G), a reference which then moves on to the rumba block at Nos. 152–54 with its (0,6) tritone partitioning of Collection I in terms of (G,D♭). Moreover, in *Oedipus*, the C-scale-on-C setting at No. 27 is preceded at No. 25 by a (G B D) triadic reiteration. And since these (G B D) triads emerge from a diatonic A-scale-on-B♭ framework (or pseudo-B♭-minor reference) not untinged by Collection I intervention, the dominantlike preparation here is similar to the "half cadence" on G that concludes the first movement of *Psalms*, preparing dominant-toniclike for the quasi-C-minor fugal exposition of the second movement. The subject at hand, rather more generally, is this neoclassically conceived dominant-toniclike association between Collection I and the C-scale (or A-scale) on C: octatonic (Collection I) and diatonic C-scale-on-C (or A-scale-on-C) interaction and the specifics of its imposition from one context to the next.

CHAPTER 13

1. Robert Craft, "A Personal Preface," p. 10. For Stravinsky's own reflections on *The Rake's Progress* as a conventional opera, see the quotation from *Themes and Episodes* prefacing chapter 9.

2. Milton Babbitt, "Remarks on the Recent Stravinsky," p. 166.

3. *Retrospectives and Conclusions*, p. 193.

4. *Expositions and Developments*, p. 93.

5. This registral fixity might bring the earlier *Three Pieces for String Quartet* to mind, or indeed any of the countless settings in which fragmental repetition is linked to the second of our two rhythmic-metric types. The problem here, however, is that the detection of "serial tendencies" of this kind, or the drawing of distinctions between what—with respect to

twentieth-century techniques applied on a non-twelve-tone basis—might be deemed significantly "serial" as opposed to significantly "nonserial," is not likely—although this is not an uninstructive task in itself—to yield much in the way of specific results, if only because all music is endowed with "serial" qualifications on the most fundamental level of perception and analytic-theoretical review. True, "nonserial" methods doubtless influence "serial" methods, and certain correspondences are worth noting. But difficulties arise in attempting to appraise any one practice (or context) as potentially more "serial" than the next (with respect to twentieth-century techniques applied on a non-twelve-tone basis).

6. The standard abbreviations are as follows: P for the Prime or "original" order of the set, series, or row; R for the Retrograde of the Prime; I for the Inversion; RI for the Retrograde of the Inversion. Transpositions are numbered upwards by semitonal count from the untransposed orders (which in many texts are numbered "–0," but here merely P, R, I, and RI). Thus, for example, since the untransposed P of the Ricercar II set begins on E, the I form beginning on C is designated I–8. The centric (C E) unit of this set is flanked in all untransposed forms by the interval of 1, a semitone in terms of B and F; the resulting tritone enclosure in application tends to intensify (C E)'s centric status.

7. "Rencontre avec Stravinsky," *Preuves* (May 1952); quoted in Eric Walter White, *Stravinsky*, p. 107.

8. *Retrospectives and Conclusions*, p. 196.

9. Its five-tone set notwithstanding, *In Memoriam* is Stravinsky's first completely serial work. The middle portion, the setting of Thomas's poem, was composed in February and March 1954, while the flanking Dirge-Canons for string quartet and four trombones were added when it was learned that Schütz's *Fili Mi Absalon*, requiring four trombones, would be included on the program featuring its premiere. (Stravinsky and Thomas met in May 1953, and had planned to collaborate on an opera. Stravinsky was in fact awaiting Thomas's arrival in Hollywood for further discussion when word came of the poet's death in New York, 9 November 1953.) The second movement of *Canticum Sacrum*, "Surge, Aquilo," is Stravinsky's first completely twelve-tone movement, while *Threni* is the first, from start to finish, completely twelve-tone work. Hence, with the exception of *In Memoriam* and *Threni*, works of the earlier stage are partially serial, in the sense of their consisting merely of movements or sections so derived (*Canticum Sacrum, Agon*), or of movements or sections where serially derived components are joined with nonserial components (as in the Ricercar II of the *Cantata* and the Coda of *Agon* at mm. 185–253).

10. Stravinsky's lengthy Webern interview with the University of Washington, "A Decade Later," appearing in Hans Moldenhaur, comp., and Demar Irving, ed., *Anton von Webern: Perspectives* (from which the quotation at the outset of this chapter derives) was slightly revised in *Themes and Episodes*, pp. 115–23 and then revised a second time in *Themes and Conclusions*, pp. 91–96. See, also in this connection, Henri Pousseur, "Stravinsky by Way of Webern," a very meticulous account of *Agon* "by way of Webern," and specifically by way of the *Variations* set. Pousseur also refers to the octatonic and diatonic implications of *Agon*'s extensive (0 1 3 4) and (0 2 3 5) tetrachordal articulation, and his account is in all respects remarkably consistent with the general premises of this inquiry.

11. *Memories and Commentaries*, p. 99.

12. *Themes and Episodes*, p. 59.

13. "Ein Ballett für zwölf Tänzer," p. 284.

14. According to Stravinsky and Craft, *Conversations with Stravinsky*, p. 19, the seventeenth-century French dance forms (along with titles) in the two middle sections of *Agon* were borrowed from De Lauze's *Apologie de la danse* (1623), and some of the music modeled after "examples" from Mersenne. The trumpet duet of the "Bransle simple" is said to have been inspired by an illustration in the De Lauze volume depicting two trumpeters heralding an ancient Bransle Simple.

15. These do not exhaust pockets of octatonic cohesion in the Adagio, however. See, although not shown in Examples 83a–b, Collection II's (F A)–(D F♯)–(B D♯)–(A♭ C) "minor-major third" succession in the lower strings at mm. 443–45, which is followed at mm. 447–49 by a similar Collection I succession.

16. The numbering of transpositions from the primal B♭–B–D–D♭ unit is ignored in Examples 83a–b. R, 1–4, and RI–4 retrograde, invert, and retrograde-invert B♭–B–D–D♭ while preserving pitch content (hence figuring as part of its "home-base" status). The within-Collection I transpositions of P and R at 3, 6, and 9, and of I and RI at (4), 7, 10, and 1 are perhaps slightly more distant in this presumed hierarchy. Also in this connection, there are at mm. 411–51 in the Adagio roughly thirty-three (0 1 3 4) tetrachordal delineations or set-statements, of which thirteen refer to Collection I, fifteen to Collection II, five to Collection III. In the concluding passage at mm. 452–62 there are twenty such statements, eight referring to Collection I, ten to Collection II, two to Collection III. These ratios reflect the Collection-I–Collection–II (0 1 3 4) tetrachordal interlock, but are also somewhat misleading in failing—obviously—to consider duration or emphasis, the longer stretches of time allotted Collection I's tetrachords, in particular its (B♭ B D♭ D) "home-base" unit.

17. In "Ein Ballett für zwölf Tänzer," Craft cites the set of the "Four Duos" and "Trios" as that also of the "Pas de deux"'s Adagio, but this is clearly unrealistic. For the commonest of serial denominators in the "Pas de deux" is the (0 1 3 4) tetrachord. And while it is true enough that all twelve pitch classes are present and accounted for in the opening three measures of the Adagio, the ordering is not that as defined by the Duos' set, and has little bearing on the Adagio itself or subsequent miniatures in the "Pas de deux." But, crucially, the (0 1 3 4) interlock as defined by the first seven set-factors of the Duos' set—as has been abundantly demonstrated—but one of several modes of (0 1 3 4) tetrachordal linkage pursued in the Adagio and throughout the "Pas de deux" as a whole.

18. Robert Craft, "A Concert for Saint Mark," p. 36.

19. The lengthy "Flood" section of *The Flood* (1962) is also a massive retrograde movement, although the original "forwards" is mirrored instantly at midpoint, while here in *Canticum* it is separated from its "backwards" by three movements (which might in fact heighten the sinister effect). In retrospect it is surprising that such literal retrogrades (of whole blocks of material) should not have occurred earlier in Stravinsky's music. The symmetrical character of pitch organization generally, the back-and-forth oscillation of configurations, along with the contradictions or reversals in rhythmic-metric identity would all seem ideally suited to such treatment. (By "literal retrograde" we naturally mean a preserved—if retrograded—rhythmic and pitch succession, in contrast to the retrograde designation of serial music, where usually only pitch-class succession is implied.)

20. The (D E F G A B♭ B C D♭ [C♯] D) pitch content of the chorus is accounted for in terms of the familiar tonally-derived, hybrid minor scales: the ascending, descending, and harmonic minor scales on D. But it should be evident that the critically "altered" pitches of this content are not tonally motivated. The D♭ is cohesively a member of Collection I's (G B♭ D♭) bass pattern; and not until the final measures of the movement does it, as a C♯, momentarily assume the guise of a "leading tone" to the D. Similarly, the B♭ adheres to the (G B♭ D♭) bass pattern, "clashes" with the B as a member of the (B♭ B D) "home-base" unit, and is succeeded in the chorus by B as part of the exposed D–B♭–(B D) succession. These are conditions hardly suggestive of a tonally oriented "flatted-sixth degree."

21. See, in addition, the opening measures of the "Basle" *Concerto in D*, Example 58a in chapter 10, where Stravinsky's stressed upbeating (including the (F F♯ A) "clash" at m. 3) is likewise unprepared and "without context," and is therefore more likely to be heard and understood as a downbeating succession. But unlike *Canticum*, the conflict is eventually resolved or "phased out" with an extra dotted quarter-note beat at No. 1. Thus, too, the opening two measures of *Agon* (not shown in Example 78), where the two, stressed, off-the-beat (C

B F) attacks are unprepared, and likely to be heard as initiating two on-the-beat groupings of four sixteenth-notes. The uncertainty arises with the trumpet's triplets on the fourth beat of m. 2, which, as a consequence of this alternative, assume an uncertain off-the-beat appearance. (The eighth-note is the beat here, with 4/8 and 3/8 measures.) In *Agon* this concealed ambiguity is not subsequently resolved, but hovers on through m. 4.

22. Roberto Gerhard, "Twelve-note Technique in Stravinsky," p. 41.

23. The simultaneities at mm. 46, 82, and 83 (referring to R and P), and those at mm. 69–71 (referring to RI and I) are exceptions. In fact, m. 46 is the first instance of "vertical serialism" in Stravinsky's music (since, of course, *Canticum* preceded *Agon*'s serial miniatures).

24. As the center of attraction, the tenor confines itself almost exclusively to P, R, and the R (1–6) and RI–8 (1–6) hexachords, so that, of a total of twenty-two hexachordal delineations, the majority, fourteen, are E♭–A hexachords. The sole exception to this confinement is I–1 at m. 86, where, almost incidentally in "Surge, Aquilo," the set's combinatorial asset is exposed: I–1 in the tenor coincides with I–9 in the flute (in canon, I–9 in augmentation of I–1). But note in this connection the closeness between P (7–12) or R (1–6) and RI–8 (1–6), not only in pitch content but also in order. Undoubtedly the preservation here of both the E♭–D♭ whole-step succession and the E♭–A boundary relationship relates intimately to the privileged status of these variants, and to the independent use of both R (1–6) and RI–8 (1–6).

25. There are differences of opinion with respect to a possible pitch-class centricity in "Surge, Aquilo": Robert Craft has suggested A, Roberto Gerhard has mentioned P's A♭–E♭/ A–E "fifth" relationships (composed of the initiating/concluding set-factors of P's hexachords), while Eric Walter White (*Stravinsky*, p. 445) has opted for a kind of G–C dominant-tonic relationship over P's hexachordal bar. These contentions are unlikely to inspire much confidence. Thus, the undeniably stressed A, although occasionally given obvious "fifth support" from the E (as in the final measures), is more characteristically identified with (qualified by or "in opposition" to) the tritone, E♭; and the E♭–A relationship is critical not only to the hierarchy of engaged set-forms, but also to the octatonic Collection III implications alluded to. White's conclusions require a more active imagination (getting beyond P and the opening few measures), especially with respect to the C, which is obviously less prominent a factor in P (7–12) than either the E♭, the A, or the E♭–A tritone. Still, were the G–C relationship to be heard and understood as part of the Collection-I–Collection-III bond noted above (as, indeed, it so characteristically is in neoclassical contexts), the inference would seem less far-fetched (although, admittedly, much of the piece would still remain unaccounted for).

CHAPTER 14

1. *Expositions and Developments*, p. 151.

2. "Working Notes for *The Flood*," *Dialogues and a Diary*, pp. 89–98. Based on a series of meetings between Stravinsky, Craft, and Balanchine, these "Notes" provide an insightful glimpse of the meticulous and resourceful planning of the participants; but a promise, alas, which remains unfulfilled.

3. *Dialogues and a Diary*, p. 89.

4. *Themes and Episodes*, p. 58.

5. The scene between God and Noah at mm. 180–247 is similarly defined: two distinct blocks, with prolonged near repeats of the instructional voices of God being placed in abrupt juxtaposition with Noah's brief speech-responses. In his "Working Notes," Stravinsky likened the dialogue to a tennis match: "The God-Noah dialogue could be seen like a tennis

game, back-and-forth from the earth-level view of Noah to the light of iconostasis, which is the visual anchor throughout *The Flood*" (*Dialogues and a Diary*, p. 93).

6. The successive entrances (or block near repeats) of Lucifer at mm. 130, 134, and 139 are also, with their metrically irregular "phrasing," in accord with the first of our two rhythmic-metric types. Indeed, the "syncopation" to which Stravinsky refers with regard to Lucifer's musical personality (as opposed to God's; see the quotation at the outset of this discussion), is in this respect not a *marked* (barred) "syncopation," but is the result of regular metric periodicity on whose "background" presence the effect of "syncopation" (with its off-the-beat/on-the-beat contradictions or reversals) depends. Both the Te Deum and Lucifer's successive entrances may be likened to the Shepherd/Messenger entrances at Nos. 139–47 and 159–67 in *Oedipus*, to which reference was made in chapter 8 (Example 53f) and again in chapter 10 (Example 63).

7. *Dialogues and a Diary*, p. 91.

8. Ibid. p. 95.

9. This list of "ten musical units" is borrowed from Claudio Spies, "Notes on Stravinsky's *Abraham and Isaac*." A word of caution is necessary, however. The serial analysis provided by Spies appeared before Stravinsky's transposition-rotation scheme had become widely known, with the consequence that, while not strictly inaccurate, his analysis, along with the serial charts furnished as a reference (with independent hexachordal rotation applied on a pitch/interval order basis), is inevitably a rather obscure approach to what has since emerged as a unique but nonetheless straightforward musical system. And while he includes *Addenda* to this effect, Spies's corrections refer to Stravinsky's "serial verticals," not really to the inappropriately devised analyses and rotation charts. It is therefore recommended that the serial references in Spies's article be replaced by Examples 92–96 in this chapter, and that his otherwise instructive commentary be heard and understood accordingly.

10. For additional comment on the *Variations* and the *Requiem Canticles* see Claudio Spies, "Notes on Stravinsky's Variations" and "Some Notes on Stravinsky's Requiem Settings." Again, however, a word of caution is necessary. In his discussion of the *Variations*, Spies correctly infers Stravinsky's habitual transposition-rotation scheme applied on a twelve-tone basis; but then, in his analysis of the monodic section of the first "variation" at mm. 6–23 and of the block of "twelve-part polyphony" at m. 23 (with near repeats at mm. 47 and 118), he inexplicably retreats to the old system of set transposition and rotation applied on a pitch/interval order basis. As earlier in his discussion of *Abraham and Isaac*, the results are needlessly cumbersome, and the reader is again advised to consult these articles using the serial charts and analysis of Examples 97, 98, and 99 in this chapter as his/her point of departure. (This is said with no intent of belittling Spies's contributions. Indeed, few studies offer such otherwise useful and informative comment, and much of Spies's terminology and numbering procedures has been adopted in this inquiry.) For a few publications of Stravinsky's own serial charts, see for the *Variations, Themes and Conclusions*, p. 64; and for the *Introitus*, Vera Stravinsky and Robert Craft, *Stravinsky in Pictures and Documents*, p. 401.

BIBLIOGRAPHY

Abraham, Gerald. *Studies in Russian Music*. London: William Reeves, 1935.

Adorno, Theodor W. *Philosophie der neuen Musik*. Tübingen: Mohr, 1949.

Arnheim, Rudolf. *Art and Visual Perception*. Berkeley and Los Angeles: University of California Press, 1969.

Austin, William W. *Music in the 20th Century*. New York: W. W. Norton, 1966.

Babbitt, Milton. "Remarks on the Recent Stravinsky." In *Perspectives on Schoenberg and Stravinsky*, edited by Benjamin Boretz and Edward T. Cone. New York: W. W. Norton, 1972.

———. "The Structure and Function of Music Theory." In *Perspectives on Contemporary Music Theory*, edited by Benjamin Boretz and Edward T. Cone. New York: W. W. Norton, 1972.

Beliaiev, Viktor. "Kastalsky and Russian Folk Polyphony." *Music and Letters* 10 (1929), p. 378.

Berger, Arthur. "Problems of Pitch Organization in Stravinsky." In *Perspectives on Schoenberg and Stravinsky*, edited by Benjamin Boretz and Edward T. Cone. New York: W. W. Norton, 1972.

———. "New Linguistic Modes and the New Theory." In *Perspectives on Contemporary Music Theory*, edited by Benjamin Boretz and Edward T. Cone. New York: W. W. Norton, 1972.

Besnois, Alexandre. *Reminiscences of the Russian Ballet*. Translated by Mary Britnieva. London: Putnam, 1941.

Boretz, Benjamin. "Meta-Variations: Studies in the Foundations of Musical Thought, Part I." *Perspectives of New Music* 8, no. 1 (1969), p. 1.

———. "Meta-Variations, Part II." *Perspectives of New Music* 8, no. 2 (1970), p. 49.

———. "The Construction of Musical Syntax (1)." *Perspectives of New Music* 9, no. 1 (1970), p. 23.

———. "Musical Syntax (II)." *Perspectives of New Music* 10, no. 1 (1970), p. 232.

———. "Meta-Variations, Part IV: Analytic Fallout (1)." *Perspectives of New Music* 11, no. 1 (1972), p. 146.

———. "Meta-Variations, Part IV: Analytic Fallout (II)." *Perspectives of New Music* 11, no. 2 (1973), p. 156.

———. "In Quest of the Rhythmic Genius." *Perspectives of New Music* 9, no. 2 (1972), p. 149.

Boulez, Pierre. *Notes of an Apprenticeship*. Translated by Herbert Weinstock. New York: Alfred A. Knopf, 1968.

Boys, Henry. "Stravinsky: The Musical Materials." *Score*, no. 4 (1951), p. 11.

———. "Note on the New *Petroushka.*" *Tempo*, no. 8 (1948), p. 15.

Bunge, Mario. *Causality.* Cambridge: Harvard University Press, 1959.

Collaer, Paul. *A History of Modern Music.* Translated by Sally Abeles. Cleveland: World, 1961.

Cone, Edward T. "The Uses of Convention: Stravinsky and His Models." In *Stravinsky: A New Appraisal of His Work,* edited by Paul Henry Lang. New York: W. W. Norton, 1963.

———. "Stravinsky: The Progress of a Method." In *Perspectives on Schoenberg and Stravinsky,* edited by Benjamin Boretz and Edward T. Cone. New York: W. W. Norton, 1972.

Corle, Edwin, ed. *Igor Stravinsky.* New York: Duell, Sloane and Pearce, 1949.

Craft, Robert. "Music and Words." In *Stravinsky in the Theatre,* edited by Minna Lederman. New York: Pellegrini & Cudahy, 1949.

———. "Reihenkompositionen: Vom *Septett* zum *Agon.*" *Musik der Zeit* 1, no. 12 (1955), p. 43.

———. "A Concert for Saint Mark." *Score,* no. 18 (1956), p. 35.

———. "A Personal Preface," *Score,* no. 20 (1957), p. 7.

———. "Ein Ballett für zwölf Tänzer." *Melos* 24 (1957), p. 284.

———. "*The Rite of Spring*: Genesis of a Masterpiece." *Perspectives of New Music* 5, no. 1 (1966), p. 20.

———. *Stravinsky: Chronicle of a Friendship, 1948–1971.* New York: Alfred A. Knopf, 1972.

———. "Stravinsky: Problems for Biographers." *New York Review of Books* (9 August 1973), p. 14.

———. "*Le Sacre* and Pierre Monteux: An Unknown Debt." *New York Review of Books* (3 April 1975), p. 33.

———, and William Harkins. "Stravinsky's Svadebka (*Les Noces*)." *New York Review of Books* (14 December 1972), p. 23.

Dray, William H. *Philosophy of History.* New Jersey: Prentice-Hall, 1964.

Drew, David. "Stravinsky's Revisions." *Score,* no. 20 (1957), p. 47.

Dushkin, Samuel. "Working with Stravinsky." In *Igor Stravinsky,* edited by Edwin Corle. New York: Duell, Sloane and Pearce, 1949.

Forte, Allen. *Contemporary Tone Structures.* New York: Columbia University Press, 1955.

———. *The Harmonic Organization of "The Rite of Spring."* New Haven: Yale University Press, 1978.

Gardiner, Patrick. *Theories of History.* New York: Free Press, 1959.

Gerhard, Roberto. "Twelve-Note Technique in Stravinsky." *Score,* no. 20 (1957), p. 38.

Grigoriev, S. L. *The Diaghilev Ballet, 1909–1929.* Translated by Vera Bowen. London: Constable, 1953.

Gurwitsh, Aron. *The Field of Consciousness.* Pittsburgh: Duquesne University Press, 1964.

Hamm, Charles, ed. *Igor Stravinsky: Petrushka.* New York: W. W. Norton, 1967.

Henle, Mary, ed. *Documents of Gestalt Psychology.* Berkeley and Los Angeles: University of California Press, 1961.

———, ed. *The Selected Papers of Wolfgang Köhler.* New York: Liveright, 1971.

Hopkins, G. W. "Stravinsky's Chords." *Tempo*, no. 76 (1966), p. 6.

Horgan, Paul. *Encounters with Stravinsky*. New York: Farrar, Straus and Giroux, 1972.

Karsavina, Tamara. "A Recollection of Stravinsky." *Tempo*, no. 8 (1948), p. 7.

Keller, Hans. "Schönberg and Stravinsky: Schönbergians and Stravinskyans." *Music Review* 15 (1954), p. 307.

———. "Rhythm: Gershwin and Stravinsky." *Score*, no. 20 (1957), p. 19.

Koffka, Kurt. *Principles of Gestalt Psychology*. New York: Harcourt Brace and World, 1935.

Lambert, Constant, *Music Ho! A Study of Music in Decline*, 3d ed. London: Faber and Faber, 1966.

Lang, Paul Henry, ed. *Stravinsky: A New Appraisal of His Work*. New York: W. W. Norton, 1963.

Lederman, Minna, ed. *Stravinsky in the Theatre*. New York: Pellegrini and Cudahy, 1949.

Libman, Lillian. *And Music at the Close: Stravinsky's Last Years*. New York: W. W. Norton, 1972.

Lifar, Serge. *Diaghilev*. London: Putnam, 1940.

Mason, Colin. "Serial Procedure in The Ricercar II of Stravinsky's *Cantata*." *Tempo*, no. 61/62 (1962), p. 6.

Mellers, Wilfrid. *Romanticism and the 20th Century*. Fairlawn, New Jersey: Essential Books, 1957.

———. "Stravinsky's *Oedipus* as 20th-Century Hero." In *Stravinsky: A New Appraisal of His Work*, edited by Paul Henry Lang. New York: W. W. Norton, 1963.

———. *Caliban Reborn*. New York: Harper and Row, 1967.

Messiaen, Olivier. *Technique de mon langage musical*. Paris: Leduc, 1944.

Meyer, Leonard B. *Emotion and Meaning in Music*. Chicago: University of Chicago Press, 1956.

Mitchell, Donald. *The Language of Modern Music*. New York: St. Martin's Press, 1970.

Moldenhauer, Hans, comp., and Demar Irvine, ed. *Anton von Webern: Perspectives*. Seattle: University of Washington Press, 1966.

Moles, Abraham. *Information Theory and Esthetic Perception*. Translated by Joel E. Cohen. Urbana: University of Illinois Press, 1968.

Morton, Lawrence. "Incongruity and Faith." In *Igor Stravinsky*, edited by Edwin Corle. New York: Duell, Sloane and Pearce, 1949.

———. "Stravinsky and Tchaikovsky: *Le Baiser de la fée*." In *Stravinsky; A New Appraisal of His Work*, edited by Paul Henry Lang. New York: W. W. Norton, 1963.

Nabokoff, Nicolas. "Christmas with Stravinsky." In *Igor Stravinsky*, edited by Edwin Corle. New York: Duell, Sloane and Pearce, 1949.

———. *Igor Stravinsky*. Berlin: Colloquium Verlag, 1964.

Perle, George. *Serial Composition and Atonality: An Introduction to the Music of Schoenberg, Berg, and Webern*. Berkeley and Los Angeles: University of California Press, 1963.

Polanyi, Michael. *Personal Knowledge*. New York: Harper and Row, 1958.

Pousseur, Henri. "Stravinsky by Way of Webern." *Perspectives of New Music* 10, no. 2 (1972), p. 13; and 11, no. 1 (1972), p. 112.

Ramuz, C. F. *Souvenirs sur Igor Stravinsky*. Lausanne: Editions Mermod, 1929.

Rimsky-Korsakov, Nicholas. *My Musical Life*. Translated by Judah A. Joffee. New York: Tudor, 1935.

Schaeffner, André. "On Stravinsky, Early and Late." *Modern Music* 12, no. 1 (1934), p. 3.

Schloezer, Boris de. "An Abridged Analysis." In *Igor Stravinsky*, edited by Edwin Corle. New York: Duell, Sloane and Pearce, 1949.

Spies, Claudio. "Notes on Stravinsky's *Abraham and Isaac*." In *Perspectives on Schoenberg and Stravinsky*, edited by Benjamin Boretz and Edward T. Cone. New York: W. W. Norton, 1972.

———. "Notes on Stravinsky's Variations." In *Perspectives on Schoenberg and Stravinsky*, edited by Benjamin Boretz and Edward T. Cone. New York: W. W. Norton, 1972.

———. "Some Notes on Stravinsky's Requiem Settings." In *Perspectives on Schoenberg and Stravinsky*, edited by Benjamin Boretz and Edward T. Cone. New York: W. W. Norton, 1972.

———. "Editions of Stravinsky's Music." In *Perspectives on Schoenberg and Stravinsky*, edited by Benjamin Boretz and Edward T. Cone. New York: W. W. Norton, 1972.

Sternfeld, Frederick W. "Some Russian Folk Songs in Stravinsky's *Petroushka*." In *Petrushka*, edited by Charles Hamm. New York: W. W. Norton, 1967.

Stravinsky, Igor. *An Autobiography*. New York: W. W. Norton, 1962. [First published as *Chroniques de ma vie*. Paris: Denoël et Steele, 1935.]

———. *Poetics of Music*. Translated by Arthur Knodel and Ingolf Dahl. Cambridge: Harvard University Press, 1947. [First published as *Poétique musicale*. Cambridge: Harvard University Press, 1942.]

———, and Robert Craft. *Conversations with Stravinsky*. New York: Doubleday, 1959.

———, and Robert Craft. *Memories and Commentaries*. New York: Doubleday, 1960.

———, and Robert Craft. *Expositions and Developments*. New York: Doubleday, 1962.

———, and Robert Craft. *Dialogues and a Diary*. New York: Doubleday, 1963.

———, and Robert Craft. *Themes and Episodes*. New York: Alfred A. Knopf, 1966.

———, and Robert Craft. *Retrospectives and Conclusions*. New York: Alfred A. Knopf, 1969.

———, and Robert Craft. *Themes and Conclusions*. London: Faber & Faber, 1972.

Stravinsky, Vera, and Robert Craft. *Stravinsky in Pictures and Documents*. New York: Simon and Schuster, 1978.

Swan, Alfred J. "The Nature of The Russian Folk-Song. *Musical Quarterly* 29 (1943), p. 498.

Tansman, Alexandre. *Igor Stravinsky: The Man and His Music*. Translated by Therese and Charles Bleefield. New York: Putnam, 1949.

Taruskin, Richard. "Russian Folk Melodies in *The Rite of Spring*." *Journal of the American Musicological Society* 33 (1980), p. 501.

Travis, Roy. "Toward a New Concept of Tonality?" *Journal of Music Theory* 3 (1959), p. 257.

Treitler, Leo. "On Historical Criticism." *Musical Quarterly* 53 (1967), p. 188.

———. "The Present as History." *Perspectives of New Music* 7, no. 2 (1969), p. 1.

van den Toorn, Pieter C. "Some Characteristics of Stravinsky's Diatonic Music." *Perspectives of New Music* 14, no. 1 (1975), p. 104; and 15, no. 2 (1977), p. 58.

Vlad, Roman. *Stravinsky.* Translated by Frederick and Anne Fuller. London: Oxford University Press, 1960.

White, Eric Walter. *Stravinsky: The Composer and His Works.* Berkeley and Los Angeles: University of California Press, 1966.

INDEX

Abraham and Isaac, xvi; in Hebrew, 248, 250, 445, 446; set-usage, 430–33; Stravinsky's reflections on, 445; compared to *The Flood*, 446–47; hexachordal transposition-rotation, 447–50

Afanasiev, Aleksandr Nikolaevich, 91, 155, 178, 247

Agon, xiv, xvi, 4, 42, 46, 196–97, 374, 451; rhythmic-metric type (2), 232, 234; influence of Webern, 383, 385; set-usage, 387, 389, 390; as a work of transition, 391, 392–97, 413–14, 479n*16*; conception of, 392–93, 496n*14*; "Pas de quatre," 392, 393–97; Prelude, 397–400; "Bransle simple," 400–03; "Bransle gay," 403–07; "Bransle double," 407–08; "Pas de deux," 408–13; compared to *Canticum Sacrum*, 415, 419–20, 421

Ansermet, Ernest, 97, 198, 200

Anthem, 430, 435

Apollo, xvi; as neoclassical ballet, 243, 254, 259, 261, 377; commission of, 485n*9*

Auden, W. H., 372, 378, 380

Babbitt, Milton, 379, 386

Babel, xvi, 44, 46, 259; analysis of, 290–94, 490n*10*; conception of, 379, 489n*9*. See also *Genesis Suite*

Bach, Johann Sebastian, 254, 333

Baiser de la fée, Le, 4, 259, 269, 485n*9*

Balakirev, Mili Alekseevich, 3, 5, 91, 468n*7*

Balanchine, George, 253, 358, 392, 437

Balmont, Konstantin, 246

Bartok, Bela, 8, 135–36, 471n*14*

Beethoven, Ludwig van, 254, 255, 260

Berceuse, 183

Berceuses du chat, 92, 158, 247

Berg, Alban, 373, 379, 382

Berger, Arthur: on the octatonic scale, xv, xix, 68–72, 463n7, 465n*15*, 477n*39*; on the "*Petroushka* chord," 52, 61, 64; on *Psalms*, 322

Berlin, 257, 372, 379

Besnois, Alexandre, 2, 462n*1*

Bitonality, xv, 63–65, 298, 314

Boretz, Benjamin, 54, 61, 212, 238, 467n*1*

Boulez, Pierre: on *Le Sacre*, 61–62, 63, 132, 181, 328, 469n*1*, 471n*13*; on rhythm, 137–38, 140, 195, 215–16, 217, 471n*16*, 481n*10*; on instrumentation, 202, 258, 373

Brahms, Johannes, 241, 254, 325

Cantata, xv; Ricercar II, 374, 378, 380, 384, 495n5, 496n6

Canticum Sacrum, xvi, 42, 46, 244, 383, 392; set-usage, 374, 385, 386, 389–91; conception of, 415–16; first movement, 416–21; second movement, "Surge, Aquilo," 421–26, 496n9, 498n*25*

Capriccio, xvi, 46, 240–41, 245, 254, 261, 269

Casella, Alfredo, 198, 199, 200

Chant funèbre, 458n2

Chromatic tendency tones, 18, 19; explained, 69–71, 262–67, 272–75, 486n*14*; in neoclassical works, 275–320 passim. *See also* Interpenetration, octatonic-diatonic; Model A and the C-scale ("minor-major third" emphasis); Neoclassicism

Cimbalom, 203, 245; in abandoned versions of *Les Noces*, 155, 158, 202, 244, 245, 474n6

Circus Polka, 353

Clarens, Switzerland, 99, 156
Collaer, Paul, xiv
Concertgebouw Orchestra, 240–41
Concertino, 157, 259
Concerto, opus 25 (Webern), 384
Concerto for Two Pianos, 205, 254, 259
Concerto in D ("Basle"), xvi, 26, 43, 45, 46, 48, 70; first movement, 275–81, 287, 322–23, 439–40, 488n3; rhythmic-metric type (1), 281–83; second movement, 283–84, 488n4; conception of, 488n1
Concerto in E♭ ("Dumbarton Oaks"), xvi, 46, 48, 254, 259, 287, 294
Cone, Edward T., 260, 466n30
Cosi fan tutte, 378
Craft, Robert: his "conversation" books with Stravinsky, xx, 9, 42, 239, 241, 258, 457n11; on *Les Noces*, 156, 157; "auditions" with Stravinsky, 211; on the serial period, 373–74, 379, 382; on *Agon*, 392; on *Canticum Sacrum*, 416, 498n25

D-scale, diatonic: descending scale, 60, 469n6; partitioning formulae, 73–76, 460n15; in *Petroushka*, 81–82, 88–89, 92–94; in *Le Sacre*, 101, 103, 116–17, 125–26, 471n13; in *Les Noces*, 159–60, 172–75; in *Canticum Sacrum*, 416, 419. *See also* Interpenetration, octatonic-diatonic
Danses concertantes, xvi, 37, 44, 46, 259; analysis of, 288–90, 318; conception of, 489n8
Debussy, Claude, 1, 207; Stravinsky's recollections of, 144–45; influence of, 145–46, 257, 258, 472n1, 473n2; *Zvezdoliki*, 473n3
Diaghilev, Sergei, 147, 258; commissions *The Firebird*, 1, 2, 8, 9; and *Petroushka*, 31, 98; and *Le Sacre*, 100, 134; and *Les Noces*, 156, 157; in Venice, 198, 199; commissions *Pulcinella*, 252, 253; visits Berlin (1912), 257, 372, 379; rupture with Stravinsky, 485n9; stages *Oedipus*, 490n16
Double Canon, 385, 430, 432, 435
Drei Satiren (Schoenberg), 379, 485n6
Duo concertante, 205

Ebony Concerto, 257, 353
Eight Easy Pieces, 198, 199, 271

Eight Instrumental Miniatures, 490n11
Elegy for J. F. K., 388, 423, 439–40
Epitaphium, xvi, 46, 388; conception of, 427–28; set-usage, 430, 431; analysis of, 433–35
Etude for Pianola, 145, 245, 246

Fanfare for a New Theater, 428
Faune et bergère, 146
Firebird, The, xvi, 31, 42, 44, 46, 144–46, 204; Stravinsky's reflections on, 1–2, 9, 17, 25; influence of Rimsky-Korsakov, 2–5, 8, 14, 20–21, 29; folksongs, 3, 29–30, 87–88, 179–80, 462n25; "basic-cell" structure, 5–7; recollections of Grigoriev, 8–9; octatonic relations in the Introduction, 11–17, 32–35; "Danse infernale," 17–25; rhythm and meter, 25–28, 142, 228; Finale, 26–28, 87–88, 179–80; "dominant sevenths," 323–25, 326, 327
Fireworks, 24, 42, 461n20
Five Fingers, The, 294, 490n11
Five Pieces for Orchestra (Schoenberg), 379
Flood, The, xvi, 26, 46, 344, 423; set-usage, 430–33; conception of, 436–37; "Te Deum," 437–41; "Working Notes," 439, 443, 444; rhythmic-metric type (1), 440–41; hexachordal transposition-rotation, 441–45; compared to *Abraham and Isaac*, 446–47
Fokine, Michel, 8, 9
Folksongs, Russian. See *Firebird, The; Petroushka*
Forte, Allen, xiv, 466n37
Four Etudes, 145
Four Norwegian Moods, 353
Four Russian Peasant Songs, 92, 158, 477n6
Fourth String Quartet (Schoenberg), 374
Freischütz, Der (Weber), 254

Genesis Suite, 373, 379, 489. See also *Babel*
Gide, André, 250
Giselle, 9
Grigoriev, S. L., 8, 25

Haydn, Franz Joseph, 255
Herman, Woody, 353
Hexachord, (0 2 3 5 7 9) diatonic, 59; partitioning formulae, 74–76, 83–84, 178–83, 476n1; in *Petroushka*, 76–84, 88–89,

126; in *The Firebird* (Finale), 87–88, 179–80, 462n24; in *Les Noces*, 160, 164–67, 172–76, 193–95, 477n6; in *Renard*, 179, 180; in *Histoire*, 181–93, 477n6, 477n7; in *Psalms*, 194–96; in *Agon*, 196–97, 394–96, 399. *See also* Interpenetration, octatonic-diatonic: Model B and the (0 2 3 5 7 9) hexachord or D-scale

Histoire du soldat, xvi, 46, 91, 92, 154, 155, 157; conception of, 178, 197–98; (0 2 3 5 7 9) hexachordal reference, 178–83; tonal alternatives, 181–82, 265, 477n7; "Soldier's March," 181–86; Scene I, 186–88; Scene II, 188–93; relations summarized, 193; as a work of transition, 198, 199–200, 392, 395, 479n16; jazz influence, 198, 200, 201–03; instrumentation, 198, 200, 201–03, 257; eclecticism, 200–01, 271; rhythmic-metric type (1), 221–23, 225–31, 481n14, 482n17, 482n18

In Memoriam Dylan Thomas, xvi, 383; set-usage, 381, 384, 421, 435; conception of, 392, 569n9

Interpenetration, octatonic-diatonic, xv, 19, 43, 66

—Model A and the A-scale: in *Psalms*, 295–98; in *Oedipus*, 302–05; in *Orpheus*, 307, 314–15, 492n24

—Model A and the C-scale (dominant-tonic relation): explained, 67–68, 267–70, 331–32

—Model A and the C-scale ("minor-major third" emphasis): explained, 69–71, 262–67, 272–75, 321, 322–23, 386n15, 387n17, 488n3; connecting-link summaries, 263, 264, 317–20

—Model B and the (0 2 3 5 7 9) hexachord or D-scale: 60, 69; connecting-link summaries, 73–76, 84–88 (*Petroushka*), 115–23, 469n1 (*Le Sacre*), 154 (*Three Pieces*), 160–62, 163–64, 172–75, 475n7 (*Les Noces*), 192–93 (*Histoire*), 271

Introitus, 386, 429, 430

Isorhythm, 430

Jazz, 198, 200–02, 257, 392, 485n3

Jeu de cartes, 259, 487n18

Juxtaposition, block, xviii, xx, 23, 26; explained, 43, 62–63, 66, 328; interplay, 63, 134–35, 176–77, 215; in *Le Sacre*, 101; in *Les Noces*, 158–59; neoclassical accommodations, 259–60, 269–70; in *Psalms*, 269–70, 348–49; linked to rhythmic-metric construction, 282–83, 342; in the *Symphonies of Wind Instruments*, 339–42; in *Agon*, 393–94; in *Canticum Sacrum*, 416; in the *Variations*, 429–30

Kallman, Chester, 378

Karsavina, Tamara, 8

Keller, Hans, 214

Kireievsky, P. V., 91, 155, 157, 247

Kirstein, Lincoln, 258, 392

Konzertstück, 31, 35, 73

Lambert, Constant, 156, 237

Lausanne, Switzerland, 198, 203

Liadov, Anatoli Konstantinovich, 5, 91

Lists 1 and 2, 44–46

Los Angeles, 373, 380

Lourié, Arthur, 258

"*Lux facta est* cadence" (*Oedipus*), 298, 299, 303–05

Maeterlinck, Maurice, 243

Mahler, Gustav, 257, 379

Mass, 46, 205, 351, 414, 415

Mavra, 157, 256

Mellers, Wilfrid: on *Histoire*, 181, 201, 218, 477n7; on *Oedipus*, 305

Mendelssohn, Felix, 254

Mengelberg, William, 241

Messiaen, Olivier, 216, 463n7

Milhaud, Darius, 373

"Minor-major third" emphasis. *See* Interpenetration, octatonic-diatonic: Model A and the C-scale; Neoclassicism

Model A. *See* Octatonic pitch collection

Model B. *See* Octatonic pitch collection

Monteux, Pierre, 97, 458n5

Monumentum Pro Gesualdo, 478n11

Morges, Switzerland, 144, 198, 204, 252, 373

Moussorgsky, Modest Petrovich, 3, 144

Movements, xvi, 382, 442; Stravinsky's reflections on, 427; set-usage, 428, 429, 430, 431

Mozart, Wolfgang Amadeus, 255, 378

Neoclassicism, xiv–xvii, 3, 4, 66–68, 69–71; origins of, 198–99, 256–58, 271; Stravinsky's reflections on, 252–55, 377; general characteristics of, 258–61; pitch relations surveyed, 261–62; Model A partitioning formulae, 261–64, 487n17; "minor-major third" emphasis, 262–67, 272–75, 317–20, 486n14, 486n15; chromatic tendency tones, 262–67, 273–75, 486n14; dominant-tonic relations, 267–69, 331–32; "relative–key" relationship, 297–98 (*Psalms*), 302, 304–05 (*Oedipus*), 307 (*Orpheus*), 378; relations summarized, 317–20, 321–23, 330–32.

Nightingale, The, 44, 45, 144, 146, 178

Nijinsky, Vaslav, 98, 100

Noces, Les, xvi, 21, 26, 43, 44, 45, 48, 70, 91–92, 237, 247, 272; compared to *Le Sacre*, 114, 159, 475n8; Stravinsky's reflections on, 155–56, 468n8; abandoned versions of, 155, 158, 202, 244, 245, 474n6; conception of, 156–58, 474n4; octatonic-diatonic relations surveyed, 158–62, 163–64; opening blocks in first tableau, 160–63, 277; rhythmic-metric type (1), 162–63; passage of transition, 164–67; explicit octatonic reference at Nos. *68–70*, 167–72, 278, 288, 475n11; rhythmic-metric type (2) at Nos. *68–70*, 170–71, 476n12; conclusion of third tableau, 172–75; relations summarized, 176–77; compared to *Histoire*, 193–95, 477n6

Nocturnes (Debussy), 146

Octatonic pitch collection: defined, xv, 5; inherited from Rimsky-Korsakov, 5, 8, 20–21, 35–37, 328–29, 461n19, 464n10; Lists 1 and 2, 42–48, 462n2, 464n13; structure of, 48–49, 53; limited to three collections, 49; Models A and B, 49–51, 56; (0,3,6,9) partitioning elements, 51–53, 57–58; structural levels, 54–56; pitch numbering, 56–59, 465n25; Model B's descending scale, 59–60, 71–72, 103–11, 470n6; Model B emphasis of the "Russian" period, 66–67, 68–69; Model A in neoclassical works, 66–68, 69–71. *See also* Interpenetration, octatonic-diatonic; Neoclassicism

Octet, xvi, 42, 46, 256; traditional forms, 259, 261; second movement (variations), 294, 333–37; conception of, 332–33

Ode, 44, 46, 294, 353

Oedipus Rex, xvi, 21, 44, 46, 377, 464n13; eclecticism, 200, 202, 258; rhythmic-metric type (1), 234–35, 299, 490n12; in Latin, 248–49; Stravinsky's reflections on, 252, 253–54, 298–99; Act II (Nos. *166–70*), 299–305, 318; rhythmic-metric type (2), 303–04; Act I (Nos. *27–45*), 366–71; conception of, 490n16

Orpheus, xvi, 46, 198, 200; traditional forms, 254, 259, 260; rhythmic-metric type (2), 233, 234; detailed analysis (Nos. *4–77*), 305–16; pitch relations summarized, 316–18, 492n22

Owl and the Pussycat, The, 428

Paris, France, 146, 199, 245, 373, 379; *Firebird* premiere, 1, 2, 9, 31

Pelléas et Mélisande (Debussy), 473n2

Pelleas und Melisande (Schoenberg), 373

Pergolesi, Giambattista. See *Pulcinella*

Perle, George, 386

Perséphone, xvi, 250, 254, 487n18

Petroushka, xiv, xvi, 1, 3, 22, 44, 45, 48, 73, 134; conception of, 31; octatonic origins of the "*Petroushka* chord," 31–37, 463n5; superimposition, 37–41; "polarity," 52; structural-level format, 53-54; "bitonality," 63–65

—first tableau: (0 2 3 5 7 9) hexachordal reference, 73–87, 179, 180, 183–85, 187, 410; octatonic (Model B) interpenetration, 73, 74, 75–76, 84–86; octatonic-diatonic relations summarized, 75–76, 83–87; accordianlike oscillation, 77–81; tonal alternatives, 81–82, 87–88, 92–95; "Danse russe," 88–90; folksongs, 90–91; chansons, 91, 200, 271; No. *5* compared to Rimsky-Korsakov version, 92–96; *1947* revision, 96–98, 243; compared to *Le Sacre*, 100–03, 126; compared to *Les Noces*, 159–60. *See also* Hexachord, (0 2 3 5 7 9) diatonic

Piano Concerto, 254, 256, 259, 333

Pianola, 203; in abandoned versions of *Les Noces*, 156, 158, 202, 244, 245; transcriptions, 245–46, 484n40

Piano Rag-Music, 96, 204, 257

Piano Sonata, 256, 259, 485n6

Pierné, Gabriel, 9

Pierrot lunaire, 145; Stravinsky's early encounter with, 257–58, 372–74, 379, 472n*1*

Pijper, Willem, 464n*11*

Poetics of Music (Poétique musicale), 61, 473n6

Polarity, 52, 61–63, 471n*13*; in rhythmic-metric construction, 215, 282–83

Polytonality. *See* Bitonality

Prelude to Genesis (Schoenberg), 373

Pribaoutki, xvi, 44, 45, 92, 157, 247; octatonic (Model B) relations, 40, 470n7

Pulcinella, xiv, xv, 4, 157; beginning of neo-classicism, 199, 242, 252–53, 256, 271

Ragtime, 46, 198, 204, 245, 257, 353

Rake's Progress, The, 45, 46, 205, 377; Stravinsky's reflections on, 255; as neo-classical opera, 372, 378–79, 380, 429, 487n*18*

Ramuz, C. F., 178, 247, 250, 258

Ravel, Maurice Joseph, 1, 2, 9, 144, 257

Relative-key relationship. *See* Neoclassicism

Renard, xvi, 44, 45, 92, 245, 377; Russian popular verse, 91, 155, 247, 248, 251; octatonic relations, 153, 470n7, 476n2; conception of, 157; (0 2 3 5 7 9) hexachordal reference, 179, 180; rhythmic-metric type (1), 223–24, 420

Requiem Canticles, xv, 146, 244, 372; block juxtaposition, 429, 430; hexachordal transposition-rotation, 432, 447, 450

Revisions, 96–98, 481n*12*

Rhythmic-metric type (1): described, 138–39, 216–18; in *Le Sacre*, 138–39; in *Les Noces*, 162–63; displacement, 217–18; in *Histoire*, 218–23, 481n*14*, 481n*15*; in *Renard*, 223–24; purpose of metric irregularity, 224–26, 482n*18*; relation to rhythmic-metric type (2), 226–28; relation to traditional patterns, 228–31, 482n*19*; in the *Symphonies of Wind Instruments*, 231–32, 341–42; in *Oedipus*, 234–35, 299; in the Concerto in D, 281–83; in *Psalms*, 350–51, 494n7; in *Agon*, 397–99, 405; in *The Flood*, 440–41

Rhythmic-metric type (2): described, 139, 216–18; in *Le Sacre* at Nos. *64–71*, 139–43, 226–28, 230–31; in *Psalms*, 140–41, 142, 195–96, 233–34, 239, in *Three Pieces*, 147–49, 474n*10*; in *Les Noces*,

170–71, 476n*12*; additional illustrations, 232–34; in *Oedipus*, 303–04; in *Canticum Sacrum*, 420–21

Rimsky-Korsakov, Andrei, 1, 200

Rimsky-Korsakov, Nikolai Andreevich, 1, 2, 144, 258; his "chromatic" / folksong approach as model for *The Firebird*, 3–5, 8, 14, 21; Stravinsky inherits the octatonic collection from, 20, 328–29, 464n*10*; octatonic passages in *Sadko*, 21, 35; folksong tradition, 29–30, 90–91, 462n25; Easter song compared to *Petroushka* at No. *5*, 92–96; as Stravinsky's teacher, 204, 458n2

Roi des étoiles, Le. *See Zvezdoliki*

Rubenstein, Artur, 96, 204

Russian Ballet, 8, 98, 156, 490n*16*

Sacre du printemps, Le, xiv, xvi, 1, 44, 45, 48, 69, 153, 240, 272–74; superimposition, 37, 40, 62, 327–28; "polarity," 61, 471n*13*; conception of, 92, 98, 99–100, 145; as ballet, 98, 100, 243; Stravinsky's recollections of, 99–100; Model B's partitioning formulae surveyed, 100–03, 469n*1*, 469n2; Model B's descending scale, 103–15; Model A's "dominant sevenths," 111–15; connecting-link summaries, 115–21, 123; detailed analysis of, 124–30; relations summarized, 131–33; interplay, 134–35; melodic invention, 135–37; rhythmic-metric type (1), 138–39, 472n*21*; rhythmic-metric type (2) at Nos. *64–71*, 139–43, 226, 227–28, 230–31, 244, 472nn*18, 19*, and *21*; compared to *Les Noces*, 156, 158, 164, 475n8

Sadko, 21, 35–37, 461nn*19* and *20*. *See also* Rimsky-Korsakov, Nikolai Andreevich

St. Petersburg, 1, 8, 145, 372, 373, 473n5

Satie, Erik, 199

Scènes de ballet, 44, 46

Schenker, Heinrich, xiv, xvii, 55

Scherzo à la russe, 353

Scherzo fantastique, xvi, 24, 42, 44, 45, 254, 354; octatonic relations, 35–37, 39, 48, 461n*21*, 463n4; as a ballet (*Les Abeilles*), 237, 243, 461n*21*

Schoenberg, Arnold, 132, 382, 388, 430; relation to Stravinsky, 211, 257–58, 379–80, 464n*1*; Stravinsky's reflections on, 372–73, 374–75. *See also Pierrot lunaire*

Searle, Humphrey, 238

Septet, 374, 378, 391

Serenade (Schoenberg), 374, 379, 485n6

Serenade in A, 256

Serial period: Stravinsky's reflections on, 372, 377; origins of, 378–81; influence of Webern, 382–85, 387; set-usage during the early stage, 389–90; later developments, 427–30; set-usage in late works, 430–33. *See also* Transposition-rotation

Sermon, A Narrative and A Prayer, A, 385, 428, 435

Sonata for Two Pianos, 353

Song of Bernadette (Werfel), 351, 353

Superimposition: explained, 23–24, 37–40, 62, 63; in *Petroushka*'s first tableau, 94, 95; in *Three Pieces*, 147, 149–50; in *Les Noces*, 159; "minor-major third" emphasis, 264; in the *Octet*, 335

Suvchinsky, Pierre, 255, 258, 379

Symphonies of Wind Instruments, xv, xvi, 4, 44, 46, 92, 157; conception of, 144, 243, 271, 337, 493n2; rhythmic-metric type (1) in opening blocks, 231–32, 283, 341–42; pitch relations, 270, 294, 337–44, 355, 363; block juxtaposition, 339–41

Symphony in C, xvi, 255, 259–60, 261, 269

Symphony in E♭, 461n21

Symphony in Three Movements, xvi, 45, 46, 47, 67, 323; triadic oscillation at Nos. *7–13*, 22, 327, 328; superimposition, 24; second movement, 70, 284–88; neoclassical accommodations, 259, 261; block juxtaposition, 269; "dominant sevenths" irregularly resolved, 327, 328; Stravinsky's reflections on, 351–52; conception of, 351–53, 489n6; first movement, 354–64; dominant-tonic relation, 362–64; compared to *Psalms*, 364, 495n10; third movement, 364–66, 495n13

Symphony of Psalms, xvi, 44, 46, 48, 252, 243; triadic oscillation, 22; block juxtaposition, 26, 269, 270, 348; octatonic-diatonic relations surveyed (first movement), 67, 268, 269, 293, 322–23, 344–50, 355; rhythmic-metric type (2) at No. *22* (third movement), 139, 142, 195–96, 216, 218; (0 2 3 5 7 9) hexachor-

dal reference at No. *22* (third movement), 195; rhythmic-metric type (1) at No. *3* (third movement), 233, 234, 239; Stravinsky's reflections on, 244, 249, 344–45, 363; second movement, 295–98, 309, 335; "dominant sevenths" irregularly resolved, 327–28, 492n3, rhythmic-metric type (1) (first movement), 350–51, 494n7

Tansman, Alexandre, xiv

Tchaikovsky, Pëtr Ilich, 2, 4, 255; folksong tradition, 5, 8, 90, 91

Third String Quartet (Bartok), 135–36

Three Japanese Lyrics, 258, 377, 472n1

"Three Movements from *Petroushka*," 96

Three Pieces for String Quartet, xvi, 45, 92, 139, 243; rhythmic-metric type (1), 147–49, 216, 236–37, 244, 474n10; Model B partitioning, 149–51, 423; diatonic intervention, 151–52; relations summarized, 152–54

Threni, 42, 46, 383; rhythmic-metric type (2), 232–33, 234; 12-tone set, 382, 385, 414, 496n9

Tierce de Picardie, 295, 302–05, 335, 492n24

"Tilimbom." See *Trois histoires pour enfants*

Toscanini, Arturo, 241

Transposition-rotation: hexachordal, 390, 428, 432–33, 441–45 (*The Flood*), 447–50 (*Abraham and Isaac*); 12-tone, 433, 450–51 (*Variations*)

Travis, Roy, xiv, 466n37

Tres Sacrae Cantiones, 478n11

Tristan und Isolde, 5

Trois histoires pour enfants, 92, 182; "Tilimbom," 182, 183, 477n4

Two Poems of Balmont, 45

Ustilug, Russia, 1, 99

Valéry, Paul, 258

Varèse, Edgard, 470n9

Variations (Webern), 376, 384, 385

Variations for orchestra, xvi, 429–30; set-usage, 430; transposition-rotation, 433, 450–51; Stravinsky's reflections on, 445–46

Venice, Italy, 146, 379, 415, 485n9
Verdi, Giuseppe, 252
Violin Concerto (Schoenberg), 374
Violin Concerto in D, 205
Vlad, Roman, xiv, 457n3, 463n7

Wagner, Richard, 4
Weber, Karl Maria Friedrich Ernst von, 254
Webern, Anton, 145, 374; Stravinsky's re-
flections on, 375–77; influence of,
382–85, 387, 421
Werfel, Franz, 258, 351
White, Eric Walter, xiv
Whiteman, Paul, 353
Whole-tone scale, 5, 123

Zorina, Vera, 353
Zvezdoliki, 44, 45, 158, 246, 473n3

I wish to acknowledge my gratitude to the following for permission to use the musical illustrations and quotations reprinted here:

Boosey and Hawkes, Inc. for *Three Pieces for String Quartet* © Copyright 1922 by Edition Russe de Musique. Copyright assigned to Boosey and Hawkes, Inc.; *Octet for Winds* © Copyright 1924 by Edition Russe de Musique. Renewed 1952. Copyright and renewal assigned to Boosey and Hawkes, Inc. Revised version copyright 1952 by Boosey and Hawkes, Inc.; *Oedipus Rex* © Copyright 1927 by Edition Russe de Musique. Renewed 1944. Copyright and renewal assigned to Boosey and Hawkes, Inc. English translation copyright 1949 by Boosey and Hawkes, Inc.; *Symphony of Psalms* © Copyright 1931 by Edition Russe de Musique. Renewed 1958. Copyright and renewal assigned to Boosey and Hawkes, Inc. Revised edition copyright 1948 by Boosey and Hawkes, Inc. Renewed 1975; *Concerto in D* ("Basle") © Copyright 1946 by Igor Stravinsky. Renewed 1973. Copyright and renewal assigned to Boosey and Hawkes, Inc.; *Orpheus* © Copyright 1947, 1948 by Boosey and Hawkes, Inc. Renewed 1974, 1975; *Agon* © Copyright 1957 by Boosey and Hawkes, Inc. *Epitaphium* © Copyright 1959 by Hawkes and Son (London) Ltd.; *The Flood* © Copyright 1962, 1963 by Boosey and Hawkes Music Publishers Ltd.; *Abraham and Isaac* © Copyright 1954 by Boosey and Hawkes Music Publishers Ltd.; *Variations for Orchestra (In Memoriam Aldous Huxley)* © Copyright 1965 by Boosey and Hawkes Music Publishers Ltd.; *Symphonies of Wind Instruments* © Copyright 1926 by Edition Russe de Musique. Copyright assigned to Boosey and Hawkes, Inc. Revised version copyright 1952 by Boosey and Hawkes, Inc.; *Canticum Sacrum* © Copyright 1956 by Boosey and Hawkes, Inc.; *Le Sacre du printemps (Rite of Spring)* © Copyright 1921 by Edition Russe de Musique. Copyright assigned 1947 to Boosey and Hawkes, Inc.; *Petroushka* © Copyright by Edition Russe de Musique. Copyright assigned to Boosey and Hawkes, Inc. Revised edition copyright 1947, 1948 by Boosey and Hawkes, Inc. Renewed 1975.

J & W Chester/Edition Wilhelm Hansen London Ltd. for *Pribaoutki, Renard,* and *Les Noces.*

B. Schott's Söhne for *Symphony in Three Movements.* Copyright 1946 by AMP, Inc. New York. Copyright assigned to B. Schott's Söhne, Mainz. Used by permission of European American Music Distributors Corporation, sole agent for B. Schott's Söhne; *Scherzo fantastique.* Copyright B. Schott's Söhne, Mainz, 1931. Used by permission of European American Music Distributors Corporation, sole U. S. agent for B. Schott's Sohne; *Babel* © Schott & Co. Ltd., London, 1952. Used by permission of European American Music Distributors Corporation, sole U.S. agent for Schott & Co. Ltd.

Alfred A. Knopf, Inc. for excerpts from *Themes and Episodes* by Robert Craft and Igor Stravinsky. Copyright © by Robert Craft and Igor Stravinsky.